Lecture Notes in Computer Science 13521

More information about this series at https://link.springer.com/bookseries/558

HCI International 2022 Thematic Areas and Affiliated Conferences

Thematic Areas

- HCI: Human-Computer Interaction
- HIMI: Human Interface and the Management of Information

Affiliated Conferences

- EPCE: 19th International Conference on Engineering Psychology and Cognitive Ergonomics
- AC: 16th International Conference on Augmented Cognition
- UAHCI: 16th International Conference on Universal Access in Human-Computer Interaction
- CCD: 14th International Conference on Cross-Cultural Design
- SCSM: 14th International Conference on Social Computing and Social Media
- VAMR: 14th International Conference on Virtual, Augmented and Mixed Reality
- DHM: 13th International Conference on Digital Human Modeling and Applications in Health, Safety, Ergonomics and Risk Management
- DUXU: 11th International Conference on Design, User Experience and Usability
- C&C: 10th International Conference on Culture and Computing
- DAPI: 10th International Conference on Distributed, Ambient and Pervasive Interactions
- HCIBGO: 9th International Conference on HCI in Business, Government and Organizations
- LCT: 9th International Conference on Learning and Collaboration Technologies
- ITAP: 8th International Conference on Human Aspects of IT for the Aged Population
- AIS: 4th International Conference on Adaptive Instructional Systems
- HCI-CPT: 4th International Conference on HCI for Cybersecurity, Privacy and Trust
- HCI-Games: 4th International Conference on HCI in Games
- MobiTAS: 4th International Conference on HCI in Mobility, Transport and Automotive Systems
- AI-HCI: 3rd International Conference on Artificial Intelligence in HCI
- MOBILE: 3rd International Conference on Design, Operation and Evaluation of Mobile Communications

Conference Proceedings – Full List of Volumes

http://2022.hci.international/proceedings

24th International Conference on Human-Computer Interaction (HCII 2022)

The full list with the Program Board Chairs and the members of the Program Boards of all thematic areas and affiliated conferences is available online at:

http://www.hci.international/board-members-2022.php

HCI International 2023

The 25th International Conference on Human-Computer Interaction, HCI International 2023, will be held jointly with the affiliated conferences at the AC Bella Sky Hotel and Bella Center, Copenhagen, Denmark, 23–28 July 2023. It will cover a broad spectrum of themes related to human-computer interaction, including theoretical issues, methods, tools, processes, and case studies in HCI design, as well as novel interaction techniques, interfaces, and applications. The proceedings will be published by Springer. More information will be available on the conference website: http://2023.hci.international/

General Chair
Constantine Stephanidis
University of Crete and ICS-FORTH
Heraklion, Crete, Greece
Email: general_chair@hcii2023.org

http://2023.hci.international/

Contents

Universal Access and Active Aging

HCI for Health and Well-being

A Recognition Model of Motion Primitives in VR-IADL Based on the Characteristics of MCI Patients and Elderly Adults

Taisei Ando[1], Takehiko Yamaguchi[1]([✉]), Tania Giovannetti[2], and Maiko Sakamoto[3]

[1] Suwa University of Science, Toyohira, Chino, Nagano 5000-1, Japan
`tk-ymgch@rs.sus.ac.jp`
[2] Temple University, Philadelphia, PA 19122, USA
[3] Saga University, 5-1-1 Nabeshima, Saga, Saga, Japan

Abstract. In recent years, studies have found that patients with mild cognitive impairment (MCI) display lower functioning in instrumental activities of daily living (IADLs) compared to healthy subjects. We have used virtual reality (VR) technology as a means to test IADLs in virtual space (VR-IADLs). Previous research has focused on motion primitives, which are the smallest units of motion in a VR-IADL task, and has developed techniques for screening for MCI based on their frequency of occurrence. As a result, this presented the possibility of screening for MCI using motion frequency analysis. However, there remains a problem in extracting motion primitives related to the characteristics of the elderly and MCI patients. The purpose of this study is to develop a model capable of identifying the motion primitives necessary for extracting motion primitives by analyzing the characteristics of the elderly and MCI patients. As a result of this evaluation, which uses the confusion matrix, it was possible to identify motion primitives with 75.5% accuracy. In the future, we plan to select feature quantities to improve recognition accuracy.

Keywords: Mild cognitive impairment · Virtual reality · Motion primitives · Machine learning

1 Introduction

1.1 Association Between IADL and MCI

Detecting mild cognitive impairment (MCI) as early as possible is important. MCI patients have been shown to experience a slight functional decline in instrumental activities of daily living (IADLs) [1]. IADLs are more complex and higher-level activities than activities of daily living (ADLs). IADLs include activities such as meal preparation, shopping, and cleaning.

In their study evaluating IADL performance, Giovannetti et al. reported a significant difference in the frequency of human errors during IADL tasks [1]. In a subjective evaluation of IADL performance, Fabiana et al. also identified a significant difference

V. G. Duffy et al. (Eds.): HCII 2022, LNCS 13521, pp. 3–12, 2022.
https://doi.org/10.1007/978-3-031-17902-0_1

in questionnaire scores for family members and caregivers [2]. Therefore, existing studies have highlighted the importance of focusing on behavioral function in addition to conventional cognitive function assessment.

The Naturalistic Action Test (NAT) is designed to evaluate the performance of IADLs [3]. For the NAT, subjects are required to complete the following three tasks: 1) Prepare toast with butter and jam. 2) Wrap a present. 3) Prepare a lunch box with sandwiches, snacks, and drinks and pack them in a school bag. The bread, jam, and other items needed to complete the task are arranged on a U-shaped table. NAT scores are independent of an individual's educational level, gender, and mobility impairment [3], and they have been shown to be significantly associated with caregiver reports of ADLs [4]. However, the NAT has several problems: 1) It is not suitable for mass screening. 2) A heavy burden is placed on examiners (clinical psychologists, etc.). 3) The food used in the experiment must be discarded.

1.2 Virtual Kitchen Challenge System

We developed an assessment tool for evaluating meal preparation using virtual reality (VR) technology [5]. This system is called the Virtual Kitchen Challenge (VKC) system, and it solves the problem of performing IADL tasks in real space. The VKC includes two types of tasks: the toast and Coffee task, which simulates preparing breakfast, and the lunchbox task, which simulates preparing lunch (Fig. 1).

Fig. 1. Toast and coffee task screenshot

The VKC also contains objects that are unrelated to the task. In the VKC, actions such as moving objects and opening a lid in real space are transformed into interactions such as dragging and touching items.

It has been shown that there is a positive correlation between the VKC and the frequency of human error in the real environment [5] (Fig. 2).

For this study, the minimum unit of operation in the VKC is defined as a motion primitive.

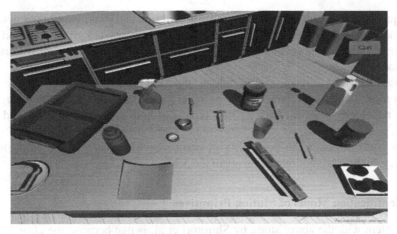

Fig. 2. Screenshot of the lunchbox task

2 Previous Research

First, this paper reviews existing studies that have examined motion primitives in the VKC context. In one study, the authors focused on motion primitives only when the screen was touched; in another study, the authors focused on motion primitives with and without a screen.

2.1 Clustering Motion Primitives Using Topic Models

In a study by Shirotori et al. focusing on the frequency of motion primitives in VKC, the authors examined whether there was a difference in the occurrence probability of motion primitives among healthy university students, elderly people, and MCI patients [6]. The author's research method consisted of two steps. First, the authors determined

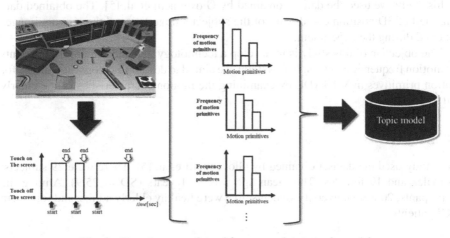

Fig. 3. Flow from creation of frequency data to topic model

the frequency data of motion primitives, such as touch and drag, using data obtained from lunchbox tasks performed by healthy university students, elderly people, and MCI patients. Next, the authors clustered the frequency data of the motion primitives using a topic model (Fig. 3).

Subsequently, healthy university students and MCI patients were divided into independent topics; however, topics specific to the elderly could not be identified, suggesting that the elderly possess characteristics typical of both university students and MCI patients.

This study suggests the possibility of screening MCI patients according to the frequency analysis of motion primitives in the VKC.

2.2 Identification Model of Motion Primitives

One problem with the above study by Shirotori et al. is that because the classification of motion primitives was performed by an observer while analyzing the moving image, the observer's subjectivity may have influenced the results.

To solve this issue, Iwashita et al. developed a model for automatically classifying motion primitives [7]. They conducted an experiment using the VKC with university students, and they measured the 3D position coordinates and moving images of study participants' fingertips. Subsequently, they calculated time-series data for fingertip speed. They segmented the data into motion primitives and defined motion primitives for each segmented segment. Iwashita et al. considered that motion in the VKC could be performed by a combination of four actions: 1) pointing, 2) resting, 3) clicking or releasing, and 4) dragging. Ensemble learning was used to model the average and variance of the velocity of each segment. As a result, it was possible to classify motion primitives with considerable accuracy.

3 Method

In this study, we used the dataset obtained by Giovannetti et al. [5]. The obtained data consisted of 3D position coordinates of the subject's fingertips and the moving images obtained during the experiment.

The objective of this study is to develop a technology that can screen MCI patients via motion frequency analysis. In this study, we aimed to develop a recognition model for motion primitives in VR-IADL by examining the motion characteristics of the elderly and MCI patients.

3.1 Subjects

This study used the dataset obtained by Giovannetti et al. [5]. There were 29 subjects: 10 males and 19 females. The mean age was 37.1 years (SD = 25.9). Among the participants, 20 were university students, five were healthy elderly adults, and four were MCI patients.

3.2 Lunchbox Task

The lunchbox task consists of three main tasks (the sandwich task, cookie task, and water bottle task) and the subtasks required to accomplish the main tasks. The main tasks and subtasks are described in detail below.

(1) **Sandwich Task**

The sandwich task consists of eight subtasks:

1. Place a piece of bread on a sheet of aluminum foil.
2. Uncover the peanut butter.
3. Scoop the peanut butter with a knife and spread it on the bread.
4. Open the lid of the blueberry jam.
5. Scoop the blueberry jam with a knife and spread it on the bread.
6. Place another slice of bread on top of the peanut butter and jam.
7. Wrap the sandwich in aluminum foil.
8. Put the wrapped sandwich into the lunchbox.

(2) **Cookie Task**

The cookie task consists of three subtasks:

1. Place three cookies on a sheet of aluminum foil.
2. Wrap the three cookies in aluminum foil.
3. Place the wrapped cookies in a lunchbox.

(3) **Water Bottle Task**

The water bottle task consists of five subtasks:

1. Open the lid of the juice container.
2. Pour the juice into a water bottle.
3. Close the inner lid of the water bottle.
4. Close the lid of the water bottle.
5. Put the water bottle in the lunchbox.

Finally, press the end button in the upper right-hand corner of the screen to end the task.

3.3 Human Cognitive Models

In this study, we utilized a human cognitive model to analyze the motion primitives of the elderly and MCI patients. The human cognitive model is shown in Fig. 4 [8].

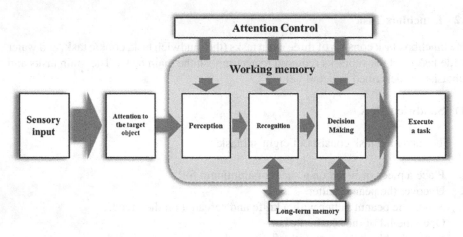

Fig. 4. Human cognitive model (modification of figure from [8])

As shown in Fig. 4, humans receive information via their sensory organs. Among the information received, humans filter out all but the necessary information; subsequently, they interpret this information based on past memories, make judgments, and then act.

Atance et al. define planning as the ability to consider several actions and their consequences and then implement actions in a sequence [9]. Based on Atance et al.'s definition, we defined motion planning as the action that occurs prior to task execution in this study.

It has been shown that when working memory, which is included in motion planning, malfunctions, the function and planning abilities necessary for executing IADLs deteriorate.

In this study, we defined new motion primitives at the stages of motion planning and task execution. We believe that defining motion primitives in this way enables us to consider the motion characteristics of the elderly and MCI patients.

3.4 Motion Primitives

In this study, we defined motion primitives at the stages of motion planning and execution. Figure 5 shows the motion primitives.

Remaining stationary and wandering are the stages of motion planning. Wandering is the act of wandering during a task before deciding what action to take next. This action was more common among the elderly and MCI patients than among university students.

The execution steps include pointing, making screen contact, releasing, and committing a micro-error (ME). ME is one of the errors of IADL tasks [10]. ME is defined as stopping when touching an object or touching an object and releasing it without doing anything. It has been shown that the respective incidence rates of ME among healthy adults and MCI patients are significantly different [10].

Screen contact refers to the act of touching a screen.

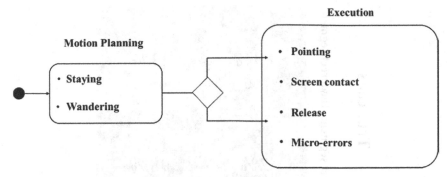

Fig. 5. Motion primitives

3.5 Segmentation of the Motion Primitives

In this study, we segmented fingertip speed time-series data into units of motion primitives using a two-step process similar to the method employed by Iwashita et al. Specifically, the segmentation was performed at zero acceleration intersection in the first stage. This method uses machine learning to rectify any incorrect segmentation that occurs during the first segmentation in the second stage. For the segment points obtained in the first stage of segmentation, a data set was created from the teacher data that was used to determine whether to subtract segments and the feature quantities of segment segments, and this was implemented via machine learning. After segmentation in the first stage, an error occurred whereby segment boundaries were drawn where segments were not needed.

3.6 Segmentation Results

In this study, segments in the inner screen and in the non-screen contact section of all the time-series data were used, and other data were excluded via preprocessing. Screen contact sections were not included in the dataset because they can be segmented as a single motion primitive.

The accuracy of segmentation was evaluated using a confusion matrix. The confusion matrix is shown in Fig. 6.

In this study, seven dimensional features, including segment interval time and segment velocity, were extracted. We created data to determine whether to subtract segments as teacher data. A data set was created from these data. In total, there were 2,370 data sets.

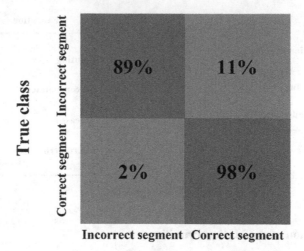

Predicted class

Fig. 6. Segmentation evaluation by confusion matrix

Using a decision tree, a segmentation accuracy of 97% was achieved. These results suggest that we have developed a motion segmentation model that accounts for the motion characteristics of the elderly and MCI patients.

3.7 Safe-Level SMOTE Data Augmentation

In this study, we defined motion primitives as data obtained by segmenting fingertip speed time-series data into units of motion primitives.

We extended the motion primitive data using the safe-level SMOTE method. Safe-level SMOTE is a data extension method used in the unbalanced classification problem [11].

In this study, we extended the data for micro-errors, releasing, and wandering operations, which had less data than the other three motion primitives. This extension allowed us to achieve a similar amount of data for all six motion primitives.

3.8 Results of Motion Primitives Recognition

In this study, we extracted five dimensional feature values, including the maximum and minimum velocity values for each segment interval. The total number of data sets was 5,764. Ensemble learning was used to model the data set.

The recognition accuracy of the motion primitives was evaluated using a confusion matrix; the results are shown in Fig. 7. The overall recognition accuracy was 75.5%.

Recognition accuracy by category was 69.2% for pointing, 86% for screen contact, 72.5% for stationary, 85.7% for wandering, 62% for ME, and 78% for releasing.

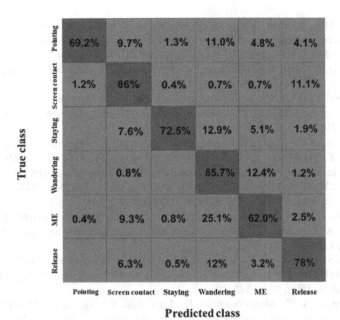

Fig. 7. Result of recognition of motion primitives by confusion matrix

The recognition result of a motion primitive depends on the segmentation result for each motion primitive. Therefore, although the accuracy of the segmentation model developed in this study was 97%, there are segments that could not be correctly segmented. We believe that this influenced the recognition results of the motion primitives.

4   Conclusion

In this study, we developed a recognition model of motion primitives in VR-IADL by considering the motion characteristics of elderly people and MCI patients using the data set obtained by Giovannetti et al. We successfully developed a model capable of recognizing motion primitives with 75.5% accuracy. We used data from five elderly patients and four MCI patients. Therefore, it cannot be claimed that this model perfectly accounts for the movement characteristics of all elderly people and MCI patients. In the future, we plan to review the features and develop more accurate models by increasing the number of subjects.

References

1. Giovannetti, T., et al.: Characterization of everyday functioning in mild cognitive impairment: a direct assessment approach. Dement. Geriatr. Cogn. Disord. **25**(4), 359–365 (2008)
2. da Cunha Cintra, F.C.M., et al.: Functional decline in the elderly with MCI: cultural adaption of the ADCS-ADL scale. Revista da Associação Médica Brasileria **63**(7), 590–599 (2017)

3. Schwartz, M.F., Segal, M., Veramonti, T., Ferraro, M., Buxbaum, L.J.: The naturalistic action test: a standardised assessment for everyday action impairment. Neuropsychological Rehabil. **12**(4), 311–339 (2002). https://doi.org/10.1080/09602010244000084

4. Giovannetti, T., Libon, D.J., Buxbaum, L.J., Schwartz, M.F.: Naturalistic action impairments in dementia. Neuropsychological **40**(8), 1220–1232 (2002)

5. Giovannetti, T., et al.: The virtual kitchen challenge: preliminary data from a novel virtual reality test of mild difficulties in everyday functioning. Aging Neuropsychol. Cogn. **26**(6), 823–841 (2019)

6. Shirotori, A., et al.: Topic model-based clustering for IADL motion primitives (2019)

7. Iwashita, Y., Yamaguchi, T., Giovannetti, T., Sakamoto, M., Ohwada, H.: Discriminative model for identifying motion primitives based on virtual reality-based IADL. In: Stephanidis, C., Antona, M., Gao, Q., Zhou, J. (eds.) HCII 2020. LNCS, vol. 12426, pp. 574–585. Springer, Cham (2020). https://doi.org/10.1007/978-3-030-60149-2_44

8. Yamaguchi, H.: https://www.dcnet.gr.jp/pdf/journal/t_2019_sousetu_190708.pdf

9. McCormack, T., Atance, C.M.: Planning in young children: a review and synthesis. Dev. Rev. **31**(1), 1–31 (2011)

10. Seligman, S., Giovannetti, T., Sestito, J., Libon, D.J.: A new approach to the characterization of subtle errors in everyday action: implications for mild cognitive impairment. Clin. Neuropsychol. **28**(1), 97–115 (2014)

11. Bunkhumpornpat, C., Sinapiromsaran, K., Lursinsap, C.: Safe-level-SMOTE: safe-level-synthetic minority over-sampling technique for handling the class imbalanced problem. In: Theeramunkong, T., Kijsirikul, B., Cercone, N., Ho, T.-B. (eds.) PAKDD 2009. LNCS (LNAI), vol. 5476, pp. 475–482. Springer, Heidelberg (2009). https://doi.org/10.1007/978-3-642-01307-2_43

Using Machine Learning to Determine Optimal Sleeping Schedules of Individual College Students

Orlando Yahir Azuara-Hernandez$^{(\boxtimes)}$ and Zachary Gillette

Swarthmore College, Swarthmore, PA 19081, USA
{oazuara1,zgillet1}@swarthmore.edu

Abstract. Sleep is one of the most important bodily functions for maintaining a healthy lifestyle, especially for teenagers and young adults. Though general guidelines for healthy sleeping habits for this age group are well documented, it is often difficult to know exactly what bed time, wake time, and total amount of sleep is best for a given individual based on their personal biological needs. Given this shortcoming in current sleep research, our goal is to create an algorithm that reliably classifies EEG sleep data in order to predict the optimal sleep schedule for an individual, specifically for a college student. In addition to this, we address the shortcomings of current sleep data by developing our own dataset of over 300 h of full night recordings for a single individual. Using this dataset, we implement and compare various ML models, and discuss limitations and areas of future work for prediction of optimal sleep.

Keywords: Machine learning · Supervised learning · Electroencephalogram (EEG) · Sleep research · Sleep data · Individualized healthcare · Optimal sleep duration

1 Introduction

1.1 Problem Statement

Sleep is a highly-important bodily function that helps maintain the health and general well-being of the human body. Additionally, sleep plays a major role in the development and well being of teens and young adults, a concept that has become significantly more recognized with the advancements in sleep research and analysis. For example, it has been observed that proper sleep provides various benefits, such as promoting growth, learning, and cognitive development, strengthening the immune system, and decreasing the chances of illnesses such as heart disease [6]. These benefits corroborate research which shows a strong correlation between high sleep quality and better academic performance, a factor which is without a doubt of great importance to many college students [23].

O. Y. Azuara-Hernandez and Z. Gillette—Both authors contributed equally to this work.

© Springer Nature Switzerland AG 2022
V. G. Duffy et al. (Eds.): HCII 2022, LNCS 13521, pp. 13–25, 2022.
https://doi.org/10.1007/978-3-031-17902-0_2

The lack of sleep, on the other hand, is tied to various health concerns such as increased risk of obesity, increased probability of taking risk-taking behaviors, and overall detrimental effects to mental health [37]. Because of the importance of proper sleeping habits for teenagers and young adults, and especially for college students, it is necessary to determine what types of sleeping patterns are best for this specific demographic.

Plenty of research has already been done on this topic[1,2,8,16,21,24,32,33, 35,36]. For instance, Chaput et al. [7] reports that young adults need more sleep than older adults. However, while these findings generally outline the optimal sleeping habits for teens and young adults, the specific needs for individuals vary depending on a large variety of biological factors as well as lifestyles. Additionally, since people naturally lead varying lifestyles, it is impossible for many individuals to follow the sleeping recommendations proposed for their demographic. College students notably fall under this category, since college life often encourages staying up to extreme hours to finish assignments and spend time with friends [12]. For the above reasons, it is necessary to devise a system that can diagnose the specific optimal sleeping patterns of an individual. Because of the usefulness such a system would provide to college students in particular, this study attempts to develop an algorithm to help college students determine their personalized optimal sleeping schedule.

1.2   Literature Review

When reviewing currently available sleep-related literature, it is apparent that such an algorithm to obtain individualized data for optimal sleep would be novel. This is seemingly the case because there is limited data available for the long-term study of an individual's sleeping patterns compared to other types of sleeping data. For instance, epidemiological data has shown chronically inadequate sleep in the general population, with various experts claiming the core sleep duration needed to be of 6 h [9]. This number has varied over the years, with a general consensus of 6 to 9 h of sleep needed by an individual [13]. However, there exists a lack of studies done on the specific sleep needs of individuals.

A sample of papers cited in Roy [32] and Craik [8] find that most sleeping studies use datasets consisting of various people whose sleep patterns are monitored for a shorter period of time. Studies such as Arnal et al. [5], Giri et al. [11], and Hou et al. [14] (and many others) have been done on sleep stage classification, the process of determining whether a person is either awake, in non-rapid eye movement sleep (NREM), or in rapid eye movement sleep (REM) at any given point during their sleep. These studies generally use Electroencephalography (EEG) technology coupled with deep learning (DL) algorithms to determine the sleep phase. Ansari et al. [4]. dives further into sleep stage classification, using EEG technology specifically with infants to help optimize their brain development during sleep. Additionally, Kemp et al. [17]. uses EEG technology to quantify how deep one's sleep is. However, because each of these studies utilize various participants with each participant studied for a shorter period of time, it is difficult to repurpose these datasets to draw conclusions pertaining to a single individual. In other words, there simply is not enough data available on any given individual to analyze their personal sleep patterns sufficiently.

Moreover, while there are a limited number of datasets available that include sufficient data for the individual to train an ML algorithm, these data sets are largely unusable for the purposes of this study. For one, because wearing EEG headsets for extended periods of time can be uncomfortable, these existing datasets are usually composed of individuals who are in critical condition and are being monitored for extended periods of time by hospital staff. Since these individuals have underlying health conditions and are generally not in the teenage and young adult demographic, their data cannot be used to train algorithms intended for the average healthy college student. Secondly, extensive data revealing a single-individual's sleeping patterns can be subject to privacy and ethical concerns. Ultimately, to the best of our knowledge, there currently exists no study which focuses on a long-term analysis of an individual, with the longest individual sleep recording from the aforementioned studies being of 3 weeks. We also reviewed the machine learning and deep learning algorithms for EEG classification to analyze our experimental data better [8,18,19,27,29,32].

1.3 Purpose of Study

For this reason, the purpose of the study is to generate long-term sleep data of a college student using a comfortable and non-intrusive EEG headset, and ultimately use the data to train a ML algorithm that can diagnose the college student's optimal sleeping patterns. If successful, the study would attempt to refine the algorithm such that it could be applied to other healthy college students to find their optimal sleeping patterns. As alluded to above, this study could be extremely beneficial to college students, since the knowledge of one's sleeping schedule can pay dividends on an individual's physical and mental health.

1.4 Research Question

Thus, the research question we intend to answer is: How can we use ML models and EEG technology to accurately detect an individual college student's optimal sleeping schedule?

2 Method

2.1 Dataset

The dataset used for this study contains 41 full nights of sleep data and was provided by an undergraduate college student (who will remain anonymous for privacy concerns). The college student is a 19 year-old Caucasian male from the United States, and is a generally healthy individual who maintains a healthy diet, drinks a sufficient amount of water, and frequently exercises. In additional to the clinical experimental devices [8,20,28], there are several consumer-grade non-invasive EEG headsets available at the time of the experiment [15,25,34]. The subject used a Muse S (Generation 2) headband for recording sleep sessions (see Fig. 1). The dataset includes a number of metrics for each of the 41 nights of sleep data. Specifically, bed time, wake time, time in bed, time asleep, sleep stages, sleep position, sleep intensity, heart rate, stillness, and a value of 1–100 representing the overall quality of a given night's sleep were recorded. Bedtime and wake time refer to the times at which the subject fell asleep and woke up for any given session, with time in bed being the difference between these two metrics and sleep duration being the amount of total time the subject was asleep. The sleep stage metric recorded the total amount of time the subject spent in each of the four sleep stages: awake, rapid eye movement (REM), light sleep, and deep. Sleep position refers to the amount of time the subject spent sleeping on each their left side, right side, back, and front. Sleep intensity measured the relative intensity of a given night's sleep. Stillness was determined by the total amount of time the subject was "active" and "relaxed" throughout the night. Lastly, the dataset includes a single statistic summarizing the quality of the subject's sleep for any given night, with a score of 75 translating roughly to an average night's sleep for the average person. This value is determined by the Muse headset's software, and is trusted to be a reasonably accurate numerical representation of the quality of a given session.

Fig. 1. Diagram of Muse S and sensors.

2.2   Note on Exportation of Dataset

When collecting data using the Muse S headset, the subject synced the headset with the official Muse mobile application, which provides an interface for viewing logged sleep sessions. In recent years, Muse removed the capability to export raw EEG files from the application, and provides no alternate method for recovering the raw EEG files. For this reason, the data that was presented in the Muse application was manually entered into a spreadsheet in .xlsx format. Thus, it should be noted that the data is preprocessed by the official Muse application.

2.3   Accessing the Dataset

For ease of reproducibility, the study's official GitHub page details the process of downloading the dataset. The page is available at https://github.com/ztgillette/optimal-sleep-algorithm.

2.4   Overview of Experimental Design

Using the set of an individual's sleep data, the intention of the experiment is to create a model that predicts the aspects of an optional night's sleep for that person. As described in the dataset section, bed time, wake time, time in bed, time asleep, sleep stages, sleep position, sleep intensity, heart rate, stillness, and a value of 1–100 representing the overall quality of a given night's sleep were recorded for a set of nights. Since a metric that represents the overall quality of sleep is provided, it is possible to apply machine learning algorithms to learn to classify certain ranges of sleep metrics with their corresponding sleep scores. In other words, machine learning can be utilized to learn what values for each of the sleep metrics correspond with better nights of sleep. Since these sets of values are determined to result in a better night's sleep, they are considered the desirable metrics that subjects would intend to emulate each night in practical use. However, given that certain metrics such as average heart rate, sleep intensity, and stillness are usually out of one's control during sleep, we are most interested in the relationship between bed time, wake time, and sleep duration and their corresponding sleep scores, since these metrics can be easily controlled by the subject. We are interested in aspects of the data that subject can control because the model can then be used as a tool to aid subjects in determining their best sleep practices. Thus, by analyzing the set of bed times, wake times, and sleep duration times that correspond to higher sleep scores, we can determine the bed times, wake times, and sleep duration that are most beneficial for the subject based on their given data.

2.5   Comparison of Algorithms

EEG data is a type of personalized time-series data [8, 19, 26]. In order to perform the experiment, the appropriate algorithm has to be selected to accurately determine which types of sleep data correspond with high sleep scores. Because the experiment requires selecting a known class for a collection of data, a supervised classification algorithm is ideal. A number of algorithms meet this criteria, including K-Nearest Neighbor (KNN), Support Vector Machine (SVM), Linear Discriminant Analysis (LDA), and Decision Tree Classifiers, among others [18, 29, 30]. Two of the most common and widely discussed algorithms used when processing EEG signals are KNN and SVM. More specifically, both KNN and SVM have been extensively used and analyzed in previous work in relation to EEG signals, with a range of results from different studies. For example, Mousa et al. [22] demonstrates a relative higher accuracy and fidelity in the KNN model when used for EEG signals compared to the SVM model. However, Amancio et al. [3] shows a greater accuracy of SVM models in comparison to KNN models.

Generally speaking, the KNN Machine learning model takes a predefined number of K samples closest to a point and predicts the label from these. The number of K samples can be user defined and a constant, or can vary based on density of points. The distance between points is usually measured in Euclidean distance. As a supervised model, KNN first computes the K nearest neighbors through training, and then uses that training to predict the nearest neighbors for a given dataset, hence categorizing data points into the predetermined labels (see Fig. 1). While SVMs are also supervised machine learning models, their implementation varies from that of KNNs. SVMs work by projecting non-linear data onto higher dimension space (also known as the kernel trick). In doing so, SVMs make it easier to classify data. Through this process, an optimal boundary between possible output can be found. This allows the algorithm to figure out how to separate or classify the data based on defined labels or outputs (see Fig. 2). Additionally, LDA is a statistical model for topic modeling. Although this topic modeling algorithm is usually used as an unsupervised form of classification, often used for preprocessing of data, it can also be used as a supervised form of classification. More specifically, LDA uses matrix factorization to solve classification problems. LDA is especially useful when needing to reduce features of a higher dimensional space onto a lower dimensional space. Hence, it is able to reduce both resources and dimensional costs (see Fig. 3). Finally, a Decision Tree Classifier (DTC) is a tree-structured classifier, where internal nodes represent the features of a dataset, branches represent the decision rules and each leaf node represents the outcome. There exists two main types of DTCs, those which have a continuous target variable - Continuous variable decision trees - and those which have a categorical target variable - Categorical variable decision trees (see Fig. 4). Hence, this study focuses on how EEG data can be precisely categorized by comparing all four of the aforementioned ML algorithms in order to assess the best approach for further research in determining optimal sleep schedules.

2.6   Implementation of the Machine Learning Algorithms

We implement SVM, KNN, LDA, and DTC models for this study. All four of the ML models are implemented using the scikit-learn machine learning library, as noted in the provided repository. Additionally, some of the ML models are implemented using specific parameters. For instance, for the SVM algorithm, we implement a SVM model using a linear kernel, creating a single hyperplane to categorize sleep data into two categories: accurate and not accurate. Due to only needing one kernel for the two categories, we can maximize scalability and practicality in using a linear SVM as opposed to a non-linear SVM algorithm. Another specific parameter that we use is for the KNN algorithm, for which we implement a KNN model using $K = 5$ as the K value.

We implement all four of the ML algorithms using a train-test split of 80/20 (see Fig. 2). We run each model 100,000 times, each iteration with a new train-test set of data, and use the mean accuracy rate to determine the algorithm performance. The accuracy rate of a given algorithm is determined by comparing the predicted overall quality score with the actual overall quality score. If the predicted overall quality value is within a certain window, we deem the given prediction accurate. We coin this term the correctness window. For instance, a predicted sleep quality score of 83 with an actual sleep quality score of 85 would fit within a correctness window of 5, as 83 is less than 5 over or under the actual score of 85 (see Fig. 3). In order to analyze and test the four ML models, we utilize a correctness window of 7.5, deeming a predicted score within that window accurate.

Dataset train-test split
300+ hours of sleep

Test data
20.0%

20.0%

80.0%

Train data
80.0%

Fig. 2. The pie chart represents an 80/20 train-test split with over 300 h of sleep collected.

Correctness Window

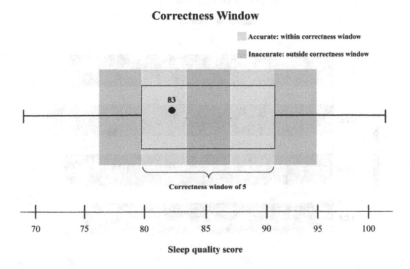

Accurate: within correctness window

Inaccurate: outside correctness window

83

Correctness window of 5

70   75   80   85   90   95   100

Sleep quality score

Fig. 3. Diagram of correctness window. A predicted sleep quality score of 83 with an actual score of 85 fits within a correctness window of 5. Hence, the predicted score is deemed accurate.

2.7 Effectiveness of the Machine Learning Algorithms

As indicated by Fig. 4, SVM is shown to be the most effective classification algorithm for our task with an accuracy rate of over 65%. The other algorithms follow in accuracy in descending order: KNN, DTC, and LDA, respectively. It is worth noting that neither ML model demonstrates a relatively high accuracy, being evident of a need for future research and the possible limitations of this study. This is further discussed in the Discussion and Conclusion. However, due to being the algorithm with the highest accuracy, SVM is used in the second part of this study.

2.8 Applying SVM

Given that SVM is shown to be the most effective classification algorithm for our task with an accuracy rate of over 65%, we select it for the task of determining the relationship between sleep metrics and their overall sleep scores. With the algorithm already trained from the previous phase of comparing the effectiveness of the algorithms on the dataset, the SVM algorithm is then used to generate the bed times, wake times, and sleep duration times that correspond to desirable sleep scores. Here, we consider "desirable" to be any sleep score that meets or exceeds a certain threshold determined by the user. In our results, we set this mark as a sleep score of 90, meaning that only bed times, wake times, and sleep duration times that resulted in a score of 90 or more would be considered in the final output.

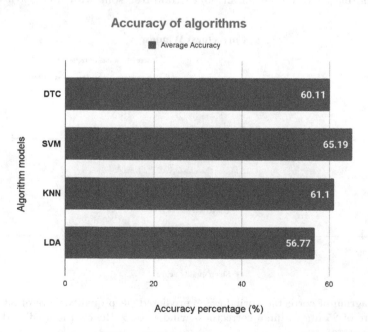

Fig. 4. Average accuracy of ML models based on a correctness window of 7.5; 100,000 total iterations.

To determine these sleep times, we first generated a set of 100,000 sample nights of sleep. Each sample night was set with data that was generated randomly using realistic values from the dataset. Specifically, for each category of data for any given sample night, a random value between the minimum and maximum for that value in the dataset was selected. By creating these 100,000 sample nights, we then could apply the trained SVM algorithm to determine which of the nights would be expected to yield a score of 90 or more. We filtered out sample nights of data that were not expected to reach an overall sleep score of 90, leaving only data that was expected to yield "desirable" scores. From this subset, we then considered only the bed times, wake times, and sleep duration values, and calculated their mean and median values. Presented in the figure below are the Sleep Prediction Results that were determined from the median values for each bed time, wake time, and sleep duration. Note, the results include a window of 15 min to provide a more logistically-attainable bed, wake, and sleep duration time.

3 Result

The predicted sleep schedule for the subject is as follows: 9 h and 30 min of sleep, with a bedtime of 1:00am with a precision of up to 15 min, and a wake time of 10:04 am with a precision of up to 15 min (see Table 1).

Table 1. Optimal sleep prediction results using a SVM classification model; 1000 iterations.

Sleep prediction results	
Optimal bedtime	1:00 AM + / − 15 min
Optimal wake time	10:04 AM + / − 15 min
Optimal sleep duration	9 h 30 min + / − 15 min

4 Discussion and Future Work

Based on the reasonable nature of our results given our dataset, as well as their correspondence with general sleep recommendations for teenagers and young adults, we believe that our algorithm is generally effective in predicting the optimal sleep schedules for teenagers and young adults. This can be compared to studies by Richards et al. [31] as well as Gillen-O'Neel et al. [10], which show that teenagers and young adults need approximately a little over 9 h of sleep.

However, we also believe that three specific improvements to our dataset would greatly improve the accuracy. Firstly, it would be greatly beneficial to collect additional nights of sleep data, since this would improve the ability of the SVM algorithm to accurately classify the sleep data with its overall sleep score. Specifically, we would like to curate upwards of 100 nights of sleep data.

On that front, a significant increase in the number of nights of data would make it possible to apply a deep learning algorithm such as CNN or RNN to the dataset. We refrained from implementing deep learning algorithms during this initial stage of research, since deep learning algorithms tend to require large amounts of data to be effective. In addition to opening the door to deep learning algorithms, adding additional nights of sleep data would also create the possibility that another machine learning algorithm (KNN, LDA, etc.) exceed SVM in accuracy. This is due to the general trait of machine learning algorithms of having varying accuracy rates depending on the size of the datasets. Secondly, it would be optimal to recruit additional subjects to partake in the study. An inherent limitation to the study as it has currently been performed is that only one subject was utilized. While our algorithm proved effective for our single subject, there is no evidence to say that such an algorithm would be effective if applied to an alternate set of sleep data from a different subject. For this reason, we intend in our future work to recruit 10–15 additional college-aged individuals so that the algorithm can be trained to be effective for generally for college students rather than for the single subject that was used in this initial stage of the experiment. Thirdly, we recognize that manually creating a dataset using preprocessed data from the Muse mobile application is neither a desired nor logistically sustainable approach for the future work of this study. For this reason, we have recently begun advising that our subject use a third-party application called Mind Monitor to record their nights of sleep, since the application allows for the raw EEG data from the Muse headset to be collected in DropBox and exported in a variety of file types.

In addition to the limitations posed by our dataset, we also want to address some potential limitations in our future work so that they can be avoided. We expect our primary limitation to be our ability to recruit additional subjects to partake in the study. One reason for this is due to the inconvenience of wearing the Muse headset while sleeping. While the Muse S headset is significantly more comfortable than other EEG-collecting head trackers, it is still an instrument that can be uncomfortable while sleeping. Additionally, since the Muse S is powered by rechargeable batteries, charging and/or battery issues often result in the headset not being fully charged when the subject desires to go to bed. Moreover, in order to get the most accurate EEG readings, it is necessary for the headset to maintain direct contact with the skin on one's head. This means that individuals with hair on the sides of their head may have significant trouble creating a sufficient connection between the headset and their skin, meaning that a close-cut haircut or a significant amount of nightly hair manipulation is necessary. In addition to inconveniences regarding the Muse headset, we also expect the length of the study to deter potential subjects. As noted in our discussion of the dataset, we plan to collect over 100 nights of sleep for each subject to ensure that the machine learning algorithms have sufficient data to train. Given that 100 nights is well over 3 months of commitment, we find it unlikely that college students would be willing to participate. An alternative that we have considered is using smart watches to track sleep data. This solution would provide a more comfortable and less invasive alternative to wearing Muse headsets. Additionally, smart watches tend to have longer and more consistent battery lives than the Muse headsets, meaning that charging-related issues would not pose as much of a barrier. Finally, due to their comfortable and easy-to-use design, it is more likely that college students would be willing to commit to months or potentially years of nightly data collection.

5 Conclusion

Given the importance of sleep in maintaining a healthy lifestyle, especially for teenagers and young adults, our research was focused on devising an algorithm to optimize sleep schedules on an individualized level. We created a dataset of over 300 h of sleep data for a single subject, and used that dataset to train four machine learning algorithms. We found that SVM proved most accurate in classifying our sleep data, and selected it as our algorithm of choice for determining the optimal bed times, wake times, and sleep duration times for the subject. Using SVM, we determined that based on the collected dataset, the subject's ideal bedtime was about 1:00am and ideal wake time was about 10:00am, with their ideal total sleep duration being around 9.5 h. While these results appear reasonable based on the dataset, we expect that a number of adjustments in our dataset would lead to increased precision. In our future work, we would like to record additional nights of data in our dataset, recruit 10–15 subjects to record nightly data, and use raw EEG data rather than preprocessed data. Ultimately, we hope that with this study we are able to provide a foundation for future work towards more accurate results, and towards more individualized sleep data collection and healthcare.

References

1. Abdulla, S., Diykh, M., Laft, R.L., Saleh, K., Deo, R.C.: Sleep EEG signal analysis based on correlation graph similarity coupled with an ensemble extreme machine learning algorithm. Expert Syst. Appl. **138**, 112790 (2019)
2. Aboalayon, K.A., Almuhammadi, W.S., Faezipour, M.: A comparison of different machine learning algorithms using single channel eeg signal for classifying human sleep stages. In: 2015 Long Island Systems, Applications and Technology, pp. 1–6. IEEE (2015)
3. Amancio, D.R., et al.: A systematic comparison of supervised classifiers. PLoS ONE **9**(4), e94137 (2014)
4. Ansari, A.H., et al.: Quiet sleep detection in preterm infants using deep convolutional neural networks. J. Neural Eng. **15**(6), 066006 (2018)
5. Arnal, P.J., et al.: Auditory closed-loop stimulation to enhance sleep quality. J. Sci. Med. Sport **20**, S95 (2017)
6. Bruce, E.S., Lunt, L., McDonagh, J.E.: Sleep in adolescents and young adults. Clin. Med. **17**(5), 424 (2017)
7. Chaput, J.P., et al.: Sleep timing, sleep consistency, and health in adults: a systematic review. Appl. Physiol. Nutr. Metab. **45**(10), S232–S247 (2020)

8. Craik, A., He, Y., Contreras-Vidal, J.L.: Deep learning for electroencephalogram (EEG) classification tasks: a review. J. Neural Eng. 16(3), 031001 (2019)
9. Ferrara, M., De Gennaro, L.: How much sleep do we need? Sleep Med. Rev. 5(2), 155–179 (2001)
10. Gillen-O'Neel, C., Huynh, V.W., Fuligni, A.J.: To study or to sleep? the academic costs of extra studying at the expense of sleep. Child Dev. 84(1), 133–142 (2013)
11. Giri, E.P., Fanany, M.I., Arymurthy, A.M.: Combining generative and discriminative neural networks for sleep stages classification. arXiv preprint arXiv:1610.01741 (2016)
12. Hershner, S.D., Chervin, R.D.: Causes and consequences of sleepiness among college students. Nat. Sci. Sleep 6, 73 (2014)
13. Hor, H., Tafti, M.: How much sleep do we need? Science 325(5942), 825–826 (2009)
14. Hou, H., et al.: Association of obstructive sleep apnea with hypertension: a systematic review and meta-analysis. J. Global Health 8(1), 010405 (2018)
15. Ienca, M., Haselager, P., Emanuel, E.J.: Brain leaks and consumer neurotechnology. Nat. Biotechnol. 36(9), 805–810 (2018)
16. Ilhan, H.O., Bilgin, G.: Sleep stage classification via ensemble and conventional machine learning methods using single channel EEG signals. Int. J. Intell. Syst. Appl. Eng 5(4), 174–184 (2017)
17. Kemp, B., Zwinderman, A.H., Tuk, B., Kamphuisen, H.A., Oberye, J.J.: Analysis of a sleep-dependent neuronal feedback loop: the slow-wave microcontinuity of the EEG. IEEE Trans. Biomed. Eng. 47(9), 1185–1194 (2000)
18. Lotte, F., et al.: A review of classification algorithms for EEG-based brain-computer interfaces: a 10 year update. J. Neural Eng. 15(3), 031005 (2018)
19. Lotte, F., Congedo, M., Lécuyer, A., Lamarche, F., Arnaldi, B.: A review of classification algorithms for EEG-based brain-computer interfaces. J. Neural Eng. 4(2), R1 (2007)
20. Lotte, F., Jeunet, C., Mladenović, J., N'Kaoua, B., Pillette, L.: A bci challenge for the signal processing community: considering the user in the loop (2018)
21. Mikkelsen, K.B., et al.: Machine-learning-derived sleep-wake staging from around-the-ear electroencephalogram outperforms manual scoring and actigraphy. J. Sleep Res. 28(2), e12786 (2019)
22. Mousa, F.A., El-Khoribi, R.A., Shoman, M.E.: EEG classification based on machine learning techniques. Int. J. Comput. Appl. 975, 8887 (2015)
23. Okano, K., Kaczmarzyk, J.R., Dave, N., Gabrieli, J.D., Grossman, J.C.: Sleep quality, duration, and consistency are associated with better academic performance in college students. NPJ Sci. Learn. 4(1), 1–5 (2019)
24. Peker, M.: An efficient sleep scoring system based on EEG signal using complex-valued machine learning algorithms. Neurocomputing 207, 165–177 (2016)
25. Portillo-Lara, R., Tahirbegi, B., Chapman, C.A., Goding, J.A., Green, R.A.: Mind the gap: State-of-the-art technologies and applications for EEG-based brain-computer interfaces. APL bioengineering 5(3), 031507 (2021)
26. Qu, X., Hall, M., Sun, Y., Sekuler, R., Hickey, T.J.: A personalized reading coach using wearable EEG sensors-a pilot study of brainwave learning analytics. In: CSEDU, vol. (2), pp. 501–507 (2018)
27. Qu, X., Liu, P., Li, Z., Hickey, T.: Multi-class time continuity voting for EEG classification. In: Frasson, C., Bamidis, P., Vlamos, P. (eds.) BFAL 2020. LNCS (LNAI), vol. 12462, pp. 24–33. Springer, Cham (2020). https://doi.org/10.1007/978-3-030-60735-7_3

28. Qu, X., Liukasemsarn, S., Tu, J., Higgins, A., Hickey, T.J., Hall, M.H.: Identifying clinically and functionally distinct groups among healthy controls and first episode psychosis patients by clustering on eeg patterns. Front. Psych. **11**, 938 (2020)
29. Qu, X., Mei, Q., Liu, P., Hickey, T.: Using EEG to distinguish between writing and typing for the same cognitive task. In: Frasson, C., Bamidis, P., Vlamos, P. (eds.) BFAL 2020. LNCS (LNAI), vol. 12462, pp. 66–74. Springer, Cham (2020). https://doi.org/10.1007/978-3-030-60735-7_7
30. Qu, X., Sun, Y., Sekuler, R., Hickey, T.: EEG markers of stem learning. In: 2018 IEEE Frontiers in Education Conference (FIE), pp. 1–9. IEEE (2018)
31. Richards, A., et al.: Sleep and cognitive performance from teens to old age: more is not better. Sleep **40**(1), zsw029 (2017)
32. Roy, Y., Banville, H., Albuquerque, I., Gramfort, A., Falk, T.H., Faubert, J.: Deep learning-based electroencephalography analysis: a systematic review. J. Neural Eng. **16**(5), 051001 (2019)
33. Santaji, S., Desai, V.: Analysis of EEG signal to classify sleep stages using machine learning. Sleep Vigilance **4**(2), 145–152 (2020)
34. Van Erp, J., Lotte, F., Tangermann, M.: Brain-computer interfaces: beyond medical applications. Computer **45**(4), 26–34 (2012)
35. Vilamala, A., Madsen, K.H., Hansen, L.K.: Deep convolutional neural networks for interpretable analysis of eeg sleep stage scoring. In: 2017 IEEE 27th international workshop on machine learning for signal processing (MLSP), pp. 1–6. IEEE (2017)
36. Vimala, V., Ramar, K., Ettappan, M.: An intelligent sleep apnea classification system based on EEG signals. J. Med. Syst. **43**(2), 1–9 (2019)
37. Worley, S.L.: The extraordinary importance of sleep: the detrimental effects of inadequate sleep on health and public safety drive an explosion of sleep research. Pharm. Ther. **43**(12), 758 (2018)

Analysis and Design of an Information System for Blood Component Donations

Hemanth Reddy Boddukuru and Deniz Cetinkaya$^{(\boxtimes)}$ (iD)

Department of Computing and Informatics, Faculty of Science and Technology,
Bournemouth University, Poole BH12 5BB, UK
{s5230646,dcetinkaya}@bournemouth.ac.uk

Abstract. In the UK, NHS Blood and Transplant (NHSBT) administers the blood and transplantation service to National Health Service (NHS), overseeing blood collection in England and transplant facilities in the United Kingdom. This research focuses on improving blood component donations by using an information system. This paper presents system analysis and user interface design of an information system for blood component donations to improve the current process. The software system requirements were gathered via a focus group consisting of employees from a Blood Donation Centre in the UK. The problem space in the component donation process was analysed and human factors has been explored for potential users of the component donation information system. Both low-fidelity and high-fidelity designs have been designed where interactive user interfaces have been made on Adobe XD tool. Usability evaluation has been performed with potential users from the focus group using a cognitive walk through to examine usability concerns and user experience of the design prototype. Conclusions and future work have been presented for potential further research opportunities.

Keywords: User experience · Usability · Component donation · Information system design · Blood component donations information system · System analysis

1 Introduction

The demand for blood and its components is increasing in many countries due to several reasons such as the rising number of trauma patients, including those involved in road traffic accidents, cancer chemotherapy, patients requiring long-term blood therapy, such as sickle cell anaemia, etc. [1]. In the UK, NHS Blood and Transplant (NHSBT) administers the blood and transplantation service to National Health Service (NHS), overseeing blood collection in England and transplant facilities in the United Kingdom.

Our research focuses on improving blood component donations in the UK by introducing a new information system to the existing process. Although, there are studies in the literature regarding the blood donation process and its

V. G. Duffy et al. (Eds.): HCII 2022, LNCS 13521, pp. 26–45, 2022.
https://doi.org/10.1007/978-3-031-17902-0_3

improvement [2–7], component donation is slightly different and not covered much in the existing studies so there are limited research about it in the context of information systems. We focus on the component donation process in the UK, but the terms are similar in other developed countries [8,9]. However, it is difficult to say that there is a common standard for all countries. WHO recommends that all blood donation activities should be coordinated at the national level through effective organization and integrated supply networks, but only 73% of the reporting countries, or 125 out of 171, had a national blood policy according to 2018 data [10].

As it is known, human blood is a complex mixture of various components such as plasma, red blood cells, white blood cells and platelets [11]. When centrifugal force is applied, distinct blood components with different relative density, sediment rate, and scale can be differentiated [12]. Since each blood component has an individual purpose, the component isolation has increased the utility of a single whole blood unit. For therapeutic effectiveness, different blood components need different storage conditions and temperatures. Alternatively, to collect specific blood components from the donors, apheresis blood donations can be performed. Apheresis is the process of separating blood components from whole blood by using special equipment [13], hence the process is also known as component donation.

NHSBT involves managing blood, organ, skin, bone marrow, and stem cell donation, storage, and transplantation, as well as exploring alternative therapies and processes. According to the NHSBT Statistical Reports [14], there are 416,381 new registrations and 131,825 new donations in 2019-2020. The numbers show that NHSBT should cope with a large amount of data and information without compromising blood safety and donor safety. Due to high volume of data, there are issues and challenges during the donation process such as the potential inconsistent or wrong data if donor data and records were manually recorded [15]. Besides, when donor information is not stored properly or data is not well-structured, then it becomes difficult to use the data in the future as well as it affects the document's legibility.

Using information technologies in the management of component donations can support effective organization and tracking with streamlining the donation process. However, information of the donors should be confidential and blood safety is a crucial factor [15]. Using technologies such as barcodes in the component donation operations can enhance patient safety and ensure quality control. A reliable and secure information system is highly beneficial to users in data management and decision making by helping with effective management of the activities and digitally recording them. Furthermore, NHSBT Board Meeting in 2019 [14] has highlighted the need for future innovations to perform the component donation operations like electronic component day sheet, electronic donor health check, and electronic component donor procedure notes. The report also stated that there are various financial and non-financial benefits such as increasing the blood donation safety by reducing the number of errors, facilitating the management of data, improving the donation process, reducing the donor journey time, improving donor satisfaction, increasing front line staff morale, and enabling the future innovations [14]. In conclusion, there is a need for an information system to perform the component donations safely and securely to enhance donor safety and satisfaction.

This paper presents system analysis and user interface design of an information system for blood component donations to improve the current process. This research aims to digitally transform all operational activities for the component donation process and digitise the paper-based component donation records. The data collected from the participants were obtained from an online questionnaire. Personas and user empathy mapping facilitated understanding the user needs and behaviours, which allowed the creation of low fidelity wire frames. High fidelity designs and user interactions are created using Adobe XD tool. The design prototype has been evaluated by usability testing and collecting feedback from potential users.

The remaining of the paper is structured as follows: Next section presents the literature review and related work. Research methods are explained in Sect. 3. Problem space contextualisation and requirements analysis are given in Sect. 4. Design process and evaluation of the study are presented in Sect. 5 and 6 respectively. Finally, conclusions and potential future work are provided.

2   Literature Review

National Health Service Blood and Transplant (NHSBT) is responsible for various blood and transplantation services, including promoting tissue donation, delivering life-saving therapeutic apheresis, and managing patient blood. NHSBT is a special health authority, and it is responsible for saving and enhancing lives by supplying blood and supporting the supply of organs and tissues to the NHS, as well as overseeing blood donation services in England and transplant services throughout the UK [16].

NHSBT was founded in 2005 to combine the functions of two different NHS organisations: UK Transplant and the National Blood Service [16]. Since then, there are now more than 25 million people on the NHS Organ Donor Register, representing 38% of the population. Currently, NHSBT have five operational responsibilities including: (1) Blood donation and supply (2) Patient blood management (3) Organ donation and transplantation (4) Tissue and eye donation and (5) Therapeutic apheresis.

Therapeutic apheresis services of NHSBT use specialised equipment to exchange, remove, or collect particular components within the blood to give life-saving and life-enhancing therapies. Harris and McKeown [16] stated that NHSBT had treated over 1,200 adults and children each year from designated treatment units located around the UK.

In this study, our main focus is on the component donations. Blood donations are most commonly classified into two types which are whole blood donations and apheresis donations [17]. During the whole blood donation, one unit of blood is extracted from a donor; it will be separated into its constituent components in the lab later. However, apheresis donations, a.k.a component donations, allow the donor to maximise their contribution and donate specific blood components based on their blood type. The unique aspect of these donations is that only required blood components can be donated, with the rest can be given back to the donor.

Healthcare providers may face multiple operational challenges to get the blood and blood components according to their therapeutic requirement. Knight et al. [18] highlighted some challenges in the blood donation process.

- *High demand*: To meet the needs of hospitals, NHSBT must collect the proper combination of blood types and blood components daily. NHSBT has to recruit over 100K new donors each year to replace those who cannot donate for various reasons.
- *Donor satisfaction*: Donors are healthy volunteers and good donor experience is crucial to keep the existing donors and recruit new ones. Staff should be professional and ensure that the donor is comfortable during the process. At the same time, they must guarantee that the blood donation process is easy.
- *Component availability*: Hospitals should assist in preserving blood donations for those who genuinely require it, ensuring that the appropriate blood component is accessible for the appropriate patient at the appropriate time. Platelets are especially sensitive because of their limited shelf life.
- *Communication*: Information flow and communication plays an important role in the daily operations of the blood donation process because NHSBT is a nationwide organisation with geographically distributed donation centres.

2.1   Component Donation Process

Component donation is more flexible to donate various blood components than a whole blood donation, but it needs more time which may be up to two hours. Component separation is performed by special equipment that separates the blood components obtained from the donor by centrifuging, stacking them by weight and separating them from the liquid [17]. The device may then take out the necessary blood components and store them in a sterile bag. For employees performing component donation operations, a complete training program is offered in the donor management, donation process and procedures, and the apheresis equipment. It allows to maximise component donations based on particular component and blood type needs. In the literature, it is suggested that component donations are to be performed in the static blood donation centres but not in the mobile blood donation units [19]. NHS Give Blood had created a short video to provide an overview of the component donation process, and the outline of the process is illustrated in Fig. 1. Component donation process starts with welcoming the donor, and then donor completes the health questionnaire. The donor should be in good health. A qualified clinical professional must do the health screening of the donors. Donors who undergo component donation procedures may be subject to additional or separate criteria compared to whole

Fig. 1. Component donation process overview.

blood donors. If the eligibility criteria is satisfied, then component donation is done, and next appointment may be booked.

Various organisations regulate the blood donation centers to offer the best quality of blood products and service. For example, NHSBT is required to comply with the Blood Safety and Quality Regulations as well as follow the donor selection guidelines of the Joint UK Blood Transfusion and Tissue Transplantation Services Professional Advisory Committee. Those guidelines specify the criteria for determining whether or not a person is qualified to donate blood. In addition, Medicines and Healthcare Products Regulatory Agency (MHRA) conducts inspections to check the process, procedures and protocols [19].

2.2   Related Work

In the literature, there are studies regarding the blood donation process and its improvement [2–7]. HL7 (Health Level Seven) specification includes fields for blood component specification and a few blood banks utilize software including component management features [20]. However, these studies do not fully cover the blood component donations, e.g. platelets donation. There is limited research in the field of information system support for component donations.

All NHSBT staff are responsible and accountable for entering data and ensure that data entry is complete and legible. NHSBT uses the PULSE software system that empowers the blood donation life cycle. All elements of blood donation and processing are handled by this management system and it is in use for many years [21]. PULSE system helps to enrol donors and manage the laboratory activities such as testing, labelling, stock tracking, supply and delivery of blood to hospitals and medical research facilities.

A new system called as 'Session Solutions' has been introduced to have a more efficient donation procedure [18], especially focusing on mobile blood donation centres which require portable handheld devices to track a donor's progress during the session. These devices offer real-time data exchange among the NHSBT and streamline the donation process. The new system is expected to enhance donor safety and donor experience by improving ineffective working practices [14]. Existing system offers some partial operational and database support for the component donations, but this is limited. Currently, staff perform the component donor recruitment, donation documentation, and future donation appointments manually. Digital transformation of the component donations strives to improve donor experience as pleasant as possible. However, there are many challenges to the change. The component donation process should enhance aspects of donor experience like scheduling, processing time, and apparent effects, as well as reduce the cost and effort.

There are different parameters that drive or discourage people from donating blood [22]. To advertise, encourage, attract, and retain blood donors, several approaches have been investigated using ICT and smart devices. Donor motivation for blood donation can be effected by altruism, self-interest, and responsiveness to direct or societal influence. In this regard, the introduction and expanding usage of digital collaboration platforms may be an effective tool for increasing blood donation, particularly among the younger generation [22].

NHSBT is looking to secure the systems by bringing in the latest and cutting-edge technologies like cloud services to provide resilience, scalability, and flexible solutions to integrate standard operating procedures of blood donation. For example, 'DonorPath' app is launched to transform risk assessment operations in organ donation to make it easier for nurses to fill in the risk profile.

The digital transformation of the component donations process should involve a multidisciplinary team to gather the requirements and design a system to enhance the donor experience and support new donor recruitment. The success of the digital transformation depends on the system compliance with the regulatory procedures. The ongoing registration of new donors and concurrently preserving previous donor records, i.e. launching a new system while maintaining the legacy one, is a challenge due to the critical nature of the process.

To the best of our knowledge, while there are systems in use for whole blood donations, research about IT support for blood component donations is limited. Our research focuses on improving blood component donations by introducing a new information system to the existing process and aim to fill in the gap in information system support for component donation process and operations.

3   Research Methods

In this study, we used Checkland's Soft Systems Methodology (SSM) as applying SSM in health domain is a proven approach and used in the literature commonly [23,24]. Checkland points out that it is useful to consider potential users' aspirations and include them at various stages of the analysis and design.

We did a qualitative study and used various methods including focus group, interviews, usability testing, etc. The software system requirements were gathered via a focus group consisting of employees from a Blood Donation Centre in the UK. The problem space in the component donation process was analysed and human factors has been explored for potential users of the component donation system. Both low-fidelity and high-fidelity designs has been designed where interactive user interfaces have been made on Adobe XD tool. Usability evaluation has been performed with potential users from the focus group using a cognitive walk through to examine usability concerns and user experience (UX) of the design prototype.

Interviews are one of the most effective ways to acquire system requirements from the potential users and domain experts. However, due to the Covid19 pandemic and social distancing measures during the research, the researcher has chosen online questionnaires to collect data from the participants. The questionnaires aim to collect targeted data of functional, non-functional and user requirements about the application early in the designing process. The user insights may support the design thinking process and drive the research to achieve the rationale. Component donors are not included in the study's target participants due to the time constraints but included as a future work. Participants are chosen from the staff members in donation centres, specifically employees from Poole Donor Centre in the UK have joined this study.

The online questionnaire was created using the Microsoft forms tool, with the sections of the participant information sheet, participant consent form and over 25 questions regarding the functional, non-functional and user requirements. Participants were contacted through social media and the online questionnaire was open from 20/04/2021 to 30/04/2021. The participants were selected and invited from those with working experience and knowledge of the component donation process. Eleven participants have participated in the online questionnaire from Poole Donor Centre who have various roles.

The data was analysed with Microsoft forms tool. The critical findings based on the participants' responses are summarised below:

- 91% of the participants required a barcode scanning feature in the system.
- 82% of the participants recommended the system should generate reconciliation reports.
- 82% of the participants suggested that signature fields should be embedded in the forms.
- 91% of the participants agreed that the system must comply with GRPD and data protection guidelines.
- 64% of the participants agreed that the system should not navigate the next screen without fulfilling mandatory fields and must display required fields.
- 64% of the participants required the blood group management feature.

while only,

- 55% of the participants required the detection of donor signatures mismatch in the donor consent form and donor health check questionnaire.
- 55% of the participants required an electronic donor health check form.
- 55% of the participants agreed that the system should be interoperable.
- 45% of the participants required a validation alert feature.
- 36% of the participants agreed to restrict the number of concurrent users.
- 36% of the participants wanted to have an aesthetic look.

The primary purpose of the online questionnaire is to gather some of the system requirements from the potential users to design an information system that can digitally transform component donations. The results from the online questionnaire have shown the significant importance of an information system that supports the component donation process because major features scored high 80% percentage or higher. According to the results, we identified that the staff prioritises facilitation of core functionality and easy to use system over advanced features or decision support because desirable features scored average 55% percentage or lower.

4 Problem Space Contextualisation and Analysis

4.1 Problem Analysis

The digital transformation of component donations and designing a new information system to support component donations is a challenging task and require a thorough analysis of the problem space. When dealing with complicated issues and enhancing project activities, driver diagrams can help to find a solution to the problem [25]. Driver diagrams, a.k.a tree diagrams, can provide what modifications are most likely to result in the desired outcomes and attainment of the aim. This problem analysis technique is suitable to get insights for designing an information system. Creating driver diagrams is beneficial during the initial phases of the study, but they should also be used throughout the study. Three stages are depicted in basic driver diagrams (aim, primary drivers and actions). Driver diagrams for more complicated goals include more layers, so each principal driver has its own set of supporting elements. Table 1 presents the analysis of the problem space.

Table 1. Driver diagram for problem analysis.

Aim	Primary drivers	Actions
Improve donor Experience	Decrease in waiting time	Appointment management
	Smooth journey of donors	Pre-booked appointments
	Efficient blood collection planning	Robust IT system
	Best use of resources	
Reduce the errors	Training for staff	Using IT
	Collaboration between the staff	Signature validation
	Mitigation of preventable errors	Barcode technology
Improve the process	Paper-based donor records Storage	Digital donor library
System usage by donors and staff	Donor health check	Electronic donation records
	Consent forms	Accessible to all parties
	Procedure notes	
Reduce the workload	Manual documentation process	Donor management
	Data Protection	Blood group management

As mentioned before, currently, staff perform the component donor recruitment, donation documentation, and future donation appointments manually. The proposed system can help to overcome the challenges of accountability in the component donations within blood donation centres. It can also help to reduce the financial burden for printing weekly Donor Health Check Forms and the storage and retrieval charges for the forms [14]. Especially, such an information system can overcome the inconsistency issues and dependencies of the paper-based donor records.

4.2 System Requirements

During the early iteration process, system requirements are gathered from the users using online questionnaires. The potential users of the system can be Donor Carers, Donor Centre Supervisors, Donor Carer Administrators, Session Nurses, Component Donors and Blood Donation Centre Managers. The system should mainly provide a digital library or repository for component donors' records and donations as well as help to manage appointments. The MoSCoW model prioritises system needs to determine needs for system design. Table 2 presents the major system requirements according to the MoSCoW model.

Table 2. System requirements.

Must	The system must perform appointment management
	The system must have a barcode scanning feature
	The system must perform session reconciliation
	The system must generate an Electronic Donor Health Check record
	The system must validate the donor's signatures
	The system must provide a signature field where required
	The system must generate an electronic donor number record
	The system must generate an electronic donation day sheet
	The system must have a blood group management feature
	The system must comply with GDPR and Data Protection Act
	The system must provide user login authentication
	The system must back up the data automatically
	The system must be available all the time
	The system must not proceed without fulfilling mandatory fields
	The system must perform all the operation without fail
Should	The system should generate electronic donor procedure notes
	The system should not restrict the number of users
	The system should be interoperable
	The system should give a response in three seconds
	The system should have an aesthetic look
	The system should provide a validation alert to the user
	The system should show the status of the process

Use case modelling is used to capture and understand the behaviour of the system. Use case modelling is helpful to know what a system needs to achieve, considering who will use it. Figure 2 illustrates a high level use case of the system where actors are the interface users like donation centre staff and donors who interact with the system for a specified use case.

5 Design Process

Designing a usable and human-centred interface can be challenging. Because the design process frequently involves many groups of individuals from many departments, creating and organising ideas to find a solution. Design plays a vital part

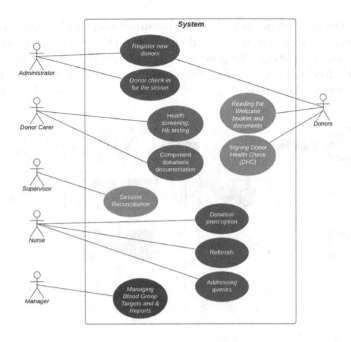

Fig. 2. Use cases of the system.

in the invention and development of meaningful processes, as well as contributing to product functionality, aesthetics, and usability [26]. A design thinking approach extends beyond goods and services to combine an understanding of technical challenges with respect for the socio-cultural environment [26].

Design thinking is an iterative approach that allows teams to understand people, question assumptions better, re-frame challenges and develop and test novel solutions [27]. Design thinking offers a problem-solving strategy centred on solutions and a set of practical techniques. It enables us to observe and empathise with the target user. By addressing the problem in human-centric ways, developing ideas in brainstorming sessions, and using a hands-on approach with design prototyping and design testing, design thinking is highly beneficial in resolving ill-defined or unknown challenges [27]. Empathy is essential in a human-centred design approach like design thinking because it helps you acquire meaningful user insights and their needs.

According to the design thinking process, a design process map has been created in this study to support the design process. A process map may assist a design team in scaling, designing quickly and maintaining brand harmony as well as aid other groups, such as project managers or developers [28]. In the design process map, there are four phases: ideation, definition, iteration, and implementation [28]. In the ideation phase, understanding the users and product strategy have foremost importance. The system's primary goal is to improve the donor experience by digitally transforming the component donation process. In the next phase, definition of the subsystems and implementation of human-centred design principles are done. In the third phase, prototyping the design solution and testing with potential users are performed. Finally, according to the user's feedback, redesigning the prototype and delivering the improved version are aimed. The steps of the design approach are depicted in Fig. 3.

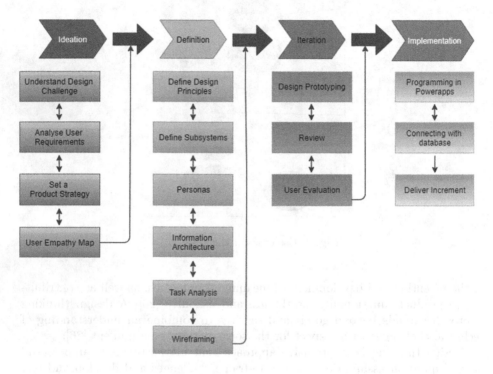

Fig. 3. Design process map.

5.1   User Empathy Mapping

Empathy mapping is used in this study to construct user personas and to identify and prioritise user requirements. It is used to find knowledge gaps and classify qualitative data obtained from the online questionnaires. User empathy maps assist the project team in comprehending the user's perspective and help to visualise user attitudes and actions. Mapping procedure identifies any gaps in current user data [29]. Five maps are developed for Donor Carer, Donor Carer Supervisor, Donor Centre Administrator, Session Nurse and Donor Centre Manager. As an example, Fig. 4 illustrates the empathy map of a Donor Carer. Empathy mapping is a collaborative visual tool that illustrates what we know about a specific user group. It externalises user knowledge to facilitate decision-making and build a shared understanding of user demands [29].

Fig. 4. Empathy mapping for Donor Carer.

The user or persona is in the centre of traditional empathy maps, which are divided into four quadrants (Says, Thinks, Does, and Feels). Empathy maps are not chronological or sequential but rather present a snapshot of who a person is as a whole [29]. In Fig. 4, the first quadrant depicts the system requirements gathered from participants during the online survey. The user's behaviours are illustrated in the other quadrants.

5.2 User Personas

Personas give user research a face, transforming data into information that improves user experience. A persona is a realistic character sketch that represents a user or a focus group. Personas condense user research results and bring them to life in a way that allows anybody to make judgments based on these personas rather than on themselves [30]. Creating fictional characters of users according to the user research should represent the users and can be utilised by the project team as a decision-making tool. Personas help people to focus, build empathy, encourage consensus, increase efficiency, and help people make better decisions. Personas also assist in developing information architecture, interaction design, visual design, content development and user evaluation in the designing process [30]. In this study, five distinct personas are being created to represent each user segment. As an example, Donor Carer persona is illustrated in Fig. 5.

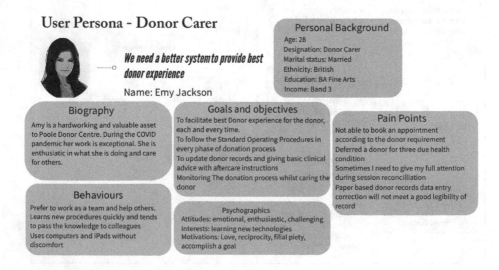

Fig. 5. Donor carer user persona.

Mulder and Yaar [30] proposed three phases in developing personas; conduct research, segment users based on research, and create a persona for each segment. In this study, the preliminary information for developing personas is obtained from online questionnaires, a design process map, and user empathy mapping.

Users have been separated into two main segments, blood donation centre staff and donors. A good persona is intended to be detailed representations of users that go beyond demographic or personal information and include such as goals, motivations, behavioural and cognitive details [31].

5.3   Wireframes Design and Information Flow

Human factors in the design process focus on how humans interact with technology [32]. There are three types of human demands that a system or device can make are cognitive, visual, and motor loads [33]. Most common human-centred design principles to decrease the user's loads are: physical ergonomics, consistency, familiarity, sense of control, efficiency error management [32]. A wireframe is a low fidelity representation of a proposed design. Wireframes link the information architecture to its user interface design [34]. Balsamiq tool is used to design the wireframes for this project. Over 25 wireframes were designed with a consistent layout. As example, four of the screen designs are shown in Fig. 6.

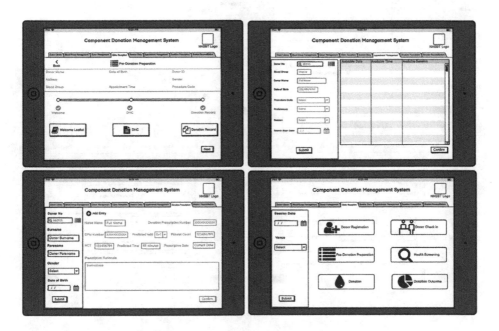

Fig. 6. Sample wireframes of the system.

There are mainly two approaches in designing information architecture for a digital product, the top-down approach and the bottom-up approach. The top-down information architecture entails building the architecture directly from the product goals and user requirements while the bottom-up approach focuses on low level components and their composition to reach the goals. Top-down method is also categorised into two approaches, narrow and deep hierarchy and broad and shallow hierarchy [34]. The broad and shallow hierarchy is used in this study to decrease cognitive load for users and to decrease the number of taps to reach the desired content. Both global navigation and local navigation are embedded in all of the user screens.

In addition to wireframes, high fidelity designs are created in Adobe XD tool. Over 50 user interface designs were prepared with a consistent layout. Four sample screen designs are illustrated in Fig. 7. The designs were made to launch the system on iPad based on user needs and research. Data elements in the design are extracted from the participants and open-source training documents such as standard operating procedures for donor procedure notes, donor health check, component day sheet, and donor centre reconciliation [14].

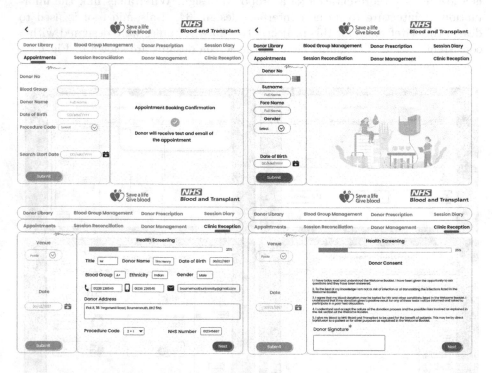

Fig. 7. User interface design with Adobe XD.

The designs generated by Adobe XD allows interactive prototyping by defining the flow between the user screens. Interactive prototype allows people to scrutinise design concepts and content [35] and so it enables stakeholders to interact with it and evaluate its usability. A high-fidelity prototype looks and functions more like the final product than a low-fidelity prototype.

6 Usability Evaluation

The need for high-quality software systems is continually growing. However, despite significant investments in software development, a wide range of software solutions cannot fulfil user-specific goals. Ouhbi et al. [36] present as study about the compliance of blood donation applications with the mobile platform usability guidelines. They report that around 35% of the applications had issues with usability. So, it is essential to evaluate a digital product to see how well people can understand and utilise it to achieve their objectives. There are various evaluation methods to find usability and user experience issues in a system. This research used the Cognitive Walk through evaluation approach to detect usability concerns in the design prototype. The cognitive walk through can be applied at every stage of product development, including conceptual design, detailed design, and implementation [37]. Users learn the new product by product exploration process, not through a training. There are several steps for a cognitive walk through evaluation and we used an adapted approach of Wilson's [37] in this study as illustrated in Fig. 8.

Fig. 8. Cognitive walk through process in this project.

Define Product Users: The project cognitive walk through evaluation starts with defining the users for the assessment. Because various personas may follow multiple pathways through the system, it is also a good idea to employ persona-matched users [37]. Considering this, we preferred to have a small group of users who took part in the online questionnaire, to evaluate the design prototype.

Create Evaluation Guidelines: We created the evaluation instructions sheet, which consists of information on the purpose of the evaluation, an overview description of the design prototype, and participants' role and responsibilities throughout the evaluation.

Develop Tasks and Action Sequences: The tasks and action sequences for each task were created based on the user personas to discover usability concerns for each component of the persona. Table 3 depicts the list of task and action sequences for the tasks used in the project. We asked four questions for each task to analyse the cognitive process and learnability of the user [38].

Summarise the Findings: Due to Covid19 pandemic and social distancing measures during the time that this project was done, we could not employ user testing but instead the Microsoft Forms tool has been used to record the responses from the users with associated participants instructions document and a link for the design prototype. Hence, only limited number of user responses were recorded to find the usability concerns of the design prototype. We summarised the findings of the usability evaluation to highlight the issues and list the actions.

Table 3. Tasks and action sequences for each task used in cognitive walk through.

Task	Action Sequence
1. Navigate to the home screen	After entering the correct login credentials
	Click on submit button
2. Print the session diary	Home screen → Click on session diary button
	Select the right venue and date
	Click on submit → Scroll down → Print
3. Edit A+ blood group targets in blood group management	Home Screen → Blood group management
	Select the right blood group and date
	Click on edit → Update → Save
4. Book a new appointment for future donations	Home screen → Appointments
	Enter or scan donor details
	Click on submit → Select date and time
	Submit → Confirm
5. Regist era new donor in the clinic reception	Home screen → Clinic reception
	Select the right venue and date
	Click on submit → Donor registration
	Enter donor details → Registration → Confirm
6. Update the donor contact details	Home screen → Donor management
	Enter or scan donor details
	Click on submit → Personal information
	Click on edit → Update → Save
7. Archive the donor record	Home screen → Donor management
	Enter or scan donor details
	Click on submit → Archive
	Click on add entry → Enter data → Confirm

7   Conclusion

This research started with exploring the existing knowledge in the component donation domain and collecting the software system requirements. This research produced a design prototype that will be used to implement a proof-of-concept implementation. The data collected from the participants' were obtained from an online questionnaire. Personas and user empathy mapping facilitated understanding the user needs and behaviours, which allowed the creation of low fidelity wire frames. High fidelity designs and user interactions are created using Adobe XD tool. We could only present some of the maps, personas, diagrams, etc. in this paper, but all of the remaining design elements as well as any other information, such as the questions in the online questionnaire, are available upon request by contacting the authors. The design prototype has been evaluated with some limitations in the participation and highlighted specific critical usability issues. Our study was validated by usability testing and collecting feedback from potential users.

Despite the interesting findings, this study has several limitations. Firstly, the sample group only targets a small number of employees from a blood donation center in the UK. Secondly, the study focused mainly on gathering requirements from the participants using an online questionnaire as a method. If a more comprehensive survey was distributed to all UK blood donation centres as well as internationally, then the research results could provide further insights. We also think that this research would benefit a future proof-of-concept implementation to validate the study more formally.

There are several potential areas for future work. First of all, developing a Microsoft Power app utilising Power Fx language may provide an opportunity to test the system and validate the approach better. Due to the pandemic and time constraints in the project, research methodology and usability evaluation methods have limitations. A more comprehensive survey as well as interviews on larger scale will improve our work. Other well-known evaluation approaches, such as Heuristics Evaluations and Pluralistic Usability Walk through, may also be used to analyse the proposed solution usability problems. The research only concentrated on designing a system to digitally transform component donations in the blood donation centre only. A potential future work to design and develop a larger system that can support other operations such as laboratory testing and blood storage will have more impact.

Acknowledgments. This study was conducted according to the ethical guidelines of Bournemouth University. In addition, the research has also been approved by the NHS Blood and Transplant with document NHSBT ID MSc-21-04 on 19/04/2021. BSCARE research group of NHSBT supported the study at an operational level. Informed consent was obtained from all subjects involved in the study. Authors would like to thank employees of the NHSBT Poole Donor Centre in the UK who joined in this study.

References

1. Martino, C., Russo, E., Santonastaso, D.P. et al.: Long-term outcomes in major trauma patients and correlations with the acute phase. World J. Emerg, Surg. **15**(6) (2020)
2. Fotopoulos, I., Palaiologou, R., Kouris, I., Koutsouris, D.: Cloud-based information system for blood donation. In: Proceedings of the XIV Mediterranean Conference on Medical and Biological Engineering and Computing. Springer (2016). https://doi.org/10.1007/978-3-319-32703-7_156
3. Mittal, N., Snotra, K.: Blood bank information system using Android application. In: Recent Developments in Control, Automation and Power Engineering (RDCAPE 2017), pp. 269–274. IEEE (2017)

4. Hu, W., Meng, H., Hu, Q., et al.: Blood donation from 2006 to 2015 in Zhejiang Province, China: annual consecutive cross-sectional studies. BMJ Open **9**(5), e023514 (2019). https://doi.org/10.1136/bmjopen-2018-023514
5. Sandaruwan, P.A.J., Dolapihilla, U.D.L., Karunathilaka, D.W.N.R., Wijayaweera, W.A.D.T.L., Rankothge, W.H., Gamage, N.D.U.: Towards an Efficient and Secure Blood Bank Management System. In: IEEE Region 10 Humanitarian Technology Conference, R10-HTC. IEEE (2020)
6. Patel, A., Tomar, D., Mourya, V., Kumar, N.S.: An enhanced framework for digital repository using bootstrap technique. In: International Conference on Advance Computing and Innovative Technologies in Engineering, pp. 711–713. IEEE (2021)
7. Nabil, M., Ihab, R., El Masry, H., Said, S., Youssef, S.: A Web-based blood donation and medical monitoring system integrating cloud services and mobile application. J. Phys. Conf. Ser. **1447**(1), 012001 (2020)
8. Zimmermann, R., et al.: A survey of blood utilization in children and adolescents in a German university hospital. Transfus. Med. **8**(3), 185–194 (1998)
9. Mowla, S.J., Sapiano, M.R.P., Jones, J.M., Berger, J.J., Basavaraju, S.V.: Supplemental findings of the 2019 National Blood Collection and utilization survey. Transfusion **61**(S2), S11–S35 (2021)
10. WHO: Blood safety and availability. https://www.who.int/news-room/fact-sheets/detail/blood-safety-and-availability. (Accessed 26 May 2022)
11. Sarode, R.: Components of Blood. University of Texas Southwestern Medical Centre. https://www.msdmanuals.com/en-gb/home/blood-disorders/biology-of-blood/components-of-blood. (Accessed 26 May 2022)
12. Basu, D., Kulkarni, R.: Overview of blood components and their preparation. Indian J. Anaesth. **58**(5), 529–537 (2014)
13. Eirini, G., Dimitrios, P.: Therapeutic apheresis: Technical modalities and therapeutic applications. Nephrolo. Renal Diseases **2**(2) (2017)
14. NHS Blood and Transplant Website. https://www.nhsbt.nhs.uk. (Accessed 26 May 2022)
15. Harjoseputro, Y.: Blood transfusion information system design for blood transfusion services unit. Int. J. Inf. Technol. Electr. Eng. **2**, 78–84 (2018)
16. Harris, A., McKeown, P.: Nursing in NHS blood and transplant: an overview. Brit. J. Nursing **28**(19), 1160–1161 (2019)
17. Carter Blood Care Website. https://www.carterbloodcare.org. (Accessed 26 May 2022)
18. Knight, S., Tartakovski, O., Harris, A.: Blood donation: key challenges. Brit. J. Nursing **28**(21) (2019)
19. Heal, S., Webster, C., Harris, A.: Blood donation: nurse roles and responsibilities. Brit. J. Nursing **28**(20) (2019)
20. HL7 Definitions. https://hl7-definition.caristix.com/v2/HL7v2.7/Fields/BPX.6. (Accessed 26 May 2022)
21. Savant Ltd. PULSE: Blood Bank Control and Management System. https://www.savant.co.uk/pulse. (Accessed 26 May 2022)
22. Torrent-Sellens, J., Salazar-Concha, C., Ficapal-Cusi, P., Saigi-Rubio, F.: Using digital platforms to promote blood donation: motivational and preliminary evidence from Latin America and Spain. Int. J. Environ. Res. Public Health **18**(8), 4270 (2021)
23. Shahzad, I., King, M., Henshaw, M.: Applying SoSE in Healthcare: the case for a soft systems methodology approach to Digital-first Primary Care. In:16th International Conference of System of Systems Engineering, SoSE 2021, pp. 37–42 (2021)

24. Augustsson, H., Churruca, K., Braithwaite, J.: Change and improvement 50 years in the making: a scoping review of the use of soft systems methodology in health-care. BMC Health Serv. Res. **20**, 1063 (2020)

25. National Health Service (NHS). Driver Diagrams: Quality, Service Improvement and Redesign Tools. https://www.england.nhs.uk/sustainableimprovement/qsir-programme/qsir-tools/. (Accessed 27 May 2022)

26. Roper, S., Micheli, P., Love, J., Vahter, P.: The role and effectiveness of design in new product development: a study of Irish manufacturers. Enter. Res. Centre **41**, 319–329 (2016)

27. Siang, T.Y.: What is Design Thinking? Interaction Design Foundation. https://www.interaction-design.org/literature/topics/design-thinking. (Accessed on 27 May 2022)

28. Bluemenrose, B.: Clarity in the design process: how to create a process map for your team (2017). https://medium.com/bridge-collection

29. Gibbons, S.: Empathy Mapping: The first step in Design Thinking. Nielsen Norman Group (2018). https://www.nngroup.com/articles/empathy-mapping

30. Mulder, S., Yaar, Z.: The User is always right: A Practical guide to creating and using Personas for the Web. New Riders, Berkeley (2006)

31. Laubheimer, P.: Personas vs. Jobs-to-Be-Done. Neilsen Norman Group (2017). https://www.nngroup.com/articles/personas-jobs-be-done

32. Babich, N.: Human Factor Principles in UX Design (2020). https://xd.adobe.com/ideas/principles/human-computer-interaction/human-factors-ux-design. (Accessed on 27 May 2022)

33. Weinschenk, S.M.: 100 Things Every Designers Needs to Know About People. New Riders, Berkeley (2011)

34. Rosenfeld, L., Morville, P., Arango, J.: Information Architecture. 4th edn. O' Reily Media, Inc. (2015)

35. Preece, J., Sharp, H., Rogers, Y.: Interaction Design: Beyond Human-Computer Interaction. 4th edn. John Wiley and Sons Ltd. Chichester

36. Ouhbi, S., Fernandez-Aleman, J.L., Pozo, J.R., Bajta, M.E., Toval, A., Idri, A.: Compliance of blood donation apps with mobile OS usability guidelines. J. Med. Syst. **39**(6), 63 (2015)

37. Wilson, C.: User Interface Inspection Methods. Elsevier Inc., Waltham (2014)

38. Bligard, L., Osvalder, A.: Enhanced cognitive walkthrough: development of the cognitive walkthrough method to better Predict, Identify, and present usability problems. Adv. Hum. Comput. Inter. **2013**(931698) (2013)

Designing and Developing a Web Application of Food Products Focusing on Plant-Based Diets for Better Health

Way Kiat Bong[✉], Abubakar Yousaf, Yuan Jing Li, and Weiqin Chen

Oslo Metropolitan University (OsloMet), St. Olavs Plass, P.O. Box 4, 0130 Oslo, Norway
{wayki,s339945,s343868,weiche}@oslomet.no

Abstract. Plant-based food products are getting more popular in the market as they are claimed to be healthier and more sustainable to the environment. However, there is a lack of platform where consumers can easily obtain nutritional information of these on-the-shelf plant-based food products. Therefore, our study aimed to design a web application where the consumers could easily access this information. To design and develop the web application, user-centered design (UCD) approach was adopted to involve health and nutrition researchers, and consumers. After three iterations of design, development, and usability evaluations of UCD process, four focus group interviews focusing more on summative data were conducted using the final version of the prototype. The findings indicate that the web application was easy to learn and use but its design could be less attractive to some users. Involvement of health and nutrition researchers throughout the UCD process ensured that the web application was perceived credible and trustworthy. Started as a research-oriented study, the web application was originally developed for the health and nutrition researchers. By extending its use to consumers, the study contributes to more understanding in involving researchers and consumers throughout a UCD process and providing considerations in designing health-related digital tools.

Keywords: User-centered design · Usability · Health · Plant-based diets

1 Introduction

Diet plays an essential role in shaping our health and well-being. Plant-based diets have been getting extensively popular among consumers. They are one of the fastest growing dietary trends globally and especially in European countries [1, 2]. By consuming plant-based diets, the consumers can make a positive impact to their own health. Plant-based food can contribute in reducing the risks of developing numerous chronic diseases, such as obesity, cancer, heart disease and so forth [3]. In addition, they are considered more effective in the treatment of fatal diseases such as chronic kidney disease [4] and hypertension [5]. They are also perceived as sustainable food that contributes to better environmental well-being [2, 3]. All these benefits are aligned with United Nation's

V. G. Duffy et al. (Eds.): HCII 2022, LNCS 13521, pp. 46–60, 2022.
https://doi.org/10.1007/978-3-031-17902-0_4

sustainable development goals such as good health and well-being (goal 3), responsible consumption and production (goal 12) and climate action (goal 13).

The review from Fehér, Gazdecki [3] identified several shortcomings in practicing plant-based diets; challenges in obtaining information about the diet was one of them. For the past 20 years, consumers found it challenging to prepare plant-based food, as there were little relevant and available information concerning what dishes were worth preparing, how to prepare them, and which ingredients could replace meat [6–8]. As plant-based diets are getting more popular, this information is getting more widespread. However, such information is yet to be extended further to market-available plant-based food products, i.e., all type of processed food products which are not raw ingredients.

Using information and communication technologies (ICT) as a platform for information sharing can reach more users in an accessible way. Many ICT tools in the form of websites and applications have been developed to promote healthier diets. Useful information and guidance are provided to the users with the aim to make wiser choice for their diets. Some of these ICT tools focused on on-the-shelf food products [9–12], and the results were promising. However, there is a lack of focus on plant-based diets among these tools. ICT tools for plant-based diets, as the other way around has paid less attention to on-the-shelf food products [8, 13]. The above-mentioned apps were either only used at national level or in countries speaking the same language. In Norway, there is no such ICT tool yet. Localization is important as the contents displaying nutritional information across food products of different brands and manufacturers, while categorizing food products based on plant-based and non-plant-based have to appear credible to the users. In this paper, food products refer to both plant-based and non-plant-based meat products and dairy products.

Besides that, too little attention has been paid in involving both researchers in health and nutrition, and consumers in the process of developing food product-related ICT tools. As experts, researchers could contribute to assisting consumers in getting the most important and relevant nutritional information of food products. Consumers as end users, have to be able to understand the information to be benefited. Thus, in this study we intended to involve both groups in designing a web application where the users could easily assess and understand information about food products sold in the market, concerning the amount of nutrients and type of food. The food products displayed in the web application were aimed to be categorized based on plant-based and non-plant-based to promote plant-based diets. Usability of this web application was crucial in ensuring the consumers find it easy to learn and use.

This study is part of a bigger project about health effects and consumer perceptions of meat substitutes. The study started with the idea from the health and nutrition researchers wanting to use the web application for their research work. At the same time, they also wished to extend the use of web application to the consumers. This was the reason why the study started with the design of a web application and not a mobile app. By the time of writing this paper, we were designing and developing a mobile app version of the web application, with the aim to offer another platform for the consumers. Through the web application, we hoped the consumers could make better choices when choosing market available food products, increase their awareness about the benefits of consuming plant-based food products (after comparing the nutrients in both plant-based and non-plant-based food products), and thus improve their diets and health.

2 Related Research

Most of the existing plant-based diet-related ICT tools in the market are either only focusing on ingredients or dishes. In a content analysis study assessing free and popular plant-based mobile health apps for Canadians, 16 apps that were included by Lee, Ahmed [14] comprised of five main types. They were recipe manager and meal planners (ten apps), food scanners (two apps), vegan community builders (two apps), restaurant identifier and sustainability-focused (one app each). None of them focused on on-the-shelf food products. In addition, Lee, Ahmed [14] pinpointed the low support of knowledge acquisition in these apps. Support of knowledge acquisition, which comes in the form of education is as one of the primary factors included in an evaluation instrument assessing quality of nutrition apps [15]. This education has to be reliable so that the users can gain correct nutrition knowledge and practice genuine health diets. Comparing other sources like crowdsourcing of food composition database and commercialized entities, academic apps are more reliable and therefore more often being used in nutritional and clinical studies [16]. Hence, to increase the credibility of diet-related ICT tools used among consumers, there is a need to include trustworthy sources, i.e., researchers.

In Thailand, Tangsripairoj, Wongkham [9] developed a mobile application named "WhatTheHealth" that aimed to guide consumers in purchasing healthier packaged food. It had functionalities such as user profile, logging food consumption, comparing between two food products, etc. These functionalities could assist consumers practicing a healthier diet to help preventing and controlling non-communicable diseases, i.e., chronic diseases that are not passed from individual to individual and mostly caused by individual lifestyles and behaviors such as diets. A French mobile app named Yuka [10], and Australian mobile app named FoodSwitch [12] offered similar functionalities. After scanning a food product's barcode, users could obtain its detailed information. This could assist them in choosing products that were healthier for their health. Foodle also offered the consumers guidance to buy healthier food [11]. The application first collected the users' grocery receipt data, and then proposed them what to buy based on the nutritional goal and historic nutrition data linked to their receipt database.

In Norway, despite being able to easily buy market-available food products on the shelves in supermarkets and shops, there is a lack of platform that can provide consumers an overview about the nutrients contained in these food products. Apps such as Yuka [10] and FoodSwitch [17] were mostly only being used in French-speaking countries, and English-speaking countries respectively. When FoodSwitch was extended to China and India, issues concerning differences in nutrition labelling occurred [17].

3 Methodology

In this study, we first adopted a UCD approach involving two user groups, i.e., researchers of health and nutrition, and consumers who were target users of the web application to design and develop the web application. Using the final version of prototype resulted from the UCD process, we then conducted four focus group interviews for a more summative evaluation.

3.1 User-Centered Design (UCD)

The two user groups we involved were very different. Studies have shown that UCD could result in producing an end product that fulfilled different needs among diverse end users [18, 19]. By adopting UCD approach, we aimed to develop the web application based on user requirements and feedback from these two user groups. Throughout the UCD process, we had a total of three iterations of design, development, and usability evaluation. At this stage, the evaluation aimed to provide formative data so that the improvements to the design could be gathered for next iteration [20].

Due to the restrictions under the COVID-19 pandemic, we conducted all usability evaluations remotely; Some were synchronous, and some were asynchronous. All participants of usability evaluation were asked to perform a series of testing tasks. The tasks were navigating to the home page, using the search function to find a food product under a particular product category (e.g., meat burgers, plant-based sausages, plant-based cheese, etc.), searching a food product under a particular product category with filters of nutrients (e.g., meatballs with less than 1000 kilojoules (kJ) of energy, plant-based nuggets with less than 15 g (g) of fat, etc.) and sorting the search results.

For synchronous evaluations, we conducted them through digital video conferencing platforms such as Zoom, Teams and Google Meet. We observed how the participants performed the tasks, asked their opinions regarding the prototype they were using, and clarified with them when we had follow-up questions based on the observation. Asynchronous participants were required to write down their notes and comments in an excel file that was provided to them together with the testing tasks. After performing the evaluation by themselves, they sent back the filled-up excel file to us. We clarified with them when the answers appeared unclear to us. Both user groups, i.e., researchers and consumers have never met during the evaluations so that we were able to compare their feedback.

3.2 Focus Group Interview

After three iterations of design, development, and usability evaluation, we conducted a series of focus group interviews to perform final evaluation with consumers of diverse background. The focus group interviews were conducted either as local evaluations, i.e., the participant and the evaluator are at the same location, or as remote evaluations. Same as usability evaluations in the UCD process, the participants were given the same series of testing task to perform using the web application (the final version of prototype) and being observed how they performed the tasks. Some were requested to use a laptop, while others were assigned to use a tablet to perform the evaluation. In addition to observation, the participants were also asked to discuss about the design of the web application when performing the testing tasks. Other questions concerning the potential of the web application were probed. For instance, "Overall, what do you think of the web application?", "Any other functionalities you would like to add?", "Any functionality shall be removed", and "Who do you think will use, or benefit from this web application?". As this evaluation was more summative than formative [21], we asked the participants to provide their System Usability Scale (SUS) scores [22] after using the web application.

3.3 Recruitment and Participants

We recruited the participants using convenience sampling [23], i.e., they were recruited as they were easily accessible. Two researchers in health and nutrition who were part of the bigger project of health effects and consumer perceptions of meat substitutes, participated in the usability evaluations throughout all iterations of UCD process in this study. 17 participants presenting the user group of consumers participated only once, either in usability evaluation during UCD process or in focus group interview. We took into the consideration of having diversified participants based on their demographic background, such as age, ICT skills, education, and diet. All participants in this study, from UCD usability evaluation to focus group interview were first briefed about the study. They were then presented with the consent form, and their consent together with some demographic information were provided prior to participating in the study.

When asking about demographic information, in addition to age, gender, education and so forth, we asked the participants to rate themselves their ICT skills (on a scale from 1 to 10; 1 is very bad and 10 is very good) and their concern and/or interest regarding nutritional information (on a scale from 1 to 10; 1 is not concerned at all and 10 is very concerned). The demographic information of all participants, and their participation are summarized in Table 1, except for the researchers in health and nutrition. Their demographic backgrounds were considered less relevant in influencing the design of the prototype, as they were the ones providing contents of the web application.

Table 1. Summary of all participants' demographic information and participation.

	Gender	Age	Occupation	Highest education	ICT skills	Diet	Concern (nutrition)	Participation
R1	–							All UCD
R2	–							iteration
C1	M	33	PhD candidate	Master	8	Vegan	8	UCD iteration 1
C2	F	36	QC specialist	PhD	7	Regular	4	
C3	M	62	Seller	High school	5	Regular	3	UCD iteration 2
C4	F	46	Housewife. Earlier web designer	Bachelor	8.5	Regular	7	
C5	F	36	PhD candidate	Master	7	Vegetarian	8	UCD iteration 3
C6	M	40	Researcher	Master	7	Vegan	7	

(continued)

Table 1. (*continued*)

	Gender	Age	Occupation	Highest education	ICT skills	Diet	Concern (nutrition)	Participation
C7	M	29	Programmer	Master	2	Regular	1	Focus group 1
C8	M	31	Retail worker	Bachelor	6	Regular	2	
C9	F	32	Retail worker	High school	4	Regular	7	
C10	F	28	Freelance illustrator	Master	3	Regular	3	
C11	F	45	Tax manager	Master	7	Regular	6	Focus group 2
C12	M	48	Senior IT advisor	Master	10	Regular	7	
C13	M	29	Reception	Bachelor	7	Vegan	1	Focus group 3
C14	F	26	Master student	Bachelor	5	Regular	4	
C15	M	27	Master student	Bachelor	4	Regular	8	
C16	M	57	Receiving disability benefit. Earlier cook	High school	2	Regular	4	Focus group 4
C17	F	65	Retired. Previously housekeeper	High school	0	Regular	1	

4 Results

4.1 Iterations of Design, Development and Usability Evaluation

In the first iteration, using user requirements given by the researchers in health and nutrition, the first version of prototype was developed. The prototype was then evaluated by both researchers and consumers. In the second and third iterations, feedback gathered in the usability evaluation in the previous iteration were used to improve the design of the prototype, and then researchers and consumers evaluated the prototype. In addition, the prototype was tested using WAVE (web accessibility evaluation tool) to ensure it met accessibility requirements from Web Content Accessibility Guideline. The final version of prototype is the web application, which is described in the Sect. 4.2.

Throughout the three usability evaluations, the common issues being raised by both researcher and consumers participants were mostly visual related, i.e., choice of colors and placement of the elements. They wanted different colors in the homepage and search results page to differentiate the two of them, despite the information displayed was already different. The placements of elements reflected on the usability aspects, which involved the functionalities of performing search, and sorting search results. They wanted the search function to be divided into two parts, basic and advanced. In terms of sorting results, they wanted the sorting to be able to perform as easy as possible, i.e., by clicking directly at the parameters offering sorting possibilities. Both user groups also provided suggestions about other functionalities that could be included in the next research. Due to time and resource constraints, we had started the implementation but yet to have them completed in the next iteration. These suggestions are presented as potential improvements, in Sect. 4.4, which is after we present the findings of focus group interview.

Other issues, which the consumer participants brought up more than researcher participants, were related to the wordings and formulation of information. For example, they would like to have more information about the amount of nutrients in relationships to the amount of food products. We then added the sentence "All nutrients displayed in the table are per 100 g of food product" to clarify better. They preferred the wordings "product type" and "product category" over "food group", as these terms were more reasonable and understandable from the consumers' perspectives. All these suggestions were first clarified with the health and nutrition researchers so that the changes to be made were correct from the perspectives of experts and not only the consumers. The roles of health and nutrition researchers as educators were observed. For instance, they provided inputs on the correct way to display nutrient value, to categorize food products, and what the consumers should pay attention to and how they should interpret the information displayed on the web application.

4.2 Web Application

The web application was named as "Nutrition database for meat and dairy products & plant-based substitutes" (see Fig. 1). It consisted of two main functionalities. First was the homepage to display all food products, with their respective amount of nutrients. These nutrients included energy in both kJ and kilocalorie (kcal), and fat, saturated fat, carbohydrates, sugar, fiber, protein, and salt in gram.

Fig. 1. Search function of the web application.

Figure 1 illustrates the second functionality, which was a search page to search food products based on two main parameters. First was product type, which included meat, meat substitutes, dairy products, and plant-based dairy products. Second was product category; as shown in Fig. 1 (product categories for meat): burger, sausages, minced meat, meatballs, nuggets, keyhole-marked and others. Keyhole-marked (nøkkelhullsmerket) is a public label for healthier foods that indicates the product contains less fat, sugar and salt, and more fiber and whole grains. The same product categories applied for meat substitutes. For both dairy and plant-based dairy products, their product categories included cheese, ice cream, yogurt, cream, milk, and others. Users could also perform advanced search by providing a range for nutrients' amount.

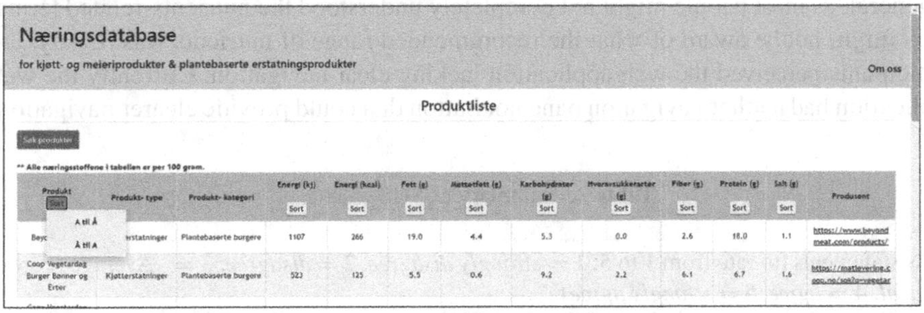

Fig. 2. Search results page and sort function of the web application.

As shown in Fig. 2, after getting the search results, the users could choose to sort the results by the food products' name alphabetically, and by each nutrient in either ascending or descending order.

4.3 Focus Group Interview

Overall, all participants managed to perform the testing tasks. Issues such as wordings and formulation of information that were encountered during the UCD process, did not occur in focus group interview. All participants agreed that the web application was simple to learn and use. They understood that the focus was about nutrients of various food products and perceived the information as clear and easy to understand. However, due to the simplicity in design, participants such as C7, C8 and C10 thought the web application could appear easy to use for older adults but less appealing and attractive for younger people. They also expressed that this kind of design could be acceptable for consumers who were more interested in nutrients of food they ate and practiced healthy diets, but not for them. As shown in Table 1, participants in this study were either very concern about food nutrition (self-rated as high as 7 and 8 out of 10) or very little (as low as 1 to 3). C7, C8 and C10 happened to be in the group who concerned less about food nutrition, and they were also in the younger user group as well (age 29, 31 and 28 respectively).

Most recommendations were associated with visual aspects, which were also subjective to individuals. However, we did observe commonalities among some participants. For instance, younger participants tended to emphasize more on visual design when providing feedback. Focus group 1 and 3 wanted the web application to be more "fashionable", which could attract their attentions more and motivate them in using it eventually. As shown in Fig. 2, buttons "Sort" in the page of search results were currently having text ("Sort", "Highest", "Lowest", "A to Å", and "Å to A"). Younger participants expressed that the icons with arrow would be sufficient.

One usability issue pointed out by all focus groups is the design of displaying food products. Its current design displayed all food products in one page. This was perceived as boring and too much information to take in. The participants in focus group 3 pointed out specifically that they would prefer a page that displays a maximum of 20 food products, and the users could press next page to view more. Another issue was concerning the advanced search. Some participants thought it was a complicated function for consumers in general, as most people might not completely understood the nutrients-related terms. They might not be aware of what the recommended range of nutrients was. Lastly, the participants perceived the web application lacking clear navigation. Currently the web application had neither navigation pane nor button that could provide clearer navigation.

Table 2. Summary of SUS results.

SUS statements (to rate from 1 to 5; 1 = *strongly disagree*, 2 = *disagree*, 3 = *neutral*, 4 = *agree*, 5 = *strongly agree*)	Average scores
1. I think that I would like to use this system frequently	1.63
2. I found the system unnecessarily complex	3.28
3. I thought the system was easy to use	3.00
4. I think that I would need the support of a technical person to be able to use this system	1.36
5. I found the various functions in this system were well integrated	2.36
6. I thought there was too much inconsistency in this system	2.36
7. I would imagine that most people would learn to use this system very quickly	4.00
8. I found the system very cumbersome to use	2.82
9. I felt very confident using the system	3.72
10. I needed to learn a lot of things before I could get going with this system	2.00

Table 2 presents the average scores of SUS questionnaires. As the average scores show, the web application scored very high in statements 7 and 9, and very low in statements 4 and 10. This aligned with the findings of observation and discussion concerning the design of the web application being simple and easy to learn and use. The score of statement 1 indicated low interest among the participants in using the web application. The reasons provided by the participants were either because they were not very interested in information about food nutrition, or they thought the web application did not appear attractive to them.

Despite being perceived as easy to learn and use, some participants thought the web application was unnecessarily complex (statement 2). Interestingly, this group of participants were all from focus group 1 and 2, and these two groups were the only two groups which compared the design of the web application with a common web application in Norway named Finn.no [24]. Finn.no is a classified advertisement digital platform where users can both advertise and search advertisements of buying and selling all kind of brand new and used items, properties, transportations, travels, and services. Finn.no offers both website and mobile app version to the users. The first thing that being compared was the search functionality. These participants wanted the search possibilities to be displayed as single items in grid view, instead of a dropdown list (refer Fig. 1). Secondly, the search result page should have displayed the search parameters that the users had selected. Lastly, we had several sort buttons on the search results page (refer Fig. 2) and the participants expressed it could be less complex by having all sorts grouped at one dropdown list like in Finn.no.

In summary, all participants in focus group interview saw the potential in this web application and appreciated its purpose as a platform to provide consumers nutritional information of market-available food products. Other findings gathered during the focus group interview were similar as those gathered during the UCD process. They were potential improvements that the project team had started working with since the UCD process started. However, they were yet to be completely implemented before the focus group interview were conducted due to concerns such as copyright, collaborations with other organizations, etc. We present these feedbacks in Sect. 4.4.

4.4 Potential Improvements

Both researcher and consumer participants in the UCD process and focus group interview would like to have images of food products instead of just pure text. When developing the web application, the project team was surveying the possibilities in having these images on the web application in relations to the concern of copyright. Other suggestions such as including information about shops which sell food products and prices were also brought up, both during the UCD and focus group interview. These suggestions could be implemented with the collaborations with food producers, shops, and supermarkets. The participants expressed that it would be beneficial if the web application could suggest them healthy food products that were on promotions.

Another functionality that most participants wanted was having a user profile. This functionality could offer users to have their own account, log in, and save the items into their own favorite list. We have evaluated this function during the UCD process concerning user interface design and its usability; the results were promising. However, due to the concern of General Data Protection Regulation (GDPR) and privacy issue when implementing it, this function was not included in the evaluations in focus group interview.

5 Discussion

The study started as a research-oriented project where the web application was originally designed and developed for the use of researchers in health and nutrition. Using user requirements provided by them, the very first prototype was made. As the nutritional information could be relevant for the consumers in assisting them in making better choice for healthier diets, and encouraging them to practice plant-based diets, these researchers wished to extend the use of the web application to the consumers. The findings show the potential of the web application, in addition to the innovation of the study; ICT tools nowadays providing guidance and information of market-available food products do not focus on plant-based food products [9–12], while ICT tools focusing on plant-based diets only focused on ingredients or recipes, and not on-the-shelves food products [6, 8].

When assessing free and popular mobile apps for supporting plant-based diets for Canadians, Lee, Ahmed [14] identified issue of lacking credible and trustworthy sources among the evaluated apps. Contributions from researchers in health and nutrition in this study was important in addressing this issue. Besides advising us about the design of the web application, their input and feedback have been used as a form of education to the consumer user group, which include what the consumers should be aware of, and the information displayed in the web application being credible and trustworthy. Such practice is important in designing and developing all kind of health-related ICT tools.

In order to impact on consumers' attitude change, information targeted to them has to appear both attractive and credible [25]. UCD approach involving both researchers in health and nutrition, and consumers was therefore adopted. Comparing feedback from researchers in health and nutrition, and consumer participants from UCD usability evaluation and focus group interview, different perspectives were observed. Researchers in health and nutrition, and consumer participants in UCD had more interest in nutritional information, while consumer participants in focus group interview had less. This resulted in more focus in elements concerning attractiveness in focus group interview than in UCD. Concerning credibility of the information, we wish to highlight the importance of health and nutrition researchers' involvement and contribution in ensuring that the web application was perceived credible and trustworthy.

Alongside to credibility of an app, Van Loo, Hoefkens [25] emphasized other factors such as attractiveness and personal motivation in making an attitude change in consumers choosing healthier and more sustainable plant-based diets. In this study, the participants in focus group interview expressed that the visual appearance of the web application was less attractive. This was reflected on their SUS scores, indicating them being less interested in using the web application. Comparing to participants in focus group interview, consumer participants in UCD process rated themselves having higher concern in nutritional information in food. Out of six of them, two of them were vegan and one was vegetarian. Other than these participants, two health and nutrition researchers participated throughout the entire UCD process. It is likely that the participants' personal motivation outweighed attractiveness of the web application during the UCD process. This then resulted in the concern of web application being less attractive was not mentioned during the UCD process but only in the focus group interview.

In the focus group interview, participants suggested other design features that could make the web application appeared more attractive to them. One of them was suggesting healthy food products that were on promotions to the users. In a review identifying factors that could contribute to promoting plant-based food consumptions, Taufik, Verain

[13] concluded that price incentive was one of the effective factors. Ball, McNaughton [26] compared three interventions to investigate effects on the consumptions of healthy food and beverages. These were intervention with a 20% price reduction, intervention with a skill-building, and a intervention of a combination of both. Information alone, i.e., newsletters about health eating combined with other skill-building resources such as opportunity to participate in an online forum, budgeting worksheets, goal-setting, and self-monitoring exercises were found ineffective in promoting the consumers to buy healthy food and beverages. On the other hand, price reduction alone and the combination of price reduction and skill-building resulted in higher consumption of healthy food and beverages. As suggested by some participants in this study, the nutritional information alone did not appear attractive enough for them. Combining this information with information about promotions could give stronger impact. In addition to food products on promotions, others suggested design included having images to illustrate the food products, indicating the consumers where they could get the food products and having a user profile where they could save the food products into their favorite list.

Some findings concerning usability perspective of the web application could be related to universal design (UD) principles. The focus group interview participants perceived the web application lacking clear navigation as it had neither navigation pane nor button that could provide clearer navigation. Besides, colors were one of the design elements wanted by both researcher and consumer participants in differentiating between the home page and the search results page. These could assist them feeling directed and knowing where they were when using the web application; supporting UD principle 4, perceptible information [27].

The participants in UCD process wanted the sort function to be simple, and we had the sort buttons at the parameters which could offer sort possibilities (refer Fig. 2). However, this design was perceived as confusing during focus group interview. The participants in the first and second focus group interviews pointed out that they preferred a design which was based on finn.no, a popular Norwegian classified advertisement digital platform. They were used to having only one dropdown list, displaying all types of sort possibilities. In addition to that, when performing search, all search possibilities could be displayed as single items in grid view, instead of a dropdown list (refer Fig. 1). These findings are in line with UD principle 3, simple and intuitive use where the design has to "*be consistent with user expectations and intuition*" [27]. Since finn.no is very popular among people living in Norway, it was understandable that they compared the design of our web application to their experiences using finn.no. Hence, using a familiar web application can be a good approach as a starting point to design a brand-new prototype. This approach is in line with the guide for better usability proposed by Nielsen [28].

6   Conclusion and Future Work

This study demonstrates a UCD process involving both health and nutrition researchers, and consumers in producing a web application that enabled the consumers to easily obtain nutritional information about plant-based and non-plant-based food products sold in the market. The UCD process involved two health and nutrition researchers and six consumers in three iterations of design, development, and evaluations. Using the final version of the prototype, evaluations focusing on summative results were conducted with eleven consumers participating in four focus group interviews. The results show that the web application was easy to learn and use, due to the simplicity in its design. However, most of the participants thought this design appeared less appealing and attractive to them. Hence, they had less interest in using it in the future. On the other hand, such design was commented could be more suitable for older adults.

In this study, a UCD approach involving experts and consumers has proven beneficial in designing a diet-related web application. By consulting the researchers in health and nutrition, we managed to convey information that is scientifically precise to the consumers via the web application. By consulting the consumers, we could ensure the information on the web application is understandable to them, and inputs on how to make the web application more attractive have been gathered. One of the implications of this study is informing the researchers, designers and developers, policymakers, and industry players about the essential considerations in providing consumers health-related ICT tools, i.e., usability, credibility, and attractiveness.

This study was undertaken to design a web application that provides nutritional information of market-available food products to consumers. By enhancing the access to this information, we hope to promote more plant-based diets among the consumers, and hence they can have a healthier diet and better health. The web application can hopefully inspire other work in promoting plant-based diets as well, as plant-based food is more sustainable [2, 3]. As the study was at its preliminary stage, we have only focused on the aspects of usability and functionality. Therefore, the future works include to further improve the web application based on the participants' feedback and incorporate proposed functionalities such as having prices, information about products on promotions, shops and supermarkets selling the products, and so forth.

Using the web application, we intend to evaluate its usage regarding user experience and impact on consumers' choice in choosing food products in a longer period of time. One limitation of this study is that we did not specifically include user groups that face risks of malnutrition, such as people with disabilities and older adults [29]. Some usability issues found in this study were related to UD principles [27]. Hence, we would highlight the importance of having the web application universally designed so that users with diverse background and needs could benefit from using it.

References

1. Alae-Carew, C., et al.: The role of plant-based alternative foods in sustainable and healthy food systems: consumption trends in the UK. Sci. Total Environ. **807**, 151041 (2022)
2. Aschemann-Witzel, J., et al.: Plant-based food and protein trend from a business perspective: markets, consumers, and the challenges and opportunities in the future. Crit. Rev. Food Sci. Nutr. **61**(18), 3119–3128 (2021)
3. Fehér, A., et al.: A comprehensive review of the benefits of and the barriers to the switch to a plant-based diet. Sustainability **12**(10), 4136 (2020)
4. Banerjee, T., Liu, Y., Crews, D.C.: Dietary patterns and CKD progression. Blood Purif. **41**(1–3), 117–122 (2016)
5. Joshi, S., Ettinger, L., Liebman, S.E.: Plant-based diets and hypertension. Am. J. Lifestyle Med. **14**(4), 397–405 (2020)

6. Lea, E., Worsley, A.: Benefits and barriers to the consumption of a vegetarian diet in Australia. Public Health Nutr **6**(5), 505–511 (2003)

7. Lea, E., Worsley, A.: Influences on meat consumption in Australia. Appetite **36**(2), 127–136 (2001)

8. Lea, E.J., Crawford, D., Worsley, A.: Public views of the benefits and barriers to the consumption of a plant-based diet. Eur. J. Clin. Nutr. **60**(7), 828–837 (2006)

9. Tangsripairoj, S., et al.: WhatTheHealth: An android application for consumers of healthy food. In: 2019 16th International Joint Conference on Computer Science and Software Engineering (JCSSE), pp. 61–66. IEEE, Thailand (2019)

10. Southey, F.: Evaluating the Yuka 'Phenomenon': How Effective Is the Scanning App in Practice?, https://www.foodnavigator.com/Article/2019/08/20/Evaluating-the-Yuka-phenom enon-How-effective-is-the-scanning-app-in-practice (2019). Last accessed 16 May 2022

11. Wayman, E., Madhvanath, S.: Nudging grocery shoppers to make healthier choices. In: Proceedings of the 9th ACM Conference on Recommender Systems, pp. 289–292. ACM, Austria (2015)

12. Dunford, E., et al.: FoodSwitch: a mobile phone app to enable consumers to make healthier food choices and crowdsourcing of national food composition data. JMIR mHealth uHealth **2**(3), e3230 (2014)

13. Taufik, D., et al.: Determinants of real-life behavioural interventions to stimulate more plant-based and less animal-based diets: a systematic review. Trends Food Sci. Technol. **93**, 281–303 (2019)

14. Lee, J., et al.: A content analysis of free, popular plant-based mobile health apps. Curr. Dev. Nutr. **5**(Supplement_2), 1003–1003 (2021)

15. DiFilippo, K.N., Huang, W., Chapman-Novakofski, K.M.: A new tool for nutrition app quality evaluation (AQEL): development, validation, and reliability testing. JMIR Mhealth Uhealth **5**(10), e163 (2017)

16. Khazen, W., et al.: Rethinking the use of mobile apps for dietary assessment in medical research. J. Med. Internet Res. **22**(6), e15619 (2020)

17. Dunford, E., Neal, B.: FoodSwitch and use of crowdsourcing to inform nutrient databases. J. Food Compos. Anal. **64**, 13–17 (2017)

18. Winter, J., Rönkkö, K., Rissanen, M.: Identifying organizational barriers—a case study of usability work when developing software in the automation industry. J. Syst. Softw. **88**, 54–73 (2014)

19. Kübler, A., Nijboer, F., Kleih, S.: Hearing the needs of clinical users. Handb. Clin. Neurol. **168**, 353–368 (2020)

20. Joyce, A.: Formative vs. Summative Evaluations (2019). https://www.nngroup.com/articles/formative-vs-summative-evaluations/. Accessed 17 May 2022

21. Nielsen, J.: 10 Usability Heuristics for User Interface Design (1994). https://www.nngroup.com/articles/ten-usability-heuristics/. Accessed 17 May 2022

22. Brooke, J.: SUS-A quick and dirty usability scale. Usability Eval. Ind. **189**(194), 4–7 (1996). Taylor & Francis Group

23. Sedgwick, P.: Convenience sampling. Bmj **347**, f6304 (2013)

24. Finn.no: FINN.no - mulighetenes marked, http://www.finn.no. Last accessed 17 May 2022

25. Van Loo, E.J., Hoefkens, C., Verbeke, W.: Healthy, sustainable and plant-based eating: perceived (mis) match and involvement-based consumer segments as targets for future policy. Food Policy **69**, 46–57 (2017)

26. Ball, K., et al.: Influence of price discounts and skill-building strategies on purchase and consumption of healthy food and beverages: outcomes of the supermarket healthy eating for life randomized controlled trial. Am. J. Clin. Nutr. **101**(5), 1055–1064 (2015)

27. Story, M.F.: Principles of Universal Design, Universal Design Handbook, 2nd edn. McGraw-Hill Professional New York, New York (2001)

28. Nielsen, J.: Usability 101: Introduction to usability (2012). https://www.nngroup.com/art
    icles/usability-101-introduction-to-usability/. Accessed 19 May 2022
29. Groce, N., et al.: Malnutrition and disability: unexplored opportunities for collaboration.
    Paediatr. Int. Child Health 34(4), 308–314 (2014)

Using Emerging Technologies to Support Wellbeing and Resilience for Pilots and Enabling the Assessment of Wellbeing Risk in Airline Safety Management Systems

Joan Cahill[✉] [ID], Paul Cullen, Sohaib Anwer, and Fiona Hegarty

Trinity College Dublin, Dublin, Ireland
cahilljo@tcd.ie

Abstract. This paper reports on the findings of two anonymous online surveys undertaken with pilots (n = 170) pertaining to pilot self-care behaviors, the use of technology to support wellbeing management, and the acceptability of sharing wellbeing information captured using mobile phone apps with aviation employers, to support the analysis of wellbeing risk in safety management systems (SMSs). New mobile phone-based apps might be implemented to support self-care for pilots as part of a phased approach to the promotion of an integrated health and safety culture, and the management of wellbeing risk in aviation safety management systems (SMS). In the short term, there is insufficient trust on behalf of pilots to support such information sharing practices. Accordingly, it is proposed that pending consent, pilots share deidentified wellbeing information using mobile phone apps (and/or a web interface), in a global repository. This repository or 'wellbeing monitor' would be accessible to the industry – providing airlines with general trends data and reports, supporting wellbeing management and risk assessment. This will help mitigate existing employee information sharing barriers, build trust, and foster an integrated health and wellbeing culture, which is the prerequisite for the future assessment of wellbeing risk within a company SMS.

Keywords: Pilots · Wellbeing · Self-care · Mobile Apps · Safety

1 Introduction

The workplace is an important setting for health protection, health promotion and disease prevention programs [1]. New perspectives on stress coping illustrate the role of both individual and organisational factors in stress coping. Individual factors (i.e., age, experience, personality) and resources (i.e., social supports, coping mechanisms), along with the physical and social resources available in the workplace (i.e., equipment, social support, leadership, safety climate) impact on the individual's ability to cope with Work Related Stress (WRS) and wellbeing challenges.

In the OECD countries, mental health conditions are the second largest cause for work disability [2] and their proportion is still increasing. At the 2021 World Economic Forum

© Springer Nature Switzerland AG 2022
V. G. Duffy et al. (Eds.): HCII 2022, LNCS 13521, pp. 61–79, 2022.
https://doi.org/10.1007/978-3-031-17902-0_5

[3], it was reported two out of three employers now have mental health (MH) as their number one priority [4]. However, it was also noted that only one in six employees feel supported by their company during the COVID 19 pandemic. The Forum's 'mental health in the workplace initiative' outlines a vision 'where all workplace leaders recognize and commit – with the right tools in place – to taking tangible and evidence-based action on mental health and wellbeing, enabling their workforces to thrive' [4].

The 2008 European Pact for Mental Health and Well-being recognizes the changing demands and increasing pressures in the workplace and encourages employers to implement additional, voluntary measures to promote mental well-being [5]. These voluntary measures highlight the need for employers to go beyond a 'compliance' based approach. However, the appetite for implementing voluntary measures to support wellbeing varies across different industries and sectors.

Aviation is subject to seasonal fluctuations in terms of ticket demands/passenger traffic. Many aviation workers (both on the ground and in the air) work antisocial and irregular working hours and have commuting lifestyles. This creates many psychosocial pressures for workers attempting to balance the demands of work life and home-based responsibilities. In 2006, Hubbard and Bor provided an informative account of the mental health issues affecting pilots and the consequences of these [6]. The last decade has seen an increase in studies focusing on Work Related Stress (WRS) and mental health issues for pilots. Prior to the COVID pandemic, there was ample evidence of work stress issues impacting on pilot wellbeing. This includes disengagement and burnout [7] and depression amongst pilots – including studies at Harvard [8] and Trinity College Dublin [9–12]. Notably, in the Trinity College Dublin study involving 2,000 commercial pilots, 92% of respondents stated that the environment in which pilots work can contribute to the onset of and/or worsen an existing a mental health issue [11, 12]. Further, the study highlights the benefits of self-care practices adopted by commercial pilots, to manage wellbeing (including mental health) and foster resilience [12]. Practices such as sleep management, managing social wellness and taking physical exercise were demonstrated to have a positive effect on pilot wellbeing, and in particular, depression severity levels [12]. However, the study highlights that at an organisational level, the culture of supporting and maintaining wellbeing for pilots falls short. Currently, there is no definitive data directly linking wellbeing risk (including mental wellbeing) to safety outcomes in aviation [9, 11]. Further, there is a dearth of evidence around wellbeing risk. Airlines are not required to collect wellbeing data on a routine basis. Wellbeing data is however being gathered in relation to pilot peer support programs. As defined by the European regulator, any wellbeing trends or insights must be anonymized/de-identified when fed back into safety systems [13].

Some argue that airlines need to think differently about (a) supporting pilot wellbeing, (b) capturing data about wellbeing (including the link between wellbeing issues and performance/safety events), and (c) using wellbeing information to assess wellbeing risk in airline safety management systems [14]. The use of apps Potentially, mobile technologies might be used to support pilot self-monitoring of wellbeing, whilst on and off duty, along with enabling wellbeing and WRS reporting, supporting an integrated health and safety risk assessment process.

This paper reports on the findings of two anonymous online surveys (referred here-after to as Survey 1 and Survey 2) undertaken with pilots. The surveys address pilot health and self-care behaviors, the use of technology to support wellbeing management, and the acceptability of sharing wellbeing information captured using mobile phone apps, with aviation employers, to support the analysis of wellbeing risk in safety management systems (SMSs). Survey 1 was undertaken with pilots, but not specific to any organization. Survey 2 was undertaken with pilots working for a European aviation organization and elicited some additional feedback on the company's wellbeing culture and respondent attitudes to reporting MH issues and seeking support. First, a background to this research is presented. Following this, the methodological approach is outlined. Survey results are then outlined. The results are then discussed. A preliminary approach to implementing the proposed mobile phone apps is then reviewed, along with a plan for how this might link to the future analysis of wellbeing information in airline safety management systems. As part of this, a proposed industry wide 'welling monitor' is suggested. Areas for further research are then examined and some conclusions drawn.

2 Background

2.1 Wellbeing, Mental Health, Quality of Life and Work Life Balance

Physical, psychological factors and social factors (including family relationships, social support, working conditions and working environment) are some of the determinants affecting a person's health and wellbeing [15]. As emphasized in the constitution of the World Health Organisation (WHO), health is more than the absence of disease [16]. Accordingly, the WHO highlight the importance of fostering and maintaining positive wellbeing and reaching one's potential, as opposed to simply preventing and managing illness. This aligns with positive psychology frameworks which are directed at human 'flourishing' [17]. The concept of 'quality of life' (QOL) is also related to that of wellbeing and 'flourishing'. Multiple factors play a role in QOL including financial security, job satisfaction, family life, health, and safety. Work life balance is a key part of QOL. Where good work life balance exists, workers can easily combine work, family commitments, and leisure. Importantly, the 'Better Life Index' includes work life balance as one of the eleven factors contributing to QOL [18]. Research indicates that occupations involving shiftwork and/or the requirement to work antisocial working hours can create imbalances in the home/work interface, leading to work family conflict [19]. Work family conflict (or work-family interference) refers to 'a form of inter-role conflict in which role pressures from the work and family domains are mutually incompatible in some respect' [19].

2.2 Occupational Health and Safety and Mental Wellbeing in the Workplace

The International Labour Organization (ILO) and the World Health Organization (WHO) define occupational health in relation to three objectives. "These are (1) the maintenance and promotion of workers' health and working capacity; (2) the improvement of working environment and work to become conducive to safety and health and (3) development of work organizations and working cultures in a direction which supports health and safety at work and in doing so also promotes a positive social climate and smooth operation and may enhance productivity of the undertakings" [20]. Tamers (2019) proposes the 'Total Worker Health' (TWH) framework, which is defined in relation to policies, programs, and practices that integrate protection from work-related safety and health hazards, with promotion of injury and illness prevention efforts to advance worker well-being [21].

2.3 Aviation Worker Wellbeing and Wellbeing Reporting

The issue of aviation worker wellbeing/mental health has received increased attention since the 2015 Germanwings Flight 9525 accident. In particular, the tragedy raised issue pertaining to the aeromedical assessment of pilots, medical confidentiality, and issues around disclosure of (MH) issues to employers. In 2018, following the Germanwings tragedy, EASA introduced new rules in relation to the management of pilot mental fitness. These rules pertain to three key areas - psychological testing of aircrew pre-employment in line flight, access to a psychological support/peer support resource, and substance abuse testing on a random basis. Many in the industry argue that these guidelines do not go far enough – pointing to the fact that the rules overlook prevention [22, 23]. Further, it is argued that the new rules do not address positive wellbeing [24]. The Trinity College Study highlights the continued stigma associated with MH issues and reporting unfit for work [11, 12]. This was corroborated in a further anonymous survey undertaken in 2020, with a broad range of aviation workers [25]. In this study approximately 1 in 4 respondents stated that they would willingly report MH issues to their employer [25].

2.4 Safety Management Systems and Safety II Approach

Over the last 15 years, airlines have been introducing safety management systems (SMS). This follows a focus on prevention as opposed to reaction, and the advancement of a proactive safety culture, in which everybody in the company is responsible for safety. The objective of a SMS is to provide a structured management approach to control safety risks in operations [26]. Safety management systems include four components – safety policy, safety assurance, safety risk management and safety promotion. Currently, the assessment of wellbeing risk primarily relates to fatigue. Critically, it does not include other aspects of the pilot's physical wellbeing (i.e., diet and physical activity), and/or other dimensions of their social and psychological wellbeing.

The Safety-I approach focuses on improving safety by examining and learning from system failures (for example, near misses, safety events and serious accidents). The Safety-II approach investigates all possible outcomes: involving normal performance (everyday routine performance), excellent performance, near-misses, accidents, and disasters [28]. As such, Safety-II focuses on all events (the full distribution profile of safety – both good and bad). In so doing, it seeks to enhance effectiveness while also addressing failure. Importantly, Safety-I and Safety-II are complementary [28].

2.5 Organisational Approaches to Addressing Wellbeing Within SMS

Some airlines are adopting more innovative approaches to addressing wellbeing [27] and linking to predictive safety management concepts and the Safety II approach [28]. This wellbeing (not simply illness) and to draw attention to mental health (i.e., mood, stress levels, attitude) and the use of coping strategies [34].

3 Methodology

3.1 Data Gathering

An anonymous online survey using the Qualtrics survey platform, was administered at two different time periods to assess the acceptability of introducing novel mobile phone apps, to support a pilot to assess and manage their wellbeing in two contexts – namely, while off duty, and on duty.

The survey design drew upon prior research undertaken by the authors pertaining to a biopsychosocial model of wellbeing, the factors that can positively and negatively influence a pilot's physical, mental, and social health, and the case for introducing new tools to enable pilots to manage their wellbeing [9–12]. Survey 1 was administered between November 2020 and January 2021 (n = 82), and targeted commercial pilots only. Respondents were recruited using social media platforms such as LinkedIn and Twitter. Survey 2 was administered between February 2021 and April 2022, and targeted staff working at a European based aviation organization, (n = 88). In this case, staff received an email from management, advertising the survey and the research objectives. The second survey included some additional questions on mental health reporting and seeking help within the organization.

This research was conducted in accordance with the Declaration of Helsinki, and the survey protocol was approved by the Ethics Committee of the School of Psychology, Trinity College Dublin (TCD) Ireland. The data protection impact assessment was approved by the Data Protection Officer at TCD.

3.2 Data Analysis

Survey questions involved categorical data only. Descriptive statistics were computed for all questions. Text analysis was undertaken for those questions eliciting additional text feedback. This involved undertaking counts in excel and the production of word clouds.

4 Results

4.1 Respondent Profiles

Survey 1 respondents were mostly male (77.63%), aged between 36–45 years (38.16%), most working between 11–15 years (20.83%), working for full-service carrier (51%), employed – permanent – full time (36%), captain rank (44%), and flying short range (43%). Survey 2 respondents were mostly male (95.24%), aged between 25 and 35 years (42.37%) and working full time (100%). The largest portion were Junior First Officers (31.33%).

involves capturing routine information about staff wellbeing levels using a combination of methods which protect employee identity and speak to concepts of 'just culture' and 'trust'. This includes the use of pulse surveys (which elicit anonymous information about crew wellbeing levels and coping methods), operational learning reviews (which capture information about the presence of safety, via confidential interviews) and making use of de-identified data from Peer Assistance Network (PAN) reports and conversations with aeromedical/psychology professionals at the airline. As argued by McCarthy [27] 'trust works both ways, as does accountability'. The objective is to channel learning via these alternative reporting methods into the airline's safety management system, so that risks relating to staff wellbeing are identified and managed. In addition, other airlines are making use of deidentified information from the analysis of peer support referrals, to gather evidence about staff wellbeing and the contributory factors to wellbeing and mental health issues [29].

2.6 Safety Reporting, Managing Privacy and Industry Co-operation

Voluntary and confidential reporting systems have been established, enabling pilots and other aviation professionals to confidentially report near misses and safety events, with the goal of improving flight safety, while protecting operational personnel. Established in the 1982, the UK Confidential Human Factors Incident Reporting Programme for aviation (CHIRP), invites safety-related reports from flight crew, air traffic control officers, licensed aircraft maintenance engineers, cabin crew and the general aviation community along with workers in the international maritime sector, including the shipping industry, fishing industry and leisure users [30]. In addition, the Air Safety Reporting System (ASRS) system developed by the Federal Aviation Authority, and operated by NASA, enables safety reporting [31]. NASA operate as a neutral third party (i.e., no enforcement authority and no relationship with airlines). Protections are in place, to ensure that reporters can come forward, without fear of a punitive outcome. The benefit of this system is that it enables the reporting of systemic safety issues – and specifically, the identification of latent system hazards, necessary to predictive risk management approaches. However, no such database exists in relation to wellbeing, and more broadly the occupational health and safety (OSH) space within aviation.

2.7 Existing Wellbeing Self-assessment Tools

Several checklists have been advanced to support pilot self-assessment of fitness to fly at an operational level. This includes two checklists developed by the Federal Aviation Authority (FAA) in the USA. That is, the I'm Safe Checklist, which supports pilot evaluation of the 'pilot' section of the 5Ps (i.e., plan, plane, pilot, passengers, and programming [32], and the Personal Minimums Checklist, which addresses four evaluation areas – the pilot, the aircraft, the environment, and external pressures [33]. The FAA's 'I'm Safe Checklist' supports pilots in relation to self-assessment of their overall readiness for flight in relation to illness, medication, stress, alcohol, fatigue, and emotion. Many in the industry highlight the need for aviation workers to help themselves (i.e., address self-care) as opposed to waiting for regulation to mandate better supports for pilots [34]. It has been suggested that this checklist might be extended to address positive

4.2   Health, Wellbeing and Self-Care

Respondents reported higher levels of physical wellbeing than mental and emotional wellbeing. 66% of Survey 1 respondents and 68% of Survey 2 respondents rated their physical health as either very good or excellent. 54% of Survey 1 respondents, and 62% of Survey 2 respondents rated their mental/emotional health as very good or excellent.

66.20% of Survey 1 respondents and 74% of Survey 2 respondents reported that they used self-care strategies to deal with stress and WRS. Respondents in both surveys provided examples of the top five coping strategies which they found most beneficial from a stress coping perspective. Taking exercise was the most frequently selected strategy in both surveys. Table 1 below details the five top selfcare strategies reported by survey respondents.

Table 1. Selfcare strategies.

#	Survey 1	Survey 2
1	Take exercise/sport (13.66%)	Exercise, sport (15.56%)
2	Socialize/spending time with family and friends (12.68%)	Spend time outdoors/nature (12.59%)
3	Focus on sleep and rest (10.24%)	Socialize/spending time with family and friends (10.74%)
4	Spend time outdoors/in nature (10.24%)	Focus on sleep and rest (9.63%)
5	Try to do things I enjoy (eating out, watch TV, play video games, hobbies etc.) (9.76%)	Try to do things I enjoy (eating out, watch TV, play video games, hobbies etc.) (8.15%)

Participants were also asked about their use of alternative/maladaptive strategies to cope with stress and WRS. A large proportion in both surveys reported using 'avoidance' as a strategy. Table 2 below details the five top maladaptive strategies, as reported by survey respondents.

Table 2. Maladaptive strategies.

#	Survey 1	Survey 2
1	Avoidance/ignore (38.10%)	Avoidance/Ignore (31.47%)
2	Self-harm (17.46%)	Alcohol (21.68%)
3	Substance misuse - alcohol (7.94%)	Withdraw from people (16.08%)
4	Screaming/throwing things/tantrums (7.94%)	Temper/lash out/aggressive behavior (10.49%)
5	Smoking (4.76%)	Disordered eating (6.29%)

4.3 Self-Care and Technologies

Many respondents reported using a mobile phone app to manage their health and well-being – 41% of survey 1 respondents and 31% of survey 2 respondents. In the case of respondents who currently do not use a mobile phone app to manage their wellbeing, nearly half noted that they would be open to doing this (44% of survey 1 respondents, and 48% of survey 2 respondents). 40% of Survey 1 respondents and 60% of survey 2 respondents reported using a wearable device (for example, Fitbit or Garmin) to track aspects of their health and wellbeing. The top three types of health data tracked was the same in both surveys. The top 3 were exercise/activity, sleep, and heart rate. In survey 1, over 50% of respondents referred to exercise/activity, while in Survey 2, 100% of respondents referred to this. Of those who are currently not using wearables, 34% of survey 1 respondents and 48% of survey 2 respondents stated that they would be open to using a wearable to manage their health. Respondents were invited to provide suggestions of the top three health factors/areas that they would like to monitor using a wearable. The same items were reported in both surveys, with exercise being rated the most important in both surveys. In relation to Survey 1, the top three were sleep, exercise/physical activity/steps, and heart rate. In Survey 2, the top three were exercise/physical activity/steps, sleep, and heart rate.

4.4 Self-Reporting Health Data

Respondents were asked whether they would be happy if the information collected using a wearable device might be integrated into an aviation worker health and wellbeing app, for the purpose of assessing wellbeing risk (pending their consent and appropriate security protections). 59% of Survey 1 respondents agreed or strongly agreed that they would be happy, while 47% of Survey 2 respondents agreed or strongly agreed that they would be happy.

77% of survey 1 respondents and 64% of survey 2 respondents reported that they would be willing to self-report certain types of health data. In both surveys, the top ranked data type was data pertaining to stress levels. Table 3 below provides feedback as to the types of information they would be willing to self-report, using a mobile phone app.

Table 3. Data willing to report.

#	Survey 1	Survey 2
1	Stress level (28.97%)	Stress level (29.67%)
2	Levels of anxiety (19.63%)	Mood (25.27%)
5	Levels of depression (15.89%)	Levels of anxiety (17.58%)

In addition, 48% of survey 1 respondents and 44% of survey 2 respondents noted that they would be happy to self-report data about social activity.

Respondents were invited to report using free text what data (if any) they would you like to be shared with their employer. In Survey 1, the word 'none' was most frequently cited. In Survey 2, the words' data' and 'health' were most frequently cited. See example word clouds below (Fig. 1, Fig. 2).

Fig. 1. Survey 1 - Data I Would Be Willing to Share with My Employer

4.5 Organisational Culture and Priorities

32% of Survey 1 respondents and 41% of Survey 2 respondents reported that their employer is interested to a 'moderate extent', in protecting their health and wellbeing.

4.6 Integration with Other System/SMS

93% of Survey 1 respondents, and 83% of Survey 2 respondents agreed or strongly agreed that fatigue risk management systems (and by implication rostering/flight planning systems) need to be extended to consider the relationship between fatigue risk and the other dimensions of a person's wellbeing.

70% of Survey 1 respondents, and 65% of Survey 2 respondents agreed or strongly agreed that existing safety management and rostering/planning systems might be augmented to make use of wellbeing/health data from an operational and risk/safety management perspective.

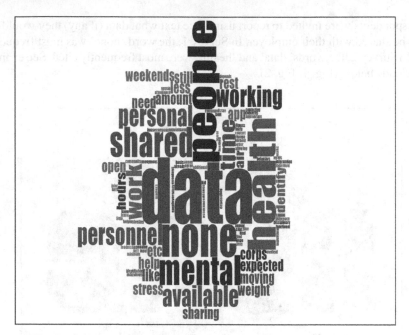

Fig. 2. Survey 2 - Data I Would Be Willing to Share with My Employer

4.7 Wellbeing Culture, Disclosing Wellbeing and Seeking Help (Survey 2 Only)

Survey 2 respondents were asked some additional questions pertaining wellbeing reporting and seeking help, along with the wellbeing culture at their company. Less than half (41%) agreed or strongly agreed that there is adequate attention to the promotion of positive wellbeing and coping at their organization. 72% agree or strongly agreed that there are low levels of speaking out and/or reporting about mental health amongst their colleagues. Over half (58%) agreed or strongly agreed that they would look for help if they had a health issue (including mental health). The top three people they would look for help included (1) a partner/spouse (27.47%), a close friend (24.73%) and a family member (15.93%). A small number indicated they would use peer support (10.44%). Just under 4% indicated that they would approach a mental health professional at their company. A very low number (32%) indicated they would willingly approach their employer with a MH issue. 22% indicated that they had approached a MH professional outside their company to obtain help.

4.8 High Level Concepts for Mobile Phone Apps and Tool Requirements

Respondents were asked several questions pertaining to the high-level requirement for a potential mobile app, to support wellbeing management for pilots. A large majority either agreed or strongly agreed that staff must be educated about the boundaries between life inside and outside of work and managing conflicting demands (84% of Survey 1 respondents, and 93% of Survey 2 respondents). 73% of Survey 1 respondents, and 86% of survey 2 respondents either agreed or strongly agreed that staff require tools to nudge them towards healthy behaviors, and to prevent the onset of problems (i.e., to keep them well). 66% of Survey 1 respondents, and 71% of Survey 2 respondents either agreed or strongly agreed that future wellbeing tools (i.e., mobile apps) should provide staff with tools/checklists to enable them to evaluate their health and wellbeing, in advance of reporting for duty. 82% of Survey 1 respondents, and 85% of Survey 2 respondents either agreed or strongly agreed that any health and wellbeing assessment provided by the wellbeing tools should include the three pillars of wellbeing (i.e., physical, psychological/emotional, and social). 68% of Survey 1 respondents, and 75% of Survey 2 respondents either agreed or strongly agreed that any health and wellbeing assessment provided by the wellbeing tools should include what I am currently doing to manage stress/work related stress.

88% of both Survey 1 and Survey 2 respondents either agreed or strongly agreed that future wellbeing tools (i.e., mobile apps) should provide the user with feedback about the state of their health and wellbeing. 86% of Survey 1 respondents, and 90% of Survey 2 respondents either agreed or strongly agreed that mobile apps should provide the user with feedback about their stress levels 68% of Survey 1 respondents, and 73% of Survey 2 respondents either agreed or strongly agreed that supporting healthy behavior requires the development of a set of targets for oneself and monitoring of one's level of achievement of the targets. 59% of Survey 1 respondents, and 47% of Survey 2 respondents either agreed or strongly agreed that future wellbeing tools (i.e., mobile apps) should provide the user with feedback about their own health and wellbeing and how it compares with others. 66% of Survey 1 respondents, and 68% of Survey 2 respondents either agreed or strongly agreed that future wellbeing tools (i.e., mobile apps) should provide access to virtual coaching/support to maintain positive wellbeing. 59% of Survey 1 respondents, and 68% of Survey 2 respondents either agreed or strongly agreed that future wellbeing tools (i.e., mobile apps) should enable the user to report challenges to their health and wellbeing that may impact on their work. 63% of Survey 1 respondents, and 68% of Survey 2 respondents either agreed or strongly agreed future wellbeing tools (i.e., mobile apps) should enable them to report wellbeing issues that contribute to safety events.

4.9 App Concepts/Tools and Functions

Respondents were rate from 1 (low) to 10 (high) the most useful functions for a mobile phone app supporting wellbeing, while off duty. Respondents across both surveys highly rated the function 'reporting of stress and wellbeing issues that impact on safety'. This feature was rated second most important by survey 1 respondents, and third most important by Survey 2 respondents. Tables 4 and 5 below provide a summary of the top three selected functions, for both the off duty and on duty apps.

Table 4. Off duty tool – functions.

#	Survey 1	Survey 2
1	Integration with airline information systems (for example, roster, health promotion information, EAP services information) (54.5%)	Provision of general resources/information and relaxation exercises (45.76)
2	Reporting of stress and wellness issues that impact on safety (52.27%)	Self-assessment tools (37.28%)
3	Wellness tracking, assessment, and reporting (47.73%)	Wellness goal setting, plans and feedback (35.59%) Reporting of stress and wellness issues that impact on safety (35.59%)

Table 5. On duty tool – functions

#	Survey 1	Survey 2
1	Enable crew self-assessment of wellbeing/state in advance of the flight (63.64%)	Provide supports in a crisis (55.87%)
2	Provide supports in a crisis (61.37)	Enable crew self-assessment of wellbeing/state in advance of the flight (43.97%)
3	Enable reporting concerning stress and wellbeing threats that impact on safety (56.82%)	Enable access to support services within the airline (38.77%)

5   Discussion

5.1   Pilot Self-Care and Stress Coping

Respondents reported higher levels of physical wellbeing than mental and emotional wellbeing. A large proportion of survey respondents (66.20% of survey 1 respondents and 74% of survey 2 respondents), reported that they are using coping strategies to manage stress and WRS. This should be both encouraged and supported by their employers. However, a significant number of respondents reported 'avoidance' as a strategy. This needs to be addressed in relation to crew training and safety promotion activities. Pilots should be encouraged to assess their own wellbeing and adopt healthy approaches to managing stress and WRS, to benefit their individual wellbeing perspective along with flight safety. In cases of mild suffering, it is likely that a self-management approach will prevent an escalation of symptoms, with consequences for the person's wellbeing and operational performance.

5.2 Use of Technologies and Health Promotion

This research indicates the overall acceptability of using mobile phone apps and wearable devices to manage pilot wellbeing. A large proportion of survey respondents reported using both mobile phone apps and wearable devices to manage their wellbeing.

Survey feedback indicates that the evaluation of wellbeing requires capturing data across the three pillars of wellbeing (i.e., biological, psychological, and social). In addition, it highlights the importance of including information about a person stress coping activity. Further, the survey indicates that pilots might benefit from nudges in relation to both self-assessing their wellbeing and managing their wellbeing (i.e., engaging in health promoting activities, or activities that deliver therapeutic benefits).

There is an opportunity to address work stress and wellbeing from a positive managerial perspective. The use of mobile phone apps might be supported by employers, in terms of enabling self-awareness and self-assessment of wellbeing and MH, along with the adoption of healthy strategies to promote positive wellbeing/resilience and manage stress and WRS. Airlines might sponsor this technology for their pilots, as part of a preventative health management approaches. This would supplement existing secondary approaches to wellbeing management (for example, wellbeing awareness training), along with tertiary approaches (for example, peer support, access to company psychologist and or access to external counselling services).

5.3 Management of Wellbeing Risk in SMS

In keeping with the literature, this study highlights the existing poor wellbeing culture within aviation. In both surveys, respondents indicated that they would be willing to self-report data using a mobile phone app, to support self-assessment of their own health and wellbeing. However, respondents also indicated that they have concerns sharing this data with their employer. In both surveys, the term 'none' was the most frequently reported term used by respondents in relation to the question of 'would you be willing to share this data with your employer'. Further, survey 2 highlights significant issues pertaining to MH stigma and disclosing MH challenges to an employer. Very low numbers agreed that they would willingly disclose wellbeing/MH challenges to their employer. However, in both surveys, a large number agreed that existing safety management systems should be extended to consider the analysis of information pertaining to wellbeing risk. This presents a quandary. The capture and use of wellbeing information in an airline SMS is perceived as required and beneficial. However, pilots do not feel safe sharing this information with their employer. In the current climate, there seems to be insufficient trust between pilots and their management, to support such reporting practices. Thus, assessing wellbeing risk within a SMS is dependent on building trust between staff and management, and making progress in terms of fostering a wellness culture within aviation.

Further, in relation to the proposed tool concepts, we would expect additional barriers in relation to collecting wellbeing information while on duty (i.e., identification and privacy). Unsurprisingly, the top three features for an on-duty tool, did not include this.

As indicated in this research, airlines will need to think differently about how wellbeing information is obtained and used, to support an integrated approach to health and safety risk assessment. A future strategy necessitates careful attention to issues of data protection, and a phased implementation approach. From an implementation perspective, trust is obtained via staff protections and safeguards. De-identifying information (i.e., protecting employees/staff) is a route to both obtaining wellbeing data (i.e., evidence), and to building a culture of wellbeing. This in turn, is a stepping-stone to the assessment of wellbeing risk in aviation SMSs.

5.4 Wellbeing Apps, Total Worker Health and Joint Responsibility

Safety management needs to be integrated with wellbeing management, as part of an integrated approach to occupational health and safety, and the adoption of a total worker health perspective [21]. Supporting pilots to manage their own wellbeing (i.e., self-assessment and self-care), while on and off duty, and enabling wellbeing reporting is the start of advancing a wellbeing culture. Moreover, it is key to advancing an integrated health and safety culture and associated process. As evidenced in this research, the design and conceptual approach to managing wellbeing underpinning the mobile phone apps follows from an integrated approach. In this respect, it is anticipated that pilots would use the apps to bolster positive wellbeing, to report on their wellbeing, along with reporting on specific wellbeing/WRS issues that impact on performance and operational safety, and to access supports where required. In the short term, wellbeing information might not be shared with employers directly. However, this might happen further down the line (see below). Importantly, if this information is shared with employers, employers have a responsibility to ensure that pilot are supported, and that safety levels are maintained. This requires aviation organizations to adopt a 'joint responsibility' approach to managing wellbeing.

6 Recommendations and Future Roadmap for Managing Wellbeing in Airline SMS

6.1 Augmenting I'm Safe Checklist and Wellbeing Assessment Using Mobile Apps

It is worth noting that pilots responded positively to the idea of using the mobile phone app to assess their own wellbeing in advance of the flight. Here, an individual pilot would assess their own wellbeing, using a mix of objective data (i.e., data gathered from wearable) and subjective data (i.e., self-reports) about their wellbeing. In the current concept (i.e., tool used on a personal basis, not integrated with work), it would be up to the individual pilot to decide how this self-assessment might be treated from a 'fitness to fly' perspective. Further, it would be up to the pilot to decide how they might share their own assessment of their wellbeing with their copilot. To note, the pilot using the app would not be required to share his/her data with anybody (the process would sit outside any organizational process). This could lead to difficult situations for different parties. For example, if a pilot showed the mobile phone app user interface to their co-pilot, and the interface indicated extreme fatigue, what would be expected of the co-pilot? Would this be different from what might be expected from a pilot verbalizing,

'I am exhausted today', without any app data? Does the availability of objective data change the requirement to ask the copilot to step down, and/or report the issue to flight operations? If there was a safety event, would the co-pilot be considered responsible? Evidently, pilots are already using apps and making such self-assessments – outside any formal process within the airline. Is this acceptable from a safety management perspective?

6.2 Assessing Wellbeing Risk in Airline SMS

As indicated in this research, a phased approach to the management of wellbeing risk in aviation SMS is required. Airlines might consider the implementation of mobile phone apps for staff as part of a broader wellbeing management roadmap.

The off-duty app might be used to promote positive wellbeing, to enable a preventative approach to wellbeing management (at an individual level), and to promote a wellbeing culture. This would foster trust and destigmatize wellbeing/MH – paving the way for an improved wellbeing reporting culture which is a prerequisite for the collection and analysis of data about wellbeing risk in an airline SMS.

Further, with the right protections in place and pilot consent, pilot wellbeing data (i.e., data harvested via the off duty mobile phone app) might be shared in a central repository. In addition, such information might be collected using web-based reporting interfaces. This might be more acceptable for pilots (i.e., protection afforded by online reporting as opposed to mobile phone app, where there are always fears of hacking). Specifically, pilots might be invited to share their deidentified wellbeing information in an industry wide 'wellbeing monitor'. Potentially, this system might collect anonymous information in five core topic areas. These are outlined in Table 6.

Table 6. Data to gather from pilots.

#	Description
1	Real time levels of wellbeing for aviation workers
2	Sources of WRS linked to the job (span biopsychosocial - that is, beyond fatigue to include psychosocial hazards)
3	The relationship between wellbeing, performance, and safety (i.e., impact of wellbeing and sources of WRS on performance - including near misses and safety events)
4	Coping methods (i.e., what self-care practices using) and what are more/less useful
5	Use of organizational supports (i.e., examples of supports) and what is most beneficial

Such a system might produce trends reports based on aggregated deidentified data. This would enable the industry to (1) better understand wellbeing for aviation workers, (2) to normalize wellbeing and MH/addressing stigma and reporting barriers (i.e., enable a safe space for sharing of wellbeing information), and (3) to drive change in the industry in terms of wellbeing culture and making use of data about real time wellbeing and WRS within an organisation's SMS, in support of (a) a preventative approach to managing wellbeing risk and psychosocial hazards (i.e., primary interventions), and (b) joined up approach to health and safety (i.e., integrated health, wellbeing and safety). Further, such a system would (4) enable airlines to consider wellbeing risk in their SMS – albeit indirectly and (5) enable pilots sharing data, to compare their wellbeing with other groups.

As indicated in Fig. 3, an online platform might be developed enabling the capture of wellbeing information (reports in), and the analysis of trends information (reports out). In terms of 'reports in', this might include data gathered from mobile phone apps (i.e., linked to wearables), and data captured using web-based reporting methods (i.e., not linked to wearables, but potentially allowing pilot to report this data, if they choose). As such, different functions might be provided for data creators (pilots providing information) and data viewers (those viewing reports). 'Reports out' might be targeted at different stakeholders. For example, (1) pilots sharing information (2) pilots not sharing information (3) airline staff [safety managers, crew rostering, human resources, occupational health and safety, training, and flight operations], (4) aeromedical examiners, (5) aviation regulator and (6) health and safety regulator.

Wellbeing Monitor

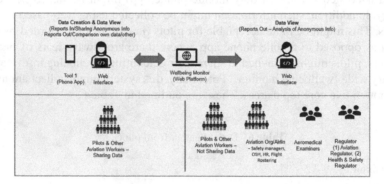

Fig. 3. Wellbeing monitor

Once a more positive wellbeing culture has been advanced, and trust has improved, this approach might be extended. That is, in the longer term, airlines might develop their own 'wellbeing monitors'. In this case, pilots providing consent might share deidentified information with their employer to assess wellbeing risk within the airline SMS. This would enable a preventative approach to wellbeing management at an organisational level. Deidentified and aggregated wellbeing data might be used within the context of the flight planning and crew scheduling/rostering processes. This aligns well with a commitment to 'just culture', to a 'learning culture' and a 'people-centric' approach. The aviation community understands the role of 'just culture' in relation to safety. Health/wellbeing and safety culture needs to be framed from this perspective (i.e., safe disclosure and psychological safety). Evidently, it is not enough to talk about 'just culture'. This needs to be enshrined in laws that protects aviation workers, so that workers can disclose problem without this impacting on their license and career progression.

7   Next Steps and Areas for Further Research

Participatory based human factors action research is required to specify the design of mobile phone app, along with the proposed wellbeing monitor for use by the industry. This will require collaboration across different stakeholders in relation to both 'reports in' (i.e., pilots sharing deidentified information) and 'reports out' for different stakeholders. In relation to the design of the off-duty wellbeing app, the algorithm producing a wellbeing scoring requires consideration. This score will need to integrate a mix of subjective (pilot self-reports) and objective reporting data (i.e., data from wearable). Potentially scores might be provided for the individual pillars. In addition, attention needs to be paid to the design of nudges. This should consider the duty status of the pilot, and the expected role of the health promoting nudges. In this context, the purpose of the nudges is not to diagnose mental ill-health. However, nudges might be used to signpost the pilot to available supports and/or specialist help if a consistent pattern of poor wellness is detected. This requires further research. Data protection issues must also be addressed. Pilots require assurances about how their data is protected and shared with the industry. Governance and oversight in relation to data protection is critical.

8   Conclusion

Airlines need to go beyond a compliance-based approach to wellbeing management for pilots, to a human centered and ethical process. This involves treating pilot wellbeing as a shared responsibility. Further, the management of wellbeing should be an integral part of the safety culture (i.e., integrated health, wellbeing, and safety culture). This starts with gathering and making use of data regarding the wellbeing of their staff, while addressing issues pertaining to trust.

In addition, aviation organizations need to rethink their objectives and approach in terms of prioritizing wellbeing, and providing appropriate wellbeing supports for pilots.

Technologies are part of addressing wellbeing management for pilots, and for addressing an integrated health and safety culture. New mobile phone apps might be implemented to support self-care for pilots as part of a phased approach to the management of wellbeing risk in aviation safety management systems (SMS), and the promotion of an integrated health and safety culture. Further, they might be considered as part of a preventative health strategy (i.e., primary intervention).

With the increasing use of operational intelligence and reporting systems involving machine learning and artificial intelligence, there is an opportunity to use technology to further enhance the Safety II approach. This depends on the ability to gather information about the wellbeing of operational personnel, both when on and off duty. However, this will only happen if there is a strong safety/reporting culture – underpinned by protections for staff, so that personal information is protected. In the short term, an industry wide wellbeing monitor enabling the collection of anonymous information pertaining to pilot WRS and wellbeing levels is required. Airlines might make use of this information, as a 'stepping-stone' to analyzing wellbeing risk in an airline SMS. The use of the proposed mobile phone apps is one of many interventions that might be considered by aviation organizations in relation to supporting employee wellbeing.

References

1. Centre for Disease Control & Prevention (CDC): Workplace health model. https://www.cdc.gov/workplacehealthpromotion/model/. Last accessed 11 Mar 2022
2. The Organisation for Economic Co-operation and Development (OECD): Mental health, disability and work. https://www.oecd.org/els/45008308.pdf. Last accessed 11 Mar 2022
3. Viola, S., Moncrieff, J.: Claims for sickness and disability benefits owing to mental disorders in the UK: trends from 1995 to 2014. BJPsych. Open **2**(1), 18–24 (2016)
4. World Economic Forum. Why this is the year we must take action on mental health. https://www.weforum.org/agenda/2019/01/lets-make-2019-the-year-we-take-action-on-mental-health/. Last accessed 11 Mar 2022
5. European Commission: European pact for mental health and wellbeing. https://ec.europa.eu/health/ph_determinants/life_style/mental/docs/pact_en.pdf. Last accessed 11 Mar 2022
6. Hubbard, T., Bor, R. (Eds.): Aviation Mental Health: Psychological Implications for Air Transportation (1st ed.). Routledge (2006). https://doi.org/10.4324/9781315568560
7. Demerouti, E., et al.: Burnout among pilots: psychosocial factors related to happiness and performance at simulator training. Ergonomics **62**(2), 233–245 (2019)
8. Wu, A.C., Donnelly-McLay, D., Weisskopf, M.G., McNeely, E., Betancourt, T.S., Allen, J.G.: Airplane pilot mental health and suicidal thoughts: a cross-sectional descriptive study via anonymous web-based survey. Environ. Health **15**(1), 121 (2016). https://doi.org/10.1186/s12940-016-0200-6.doi:10.1186/s12940-016-0200-6
9. Cahill, J., Cullen, P., Gaynor, K.: Estimating the impact of work-related stress on pilot wellbeing and flight safety. In: Proceedings of the 2nd International Symposium on Human Mental Workload: Models and Applications (H-WORKLOAD 2018), Amsterdam, 20–21 Sept 2018, Netherlands Aerospace Centre (NLR), The Netherlands (2018)
10. Cullen, P., Cahill, J., Gaynor, K.: A qualitative study exploring well-being and the potential impact of work-related stress among commercial airline pilots. Aviation Psychol. Hum. Fact. (2021)
11. Cahill, J., Cullen, P., Gaynor, R.: Interventions to support the management of WRS & wellbeing issues for commercial pilots. Cogn. Technol. Work **22**, 517–547 (2019)
12. Cahill, J., Cullen, P., Anwer, S., Wilson, S., Gaynor, K.: Pilot work related stress (WRS), Effects on Wellbeing (Including Mental Health) & Coping Methods. (2021). Int. J. Aerosp. Psychol. **31**(2), 87–109 (2021)
13. European Union Aviation Safety Agency (EASA): Commission Regulation (EU) No 965/2012 on Air Operations and associated EASA Decisions (AMC, GM and CS-FTL.1), Consolidated version for Easy Access Rules, Revision 12 Mar 2019. Part ORO, Annex II, Part ORO, ORO.GEN.200 Management Systems and associated Acceptable Means of Compliance (AMCs) and Guidance Material (GMs) (2019). https://www.easa.europa.eu/sites/default/files/dfu/Air%20OPS%20Easy%20Access%20Rules_Rev.12_March%202019.pdf
14. Cahill, J., Cullen, P., Anwer, S., Gaynor, K., Wilson, S.: The requirements for new tools for use by pilots and the aviation industry to manage risks pertaining to work-related stress (WRS) and wellbeing, and the ensuing impact on performance and safety. Technol. **8**, 40 (2020)
15. Engel, G.L.: The need for a new medical model: a challenge for biomedicine. Science **196**(4286), 129–36. https://doi.org/10.1126/science.847460. PMID: 847460 (1977)
16. World Health Organisation: Constitution of the World Health Organisation (2006). https://www.who.int/about/governance/constitution#:~:text=Constitution%20WHO%20remains%20firmly%20committed%20to%20the%20principles,not%20merely%20the%20absence%20of%20disease%20or%20infirmit
17. Seligman, M.E.: Flourish: A New Understanding of Happiness and Wellbeing and How to Achieve Them. Nicholas Brealey, London (2011)

18. The Organisation for Economic Co-operation and Development (OECD): Better life index. https://www.oecdbetterlifeindex.org/topics/life-satisfaction/#:~:text=Surveys%2C%20in%20particular%2C%20are%20used,measure%20life%20satisfaction%20and%20happiness.&text=Life%20satisfaction%20measures%20how%20people,OECD%20gave%20it%20a%206.5

19. Greenhaus, J., Beutell, N.: Sources of conflict between work and family roles. Acad. Manag. Rev. **10**(1) (1985)

20. International Labour Organisation (ILO): WHO & ILO joint statement on occupational health services & practices (2012). https://archive.ph/20120904021458/http://www.ilo.org/safework_bookshelf/english?content&nd=857170174

21. Tamers, S.L., Chosewood, L.C., Childress, A., Hudson, H., Nigam, J., Chang, C.C.: Total Worker Health® 2014–2018: the novel approach to worker safety, health, and well-being evolves. Int. J. Environ. Res. Public Health **16**(3), 321 (2019)

22. Atherton, M.: A question of psychology. Downloaded from: https://www.aerosociety.com/news/a-question-of-psychology/ on 6 Mar 2019

23. Dickens: Beyond Germanwings Flight 9525: pilot mental health and safety. Presentation to the European Association of Aviation Psychologists (EAAP). https://irp-cdn.multiscreensite.com/7d6d5c94/files/uploaded/Paul%20Dickens%20article.pdf

24. British Psychological Society x Aviation and aerospace psychology: Pilot mental health and wellbeing (2019). https://www.bps.org.uk/sites/bps.org.uk/files/Policy/Policy%20-%20Files/Aviation%20and%20aerospace%20psychology%20-%20pilot%20mental%20health%20and%20wellbeing.pdf

25. Cahill, J., Cullen, P., Anwer, S., Gaynor, K.: The Impact of the COVID 19 Pandemic on Aviation Workers & The Aviation System. Federal Aviation Authority (FAA) Human Factors Maintenance Quarterly, Dec 2020, vol. 8, no. 4 (2020). https://www.faa.gov/about/initiatives/maintenance_hf/fatigue/publications/

26. Skybrary: Safety Management (2021). https://skybrary.aero/enhancing-safety/safety-management

27. McCarthy, P.: Operational learning reviews. In: Proceedings of the Human Computer International Conference (2020)

28. Hollnagel, E.: Safety-I and safety-II: The Past and Future of Safety Management. In Safety-I and Safety-II: The Past and Future of Safety Management. Ashgate, Farnham, UK (2014)

29. Phoenix, N.: Peer support in aviation. Presentation at 2021 RaeS Annual Conference (2021). https://kurahumanfactors.com/kura-human-factors-sponsor-raes-conference/

30. The UK Confidential Human Factors Incident Reporting System: About Us. https://www.chirp.co.uk/about-us/chirp-aviation#:~:text=The%20aim%20of%20the%20UK%20Confidential%20Human%20Factors,all%20individuals%20employed%20in%2C%20or%20associated%20with%2C%20aviation

31. Aviation Safety Reporting System: https://asrs.arc.nasa.gov/

32. Federal Aviation Authority: Single-pilot crew resource management. https://www.faa.gov/news/safety_briefing/2015/media/SE_Topic_15_03.pdf

33. Federal Aviation Authority: Personal Minimums Checklist. https://www.faa.gov/training_testing/training/fits/guidance/media/personal%20minimums%20checklist.pdf

34. Cahill, J., Cullen, P., Anwer, S., Gaynor, K., Wilson, S.: The requirements for new tools for use by pilots and the aviation industry to manage risks pertaining to work-related stress (WRS) and wellbeing, and the ensuing impact on performance and safety. Technol. **8**(3) (2020)

Development of a System to Support Operators When a Ventilator Alarm Happens

Jun Hamaguchi[1]([✉]) and Sakae Yamamoto[2]

[1] Tohto University, Mihama, Chiba, Japan
jun.hamaguchi@tohto.ac.jp
[2] Tokyo University of Science, Katsushika, Tokyo, Japan

Abstract. Objective: This paper researches the behavior of ventilator operators from a cognitive perspective. Especially, based on the performance of the operator when an alarm happens, the system is built to support the operator's decisions. **Introduction:** Because of Covid-19, more operators were needed who could correctly operate the ventilator. Even inexperienced operators might operate the ventilator. Therefore, training support systems such as simulators that could simulate alarm situations are needed to train operators of the ventilator. An Operations Information Screen (OIS) was created that included logical decisions. The OIS is used to investigate the behavior of the inexperienced operators during ventilator alarms. **Methods:** The participants are the seven the IG operators in the previous study. The IG operator's behavior during a ventilator alarm using the OIS is video recorded. The verbal protocol data are also recorded to examine the thinking during the manipulation. After the experiment, the video recordings were reviewed with the participants and interviewed about the reasons for their speeches and behaviors. **Results:** From the analysis of the behavior and the verbal protocol, it was found to be a logical behavior. And, there was no behavior based on assumptions. An inexperienced operator could use the OIS to experience and learn the decisions of a skilled operator. The OIS could be used for education and training to learn the operating procedures performed by skilled operators in a short period of time. **Applications:** The results of this study are for alarms with machine side factors. Currently, the operators' behavior is being analyzed for alarms caused by patient changes, and the OIS is being developed.

Keywords: Ventilator · Cognition · Support system · Assumption · Logical actions · Motion study

1 Introduction

1.1 Background of Research

Medical equipment ventilators (the ventilator) are important as life support systems. As a patient's respiratory condition becomes more severe, specialized medical equipment such as the ventilator is generally used.

The primary troubles related to the ventilator are 1) the ventilator stops working during operation, 2) problems with the patient's tube, and 3) improper setting of alarms

© Springer Nature Switzerland AG 2022
V. G. Duffy et al. (Eds.): HCII 2022, LNCS 13521, pp. 80–91, 2022.
https://doi.org/10.1007/978-3-031-17902-0_6

[1]. Alarms for these malfunctions include minute volume of ventilation, airway pressure, apnea, respiratory rate, gas supply, oxygen concentration, and power supply. The types of ventilator alarms are shown in Fig. 1. There are two causes of ventilator alarms. First, a change in the patient's respiratory state can cause the alarm. The other is a factor on the equipment itself. The minute volume of ventilation alarm ("MV alarm") is particularly important because it often happens in clinical settings and could affect the patient's life if not correctly operated.

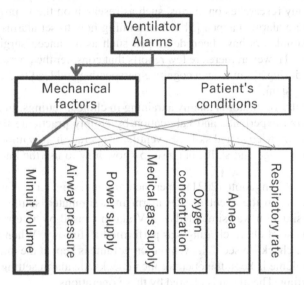

Fig. 1. Types of ventilator alarms

In Japan, the third report of the Medical Accident Information Collection Project (2005) [2] reported many cases in which the operation when an alarm happening caused an impact on the patient. The 65th Report on Medical Accident Information Collection Project (2021) [3], there is a report on ventilator circuit connection, but no investigate specific to ventilator alarms. However, there are often potential errors related to alarms that are not reported in clinical settings. Peters (2008) describe ventilator-related deaths and injuries that include inappropriate handling of alarms [4].

If operation during an alarm is incorrect or late, early recovery from the abnormal condition will not be possible. This can have severe impact on the patient.

When the ventilator alarm is activated, the operator needs to get the ventilator into the correct condition as soon as possible. Even operators with basic knowledge and operating skills for the ventilator need habituation and experience in alarm operation. Therefore, it is said that enough training is necessary.

In intensive care units, where patients are critically ill, the occupations that operate the ventilator include medical doctors, nurses, and specialized technicians. Of these, nurses who keep the patients care day and night, are most involved in operating the ventilator. Therefore, nurses often operate the ventilator during alarm conditions.

In clinical settings, there are enough ventilator equipment for the patients. On the other hand, there are operators with basic knowledge and skills, but not so many with experience and habituation. However, with the impact of Covid-19, it became necessary to increase the operators who could manage the ventilators correctly. In the past, there was no need for more operators as soon as possible. Because of this, operations during ventilator alarms were mainly trained through experience. Therefore, no simulated training procedure has been established. Thus, a training support system such as a simulator that can simulate alarm situations is needed to train the ventilator operators.

There are many researches on alarms, such as research on the improvement of the environment where alarms happen [5] and examining how to set alarms [6]. In recent years, medical simulators have been developed such as advanced surgical skills and patient simulators. However, there are few reports that consider the operator's operation of the ventilator during alarm from a cognitive perspective and lead to the development such as training system.

Operation of the ventilator is mainly a training in clinical settings. In the past, operators have acquired experience and habituation by simply practicing the "operation" after learning the knowledge and skills. In ventilator operation, it is important not only to having the knowledge and skills, but also to know how to use the knowledge in the situation.

Hamaguchi and Yamamoto (2021) experimentally investigated how ventilator operators would operate in the event of MV alarm in a simulated setting [7, 8]. In the experiment, the situation was simulated as MV alarm caused by an error in the alarm setting. The process of alarm clearing was performed as follows. When an alarm happens, the operator checks to see if the ventilation volume is kept at the initial setting. As the ventilation volume is kept, the operator then checks the alarm setting and adjusts it to the correct setting. The alarm is cleared by these operations.

The operator's behavior during the operation was video-recorded. From the recordings, behaviors were categorized in detail and analyzed. In addition, verbal protocols were recorded to clarify the operator's thinking during the operation. These recordings were analyzed from a cognitive perspective [6, 7]. The cooperation of nurses working in intensive care units ("ICU"), where the ventilator is often operated, was obtained.

The ventilator alarms usually should be cleared within 45 s. However, it was found that there were two groups: Proficient Group (PG) 6 participants who could clear the alarm within 40 s and Novice Group (NG) 7 participants who needed more time.

PGs had an average of 8.5 years (SD.: 3.9 years) of ICU experience, while NGs had an average of 1.6 years (SD., 0.7 years). The coefficient of variation was 0.46 for the PGs and 0.44 for the NGs, and there was no significant difference between the PGs and NGs in the dispersion of years of ICU experience. On the other hand, the time required to clear the alarm (operation time) averaged 34.3 s (SD.: 5.85 s) for the PG and 96.3 s (SD., 26.2 s) for the NG. The coefficient of variation was 0.17 for PG and 0.27 for NG, with NG showing significant dispersion in operating time. The reason for this is not simply that the NGs had less years of experience, but that differences in training and knowledge, as well as thinking about alarm operation, influenced the results. It is important to investigate these reasons behind the behavior.

Thus, the cognitive model of the operator during the minute ventilation volume alarm was created based on the analysis of the behavior and verbalization of the PG and the NG. The cognitive model is shown in Fig. 2 PG logically decided the information from the ventilator and cleared the alarm condition within 40 s. On the other hand, NG repeated incorrect behaviors through assumptions (Fig. 2. Single-dotted line), and it took more than 60 s to clear the alarm.

The ventilator alarm operation has a time limit, besides, the patient's life is critical. Therefore, it is important for the time to clear the alarm be quick. Furthermore, it is necessary to prevent the operator from operating the ventilator on assumption.

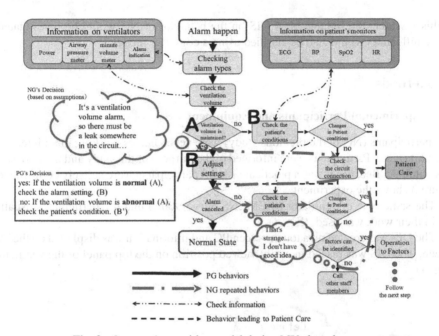

Fig. 2. Operator's cognitive model during MV alarm happen

The analysis of the PG operator's verbal protocols and interviews after the experiment showed that the PG makes the following decisions.

A. Whether the set ventilation volume is kept (A in Fig. 2).
B. If ventilation volume is keeping, check the setting (B in Fig. 2).
B'. If ventilation volume is not keeping, first check the patient's condition (B' in Fig. 2).

Thus, the PG selects the next behavior (B or B') to take based on A's decision.

These PG's decision A and the behavior to be taken from the result of the decision (operation details) B provide to the NG. In this way, we thought that the NG might not behave based on assumptions (single dotted line in Fig. 2).

Thus, we created the Operating Information Screen (OIS) as follows.

α Screen: The screen displays what the PG determines during alarm operation (A in Fig. 2).

β screen: The screen displays the operation procedure (B in Fig. 2) appropriate for the decision of A.

In the experiment, OIS was used to study NG's behavior in the ventilator alarm happened.

2 Objective

In this research, the influences of OIS on the behavior of NG would be investigated. These influences would also be clarified using a cognitive model.

3 Methods

3.1 Experimental Participants and Equipment

The participants (NG in the previous study) were seven nurses working in an intensive care unit (ICU). Participants were informed of the purpose of the study and their consent was obtained. Because it was a practical task, all participants were actively cooperative. Figure 3 shows the experiment.

The same type of ventilator (SIEMENS Servo 900C) that the participants usually use in their work was used. (Fig. 4).

The OIS was created on a touch-screen PC and information was displayed on the PC screen. The OIS was placed in easily viewed position on the top panel of the ventilator (Fig. 4).

Fig. 3. Experimental setting

Fig. 4. Experimental equipment

3.2   Experimental Environment (Situation of Simulation)

Since this experiment was a simulation using only a ventilator, the patient's vital signs were not displayed. Therefore, the participants were informed before the experiment that there would be no change in the patient's vital signs.

3.3   Alarms Types

In the experiment, the "MV alarm," that can have severe influence on the patient's life, was alarmed. In simulations of patients on ventilators, it is difficult to express changes in patient conditions. Therefore, the experiment focused on factors on the equipment itself. Among the causes of MV alarms, "alarm setting errors," which are difficult to notice, was selected as the cause.

3.4   About the Data to Be Obtained

The time from the ventilator alarm happens to the normal condition recovered ("Operation Time") was measured. To categorize the behavior during the operation, the operator's behaviors were recorded with a video camera and analyzed. Also, the speech data was recorded to find out what the operators were thinking during the operation. Post-experimental interviews confirmed the reasons for the behavior without speech.

3.5   About the OIS

How OIS Works. The OIS works as follows. When a MV alarm happens, the alpha screen is displayed. The operator checks the ventilation volume conditions based on the information on the alpha screen. If the ventilation volume is maintained, the operator touches "yes". If "yes" is touched, information on adjusting the settings error is displayed on the β screen. After adjusting the settings displayed on the β screen, confirm that the alarm clears. If the condition is normal, touch "yes" on the Beta screen and to exit.

As shown above, the OIS is designed to allow the user to select "yes" or "no" to go to the next screen. The OIS is also designed to display a screen that matches the selection if the operator selects the other.

About the Alpha Screen. Based on the behavioral analysis of PGs in previous researches, in the case of MV alarms, PGs first check the ventilation volume conditions. Thus, the alpha screen (Fig. 5) was designed to decide whether the ventilation rate is being maintained (yes) or not (no).

About the Beta Screen. After the operator decided the condition of the ventilation volume, the next screen show the possible causes and how to operate the ventilator alarm settings. This was the beta screen (Fig. 6). In addition, the beta screen shows information to determine that the alarm was cleared after the operation.

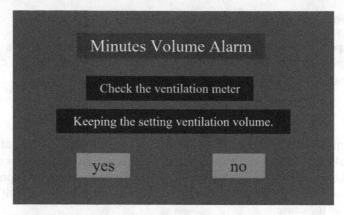

Fig. 5. Contents of the alpha screen

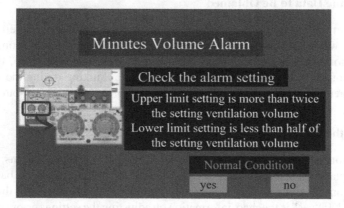

Fig. 6. Contents of the beta screen

4 Results and Discussion

4.1 About Behavior Analysis

Categories of Behavior. NG's behavior was analyzed. The flow of behaviors of ventilator alarm manipulation was categorized in detail. The operating behaviors of the α and β screens of the created OIS were incorporated into the elements categorized in the previous study by Hamaguchi and Yamamoto (2021). The results were shown in the behavior transitions.

The categories of behavior are shown in Table 1.The behaviors a) to h) are ordered in the case of proper operation of the task. The behaviors from i) to l) are not necessary for this task, and the order is not important. In addition, no participant in this experiment performed steps i) through l). (α) and (β) show how to operate the OIS created in this study.

Table 1. Categories of behavior in MV alarm operation.

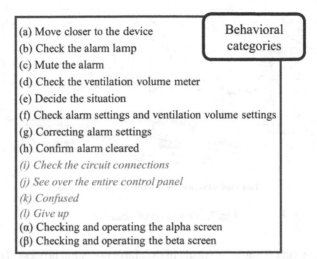

(a) Move closer to the device

(b) Check the alarm lamp

(c) Mute the alarm

(d) Check the ventilation volume meter

(e) Decide the situation

(f) Check alarm settings and ventilation volume settings

(g) Correcting alarm settings

(h) Confirm alarm cleared

(i) Check the circuit connections

(j) See over the entire control panel

(k) Confused

(l) Give up

(α) Checking and operating the alpha screen

(β) Checking and operating the beta screen

Transitions in Behavior. These categories of behavior were set on the vertical axis. The flow of behaviors by time was then shown in a graph (See Fig. 7).

NG with using the OIS was found to have a behavior pattern such as the solid line shown in the behavioral transitions in Fig. 7. The average operation time was 38.2 s (SD.: 5.1 s).

The behavioral transitions for NG using OIS are as follows. The operator goes to the side of the equipment when an alarm goes off (a). Next, the operator checks the alpha screen (α). The operator checks the content shown on the screen (ventilation volume condition check) and decides on the ventilation volume condition (d). The correct operation based on the decision is displayed on the β screen (β), and the operator operates the alarm settings based on this information (f) (g). After adjusting the alarm settings, the operator confirms the alarm clear and completes the operation (h).

4.1.1 Analysis of Behavior

From the confirmation of the ventilation rate shown in the α screen (Fig. 7(d)) to the operation of the operation contents shown in the β screen (Fig. 7(g)), the same decision as the PG (to adjust the settings if the ventilation volume is maintained) could be done. This means that there were no behaviors based on the assumption that "MV alarm is disconnect somewhere in the circuit" and no more behaviors such as giving up on the task (dotted line in Fig. 7). Furthermore, the operation time also improved. However, two of the seven operators took more than 40 s to solve the task, suggesting the need for continued training in thinking.

From the behavior transition, there were no false operations and the operation time was shorter, so it can be said that using OIS is effective in reducing the operation time. However, alarm operation is not only a speedy operation, but also needs to be correct. It is

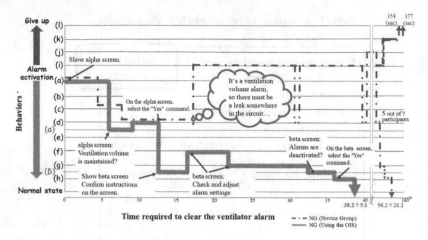

Fig. 7. Transition of behavior

important that correct decisions are made in the alarm operation process. Therefore, it is necessary to examine what is being decided at what moment during the alarm operation. In order to find out the cognitive process during the alarm operation, the operator's verbal data was analyzed.

4.2 About Behavior Analysis

Findings from the Cognitive Model. Based on the results of the analysis of NG's behaviors and speeches, a cognitive model was created. (See Fig. 8).

When a MV alarm happens, the next operation to be performed depends on the ventilation volume conditions. Therefore, it is very important to quickly and correctly decide the ventilation volume conditions.

NG no more takes false operations after deciding the ventilation volume conditions (Fig. 8.1-pointed line). This could be considered as a result of deciding the ventilation volume condition on the α screen, and then getting the next necessary information on the β screen, so that the correct operation could be done.

Analysis of Speech Data. The data on NG behavior and speech in previous studies [7, 8] by Hamaguchi and Yamamoto (2021) were reanalyzed. NG operators repeated false behaviors even though the NG operators were able to correctly make decisions about the ventilation volume conditions. In the speech data, the speech was "The patient is ventilated, but it is a ventilation volume alarm, so let's check the circuit connection." This means that there is an assumption that "MV alarm is disconnect somewhere in the circuit." This assumption leads to repeated operations that have nothing to do with the cause of the alarm. However, while repeating the operation, the correct operation was remembered. It took a long time, but the problem was solved. In the speech data, the speech was "Maybe it's a setting?" This shows that the NG has knowledge that one of the causes of the MV alarm is the setting of the alarm. From this, the NG operator could have cleared the alarm with the correct operation if the NG operators had been able to sort out their knowledge by making a decision on the ventilation volume condition.

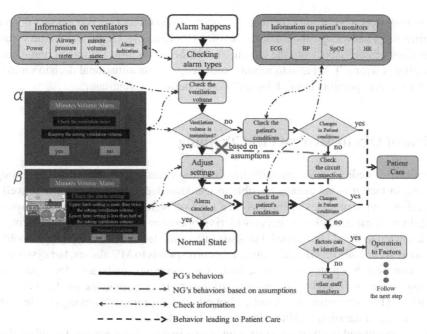

Fig. 8. Cognitive model for operation of MV alarms using OIS

J. Reason (1990) states that errors are most likely to occur at the rule-based (RB) level when information from the surroundings is forced to fit the rules of "trouble operation" with which one is well versed [9]. In this experiment, it can be assumed that errors are occurring at the RB level. Because there is trying to match the operator's routine-like rule that "the minute-hour ventilation rate alarm checks the circuit connections. This research has not been analyzed from the perspective of errors. In the future, we are considering analysis including the perspective of errors.

Analysis of Post-experimental Interviews. After the experiment, participants were interviewed about the OIS. In the interviews, participants commented that they were willing to follow the information on the screen. This showed that the operators would consciously were willing to follow the contents of the screen when there was an information screen. This can lead to depending on the screen. In other words, there is a risk that operators might only behave as the information shows without thinking about the situation or the cause of the problem.

Suchman (1987) discusses teaching information to the operator. If one of the teachings is misunderstood, the errors would go on unnoticed. The meaning of being shown the next screen is that the previous action was understood and considered appropriate, and the display of the next teaching confirms not only the correctness of the previous action in the narrow sense, but also the correctness of all the actions indicated in the earlier teaching [10]. In the information screen created, it should be considered that if the operator makes a mistake and goes on to the next screen, it will be even more difficult to resolve the problem. It should also considered that displaying information does not always result in a correct behavior to resolve the problem.

For operators who are not experienced in operating ventilators, it is necessary not only to learn a lot of knowledge about alarm operation (for example, "If the ventilation volume alarm goes off, air leaks from the circuit" or "If the ventilation volume is maintained, the setting is wrong"), but also to acquire knowledge about situational decision making in order for the operators to think logically and operate the ventilator.

5 Use of OIS in Medical Field Training

Education in medical care generally involves the acquisition of knowledge through lectures. In fact, it is not always possible to use knowledge learned in lectures well in a situation, and sometimes operations take time or behavior is based on assumptions [7, 8]. In medical education, when considering operations in the event of an alarm, not only knowledge should be learned, but also situational decisions and thinking should be learned as well. The OIS created in this study corresponds to MV alarms, but systems for other alarms can be created in the same form. These systems can be used for experiential learning by inexperienced operators of ventilators to train them in the thinking of alarm operation. Then, practicing in a simulated situation will provide "thinking training" that links situational decision making with learned knowledge.

The OIS created in this study corresponds to minute volume alarms, but other alarm systems could be created in the same form. These systems could be used by inexperienced operators of ventilators for experiential learning under simulated situations to train thinking about alarm operation.

6 Application

The ventilator is used more often due to COVID-19. Therefore, Operators that could correctly operate the ventilator are more and more needed. Based on the experience of COVID-19, it is expected that similar situations could occur also in the near future. It is important to learn the skills and be prepared through continuous training.

The ventilator was the focus of this study. In addition to a ventilator, an ECMO (Extracorporeal Membrane Oxygenator) device may be used in the treatment of Covid-19. ECMO patients are managed in the ICU and are observed with various monitoring. According to Vuylsteke (2017), bedside observation by nurses trained in ECMO is very important and it is important to be aware of possible problems so that they can respond quickly in the event of an alarm [11]. The experimental methods and results of this study can also be used for medical equipment that need advanced technology, such as ECMO devices. It is planned to study these devices from various perspectives in the future.

The operating supports such as the OIS created in this study are considered to be useful measures in training. However, when the operation support is used in clinical practice, the operator may become dependent on it and may not be able to operate the device properly without it. The needs and methods of the support would be considered in future studies.

7 Conclusions

The influence of OIS (the alpha and the beta screens) on NG behavior was investigated. The use of the OIS was able to do away with the behavior based on NG's assumptions. However, it was also found that NGs could be dependent on the OIS. The OIS could be used for experiential learning for inexperienced operators of the ventilator and to train operators in the thinking of alarm operation.

References

1. 2001 and 2002 Ministry of Health, Labor and Welfare Science Research and Special Research Project. Guideline on Alarm System for User of Medical Devices, First Edition (2003). In Japan
2. Japan Council for Quality Health Care, Medical Accident Prevention Center: Medical Accident Information Collection Business 3rd Report (2005). In Japan
3. Japan Council for Quality Health Care, Medical Accident Prevention Center: Medical Accident Information Collection Business 65th Report (2021). In Japan
4. George, A.P., Barbara, J.P.: Medical Error and Patient Safety, pp. 114–115. CRC Press, Taylor & Francis Group (2008)
5. Phillips, J.: Clinical alarms; improving efficiency and effectiveness. Crit Care Nurs **28**(4), 317–323 (2005)
6. Block, F.E., Jr., Nuutinen, L., Ballast, B.: Optimization of alarms: a study on alarm limits, alarm sounds, and false alarms, intended to reduce annoyance. J. Clin. Monit. Comput. **15**, 75–83 (1999)
7. Hamaguchi, J., Yamamoto, S.: Research on system design to support medical staff in case of ventilator alarms. In: Human-Automation Interaction: manufacturing, Services & User Experience, Springer ACES Series, (To be published) (2021)
8. Jun, H., Sakae, Y.: A modeling research on how to solve ventilator alarms from behavioral and cognitive perspectives, Springer LNCS Series, (HCI International 2021) (2021)
9. James, R.: Human error. The Press Syndicate of the University of Cambridge, New York (1990)
10. Suchman, L.A.: Plan And Situated Actions, vol. 6.4, pp. 102–104. Cambridge University Press (1987)
11. Vuylsteke, A., Brodie, D., Combes, A., Fowles, J.-A., Peek, G.: ECMO in the Adult Patient. Cambridge University Press, UK (2017). https://doi.org/10.1017/9781139088251

Voice-Assisted Food Recall Using Voice Assistants

Xiaohui Liang[1]([✉]), John A. Batsis[2], Jing Yuan[1], Youxiang Zhu[1],
Tiffany M. Driesse[2], and Josh Schultz[1]

[1] University of Massachusetts Boston, Boston, MA 02125, USA
xiaohui.liang@umb.edu
[2] University of North Carolina at Chapel Hill, Chapel Hill, NC 27599, USA

Abstract. In this paper, we design a voice-assisted food recall tool that can be implemented on voice assistants of smart speakers and smartphones, enabling frequent, quick, and real-time self-administered food recall. We envision that voice-assisted food recall can improve the accuracy and usability of the web-based Automated Self-administered 24-h Assessment (ASA-24). ASA-24 was developed by the National Cancer Institute in 2010 and has been widely used in clinical and research settings, but has low compliance and completion rates for at-home users. Specifically, we designed a prototype using nine ASA-24 general questions, two free-recall questions, five ASA-24 detailed questions, and three clarifying strategies. The integration of the ASA-24 questions ensures that the output of the prototype will align with the output of the ASA-24, so as to connect to the ASA-24 for nutrition profile analysis. We recruited twenty young adults and twenty older adults to evaluate this prototype, with each using it to recall three meals. We evaluated participants' performance per different types of questions and strategies, and analyzed the strength and weaknesses of the voice-assisted food recall. The mean success rate and session time of a single meal was (96.4%, 141.4 s) for young adults and (88.6%, 165.4 s) for older adults. The voice-assisted recall session time is significantly shorter than the ASA-24 single-meal session time, and the relevance of voice responses are determined to be high. We conducted questionnaires and interviews to obtain participants' feedback on the feasibility and acceptability of the prototype. 65% of young and 60% of older participants prefer voice-assisted food recall over web-based food recall, showing promising feasibility and acceptance of our initial voice-assisted food recall prototype. Future works include validation of the food recall content, development of food-customized speech recognition and natural language understanding techniques to enhance accuracy, and integration of human-like assistance to improve usability.

Keywords: Food recall · Voice assistants · Prototype · Usability

Supported by US National Institutes of Health National Institute on Aging, under grant No. 1R01AG067416.

1   Introduction

Dietary data is critical for personalizing nutritional interventions and monitoring ongoing dietary change [1,13]. Cinlicians and researchers have used conventional 24-h diet recalls, including the National Cancer Institute (NCI) web-based automated self-administered 24-h dietary assessment (ASA-24) [16], Nutrition Data System for Research [22], and INTAKE24 [31]. However, these self-administered, paper or web-based recalls are time-consuming (about 45 min for a 24-h recall), are not conducted in real-time, are subject to recall or reporting bias, and are difficult to use. We have gathered ASA-24 data for nutrition monitoring in our preivous studies [3–5], where we observed the usability problem of the ASA-24. We then exclusively conducted a usability study on the ASA-24 in both self-administered and Research Assistant (RA) guided settings. We found that the guidance from RA was useful, but the RA-guided ASA-24 sessions were still long and complex. Newer food recall tools must address these known accuracy and usability challenges.

Current technologies of food recall are using smartphone apps, such as, Noom and MyFitnessPal. Their main goal is to promote self-monitoring and provide in-app guidance [23]. However, the recall content from these apps might not be accurate and the use of smartphone might not be efficient for certain groups of users or in certain conditions. For example, adults with visual or dexterity barriers would have difficulties in using smartphone apps [26]. Research on food monitoring technologies include wearable sensors, such as putting motion sensor on neck or ear, and environmental sensors, such as using cameras to take food images [2,6,7,14,17,18,25]. However, these research methods have not been validated and they face usability barriers for real-world use.

Voice assistants are a promising tool for assessing diet. Voice assistants enable users to speak voice commands to interact with a large number of in-home and third-party services over their smart speakers and smartphones [12]. The total audience of smart speakers in the US reaches 51% of Americans [20]; 22% of owners are age > 55 [34]; and more than 60% of owners use smart speakers every day, with an average of 2.79 uses per day (0.33 for voice assistant at smartphone) [19]. Voice assistants can be HIPAA-compliant [30] and provide healthcare services, such as, scheduling clinical visits and monitoring vital signs [32]. Using voice assistants for food recall can be performed at a closer time to cooking or eating, thus allowing for frequent, quick, and real-time reporting with less recall bias. In this paper, we will design the first prototype of the voice-assisted food recall and evaluate the prototype with both young and older adults.

An effective voice-assisted food recall tool requires three key components: (a) adaptive questioning (b) response recognition, and (c) clarifying strategies to cope with conversation failure. We designed our voice-assisted food recall tool using three types of questions: i) ASA-24 general questions, ii) free-recall questions, and iii) ASA-24 detailed questions. The ASA-24 general questions are commonly used food recall questions from the ASA-24, such as type of meal, food-consumption location, and food source. Each question will be repeated per recall session. The free-recall questions allow users to freely form recall utterances with multiple food items, thus maximizing the usability and efficiency of voice interaction. Lastly, the ASA-24 detailed questions aim to gather missing details and thus are determined based on previously obtained food items. After matching the obtained items with the ASA-24 database, if further details are missing, detailed questions from the ASA-24 will be asked. Both the ASA-24 general questions and ASA-24 detailed questions will require the participant's answer to match a pre-defined item in the ASA-24 database. When a non-match incident occurs, clarifying strategies will be invoked to find a match. Our contributions are three-fold.

First, we designed a voice-assisted food recall using nine ASA-24 general questions, two free-recall questions, five ASA-24 detailed questions, and three clarifying strategies. Most questions were selected from the ASA-24 to ensure the relevance of the answers to the ASA-24 and allow for future integration with nutrition modules to ascertain diet quality and patterns.

Second, we recruited twenty young adults and twenty older adults to evaluate this prototype. Each participant used the prototype to recall three meals (breakfast, lunch, and dinner), and went through a Wizard-of-Oz (WoZ) session to experience the three clarifying strategies triggered towards the ASA-24 detailed questions. We designed questionnaires and interviews to obtain their feedback on the acceptability and feasibility of the prototype.

Third, we evaluated the voice-assisted food recall prototype by analyzing the participants' performances per question and their feedback via questionnaires and interviews. The average success rates of completing a single-meal session were 96.4% for young adults and 88.6% for older adults, and the lengths of the session were 141.4 s and 165.4 s, which are significantly shorter than the ASA-24 single-meal session. Both young and older adults agreed that using voice-assisted recall is preferred to web-based recall. In addition, the voice-assisted recall was preferred in both the eating/cooking scenario and the repeated-use scenario.

2   Voice-Assisted Food Recall

We first present an overview of the voice-assisted food recall, and then describe the ASA-24 general questions, the free-recall questions, the ASA-24 detailed questions, and the clarifying strategies.

2.1   Overview

Our voice-assisted food recall tool provides a convenient and easy-to-access voice interface for users to input food data. The food data collected by our tool will be sent to the ASA-24 for the nutrition profile analysis. We thus start to incorporate the ASA-24 questions to ensure the output of the voice-assisted food recall aligns with the output of the ASA-24.

We studied the ASA-24[1] and its seven steps for completing a 24-h food recall. As shown in Fig. 1, the seven steps are i) meal-based quick list, ii) meal gap

---

[1] https://epi.grants.cancer.gov/asa24/.

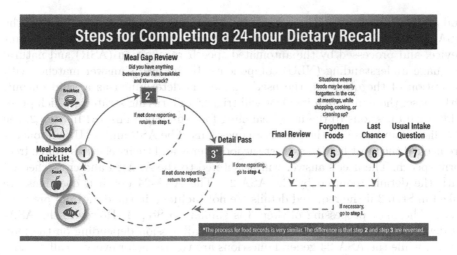

Fig. 1. ASA-24's seven steps for completing a 24-h Dietary Recall

review, iii) detail pass, iv) final review, v) forgotten foods, vi) last chance, and vii) usual intake question. We observed that the ASA-24 questioning contains multiple loops, i.e., allowing users to revisit Step 1 in multiple conditions in the case that they recall some food or details later in the session. Besides, the ASA-24 asks about the general information of meals before the detailed information. Step 1 "meal-based quick list" and Step 2 "meal gap review" gather general information of all meals before Step 3 "detail pass" targeting the details of a single meal. In addition, the ASA-24 reminds users about forgotten foods, such as water, cookies, fruits, which happens after Step 4 "final review". These foods are considered easily forgotten in situations, such as, in the car or at meetings. Lastly, the ASA-24 shows on the screen a list of meals and meal gaps in Step 2 and Step 4, and images of meals, details, and portion size in Step 3. The visual information further assists users in the recall process.

Our voice-assisted food recall incorporated some ASA-24 features, including loops in the questioning, separating general and detailed questions, and reminding about forgotten foods. However, the current prototype solely relies on voice interactions and does not support visual information. Voice assistants with screens can provide visual information, which would require further human-interaction visualization research in the future. We implemented our voice-assisted food recall prototype as an Alexa skill and used an Amazon Echo smart speaker in our evaluation. We chose the Amazon platform as Amazon is leading the smart speaker market in the United States. Recent statistics show that in the United States in 2021, the smart speaker market shares are 66%, 8%, 26% for Amazon Alexa, Apple Siri, and Google Assistant, respectively [20].

We introduce our voice-assisted food recall according to three questioning modules: ASA-24 general questions, free-recall questions, and ASA-24 detailed questions. As shown in Fig. 2, a user using the voice-assisted food recall listens and answers questions in three steps. In Step 1, the user listens and answers the ASA-24 general questions. The user's answer is recorded by the voice assistant device, and processed by the automated speech recognition (ASR) and natural language understanding (NLU) components. If the user's answer matches with an option of the question, the user's answer is determined as a valid output. Otherwise, the non-match incident will trigger a clarifying strategy, which poses additional questions to the user, searching for a matched answer. In Step 2, the user listens and answers the free-recall questions. The ASR and NLU components are needed the most here to extract the food items and their relations from a free-form speech. The user's answer will be entered to the ASA-24 and cross-checked with the details required by the ASA-24. The ASA-24 detailed questions are asked in Step 3 if the required details are not included in the data from previous steps. The data processing of Step 3 is similar to Step 1. However, the ASA-24 detailed questions may be different per recall session depending on the food intake, while the ASA-24 general questions are the same for every recall session. Thus, the clarifying strategies are more likely to be triggered in Step 3. In the evaluation of the prototype, we focused on understanding the participants' voice interaction experience in using the prototype. We employed the ASR and NLU components from the existing Alexa system, and set the prototype to accept any recognized speech so the technical challenges of speech would minimally affect the usability. We chose to analyze the relevance of the participants' answers to the food items after the participants' sessions. Only the "yes" and "no" questions will require a recognized "yes" or "no" in real-time. In the following, we describe the implementation details according to the three questioning modules.

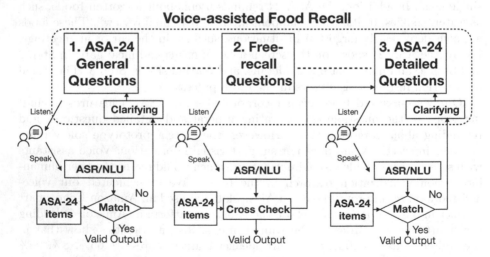

Fig. 2. Three questioning modules. ASR: Automated Speech Recognition. NLU: Natural Language Understanding.

2.2 ASA-24 General Questions

We included 9 ASA-24 general questions in our voice-assisted food recall, as shown in Table 1. (Q1, Q2, Q3, Q4, Q5) were selected from the ASA-24 Steps 1–3 (Q6, Q7, Q8) were from the ASA-24 Step 5, and Q9 was from the ASA-24 Step 7. Similar to the ASA-24, we set a loop at Q5. These questions are considered general questions because they are repeated for every recall session. We also consider that the completion rates of these questions are high, because not only users' experiences are accumulated with repeated uses, but also the ASR and NLU components can adapt to users' personalized speech behaviors and food patterns in the long run.

2.3 Free-Recall Questions

The free-recall questions allow users to freely form recall utterances with multiple food items, thus maximizing the usability and efficiency of the voice interaction. The success of the free-recall questions depends on effective ASR and NLU components. Effective extraction of items from the free-recall utterances leads to a minimum number of necessary ASA-24 detailed questions in Step 3. However, ineffective extraction will create confusion in mutual understanding and require additional user effort to clarify and negatively impact usability and efficiency. Other than the extraction, the success of the free-recall questions also depends on the users' response behavior. Users may say short answers with fewer items and then encounter more ASA-24 detailed questions in Step 3, or they may say more items and encounter fewer questions. The response behaviors may differ across users, and the response behavior of a user may change over time. The behavior is highly related to their food patterns and their personal voice assistant experiences. We specifically studied two free-recall questions Q10 and Q11, as shown in Table 1, and we inserted the two questions into the sequence of the 9 ASA-24 general questions. Note that, questions Q10 and Q11 are triggered only if a user answers "yes" to Q6, Q7, and Q8.

2.4 ASA-24 Detailed Questions

ASA-24 detailed questions focus on querying the details of a specific food item, e.g., a pizza or a sandwich. The ASA-24 uses the United States Department of Agriculture's Food and Nutrient Database for Dietary Studies [24]. A user's answer to an ASA-24 question must match to an item from the database. For example, with pizza, the question "What kind was it?" has the options of "plain cheese," "pepperoni," "meat other than pepperoni," "Vegetable, Fruit," "Supreme," "Seafood," etc. The question also has the options of "other" and "don't know." The user's answer must match with one of these options to be considered valid. We specifically studied five detailed questions, each in a representative category. In Table 2, we show the selected detailed questions from the ASA-24 Step 3 after entering "burger" into the ASA-24.

Table 1. ASA-24 general questions and free-recall questions

	ASA-24 general questions		Free-recall questions
Q1	Would you like to report breakfast, lunch, or dinner?		
Q2	Where did you eat this meal?		
Q3	Was this meal homemade or where was it purchased?		
		Q10	*What did you have for this meal?*
		Q11	*Can you provide more details about this food. For example, ingredient, kind, or size?*
Q4	How much of the meal did you actually eat?		
Q5	Have you entered all details for this meal? [If no, goto Q1]		
Q6	Certain foods and drinks are frequently forgotten, did you have any other water, coffee, tea, soft drinks, milk, juice, beer, wine?		
			If yes goto Q6:
		Q10	*What did you have for this meal?*
		Q11	*Can you provide more details about this food. For example, ingredient, kind, or size?*
Q7	Did you have any other cookies, candy, ice cream, sweets, fruits, vegetables, or cheeses?		
			If yes goto Q7:
		Q10	*What did you have for this meal?*
		Q11	*Can you provide more details about this food. For example, ingredient, kind, or size?*
Q8	Did you have any other chips, crackers, popcorn, pretzels, nuts, bread, rolls, tortillas, or other snack foods?		
			If yes goto Q8:
		Q10	*What did you have for this meal?*
		Q11	*Can you provide more details about this food. For example, ingredient, kind, or size?*
Q9	Did you eat much more, about the same, or much less than usual?		

Table 2. ASA-24 detailed questions of "Burger"

	Type	ASA-24 detailed questions
Q12	Where	Where did you get this food (or most of the ingredients for it)?
Q13	Kind	What kind of burger?
Q14	Ingredient	Were there any other ingredients on the burger?
Q15	Size	What size was the meat?
Q16	Amount	How much of the burger did you actually eat?

2.5 Clarifying Strategies

While the web-based food recall tool (e.g., ASA-24) shows all the options of the questions on the screen so users can visually see, choose, and confirm, our voice-assisted food recall does not support visual information in this initial stage and may encounter a non-match incident. To address this challenge, we equipped the ASA-24 questions with clarifying strategies. If a user provides an answer that does not match any option, the clarifying strategies are further used to resolve this non-match incident. Specifically, we designed three clarifying strategies to provide option hints. We implemented three strategies in a fair situation in that each strategy provides at most nine option hints.

Strategy 1: Read a list of nine options, stop when the user interrupts, and resume the reading after determining a non-match incident. The process ends if either a match is found or all nine options have been read.

Strategy 2: Read three options at a time, ask the user the original question. The process ends if either a match is found or all nine options have been read.

Strategy 3: Read one option at a time, and ask the user a "yes" or "no" question to confirm if the provided option hint is the right one. The process ends if either the user's answer is "yes" or all nine options have been read.

Overall, strategy 1 is the quickest process, but the user may miss the option hints while recalling. Strategy 3 is the slowest process, and the user only needs to answer "yes" or "no". Strategy 2 is somewhere between 1 and 3.

3 Experiment

To evaluate our voice-assisted food recall prototype, we recruited 20 young adults at the University of Massachusetts Boston (UMB) and 20 older adults aged 65+ through our collaboration partners of the University of North Carolina (UNC) at Chapel Hill. All participants are English-speaking. At UNC, an RA has confirmed eligibility and conducted a Callahan screen (≥ 3 is an ability to consent) [11]. To overcome the COVID-19 crisis, we designed and conducted our experiments in a virtual setting such that participants and our RAs could perform all evaluation activities through Zoom.

3.1 Recruitment

To recruit young adults, we have sent emails to students currently enrolled at UMB. In the first email, we briefly described our research goal, i.e., to investigate the feasibility of using voice assistant systems like Amazon Alexa for collecting food recall data. We expressed that we aim to recruit young adults (age 18–40) that are willing to spend 60–90 min of Zoom session at a mutually agreed time. The evaluation activities include interaction with the voice-assisted food recall prototype on an Alexa Echo device. We will record their voice during the session. Then, we will have each participant complete some surveys and take part in a short interview. In return, each participant will receive a $25 Amazon gift card as a token of thanks. From students who replied to our first email, we further asked about their first language and second language. We asked three foods that they are most familiar with. The three foods will be used by our RA to obtain ASA-24 detailed questions and options in advance, generate audio files from texts, and prepare the control interface for the WoZ experiment. As our experiment was carried out in a virtual setting, we instructed the participants to use computers or laptops and find a quiet place with a reliable Internet connection to participate in the evaluation activities. Our research activities at UMB have been approved by the IRB of UMB. Students will sign the consent to conduct the activities.

To recruit older adults, our UNC team used community-based research efforts, advertisements, worked collaboratively with colleagues, screening schedules, informed colleagues of upcoming research studies at faculty meetings, and directly recruited his practice's patients and friends of those patients. He also used resources available at UNC through the Center for Aging and Health to facilitate recruitment (NCTracs, Researchmatch.org). In addition, competence to provide informed consent will be assured by a review of personal history or medical record and the Callahan Cognitive screener score ≥ 3 prior to informed consent evaluation (by phone). Individuals with a diagnosis of dementia or a failed Callahan screener will be excluded. Our research activities at UNC have been approved by the IRB of UNC.

3.2 Prototype Evaluation

In a controlled study, participants were invited to perform a set of specific tasks under the instructions given by the RA. Our evaluation was conducted remotely due to the COVID-19 pandemic, as shown in Fig. 3. An RA set up a laptop, an Alexa Echo Dot device, speaker, camera, and microphone devices physically in an office. The RA then used the laptop to set up a Zoom session with participants who used their own computers. The participant's computer received the audio of the commands from the participant and transmitted the audio to the RA's laptop over the Zoom session. The RA's laptop then played the command audio at a speaker device close to the Alexa device. The Alexa device received the command audio and played the response audio at its speaker. The RA's laptop received the response audio and transmitted it to the participant's computer over the Zoom session. In such a way, the participant successfully interacted with the remote Alexa on the RA's side. During the session, the participant's computer and the RA's laptop share a camera view of the participant's face and a camera view of the Alexa Echo Dot device.

Evaluation on ASA-24 General Questions and Free-Recall Questions.
The ASA-24 general questions and free-recall questions are implemented in an Alexa skill in a sequence introduced in Sects. 3.2 and 3.3. The RA introduced the questions by showing them on a shared screen. The RA reminded participants that some questions take any answers while others only accept pre-defined answers. Each participant recalled three meals they had in the previous 24 h, including breakfast, lunch, and dinner. The RA assists the process at participants' requests during the session.

Evaluation on ASA-24 Detailed Questions and Clarifying Strategies.
The ASA-detailed questions and clarifying strategies were implemented in a WoZ experiment. WoZ experiments are mainly used to analyze an unimplemented or partially implemented computer application for design improvements. Study participants interact with a seemingly autonomous application whose unimplemented functions are actually simulated by a human operator, known as the Wizard. To make the interactions convincing, the Wizard performed practice sessions with members of our research team before conducting the WoZ studies. Every participant was asked to interact with three Wizards using the three strategies. The order in which participants were asked to interact with the question sets was randomized to control for ordering effects. Semi-structured interviews will be used to ascertain the feasibility and usability of each clarifying strategy. Specifically, our RA has entered the seven common foods into the ASA-24 to gather five detailed questions per each food and the options of these questions. The seven foods are obtained from the participants' replies to our recruitment emails, and they are pizza, salad, sandwich, burger, chocolate cake, macaroni and cheese, and sushi. The five questions are related to the food's source, kind, ingredient, size, and consumed amount. After we gathered questions and options, we converted text files to audio files. Our RA has been trained to play the audio files according to the needed questions and strategies.

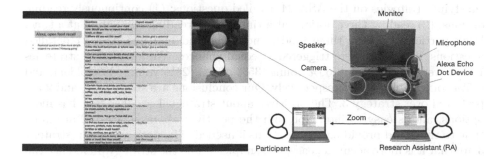

Fig. 3. Virtual evaluation of voice-assisted food recall

4 Results

In this section, we analyze the participants' performance in their recall sessions and show the results from the questionnaires and interviews.

4.1 Performance Evaluation

Overall, the mean success rate and session time of a single meal was (96.4%, 141.4 s) for young and (88.6%, 165.4 s) for older adults, significantly shorter than the ASA-24 single-meal (about 15 min). We then analyzed their performance according to the three types of questions.

ASA-24 General Questions. We found that participants can provide relevant answers to 90.5% (young) and 93.2% (older) of the questions being asked, which emphasizes that the general questions are relatively easy to understand and respond to. The questions "How much of the food did you actually eat?" and "Was this food homemade or where was it purchased?" resulted in most of the conversation failure; the reason is that the responses to these two questions have various forms and pose a greater challenge to speech processing. If the Alexa device does not recognize any response, it will repeat the question at first and end the process after several failures. The results were consistent between young and older adults.

Free-Recall Questions. We measured the words and audio length of the users' answers to the free-recall questions. We found on average, young adults respond to a free-recall question with 4.2 words and 2.8 s, and older adults respond with 2.8 words and 2.3 s. On the one hand, we told participants that the Alexa implementation limits the maximum length of the responses. On the other hand, participants used the prototype for the first time and may lack confidence in the device accurately recognizing their responses. When participants become more familiar and confident with the tool, we envision that they will provide longer and more recognizable responses.

ASA-24 Detailed Questions and Clarifying Strategies. We tested three clarifying strategies on the ASA-24 detailed questions: (1) continuously reading options; (2) reading three options at a time; or (3) reading one option at a time. Each participant chose three foods, and each food had five ASA-24 detailed questions. Strategies were triggered at equal chances. We found that strategies 1, 2, 3 were preferred by (60% young, 35% older) (25% young, 45% older), and (15% young, 20% older), respectively. Our conclusions are strategies 1 and 2 are preferred over strategy 3. The positives about strategy 1 are it is fast, has more options, and is easy to interrupt, and the positives about strategy 2 are more time to think and providing more options if needed. The positives about strategy 3 are that it is more accurate, easy, and simple. While the strategy preference can vary per type of question and food, the preference shows consistency in personal behavior and thus the voice-assisted food recall tool can learn and adapt personal preferences on the strategies.

4.2   Feedback from Participants

Participants finished a System Usability Scale (SUS) questionnaire [8] and a Technology Comparison questionnaire. We customized the SUS's questions to the voice-assisted food recall context. In addition, we used the following five questions in a Technology Comparison Questionnaire to obtain participants' feedback on comparing web-based food recall and voice-assisted food recall. They are 5-point Likert questions.

- If I am cooking or eating meals at home, describe the easiness of performing the voice-assisted food recall.
- If I am cooking or eating meals at home, describe the easiness of performing the web-based food recall
- The use of voice-assisted food recall can be more often than the web-based food recall
- I prefer using voice technology to report food compared to using web apps to report food
- I agree as AI technology advances, the voice-assisted food recall will become effective and widely acceptable

Table 3. System Usability Scale questionnaire and Technology Comparison questionnaire. SUS score ranges from 0–100. Scales range from 1–5 difficult to easy or strongly disagree to strongly agree.

Age	Young	Older
	18–40	65+
System Usability Scale	65.3	58.1
Positive about voice recall	4.2	3.7
Prefer voice recall to web	3.6	3.1
Voice recall while eat/cook	3.6	3.3
Web recall while eat/cook	3.1	3.4
Prefer voice for repeated use	3.5	3.0

As shown in Table 3, we found the SUS score of the voice-assisted food recall among older adults is 58.1, which is between 56 for the self-administered ASA-24 and 60 for the RA-guided ASA-24. The SUS score of the voice-assisted food recall among young adults is 65.3, much higher than older adults. Both young and older adults feel positive about the future of voice-assisted food recall with AI advancement. In comparison, young adults feel more positive than older adults (4.2 > 3.7). In terms of the easiness of performing voice-assisted food recall and web-based food recall, both groups prefer using voice technology compared to using the web to report food (3.6 young and 3.1 older). Additionally, 65% of young and 60% of older participants prefer voice-based diet recall. If the food recall was conducted while eating or cooking, young adults agree that it is easier to perform voice-assisted food recall (3.6) than web-based (3.1). Older adults thought the easiness scores of performing the two types of recalls while eating or cooking were similar, 3.3 for voice and 3.4 for web. If the food recall was needed for repeated use in the long term, young adults prefer voice to web (3.5), while older adults do not choose sides (3.0). The feedback we received from the participants was based on the evaluation of our initial voice-assisted food recall prototype and their previous experiences of using web apps. The output of the voice-assisted food recall was checked in terms of relevance, but not cross-checked with the output of the web-based food recall for accuracy. This initial feedback reveals promising feasibility and acceptance of the voice-assisted food recall.

5   Challenges

Virtual Settings. In a virtual setting, participants' devices, network conditions, and physical environments are not controllable. We conducted a pre-test phase to ensure that the participants' devices (speakers and microphones) could meet the requirements of the virtual experiments, i.e., the participant can join in a Zoom meeting and effectively interact with the Alexa device on the RA's side. We also advised participants to conduct the experiment in a quiet place. Nevertheless, we found some participants had difficulty interacting with the Alexa devices due to low voice quality or background noise and were unable to pass the pre-test phase. We had to drop them from the study.

Technical Limitations. In our sessions, our RA explained to participants the procedure, the sequence, the options of questions, and then the RA showed a demo session using the voice-assisted food recall tool. However, participants may not be able to follow the instructions in their self-administered sessions. For example, they misunderstood the questions or did not say "yes" or "no" to a "yes" or "no" question. Furthermore, we adopted the ASR and NLU components from the Alexa system, which are limited to processing long and free-form responses. The RA explained to the participants certain restrictions, but some participants tend to forget the restrictions in the first couple of attempts. For each participant performing the food recall on one meal, a maximum of 3 times of failures are allowed. If 3 times of failure are reached, the participant is required to move on to the food recall of the next meal.

WoZ Experiment. In our WoZ experiment, the audio files of the questions, the options, and the clarifying strategies were synthesized from the texts, and played through the Zoom. Our RA needs to mute the microphone such that the participant would not hear keyboard and mouse click sounds. If audio files were played by mistake, our RA will play the right one and pretend it was a mistake made by the machine. In a situation where the RA must interfere, the RA informs the participant that he or she pauses and resumes the interaction. In some cases, even if the RA understands the user's response and finds a match, the RA will pretend not and trigger the clarifying strategies for the testing purpose.

6   Conclusion

In this paper, we proposed a voice-assisted food recall tool that can be self-administered by users using voice assistants on their smart speakers or smartphones. Our voice-assisted recall tool employs ASA-24 general questions, free-recall questions, and ASA-24 detailed questions to ensure the output aligned with the ASA-24. The free-recall questions allow users to freely form recall utterances with multiple food items, thus maximizing the usability and efficiency of voice interaction. In addition, clarifying strategies were designed to assist in finding a matched item when a non-matched incident occurs. We conducted an evaluation over 20 young adults and 20 older adults. We analyzed their performance in the recall sessions and summarized their feedback from questionnaires and interviews. Our design and evaluation demonstrated promising feasibility and acceptance of our initial prototype of the voice-assisted food recall.

Future research in voice-assisted food recall aims to improve the accuracy and usability of the proposed prototype, including the integration of food knowledge graphs [33], food-customized speech recognition and natural language understanding techniques to improve accuracy, and the integration of human-like assistance from RA-guided ASA-24 sessions to enhance usability. Task-based conversational AI has been successfully used in flight bookings, online shopping, bus schedules, and tasks of voice assistant [9,10,15,21,29,35]. In addition, question and answering techniques from natural language research have been advanced significantly to achieve higher accuracy than humans [27,28,36]. In the meantime, we will work with the ASA-24 researchers for the future integration of the voice-assisted food recall with nutrition modules to ascertain diet quality and patterns.

References

1. Dietary guidelines for americans: 2020–2025. US Department of Agriculture (9) (2020)
2. Alharbi, R., Stump, T., Vafaie, N., Pfammatter, A., Spring, B., Alshurafa, N.: I can't be myself: effects of wearable cameras on the capture of authentic behavior in the wild. Proc. ACM Interact. Mobile Wearable Ubiquit. Technol. **2**(3), 1–40 (2018)
3. Batsis, J.A., et al.: Feasibility and acceptability of a technology-based, rural weight management intervention in older adults with obesity. BMC Geriatr. **21**(1), 1–13 (2021)
4. Batsis, J.A., et al.: A weight loss intervention augmented by a wearable device in rural older adults with obesity: a feasibility study. J. Geront. Ser. A **76**(1), 95–100 (2021)
5. Batsis, J.A., et al.: A community-based feasibility study of weight-loss in rural, older adults with obesity. J. Nutrit. Geront. Geriat. **39**(3–4), 192–204 (2020)
6. Bedri, A., et al.: Earbit: using wearable sensors to detect eating episodes in unconstrained environments. Proc. ACM Interact. Mobile Wearable Ubiquit. Technol. **1**(3), 1–20 (2017)

7. Bi, S., et al.: Measuring children's eating behavior with a wearable device. In: 2020 IEEE International Conference on Healthcare Informatics (ICHI), pp. 1–11. IEEE (2020)

8. Brooke, J.: SUS: A 'Quick and Dirty' Usability Scale. Usability evaluation in industry 189(3) (1996)

9. Budzianowski, P., Vulić, I.: Hello, it's gpt-2-how can i help you? towards the use of pretrained language models for task-oriented dialogue systems. arXiv preprint arXiv:1907.05774 (2019)

10. Budzianowski, P., et al.: Multiwoz-a large-scale multi-domain wizard-of-oz dataset for task-oriented dialogue modelling. arXiv preprint arXiv:1810.00278 (2018)

11. Callahan, C.M., Unverzagt, F.W., Hui, S.L., Perkins, A.J., Hendrie, H.C.: Six-item screener to identify cognitive impairment among potential subjects for clinical research. Med. Care 40, 771–781 (2002)

12. Canalys, R.F.: 56 million smart speaker sales in 2018 says canalys. https://www.voicebot.ai/2018/01/07/56-million-smart-speaker-sales-2018-says-canalys/

13. Estruch, R., et al.: Primary prevention of cardiovascular disease with a mediterranean diet. N. Engl. J. Med. 368(14), 1279–1290 (2013)

14. Farooq, M., Sazonov, E.: Accelerometer-based detection of food intake in free-living individuals. IEEE Sens. J. 18(9), 3752–3758 (2018)

15. Goyal, A., Metallinou, A., Matsoukas, S.: Fast and scalable expansion of natural language understanding functionality for intelligent agents. arXiv preprint arXiv:1805.01542 (2018)

16. Harnack, L., Stevens, M., Van Heel, N., Schakel, S., Dwyer, J.T., Himes, J.: A computer-based approach for assessing dietary supplement use in conjunction with dietary recalls. J. Food Compos. Anal. 21, S78–S82 (2008)

17. Hossain, D., Ghosh, T., Sazonov, E.: Automatic count of bites and chews from videos of eating episodes. IEEE Access 8, 101934–101945 (2020)

18. Jia, W., et al.: Automatic food detection in egocentric images using artificial intelligence technology. Public Health Nutr. 22(7), 1168–1179 (2019)

19. Kinsella, B.: Smart speaker owners use voice assistants nearly 3 times per day (2018). https://voicebot.ai/2018/04/02/smart-speaker-owners-use-voice-assistants-nearly-3-times-per-day/

20. Laricchia, F.: Share of voice assistant users in the U.S. 2020 by device (2021). https://www.statista.com/statistics/1171363/share-of-voice-assistant-users-in-the-us-by-device/

21. Mamatha, M., et al.: Chatbot for e-commerce assistance: based on rasa. Turkish J. Comput. Math. Educ. (TURCOMAT) 12(11), 6173–6179 (2021)

22. Miller, P.E., Mitchell, D.C., Harala, P.L., Pettit, J.M., Smiciklas-Wright, H., Hartman, T.J.: Development and evaluation of a method for calculating the healthy eating index-2005 using the nutrition data system for research. Public Health Nutr. 14(2), 306–313 (2011)

23. Mitchell, E.S., et al.: Self-reported nutritional factors are associated with weight loss at 18 months in a self-managed commercial program with food categorization system: Observational study. Nutrients 13(5), 1733 (2021)

24. Montville, J.B., et al.: Usda food and nutrient database for dietary studies (fndds), 5.0. Procedia Food Science 2, 99–112 (2013)

25. Nyamukuru, M.T., Odame, K.M.: Tiny eats: eating detection on a microcontroller. In: 2020 IEEE Second Workshop on Machine Learning on Edge in Sensor Systems (SenSys-ML), pp. 19–23. IEEE (2020)

26. Radcliffe, E., Lippincott, B., Anderson, R., Jones, M.: A pilot evaluation of mhealth app accessibility for three top-rated weight management apps by people with disabilities. Int. J. Environ. Res. Public Health **18**(7), 3669 (2021)
27. Raffel, C., et al.: Exploring the limits of transfer learning with a unified text-to-text transformer. arXiv preprint arXiv:1910.10683 (2019)
28. Rajpurkar, P., Zhang, J., Lopyrev, K., Liang, P.: Squad: 100,000+ questions for machine comprehension of text. arXiv preprint arXiv:1606.05250 (2016)
29. Ram, A., et al.: Conversational ai: The science behind the alexa prize. arXiv preprint arXiv:1801.03604 (2018)
30. Ross, C.: Amazon Alexa is now HIPAA-compliant. Tech giant says health data can now be accessed securely (2021). https://www.statnews.com/2019/04/04/amazon-alexa-hipaa-compliant/
31. Simpson, E., et al.: Iterative development of an online dietary recall tool: Intake24. Nutrients **9**(2), 118 (2017)
32. Tuohy, J.P.: Amazon Alexa's new elder care service launches today (2021). https://www.theverge.com/2021/12/7/22822026/amazon-alexa-together-elder-care-price-features-release-date
33. Wang, Q., Mao, Z., Wang, B., Guo, L.: Knowledge graph embedding: a survey of approaches and applications. IEEE Trans. Knowl. Data Eng. **29**(12), 2724–2743 (2017)
34. Weinschenk, C.: Smart Speaker Research Finds Strong Adoption by Seniors (2021). https://www.telecompetitor.com/smart-speaker-research-finds-strong-adoption-by-seniors/
35. Yan, Z., Duan, N., Chen, P., Zhou, M., Zhou, J., Li, Z.: Building task-oriented dialogue systems for online shopping. In: Thirty-First AAAI Conference on Artificial Intelligence (2017)
36. Yang, Z., Dai, Z., Yang, Y., Carbonell, J., Salakhutdinov, R.R., Le, Q.V.: Xlnet: Generalized autoregressive pretraining for language understanding. In: Advances in Neural Information Processing Systems, vol. 32 (2019)

Virtual Assistant as an Emotional Support for the Academic Stress for Students of Higher School: A Literature Review

Alexis Lucero Fredes[1], Sandra Cano[1(✉)], Claudio Cubillos[1], and María Elena Díaz[2]

[1] School of Computer Engineering, Pontificia Universidad Católica de Valparaíso, Valparaíso, Chile
Sandra.cano@pucv.cl
[2] Psychology, Universidad de San Buenaventura Cali, Cali, Colombia

Abstract. Mental healthcare has seen numerous benefits from interactive technologies and artificial intelligence. Virtual Assistant is a conversational agent, also called chatbots, which are being of great interest to researchers in different areas such as: psychology, marketing, education, among others. Virtual Assistants are trained to converse and interact with a person using speech, typing and visual languages through natural language techniques. Therefore, they have the potential to be a support tool for people. This study is focused to make a literature search in Scopus, Web of Science (WoS), and IEEE Xplore digital databases to answer questions in how virtual assistant can support the academic stress.

Keywords: Mental health · Virtual assistant · Academic stress · Higher school · Conversational agents

1 Introduction

Mental healthcare has seen numerous benefits from interactive technologies and artificial intelligence [1]. Virtual Assistant is a conversational agent, also called chatbots, which are being of great interest to researchers in different areas such as: psychology [2], marketing, education [3], among others. Conversational agents are interfacing whose communication can be through speech, writing and visual language, where different users interact with the agent. Therefore, from Human Computer Interaction (HCI) line research, there has been interest in how to design an intelligent virtual agent that emotionally supports [4].

Nowadays, students experience academic stress when the amount of academic workload greater. Stress is the human body's natural response to daily pressures and threats to one's well-being [5]. Stress can be positive or negative, the negative stress occurs when one feels overwhelmed and is unable to cope with the pressures from situations or life events that have become unmanageable. Negative stress includes decreased attention and concentration, difficulty in making decisions, challenges with interpersonal relationships and continued feelings of fear or anger. These symptoms can lead to anxiety or depression [6].

© Springer Nature Switzerland AG 2022
V. G. Duffy et al. (Eds.): HCII 2022, LNCS 13521, pp. 108–118, 2022.
https://doi.org/10.1007/978-3-031-17902-0_8

Virtual Assistants are trained to converse and interact with a person using speech, typing and visual languages through natural language techniques. Therefore, they have the potential to be a support tool for people. This study is focused to make a literature search in Scopus, Web of Science (WoS), and IEEE Xplore digital databases to answer questions in how to design a virtual assistant that can support the mental health to undergraduate students.

However, there is a heterogeneity of the studies of conversational agents focused to the mental health. Our study is centered in academic stress.

2 Background

2.1 Academic Stress

Stress can be defined as the body's non-specific response to demands made upon it or to disturbing events in the environment [5]. Academic stress commonly occurs in first year students [7] when they enter college. It also occurs in exams, academic overload caused by homework or difficulties in understanding or obtaining a good grade in a course. Academic stress can be defined as the body's responses to academic-related demands that exceed adaptive capabilities of students [8]. However, Muñoz [9] mentions that stress in university students is generated by (1) related to evaluation processes; (2) those with work overload; (3) other conditions related to the teaching-learning process.

Coping with stress may also be different from a gender perspective, as mentioned by De Miguel and García [10], in that females tend to implement coping strategies focused on emotion and social support, whereas males' resort to avoidance and evasion. According to De Miguel and García [10], coping strategies can be active or passive. Active coping strategies are aimed at solving a problem by modifying the stressor effect. Passive coping strategies are avoidance behaviors.

On another hand Lumley and Provenzano [11] mention that "stress can affect the academic functioning of university students, interfering with adaptive behaviors such as dedication to study and class attendance or hindering essential cognitive processes such as attention and concentration".

Studies have found that stress can be augmented when students leave their parents and attend university for the first time, which is commonly manifested among first-year college students [7]. Another factor that it induces stress is the highly competitive educational environment existing in the preparatory years.

In general, it should be noted that in the measurement of stress perception in the university academic context, instruments that could be called "generic", such as the PSS (Perceived Stress Scale), have been used [12]. However, stress is not induced in the same way for each student, and some university courses are activated at a higher level. Therefore Cabanach et al. [13] designed a study to evaluate the academic environment stressors. Academic Stressors Scale of the Academic Stressor Questionnaire (ECEA) proposed by Cabanach et al. [14], which is composed by 54 items which reflected the main stressors to face by university students in the academic setting.

2.2 Virtual Assistants

Virtual assistants are increasingly being designed for the healthcare area. However, the experience when interacting with these assistants may not be a positive one if they are not designed according to the user's needs and preferences. According to the literature found they can also be called chatbots. Some studies found include methods such as tracking medications and physical activity adherence providing cognitive behavioural therapy and lifestyle recommendations.

Virtual Assistants proposed use artificial intelligence (AI) and they are emerging in the field of psychology [15]. Affective chatbots have been proposed to support anxiety and depression, such as Woebot [16] a chatbot based on the cognitive behavioral therapy (CBT), which was developed to reduce anxiety and depressive symptoms. Woebot can be used on a mobile device. Each interaction begins with a general inquiry about context, and mood (e.g. how are you feeling today?) with responses provided as words or emoji images to present empathy during the conversation. In addition, Woebot explains very briefly about CBT, also send notifications to the user to speak with him/her all days. Woebot allows to interact with the user during several days.

Another virtual assistant is Wysa that uses CBT, behavioral reinforcement, and mindfulness techniques to support patients with depression [17]. Wysa is on AI-based emotionally intelligent using a text-based conversational interface. Wysa uses evidence-based self-help practices, behavioral reinforcement, mindfulness, and guided micro actions and tools to encourage users to build emotional resilience skills. Yana is an agent conversational developed in Spanish language [18]. YANA ((You are not Alone) is developed in Chatterbot, is a Python library that generates automatic responses to a user's input, using machine learning algorithms to automate conversations. The conversations are grouped by categories such as: general conversations, money, emotions, AI, psychology, trivia, greeting, jokes, and profile. Yana has a database local and unique for each user, this database is based on the python sqlite3 library. MYLO (Manage Your Life Online (MYLO) [19] is a chatbot focused on problem solving based on CBT and elements of positive psychology [20]. Tess is a chatbot design for pediatric obesity and prediabetes treatment [21], which was used for support mental health in students [22], based on CBT [23], emotion-focused therapy [24], solution-focused brief therapy [25] and motivational interviewing [26]. This chatbot includes symptoms of depression and anxiety in university students, which was evaluated to 181 Argentinian college students aged 18 to 33.

3 Method Research

To guide this research, a review literature method was applied based on framework on literature review proposed by [27, 28], which sets out the stages to be followed such as: (1) identify the research questions; (2) Identify relevant studies; (3) Study selection; (4) Charting the data.

3.1 Identify the Research Questions

– RQ1: What is a Virtual Assistant or Chatbot?

- RQ2: What therapy theories included in the virtual assistants?
- RQ3: What are virtual assistants developed for mental health?

3.2 Identify Relevant Studies

Using the keywords "mental health" and ("virtual assistants" or "chatbots") were found in SCOPUS 129 documents by subject area, including Computer science (67), Medicine (55), Mathematics (19), Engineering (17), Social Sciences (14), Psychology (10), among others. Scopus were found documents from 2010 to 2022. WoS database were used keyword "mental health" and "virtual assistant", where were found 4 documents using google assistant, Amazon Alexa, and Microsoft Cortana. Documents found are by subject area such as health care sciences services (2), medical informatics (2), communication (1) and robotics (1). In IEEE Xplore using keywords "mental health" and "virtual assistant" were found 3 documents from 2016 to 2021. Meanwhile using the keywords "mental health" and "chatbots" were found 14 documents from 2019 to 2021. Most of the articles found were focused emotion recognition (4), natural language processing (4), health care (3) and human computer interaction (3).

Research found was conducted in the United States, the United Kingdom, Germany, and Australia. However, no relevant studies have been reported in Latin America. The research contains the following terms (see Table 1) that were considered for the search. The search for the terms was applied in "article title, abstract and keywords".

Table 1. List of keywords used.

Research keywords
"Virtual assistants" AND "mental health"
"Chatbots" AND "mental stress"
"Conversational agents" AND "mental health"

3.3 Study Selection

Evaluating virtual assistant developed and that can be included in approaches such as education and healthcare. Therefore, the studies most relevant for our study are shown in Table 2, where a search was made in Scopus, WoS and IEEE Xplore digital databases.

Answering the research questions:

RQ1: What is a Virtual Assistant?
Virtual assistant, they also are called as chatbot, which are software applications that interact with humans through verbal or written conversation. Chatbot are based on branch of artificial intelligence called Natural Language Processing (NLP). Therefore, is a subfield of linguist, computer science and artificial intelligence.

Table 2. Summary of published research on chatbots for mental health.

Article	Objective	Technology	Theories	Public
[29]	Development of a chatbot for mental health	Dialogflow created by google	–	–
[30]	Development of a chatbot for mental health	Facebook messenger	Psychodynamic or interpersonal therapy	–
[31]	Regarding how to design chatbots for mental health	–	–	Youths (aged 16–18)
[32]	Describing how intelligent cognitive assistant technology can be used as support to reduce stress, anciety and depression	–	Personality-based user model, personalized strategies, machine learning	–
[33]	PRERONA, a chatbot designed to help depression	–	–	–
[16]	Chatbot "Woebot" has been designed using Facebook messenger	–	Cognitive Behavioral Therapy	all
[34]	Chatbots for a mental health intervention, especially alcohol drinking habits assessment	AIML	1- Initiation conversation 2- providing alchol education 3- Performing an assessment 4- Concluding the conversation	18–25 years

NLU includes two steps Natural Language Understanding (NLU) and Natural Language Generation (NLG). NLU helps in understanding the dialogue of the user (known as an intent). Meanwhile NLG helps generating the right response for the given intent. Therefore, machine learning algorithms are used to generate a response correct according to the intention.

In literature found chatbots is like virtual assistants, which allow users to access data and services through a conversational interface, where the interaction is conducted by written communication.

K. Lister et al. [35] mention that chatbots are defined as conversation systems that interact with human users using concepts of natural language [X], where is included in areas such as: customer service, entertainment, education, and therapy. The interaction can be through text chat or voice. Normally, interfaces with voice are called Voice User Interfaces (VUIs) some systems are specialized for interactions in home as: Amazon Alexa and Siri Google.

Meanwhile Wahde and Virgolin [36] mention the term conversational agents (CAs), also known as intelligent virtual agents (IVAs), which define as computer programs designed for natural conversational with human users. However, in literature found many authors refer such systems as chatbots, but they mention that it is incorrect because chatbots do just that, chat, while conversational agents are task-oriented are normally used for more serious and complex tasks. Also, they mention that CAs have two categories, which can change according to the input and output modalities used (e.g., text, speech, etc.) Another definition is given by A. Abd-alrazaq et al. [37], where chatbots are systems that can converse and interact with humans' users using spoken, written, and visual languages.

RQ2: What therapy theories included in the virtual assistants for mental health?
Cognitive behavioral therapy (CBT) explores between thoughts, emotions, and behaviors are influenced by their perceptions of events. This approach is based on the cognitive model of mental illness, which was proposed by Beck [38]. Therefore, how people feel is determined by the way in which they interpret situations. CBT is structured and time-limited treatment. Typically, between 5 to 20 sessions. CBT aims to change how a person thinks (cognitive) and what they do (behaviors). Therefore, CBT uses cognitive and behavioral techniques [39].

Another theory is Perceptual Control Theory (PCT) can be used as a framework for developing interventions to influence and change behavior [40]. PCT is a model of behavior based on the properties of negative feedback control loops. The central ideas in PCT are: (1) people as perception controlling beings; (2) people as beings who self-organize/reorganize the nervous system when necessary [41].

A psychological therapy is Method of Levels (MOL) based on perceptual control theory. MOL has been tested empirically used in mental health problems such as depression, anxiety, panic, eating disorder and comorbid presentations. Also, it is associated with significant improvements in stress and self-reported level of distress when used as an intervention in primary and secondary care settings [42]. MOL is a way as talk to people, a way of helping people listen to themselves. MOL allows the user to lead the focus of the session and helps the user to shift and sustain their awareness to the source of the conflict that underlies their difficulties.

Emotionally Focused Therapy (EFT) is based on three stages such as (1) stabilization: therapist facilitates secure environment for the couple to confront the way that trauma has defined their relationship and own sense of self; (2) expanding and restructuring the emotional experience; (3) Integration: Assist the couple integrate new emotional experience and self-concepts [43].

RQ3: What are virtual assistants developed for mental health?
Table 3 shows a summary related with different virtual assistants developed for mental health.

Table 3. Virtual Assistants for mental Health

Virtual Assistant	Mental Health	Therapy-based	Language	Public	Interaction	Technology
Woebot [16]	Depressión and anxiety	CBT, IBT (Interpersonal Psychotherapy), DBT (Dialectical Behavioral Therapy)	English	>18 years	Textual	Smartphone app for Android and IOs
MYLO [19]	Distress, depression, anxiety, and stress	MOL, PCT	English	Students	Textual	Web
YANA [18]	depression	CBT	Spanish	All	Textual	Mobile application developed in Python
Wysa [17]	Stress, Anxiety and Depression	Evidence-based therapies such as CBT, behavioral reinforcement, and mindfulness	English	ALL	Textual	Mobile application
Tess [44]	Symptoms of depression and anxiety	CBT, machine learning and emotion algorithms	English	>18 years	Textual	Facebook messenger, slack

3.4 Charting the Data

Figure 1 shows a map based on bibliographic data with keywords "mental health" and "virtual assistants" or "chatbots "in two databases such as WoS and SCOPUS using VOSViewer, a software tool constructing and visualizing bibliometric networks using keyword selected. Each colour represents one cluster, curved lines are relationships associated with keywords and density is related with occurrences. It is observed that the terms mental health and chatbots are related with depression and anxiety. However, chatbots or virtual assistants focused to academic stress were not found.

On another hand, the literature reviewed show studies from 2010 to 2021. However, since the Covid-19 global pandemic, these virtual assistant studies focused on mental health began to increase (e.g., 2022 (6), 2021 (67), 2020 (28)). In addition, research found was conducted in the United States, the United Kingdom, Germany, and Australia. However, no relevant studies have been reported in Latin America. Studies also focused more on conference paper.

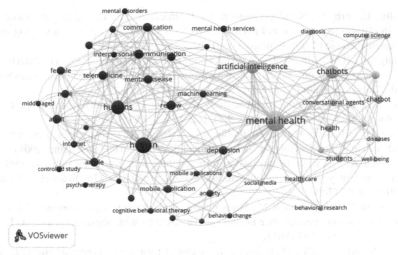

Fig. 1. Analysis of keywords cluster (in colours). VOSViewer analysed the keywords of the selected articles that are used together.

4 Conclusions

Virtual assistants can be an alternative for emotional support. They are being developed as therapists to support a user's mental health. In turn, the development of a chatbot involves considering certain aspects of dialogue design to empathize with the user.

In addition, design guidelines for chatbots are generally heterogeneous and are largely based on common knowledge rather than empirical evidence. It was also found that most of the studies are more focused towards anxiety and depression, but not academic stress. In turn, most of these proposed chatbots follow the CBT approach. Most of the studies found do not explore the user experience of interacting with this type of intelligent interfaces, which is closely related to features in the dialog design.

References

1. Horgan, D., Romao, M., Morré, S.A., Kalra, D.: Artificial intelligence: power for civilisation – and for better healthcare. Public Health Genomics **22**(5–6), 145–161 (2019). https://doi.org/ 10.1159/000504785
2. Curtis, R.G., et al.: Improving user experience of virtual health assistants: scoping review. J. Med. Internet Res. **23**(12), e31737 (2021). https://doi.org/10.2196/31737
3. Villegas-Ch, W., García-Ortiz, J., Mullo-Ca, K., Sánchez-Viteri, S., Roman-Cañizares, M.: Implementation of a virtual assistant for the academic management of a university with the use of artificial intelligence. Future Internet **13**(4), 97 (2021). https://doi.org/10.3390/fi1304 0097
4. Doherty, G., Coyle, D., Matthews, M.: Design and evaluation guidelines for mental health technologies. Interact. Comput. **22**(4), 243–252 (2010). https://doi.org/10.1016/j.intcom. 2010.02.006
5. Lazarus, R.S., Folkman, S.: Stress, Appraisal and Coping. Springer, New York. Versión en castellano: Estrés y procesos cognitivos. Barcelona: Martínez Roca, 1.986 (1984)

6. Bendig, E., Erb, B., Schulze-Thuesing, L., Baumeister, H.: The next generation: chatbots in clinical psychology and psychotherapy to foster mental health – a scoping review. Verhaltenstherapie (2019). https://doi.org/10.1159/000501812(2019)

7. Abdulghani, H.M., AlKanhal, A.A., Mahmoud, E.S., Ponnamperuma, G.G., Alfaris, E.A.: Stress and its effects on medical students: a cross-sectional study at a college of medicine in Saudi Arabia. J. Health Popul. Nutr. 29(5), 516–22 (2011)

8. Wilks, S.E.: Resilience amid academic stress: the moderating impact of social support among social work students. Adv. Soc. Work 9(2), 106–125 (2008)

9. Muñoz, F.J.: El Estrés Académico: Problemas y Soluciones Desde una Perspectiva Psicosocial. Servicio de Publicaciones de la Universidad de Huelva, Huelva, España (2004)

10. De Miguel, A., García, L.: Estrategias de afrontamiento: un estudio comparativo con enfermos físicos crónicos y personas sin enfermedad crónica. Análisis y Modificación de Conducta 26(105), 29–55 (2000)

11. Lumley, M.A., Provenzano, K.M.: Stress management through written emotional disclosure improves academic performance among college students with physical symptoms. J. Educ. Psychol. 95(3), 641–649 (2003)

12. Cohen, S., Kamarck, T., Mermelstein, R.: A global measure of perceived stress. J. Health Soc. Behav. 24(4), 385 (1983). https://doi.org/10.2307/2136404

13. Cabanach, R.G., Souto-Gestal, A., Franco, V.: Escala de estresores académicos para la evaluación de los estresores académicos en estudiantes universitarios. Rev. Iberoam. Psicol. y Salud 7(2), 41–50 (2016). https://doi.org/10.1016/j.rips.2016.05.001

14. Cabanach, R.G., Valle, A., Rodríguez, S., Piñeiro, I.: Variables explicativas del estrés en estudiantes universitarios: construcción de una escala de medida. Comunicación V Congreso Internacional de Psicología y Educación: Los retos del futuro. Oviedo, 23–25 de abril de 2008. (2008)

15. Bendig, E., Erb, B., Schulze-Thuesing, L., Baumeister, H.: The next generation: chatbots in clinical psychology and psychotherapy to foster mental health – a scoping review. Verhaltenstherapie (2019). https://doi.org/10.1159/000501812

16. Fitzpatrick, K.K., Darcy, A., Vierhile, M.: Delivering cognitive behavior therapy to young adults with symptoms of depression and anxiety using a fully automated conversational agent (Woebot): a randomized controlled trial. JMIR Ment. Health 4(2), e19 (2017). https://doi.org/10.2196/mental.7785

17. Inkster, B., Sarda, S., Subramanian, V.: An empathy-driven, conversational artificial intelligence agent (Wysa) for digital mental well-being: real-world data evaluation mixed-methods study. JMIR mHealth and uHealth 6(11), e12106 (2018). https://doi.org/10.2196/12106

18. https://play.google.com/store/apps/details?id=com.yanaapp&hl=es_CL&gl=US.   last Accessed 18 Feb 2022

19. Gaffney, H., Mansell, W., Edwards, R., Wright, J.: Manage Your Life Online (MYLO): a pilot trial of a conversational computer-based intervention for problem solving in a student sample. Behav. Cogn. Psychother. 42(6), 731–746 (2014). https://doi.org/10.1017/S13524 6581300060X

20. Ly, K.H., Ly, A.-M., Andersson, G.: A fully automated conversational agent for promoting mental well-being: A pilot RCT using mixed methods. Internet Interv. 10, 39–46 (2017). https://doi.org/10.1016/j.invent.2017.10.002/

21. Stephens, T.N., Joerin, A., Rauws, M., Werk, L.N.: Feasibility of pediatric obesity and prediabetes treatment support through Tess, the AI behavioral coaching chatbot. Transl. Behav. Med. 9(3), 440–447 (2019). https://doi.org/10.1093/tbm/ibz043

22. Klos, M.C., Escoredo, M., Joerin, A., Lemos, V.N., Rauws, M., Bunge, E.L.: Artificial intelligence–based chatbot for anxiety and depression in university students: pilot randomized controlled trial. JMIR Form. Res. 5(8), e20678 (2021). https://doi.org/10.2196/20678

23. Beck, J.: Cognitive Behavior Therapy: Basics and Beyond, 2nd edn. The Guilford Press, New York City (2011)
24. Greenberg, L.: Emotion-Focused Therapy: Coaching Clients to Work Through Their Feelings. American Psychological Association, Washington, DC (2002)
25. Pichot, T., Dolan, Y.: Solution-Focused Brief Therapy: Its Effective Use in Agency Settings. Haworth Marriage and the Family. Routledge, New York (2003)
26. Rollnick, S., Miller, W.R.: What is motivational interviewing? Behav. Cogn. Psychother. **23**(4), 325–334 (2009). https://doi.org/10.1017/S135246580001643X
27. Arksey, H., O'Malley, L.: Scoping studies: towards a methodological framework. Int. J. Soc. Res. Methodol. **8**(1), 19–32 (2005). https://doi.org/10.1080/1364557032000119616
28. Kitchenham, B.A.: Procedures for Undertaking Systematic Reviews. Joint Technical report, Computer Science Department, Keele University (TR/SE- 0401) and National ICT Australia Ltd. (0400011T.1) (2004)
29. Dhanasekar, V., Preethi, Y., S, V., R, P.J.I., M, B.P.: A Chatbot to promote students mental health through emotion recognition. In: 2021 Third International Conference on Inventive Research in Computing Applications (ICIRCA), 2021, pp. 1412–1416 (2021). https://doi.org/10.1109/ICIRCA51532.2021.9544838
30. Yang, P., Fu, W.: Mindbot: a social-based medical virtual assistant. IEEE International Conference on Healthcare Informatics (ICHI) **2016**, 319 (2016). https://doi.org/10.1109/ICHI.2016.105.8
31. Høiland, C.G., Følstad, A., Karahasanovic, A.: Hi, can I help? Exploring how to design a mental health chatbot for youths. Hum. Technol. **16**(2), 139–169 (2020). https://doi.org/10.17011/ht/urn.202008245640
32. Kolenik, T., et al.: Designing an intelligent cognitive assistant as persuasive technology for stress, anxiety and depression relief. PERSUASIVE (2020)
33. Hussna, A.U., Laz, A.N.K., Sikder, M.S., Uddin, J., Tinmaz, H., Esfar-E-Alam, A.M.: PRERONA: mental health bengali chatbot for digital counselling. In: Singh, M., Kang, D.-K., Lee, J.-H., Tiwary, U.S., Singh, D., Chung, W.-Y. (eds.) IHCI 2020. LNCS, vol. 12615, pp. 274–286. Springer, Cham (2021). https://doi.org/10.1007/978-3-030-68449-5_28
34. Elmasri, D., Maeder, A.: A conversational agent for an online mental health intervention. In: Ascoli, G.A., Hawrylycz, M., Ali, H., Khazanchi, D., Shi, Y. (eds.) BIH 2016. LNCS (LNAI), vol. 9919, pp. 243–251. Springer, Cham (2016). https://doi.org/10.1007/978-3-319-47103-7_24
35. Lister, K., Coughlan, T., Iniesto, F., Freear, N., Devine, P.: Accessible conversational user interfaces: considerations for design. In: Proceedings of the 17th International Web for All Conference (W4A '20). Association for Computing Machinery, New York, NY, USA, Article 5, pp. 1–11 (2020). https://doi.org/10.1145/3371300.3383343
36. Wahde, M., Virgolin, M.: Conversational agents: theory and applications. ArXiv, abs/2202.03164 (2022)
37. Abd-alrazaq, A.A., Alajlani, M., Alalwan, A.A., Bewick, B.M., Gardner, P., Househ, M.: An overview of the features of chatbots in mental health: a scoping review. Int. J. Med. Inform. **132**, 103978 (2019). https://doi.org/10.1016/j.ijmedinf.2019.103978
38. Beck, J.S.: Cognitive Therapy: Basics and Beyond. Guildford Press, New York (1964)
39. Fenn, K., Byrne, M.: The key principles of cognitive behavioural therapy. InnovAiT: Education and Inspiration for General Practice **6**(9), 579–585 (2013). https://doi.org/10.1177/1755738012471029
40. Powers, W.T.: Behavior: The Control of Perception. Benchmark Publications, New Canaan, United States (1973)
41. Marken, R.S., Mansell, W.: Perceptual control as a unifying concept in psychology. Rev. Gen. Psychol. **17**(2), 190–195 (2013). https://doi.org/10.1037/a0032933

42. Carey, T.A., Carey, M., Mullan, R.J., Spratt, C.G., Spratt, M.B.: Assessing the statistical and personal significance of the method of levels. Behav. Cogn. Psychother. **37**, 311–324 (2009)
43. Soltani, M., Shairi, M.R., Roshan, R., Rahimi, C.R.: The impact of emotionally focused therapy on emotional distress in infertile couples. Int. J. Fertil. Steril. **7**(4), 337–344 (2014)
44. Fulmer, R., Joerin, A., Gentile, B., Lakerink, L., Rauws, M.: Using psychological artificial intelligence (Tess) to relieve symptoms of depression and anxiety: randomized controlled trial. JMIR Mental Health **5**(4), e64 (2018). https://doi.org/10.2196/mental.9782

Hierarchical Binary Classifiers for Sleep Stage Classification

Erebus Oh and Kenneth Barkdoll[✉]

Swarthmore College, Swarthmore, PA 19081, USA
kbarkdo1@swarthmore.edu

Abstract. This paper examines the benefits and shortfalls of using local binary "one-vs.-all" classifiers with a variety of models in different hierarchical layouts in order to classify sleep stages using raw signal inputs in 30-s increments. Although under-performing more advanced algorithms, our best hierarchies outperform a Random Forest multi-class classifier, indicating the potential of binary classifiers in future work. This paper lays the groundwork for developing more advanced hierarchical classifiers using pre-trained binary classifiers.

Keywords: Human computer interface · Machine learning · Binary classifiers · Sleep · Sleep stage classification · Hierarchical classification · Decision trees · Support vector machines · Voting classifiers · Human-centered AI · Sleep · Healthcare · EEG analysis

1 Introduction

1.1 Problem Statement

Sleep is essential for human health and wellness. Inadequate or poor sleep affects one's psychological state, learning abilities, and judgement. Furthermore, long-term damage may be done causing widespread diseases such as obesity and cardiovascular disease [1]. Approximately 50 to 70 million people in the US suffer from sleep disorder [4]. Thus, being able to track and evaluate sleep is essential for diagnosing and treating many health conditions. Traditional sleep stage recordings are done with a polysomnogram, which tracks eye movements, muscles activity, breathing, heart rate, and electrical brain signals. This is uncomfortable and complicated to set up, making it impractical for continual sleep monitoring. There is a need to have a diagnostic tool that can more easily analyze sleep, such as by using only the brain's electrical activity (via EEG signals). Sleep

© Springer Nature Switzerland AG 2022
V. G. Duffy et al. (Eds.): HCII 2022, LNCS 13521, pp. 119–129, 2022.
https://doi.org/10.1007/978-3-031-17902-0_9

stage analysis is important because it is known that individual sleep stages have unique benefits. For example, it is believed that both REM and NREM sleep are necessary for adequate memory consolidation, and thus being about to analyze the distributions of these patterns may help in detecting the presence of potential causes of memory issues [6].

1.2   Literature Review

Sleep occurs in stages that provide important information about sleep quality, but also lend themselves to classification using machine learning [15,18]. Waking EEG signals are immensely chaotic, but this data becomes more periodic as sleep occurs. As people fall asleep, they transition for approximately 1–5 minutes into NREM1 sleep, which is characterized by a decrease in high frequency "alpha" waves and an increase in low-amplitude mixed-frequency activity [15]. NREM2 sleep is deeper sleep, characterized by slow, intermittent delta waves in EEG signals, that serve as precursors to the stage of NREM3 sleep, which can be delineated by the high prevalence of low-frequency, high-amplitude delta waves [13]. The final stage is the chaotic REM sleep. This presents a challenge as EEG signals in REM can be hard to differentiation from similar waking signals [15]. This presents challenges with classification that we will have to address.

Machine learning has been known to be able to learn large and complicated data sets. In addition, it has been known to classify chaotic and periodic systems with high accuracy [18]. While the idea of using machine learning to classify sleep has been explored, it has not seen nearly the same attention for classification that other areas of machine learning EEG classification have received [7]. Because of this, attempts to classify sleep have seen little standardization towards a good predictive model for classification. In addition there are a series of non-network ways of analyzing sleep.

Current human expert analysis uses visual data of neurophysiological signals (polysomnograms) analyzed by trained specialists [11]. This is incredibly slow and fails to allow large scale, continual sleep stage tracking. So far, attempts made to classify sleep have approached the task using a range of machine learning systems. A signal-analysis based process achieved an overall accuracy of 92.31% using binary one-against-all classifiers after heavy signal processing [2], amongst other methods, with an 80–20% training-testing split of their dataset. The individual sensitivities of their binary classifiers ranged from 98.31% (Wake) to 36.22% (REM), and specificities ranged from 99.63% (Wake) to 97.34% (N1). Binary classifiers have computationally efficient implementations and work better with smaller amounts of data than other algorithms (as would be required for cost-acceptable individualized care [14]), though the use of the preprocessing methods seen in prior binary-classifier work is complex and computationally intensive, making raw signal data a valuable, if difficult, input for machine learning classification. A method that uses raw signal data and potentially decreases computational power would allow for processing to be done on a smaller scale, possibly in wearable electronics or on a patient-to-patient basis, removing the need to transmit sensitive patient data to external computing systems. The use of raw signal data is an underdeveloped area of research owing to the complexity and noisiness of raw inputs, however it is worth investigating for our research due to the computational benefits of eliminating pre-processing.

Meanwhile, the other multi-class machine learning approaches vary in effectiveness. Convolutional neural networks have been used to achieve an overall accuracy of 86% [19], and other studies used a Random Forest algorithm to achieve an overall 91% classification accuracy [3]. With all this work, our review pointed to a number of algorithms with high efficacy for our study. Based on their use in the machine learning classification of sleep and other EEG tasks, algorithms worth investigation include Support Vector Machines [7,8,10,17], Linear Discriminant Analysis [17], Naive Bayes [8], K-Nearest Neighbors [16], and Adaptive Boosting [5]. In addition these algorithms are functionally implementable on consumer machinery, making them viable for both reproduction and realistic for patient use.

1.3 Purpose of Study

This paper pursues a more computationally efficient machine learning algorithm for sleep stage detection. In addition, our work highlights where our machine learning algorithms struggle to classify sleep and investigates the efficacy of using raw signal data.

1.4 Research Questions

What are the best binary one-vs.-all classification algorithms for each sleep stage? Can pre-trained binary classifiers be arranged into efficient hierarchical classification models for individualized sleep stage classification?

2 Dataset

The Sleep-EDF database [12] is an open source sleep EEG database compiled from two separate studies. It consists of 197 whole-night sleep recordings consisting of EEG, EOG, and chin EMG data, and event markers. In addition, a number of the recordings also have respiration and body temperature recordings.

All of this data was classified by trained professionals and compiled into hypnograms that tracked sleep patterns. We use the records of 82 healthy Caucasian adults across a range of ages from 25 to 101 without any known sleep conditions or medications. Each record contained two nights of sleep per patient. During this time, they were recorded by EEGs sampling 100 Hz. This study does not attempt to classify the sleep of the other subjects in the Sleep-EDF database who were undergoing a drug trial.

3   Methods and Experimental Design

The raw data for our experiment was taken from the Sleep-EDF database [12] and used code from a prior experiment [9] to divide every sleep recording into 30 s chunks. The samples did not undergo any other preprocessing, filtering, or extraction procedures. Next we sorted the data by class, and noted that it was uneven, requiring special care [14]. The data distribution across sleep stages is visible in Fig. 1. Because of this, we used class-weighted training methods to train our binary classifiers to alleviate bias.

To determine the best algorithms for one-vs.-all binary classification for each sleep stage, six different algorithms were tested—one being a custom voting classifier based on the other five. For each stage of sleep we trained five algorithms (a Support Vector Machine with a Radial Basis Function, a Linear Discriminant Analysis algorithm, a Naive Bayes classifier, an Adaptive Boosting classifier, and a k-Nearest Neighbors classifier). The performance of these classifiers is encoded in Fig. 2. From these algorithms, we also created custom voting classifiers, weighting the best algorithms for each stage disproportionately—these weights are visible in Fig. 3. These voting classifiers were tested and their performance was compared to the initial algorithms (the custom voting classifier performance is visible as "Voting" in Fig. 2). The best performing algorithms are visible in Fig. 4. The exact sensitivity and specificity of each of these is shown in Fig. 5.

Using these tables, and a series of other methods, hierarchical arrangements of these binary classifiers were developed. In a binary classifier hierarchy, the aim is to have the initial classifiers accurately prevent lower binary classifiers from misclassifying data as a "false positive"—ex. a classifier made to select N3 sleep samples accidentally selecting an N1 sleep samples—by eliminating those samples from the dataset (once a sample has been classified as a specific sleep stage it is eliminated from the data stream and given that classification). The first hierarchy was built based on an intuitive understanding of the differences in sleep stages from academic literature, thus first came the Wake classifier, as waking sleep is chaotic and very active, unlike most sleep. Next came the REM classifier, since REM sleep is the most chaotic of the sleep stages, and thus the REM classifier was anticipated to have high accuracy since it would not be able to confuse Wake signals (having already been filtered out). After the REM classifier was the N1 classifier. N1 sleep is seen as a transitional period from wakefulness to sleep, and therefore is likely difficult to classify and easy to confuse with Waking signals. Then came the N2 and N3 classifiers, since N2 is the next most similar to N1, and N3 is the most distinct. Thus, the hope is that conventional knowledge about sleep would point to the most likely issues for machine learning algorithms, and each successive classifier will have less potentially problematic data to classify. This classifier schema can be seen as "Intuitive Binary Hierarchy" in Fig. 6.

The next hierarchy followed the same logic of eliminating confounding data, though using dataset size, placing the classifiers in the order corresponding to the size of each sleep stage dataset ("Size Binary Hierarchy" in Fig. 6). The third hierarchy places the classifiers in order of accuracy ("Accuracy Binary Classi-fier") Fig. 4 and the fourth hierarchy places the binary classifiers in order of their sensitivity Fig. 5 ("Sensitivity Binary Classifier")—the inspiration being that the most sensitive classifiers would be the most accurate at removing data correctly. In addition to these binary hierarchies, we developed a traditional multi-class Random Forest classifier as a baseline for comparison to our hierarchies. The accuracy of these hierarchies, and the "Multi-Class" Random Forest classifier are recorded in Fig. 7.

4   Results

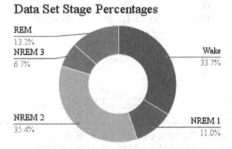

Fig. 1. Data set sleep stage distribution

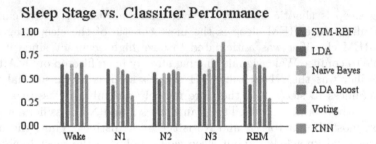

Fig. 2. Sleep stage vs. classifier performance

	Predicted by Network				
Voting Weights	Wake	N1	N2	N3	REM
SVM-RBF	1.5	1.5	1.5	1	1.5
LDA	0	0	0	0	0
Naive Bayes	1.5	1.5	0	0	1
ADA Boost	1	1	1	1	1
KNN	0	0	1.5	2	0

Fig. 3. Voting classifier weights

Stage	Classifier	Performance
Wake	Custom Voting	68.42%
NREM 1	Naive Bayes	62.64%
NREM 2	Custom Voting	60.07%
NREM 3	KNN	89.59%
REM	SVM RBF	68.66%

Fig. 4. Best binary classifier performance

	Predicted by Network				
Classifier	Wake	N1	N2	N3	REM
Specificity	74.42%	62.13%	66.95%	96.81%	68.48%
Sensitivity	55.11%	68.79%	47.45%	3.60%	66.22%
Accuracy	68.03%	62.85%	60.28%	89.54%	68.16%

Fig. 5. Best binary classifier performance (detailed)

Intuitive Binary Hierarchy

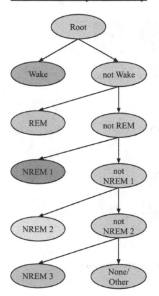

Size Binary Hierarchy

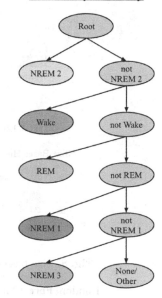

Accuracy Binary Hierarchy

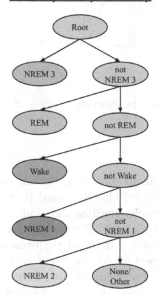

Sensitivity Binary Hierarchy

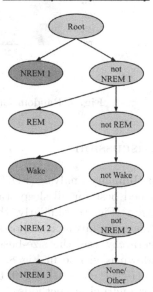

Fig. 6. Hierarchy layouts

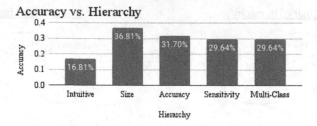

Fig. 7. Hierarchy accuracy

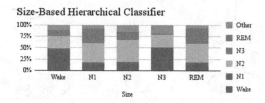

Fig. 8. Size-based hierarchical classifier performance

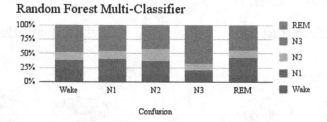

Fig. 9. Random forest multi-class classifier performance

5   Discussion

Our preliminary analysis (Fig. 2) indicated there was no specific algorithm that performed best for all sleep stages, instead each binary classifier used its own algorithm (Fig. 4). Similarly, the variation in hierarchy performance indicates that hierarchy layout is important to overall performance 7. The best performing hierarchy was the size-based hierarchy, for which a detailed performance breakdown is visible in Fig. 8. In addition, it outperformed the Random Forest multi-class classifier Fig. 9, though it failed to outperform the 86% accuracy of prior multi-class methods [19]. It should also be noted that our binary classifiers failed to outperform prior binary classifiers as well [2]. Increased binary classifier performance would likely increase hierarchy accuracy. Interestingly, the size-based hierarchy significantly outperforms the "intuitive" hierarchy, indicating that hierarchy layout, and the subsequent filtering of samples that facilitates, is important to overall performance.

Though the overall performance of the size-based hierarchy is better than the Random Forest classifier, the more detailed graphics indicate the perils of our arranged hierarchical classification. The classifier seems to be heavily biased towards classifying signals as wake, N2, and REM, with very little sleep classified as N1 or N3. As it is important to note, N2, wake, and REM also happen to be the first three classifiers in the hierarchy. Inversely, the Random Forest Classifier seems to have a slight bias towards REM sleep, but has a much more even distribution of the five classes across the hierarchies—it is significantly more accurate at classifying the deepest (and widely seen as most distinct) period of sleep: N3. This indicates a number of things. Firstly, it may mean that the accuracy of our size-based hierarchy is partially a result of the fact that we biased that hierarchy towards the most common of the sleep stages. Secondly, it may indicate that certain samples have an increased likelihood of being classified as multiple sleep stages by multiple binary classifiers (effectively the opposite of "other", which consists of samples for whom no binary classifier selects that sample as the stage it is classifying—samples classified as "none" by ever one-vs.-all classifier). This requires further investigation, and indicates that if different classifiers have similar "one" and "all" pools despite being designed to classify different classes, hierarchical classification may have limited potential. This also indicates that hierarchy layout is an important tool if classification demands the minimization of specific error types. For example, if it were found that a minimum amount of REM sleep was critical to safe driving for a professional driver who tracked their sleep, a "false positive" for REM would potentially be more problematic than a false negative (the under-classification of sleep as REM). Thus, putting the REM sleep classifier higher in the hierarchy could be negligent for their use case as it increases the chance for a false positive REM classification, just as the size-based hierarchy is biased towards N2 false positives.

Thus, although our binary classifier does outperform our multi-class classifier, and better binary classifiers may outperform stronger multi-class classifiers, it is clear that our implementation does suffer from some issues biasing hierarchies towards certain sleep stages.

6   Conclusions and Future Work

This study provides ample territory for future work. It indicates that hierarchical classification using pre-trained binary classifiers can outperform traditional multi-class classifiers on raw data, but also can introduce bias based on the characteristics of the binary classifiers and the dataset. It also indicates that hierarchy layout is important to overall accuracy. Future work should focus on both better understanding the properties of binary classification hierarchies, and on improving the accuracy of our algorithms. It is clear from our work that the raw data cannot be classified well by binary classifiers. Instead, just as preprocessing appears to greatly improve the accuracy of other algorithms, so too may it improve the performance of binary hierarchical classification when implemented for the binary classifiers. Immediate followup work should also investigate other binary classification hierarchies, perhaps based on other performance metrics, such as specificity, or based on the unique characteristics of the binary classifiers upon closer inspection (if one binary classifier, such as N3, were to consistently classify N2 sleep as N3, then it would be possible to increase its accuracy by putting it after the N2 classifier—this is a more granular approach to the general intent behind accuracy and sensitivity based hierarchies). More detailed breakdowns of algorithm performance would provide better insights in this area. In addition, it may be worth investigating custom-trained algorithms for their positions in the hierarchy, although in this scenario hierarchy layout would have to be determined by the inherent characteristics of the dataset. For example, REM sleep and Waking signals are believed to be very similar by sleep experts, and thus a "REM & Wake vs. Other" binary classifier could provide a valuable tool in hierarchical classification, though this would require knowing that specific decision would be a valuable node in the tree—this demands prior knowledge of the dataset. Finally, by training and testing classifiers for each subject, we are working with intra-patient accuracies. In order for widespread use without individual sleep scoring for each patient, inter-patient classifiers are much needed for widespread implementation.

References

1. Consequences of insufficient sleep. https://healthysleep.med.harvard.edu/healthy/matters/consequences
2. Aboalayon, K.A.I., Faezipour, M., Almuhammadi, W.S., Moslehpour, S.: Sleep stage classification using EEG signal analysis: a comprehensive survey and new investigation. Entropy 18(9), 272 (2016)
3. Bakmeedeniya, T.: Random forest approach for sleep stage classification. 10, 768 (2020). https://doi.org/10.29322/IJSRP.10.05.2020.p10189
4. CDC: Sleep and sleep disorders. https://www.sleepassociation.org/about-sleep/sleep-statistics/
5. Chen, Y., Chang, R., Guo, J.: Emotion recognition of EEG signals based on the ensemble learning method: Adaboost. Math. Problems Eng. 2021, 1–12 (2021)
6. of Communcations, O., Liason, P.: Brain basics: sleep disorders. https://www.ninds.nih.gov/Disorders/Patient-Caregiver-Education/Understanding-Sleep#10
7. Craik, A., He, Y., Contreras-Vidal, J.L.: Deep learning for electroencephalogram (EEG) classification tasks: a review. J. Neural Eng. 16(3), 031001 (2019)
8. Dabas, H., Sethi, C., Dua, C., Dalawat, M., Sethia, D.: Emotion classification using EEG signals. In: Proceedings of the 2018 2nd International Conference on Computer Science and Artificial Intelligence, pp. 380–384 (2018)
9. Eldele, E., et al.: An attention-based deep learning approach for sleep stage classification with single-channel EEG. IEEE Trans. Neural Syst. Rehab. Eng. 29, 809–818 (2021). https://doi.org/10.1109/TNSRE.2021.3076234
10. Hsu, C.W., Lin, C.J.: A comparison of methods for multiclass support vector machines. IEEE Trans. Neural Netw. 13(2), 415–425 (2002). https://doi.org/10.1109/72.991427
11. Keenan, S.A.: Polysomnographic technique: an overview. Sleep Disorders Medicine, pp. 79–94 (1994)

12. Kemp, B., Zwinderman, A., Tuk, B., Kamphuisen, H., Oberye, J.: Analysis of a sleep-dependent neuronal feedback loop: the slow-wave microcontinuity of the EEG. IEEE Trans. Biomed. Eng. **47**(9), 1185–1194 (2000). https://doi.org/10.1109/10.867928

13. McCarley, R.W., Sinton, C.M.: Neurobiology of sleep and wakefulness. Scholarpedia **3**(4), 3313 (2008). https://doi.org/10.4249/scholarpedia.3313

14. Mousavi, S., Afghah, F., Acharya, U.R.: SleepEEGNet: automated sleep stage scoring with sequence to sequence deep learning approach. PloS one **14**(5), e0216456 (2019)

15. Patel, A.K., Reddy, V., Araujo, J.F.: Physiology, Sleep Stages. In: StatPearls [Internet] (2021)

16. Sha'abani, M.N.A.H., Fuad, N., Jamal, N., Ismail, M.F.: kNN and SVM classification for EEG: a review. In: Kasruddin Nasir, A.N., et al. (eds.) InECCE2019. LNEE, vol. 632, pp. 555–565. Springer, Singapore (2020). https://doi.org/10.1007/978-981-15-2317-5_47

17. Subasi, A., Ismail Gursoy, M.: EEG signal classification using PCA, ICA, LDA and support vector machines. Expert Syst. Appl. **37**(12), 8659–8666 (2010). https://doi.org/10.1016/j.eswa.2010.06.065. https://www.sciencedirect.com/science/article/pii/S0957417410005695

18. Uzun, S.: Machine learning-based classification of time series of chaotic systems. Eur. Phys. J. Spec. Top. , 1–11 (2021). https://doi.org/10.1140/epjs/s11734-021-00346-z

19. Vilamala, A., Madsen, K.H., Hansen, L.K.: Deep convolutional neural networks for interpretable analysis of EEG sleep stage scoring. In: 2017 IEEE 27th International Workshop on Machine Learning for Signal Processing (MLSP), pp. 1–6. IEEE (2017)

Development of VR Exposure Therapy Support System for Social Anxiety Utilizing Anxiety Levels Estimated by Physiological Indices

Mieko Ohsuga[✉] and Haruya Koba

Osaka Institute of Technology, Osaka 530-8568, Japan
Mieko.Ohsuga@oit.ac.jp

Abstract. VR (Virtual Reality) exposure therapy is used as a treatment for social anxiety. To increase the effectiveness of the treatment and prevent patients from dropping out of treatment, we proposed an additional function to maintain the patient's anxiety level at an appropriate level during exposure therapy. The anxiety level is estimated using physiological indices obtained from electrocardiogram, finger skin conductance and respiration that can be measured without giving an excessive burden to the patient, and adjusted by selecting the questions and the actions of the virtual interviewer. We designed the system from the user's point of view, and developed an estimation equation for anxiety levels, built the experimental environment, VR interview room with avatars, and a control interface for the experimenter. After preliminary experiments and improvement, the functions and user interface, an assessment experiment was conducted in a remote environment, simulating a job-hunting interview with the cooperation of the employment counselors. Although the number of participants was small, the proposed method showed the possibility of adjusting anxiety levels.

Keywords: VR exposure therapy · Social anxiety disorder · Physiological indices

1 Introduction

Virtual Reality (VR) is now used not only for entertainment purposes but also in many scientific and engineering fields, demonstrating its usefulness and potential. In particular, VR therapy for mental care has been actively researched and practiced [1]. This is largely due to advances in devices such as head-mounted displays (HMDs) and computing and rendering engines, which have eliminated the need for expensive and large-scale systems. VR-based treatment in small clinics and at home is expected to become popular in the future.

This paper focuses on social anxiety disorder (SAD), which is characterized by an excessive fear of negative evaluation and rejection by other people and a consistent fear of embarrassment or humiliation [2]. Like Phobia and other anxiety disorders, SAD patients are also treated with VR exposure therapy (VRET). Chesham et al. [3] conducted a meta-analysis of the VRET on social anxiety and showed significant effect

© Springer Nature Switzerland AG 2022
V. G. Duffy et al. (Eds.): HCII 2022, LNCS 13521, pp. 130–141, 2022.
https://doi.org/10.1007/978-3-031-17902-0_10

sizes compared to the wait-list group and no difference from placebo treatment or in-vivo, image exposure. Carl et al. [4] conducted a meta-analysis of the benefits of VRET for social anxiety and related disorders and found that patients who also received VRET showed more significant reductions in anxiety compared to patients in the wait-list group and no difference from placebo treatment or in-vivo exposure. Emmelkamp et al. [5] compared VRET with cognitive behavioral therapy (CBT) and found no difference in effectiveness, noting that there are few studies comparing VRET alone. In summary, VRET is more effective than nothing, but has no clear significance over other therapies. However, it has not been denied that VRET is as effective as other therapies, and VRET unlike imaging therapy, has the advantages of allowing the therapist to share exposure images with the patient and of being more controllable and safer than real-life exposure. Furthermore, 76% of patients chose VRET over in-vivo treatment, suggesting that it is worthwhile to further improve this method and to test its effectiveness.

It has been reported that accustomed methods starting with relatively weak anxiety may cause a recurrence of symptoms, and that starting with strong anxiety may increase the efficacy of treatment but increase the patient's feelings of rejection of treatment [6, 7]. Therefore, we proposed a VRET system that estimates anxiety levels and modifies VR contents to keep them at appropriate levels and we showed the possibility to estimate the patient's anxiety level from heart rate (HR), respiration, and finger skin conductance (SC) which can be measured without giving excessive and additional burden to users [8, 9]. Subsequently, Mahmoudi-Nejad [10] and Mevlevioğlu et al. [11] presented similar frameworks, but they only implemented a part of functions. The purpose of this study is to develop a method to optimize the patient's anxiety level, and to implement and to assess a VRET system equipped with this method.

2 System Design

Figure 1 shows the system configuration of the proposed system. It targets patients with SAD, especially those who are anxious about communicative situations such as public speech, and those who tend to pre-disposition to such anxiety. In VRET, we hypothesized that it is important to estimate the patient's anxiety level during therapy and control it appropriately in order to reduce the patient's resistance to therapy, decrease the withdrawal rate, make the therapy more effective, and prevent relapse of symptoms. The patient wears an HMD and is presented with a virtual space in which to conduct an interview or public speech. The HMD is used to give the patient a sense of immersion and autonomy and to perform head-tracking. The real-time estimation of anxiety level is based on physiological parameters measured by a wearable device that does not overburden the patient, specifically HR, respiration, and SC. The anxiety level is adjusted by adaptively manipulating the contents of the VR space, the facial expressions, gestures, questions, and statements of the virtual interviewers and audience members.

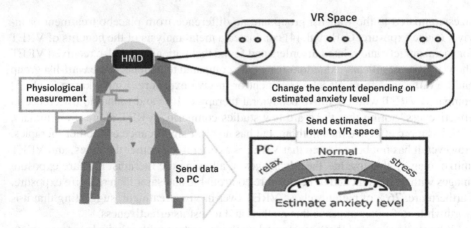

Fig. 1. System configuration of the proposed system (revised from [8])

3 Previous Work

In our previous studies [8, 9], we have developed a method for estimating the anxiety level of participants based on physiological indices. The following is an overview of the development procedure. First, we conducted an experiment in which the author was subjected to a simulated job interview in a real space. Subjective ratings, HR, and Skin Conductance Level (SCL) increased, and Respiratory Gravity Frequency (GF) decreased, confirming that the simulated interview can cause anxiety. We then measured similar physiological indices during VR simulated interviews for nine healthy male university students (Ethics Review Approval Number 2019–34). After the experiment, the mean values of the physiological indices during the period without speech immediately before the rating were obtained, and a principal component analysis (PCA) was performed with different combinations of indices that showed significant differences between the resting and interview times by the paired t-test, and the set with the highest cumulative contribution ratio was selected.

The selected set was HR, Low Frequency component of Heart Rate Variability (HRVLF), Respiratory Frequency component of Heart Rate Variability (HRVRF), GF, SCL and Skin Conductance Response (SCR). The results of varimax rotation using up to the second component showed that the first component was interpreted as sympathetic nervous system activation and the second component was a respiratory-related component (Table 1). Since the relationship between the first principal component scores and subjective ratings at rest and during the interview was observed, an equation for estimating anxiety level was developed using these scores.

Table 1. Principal component loadings of the two principal components after varimax rotation (revised from [9])

	First Principle Component	Second Principle component
HR	**0.47**	-0.078
HRVLF	0.33	**0.40**
HRVRF	-0.18	**0.68**
GF	-0.007	**-0.61**
SCL	**0.53**	0.003
SCR	**0.60**	0.038
Cumulative Contribution Rate (%)	33.54	57.52

The mean and standard deviation of each indicator used in the PCA were used to calculate the inner product of the Z-scored index values and the first PCA loadings, which was defined as the estimate of the anxiety level (Eq. 1).

$$Estimated\ Anxiety\ Level = (x - \mu)/\sigma \cdot coeff \qquad (1)$$

x: *index values*, σ: *standard deviations of* x, μ: *mean values of* x
coeff: first principal component loadings

Since a significant positive correlation was obtained between the anxiety level calculated by this method and the subjective rating of the participants with large changes in subjective rating, we decided to adopt and implement this method.

4 Preparations of Experiment

4.1 Development of a Remote Environment for Experiments

A remote experimental environment was developed to allow experiments to be conducted even under the Covid-19 pandemic (Fig. 2). The participant and the experimenter are assumed to be in remote locations. On the participant's site, a virtual space is generated using Unity on PC1, and images are presented to the HMD worn by the participant. The physiological data is sent to PC2, where it is quantified and the estimated anxiety level is calculated, and the time-series changes are displayed on the screen. The experimenter refers to this by sharing the screen with the operator PC3 on the experimenter's site. The operator PC issues a command to change the contents of the VR space and adjust the anxiety level, and PC1 receives this command and changes the appearance and gestures of the interviewer avatar. PUN2 (Photon Unity Networking 2), a SaaS service provided by Exit Games for development in the Unity environment, was used for communication between PC2 and PC1.

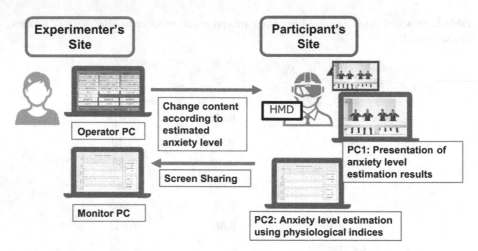

Fig. 2. Prepared remote experimental environment

4.2 Preliminary Experiment

Experiments were conducted using the prepared experimental environment to confirm whether the anxiety level could be optimized and to identify points for improvement of the system (Approval No.2020–29).

Participants

One healthy male undergraduate student and one male graduate student who gave written informed consent participated in the experiment. The experimenter and the participant were in separate rooms, and the HMD and each sensor were worn by the participants themselves, as instructed by the experimenter.

Experimental Procedure

One week before the experiment, participants were asked about their usual anxieties, especially about questions or situations that made them anxious during the interview. On the day of the experiment, a simulated interview was conducted in the VR space for about 20 min after a 6-min closed-eye resting period, including 3 min for sensor calibration and 3-min pre-rest, followed by a 3-min post-rest period was conducted. After the experiment, each participant was asked to verbally answer the experimenter's questions. Each physiological index and the estimated anxiety level during the period without speech were examined.

Pre-interview

First participant (Pt. 1-A) had been accepted to graduate school and had no experience in job hunting, but had experience with admissions interviews. In the pre-interview, he answered, "I don't feel anxious in normal conversation, and I don't get nervous in interviews," but "I just get scared when they stare at me silently. I feel comfortable if the interviewer is taking notes."

The second participant (Pt. 1-B) was a student in master's cource who had just finished his job search. In the pre-interview, he responded, "I should not have any difficulty in communicating with others, but I was nervous at job interviews and felt anxious depending on the questions asked." He also stated that, unlike Pt. 1-A, he was nervous when the interviewer was taking notes. In order to provoking and easing of anxiety, this participant was presented with an expanded list of questions and asked to rate the ease of answering them on an 11-point scale, modeled after the anxiety hierarchy chart used in clinical practice.

Scenario

We scheduled a 10-min interview and prepared the questions corresponding to each anxiety level for Pt. 1-A. The target anxiety levels were set to 5 and 6, and when the estimated anxiety level was lower than that, the virtual interviewer was made to "make the participant stare"; when the estimated anxiety level was higher than that, the virtual interviewer was made to respond favorably, such as "You worked very hard on this," with the actions such as "nod" and "take notes."

Interviews of about 20 min were planned for Pt. 1-B, and prepard questions similar as Pt. 1-A, but with more variety for each anxiety hierarchy. If the anxiety level was decreasing, the virtual interviewer's "take notes" action was taken, and if it was increasing, "nod" action was increased.

Results

Figures 3 and 4 show the estimated anxiety levels and the interviewer's questions and actions during the interval when each participant was not speaking, i.e., when the participant was listening to the interviewer's question and until the response.

For Pt. 1-A, the anxiety level was estimated to be "0" immediately after the interview began, so all of the interviewer's actions were stopped, and only the "staring" action was used. After the fifth question, the estimated anxiety level rose sharply, so the interviewer's actions were changed to "nodding" and "taking notes," but the interview ended without any change in the estimated anxiety level. The results showed that the anxiety was aroused, but not reduced. This result suggested the need to enhance the anxiety-relieving contents.

Pt.1-B were generally able to maintain his target anxiety level during the 8–16-min interval from the beginning of the interview. His estimated anxiety level rose sharply immediately after the question on "research theme" and dropped after that on "usual life with Covid-19", showing low estimated anxiety until the end of the interview.

In the post-experiment interview, the participant told, "The interviewers responded more than I expected, and I felt uneasy when I was asked questions I did not expect." He added, "However, I gradually got used to the interview situation and became less and less nervous." Regarding the virtual interviewers, he commented that he was concerned that one of the interviewers was too muscular. Although the anxiety arousal became insufficient toward the end of the interview due to acclimation, the target anxiety level was maintained until the middle of the interview. The results indicated the significance of conducting interviews that imitate the anxiety hierarchy table and enriching the content of the questions. It was also found that the appearance of the interviewers needed to be reconsidered.

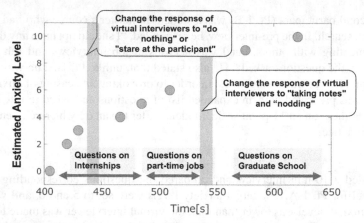

Fig. 3. The estimated anxiety levels and the interviewer's questions and actions during the interval (Pt.1-A)

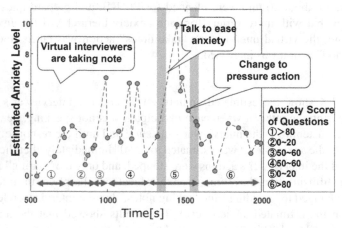

Fig. 4. The estimated anxiety levels and the interviewer's questions and actions during the interval (Pt.1-B)

4.3 Expert's Opinion

When we explained the results of the experiment to Dr. Naoki Takebayashi, Director of Natural Psychosomatic Medicine, and asked for his comments, he gave us an idea to end the interview once and resume it in a virtual space with a relaxing atmosphere for the patient when his/her anxiety became too high, as in the case of Pt. 1-A.

5 User Interface Implementation and Improvement

We designed a User Interface (UI) that can be operated intuitively by counselors in a clinical setting. A Japanese cloud service for voice synthesis called "Ondoku-san" [12] was introduced to make the interviewer's speech after the synthesized voice could induce anxiety as well as an inarticulate voice. The reason for the choice of synthetic voice was to save time and effort in recording the voice, and to make it easier to prepare and change patterns of speech according to the participant's anxiety characteristics.

Before the assessment experiment, the UI was tested by two collaborators who were working as counselors, and improvements were made by asking them about items that were difficult to use or see (Fig. 5). In addition, "yawning", "frowning", "elbowing", "looking down", and "tapping on the desk" were added to the virtual interviewer's actions.

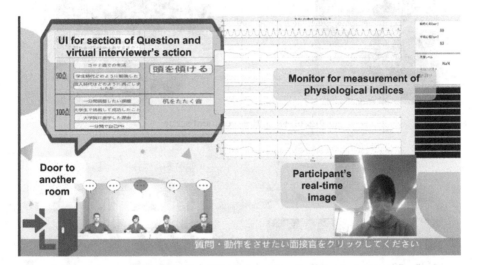

Fig. 5. Improved user interface

6   Assessment of Anxiety Level Optimization Methods

We asked people who counsel job-hunting activities to act as interviewers, and examined whether the developed system could be used to manipulate and optimize the interviewees' anxiety levels (Approval No.2020–29).

6.1   Participants and Experimental Environment

Three male university students participated in the experiment with written informed consent. Each participant and the experimenter (one of the authors) were separated by a partition of at least 2 m in the experimental room with adequate ventilation. Two experiment collaborators (counselors) participated in the experiment and controlled the VR space by manipulating the UI displayed on a laptop computer in a separate room (Fig. 6).

Four virtual interviewers (avatars) were placed in the VR interview room. The movements of three avatars were automatically updated every second according to the participant's anxiety level, and the counselor operated one avatar's movements, questions, and responses. A VR interview room with only one interviewer close to the participant's age was provided to ease anxiety levels if they rose too high (Fig. 7).

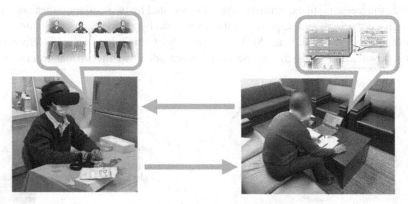

Fig. 6. Remote experiment scene

Fig. 7. Separate room with only one virtual interviewer for continued high anxiety

6.2 Experimental Procedure

A pre-experiment interview was conducted one week prior to the experiment to make an anxiety hierarchy table. The interviewer asked 17 questionnaires, 11 of which were selected based on ease of answer, and the participants were asked to score the anxiety level caused by the questionnaire on a scale of 0 to 100. Eleven types of interviewer behavior were selected and scored from 0 to 100. On the day of the experiment, a simulated interview was conducted in the VR space for about 20 min after a 6-min closed-eye resting period, including 3-min sensor calibration and 3-min pre-rest. After the interview, a 3-min post-rest period was conducted.

After the experiment, each participant was asked to verbally answer the following questions: "Did the interview in the VR space make you feel anxious?", "Did the movements of the interviewer avatar make you feel anxious or uncomfortable?", "Did the content of the questions make you feel anxious?", and "Did the intensity of the questions seem to change with your anxiety level?" Experimental collaborators who played the role of counselors were also interviewed about whether the UI they used was easy to use.

6.3   Results

The experiment for the first participant (2-A) failed due to a poor connection between the HMD and the PC, so only participants 2-B and 2-C were analyzed.

Anxiety Level During the Interview

The time series data of the interviewer's questions, the anxiety levels estimated and displayed in real time, and the anxiety levels rescaled after the experiment are shown in Figs. 8 and 9.

Although Pt. 2-B developed high anxiety just before and at the end of the interview, he maintained the target anxiety level (4–6) until about 18 min after the start of the experiment. Pt. 2-C's anxiety peaked immediately after the interview began, but after the "self-introduction" item was asked, his anxiety level decreased and remained moderate until the end of the interview.

Post-experiment Oral Questioning

In the post-experiment questions, both participants stated that they had questions that were easy to answer followed by questions that were difficult to answer, suggesting that they were generally able to maintain a certain level of tension during the interview. Pt. 2-B reported that the appearance of one interviewer avatar scared him and made him feel anxious, and Pt. 2-C reported that he sometimes laughed and was annoyed by the interviewer avatar's gestures.

One of the collaborators reported that the change in anxiety level could not be grasped when the it reached 10 or higher, and that there was sometimes a delay in button operation due to unfamiliarity with the UI operation.

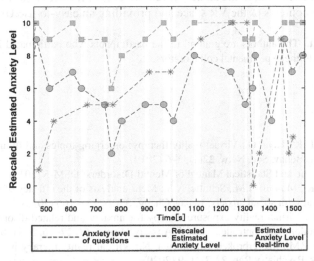

Fig. 8. The time series data of the interviewer's questions, the anxiety levels estimated and displayed in real time, and the anxiety levels rescaled after the experiment (2-B)

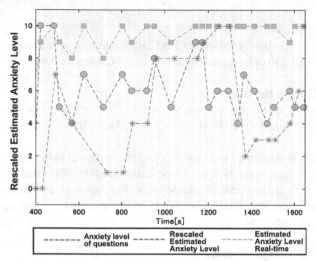

Fig. 9. The time series data of the interviewer's questions, the anxiety levels estimated and displayed in real time, and the anxiety levels rescaled after the experiment (2-C)

7 Conclusions

In this study, we developed and evaluated a VR exposure therapy using an anxiety level optimization method that changes the exposure content according to the estimated anxiety level based on physiological measurements. The results suggest the possibility of optimizing the anxiety level of patients by selecting questions and virtual interviewer's attitude according to the anxiety level. We expect further anxiety optimization by enriching the contents of the VR space and providing an easy-to-use UI.

Acknowledgment. The authors are grateful to the participants who participated in the experiments and thanks to the experimental collaborators.

References

1. Wiederhold, B.K., Riva, G.: Virtual reality therapy: emerging topics and future challenges. Cyberpsychol. Behav. Soc. Netw. **22**(1), 3–6 (2019)
2. APA: Diagnostic and Statistical Manual of Mental Disorders: DSM-5 (2013)
3. Chesham, R.K., Malouff, J.M., Schutte, N.S.: Meta-analysis of the efficacy of virtual reality exposure therapy for social anxiety. Behav. Chang. **35**(3), 152–166 (2018)
4. Carl, E., et al.: Virtual reality exposure therapy for anxiety and related disorders: A meta-analysis of randomized controlled trials. J. Anxiety Disord. **61**, 27–36, 3–6 (2019)
5. Emmelkamp, P.M., Meyerbröker, K., Morina, N.: Virtual reality therapy in social anxiety disorder. Curr. Psychiatry Rep. **22**(7), 1–9 (2020)
6. Sisemore, T.A.: The Clinician's Guide to Exposure Therapies for Anxiety Spectrum Disorders: Integrating Techniques and Applications from CBT, DBT, and ACT, New Harbinger Publications (2012)

7. Craske, M.G., et al.: Maximizing exposure therapy: an inhibitory learning approach. Behav. Res. Ther. **58**, 10–23 (2014)
8. Koba, H., Ohsuga, M.: Toward the estimation of anxiety levels using physiological measures in a virtual reality exposure therapy system. Engineering in Medicine and Biology Society (2020)
9. Koba, H., Ohsuga, M.: Estimation of anxiety level using physiological measures for virtual reality exposure therapy system. In: Joint Conference of the Asian Council on Ergonomics and Design and the Southeast Asian Network of Ergonomics Societies, pp. 15–22. Springer, Cham (2020)
10. Mahmoudi-Nejad, A.: Automated personalized exposure therapy based on physiological measures using experience-driven procedural content generation. In: Proceedings of the AAAI Conference on Artificial Intelligence and Interactive Digital Entertainment, vol. 17, No. 1, pp. 232–235 (2021)
11. Mevlevioğlu, D., Murphy, D., Tabirca, S.: Real-time anxiety prediction in virtual reality exposure therapy. In: ACM International Conference on Interactive Media Experiences, Adjunct Proceedings, pp.21–23 (2021)
12. COMOMO: ONDOKU-san. https://ondoku3.com/ja/. Last Accessed 28 May 2022

Self-determined and Informed Use of Personal Health Records: Assessment of Attitudes and Learning Requirements Among Older Adults

Luis Perotti(✉) ⓘ and Anika Heimann-Steinert ⓘ

Geriatrics Research Group, Charité - Universitätsmedizin Berlin, corporate member of Freie Universität Berlin and Humboldt-Universität Zu Berlin, Reinickendorfer Str. 61, 13347 Berlin, Germany
{luis.perotti,anika.heimann-steinert}@charite.de

Abstract. Personal Health Records (PHR) offer the opportunity for improved care for patients. Older adults, who often face a larger number of chronic diseases, could particularly benefit from the use of PHR. However, confident and self-determined use requires a high degree of digital and content-related competence. The object of this paper is to assess the attitudes and experiences of older adults in connection to the PHR and their requirements towards an eLearning system for appropriate PHR use. To answer the research questions, semi-structured interviews with older adults (aged ≥ 65 years) were conducted. A focus group was also set up, consisting of older adults. Sociodemographic data, previous knowledge about the PHR and willingness to use technology were additionally collected using validated and self-developed questionnaires. While previous knowledge about the PHR was relatively low within the study population, general attitudes towards the PHR were mostly positive. The study participants mainly expressed hope for improved care and concerns about possible incomprehensibility of the content. In terms of learning content, information about access rights and data security were the aspects most frequently mentioned. A high demand for a learning platform enabling the target group to use the PHR successfully was evident. Such a platform could facilitate implementation of the PHR and help older adults to actively participate in their healthcare. At the same time, the specific requirements of older adults should be considered during development.

Keywords: Personal health record · eLearning · Older adults

Abbreviations

PHR   Personal health record

© Springer Nature Switzerland AG 2022
V. G. Duffy et al. (Eds.): HCII 2022, LNCS 13521, pp. 142–157, 2022.
https://doi.org/10.1007/978-3-031-17902-0_11

1   Background

Personal Health Records (PHR for short) are intended to make processes in the health-care system more efficient and transparent. For this purpose, data and documents are to be exchanged between service providers and the patient. The benefits of PHR use include improved cooperation, reduced duplicate examinations and improved patient care, especially for patients with chronic diseases [5, 17]. The German PHR will be developed and released in stages and will store diagnoses, medical findings, medica-tion plans, vaccination information, X-rays and other patient data. In its conception, the PHR was designed to consider the patient as the central administrator of his or her data. Use of the record is voluntary. The user decides whether a service provider may access his or her record, add content or view specific documents. Similarly, the user can independently add documents into his or her record and delete any file at will [23]. These measures are intended to protect the user's privacy. At the same time, the PHR can only be used effectively if service providers can access such documents in as much detail as needed [21]. As a result, adequate use of the PHR requires a consider-able degree of competence on the side of end users in managing their data. On the one hand, competence or knowledge about the contents of the record is needed. Deciding which document should be accessible by which healthcare provider (and precisely when) implies that the user has an understanding of the content of each document and of how the involved parties in the healthcare system work together. Only with this knowledge, it is possible to make informed and self-determined decisions. On the other hand, due to the PHR being a digital service, skills in handling digital devices and software in general are required. As a result, the advantages and disadvantages of introducing the PHR are being widely discussed. Positive effects such as the chance to promote patient empowerment and increased participation are mentioned in the literature, as well as the danger of overburdening the user [2].

With a higher prevalence of chronic diseases, corresponding increase in contact with healthcare providers and a longer history of illness, older people have the potential to accumulate a particularly large amount of data in their PHR. At the same time, introduction of the PHR may be particularly beneficial for them. It offers the prospect of a better overview of their therapies, some of which are complex and involve several service providers and improved communication. However, the data and access rights of individual service providers must also be managed by the patient, which often poses challenges for older people [16]. Many older adults have limited experience of handling digital technologies, which could be a barrier to accessing and using the PHR. The training or empowerment of all users of the PHR was laid down by the German legislature and responsibility was transferred to the GKV Spitzenverband, which is the association of health insurance companies in Germany [22]. The PHR has been released in January 2021. However, the GKV Spitzenverband has not yet provided guidelines for health insurance companies, despite the high demand for supplementary offers to empower users with the skills and knowledge necessary to use the PHR.

In order to address this problem, the "ePA Coach" project was founded. The project aims to develop an eLearning platform, enabling older adults to use the PHR in a self-determined and informed way. Users of the service will be able to learn the necessary skills and knowledge needed to use the PHR. Elements of microlearning, gamification and AI algorithms will be integrated in order to increase learning motivation and to make the platform as effective as possible. Studies show that gamification (especially in the context of social gaming) can be a suitable approach to increase user motivation and engagement with technology among older adults [7]. Another essential part of the project is the development of the eLearning platform through a participatory and iterative process with representatives of the target group. This will ensure that the needs of the target group are precisely identified and considered during development of the service. This will raise the accessibility and effectiveness of the eLearning platform. The basis for this approach is provided by studies in other countries that introduced digital health records several years ago. In these countries, research is available concerning the actual use of PHR after implementation. These studies show that overall use of digital health records is low, mainly due to the insufficient attention paid to users' needs [21]. Clear communication has been identified as being particularly important, along with recognition of the benefits of PHR for older people, as this has been a key factor in poor uptake of PHR in other countries [15]. Furthermore, perceived usefulness from a user's perspective is described as a driving factor for using the PHR [12].

Digital services for communication and information seeking are widely used by older adults in Germany. At the same time, use of these services for health-related purposes is less common, mostly due to a sense of mistrust about the quality of information found on the internet. Older adults tend to turn to healthcare providers to get the health information they need [1]. In the context of implementation of the PHR in Germany, this fact could put an additional burden on the healthcare system, when people start seeking out doctors or pharmacists to get help in using the PHR. This will increase the need for an additional service which is independent from healthcare providers and which can help older adults acquire the skills needed for appropriate PHR use.

Against the background of this topic, we assessed the attitudes and existing knowledge of older adults in the context of the PHR and their requirements for an eLearning system for handling the PHR. It was also our intention to consider health-information-seeking behavior, prior knowledge and attitudes towards the PHR. Furthermore, general use of technology by the study participants was to be recorded.

The main research questions which the presented study sought to answer are as follows:

(1) What attitudes do older adults have towards the Personal Health Record and what experience have they had with it?
(2) What requirements do older adults have towards an eLearning system for appropriate PHR use?

2   Methods

2.1   General

The user-centered design process is an important instrument for target-group-oriented development of technical assistance systems [19]. Accordingly, at the beginning of the development of the eLearning platform within the research project "ePA Coach", a requirements analysis was conducted with representatives of the target group of older adults. An explorative, qualitative approach was chosen for the requirements analysis. In addition, sociodemographic data relating to the sample were collected using questionnaires.

The Ethics Committee of the Charité – Universitätsmedizin Berlin approved the methodological approach and the study was registered in the German Register for Clinical Studies.

2.2 Procedure and Materials

Interviews
To answer the research questions, semi-structured guideline-based interviews and a focus group discussion with older adults (aged $\geq$ 65 years) were conducted. Collection of sociodemographic data, previous knowledge about the PHR and willingness to use technology was additionally carried out by means of a survey, using standardized validated questionnaires and self-developed questionnaires.

The goal of the qualitative interviews was to learn more about the attitudes of older adults towards the PHR and to collect requirements for an eLearning system. For this purpose, older adults were recruited via mail using the database of the Geriatrics Research Group of Charité – Universitätsmedizin Berlin. To be included in the study, participants had to be over 65 years old and had to be able to give their informed consent. Exclusion criteria were severe cognitive impairment, severe sensory impairment or having a legal representative.

The potential study participants were informed about the study and had the chance to ask questions. After examination of the inclusion and exclusion criteria, an interview date was agreed upon at least 24 h after the clarifying discussion. At the beginning of the study, the subjects were contacted again and their signed consent was obtained.

The interview guide used for the one-on-one interviews contained two main topics:

1. The PHR in general (attitude, previous knowledge, advantages and disadvantages and the need for information);
2. The eLearning system (content, presentation, device, training and support).

The semi-structured interview guide included 25 main questions with up to four supplementary questions. In addition, the study included completion of three questionnaires: 1. a self-developed questionnaire on current technology use and previous experience of the PHR; 2. a questionnaire on technology commitment [11] and 3. a questionnaire on use of mobile devices (Mobile Device Proficiency Questionnaire [18]). The interview guide was tested in a pretest with an older adult. The focus was on comprehensibility and duration of the interview.

In total eight participants took part in the one-on-one interviews. The interview and answering of the questionnaires took about 1 to 1.5 h for the participants. Both authors (one male, one female) conducted the interviews. The interviews were recorded, transcribed, and evaluated by both authors. Field notes were made during the interview. Both authors have expertise in the fields of qualitative research, public health, and geriatric and usability research. Analysis of the transcripts was carried out after the content analysis in accordance with Mayring [10] and with the help of Atlas.ti 8 analysis software.

The coding was done manually by both authors independently according to the four-eye principle. In total, 29 codes were assigned. The quotes of the study participants used in this paper were translated from German into English.

Focus Group

A focus group discussion was conducted with eight representatives of the target group. The aim of the focus group interview was to verify the previously collected requirements and to supplement these. Older adults from the Senior Research Group in Berlin took part in the focus group. At the beginning, the participants were introduced to the project. Afterwards, initial results from the interviews were presented (e.g., requirements for the layout of the eLearning system) and discussed with the group. The participants' statements were recorded and evaluated. Furthermore, additional requirements were developed and included. The focus group participants filled in the same questionnaires as those who participated in the individual interviews. Two participants refused to fill in the questionnaires.

3   Results

3.1   Study Sample

In total, 16 subjects were included in the study. Eight took part in the one-on-one interviews and eight more were part of the focus group. The subjects were between 65 and 85 years old and were well educated (mostly to a higher educational level, see Table 1). Thirteen subjects had already heard about the PHR prior to the study. The internet and computer were used often by almost every study participant and the technology commitment scores were on the upper level (Table 2).

Table 1. Study sample characteristics

Sociodemographic data	Interview (n = 8)	Focus group (n = 8)	Total (n = 16)
Age (Ø years, min-max)	75.4 (69–84)	74.1 (65–78)	74.8 (65–84)
Sex	male = 4 female = 4	male = 4 female = 4	male = 8 female = 8

3.2   Expectations Towards the PHR

The general attitude towards the PHR among the majority of respondents was positive. Respondents indicated that they would welcome its introduction and could well imagine using it. However, some respondents were skeptical regarding the introduction of the PHR. One respondent feared that the PHR could be very confusing due to the large amount of data available. Only one respondent had a negative attitude towards introduction of the PHR. This respondent did not see any benefit in its use and could not yet "recognize its advantage" (female, 74 years).

Table 2. Technology usage

	Interview (n = 8)	Focus group (n = 6*)	Total (n = 16)
Internet usage	often = 8 occasionally = 0 rarely = 0 never = 0	often = 6 occasionally = 0 rarely = 0 never = 0	often = 14 occasionally = 0 rarely = 0 never = 0
Computer usage	often = 7 occasionally = 0 rarely = 0 never = 1	often = 6 occasionally = 0 rarely = 0 never = 0	often = 13 occasionally = 0 rarely = 0 never = 1
Technology commitment (Ø score, min-max)	3.89 (3.0–4.4)	4.23 (4.1–4.4)	4.04 (3.0–4.4)

* Two participants refused to fill in the questionnaires

The participants were specifically asked about their attitude towards data security in relation to the PHR. None of the respondents saw the topic of data security as a worrisome issue that could hinder rollout of the PHR. The majority of participants estimated the risk of data misuse as low (n = 5).

Three participants felt that data protection was an important issue, with the security of their own data being a basic prerequisite for using the PHR. For them, the priority was ensuring that only authorized persons have access to their own data.

3.3 Advantages and Disadvantages of the PHR

The participants were asked to name the advantages and disadvantages they associated with introduction and use of the PHR. In terms of the advantages, many factors were mentioned by the respondents. One of the most frequently mentioned advantages was improved communication, which five of the eight respondents from the individual interviews hoped might be achieved with the PHR. This included both communication between the various service providers in healthcare and doctor-patient communication.

"I also think it's good. You have a few more problems when you get older; that's just the way it is, that's all. And when everyone communicates well with each other, especially when it comes to test results, X-ray examinations, all those things that happen around or with people, I think it's good if you can do it electronically, if the doctor treating you has it on site and can put it all together." (female, 74 years).

The reason for this, according to the respondents, is simply the possibility of forwarding data and that all information is thus bundled centrally in one place. In this context, three respondents assumed that central storage of data in the PHR would lead to the avoidance of duplicate examinations. One respondent saw an advantage to centralized storage in terms of the availability of all relevant data in an emergency.

"[...] and if I'm involved in some kind of emergency, then this can be checked there in the hospital – so I imagine that – also really fast [...], what I suffer from or which medication I must take, so this does not have to be queried, since I'm no longer able to do it." (female, 79 years).

Furthermore, most respondents assumed that time and financial resources could be saved by introduction of the PHR, in terms of physicians and the entire healthcare system (n = 6). Two respondents saw an advantage in the fact that the PHR itself could give them an overview of their health data and allow family members to access this information.

Three participants also expected that it would give them some peace of mind, as patients will no longer have to rely on their memory (e.g., regarding the medication plan), which will, in turn, improve patient safety.

The participants were also asked what disadvantages or concerns they saw in provision of a Personal Health Record and in its use. Overall, however, very few statements were made on this subject.

"Well, if the person can influence what is written on it, then... I [would see] fewer disadvantages." (female, 69 years).

Two test persons feared that the content contained in the PHR might be incomprehensible. In this context, one respondent stated that it will involve a large amount of data, especially in the case of older people, so that the file would be very extensive. One respondent feared that with introduction of the PHR, less attention would be paid to the individual patient, since all the preliminary information relating to them would already be available. One respondent expressed concern about misuse. Two respondents stated that they currently had no concerns or saw no disadvantages.

3.4 Previous Knowledge

The older adults were asked where they usually obtained information on health-related issues from. Physicians, magazines (daily newspapers, pharmacy magazines and pensioners' magazines) and the internet were mentioned as the most common source of information and were each used by three test persons. At the same time, two elderly people noted that they considered the internet to be a dubious source as it often contains contradictory information. Furthermore, the older adults informed themselves via pharmacists (n = 2) and books (n = 2).

In addition, in the subject area "Previous Knowledge", participants were asked about their previous experience with the PHR. All respondents stated that they had already heard about the PHR prior to the study. According to their statements, the respondents had heard or read about it on the internet (n = 4), in the press (n = 3) and in television reports (n = 2), as well as in magazines and in information material from their doctor's office (n = 1 in each case, with multiple answers possible).

"Not so much heard, but I've read a lot about it and have read with particular interest if it described what is being planned for it." (male, 74 years).

When asked what they already knew about the PHR, the answers were very heterogeneous. Four respondents stated that they had read that the PHR was to be introduced.

Two participants were able to provide information about what data would be included. Test results and prescribed medication were given as examples.

"Actually, only that it is being introduced. I didn't think it was even on the agenda for the near future. But that everyone can see all the findings, that yes. And that was actually the information I had." (female, 74 years).

One respondent stated that he had already heard about the advantages and disadvantages of the PHR and suspected that every healthcare provider would have access to the stored data (with different stakeholders possibly being given access to the stored data).

3.5 Data Security

The participants were specifically asked about data security in relation to the PHR. None of the respondents saw the topic of data protection as a worrisome issue that could hinder rollout of the PHR. The majority of participants estimated the risk of data misuse as low (n = 5).

"No, not really, because I think we are well-secured here in Germany. They are very careful and sometimes that is even a hindrance, but I think that it is necessary and good." (female, 75 years).

Three participants felt that data protection was an important issue, with the security of their own data being a basic prerequisite for using the PHR. For them, the priority was ensuring that only authorized persons have access to their own data.

The respondents' low level of concern in connection with data protection issues can be attributed to various reasons. On the one hand, half of the respondents mentioned that there is always a risk of data misuse when using digital systems anyway (n = 4). One the other hand this was not perceived as greater for the PHR than when using a smartphone. Two of the respondents also mentioned that they considered the probability of their data being stolen to be very low. Three of the respondents stated that they considered the public debate on this topic to be exaggerated and that it is rather obstructive for some developments. Other factors mentioned were that a great deal of attention is paid to data protection in Germany and that responsible authorities can be relied upon (n = 3). This was evident, for example, in the case of the German "Corona-Warnapp" (an application for contact tracing in connection with the COVID-19 pandemic), which two of the participants cited as a good example of how a government-appointed app can function in a data-protection-compliant manner. The positive impression of the "Corona-Warnapp" was enhanced by the fact that problems with the system and during development were communicated transparently from the very beginning (n = 1).

3.6 Learning Content

Furthermore, the respondents were asked to name topics on which they would like to receive further information and which would help them to handle the data in their PHR with confidence. Respondents noted that they still knew too little about the PHR to be able to respond in more detail. Six of the eight respondents expressed that they would like to know more about access rights, i.e., who has access to the data stored in the PHR from the outset and how access rights can be managed for different actors in the healthcare system (adding and removing access rights).

> *"That, yes; who has access, how access is enabled and how I can decide who can see or use what."* (female, 79 years).

One respondent was concerned about whether employers would have access to the stored health data. In this context, two participants reported also wanting to be informed about who can access data and whether data can be added by the users themselves. Three respondents were interested in how their own access or initial activation will be carried out. Two respondents wanted to know what kind of data can be stored in the PHR. One respondent expressed uncertainty as to whether only the most recent health data are stored or all data *"from the cradle to the grave"*. Two respondents were also interested in the topic area "Security Information and Protective Measures"; i.e., they wanted to know what they could do themselves to protect their data, but also what measures are already being taken to protect their stored data. One respondent named, as possible learning topics, whether/how data in the PHR can be deleted, whether changes will be made to the insurance card, and what the overarching goal of the PHR is.

Focus group respondents also indicated that they would like to be informed about the time period between a physician visit and the uploading of data to the PHR, whether there will be an obligation to upload certain data, who is responsible for the correctness and completeness of the uploaded data, and what the procedure is when changing health insurers. Furthermore, respondents in the focus group wanted help in assessing which data might be relevant for which physician.

3.7 Layout of the eLearning Platform

The respondents felt that the presentation of the content covered in the eLearning system is an important factor relating to the usability of the system. The vast majority said that the content should have a clear structure (in the form of diagrams etc.) (n = 6). In particular, content relationships and sequences should be highlighted. Seven of the eight participants preferred to have content presented as small sections, with reduced information. This format was perceived as being easier to read than long passages.

> *"Explained as concisely as possible and not too much, yes. If what was already explained is explained again, that would be too much."* (male, 74 years).

Furthermore, the topic of accessibility and the low threshold of the eLearning system was discussed. In this context, simple language, easy comprehensibility of texts, the use of images and videos, and clear, unambiguous language were mentioned by five of the respondents and were considered the most important points that should be taken into account during development. Likewise, the desire to avoid use of foreign language was expressed (n = 3). As possible functions that could increase learning success during use, it was mentioned that most content should only be explained superficially with the possibility of accessing more in-depth information via a link (n = 5). Explanation of various terms (in a glossary) was mentioned as a useful addition. One respondent also stated that the learning speed should be individually adaptable and that individual topics should be repeatable.

There was no clear preference among the respondents as to the form in which the content should be presented. Five respondents indicated that they would prefer the use of text, while five respondents also indicated that they would consider using videos if these remained short. One respondent was completely opposed to videos while half (n = 4) indicated that pictures and graphics should be included. Three participants stated that they could imagine being guided through the application in the eLearning system by a virtual trainer, but that this trainer should not appear "silly" (n = 1).

The focus group added that there should be an export function for the content so that it could be printed out if necessary. Furthermore, respondents in the focus group wanted to have an additional summary at the end of each chapter to increase the clarity.

Most participants stated that they would prefer a neutral, simple design for the eLearning system (n = 5). Too many and overly bright colors should not be used as these would be distracting (n = 4). Only one respondent was in favor of very strong colors, as these would increase users' interest level. However, highlighting important content using color seemed to make sense to some (n = 3) and would support readability. Likewise, two participants indicated that bold text would also be appropriate for this purpose. With regard to the use of text, two respondents indicated that they considered a large font size to be important (at least 14p). Another respondent stated that an adjustable font size would be necessary. Two participants mentioned that the text should have a color contrast with the background. Other points mentioned were that the background should be bright (n = 1) and that a serious-looking font (n = 1) and simplifying symbols would be useful (n = 1).

3.8 Gamification Elements Within the eLearning Platform

Within this topic, participants were asked about possible playful and motivational elements within the eLearning system. This involved the need for a rewarding system, comparison with other users, and the possibility to comment on or rating learning content.

Of the eight participants interviewed, seven commented on whether they would like to see integration of a reward system that would reward them for completed learning units and increase users' motivation. Five of the participants fundamentally rejected the idea that any form of rewarding system should be integrated into the eLearning system.

"No. There are so many points and stars already." (female, 74 years).

Two other respondents could imagine gamification elements having a motivating effect but, at the same time, expressed that they themselves did not need motivational elements.

"I don't need it, but I do think it motivates a lot of people." (female, 75 years).

The majority of participants (n = 6) rejected the idea of a rewarding system based on gathering points or other rewards such as stars. One respondent could imagine monitoring learning success by means of a quiz. Another participant pointed out that use of the eLearning system could be connected to the bonus program of some health insurance companies, which could lead to an increase in motivation.

Furthermore, the older adults were asked about their attitude towards a rating or commenting function. Four of the respondents answered that they would definitely be interested in rating the content they have accessed, in order to give the creators of the texts/videos feedback on the quality and usefulness.

"You could include that, yes – feedback on how well that succeeded in conveying [the information], e.g., if it benefited you or not. Some questions only require a yes or no answer. You can find this everywhere on the internet: Did it help you when you looked up something or somewhere when you had a question?" (male, 84 years).

One respondent emphasized, however, that such a function would have to be voluntary. Three other participants, in contrast, stated that they were against the introduction of a rating or commenting system because they saw no need for it and would not use it.

Regarding the topic "Comparison with Other Users", the seniors were asked whether they would like to compare their learning results or learning success within the learning program with others. Only two of the eight participants commented on this. Both rejected comparison with others.

"Yes, maybe for some this is interesting, [but] for me, less so. I just want to know if I can do it or not, yes." (female, 75 years).

3.9 Support for the eLearning Platform

Within the topic "Operational Support", participants were asked in what setting they would like to be taught how to use the eLearning system once it is fully developed. Five respondents indicated that they would like to learn how to use the system in a group training setting.

"Personally, in a group, in a smaller group, I would like it best." (74 years, male).

Two participants specifically mentioned a group size of five to ten participants, or eight people, respectively. The advantages of group training were given as being that an exchange with like-minded people could take place, other participants' questions could be addressed, and a personal exchange could take place. In the opinion of the older adults, group training should allow for hands-on practice. One respondent suggested visualizing the training with a presentation. Online training was not preferred by any of the respondents. Two respondents stated that an additional manual or printed material would be helpful. One respondent stated that a manual would be sufficient. This respondent saw a manual as having the advantage of enabling individuals to easily and quickly pass on information to relatives or friends. One respondent declined printed material or would print out the information himself/herself if needed.

Furthermore, the respondents were then asked what form of help functions there should be within the eLearning system.

The majority of respondents stated that they would be happy to resolve technical or content-related difficulties over the phone (n = 6). This kind of problem-solving was perceived as being easier because questions and comments can be addressed directly.

"Yeah, so maybe if it seems a little weird or not right, or I can't do it, I would want to maybe have a phone number where I could then call and together, both sides could resolve it." (female, 74 years).

Likewise, six participants could imagine making use of a "frequently asked questions" service. However, such a function should be reduced, i.e., not containing too much information. At the same time, one participant stated that it was her experience that such frequently asked questions often did not provide the exact answer he or she was looking for. Five respondents mentioned Email as being another way of contacting a support service. This was described as being helpful because it could enable a quick response to be obtained for information needed with regard to one's own problem and it could be used at weekends and at night.

Other possible contact points for help with problems were named as being one's own family (n = 1), a chat function (n = 1), and a forum for questions (n = 1).

Respondents in the focus group additionally mentioned the desire to have a specific person to contact for concrete content-related issues.

4 Discussion

In the present study, the attitudes of older adults towards implementation and use of the PHR were examined, as well as the learning requirements of older adults in order to learn how to independently use the PHR. All participants reported that they were interested in the PHR and had been looking for information about it and its implementation in Germany prior to this study. At the same time, little knowledge about it was evident among the participants, who reported difficulties in gathering adequate information about the German version of the PHR. Paccoud et al. state that individuals aged 65 or above are associated with a lower desire to use the PHR. This was not found to be the case in the study participants presented here [14]. When considering experiences of PHR implementation in other countries, it becomes clear that a lack of accessible information could threaten successful implementation of the PHR with the target group of older adults. Price et al. and Ose et al. identified clear communication about the usefulness of the PHR [13] and attention to users' needs [15] as key factors in this regard in their research. Measures to inform older adults about usage and PHR content is therefore crucial to avoid non-use of this service. Non-use of the PHR could therefore lead to a waste of health-system resources [4].

The participants in this study also expressed a considerable number of perceived advantages to proper use of the PHR. Although this may not be true for the whole target population, it hints at the possibility that older adults see a large potential benefit in implementation of the PHR. This may be important because the general attitude of older adults towards the PHR prior to its implementation might be an important factor, which exerts a large effect on actual usage behavior. As studies like the research by Hussein show, there is a high correlation between attitude and intention to use in the context of new digital systems and technology in mHealth [6]. A lack of helpful information and resulting frustration and confusion in the context of the PHR may compromise the positive attitude of older adults who actually see the PHR as an opportunity for improved healthcare. This problem is particularly important for a system like the PHR, which considers users to be the central actors and relies on them to participate actively in its use. Due to the PHR being released in Germany without a broad program in place to provide older adults with key information, this survey of user attitudes and experiences strengthens the identified need for a designated learning solution.

Most of the older adults in this study reported using technology very frequently and did not report any mayor difficulties using digital devices or software. Yet this cannot be considered as a representative fact for the whole population of older adults in Germany. The target population is very diverse and technology usage differs within different age groups and places of residence, with a large difference existing between rural and urban areas [3].

The study participants identified various skills and competences which they would like to get further information about. It became clear that the participants had very diverse knowledge about medical procedures, the basic functionality of the PHR, and the data to be stored in it. The older adults reported a high demand for these kinds of skills and knowledge to be taught.

The "ePA Coach" eLearning platform should consider the needs of older adults and adopt their preferences in as many aspects as possible. The key factor identified by the study participants when asked about their wishes for and expectations of the eLearning program was usability. Information within the system should be presented in an easy-to-understand way for older adults and should be clearly structured. Criteria for a low-threshold information transfer for older adults could be identified: short sentences; no use of foreign words; reduced information; and small, repeatable learning segments (a microlearning approach) etc. Similar aspects have been identified in other literature [8]. The design and presentation preferences expressed by the target group in relation to the platform were also similar to those found in the literature [9]: a strong color contrast between text and background; a large, adaptable font size; and a high level of clarity etc.

In general, the study participants reported that they wanted the eLearning system to look and feel plain, practical and neutral, and thereby be serious and reliable. At the same time, most of the older adults spoke out against the integration of too many gamification elements in the eLearning platform. Although gamification elements are specifically described as being an appropriate and effective way to raise motivation in older adults [7], the interviewees in this survey were skeptical about incorporation of gamification elements. A possible explanation could be that the eLearning program is designed to inform users about health-related issues involving sensitive data and is related to an application developed by the state. These factors were stated as the most important elements for the platform to appear trustworthy. Usually valid preferences (among older adults) for learning systems and software in general may not be applicable in this context, where the reliability of the content is a top priority.

Although many of the study participants had sought information about health-related issues online, they reported having experienced difficulty identifying reliable sources on the internet. They expressed the feeling that much of the content that can be found online does not seem trustworthy and needs to be scrutinized. This previous experience with online information in the context of health issues may have led to skepticism and influenced the participants' reported requirement for the learning platform to appear as serious and trustworthy as possible.

Against this background, it was surprising that none of the study participants had major concerns about the safety of their data within the PHR. Although there was a clear demand for the eLearning platform to be informative about potential data-security measures and issues, the older adults expressed a high level of trust in the PHR developers' ability to create a safe system. While data security is frequently discussed in the public domain, it does not seem to be a particular concern for the participants of this study. This finding contrasts with other literature such as the study conducted by Ware et al., in which older adults expressed concerns about data security associated with eHealth technologies [20].

5 Limitations

Although a number of measures were taken during the design of the study to avoid potential bias, there are some limitations to be considered when interpreting the presented results. Overall, the study participants were well educated and had an affinity for technology. The results are therefore not valid for the target group in general. Furthermore, the study population was rather small and not very diverse in terms of education level and interest in the PHR.

6 Conclusions

A high demand for learning content about important information related to the PHR and its content and skills as well as competences in connection with the PHR and its use for older adults was present in this study. A platform empowering older adults in this context could play an important role in a successful implementation of the PHR in the healthcare of older adults. The eLearning platform to be developed should focus on mediation of important information and skills needed in order to use the PHR and consider the specific needs and preferences of older adults.

Conflict of Interest. The authors declare that they have no financial or personal relationships that may influence their work and no conflict of interest.

Compliance with ethical standards. Ethical approval to conduct the study was obtained from the Ethics Committee of the Charité – Universitätsmedizin Berlin (EA1/142/20). All procedures performed involving human participants were undertaken in accordance with the ethical standards of the relevant research committee and in accordance with the 1964 Declaration of Helsinki and its later amendments or comparable ethical standards. Informed consent was obtained from all individual participants included in the study.

References

1. Chaudhuri, S., et al.: Examining health information-seeking behaviors of older adults. CIN Comput. Inform. Nurs. **31**(11), 547–553 (2013). https://doi.org/10.1097/01.NCN.000043 2131.92020.42
2. Crameri, K.-A., Maher, L., Van Dam, P., Prior, S.: Personal electronic healthcare records: what influences consumers to engage with their clinical data online? A literature review. Health Inf. Manag. J. **51**(1), 3–12 (2020). https://doi.org/10.1177/1833358319895369
3. Greenberg, A.J., et al.: Differences in access to and use of electronic personal health information between rural and urban residents in the united states: ePHI use in rural and urban patients. J. Rural Health. **34**, s30–s38 (2018). https://doi.org/10.1111/jrh.12228
4. Greenhalgh, T., Hinder, S., Stramer, K., Bratan, T., Russell, J.: Adoption, non-adoption, and abandonment of a personal electronic health record: case study of HealthSpace. BMJ **341**(nov16 1), c5814–c5814 (2010). https://doi.org/10.1136/bmj.c5814
5. Hong, M.K., et al.: Adolescent and caregiver use of a tethered personal health record system. AMIA. Annu. Symp. Proc. **2016**, 628–637 (2017)
6. Hussein, Z., et al.: Consumer attitude: does it influencing the intention to use mHealth? Procedia Comput. Sci. **105**, 340–344 (2017). https://doi.org/10.1016/j.procs.2017.01.231
7. Koivisto, J., Malik, A.: gamification for older adults: a systematic literature review. Gerontologist **61**(7), e360–e372 (2021). https://doi.org/10.1093/geront/gnaa047
8. Kuerbis, A., Mulliken, A., Muench, F., Moore, A.A., Gardner, D.: Older adults and mobile technology: factors that enhance and inhibit utilization in the context of behavioral health. Mental Health and Addiction Research **2**, 2 (2017). https://doi.org/10.15761/MHAR.1000136
9. Mannheim, I., et al.: Inclusion of older adults in the research and design of digital technology. Int. J. Environ. Res. Public Health **16**(19), 3718 (2019). https://doi.org/10.3390/ijerph161 93718
10. Mayring, P.: Qualitative content analysis: theoretical background and procedures. In: Bikner-Ahsbahs, A., Knipping, C., Presmeg, N. (eds.) Approaches to Qualitative Research in Mathematics Education, pp. 365–380. Springer Netherlands, Dordrecht (2015). https://doi.org/10.1007/978-94-017-9181-6_13
11. Neyer, F.J., et al.: Kurzskala technikbereitschaft (TB, technology commitment). Zusammenstellung Sozialwissenschaftlicher Items Skalen ZIS (2016). https://doi.org/10.6102/ZIS244
12. Niazkhani, Z., Toni, E., Cheshmekaboodi, M., Georgiou, A., Pirnejad, H.: Barriers to patient, provider, and caregiver adoption and use of electronic personal health records in chronic care: a systematic review. BMC Medical Inform. Decis. Mak. **20**(1), 153 (2020). https://doi.org/10.1186/s12911-020-01159-1
13. Ose, D., et al.: A personal electronic health record: study protocol of a feasibility study on implementation in a real-world health care setting. JMIR Res. Protoc. **6**(3), e33 (2017). https://doi.org/10.2196/resprot.6314
14. Paccoud, I., et al.: Socioeconomic and behavioural factors associated with access to and use of Personal Health Records. BMC Medical Inform. Decis. Mak. **21**(1), 18 (2021). https://doi.org/10.1186/s12911-020-01383-9
15. Price, M.M., et al.: Older adults' perceptions of usefulness of personal health records. Univers. Access Inf. Soc. **12**(2), 191–204 (2013). https://doi.org/10.1007/s10209-012-0275-y
16. Pushpangadan, S., Seckman, C.: Consumer perspective on personal health records: a review of the literature. Online J. Nurs. Inform. **19** (2015)
17. Robotham, D., Mayhew, M., Rose, D., Wykes, T.: Electronic personal health records for people with severe mental illness; a feasibility study. BMC Psychiatry **15**(1), 192 (2015). https://doi.org/10.1186/s12888-015-0558-y

18. Roque, N.A., Boot, W.R.: A new tool for assessing mobile device proficiency in older adults: the mobile device proficiency questionnaire. J. Appl. Gerontol. **37**(2), 131–156 (2016). https://doi.org/10.1177/0733464816642582
19. Shluzas, L.A., Steinert, M., Katila, R.: User-centered innovation for the design and development of complex products and systems. In: Leifer, L., Plattner, H., Meinel, C. (eds.) Design Thinking Research, pp. 135–149. Springer International Publishing, Cham (2014). https://doi.org/10.1007/978-3-319-01303-9_10
20. Ware, P., et al.: Using eHealth technologies: interests, preferences, and concerns of older adults. Interact. J. Med. Res. **6**(1), e3 (2017). https://doi.org/10.2196/ijmr.4447
21. Weis, A., et al.: Caregivers' role in using a personal electronic health record: a qualitative study of cancer patients and caregivers in Germany. BMC Med. Inform. Decis. Mak. **20**(1), 258 (2020). https://doi.org/10.1186/s12911-020-01172-4
22. § 20k SGB V Förderung der digitalen Gesundheitskompetenz. https://www.sozialgesetzbuch-sgb.de/sgbv/20k.html. Last Accessed 14 Jan 2021
23. Fragen und Antworten zur elektronischen Patientenakte. https://www.bundesgesundheitsministerium.de/elektronische-patientenakte.html. Last Accessed 14 Oct 2020

Expert Requirements for an Ultrasound-Based Wearable Using Deep Learning for Exercise Feedback in Older Chronic Back Pain Patients

Oskar Stamm[(✉)] [iD] and Luis Perotti [iD]

Department of Geriatrics and Medical Gerontology, Charité – Universitätsmedizin Berlin,
Corporate Member of Freie Universität Berlin and Humboldt-Universität Zu Berlin,
Reinickendorfer Straße 61, 13347 Berlin, Germany
{oskar.stamm,luis.perotti}@charite.de

Abstract. The use of segmental stabilization exercises (SSE) is an integral part of physiotherapy treatment for patients with chronic back pain. SSE is based on learning the selective contraction of deep muscles. Learning can be supported by the use of ultrasound imaging as feedback of muscle contraction. In the ULTRAWEAR project, a mobile ultrasound system will be developed providing biofeedback on SSE execution. The interpretation of ultrasound images requires a lot of experience and knowledge of cross-sectional anatomy. Therefore, the goal of the project is to use AI image recognition software to detect and display anatomical structures as well as contraction states of muscles within the ultrasound image. This paper presents the results of a survey, in which we collected expert requirements and attitudes regarding the system to be developed. A total of 6 individual interviews were conducted with physiotherapists and medical physicians having extensive experience in the use of imaging ultrasound. In terms of technical specifications, the experts expressed essential requirements about the penetration depth, field of view, and image quality of the ultrasound system. In addition, important aspects for adequate transducer positioning as well as for reliable AI detection of the musculature could be elaborated. Likewise, suggestions for the design of the UI for both the therapists and patients were recorded. The results of this expert survey are an important part of the further development of the ULTRAWEAR project and may help others developing an ultrasound system for use in the therapeutic setting.

Keywords: Imaging-ultrasound · Biofeedback · Physical therapy · Artificial intelligence

1 Introduction

1.1 Background

The prevalence of chronic back pain (CBP) increases significantly with age in the German population, more than a quarter of people over 70 years have CBP (28%) [26]. The sample in the study was asked about back pain, which persisted for three months or longer and

V. G. Duffy et al. (Eds.): HCII 2022, LNCS 13521, pp. 158–173, 2022.
https://doi.org/10.1007/978-3-031-17902-0_12

occurred almost daily. The established definition of chronic back pain also provides the persistence of pain lasting longer than 3 months. In most cases, the pain is "non specific", which means it has a mechanical origin [23]. Exercise therapy has been proved to be effective in reducing pain and functional limitations [9, 19].

In CBP patients segmental stabilization exercises (SSE) can be more effective than medical treatment and as effective as other physical therapy treatments in reducing pain [14]. The systematic reviews suggest that specific SSE are effective in reducing pain and disability in chronic low back pain [4]. The aim of SSE is to improve active lumbar-pelvic stability (transverse abdominal muscle, multifidus muscle, pelvic floor, and diaphragm) and thus protect the joints from compressive forces [12, 21, 22]. One of the main exercises for low back pain is an abdominal drawing-in maneuver (ADIM), which is a training for facilitating the isolated contraction of the transverse abdominal muscle (TrA) [21]. This is challenging for many patients at first, as the superficial musculature usually contracts at the same time. For adequate training of the lumbar multifidus (LM), it is important to realize that only small degrees of maximal voluntary contraction is necessary to create an optimal segmental stabilization.

These exercises are usually learned in physiotherapeutic sessions with a therapist. To control the accurate execution of the involved deep musculature is challenging for physical therapists and patients, besides palpation, imaging ultrasound has been used in practice [18]. In the past, size and cost was a limiting factor in imaging ultrasound equipment acquisition in physical therapy facilities. Since ultrasound imaging is becoming more affordable, it is now increasingly integrated into physiotherapy practice [20]. In physical therapy, there is a need for objective data. Therefore, in SSE, real-time ultrasound imaging is used during training for a more precise recognition of contraction [20]. Intra- and inter-rater reliability of the ultrasound measurement of TrA thickness in asymptomatic, trained subjects, indicates an acceptable levels of intra and inter-rater reliability with ICCs between 0.86–0.95 (intra-rater) and 0.86–0.92 (inter-rater)[8]. The application of ultrasound in SSE provides a means of quantifying training progress, but is not yet widely used.

1.2 Related Work

Rehabilitative ultrasound imaging (RUSI) is used as a biofeedback method for enhancing motor performance and motor learning of selected trunk muscles in people with low back pain (LBP) [10, 16]. Studies indicate an improved contraction of the TrA when using real-time ultrasonography together with verbal feedback. Low changes in contraction thickness showed a nonagreement with a pressure cushion [2, 15]. Furthermore, real-time ultrasound feedback can decrease the number of trials needed to consistently perform the ADIM [11]. However, there has been little research on patient-friendly user-interfaces. The traditional SSE in combination with RUSI is performed in a lying position with a stationary ultrasound equipment. Novel pocket handheld ultrasound allows quick and low-cost use [1, 25]. However, these devices are still cabled to the smartphone or tablet, which makes imaging under physical activity more difficult. Another wireless ultrasound system is used for monitoring the contraction state of muscles, but is not used for feedback on SSE [13]. An ultrasound device as a wearable for physiotherapy has not yet been developed. First studies with handheld devices attached to the body allow ultrasound imaging during function, such as standing or gait, or squatting. The functional activation ratio provides a novel approach to assessing muscle thickness in increasingly functional positions and tasks [17].

1.3 Conceptual Framework

The goal of the ULTRAWEAR project is to develop a portable wireless device that transmits a real-time ultrasound image of the deep abdominal and back muscles during SSE. The goal is to monitor the correct performance of segmental stabilization training by the wearable. In order to provide precise feedback on the successful exercise execution the system will recognize the muscular structures and their state of tension via AI. The ULTRAWEAR system will be designed as low-cost hardware, consisting of a wireless transducer and mobile terminal. The system being developed is intended for use in the setting of physical therapy practices and rehabilitation centers by older CBP patients under physical therapy supervision.

This paper aims to gather expert requirements on how the system can assist therapists in providing biofeedback on SSE execution via rehabilitative ultrasound imaging and also facilitate the learning of muscle control for the patient. Furthermore, the paper is intended to provide assistance for developers who are also designing ultrasound-based wearables.

2 Methods

2.1 Procedure

The present study was conducted as part of the research project ULTRAWEAR financed by the German Federal Ministry of Education and Research (BMBF). In order to identify requirements for an ultrasound-based wearable for exercise therapy we conducted expert interviews (n = 6). In the qualitative research design all interviews were performed according to a semi-structured guideline, developed by the researchers. The guideline consisted of four parts: segmental stabilization, implementation of ultrasound in a therapy program, use of the system in a therapy setting and use of the system in a home setting. During the interview the experts were asked to give an assessment of the UI based on screenshots from a previous project of the project partners. The screenshot served as illustrative material, even though it was from a project that showed a portable ultrasound research system for use in automated bladder monitoring [5], it was a good basis for discussion.

The authors of the paper conducted the interviews. The two interviewers have expertise in medical technology, physical therapy and public health. The experts were recruited via email and were selected by a purposive sampling. The sample consisted of a radiologist, a sports physician, and four physical therapists, who had extensive experience in the use of ultrasound systems. The participants had 24 h to give their final decision with regard to the agreement of the study. All participants gave written informed consent prior to the study participation. No expert refused to participate or dropped out.

2.2 Data Analysis

The interviews were conducted at DFNconf - The Conference Service in the German Research Network and were recorded with the consent of the experts to allow later transcription. The duration of the interviews was one hour. A summarizing content analysis by Mayring [12] was applied for the data analysis. Each of the six semi-structured interviews was partially transcribed using a protocol to summarize the most important contents of the interviews. After completion, two researchers analyzed the interviews according to the principles of Mayring's systematic structured content analysis.

3 Results

3.1 Participants

Interviews were conducted with a total of 6 experts who had extensive practical experience in the use of ultrasound systems for deep abdominal and back muscle imaging. The experts were recruited from different medical professions. These included a clinical radiologist (male), a sports medicine physician (male), and four physical therapists. The physical therapists included two owners of physical therapy practices with a focus on ultrasound diagnosis (both male); a teaching physical therapist with a PhD (female) who is a leading expert in segmental stabilization; and a head of a physical therapy facility for chronic back pain patients (male).

All of the experts had many years of experience in the use of ultrasound imaging in the field of diagnostics. Three of the experts reported using ultrasound imaging as biofeedback with patients to help them learn to control specific target muscles. The other experts used ultrasound imaging only in the area of diagnostics. The experts used systems from the high-end segment as well as low-cost devices. All respondents used expensive high-resolution systems. Three experts mentioned that they also work with portable handheld solutions. It was emphasized that the use of mobile systems is practical for getting quickly available images, which would also allow the system to be used outside of the practice setting. The low initial cost of such systems was also a positive factor for using mobile systems. On the other hand, the image quality of many of the mobile ultrasound systems is not sufficient for diagnostic purposes according to the experts.

3.2 Attitude Towards the Use of Ultrasound Imaging as Biofeedback in Chronic Back Pain Patients

According to the experts interviewed, the use of SSE in patients with CBP is particularly useful at the beginning of physiotherapeutic treatment. At this point, the exercises can be used to learn the correct control of the deep abdominal and back muscles. This is particularly important for patients with a lack of perception of one's own body. In this way, the patient can overcome the pain blockade and thus learn how to contract the target musculature despite initial pain.

"Segmental stabilization should be used early in the treatment process to break the pain cycle early. To learn proper activation and movement." (sports medicine physician, male).

Two experts described their experience with patients when they received visual feedback via ultrasound imaging about the contraction state of their muscles. Patients seemed to gain a deeper understanding of their musculature. However, this extrinsic feedback via the imaging also led to an improved feeling and control about one's own musculature in the longer term (intrinsic feedback).

"Often patients say, 'Now I finally understand what to do.' or 'Now I can see what the right thing to do is.'. I, as a therapist, can palpate and say, 'You're doing it right.' But seeing it for yourself helps tremendously. That reduces learning time infinitely, that reduces therapy time infinitely." (physical therapist, female).

The experts explained that such biofeedback of the state of the musculature using ultrasound is useful to learn to execute and maintain a correct contraction and is widely used in the area of the pelvic floor musculature. In the musculoskeletal area, ultrasound imaging is rarely used as biofeedback for patients.

"While ultrasound is widely used in pelvic floor muscles, there is little use of US in the musculoskeletal area because few validating studies exist. [...] More physical therapists should use this effective method." (physical therapist, female).

The experts considered SSE, which can be performed in a lying position, to be particularly effective at the beginning of therapy. This is gentle for the patients, they stated, and the isolated and static exercises allow ultrasound to be used particularly effective as biofeedback. However, three of the experts pointed out that the isolated exercises within segmental stabilization are only useful and effective at the beginning of pain therapy. In the further process of the therapy, more emphasis should be placed on functional and holistic exercises.

"Segmental stabilization is always just the starting point and only the beginning of the therapy. [...] In the treatment, we quickly switch from local and isolated exercises, out of the treatment room, to a proactive context. Functional exercises like push-ups and squats are good, where the stabilizing musculature is integrated." (physical therapist, male).

3.3 Attitude Towards New Technology in the Field of Physiotherapy

All experts expressed that they had a positive attitude towards the use of novel technology in therapy in general, but also of AI-assisted ultrasound systems in particular. They saw the integration of technologies into physiotherapy as an important and future-oriented trend.

"I'm a big fan of the use of AI, and I think that its use is going to increase in the next few years. If you use ultrasound in a reasonably standardized way, you have a lot of good opportunities." (clinical radiologist, male).

Device-based therapies would have an impact on both treatment effectiveness and patient attitudes.

"Device-based therapies have a positive impact, and patients feel safe and in control." (physical therapist, male).

Although all experts emphasized the potential of using technology in physical therapy, two experts indicated that its use, however, must be tied to evidence and proof of efficacy to ensure medically appropriate use. In this context, cost-effectiveness must also be taken into account.

"There is a need, but ultimately you have to look at the extent to which the application is medically appropriate and researched." (sports medicine physician, male).

One expert raised the concern that there were many physical therapists with low affinity for technology, who would be much more critical regarding its use in treatment.

3.4 Use of Multiple Transducers

Regarding the number of transducers that should be used in imaging, two experts emphasized that it might be useful to obtain ultrasound images of the deep abdominal or dorsal muscles bilaterally during exercise performance, as this would allow the interplay of muscles to be observed as they co-contract.

"Later, it's about displaying muscles in movements and there will be co-contraction. It's no use if only one side is activated". (sports medicine physician, male).

It is also conceivable that the antagonists Mm. Multifidi and the M. transversus abdominis should be visualized simultaneously to observe their interaction.

"I could imagine using ultrasound with the multifidi and deep abdominal muscles in parallel, and preferably the pelvic floor as well." (physical therapist, female).

On the other hand, one expert spoke against the use of multiple transducers and suggested that neither the physical therapist nor the patient could concentrate on the images of two muscles at the same time. This would not be feasible during the exercises.

"You always want to have everything, but it will be impossible to display both. You end up needing two transducers. The physical therapist or patient will never be able to focus on two muscle groups at the same time. In ultrasound, it's hard enough to see and interpret things." (clinical radiologist, male).

In addition, the expert mentioned the concern that, especially regarding older adults, the lower affinity for technology should be taken into account when considering the simultaneous imaging of several muscles at the same time.

3.5 Transducer Positioning

According to the experts, the representation of muscle contraction using ultrasound should include imaging in at least two scanning planes. A longitudinal scanning plane of the muscle would show the sliding movement of the muscle, while the scanning plane shows the increase in thickness during contraction. However, this is said to be difficult to realize within the application scenario targeted in the ULTRAWEAR project, since several transducers would be needed simultaneously. Alternatively, the transducer would need to be constantly realigned.

"For the feedback of the contraction state of the muscle, the parasagittal section is sufficient." (physical therapist, male).

Thus, an optimal scanning plane must be found for the transverse abdominis muscle and the multifidi muscles, on which the contraction is visible.

Furthermore, for the reproducibility of measurements and the interrater reliability, the experts emphasized that it is important that individual exercise sessions are performed with the transducer being placed at a constant position. In this regard, it was said to be essential to map stationary landmarks in the ultrasound image as a reference in parallel to the muscles that can be displaced.

"You need anatomical landmarks. Every physician and every tracking software needs bony landmarks like the processus transversus of the spine or the processus costalis and they need to know that the section is correct. Only then it is standardizable and reproducible." (clinical radiologist, male).

Positioning of the Transducer for Imaging of the Deep Abdominal Muscles
For ultrasound imaging of the deep abdominal musculature, rotational movements of the upper body were perceived as particularly problematic and could lead to an unstable connection of the transducer to the body surface. Therefore, five of the experts were in favor of the transducer being placed at the height of the umbilicus, whereby the umbilicus itself should be viewed critically as a sole reference point.

"The umbilicus as a landmark is dangerous. It varies depending on the volume of the patient. And depending on the positioning of the patient. Whether he is sitting or lying for example." (physical therapist, male)

When imaging the transversus abdominis muscle, the experts advised that the final positioning must be determined via a searching motion. The transducer should be positioned at the iliac crest and then shifted cranially so that it ends up being located between the anterior superior iliac spine (ASIS) and the lower edge of the costal arch. From there, the transducer should be moved medially. Thus, orientation to the umbilicus could be avoided.

"From the Crista iliaca you should go cranial with the transducer and leave it right in the middle of the ribs and the iliac crest. Then you continue towards the umbilicus and place the transducer in a horizontal position. Sometimes not horizontal, but slightly turned inwards towards caudally." (physical therapist, female).

The experts stated that the deep abdominal muscles must be visualized in the transverse section to display the increase in muscle thickness during contraction.

Positioning of the Transducer for Imaging of the Deep Back Muscles
The attachment of the ultrasound transducer for visualization of the multifidi muscles was said to be difficult to ensure, especially because of the furrow along the spinous process. A bilateral visualization of the multifidi muscles would be preferable, using both a transversal and a longitudinal scanning plane of the muscles.

"The muscle is located bilaterally on the spinous process. I place the ultrasound transducer over both sides to visualize the sagittal scanning plane from posterior to anterior and the thickness of the muscle." (physical therapist, male).

"Transverse process should be used as a landmark. Then use the ultrasound bilaterally. What does the other side look like? The simultaneous visualization of 2 muscles is very interesting." (physical therapist, male).

According to one expert, when controlling the correct execution within SSE, it is sufficient to look at only one scanning plane of the musculature.

"Once relaxed and once tensed to determine the increase in muscle diameter and height. But for segmental stabilization, an image of muscle diameter, a parasagittal image, would be sufficient." (physical therapist, male).

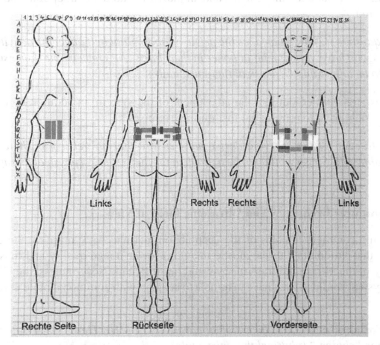

Fig. 1. Coordinate system shown to the experts for the determination of the transducer positioning and marked areas by the experts.

Thus, an observation in the transverse scanning plane was said to be particularly suitable, in which the muscle thickness can be determined.

The experts were asked about where the transducer should be placed on the patient's body surface to ensure optimal imaging of the target musculature. The specified positions are shown in Fig. 1.

3.6 Attachment of the Ultrasound Transducer

A proper and stable attachment of the ultrasound transducer to the body surface was crucial for the experts, to ensure good imaging quality, especially during dynamic exercises.

"The most important issue is a good connection over the course of time. The transducer must not slip, otherwise, the image will no longer match. Then the AI software will have a hard time detecting points or making any statement. A homogeneous image in dynamic exercises is technically challenging." *(clinical radiologist, male).*

Furthermore, two experts emphasized that the transducer to be developed within the ULTRAWEAR project must be both small and compact. It must adhere well to the body of patients during exercises. The latter could be achieved by inserting the system into a belt or by using adhesive connection. However, there was concern that the use of a belt could restrict the patient's movements and an individual adjustment option would have to be ensured.

"The question is, how much does the pelvic or abdominal belt affect the activity of women who have very dominant bones in their back? All conceivable dimensions need to be adjustable." *(physical therapist, male).*

The experts pointed out that the attachment of the system, in addition to a certain stability, would have to prevent gel loss during exercises.

"Construction of the carrying device must ensure that no gel leaks. There are sprayable gels. So gel would not be a problem for the system." *(physical therapist, male).*

3.7 Transducer Frequency and Ultrasonic Field of View

For imaging contraction states of the deep abdominal and back muscles, the experts indicated that (in contrast to diagnostic imaging) lower image quality and thus lower frequency of the ultrasound transducer would be sufficient. Nevertheless, the ULTRA-WEAR system would at least have to be able to keep up with common mobile ultrasound systems.

"Similar ultrasound transducers often have 8 to 15 MHz. Here 6–8 MHz would be a good choice." *(physical therapist, male).*

A global penetration depth of the ultrasound system required to visualize the target muscles could not be determined but was considered to be rather individual, since the degree of muscular training, the patient's height, and intermuscular as well as subcutaneous fat deposits would have a considerable influence on the ultrasound image.

"2 to 3 cm are definitely necessary. For the multifidi, perhaps 5 cm, because the erector spinae lies above it." (sports medicine physician, male).

One expert commented that a footprint of approximately 60 mm in total would be sufficient for imaging the deep abdominal and dorsal muscles in most patients.

3.8 Differences in Ultrasound Imaging in Young Vs. Older Patients

All experts emphasized that the degree of training of the musculature and the representation in the ultrasound image is very individual, even in the target group of older adults. The age and athleticism of the patients would certainly influence the echogenicity of the musculature. On the whole, however, certain atrophy of the musculature is noticeable in many people of advanced age.

The presence of fatty tissue, both in the form of subcutaneous deposits and deposits within the muscles, was mentioned as a challenge for ultrasound imaging.

"Body fat is a big issue. Subcutaneous fat is a problem, especially on the abdomen." (physical therapist, female).

"Older people often do not provide the same image quality as younger patients due to degeneration, atrophy or a higher percentage of fat in the muscles." (clinical radiologist, male).

In particular, intramuscular fat deposits would affect the visualization of the musculature in the ultrasound image. However, the experts emphasized that the identification of the fat tissue provides important information regarding the condition of the musculature. One expert commented that the analysis of muscle condition may be possible via grayscale analyses in the ultrasound image.

"A qualitative analysis of the musculature is possible via grayscale analysis in ultrasound. Differences between the shades of gray provide information about the musculature being displayed. The grayscale volume shows the difference between hypoechogenic and hyperechogenic shading. Damage and fatty tissue in the muscle can thus be made visible." (physical therapist, male).

3.9 Recognition of Muscular Status Through Artificial Intelligence

There was no common understanding among the experts about the extent to which the use of ultrasound in imaging the deep abdominal and back muscles would be difficult to learn for aspiring physical therapists and other medical professionals. Whereas one expert said that the ultrasound imaging of the musculature could be easily learned by means of a training course, another expert emphasized that many (especially inexperienced) physical therapists have little knowledge in the field of ultrasound-imaging anatomy.

"You have to be able to orient yourself, distinguish 'up' and 'down', and be able to visualize different planes. Recognition can be frustrating." (physical therapist, male).

However, all experts saw AI-assisted detection of target muscles as an important asset for deep abdominal and back muscle imaging as biofeedback in physical therapy.

"This is essential. Musculoskeletal ultrasound diagnosis is not that easy. You think it's pathology and then you tilt the transducer just 2 mm and it looks completely different. Even to radiologists, every muscle looks different. Artificial intelligence can easily recognize structures, but the correct scanning plane must always be found perfectly. Only if you always find the same point will it be feasible." (clinical radiologist, male).

Three of the experts expressed concerns about the use of automated muscle recognition, however. For example, one expert said that muscle recognition in the dynamic environment of a physical therapy exercise would be very difficult and almost impossible for AI to solve. Two other experts expressed that AI support could not replace the anatomical training of the user and may negatively impact the understanding in the area of imaging anatomy.

"It can have a negative impact on the learning behavior. You don't have to deal with it anymore, and maybe you don't." (physical therapist, male).

3.10 Evaluation of the Presented ULTRAWEAR User Interface

The experts were presented with the current user interface of the ULTRAWEAR system for feedback (see Fig. 2). The first impression of all experts was that the UI seemed too cluttered and complicated.

"It's a lot, I have to say. [...] For me, at first glance, there are too many parameters. You get so overloaded with information that you can't concentrate on the essentials." (clinical radiologist, male).

Many of the buttons and setting options of the UI did not seem necessary for the experts. For example, the graph displaying the transducer frequencies over time was perceived as not helpful for the usage scenario. The purpose of some of the control options was also not immediately apparent to the experts, especially since the terminology seemed technical and the functions were not available in conventional ultrasound systems. The experts stated that a large part of the settings should be preset or automatically adjusted by the system.

"The parameters are the same as in my practice. The only difference is that everything is pre-adjusted for me. An automatic setting option for the transversus abdominis and the multifidi would be good. [...] But a manual setting must also be available if, for example, a patient with a lot of subcutaneous fat tissue or a patient with a lot of muscle tissue comes in. So that I can get to the individual settings there." (physical therapist, male).

Once imaging adjustments would need to be manually adjusted to individual patients, it should be possible to do so using a minimalistic and easy-to-understand UI.

"When starting, there would have to be just two or three settings options, and then if you want to refine it, you go into a menu like that. I'm a fan of everything being simple and straightforward. I'm an Apple fan, so it should be like that, for example." (physical therapist, male).

Only one expert wanted to retain all the options to adjust the settings independently.

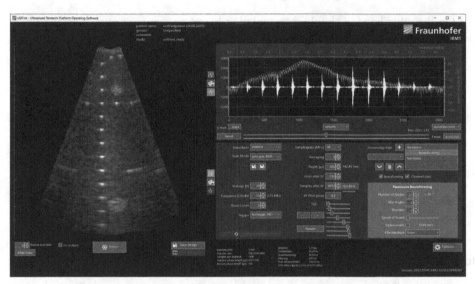

Fig. 2. Screenshot of a portable ultrasound research system [5], which served as a basis for discussion of UI design.

3.11 Suggestions for Improvement of the User Interface

The setting variables that the experts said were indispensable in the UI were a funcion for freezing the currently displayed image, the adjustment of the penetration depth and gain. There should still be an automatic TGC and autofocus, according to the experts. However, the latter should be adaptable to the individual patient if needed.

Two experts commented that for use of the ultrasound image as biofeedback for patients, the presentation of the raw ultrasound image and the UI with the adjustment options were too complicated. Instead, there should be a second UI that is used in interaction with the patient and is designed to be much simpler. The patient should not see the ultrasound image of his musculature, which is often difficult to understand and interpret. Rather, the second UI should visualize the muscle contractions abstractly through a simplified representation.

"I'd like it to be not so medical, but more playful and entertaining, simple. You need software that motivates patients to stick with it and supports them." (physical therapist, male).

On the one hand, the possibility of implementation in the form of a simple game was mentioned.

"Pelvic floor therapists have this system where patients sit on it. It's "Atari-like". Like a fish goes up or down and with bees and balloons. [...] You'd need software on top of it to keep the patient engaged." (physical therapist, male).

On the other hand, a simple representation based on common medical technology would be conceivable.

"There should be a consistent language. I think colors like green, yellow and red are a good idea. You can also try an amplitude display or you can do it with a kind of tachometer display. But it should not be too sensitive. Do not show the decimal point, but ranges. So it's easier for the patient and leads to less frustration." (sports medicine physician, male).

Lastly, the possibility of choosing a presentation form that shows the anatomical structures visible on the ultrasound image in a schematic version was mentioned.

"You could show the muscles on the skeleton that should be activated now." (sports medicine physician, male).

However, when designing a gamified or simplified presentation, care must be taken to ensure that it remains serious and confidence-inspiring.

"There would have to be a good level of gamification. Medical apps are often too cheesy. I find too gamified mediation problematic, as it can quickly come across as unserious. It shouldn't give too much information at once and thus become too complex." (sports medicine physician, male).

4 Discussion

The aim of the study was to determine expert requirements for a wearable that assists therapists in providing biofeedback on SSE execution using rehabilitative ultrasound imaging and also facilitate the learning of muscle control for the patient.

The experts emphasized the benefits of SSE especially in the beginning of therapy, in the further process functional exercises should be crucial. Studies indicate a significant increase in thickness in TrA during Pilates exercises performed [3]. Furthermore, a 1-year follow-up case series study showed multifidus thickness increases in participants who practice other exercise types in conjunction with Pilates [6]. Especially in cases of free movement in space, ultrasound-based feedback with a wearable would bring novelty value and enable feedback that is not yet possible. All experts expressed a positive attitude towards the use of novel technology in therapy and AI-assisted ultrasound systems in particular. The results showed a recommendation of positioning that is also consistent with other studies [11, 16]. A transducer frequency of 6–8 MHz was recommended, which is in the lower range of RUSI [27] and of the frequencies of the handheld devices [28].

The experts expressed important concerns that should be considered during the development, e.g. a proper and stable attachment of the ultrasound transducer to the body surface was important for the experts. First feasibility studies of a new ultrasound probe fixator indicate hands-free echocardiographic monitoring during exercise [24]. Regarding the UI, the experts explained that a large part of the settings should be preset or automatically adjusted by the system. The expert mentioned the concern that, especially regarding older adults, the lower affinity for technology should be also taken into account. Barriers for using technology can be: lack of knowledge, negative attitudes, and age-related changes such as vision and hearing loss and fine motor difficulties [7].

5 Conclusion

Overall, the interviews with the experts provided valuable insights for the further development of the ULTRAWEAR system. With regard to the technical specifications, the depth of imaging penetration and frequency of the ultrasonic transducer were discussed for appropriate imaging quality. The results of the interviews will be useful for the further design of the UI. The importance of presentation and communication of information on exercise execution for both the physical therapists and patients were emphasized. Comprehensibility and usability of the UI and the system in general were particularly emphasized.

References

1. Cardim, N., et al.: The use of handheld ultrasound devices: a position statement of the European Association of Cardiovascular Imaging (2018 update). Eur. Heart J. - Cardiovasc. Imaging **20**(3), 245–252 (2019). https://doi.org/10.1093/ehjci/jey145
2. De la Fuente, C., et al.: Intrasession real-time ultrasonography feedback improves the quality of transverse abdominis contraction. J. Manipulative Physiol. Ther. **43**(8), 816–823 (2020). https://doi.org/10.1016/j.jmpt.2019.10.017
3. Endleman, I., Critchley, D.J.: Transversus abdominis and obliquus internus activity during pilates exercises: measurement with ultrasound scanning. Arch. Phys. Med. Rehabil. **89**(11), 2205–2212 (2008). https://doi.org/10.1016/j.apmr.2008.04.025
4. Ferreira, P.H., et al.: Specific stabilisation exercise for spinal and pelvic pain: a systematic review. Aust. J. Physiother. **52**(2), 79–88 (2006). https://doi.org/10.1016/S0004-9514(06)700 43-5
5. Fournelle, M., et al.: Portable ultrasound research system for use in automated bladder monitoring with machine-learning-based segmentation. Sensors. **21**(19), 6481 (2021). https://doi.org/10.3390/s21196481
6. Gala-Alarcón, P., et al.: Ultrasound evaluation of the abdominal wall and lumbar multifidus muscles in participants who practice pilates: a 1-year follow-up case series. J. Manipulative Physiol. Ther. **41**(5), 434–444 (2018). https://doi.org/10.1016/j.jmpt.2017.10.007
7. Gitlow, L.: Technology use by older adults and barriers to using technology. Phys. Occup. Ther. Geriatr. **32**(3), 271–280 (2014). https://doi.org/10.3109/02703181.2014.946640

8. Gnat, R., et al.: Reliability of real-time ultrasound measurement of transversus abdominis thickness in healthy trained subjects. Eur. Spine J. **21**(8), 1508–1515 (2012). https://doi.org/10.1007/s00586-012-2184-4

9. Hayden, J.A., Ellis, J., Ogilvie, R., Malmivaara, A., van Tulder, M.W.: Exercise therapy for chronic low back pain. Cochrane Database Syst. Rev. **9**(9), CD009790 (2021). https://doi.org/10.1002/14651858.CD009790.pub2

10. Henry, S.M., Teyhen, D.S.: Ultrasound imaging as a feedback tool in the rehabilitation of trunk muscle dysfunction for people with low back pain. J. Orthop. Sports Phys. Ther. **37**(10), 627–634 (2007). https://doi.org/10.2519/jospt.2007.2555

11. Henry, S.M., Westervelt, K.C.: The use of real-time ultrasound feedback in teaching abdominal hollowing exercises to healthy subjects. Res. Rep. **35**(6), 338–345 (2005)

12. Hides, J., et al.: The relationship of transversus abdominis and lumbar multifidus clinical muscle tests in patients with chronic low back pain. Man. Ther. **16**(6), 573–577 (2011). https://doi.org/10.1016/j.math.2011.05.007

13. Huang, Z.-H., Ma, C.Z.-H., Wang, L.-K., Wang, X.-Y., Siu-Ngor, F., Zheng, Y.-P.: Real-time visual biofeedback via wearable ultrasound imaging can enhance the muscle contraction training outcome of young adults. J. Strength Cond. Res. **36**(4), 941–947 (2022). https://doi.org/10.1519/JSC.0000000000004230

14. Kriese, M., Clijsen, R., Taeymans, J., Cabri, J.: Segmental stabilization in low back pain: a systematic review. Sportverletz. Sportschaden Organ Ges. Orthopadisch-Traumatol. Sportmed. **24**(1), 17–25 (2010). https://doi.org/10.1055/s-0030-1251512

15. de Paula, P.O., et al.: Reproducibility of the pressure biofeedback unit in measuring transversus abdominis muscle activity in patients with chronic nonspecific low back pain. J. Bodywork Mov. Ther. **16**(2), 251–257 (2012). https://doi.org/10.1016/j.jbmt.2011.06.003

16. Lin, S., et al.: Effect of real-time ultrasound imaging for biofeedback on trunk muscle contraction in healthy subjects: a preliminary study. BMC Musculoskelet. Disord. **22**(1), 142 (2021). https://doi.org/10.1186/s12891-021-04006-0

17. Mangum, L.C., et al.: Ultrasound assessment of the transverse abdominis during functional movement: transverse abdominis during movement. J. Ultrasound Med. **37**(5), 1225–1231 (2018). https://doi.org/10.1002/jum.14466

18. Mannion, A.F., et al.: Muscle thickness changes during abdominal hollowing: an assessment of between-day measurement error in controls and patients with chronic low back pain. Eur. Spine J. **17**(4), 494–501 (2008). https://doi.org/10.1007/s00586-008-0589-x

19. van Middelkoop, M., et al.: A systematic review on the effectiveness of physical and rehabilitation interventions for chronic non-specific low back pain. Eur. Spine J. **20**(1), 19–39 (2011). https://doi.org/10.1007/s00586-010-1518-3

20. Potter, C.L., Cairns, M.C., Stokes, M.: Use of ultrasound imaging by physiotherapists: A pilot study to survey use, skills and training. Manual Therapy **17**(1), 39–46 (2012). https://doi.org/10.1016/j.math.2011.08.005

21. Richardson, C.: Therapeutic Exercise for Spinal Segmental Stabilization: In Lower Back Pain. Churchill Livingstone, Edinburgh (1998)

22. Richardson, C.A., et al.: The relation between the transversus abdominis muscles, sacroiliac joint mechanics, and low back pain. Spine **27**(4), 399–405 (2002). https://doi.org/10.1097/00007632-200202150-00015

23. Rozenberg, S.: Chronic low back pain: definition and treatment. Rev. Prat. **58**(3), 265–272 (2008)

24. Salden, O.A.E., van Everdingen, W.M., Spee, R., Doevendans, P.A., Cramer, M.J.: How i do it: feasibility of a new ultrasound probe fixator to facilitate high quality stress echocardiography. Cardiovasc. Ultrasound **16**, 6 (2018). https://doi.org/10.1186/s12947-018-0124-0

25. Solomon, S.D., Saldana, F.: Point-of-care ultrasound in medical education — stop listening and look. N. Engl. J. Med. **370**(12), 1083–1085 (2014). https://doi.org/10.1056/NEJMp1 311944

26. Von Der Lippe, E. et al.: Prävalenz von Rücken- und Nackenschmerzen in Deutschland. Ergebnisse der Krankheitslast-Studie BURDEN 2020. J. Health Monit. **6**(S3), 1–14 (2021)

27. Whittaker, J., et al.: Rehabilitative ultrasound imaging: understanding the technology and its applications. J. Orthop. Sports Phys. Ther. **37**, 434–449 (2007). https://doi.org/10.2519/jospt. 2007.2350

28. Zardi, E.M., et al.: Accuracy and performance of a new handheld ultrasound machine with wireless system. Sci. Rep. **9**(1), 14599 (2019). https://doi.org/10.1038/s41598-019-51160-6

Wild Intercepts: A Novel Approach to Usability Testing of a 'Citizen Science' Portal, Developed for Understanding the 'Burdens of Pain' Among Citizens

Bhairavi Warke[1]([⊠]) [iD], Diane Gromala[1], Ankit Gupta[1], Christopher Shaw[1],
and Linda Li[2]

[1] School of Interactive Arts and Technology, Simon Fraser University,
Surrey, BC V3T 0A3, Canada
{bwarke,gromala,aga53,shaw}@sfu.ca
[2] Department of Physical Therapy, University of British Columbia,
Vancouver, BC V6T 1Z3, Canada
lli@arthritisresearch.ca

Abstract. Whether acute or chronic, pain can significantly impact a person's biopsychosocial quality of life. To better understand the effects of pain on day-to-day life, i.e., the 'burdens of pain', our team of researchers and patient-partners developed an online portal using a 'Citizen Science' approach that collects information about living with pain from the public in British Columbia (BC). To test the initial version of the Citizen Science for Burdens of Pain (CS-BoP) portal, we needed to find participants as diverse as the population of BC. Including diverse and marginalized voices in research continues to be a challenge, so we set-up a booth at a busy mall in the suburbs of Vancouver, BC. And over a period of two days, we asked 30 mall visitors to test the portal in their spare time, followed by a short interview and survey. This usability study, called *Wild Intercepts*, was intended to help us gain an understanding of people's first impressions and perceptions about the desirability and ease of use of the portal in a short timeframe. *Wild Intercepts* was not only successful in including diverse voices that represent the diversity of BC, but the busy and chaotic environment of the mall also helped us better understand these participants' unique contexts, needs and motivations for sharing their experience with pain on a web portal in their busy day-to-day lives. This paper reflects upon our implementation and implications of the *Wild Intercepts* approach that may benefit similar research in human-computer-interaction, design and technology.

Keywords: In the wild · Field research · Usability study · Interaction design

---

In the context of this research, the term 'citizens' refers to all members of the public residing in Canada irrespective of their immigration status.

© Springer Nature Switzerland AG 2022
V. G. Duffy et al. (Eds.): HCII 2022, LNCS 13521, pp. 174–190, 2022.
https://doi.org/10.1007/978-3-031-17902-0_13

1 Introduction

Pain is a common experience, one that is crucial to life. Whether acute or chronic, pain can affect day-to-day life—not just physiologically, but psychologically and socially as well. Thus, lowering a person's quality of life (QoL) [1, 2]. Although pain symptoms are often seen as indicators of underlying condition(s) that can be diagnosed and treated, we know little about how burdensome they can be to live with. The effects of pain symptoms on an individual's life is termed as the 'burden of pain' [1, 3, 4]. Researchers at the University of British Columbia (UBC) wanted to better understand this burden of pain symptoms from perspectives beyond clinical contexts. Along with the Pain Studies Lab and patient-partners, they developed a Citizen Science web portal that captures such data from members of the public in British Columbia (BC) called 'Citizen Science for Burdens of Pain' (CS-BoP). Citizen Science is a practice that involves people who voluntarily contribute to research activities, from collecting samples and recording data or observations, to sometimes helping with data analysis [5–7].

By engaging citizens* in contributing, co-analyzing, and discovering information about their pain symptoms and their impact on individual's lives, researchers may gain insights into aspects of pain that merit further investigation and increase awareness of these under-explored burdens, while creating an online community of people with shared, hard-to-quantify lived experiences. Once an initial prototype of this Citizen Science portal was developed, we tested it at a busy mall in a large suburb of Vancouver – the Central City mall in Surrey, BC. Over a period of two days, we asked 30 adult mall visitors to test and evaluate the usability of the web portal, what we call *Wild Intercepts*. This usability study was an important step in gaining firsthand perspectives from the intended users: the general public. Our goal was to gain first impressions about ease-of-use and navigation; clarity in communication of purpose, tasks, and privacy and security issues; and overall appeal. Participants provided critical insights into the usability needs of the diverse populations of BC from the CS-BoP. A deeper analysis of the *Wild Intercepts* approach revealed additional merits.

Wild Intercepts draws upon field studies that are typically conducted to understand a phenomenon that occurs in a specific environment, or to test new designs intended for use in a specific context [8–11]. However, in this case, the CS-BoP is not intended for use in a mall per se. Rather, we chose a mall in Surrey because it attracts a wide range of local people who differ in age, gender, ethnicity, tech-literacy, health-status, and socio-economic level. The success of CS-BoP depends on engaging a diverse group of people who have equally diverse experiences with pain, and a busy suburban mall was one place to find diverse people. Importantly, this is not an upscale shopping center with high end stores, but a local mall with grocery, clothing, dollar, and chain stores, located next to a busy public transit hub.

In prior studies, mounting posters or ads in such public settings to recruit participants has limited participants to students, educated middle-class people, tech-savvy people, people who are interested in pain research, or people with prior experience with research studies. Existing literature on the challenges of recruiting participants for research studies discuss similar limitations with conventional recruitment strategies [12–15]. Further, people who respond to recruitment posters or ads must take the initiative to contact researchers. Moreover, they may come with prior interpretations or expectations about

'Citizen Science', or 'Pain' based on the limited information that they saw on the posters or ads. We were able to bypass these potential limitations by asking strangers with no prior knowledge of the portal to spend their spare time testing it, without mulling over it, or taking extra steps to participate.

Typical usability studies involve focus groups or interviews that may last an hour or longer. Standing or sitting at an open booth in a busy mall forced us to limit interactions with each person to 15 min—the duration we expect citizen scientists would spend using the portal per visit. This short exposure duration helped us identify issues that prohibited users from comprehending and completing set-tasks in the portal in a short timeframe, and in a situation that competed for their attention, much like at home.

All sessions were audio-recorded and transcribed, and the data was analyzed by researchers through thematic coding. The data gathered using the *Wild Intercepts* approach was rich and detailed. It helped us uncover deeper insights about specific features of the portal and highlighted significant opportunities for improvement. The resulting themes were then coalesced into three principles that will guide future iterations of the portal.

This paper contributes a novel approach to usability studies, *Wild Intercepts*, for web portals designed to solicit information from diverse people. With *Wild Intercepts*, we uncovered new dimensions of harnessing the power of "in the wild" research, going beyond typical field studies and overcoming some of the limitations of lab studies. This approach may help UI/UX researchers explore novel ways to engage participants in research, and to study features intended for a wide range of users.

2 Background

2.1 Citizen Science Portal for Burdens of Pain (CS-BoP)

Pain is a complex experience that cannot be easily explained, especially when are no visible signs of it. Thus, assessing its impact on a person's quality of life and their biopsychosocial 'lived experience' is of utmost importance. Pain symptoms are often primary indicators of an injury or condition. This short-term or acute pain usually ends once a person heals. However, in many cases the pain response system itself can malfunction, resulting in persistent, long-term pain, termed "chronic pain". Living with chronic or acute pain can have significant impacts on one's biopsychosocial Quality of Life [1, 2]. Acute and chronic pain can also affect work, family life, and social engagement. These effects of pain symptoms on an individual's life are called the 'burden of pain' [1, 3, 4]. Because pain has been primarily understood in the context of a symptom of a medical condition, it is an on-going challenge for health researchers to understand more fully what this burden of pain may mean. This is especially relevant because chronic pain is widespread [1], and because the opioid crisis is still a major issue in North America.

The term 'Citizen Science' refers to a collaborative approach that involves professional scientists who engage members of the public—citizens*— in collecting and analyzing data in ways that may lead to scientific discovery [5–7]. Multiple citizen science projects are underway around the world that focus on exploration of environmental changes, studying natural habitat like plant and animal species, education, health, and public policy. It leverages experiences of the public to gather information about a phenomenon; in turn, the collected information promises to satisfy contributors' own curiosity about the phenomenon or provides a sense of belonging or working toward a common goal [5, 6, 16]. Our team of health researchers/clinicians, patient-partners and designers are exploring a Citizen Science approach to collecting diverse and contextual information about the 'burdens of pain' by asking citizens to share information about their pain-related experiences, and in turn providing them with a rich resource of data gathered from others who experience pain and its effects in various ways. The long-term goal of this project is to create a community of citizens and pain researchers who can inform each other to develop research questions that may help us better understand and address the 'burdens of pain.'

We wanted to develop a web portal that uses the Citizen Science approach to gather information about the 'burdens of pain' from people living across Canada. Similar projects, like "Cloudy with a Chance of Pain," developed in the UK, inspired this project [17]. To kick-off this project, the research team and their patient-partners first conducted a participatory workshop [18–20]. Participatory research methods are at the crux of inclusive design, an approach we deemed indispensable for the CS-BoP [21–23]. The aim of this workshop was to set the stage for the Citizen Science portal by first identifying its requirements, which had to be responsive to the complexities of articulating the multiple aspects of pain. Participants contributed information related to their own current or past pain symptoms and identified the benefits and drawbacks of four data collection methods tested in this workshop [24]. The outcomes of this participatory workshop guided the development of the subsequent web portal.

The first iteration of this platform has three main levels: the first level asks users for information about their pain symptoms, the locations and duration of pain; and where relevant, diagnosis and professional consultations [25, 26]; the second level focuses on pain intensity and effects on day-to-day activities and quality of life [27]; and the third level enables users to share their story in prose. The home page gives an overview of 'Citizen Science' and 'burdens of pain' and assures citizens that their information is secure and anonymized.

 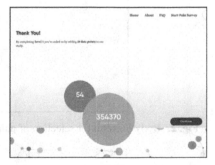

Fig. 1. Left: the first page of the Citizen Science platform. Right: a citizen's initial online contribution depicted as 'datapoints'. Citizens can return to contribute more information and see their data points increase. (https://patientscientist.ca/)

Since pain is notoriously difficult to articulate [28], we included tools on each level to help citizens describe aspects of their pain and to help motivate users to continue to subsequent levels. In level one, for example, citizens can click on a body diagram to select the location of their pain (see Fig. 2); dropdown menus help them articulate more characteristics of that pain (see Fig. 4). As an incentive, the platform gives users a visual sense that the information they contribute has potential value in helping others – this is represented by "datapoints" (Fig. 1). Datapoints are represented as colored circles; each has a numerical value, and its size grows larger as the value increases. A point is assigned for each piece of data or answer that the user provides. Datapoints are conceived of as adaptive over time: as the number of citizens' contributions grow and continual analysis reveals more insights, the value of specific datapoints will change accordingly.

Textual, audio or video stories were designed to work as social and psychological 'tools' that may help citizens articulate their own experiences and potentially feel a sense of kinship or belonging among others who may share similar experiences with pain. For instance, just before a user moves to the next level, a story shared by a fellow citizen appears on the screen. Users can either log on as guests to enter their information anonymously if they so choose. If they choose to register using their email, they can leave midway and return to the portal anytime. The objective is to help motivate people to enter information about their pain symptoms regularly so that they may discern patterns in their own experiences over time, but also to add enough datapoints so that the data collected from multiple users can be analyzed and visualized to better understand the 'burdens of pain' on a larger scale.

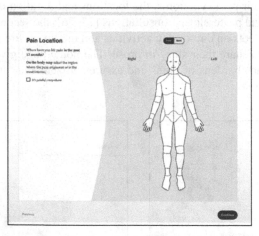

Fig. 2. Body diagram for selection of pain locations. (https://patientscientist.ca/)

2.2 *Wild Intercepts* Usability Study

Once the initial functional prototype of the CS-BoP was developed, we wanted to test it for usability. We needed to engage a quickly accessible sampling of citizens that was as diverse as the intended users of the portal. Some of the challenges to recruiting these intended users were:

1. The population of British Columbia is culturally and ethnically very diverse. It is difficult to include perspectives of the less privileged citizens, from recent immigrants and asylum seekers to people with disabilities, lower socio-economic backgrounds, and racial minorities in research– a known challenge for researchers in the context of North America [13–15].
2. Lab tests limit the kind of participants who may contribute to a study. Lab studies often advertise a call for recruitment of participants via posters, social media posts, email newsletters, etc. where it may grab attention of someone who is either interested in the research topic or the monetary compensation, if any. Moreover, the prospective participant must take the initiative to make the initial contact with the researchers which can often be a limitation for marginalized populations [12, 14, 15, 29]. As a result, and similar to what our prior experience suggests, most participants in lab studies tend to be students, educated middle-class, and tech-savvy people [12].
3. Lab studies usually require a comparatively long and more restricted timeframe. Typically, studies involve activities, interviews, focus groups, etc. which require the participants to take an hour or more out of their schedules, especially if travelling to and from a research lab is required. This can also be a factor that limits participation of diverse groups [13–15].

To overcome these challenges, we looked at field studies, mainly "In the Wild" research, as a possible way to reach participants where they are. As Rogers suggests [10],

"In the lab, participants are brought to the experiment and shown their place by a researcher or assistant and then provided with instructions on what they have to do. There is always someone at hand to explain the purpose and functionality of the application. This form of scaffolding is largely absent in the wild: The locus of control shifts from the experimenter to the participant."

But our next question was – where do we find participants as diverse people as the people of BC? We deemed that an intercept study in a busy public venue would be appropriate for evaluating the usability of the CS-BoP [9, 11, 13, 20, 23]. We chose the Central City Mall in Surrey that is centrally located in a neighborhood with government offices that serve immigrants, unemployed and retired workers, commercial businesses, banks, and social services organizations – whose visitors have ready access to both personal and public transit. Moreover, the mall is strategically located in a city that is at the crossroads of an urban center and an ethnically diverse suburb. Unlike upscale urban malls with high-end brands, the Central City mall is a mixed-use development that houses 140 retail stores, restaurants, services, Simon Fraser University campus, and a AAA office tower [30]. It includes grocery stores, grooming services, restaurants, convenience, and discount stores. Our researchers, armed with laptops, set up in a large, open booth located by a busy crossing point in the mall. This booth was constructed by the mall authorities to host community groups and boost community engagement. We engaged passers-by in conversations about the study and requested their participation. A total of 30 mall visitors between the ages 22–76 years participated in the study.

Participants tested the platform and were interviewed in a timeframe of approximately 15 min. They also responded to a set of survey questions after the interview.

Field studies focus on observing or engaging people or certain phenomenon within the specific context that cannot accurately be replicated in labs [9–11]. Field studies implement an ethnographic approach to explore how naturally occurring factors may influence design decisions. According to Koskinen et al. [9],

"Field researchers work with 'context' in an opposite way from researchers in a lab. Rather than bringing things of interest into the lab for experimental studies, field researchers go after these things in natural settings, that is, in a place where some part of a design is supposed to be used."

There is growing interest in Human-Computer-Interaction (HCI) research communities to complement lab-studies with 'In the Wild' - field studies [9–11, 31, 32]. Undertaking some or all aspects of the design, development, and evaluation phases of research 'in the wild' can help HCI researchers better understand the context, environment, and communities where the technological interventions that they develop will be used. Rogers adds that [10],

"The outcome of conducting in the-wild studies can be most revealing, demonstrating quite different results from those arising out of lab studies. In particular, they have shown how people come to understand and appropriate technologies on their own terms and for their own situated purposes."

The *Wild Intercepts* approach draws heavily upon field studies and 'In the Wild' research, but we step away from typical field studies in the aspect that the CS-BoP is not intended for use at a mall, instead the mall was identified as a place where the intended users can be found. The 'context' in this case is not the physical location but the characteristics of that location that enable us to engage with the diverse populations whose voices are crucial in the development of the CS-BoP. While field studies often take a long time, with hours of observations and participant interactions; *Wild Intercepts* is a fast-paced approach to capturing first-impressions and quick feedback within a short timeframe. Moreover, the *Wild Intercepts* approach addresses the above-mentioned challenges with lab studies, as discussed in the outcomes.

3 Methodology

We obtained permissions from the Central City Mall's Administrators to set-up a booth, which also doubles as a community engagement booth, at the primary intersecting corridors near a food court to be visible to maximum foot traffic. A team of four researchers connected two laptops with the initial functional version of the CS-BoP and put up a poster to attract passers-by. A total of 30 participants were recruited for this study over a period of two days. In the mornings, when the mall was less busy, the researchers walked up to people who strolled by the booth or were waiting and requested them to consider participating in the study. As the mall got busier in the evenings, we found it easier to attract more participants, especially if they saw a few people standing by the booth testing the portal (Fig. 3).

During the study, we first walked the participants through the study procedure. Upon obtaining their signed consent, the participants were assigned an identification number at

Fig. 3. Mall visitors testing the first iteration of the CS-BoP at the booth

random to anonymize their data. They were asked to log in using a dummy email address, and then fill in information as they would "in real life" (see Fig. 4). They "talked through" as they used the platform and responded to a semi-structured interview. The interview questions focused on 1) initial impressions of the portal 2) the ease of comprehension and use, 3) willingness to share such information, 4) desired frequency of use, and 5) privacy or security concerns. The researchers documented the process by audio recording the talk-through and interviews, and by taking notes of their own observations. The participants answered a short survey rating their experience with the portal in terms of 1) complexity, 2) need for technical support or training, 3) consistency across the different pain-related questionnaires, and 4) overall level of confidence in using the portal. In the 15–20 min that each person spent with us, most participants were able to complete the first level of CS-BoP that asked them for information about their pain symptoms, the locations and duration of pain; and where relevant, diagnosis and professional consultations. At the end of the study, they were offered a small compensation, in the form of a gift card to a nearby chain coffee shop, for their contribution.

The audio recordings were transcribed, and observation notes were compiled. Data from 3 participants was excluded because it was incomplete. Data collected from the other 27 participants was analyzed following Wolcott's approach to qualitative data analysis—description, analysis and interpretation [33]. The observations and quotations were clustered by the three researchers into themes based on emerging patterns of similarity in behavior or perceptions and compared with survey results for additional depth and context. Themes were then grouped by affinity and iteratively re-framed to reveal possible connections between them, and to contextualize any unexpected revelations [33, 34]. Three key principles emerged from these themes that will help guide the future iterations of this portal.

3.1 Ethical Concerns

This study was exempted from ethics review by the Simon Fraser University's Research Ethics Board (SFU-REB) as they deemed it to be a 'quality improvement' study, in accordance with Article 2.5 of the TCPS2 Policy [35, 36]. However, from our prior experience with conducting such usability studies, we followed standard measures with data collection and anonymization, privacy and security of participant information, and storage/destruction of data that were also outlined in the Informed Consent forms signed by all participants prior to starting the study. Participants were provided a dummy email address to log in to CS-BoP and assigned a random identification number at the beginning of the study which was used to label the audio recordings, survey responses and researcher notes. No master list that links the random identification numbers to participants' personal information was ever created. We also obtained permission from the Central City Mall authorities, Blackwood Partners Management Corporation, to use the community booth for two days.

Future work with *Wild Intercepts* may differ in research objectives and purpose and may need to undergo an ethics review. Researchers must consult their institution's ethics review committee for proper guidance and approvals.

4 Outcomes

4.1 Findings from the *Wild Intercepts* Study for the CS-BoP

This study revealed important considerations for the design of the Citizen Science platform that could have easily been overlooked by researchers, had it not involved diverse users. It is important to note that all but two participants used a laptop or computer every day and were hence comfortable with using a laptop for testing the CS-BoP. Although the two participants didn't use a computer every day, they used smartphones daily. The participants were between the ages 22–76 with a median age of 37 and they self-identified with several ethnicities, sexual orientations, and technical proficiencies. They had a wide range of occupations including administration, finance, customer service, government officers, homemakers, caregivers, and retirees. 17 of the 30 participants identified themselves as women and only 3 participants were students. Data from three of the 30 participants was excluded from analysis because it was incomplete.

From coding the observations, interviews and survey responses, three main principles emerged. Termed here "guiding principles," these helped us better understand the users' perceptions about the portal, the benefits and the drawbacks of the current design, and necessary considerations for improving CS-BoP's design and user experience. The three guiding principles are as follows:

Build Trust with Clarity

Clearly visualized purpose and definitions provide a sense of authencity. Several participants found that information about the platform (see Fig. 1) was unclear or difficult to follow. They were either unaware of what 'citizen science' meant or uncertain about how the platform worked. They desired clearer and more succinct information upfront about the purpose, functionality, and benefit of engaging with the website. For example, participant #7 said,

"… it says, 'anyone can be a Citizen Scientist' and 'the platform allows voices to be heard.' But I am still not sure what that term 'Citizen Science' means. I don't know what symptoms we're talking about. Say it at the beginning, directly, to the point."

Participants demonstrated more willingness to share information once they grasped the concept and goal of the CS-BoP. However, they desired more visuals that enticed and stimulated curiosity about the 'Citizen Science' and 'burdens of pain.' Participant #13 suggested,

"I want to see that visual image because it communicates to the self-conscious more primitively than having it spelled out and explained. Like (image for) 'This is a story of feeling pain, feeling disempowered, feeling alienated, feeling alone' and then a shift to 'Oh, this is a story of healing. This is a story of empowerment.' Seeing that journey, I think would be very impactful."

Interest and confidence in participation rely on upfront knowledge of time investment and responsive tracking through the process. The amount of time it would take to complete all levels once logged-in was an important factor in participants' estimation of how often they might use the platform. Additionally, they expressed a need for flexibility to select the level and type of questions to answer based on the characteristics of their symptoms that seemed relevant and important to them. They felt more confident and a greater sense of control if they could anticipate what was coming and how much time it would need so that they could plan other tasks in their day around it or leave and return at another time. Additionally, levels that took longer than 5–7 min to answer were deemed as 'discouraging'—mainly attributed to the repetitive nature of questions and the lack of responsive feedback at each step reminding them of the bigger picture, i.e., benefits of contributing to CS-BoP. To illustrate this, participant #30 said:

"I have seen some interfaces where the progress bar on top moves as you move (i.e., click on it) – you see where you are, where you have been and what is coming next. Like buying something on Amazon. I don't have a diagnosis (referring to a specific question), so I think here (points to the subsequent level) will be the perfect place to put that information, but I also don't know that's coming next, so I cannot make that decision."

Participant #29 added,

"I usually like an indication at the start that 'this would take approximately 15 minutes to complete,' because I know I have 5 minutes. I am just wasting time before a meeting. And then if it takes 20 minutes, I have to stop and close the browser. I generally find though that surveys that I have to pause, I just forget to come back to later."

Upfront display of privacy and security details ensure reliability. Most participants were accustomed to clicking through standard privacy and security disclaimers on other online portals, few mentioned any concerns about data privacy and security. Most of the concerns were related to data sharing with third-party organizations for profit. They wanted more transparent information about data storage and management indicated upfront. As participant #7 said,

"If the data is being sold, then that needs to be disclosed to me. May be advertise that very clearly like — 'This information is only used strictly for medical purposes; we won't be selling your information.'"

Help Me Help Others
'I don't have a story, but I do have a history'– Allow flexibility to incorporate diverse stories. When we first asked any participant to test the website by sharing their 'story' with pain, most seemed to believe that they didn't have a 'story' worth telling. But as they engaged with the platform and "talked through" using it, they seemed more willing to explain their journey with a painful injury or conditions from decades ago, or more recent health-related challenges they face. Some also discussed stressful experiences

with treatments, doctors' visits, not being believed, and wanted to share tips and tricks that worked for them. However, this iteration of the platform limited their ability to share this 'history' in their own way. To provide an example, at the start of the study, participant #22 began by saying "I don't have much of a pain story," but over the course of the next few minutes discussed experiences with heart disease and related chest pain, neck surgery that led to bronchitis, and current issues with arthritis and migraines. The participant elaborated,

"I am in pain all the time, but the doctors won't give me pain relief because they think I am looking for a fix. It's really bad and causes a lot of anxiety. I haven't got a life anymore. I can't drive or go to work anymore. I am too scared to go out in case I faint and fall down, which is very embarrassing. So, I just stay at home and hope for the best."

Such personal stories really help in capturing the biopsychosocial dimensions of the burdens of pain, but users needed to feel encouraged and supported with better affordances of the CS-BoP to communicate with minimum effort.

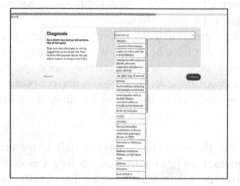 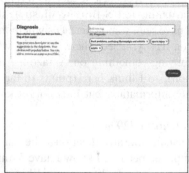

Fig. 4. Left: One of the questions on the Citizen Science platform allows users to select options from a list or to type it in. Right: Selected or typed responses appear as 'tags' right below the question. The progress bar on top shows how many questions the user has completed in that level. (https://patientscientist.ca/)

Simplify format without compromising details or excessive repetition. Most participants found the platform easy to use and follow through. However, some indicated that the similarity in layout from one question to next often made it difficult for them to distinguish between the content of the questions. Moreover, the lengthy drop-down lists and mixed formats of questions led to confusion. For example, one of the questions about existing conditions allows users to select a condition from a drop-down list or to type for a condition that may not be listed. All selected conditions were displayed as individual tags on the screen (see Fig. 4). When explaining their concerns about this layout, participant #24 said,

"It's a little confusing. 'Tag all that apply?' A lot of people are not going to get that. People are just used to clicking on the arrow and selecting from a drop down. My mom probably doesn't even know what 'tag' is … she would go 'What am I supposed to do?' (clicks around) 'It doesn't work!' and she would leave the site."

In other areas, participants wanted to provide more details that were important to them. For instance, most participants found the body diagram (see Fig. 2) to be helpful when their pain had an identifiable location, but they felt they need more detailed, clickable zones so that they could narrow down to specific areas like tailbone, neck, eye, nose and so on. It was evident that users need more flexibility in the system that allows them to provide enough detail, but in ways that prevent them from feeling overwhelmed.

Count Positive Experiences too, because they count. Participants wanted to share stories of success, of positive aspects of their health and life. They strongly believed that sharing positive experiences was just as important as explaining the negative impacts of their pain symptoms to better understand the broader effects on their Quality of Life. Participant #13 said,

"The word 'burden' has a negative priming. In my mind, I feel, 'Oh, this is going to be like a sob story rolodex.' I am just listing symptoms. I don't think it addresses the fact that I have emotional tools and day-to-day rituals that I utilize to deal with these issues. So, if someone looked at this (their data) objectively, it would be like, 'This girl's a mess!' Whereas I don't feel that way at all. I feel quite healthy and balanced and very proactive about my health."

Emphasize the Greater Good

Concrete examples of the ultimate benefit are a bigger incentive than numerical scores. Many participants struggled with the concept of 'datapoints' and hence did not feel adequately incentivized by them to continue contributing their information (Fig. 1). They needed more concrete results of their contribution to be available for viewing, like how their data helped researchers or people similar to themselves. Most of them were inclined to use the platform more frequently if it were for the 'greater good' than just tracking their own data. Participant #19 said,

"What do you get with datapoints? Anything, or is it just a number? I do tweet memes (on Twitter) and it's nice to see retweets and likes, so if you put a story and you find out that you helped 20 people (from the 'likes') or 100 people found this helpful that would encourage more people to do it. Points gets kind of abstract."

Need to be assured that 'we're in this together.' Along with helping others, another main incentive for participants was to build a community of people in similar situations as them. Since the platform asks users to enter information such as their age, health conditions, geographical location, etc. at the beginning, participants expressed the need to be able to find individuals they can relate with, to feel like they belong and that they are not alone. To provide users this gratification, the system needs to clearly show what happens to the data they contribute, not just through user 'stories,' but interactive visualizations of data gathered from multiple users that can be sorted to find details provided by users like themselves. Participant #13 said,

"I would use this to feel a sense of pride, or a sense of satisfaction in sharing a story. So, just having my voice heard, and being seen, and witnessed is gratifying, just on an egoic level. And then just that simple human camaraderie of knowing that your story has helped someone's pain."

4.2 Learnings from the *Wild Intercepts* Approach

Although the above findings are specific to the first iteration of the CS-BoP that the participants saw, upon taking a closer look, we see that the three principles and underlying themes demonstrate significant level of detail and contextual depth that would have been impossible to get in such a short period of time without *Wild Intercepts*. It also helped us address some of the challenges with lab studies, mentioned before. The researchers made notes about their observations and experiences with using the *Wild Intercepts* approach, and its benefits and limitations are discussed below:

1. The *Wild Intercepts* approach was extremely effective in including diverse perspectives of the residents of British Columbia, from government employees to retirees, people with disabilities, mixed socio-economic levels, varied technical proficiencies, and so on. Recruiting such a diversity of participants was identified as one of the key challenges and a necessity for evaluating the usability of the CS-BoP and *Wild Intercepts* helped us overcome this challenge. However, we encountered few participants who could not complete the study due to lack of time, other pressing responsibilities, or inability to stand at the booth for long. Additionally, in the mornings, we struggled to attract the attention of older adults. We believe that the researchers, who were university students in their mid 20s, standing by the booth with laptops and voice recorders may have had an influence on this. But as the day went by and more people from different ages started coming to the booth, we saw an increase in participation from older adults.
2. When the CS-BoP was developed, we anticipated that users would spend 10–15 min of their spare time to enter information about their pain as often as they would like to track it. With the *Wild Intercepts* approach, participants were limited to 15–20 min per session, which is the maximum amount of time we could realistically ask people to stand at a booth. This enabled us to observe how many levels they were able to complete within that duration and at what stages they started to lose interest in the portal.
3. An unexpected revelation was that the busy bustling mall provided a tumultuous environment, similar to what one would experience at their home, work, or between chores. We anticipate that users may have to deal with similarly chaotic scenarios when they visit the CS-BoP in their day-to-day lives. *Wild Intercepts* at the Central City Mall helped us observe how people comprehend and complete tasks on the CS-BoP despite the distractions around them.
4. Most participants were visiting their neighborhood mall for routine errands and spending their spare time to test the platform for a relatively insignificant monetary compensation. As a result, they seemed be more relaxed and at ease to communicate freely and provide their honest feedback without mulling over it or mincing words. The 15-min time limitation and the casual public setting helped participants escape the daunting atmosphere in research labs and any possible handholding by researchers. The researchers didn't have much time to develop a rapport with these participants. And although this may be a drawback for studies where participant retention over longer periods is required [15, 29], in this case, it was beneficial to get their raw, first impressions without hesitation or bias.

The Wild Intercepts approach helped us overcome many of the challenges we anticipated with a lab-based study. It provided us with a better understanding of the usability of CS-BoP and the perceptions of the 'citizens' who would use it. We believe that Wild Intercepts shows great potential to be used as a quick evaluation tool by HCI researchers for initial concepts and prototypes and yield rich insights within the situated contexts of the people that they are designed for.

5 Conclusion

The *Wild Intercepts* approach shows promise in widening the scope of research through involvement of larger audiences and pushing the boundaries of typical lab research[9, 10, 31]. Most usability studies require large time investment in recruitment of participants and conducting activities and interviews to get more nuanced and in-depth insights, which may be more appropriate for later, more finished versions of technological interventions. *Wild Intercepts* is an effective approach to conduct quick and rapid usability studies with the initial versions and in-between prototypes. The key features of this approach are: 1) Low participant overhead: Participants spent about 15 min in the study after 1–2 min of contemplation. Unlike lab studies, participants spent no time on transportation or scheduling or other overhead tasks. 2) Broader demographic range: The age, ethnicity and professional experience of participants comes close to matching that of the general public. Our observation was that there is a stronger similarity to the general public than we have often observed in our own lab studies. *Wild Intercepts* may have farther and wider implications in HCI, design and technology which are yet to be explored.

This study proved to be of crucial importance in the evolution of the Citizen Science web portal for 'burdens of pain' and building community-based tools for engaging citizens in research activities. Key usability principles were observed in our study: the need for clear communication of goals, the need to enable users to predict how long a task will take, the need for clear communication of data security, and the need to clearly demonstrate the benefits to research and community. Because CS-BoP was aimed at collecting health information, the goal of CS-BoP to use the data to help others was paramount. We found that participants were very interested in helping foster the public good through using CS-BoP. The findings from this research provide a substantial understanding and the much-needed insight into design strategies necessary to improve the user experience of the existing portal to enhance adaptability for diverse users and encourage continuous engagement necessary for its sustenance and growth.

We plan to conduct more in-depth usability studies in future with the improved version of CS-BoP focusing on motivations for returning to the portal and continued use, visualizing gathered data, and community building for the greater good. We believe that the outcomes of this study and the analysis of the *Wild Intercepts* approach may also help inform the design and validation of similar such technologies targeted towards diverse populations.

Acknowledgements. We thank Cheryl Kohen, Delia Cooper, and Sunny Loo for the important contributions as patient partners. We would also like to acknowledge Blackwood Partners Managing Corporation and researchers at the Pain Studies Lab – Shiyi (Sherry) Wang, Jinghan (Celia) Zhang, Pegah Kiaei, and Christopher Wong for their help and support during this research. In addition, we thank Alison Hoens, Stephanie Therrien, and Amrit Sandhu for their critical roles in the development of the Citizen Science portal.

This project is supported by an operating grant provided by the BC SUPPORT (Support for People & Patient-Oriented Research & Trials) Unit (KTIS-005), and NSERC (Natural, Scientific and Engineering Research Council of Canada) R611484.

References

1. Duenas, M., Ojeda, B., Salazar, A., Mico, J.A., Failde, I.: A review of chronic pain impact on patients, their social environment and the health care system. JPR **9**, 457–467 (2016). https://doi.org/10.2147/JPR.S105892
2. Gatchel, R.J., Peng, Y.B., Peters, M.L., Fuchs, P.N., Turk, D.C.: The biopsychosocial approach to chronic pain: scientific advances and future directions. Psychol. Bull. **133**, 581–624 (2007). https://doi.org/10.1037/0033-2909.133.4.581
3. Cleeland, C.S.: Symptom burden: multiple symptoms and their impact as patient-reported outcomes. JNCI Monogr. **2007**, 16–21 (2007). https://doi.org/10.1093/jncimonographs/lgm005
4. Kowal, J., Wilson, K.G., McWilliams, L.A., Péloquin, K., Duong, D.: Self-perceived burden in chronic pain: relevance, prevalence, and predictors. Pain **153**, 1735–1741 (2012). https://doi.org/10.1016/j.pain.2012.05.009
5. Irwin, A., Staff, I.A: Citizen Science: A Study of People, Expertise and Sustainable Development. Psychology Press (1995)
6. Law, E., et al.: The science of citizen science: theories, methodologies and platforms. In: Companion of the 2017 ACM Conference on Computer Supported Cooperative Work and Social Computing, pp. 395–400. ACM, Portland Oregon USA (2017). https://doi.org/10.1145/3022198.3022652
7. Oliveira, N., Jun, E., Reinecke, K.: Citizen Science Opportunities in Volunteer-Based Online Experiments. In: Proceedings of the 2017 CHI Conference on Human Factors in Computing Systems, pp. 6800–6812. ACM, Denver Colorado USA (2017). https://doi.org/10.1145/3025453.3025473
8. Furniss, D., Randell, R., O'Kane, A.A., Taneva, S.: Fieldwork for Healthcare: Guidance for Investigating Human Factors in Computing Systems. Morgan & Claypool Publishers (2014)
9. Koskinen, I., Zimmerman, J., Binder, T., Redstrom, J., Wensveen, S.: Design research through practice: from the lab, field, and showroom. IEEE Trans. Profess. Commun. **56**(3), 262–263 (2013). https://doi.org/10.1109/TPC.2013.2274109
10. Rogers, Y.: Interaction design gone wild: striving for wild theory. Interactions **18**(4), 58–62 (2011). https://doi.org/10.1145/1978822.1978834
11. Crabtree, A., et al.: Doing innovation in the wild. In: Proceedings of the Biannual Conference of the Italian Chapter of SIGCHI on - CHItaly '13, pp. 1–9. ACM Press, Trento, Italy (2013). https://doi.org/10.1145/2499149.2499150
12. Khatamian Far, P.: Challenges of recruitment and retention of university students as research participants: lessons learned from a pilot study. J. Aust. Libr. Inform. Assoc. **67**, 278–292 (2018). https://doi.org/10.1080/24750158.2018.1500436

13. Miller, K.W., Wilder, L.B., Stillman, F.A., Becker, D.M.: The feasibility of a street-intercept survey method in an African-American community. Am. J. Public Health **87**, 655–658 (1997). https://doi.org/10.2105/AJPH.87.4.655

14. Newington, L., Metcalfe, A.: Factors influencing recruitment to research: qualitative study of the experiences and perceptions of research teams. BMC Med. Res. Methodol. **14**, 10 (2014). https://doi.org/10.1186/1471-2288-14-10

15. Yancey, A.K., Ortega, A.N., Kumanyika, S.K.: Effective Recruitment And Retention Of Minority Research Participants. Annu. Rev. Public Health. **27**, 1–28 (2006). https://doi.org/10.1146/annurev.publhealth.27.021405.102113

16. Preece, J., Bowser, A.: What HCI can do for citizen science. In: CHI '14 Extended Abstracts on Human Factors in Computing Systems, pp. 1059–1060. ACM, Toronto Ontario Canada (2014). https://doi.org/10.1145/2559206.2590805

17. Cloudy with a chance of pain - Home, 26 January 2016 . https://www.cloudywithachanceofpain.com/. Last accessed 24 May 2022

18. Donetto, S., Pierri, P., Tsianakas, V., Robert, G.: Experience-based co-design and healthcare improvement: realizing participatory design in the public sector. Des. J. **18**, 227–248 (2015). https://doi.org/10.2752/175630615X14212498964312

19. Bjögvinsson, E., Ehn, P., Hillgren, P.-A.: Design things and design thinking: contemporary participatory design challenges. Des. Issues **28**, 101–116 (2012). https://doi.org/10.1162/DESI_a_00165

20. Hanington, B., Martin, B.: Universal Methods of Design: 100 Ways to Research Complex Problems, Develop Innovative Ideas, and Design Effective Solutions. Rockport Publishers (2012)

21. Holmes, K.: Mismatch: How Inclusion Shapes Design. The MIT Press (2018)

22. Newell, A.F., Gregor, P., Morgan, M., Pullin, G., Macaulay, C.: User-sensitive inclusive design. Univ. Access Inf. Soc. **10**, 235–243 (2011). https://doi.org/10.1007/s10209-010-0203-y

23. Laura Ramírez Galleguillos, M., Coşkun, A.: How do i matter? a review of the participatory design practice with less privileged participants. In: Proceedings of the 16th Participatory Design Conference 2020 - Participation(s) Otherwise, vol. 1. pp. 137–147. ACM, Manizales Colombia (2020). https://doi.org/10.1145/3385010.3385018

24. Warke, B., et al.: The Burden of Pain Symptoms: A prototype for citizens of British Columbia. In: PAINWeek Abstract Book 2019. Postgraduate Medicine, pp. 10–11

25. Melzack, R., Raja, S.N.: The McGill pain questionnaire. Anesthesiology **103**, 199–202 (2005). https://doi.org/10.1097/00000542-200507000-00028

26. World Organization of National Colleges, Academies, and Academic Associations of General Practitioners/Family Physicians ed: ICPC-2: international classification of primary care. Oxford University Press, Oxford , New York (1998)

27. World Health Organization: International classification of functioning, disability and health: ICF. World Health Organization, Geneva (2001)

28. Scarry, E.: The Body in Pain: The Making and Unmaking of the World. Oxford Paperbacks (1987)

29. Dennis, B.P., Neese, J.B.: Recruitment and retention of African American elders into community-based research: lessons learned. Arch. Psychiatr. Nurs. **14**, 3–11 (2000). https://doi.org/10.1016/S0883-9417(00)80003-5

30. Central City - 102 Ave & King George Blvd, https://centralcity.ca/home-2-2/. Last accessed 26 May 2022

31. Chamberlain, A., Crabtree, A., Rodden, T., Jones, M., Rogers, Y.: Research in the wild: understanding "in the wild" approaches to design and development. In: Proceedings of the Designing Interactive Systems Conference on - DIS '12. p. 795. ACM Press, Newcastle Upon Tyne, United Kingdom (2012). https://doi.org/10.1145/2317956.2318078

32. Schlögl, S., Buricic, J., Pycha, M.: Wearables in the wild: advocating real-life user studies. In: Proceedings of the 17th International Conference on Human-Computer Interaction with Mobile Devices and Services Adjunct, pp. 966–969. ACM, Copenhagen Denmark (2015). https://doi.org/10.1145/2786567.2794312

33. Wolcott, H.F.: Transforming Qualitative Data: Description, Analysis, and Interpretation. SAGE (1994)

34. Creswell, J.W., Poth, C.N.: Qualitative Inquiry & Research Design: Choosing Among Five Approaches. SAGE, Los Angeles (2018)

35. Government of Canada, I.A.P. on R.E.: Tri-Council Policy Statement: Ethical Conduct for Research Involving Humans – TCPS 2 (2018) – Chapter 2: Scope and Approach, 23 September 2019. https://ethics.gc.ca/eng/tcps2-eptc2_2018_chapter2-chapitre2.html. Last accessed 24 May 2022

36. Do I Require Ethics Approval? 28 January 2022. http://www.sfu.ca/research/researcher-res ources/ethics-human-research/do-i-require-ethics-approval. Last accessed 24 May 2022

Detecting Depression, Anxiety and Mental Stress in One Sequential Model with Multi-task Learning

Shen Zhang[1,2], Mei Tu[2(✉)], Yueru Yan[2,3], Yimeng Zhuang[2], Likun Ge[4], and Gaoxia Wei[4]

[1] School of Software, Beihang University, Beijing, China
zhangshen95726@buaa.edu.cn
[2] Samsung Research China-Beijing (SRC-B), Beijing, China
{mei.tu,ym.zhuang}@samsung.com
[3] School of Statistics, Beijing Normal University, Beijing, China
202122011155@mail.bnu.edu.cn
[4] CAS Key Lab of Behavioral Science, Institute of Psychology, Beijing, China
{gelk,weigx}@psych.ac.cn

Abstract. Recent studies employing mobile data to detect psychological disorders have made great progress. Mobile devices record user's behavior data and physical signals continuously. Such data are able to detect symptoms of mental disorders like depression, anxiety and stress via machine learning models. However, existing researches mainly focus on independently detecting one of these disorders, ignoring the symptom relationship among them. Besides, current studies using statistical features accumulated in a period of time lose the time correlation within data, which makes it difficult to predict future symptoms. Instead, in this paper, we firstly propose a parameter sharing model with multi-task learning to transfer the common representation of three symptoms of mental disorders, and we use biRNN approach to predict these disorders by using mobile sequential features. We obtain 175 participants completing collection for at least 2 weeks with weekly questionnaire. In the experiments, our proposed sharing model achieves average overall accuracy of 0.78 and average AUC of 0.78, outperforming three single-task model and machine learning methods that use statistical features significantly. These results suggest that multi-task learning with the sequential feature enables detecting severity of depression, anxiety and stress symptoms.

Keywords: Depression detection · Anxiety detection · Stress detection · Parameter sharing

1 Introduction

Depression, anxiety and excessive mental stress are three common symptoms of mental disorders in modern life, which threaten people's health and affect their

---

S. Zhang—This work was done during intership in SRC-Beijing.

work and quality of life heavily. It is estimated that 350 million people suffer from depression worldwide [32], and anxiety disorders are affecting 40 million adults in the United States age 18 and older, or 18.1 of the population every year [2]. In the first year of the COVID-19 pandemic, global prevalence of anxiety and depression increased by a massive 25 [33].

Existing studies that employ behavior features to detect symptoms of mental disorders, including depression, anxiety and stress have achieved promising results [1,4,7,9,16,18,21,24,26,27]. Typically, such studies extract behavior features or physical signals from mobile devices and wearable bands, and then detect the symptoms of mental disorder the participants may have via machine learning methods. However, previous detection work only focus on symptoms of one of these disorders, seldom considering the correlation between depression, anxiety and mental stress. As different types of mental disorders in conceptual-level, anxiety and depression share a significant nonspecific component encompassing general affective distress and other common symptoms [8]. And people who suffer from the symptoms of anxiety are also prone to depression [19]. Taken into consideration of the latent mechanism between the three symptoms of mental disorders, predicting these three types of disorder simultaneously ensures a more comprehensive understanding of our mental health.

This study aims to detect three symptoms of mental disorders-depression, anxiety and mental stress-simultaneously by using sequential data collected from mobile phones. We propose to learn a multi-task model based on the hypothesis that depression, anxiety and mental stress are strongly correlated. To the best of our knowledge, our work is the first to explore a multi-task framework for mental disorders prediction.

2   Related Work

2.1   Depression, Anxiety and Stress Detection

Some work has shown promising results in this area [1,4,7,9,16,18,21,24,26,27] and various machine learning methods have been constructed to enhance prediction performance in depression, anxiety and stress detection, such as logistic regression [10], SVM [6,10,24,28], DT [6,24,28], random forest [10,21,24] and MLP [6,36]. By adopting various machine learning classification algorithms, researchers found that people with depression have fewer saved contacts and spend more time on mobile devices to make and receive fewer and shorter calls [25]. In an exploratory study, the circadian movement, normalized entropy, location variance, phone usage duration and phone usage frequency were found to be correlated with depressive symptoms severity [26]. Considering emotion is continuous and easy to change, a research utilized smartphone sensor data gathered within the context of daily life to predict momentary anxiety with a deep learning model by adopting LSTM as the minimum neural units [15].

However, few studies has been conducted using bi-directional RNN to fully utilize the sequential data. This research shows that biRNN model outperforms traditional algorithms, like SVM and Random-Forest in detection depression, anxiety and stress.

2.2 Multi-task Learning

Multi-task learning (MTL) is an approach to improve the generalization by leveraging multiple related tasks information [5]. Some studies based on a priori knowledge of task relevance [12,23] show that superiority in using features of similar tasks to achieve prediction of each task in parallel. Optimal multitasking methods on different datasets need to be explored [3,13,34,35]. Although depression, anxiety and stress are related tasks, the prediction of depression, anxiety and stress in parallel has not been fully studied. In this paper, we compare soft parameter structure and hard parameter structure in symptoms of mental disorders prediction.

3   Methods

3.1   Date Collection and Preprocessing

We recruited 256 adult participants from December 2021 to March 2022. Participants were asked to keep the smart phone and wristband throughout the day for at least 2 weeks. The following features were collected from participants including: (1)mobile usage information: app usage frequency, app usage time, entertainment and social app usage frequency, entertainment and social app usage time, SMS amount, phone usage frequency, phone usage time, incoming phone calls, dialing phone calls, incoming phone calls time, dialing phone calls time, phone calls from acquaintances, phone calls from acquaintances time (2)diet information: diet frequency, calorie intake (3)sleeping information: deep sleeping time, shallow sleeping time, wake up time between 11pm. and 7am., sleeping time (4)moving behaviour information: distance, steps, walking time, running time, running distance, calorie-consumption (5)location information: location variance [26], number of different places.

During the study, participants were asked to complete the Depression Anxiety and Stress Scale-21 [22] (DASS-21) questionnaire every 4 to 7 days which is used to measure depression, anxiety, and stress symptom severity. The scoring criteria are shown in the Table 1. For each task, we regard it as a binary classification. Participants will be labelled as 0 if he or she is classified as Normal via DASS-21, otherwise will be labelled as 1.

3.2   Sequential Samples

Based on the submission date of DASS-21, we collected the features of that day and the previous four consecutive days (see Fig. 1). Features of each day are described in Sect. 3.1. If some a feature is not correctly collected or the feature is blank due to problems such as device connection or participant's personal

Table 1. Severity levels

Level	Depression	Anxiety	Stress
Normal	0–9	0–7	0–14
Mild	10–13	8–9	15–18
Moderate	14–20	10–14	19–25
Severe	21–27	15–19	26–33
Extremely severe	28+	20+	33+

reasons, we treat the feature as an invalid feature. For those samples that are not complied with the validness of features, we drop them in the training data. Finally, we get 263 sequential samples.

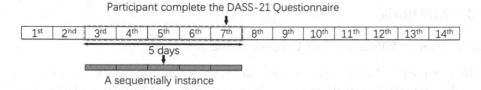

Fig. 1. Sequentially samples collection

3.3 Multi-task BiRNN

In this work, we employ bidirectional recurrent neural network (biRNN) as a base structure for detection model. biRNN is widely used in many sequential classification tasks. It is able to capture the sequential information from forward and backward direction. As the behavior features are sequentially connected, it is natural to utilize RNN model to extract high-level behavior features.

Moreover, as we know the symptoms of depression, anxiety and stress are tightly connected, the behavior features that represent depressive symptoms also likely present anxiety, such as sleep disorder. This inspires us to share model parameters among multiple detection tasks.

In multi-task learning, different branches are usually used to solve specific tasks [5]. Figure 2(b) and (c) illustrates overview of our multi-task biRNN structures, which are two types of modeling sharing. They have the same inputs and three outputs. These inputs are fully connected to four hidden layers(Dense 1.1–1.4) which connect to a shared biRNN. The biRNN connects to three separate hidden layers. Before the output layers, we add a hidden layer Dense and sigmoid activation function in the output layer for each task. Figure 2(a) shows a single task structure with only one output.

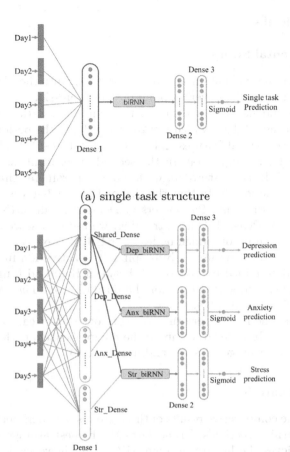

(a) single task structure

(b) soft sharing structure

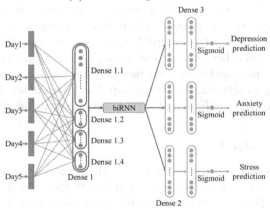

(c) hard sharing structure

Fig. 2. Models structure

4   Experiments

4.1   Experimental Setup

The ratio of training, validation and testing data against the all data set is of 0.6:0.2:0.2, and use random oversampling on the depression label. The balance rate of positive and negative samples in the validation data and test data is consistent with original data, which is 0.25. To evaluate the performance of prediction between sequential features and statistical features, LR, MLP, SVM, DT and RF are used for comparison. In the second experiment, single task models are considered. In the last group, we use a soft parameter sharing structure for multi-task prediction. Note that the size of Dense 1.1–1.4 is 7:3:3:3 in hard parameter sharing structure. Parameters of Dense 2 in all biRNN structure is twice than those of Dense 3. During training, we use grid search for the architecture with the number of hidden nodes 32, 64, 128. Next, we choose 0.001 as the initial learning rate and use earlystopping. The activation function for each hidden layer is determined by grid search between Relu and tanh. In addition, to avoid overfitting, dropout is used for the optimization. The search space for dropout rate is 0.2, 0.3, 0.4, 0.5.

For each task, the model performance score on test set can be measured by F1 score and AUC. In order to compare the comprehensive performance in the three tasks, we use average F1 score and average AUC.

4.2   Model Analysis

Table 2 shows the comparative results of three groups of experiments. Among the five machine learning methods, RF achieves the highest average F1-score(0.71) while MLP achieves the highest average AUC(0.58), however, both were lower than the performance of single biRNN (best avg. F1=0.76, best avg. AUC=0.74). Using time-series data for prediction increases the amount of training data, and we believe that the time-series information enhances the prediction performance. The result, that the comprehensive performance of hard parameter sharing biRNN model is better than that of single biRNN, proves what is learned for single task can improve the performance of other tasks. Compared to the soft parameter sharing structure in the last group, hard parameter sharing structure is more suitable for the prediction of depression, anxiety and stress severity.

4.3   Samples Analysis

Although the experimental results show that the comprehensive performance of the multi-task structure is better, we would like to know on which samples the multi-task model performs better than the single-task model. Table 3 demonstrates the performance of three single task models and multi-task models on the test set. The test set contains four types of samples((Depression label = 0, Anxiety label = 0, Stress label = 0) (Depression label = 0, Anxiety label = 1, Stress label = 0) (Depression label = 1, Anxiety label = 1, Stress label = 0) (Depression

Table 2. Comparative result

	Dep acc	Anx acc	Str acc	Avg. f1	Avg. AUC
LR	0.65	0.57	0.63	0.62	0.56
SVM	0.57	0.55	0.57	0.56	0.53
MLP	0.67	0.67	0.67	0.67	0.58
DT	0.60	0.55	0.65	0.60	0.50
RF	0.72	0.63	0.78	0.71	0.55
Single biRNN(best avg. F1)	0.77	0.70	0.82	0.76	0.66
Single biRNN(best avg. AUC)	0.57	**0.75**	0.77	0.69	0.74
Soft parameter sharing biRNN	0.77	0.68	0.75	0.73	0.77
Hard parameter sharing biRNN	**0.82**	0.70	**0.82**	**0.78**	**0.78**

label = 1, Anxiety label = 1, Stress label = 1)). The multitask model outperforms the single task model in prediction on the samples with the same labels, which is consistent with the premise that the multi-task model is applicable to the related tasks.

Table 3. Samples analysis

Participants labels(D, A, S)	Amount	Single	Soft sharing	Hard sharing
0,1,0	5	2	0	0
1,1,0	2	0	0	0
0,0,0	39	26	35	32
1,1,1	14	3	1	5

4.4 Hyperparameter Analysis

In this section, we mainly discuss the hyper-parameters in our model. We varied our best model in different ways, measuring the change in performance on testing data. The hyper-parameters consists of (A)b_s: batch size; (B)d_1, d_{biRNN}, d_2, d_3: dimension of Dense 1, biRNN, Dense 2 and Dense 3; (C)dropout; (D)act_1, act_2, act_3: the activation function of Dense 1, Dense 2 and Dense 3. In our experiments, d_3 is equal to d_{biRNN}. These results are presented in Table 4.

In Table 4 rows Hard sharing(7-3-3-3)(A), we vary the number of batch size to observe the result. While batch size = 4 is 0.9 avg.f1 and 0.9 avg.AUC worse than the best setting, quality also drops off with too large batch size. In Table 4 rows Hard sharing(7-3-3-3)(B), we observe that increasing the dense1, dense2, biRNN nodes which hurts model quality. We further observe in rows Hard sharing(7-3-3-3)(C) that, as expected, dropout is helpful in avoiding over-fitting, and 0.2 is better. In rows Hard sharing(7-3-3-3)(D) we replace our activation function with Relu, and observe worse results in this group. Finally we observe varied model

Table 4. Hyperparameter Analysis

		b_s	d_1	act_1	d_{biRNN}	Dropout	d_2	act_2	d_3	act_3	Avg.f1	Avg.AUC
Hard (7-3-3-3)	Best	8	32	tanh	16	0.2	64	tanh	16	tanh	**0.78**	**0.78**
	(A)	4	32	tanh	16	0.2	64	tanh	16	tanh	0.69	0.69
		16	32	tanh	16	0.2	64	tanh	16	tanh	0.69	0.67
		32	32	tanh	16	0.2	64	tanh	16	tanh	0.69	0.67
	(B)	8	64	tanh	16	0.2	64	tanh	16	tanh	0.71	0.62
		8	128	tanh	16	0.2	64	tanh	16	tanh	0.66	0.62
		8	32	tanh	16	0.2	32	tanh	16	tanh	0.67	0.69
		8	32	tanh	32	0.2	128	tanh	32	tanh	0.62	0.61
		8	32	tanh	64	0.2	256	tanh	64	tanh	0.70	0.63
		8	32	tanh	128	0.2	512	tanh	128	tanh	0.70	0.62
	(C)	8	32	tanh	16	0.0	64	tanh	16	tanh	0.68	0.75
		8	32	tanh	16	0.3	64	tanh	16	tanh	0.69	0.68
		8	32	tanh	16	0.4	64	tanh	16	tanh	0.69	0.75
		8	32	tanh	16	0.5	64	tanh	16	tanh	0.74	0.71
	(D)	8	32	Relu	16	0.2	64	tanh	16	tanh	0.64	0.68
		8	32	tanh	16	0.2	64	Relu	16	tanh	0.68	0.59
		8	32	tanh	16	0.2	64	tanh	16	Relu	0.67	0.65
Hard (5-4-4-3)		8	32	tanh	16	0.2	64	tanh	16	tanh	0.72	0.71
		32	64	tanh	64	0.3	128	tanh	64	tanh	0.73	0.71
Soft (7-3-3-3)		8	32	tanh	16	0.2	64	tanh	16	tanh	0.72	0.75
		32	64	tanh	64	0.3	128	tanh	64	tanh	0.73	0.77

structures that hard sharing model, which the size of Dense 1.1–1.4 is 7:3:3:3 is superior to the other two model.

5   Conclusion

In this study, a multi-task sequential model that combines the hard parameter sharing structure and biRNN is proposed to achieve a superior prediction performance for three symptoms of mental disorders. The experimental results show that multi-task framework can be applied in the prediction of relevant mental tasks. Compared to statistical features, time sequential features perform better in this depression/anxiety/stress detection task. The future work will focus on using shorter sequential features for prediction. Lastly, our proposed method may be extended to other disorder detection.

References

1. Ahuja, R., Banga, A.: Mental stress detection in university students using machine learning algorithms. Procedia Comput. Sci. **152**, 349–353 (2019)
2. Anxiety and Depression Association of America (2021)

3. Bakker, B.J., Heskes, T.M.: Task clustering and gating for Bayesian multitask learning (2003)
4. Ben-Zeev, D., et al.: Next-generation psychiatric assessment: using smartphone sensors to monitor behavior and mental health. Psychiatric Rehab. J. **38**(3), 218 (2015)
5. Caruana, R.: Multitask learning. Mach. Learn. **28**(1), 41–75 (1997)
6. Chauhan, M., Shivani, V.V., Dipak, D.: Effective stress detection using physiological parameters. In: 2017 International Conference on Innovations in Information, Embedded and Communication Systems (ICIIECS). IEEE (2017)
7. Chikersal, P., et al.: Detecting depression and predicting its onset using longitudinal symptoms captured by passive sensing: a machine learning approach with robust feature selection. ACM Trans. Comput. Hum. Interact. (TOCHI) **28**(1), 1–41 (2021)
8. Clark, L.A., David, W.: Tripartite model of anxiety and depression: psychometric evidence and taxonomic implications. J. Abnormal Psychol. **100**(3), 316 (1991)
9. Doryab, A., et al.: Detection of behavior change in people with depression. In: Workshops at the Twenty-Eighth AAAI Conference on Artificial Intelligence (2014)
10. Egilmez, B., et al.: UStress: understanding college student subjective stress using wrist-based passive sensing. In: 2017 IEEE International Conference on Pervasive Computing and Communications Workshops (PerCom Workshops). IEEE (2017)
11. Daniel, E., Golberstein, E., Hunt, J.B.: Mental health and academic success in college. BE J. Econ. Anal. Policy **9**, 40 (2009)
12. Theodoros, E., Pontil, M.: Regularized multi-task learning. In: Proceedings of the Tenth ACM SIGKDD International Conference on Knowledge Discovery and Data Mining (2004)
13. Theodoros, E., et al.: Learning multiple tasks with kernel methods. J. Mach. Learn. Res. **6**(4), 615–637 (2005)
14. Ahmad, F.A., et al.: Behavior vs. introspection: refining prediction of clinical depression via smartphone sensing data. In: 2016 IEEE Wireless Health (WH). IEEE (2016)
15. Jacobson, N.C., Bhattacharya, S.: Digital biomarkers of anxiety disorder symptom changes: Personalized deep learning models using smartphone sensors accurately predict anxiety symptoms from ecological momentary assessments. Behav. Res. Therapy **149**, 104013 (2022)
16. Raghavendra, K., et al.: Associating internet usage with depressive behavior among college students. IEEE Technol. Soc. Mag. **31**(4), 73–80 (2012)
17. Kemeny, M.E.: The psychobiology of stress. Curr. Direct. Psychol. Sci. **12**(4), 124–129 (2003)
18. Canzian L., Musolesi, M.: Trajectories of depression: unobtrusive monitoring of depressive states by means of smartphone mobility traces analysis. In: Proceedings of the 2015 ACM International Joint Conference on Pervasive and Ubiquitous Computing, pp. 1293–1304. ACM (2015)
19. Andrea Feijo, M., et al.: Depression and stress: is there an endophenotype? Braz. J. Psychiatry **29**, s13–s18 (2007)
20. Miranda, D., Favela, J., Arnrich, B.: Detecting anxiety states when caring for people with dementia. Methods Inf. Med. **56**(01), 55–62 (2017)
21. Rajdeep Kumar, N., Thapliyal, H.: Machine learning-based anxiety detection in older adults using wristband sensors and context feature. SN Comput. Sci. **2**(5), 1–12 (2021)
22. Norton, P.J.: Depression anxiety and stress scales (DASS-21): psychometric analysis across four racial groups. Anxiety Stress Coping **20**(3), 253–265 (2007)

23. Shibin, P., Weinberger, K.Q.: Large margin multi-task metric learning. In: Advances in Neural Information Processing Systems, vol. 23 (2010)
24. Priya, A., Garg, S., Tigga, N.P.: Predicting anxiety, depression and stress in modern life using machine learning algorithms. Procedia Comput. Sci. **167**, 1258–1267 (2020)
25. Razavi, R., Gharipour, A., Gharipour, M.: Depression screening using mobile phone usage metadata: a machine learning approach. J. Am. Med. Inf. Assoc. **27**(4), 522–530 (2020)
26. Sohrab, S., et al.: Mobile phone sensor correlates of depressive symptom severity in daily-life behavior: an exploratory study. J. Med. Internet Res. **17**(7), e4273 (2015)
27. Sohrab, S., et al.: The relationship between mobile phone location sensor data and depressive symptom severity. PeerJ **4**, e2537 (2016)
28. Sun, F.-T., Kuo, C., Cheng, H.-T., Buthpitiya, S., Collins, P., Griss, M.: Activity-aware mental stress detection using physiological sensors. In: Gris, M., Yang, G. (eds.) MobiCASE 2010. LNICST, vol. 76, pp. 211–230. Springer, Heidelberg (2012). https://doi.org/10.1007/978-3-642-29336-8_12
29. Fabian, W., et al.: Mobile sensing and support for people with depression: a pilot trial in the wild. JMIR mHealth uHealth **4**(3), e5960 (2016)
30. Wang, R., et al.: StudentLife: assessing mental health, academic performance and behavioral trends of college students using smartphones. In: Proceedings of the 2014 ACM International Joint Conference on Pervasive and Ubiquitous Computing (2014)
31. Wang, R., et al.: Tracking depression dynamics in college students using mobile phone and wearable sensing. Proc. ACM Interact. Mobile Wearable Ubiquitous Technol. **2**(1), 1–26 (2018)
32. World Health Organization. World health statistics 2010. World Health Organization (2010)
33. World Health Organization. Mental health and COVID-19: early evidence of the pandemic's impact: scientific brief. Mental health and COVID-19: early evidence of the pandemic's impact: scientific brief, 2 March 2022 (2022)
34. Zhang, Y., Yang, Q.: A survey on multi-task learning. IEEE Trans. Knowl. Data Eng. (2021)
35. Zhong, W., Kwok, J.: Convex multitask learning with flexible task clusters. arXiv preprint arXiv:1206.4601 (2012)
36. Pamela, Z., et al.: Stress detection through electrodermal activity (EDA) and electrocardiogram (ECG) analysis in car drivers. In: 2019 27th European Signal Processing Conference (EUSIPCO). IEEE (2019)

The Impact of Virtual Reality Toward Telemedicine: A Qualitative Study

Fan Zhao[1(✉)], Dustin Sochacki[1(✉)], Jonathan Witenko[2(✉)], and Rachel Kogan[1]

[1] Florida Gulf Coast University, Fort Myers, FL 33965, USA
fzhao@fgcu.edu, rbrener5198@eagle.fgcu.edu
[2] Lee Health, Fort Myers, FL 33991, USA

Abstract. Telemedicine is quickly becoming an essential asset in the healthcare industry today. After COVID, the combination of virtual reality (VR) technology and telemedicine is quickly becoming a safe and effective solution for patients. Despite the advantages of employing VR in medical education and treatment, various problems and limits lead to the technology's ineffectiveness or misuse. As a result, addressing potential problems associated with VR could be beneficial in the strategic decision-making process for implementing and developing this technology in the healthcare industry. This research used case study method to identify current issues of VR technology adoption at a large US hospital system. The findings of this qualitative study explore potential concerns and limitations of current VR technology. Suggestions and insights are highlighted to benefit researchers and practitioners.

Keywords: Virtual reality · Health care · Telemedicine

1 Introduction

Today, national health sectors have an ever-increasing set of costs attributable to the growing shortage of doctors and nurses relative to the general population. The increase of life expectancy concurrently raises the costs of medical care by an estimated 3% to total costs for each year of life expectancy [1]. In addition, due to increases in information and technology, patients have a greater detection of diseases. All these factors contribute to the need for a better system for doctors to interact with their patients.

Medicine is a data-rich enterprise and changing health care infrastructure from traditional paper-based medical records into an electronic health record and is a way to help optimize care in a way to make it accessible wherever and whenever it is required through telemedicine [2].

An increase in care and accessibility is vital for all people, especially those who suffer from chronic disease. Some 50 percent of patients living in the U.S. have one or more chronic diseases, which accounts for two-thirds of the health care system's financial burden [3]. Telemedicine is helpful for those with chronic, long-term conditions, as they are often required to visit doctor's offices more often and for more extended periods. There are also more in-depth care plans to follow, which need continuous updating.

© Springer Nature Switzerland AG 2022
V. G. Duffy et al. (Eds.): HCII 2022, LNCS 13521, pp. 201–214, 2022.
https://doi.org/10.1007/978-3-031-17902-0_15

A 2010 study also showed that patients using telemedicine were more participatory in managing their care [4].

Further care and accessibilities needs lie within the rural areas of the United States. Thirty-four of South Dakota's counties are classified as frontier, having populations of less than six people per square mile [5]. Ruralism hinders the patients' access to care and the caregiver's access to patients. Patients in rural communities often don't have access to doctors who have specialized expertise for a particular ailment a patient might have but cannot get access to. As such, it is difficult for both providers and patients to meet in a formal care setting. Telemedicine can bridge the gap. However, data from 4,727 facilities in Iowa showed that two-thirds of the rural hospitals did not offer any telemedicine services in 2014 [5]. Therefore, there is still a long way to go in this regard.

Using telemedicine also has an economic advantage. A study conducted with Parkinson's disease patients through the Veterans Health Administration was able to save 1,500 travel hours. Of which included 100,000 km of travel and over $37,000 USB in travel and lodging costs for 34 patients through 100 follow-up visits from those patients [6].

Computer-generated visuals and material are trying to replicate a real presence through sensory capabilities; medical experts create and apply this technology for training, diagnosis, and virtual therapy during a critical crisis [7]. VR has prompted a lot of discussion in the field of computer science. As a cutting-edge computer simulation system, Virtual reality (VR) technology has advanced tremendously in scientific study, education, and our daily life. The ability to use VR to augment health care services for clinical settings gives advantages over traditional processes. Those processes are clinical care and health education [8].

VR would have a net positive impact on patients in clinical care because of the increase of immersion of the medium [9]. As there have already been successful results on lesser mediums in regards to telemedicine (such as e-mail and apps), increasing the immersion will only increase patient engagement [8]. For health education, VR would be able to facilitate a deeper understanding of health systems to students learning within the field. By using a VR headset, the student would be able to maneuver around virtual cadavers and possibly even be able to complete dissection.

Numeric research articles have explained the potential applications of VR in health care and telemedicine [10, 11]. However, few of them describe the current issues and problems from a real scenario of the hospital perspective when adopting VR in telemedicine. This study tries to identify some potential issues of VR adoptions in telemedicine and give suggestions to the future directions to researchers and practitioners.

2 Literature Review

2.1 Immersive Technology

Immersive technology was introduced over half-decade ago by researchers in human-computer Interaction [12]. According to a generic definition by Milgram and Kishin [13], immersive technology includes three unique technologies such as augmented reality (AR), augmented virtuality, and virtual reality (VR). Augmented reality and augmented virtuality together were named mixed reality (see Fig. 1 for the reality-virtuality continuum). Researchers are currently more likely to define augmented virtuality as Mixed reality, whereas AR is the fusion of real and virtual environments.

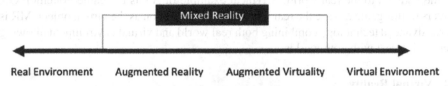

Real Environment   Augmented Reality   Augmented Virtuality   Virtual Environment

Fig. 1. Reality-virtually continuum (Milgram and Kishino 1994).

Computer-based simulation technology, such as VR, plays an important role in current higher education. VR has been described as the learning and education supportive technology of the new century [14]. VR uses graphic systems combined with various interface devices to give the effect immersion in an interactive virtual environment [15]. Presence in a virtual environment gives users a feeling of being in a virtually mediated location similar to the real location. Users' feeling or sense of this presence is a critical factor linking their perceptions, intentions and actions in the virtual environment. The level of this presence determines the engagement of the users in the VR. VR technology has a variety of unique properties along with different terms that users are utilizing. From dimensional perspective, it could be 2D, 3D VR technology. From immersive perspective, it could be non-immersive or immersive technology. From image or animation

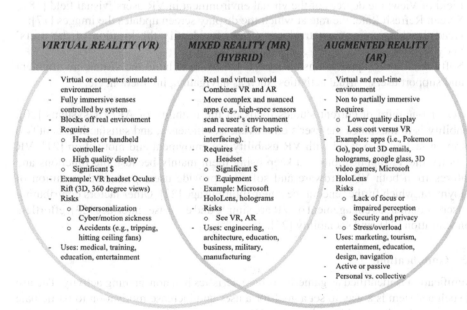

Fig. 2. Comparison of VR, AR, and MR [9]

perspective, it could be AR, VR, and Mixed Reality (MR). Figure 2 shows the differences among the three technologies. Along with VR, there are two other similar technologies named AR and MR. In both AR and MR, real world is not isolated but mixed with the virtual world. In AR, users mainly interact with the real world and the virtual objects are the adds-on to the real world. A typical example of AR is the game Pokemon Go. Players of this game can see the real world plus the Pokemon as the virtual object. MR is more advanced technology combining both real world and virtual environment allowing users to interact with both worlds.

2.2 Virtual Reality

Immersion is a new term in VR describing the level of users' involvement experiences in the virtual environment [14]. Immersive VR (IVR) technology tends to "disconnect"users from the real world and replace the real world with the virtual world created in the virtual environment. **From** a user's perspective, immersive VR excludes the physical real world and provides an isolated perception of his/her sense from the reality by changing surrounding environment [16]. The typical immersive VR is mediated through head mounted displays (HMD), such as HTC glasses or Oculus Rift, allowing users to experience the desired degree of immersion. Combining with dimensions of VR, the effectiveness of 2D immersive VR can only show images and 2D videos to the users which is lack of depth perception. Therefore, current trend of VR technology is to adopt 3D technology with immersion giving users more realistic and immersive feelings in the virtual world. Additional VR technology includes the following characteristics:

- Screen Resolution: number of pixels the VR glass screen displays per frame [17];
- Field of View: the degrees of the virtual environment in VR users' visual field [18];
- Screen Refresh Rate: the rate at which the display screen updates the images [17];
- Head Tracking: movement tracking system to identify the location of the users' body[19];
- Software for VR: applications utilize VR hardware to build the virtual environment and support users' virtual activities, such as navigation, interaction, etc.

Over one-third of current studies focus on the usability of AR/VR systems [20]. Usability is to maximize the user's effectiveness, efficiency, and satisfaction, andtTwo common factors associated with VR usability are enjoyment and motivation [21]. VR users try the VR applications and keep using them mainly because the functions and features from both VR hardware and software provide users perceived cognition of enjoyment, which further encourages their future usage [22]. Other factors contributing to users' continuous engagement of VR are simple and easy user interface [23], effortless concentration [24], and sociability [25].

2.3 Gamification

Gamification is identified as game-like characteristics in a non-gaming activity. The use of such a system is a way to set a goal for a user and increase motivation to participate in a series of tasks to achieve that goal. There are seven advantages of gamification for health and well-being [26]:

- Intrinsic motivation: inherited from game design, gamified system evokes users' intrinsic motivation;
- Broad accessibility: with the populations of mobile games, users can adopt gamified systems not only from computers but also from all other mobile devices;
- Broad appeal: gamified systems are attracting wider populations other than just young people;
- Broad applicability: gamified systems were adopted to treat multiple health risks covering from physical activity, diet management, and rehabilitation, to cancer;
- Cost-benefit efficiency: gamified systems can be efficiently engaged in the current health system as the health treatment methods with lower cost and scalable development design;
- Everyday life fit: gamified systems can be utilized, adopted, and tracked easily in patients' daily life with mobile devices;
- Supporting well-being: the positive perceived feelings generated from gamified systems, such as enjoyment, satisfaction, and other positive emotions, can directly contribute to patients' well-being health.

More and more gamification applications have been applied with VR applications [27, 28]. In the field of healthcare, gamification can help patients increase their motivation to hit their goals to see the best possible outcomes for their recovery [26].

2.4   VR Applications in Telemedicine

Pedagogical use of VR simulations has been adopted in various education areas such as healthcare [29–31], construction [32], military [33], and other higher education majors [34–36] to improve training effectiveness and avoid potential training risks. The success of VR applications in education depends on the users' feeling of "sense of presence", which gives the users a "real world" sensation and deceives the users' feeling on human behavioral parameters with the effects of 3D immersive environment [37]. In recent years, VR technology shows overwhelming advantages in training programs and education, such as schedule flexibility by self-learning, not limited to certain training locations, repeatedly and individually experiment practices, etc. [38–40]. It becomes an innovative method to provide a unique educational supplement to the in-class lectures and strengthen the students' inquired-based learning experiences, especially in laboratory education [41].

Recent studies have explored the potential to apply VR gamification in health care, especially telemedicine [27, 41]. For example, in telemedicine, one of the powerful ways a patient can deal with past trauma is through a powerful technological intervention known as Avatar Therapy [42]. Avatar therapy is utilized in the form of telemedicine through virtual environments. These environments are used as a safe space in which patients can work through interpersonal troubles, trauma caused by past events, and understand emotions that certain situations may be caused by the virtual experience [43]. In a post COVID-19 pandemic situation, rehabilitation for regular patients has had to adapt to give those patients the care they need and keep them safe from infection in a healthcare environment from those with spreadable infection. At-home rehabilitation was the obvious solution. In the case of post-stroke elderly patients using VR systems to help in their at-home rehabilitation has been a major tool to keep them safe at home while getting the care that they need [44]. Table 1 lists some recents studies with VR gamification in health care.

Table 1. Recent studies with VR gamification in health care.

Medical area	Applications	References
Virtual surgery	Dentistry oral surgery; Provide surgery at different locations;	[45, 46]
Planning of operation	Plan for surgical treatment	[47, 48]
Diagnosis	Chronic obstructive pulmonary; Identify breathing problems; Track body movement data; Track and save health data;	[49–51]
Rehabilitation	Virtual rehabilitation environment	[52, 53]
Education & Training	Anatomical education; Cardiovascular system cardiology; Emergency medicine; Gastroenterology Hepatology; Neurosciences Neurology; Orthopedics; Otorhinolaryngology; Practice surgical procedure; Urology nephrology	[46, 54–61]
Respiratory system	Biofeedback in affective computing and VR solutions for health and wellness	[62]
Acoustics	Virtual Acoustic interventions	[63]
Psychiatry	VR therapy in the management of dis orders associated with child and adole cence psychiatry	[64]
Physical therapy	Virtual exercise; Improve efficiency of psychotherapy	[65]
Mental illness	Low-cost and safe virtual treatment	[66]
Pain relief	Reduce Limb pain; Reduce trauma pain	[67, 68]
Reduce depression	Virtual environment to treat depression	[69]

VR gamification gives trainees a safe place to polish their skills and offer patients better treatment without harm [68]. Many health care facilities have adopted it for the satisfaction of both medical staff and patients. As such [70], VR technology brings medical training programs with the following advantages:

• It can simulate complex environments to test different innovative ideas repeatedly;

- Training programs can ignore geographical and time constraints that trainees can practice their skills with VR any time anywhere;
- It collects all the training performance data about trainees, and trainer's can review the data and give appropriate feedback.

Javaid and Haleem [11] also summarize some VR benefits in the medical field (Fig. 3). VR provides a powerful platform to support the improvement of current telemedicine development.

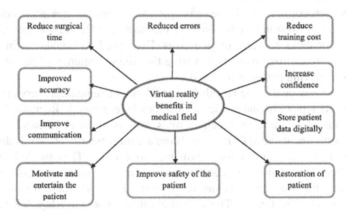

Fig. 3. VR benefits

3 Case Description

This research adopts a case study method to collect data and discuss the research question. We conducted several in-depth interviews with Mr. Jonathan Witenko, the System Director of Virtual Health & Telemedicine at Lee Health. Lee Health was founded in 1916 and governed by a publicly elected 10-member Board of Directors. Lee Health is one of the largest public health systems in the U.S. and one of the largest not-for-profit public health systems and Safety Net Hospital in Florida that receives no direct tax support. There are more than 1.5 million patient contacts each year in Lee Health. It has four acute care hospitals and more than 14,000 employees with 750+ primary and specialty care physicians and advanced practitioners in 80- + practice locations throughout Southwest Florida. Lee Health owns several special hospitals and centers. Golisano Children's Hospital of Southwest Florida is a 134-bed pediatric hospital opened in 1994 within HealthPark Medical Center. With new 7-story facility opened in 2017, it is the only comprehensive children's hospital with Level II and Level III Neonatal Intensive Care Units between Tampa and Miami. The Rehabilitation Hospital has a 60-bed comprehensive inpatient rehabilitation facility located within Lee Memorial Hospital.

Mr. Witenko has been working with Lee Health for over 10 years and is currently the director in charge of both telemedicine and virtual Health. Speaking with Jon gave us the opportunity to understand first-hand the real-world applications of telemedicine and VR with the challenges Lee Health is facing to.

Lee Health's first implementation of telemedicine was in 2014, when the technology was identified as a possible solution to an urgent care problem. The problem was that possible stroke patients needed to be seen by a neurologist as soon as possible so a visual diagnosis could be performed, and an anti-stroke medication could be prescribed. With only one neurologist on duty at Lee Health, it could take hours for the doctor to get to the patient. After adopting telemedicine at Lee Health, a doctor would be able to connect to the patient within minutes. Using video conferencing technology, doctors performed the requisite visual diagnosis and prescribed the medication if needed, getting the patient treatment much sooner than before.

This new protocol not only helped save patients' lives, but it was also cheaper for the patients. The downside to this adoption was that Lee Health was not able to bill the insurance for these non-face-to-face visits. Even so, Lee Health continued to use telemedicine to treat stroke patients, realizing that the expediency of patient care was paramount to receiving payment for a bill.

Over the last few years, Lee Health further adopted telemedicine services for additional urgent care situations and inside the hospitals in its network. Recently, Lee Health started their VR applications in three programs. One is in the children's hospital. Lee Health has a department called Child Life. There are three treatments in this department, including music therapy, distraction treatment, and gaming. They use VR technology to help children distract from pain and recover from their surgeries. The results was obviously better that the use of movies on the iPad. However, there was no statistical data support for the benefits yet. The second application was to adopt VR technology in the addiction unit at Lee Health. Patients play VR games to reduce the pain from the addiction. The unit reported that patients were able to focus and actually lowered their recovery time from six days to four days. The last one is for physical therapy. Patients completed their exercises in a virtual environment to shorten their surgery recovery, stroke recovery, etc. Doctors stated that this program was very helpful. However, since Lee Health just started this physical theropy program, there was insufficient data to statistically support this conclusion.

4 Case Analysis and Discussion

The main purpose of adopting VR technology in the health sector is to improve various medical treatments effectively and efficiently. To recognize the opportunities and challenges of VR, we need to consider all groups involved in this technology application, such as VR manufacturers, software developers, patients, and medical workers including doctors, nurses, and clinical IT employees.

4.1 VR Hardware

Current VR technology is still at its early stage. There are several issues with the hardware of VR technology. First, as we mentioned in the literature review, the usability of current VR technology does not fully satisfy patients' requirements [7]. Most of the current VR devices were designed based on technology-oriented approaches, making learning and usage complex and difficult [70, 71]. The need for user-friendly VR applications requires a user-centered design with both technology and user perspectives.

Mr. Witenko emphasized that "People just could affordable from body perspective, only less than 30 min, which means, I think that one of the purposes of gaming is to let the user or end users engaged with the game and so forgot about the time or distracted from everything else. But if you only give them 30 min, that's not typically long enough for many medical treatments." Side effects have been reported as one of the most significant issues of current VR technology [72, 73]. As the second issue from VR technology, the short-term side effects include nausea, vomiting, eye fatigue, dizziness, ataxia, etc. These symptoms were summarized as cybersickness which is due to the conflict between patients' body sensory inputs, such as visual and body movement [74]. The long-term side effects include situational instability, turbulent movements, perceptual-motor disorders, sleepiness, decreased stimuli, etc. These symptoms were addressed as perceptuomotor after-effects which is due to delays in the readaptation of the patients' sensory and motor system after frequent body adaptions/adjustments in a virtual environment [75].

4.2 VR Software

According to Mr. Witenko, VR technology showed slightly better results to distract children from their surgeries. "We used VR glasses, and they've done the same thing as before that we give the kids an iPad as they're going to surgery, and their outcomes are better just because they're not thinking about, oh, my goodness, I'm going to have surgery. There's nothing magical about the VR software." From the interview, we notice that current VR software development does not satisfy the requirements of both health care providers and patients. Health care providers want varieties of VR games. Mr. Witenko pointed out that, currently in the Children's Hopital, since there is only one short VR game, "patients just feel cool at the beginning, but this feeling disappeared quickly and no further help to distract patients from the game for enough time." Therefore, VR software providers should develop enough games to fit in requirements of various medical treatments with multiple scenarios.

Additionally, the feeling of presence in current VR devices is still different far from reality [7], which significantly reduced patients' immersive perceptions in the virtual environments. To give patients more immersive feelings in the virtual environment, as Mr. Witenko stated, the VR software should be able to show the game "in a fully interactive and close-to-real environment." With this essential feature, "VR should be more helpful because it's emerging the users in a different environment. So if they're watching a movie with an iPad, they're still be possible to be distracted by somewhere outside the movies. But in the VR world, you kind of closed and you're more easily concentrated. Yeah, because it's engaging. It's not just a passive, you've got to be an active participant in the virtual world."

Thirdly, Mr. Witenko emphasized that he could not find a VR software vendor who could provide him with useful and effective games fulfilling any of his treatment requirements. "I understand that there are some VR games that could guide you to fishing or golf or whatever, but for the hospital, for the kids, which game you use to distract them, or did you try different games? Or you just use the one type of game or you ask the kids to choose three different options, and I don't even find out what the software is. So the challenge was the guy who was running it left, and so the new guy who's picking it up hasn't even started on it. So it's been this gap of knowledge." The collaborations between the software vendors and health care providers are needed to provide more professional and effective VR games for patients.

Lastly, the current VR market is chaotic with multiple hardware, software, standards, and settings. Just like Mr. Witendo described that "one treatment needs three different software. This is three different hardware from different vendors. It's different mainte-nance. I went to all three vendors and I said, I want you to be my VR guy. And they're like, yeah, we don't do any of those others. So it's tough now for me to build a program around it, and they're totally standalone." There is a need to establish a mature market with a VR technology standard [70].

4.3 Patients

Individual patient's demographics, such as gender, age, etc., personality, and other unique psychological, cognitive, physical, and functional characteristics may cause VR treat-ment results differently. From an ethical perspective, health care providers need to be aware of the potential risks of VR technology. For example, the VR game content for children should strictly follow federal and state regulations. Furthermore, VR treat-ments should consider individual psychological differences and levels of symptoms, as Mr. Witendo addressed, "patients with addiction are a little bit sensitive due to the nature of it."

4.4 Medical Worker

Medical workers include doctors, nurses, and clinical IT employees. They have to work closely to implement the VR technology successfully. Additionally, they need to be trained by the vendors to properly set up and operate VR hardware and software. Insufficient training may cause adverse consequences of treatment [75].

4.5 Research Data Support

Previous research [69] identified that most of the current VR studies in health care focused on VR training and education programs. A lack of empirical research on VR technology applications in the health sector limited VR adoption in hospitals and clinics [7]. One of the reasons Lee Health did not expand their VR applcations over more departments was that there was no empirical data showing the effects of the treatment with VR technology. Mr. Witendo gave two examples of the data support. First, "the amount of sedation a kid needs to go under based on your body weight. Let's assume it's 100 mg. If I can distract them, what if I can put them under with only 50 mg? And that means there's less amount of medicine, so it's cheaper for the system, but the recovery time is quicker because the kid doesn't took full dose of the medicine. It's less risk to give them half medicine. Plus they recover from the surgery and the sedation sooner." Second, "If we know the VR technology improves our treatment 12% more efficient. It's leading to better outcomes, better financial results, lower length of stay, better satisfaction. However, right now, we're just doing it because it's cool. So right now I can't take any action on it because I don't have any data." According to Mr. Witendo, they are collecting data from the current three units about the effectiveness of VR technology and hope the results can support their future investment in VR applications.

5   Conclusions

Telemedicine has some time before it is fully implemented into health networks worldwide. The rise of Covid-19 has accelerated the use of VR technology and has made a leap in providing care to patients remotely for their safety, convenience, and savings. This research uses a case study at Lee Health to extend previous studies on VR applications in the health sector. Combining with our literature review, this qualitative study summarizes vital concerns of current adoptions of VR technology in a hospital system. The findings may be beneficial to VR researchers for their future study, VR manufacturers with their next VR product, VR software vendors for their new VR applications, and health care facilities who are planning to establish or expand their treatment adoptions with VR technology.

References

1. Pereira, F.: Business models for telehealth in the US: analyses and insights. Smart Homecare Technol. TeleHealth **4**, 13–29 (2017)
2. El-Miedany, Y.: Telehealth and telemedicine: how the digital era is changing standard health care. Smart Homecare Technol. TeleHealth **4**, 43–51 (2017)
3. Dinesen, B., et al.: Personalized telehealth in the future: a global research agenda. J. Med. Internet Res. **18**(3), 1–17 (2016)
4. Davis, R.M., Hitch, A.D., Salaam, M.M., Herman, W.H., Zimmer-Galler, I.E., Mayer-Davis, E.J.: Telehealth improves diabetes self-management in an underserved community. Diab. Care **33**(8), 1712–1717 (2010)
5. Nelson, R.: Telemedicine and Telehealth. AJN, Am. J. Nurs. **117**(6), 17–18 (2017)
6. Eisenberg, J., Hou, J.G., Barbour, P.: Current perspectives on the role of telemedicine in the management of Parkinson's disease. Smart Homecare Technol. TeleHealth **5**, 1–12 (2018)
7. Yu, W., Wen, L., Zhao, L.-A., Liu, X., Wang, B., Yang, H.: The applications of virtual reality technology in medical education: a review and mini-research. J. Phys.: Conf. Ser. **1176**(2), 1–5 (2019)
8. Riva, G.: From telehealth to E-Health: internet and distributed virtual reality in health care. Cyberpsychol. Behav. **3**(6), 989–998 (2000)
9. Hilty, D.M., et al.: A review of telepresence, virtual reality, and augmented reality applied to clinical care. J. Technol. Behav. Sci. **5**(2), 178–205 (2020)
10. O'Connor, S.: Virtual reality and avatars in health care. Clin. Nurs. Res. **28**(5), 523–528 (2019)
11. Javaid, M., Haleem, A.: Virtual reality applications toward medical field. Clin. Epidemiol. Global Health **8**(2), 600–605 (2020)
12. Sutherland, I.E.: Sketchpad a man-machine graphical communication system. Simulation **2**(5), R-3-R−20 (1964)

13. Milgram, P., Kishino, F.: A taxonomy of mixed reality visual displays. IEICE – Trans. Info. Syst. **77**(12), 1321–1329 (1994)
14. Jensen, L., Konradsen, F.: A review of the use of virtual reality head-mounted displays in education and training. Educ. Inf. Technol. **23**(4), 1515–1529 (2017)
15. Pan, Z., Cheok, A.D., Yang, H., Zhu, J., Shi, J.: Virtual reality and mixed reality for virtual learning environments. Comput. Graph. **30**(1), 20–28 (2006)
16. Slater, M., Wilbur, S.: A framework for immersive virtual environments (five): speculations on the role of presence in virtual environments. Presence: Teleoperators Virtual Env. **6**(6), 603–616 (1997). https://doi.org/10.1162/pres.1997.6.6.603
17. Kourtesis, P., Collina, S., Doumas, L.A., MacPherson, S.E.: Technological competence is a pre-condition for effective implementation of virtual reality head mounted displays in Human neuroscience: a technological review and meta-analysis. Front. Hum. Neurosci. **13**, 342 (2019)
18. Cummings, J.J., Bailenson, J.N.: How immersive is enough? a meta-analysis of the effect of immersive technology on user presence. Media Psychol. **19**(2), 272–309 (2015)
19. Slater, M.: Immersion and the illusion of presence in virtual reality. Br. J. Psychol. **109**(3), 431–433 (2018)
20. Carroll, J., Hopper, L., Farrelly, A.M., Lombard-Vance, R., Bamidis, P.D., Konstantinidis, E.I.: A scoping review of augmented/virtual reality health and wellbeing interventions for older adults: redefining immersive virtual reality. Front. Virtual Reality **2**, 61 (2021)
21. de Klerk, R., Duarte, A.M., Medeiros, D.P., Duarte, J.P., Jorge, J., Lopes, D.S.: Usability studies on building early stage architectural models in virtual reality. Autom. Constr. **103**, 104–116 (2019)
22. Pallavicini, F., Pepe, A., Minissi, M.E.: Gaming in virtual reality: what changes in terms of usability, emotional response and sense of presence compared to non-immersive video games? Simul. Gaming **50**(2), 136–159 (2019)
23. Corno, G., Bouchard, S., Forget, H.: Usability assessment of the virtual multitasking test (V-mt) for elderly people. Annu. Rev. Cyberther. Telemed. **12**, 168–172 (2014)
24. Manera, V., et al.: A feasibility study with image-based rendered virtual reality in patients with mild cognitive impairment and dementia. PLoS ONE **11**(3), 1–14 (2016)
25. Holopainen, J., Mattila, O., Parvinen, P., Pöyry, E., Tuunanen, T.: Sociability in virtual reality. ACM Trans. Soc. Comput. **4**(1), 1–21 (2021)
26. Johnston, E., Olivas, G., Steele, P., Smith, C., Bailey, L.: Exploring pedagogical foundations of existing virtual reality educational applications: a content analysis study. J. Educ. Technol. Syst. **46**(4), 414–439 (2017)
27. Berton, A., et al.: Virtual reality, augmented reality, gamification, and telerehabilitation: psychological impact on orthopedic patients' rehabilitation. J. Clin. Med. **9**(8), 2567 (2020)
28. Pinto, R.D., Peixoto, B., Melo, M., Cabral, L., Bessa, M.: Foreign language learning gamification using virtual reality—a systematic review of empirical research. Educ. Sci. **11**(5), 222 (2021)
29. Arane, K., Behboudi, A., Goldman, R.D.: Virtual reality for pain and anxiety management in children. Can. Fam. Physician Medecin de famille canadien **63**(12), 932–934 (2017)
30. Scapin, S., et al.: Virtual reality in the treatment of burn patients: a systematic review. Burns **44**(6), 1403–1416 (2018)
31. Shetty, V., Suresh, L.R., Hegde, A.M.: Effect of virtual reality distraction on pain and anxiety during dental treatment in 5 to 8 year old children. J. Clin. Pediatr. Dent. **43**(2), 97–102 (2019)
32. Wang, P., Wu, P., Wang, J., Chi, H.-L., Wang, X.: A critical review of the use of virtual reality in construction engineering education and training. Int. J. Environ. Res. Public Health **15**(6), 1204 (2018)
33. Ahir, K., Govani, K., Gajera, R., Shah, M.: Application on virtual reality for enhanced education learning, military training and sports. Augmented Hum. Res. **5**(1), 1–9 (2019)

34. Innocenti, E.D., et al.: Mobile virtual reality for musical genre learning in primary education. Comput. Educ. **139**, 102–117 (2019)
35. Radianti, J., Majchrzak, T.A., Fromm, J., Wohlgenannt, I.: A systematic review of immersive virtual reality applications for higher education: design Elements, lessons learned, and research agenda. Comput. Educ. **147**, 103778 (2020)
36. Kober, S.E., Kurzmann, J., Neuper, C.: Cortical correlate of spatial presence in 2D and 3D interactive virtual reality: an EEG study. Int. J. Psychophysiol. **83**(3), 365–374 (2012)
37. Cheng, M.-T., Lin, Y.-W., She, H.-C.: Learning through playing Virtual age: exploring the interactions among student concept learning, gaming performance, in-game behaviors, and the use of in-game characters. Comput. Educ. **86**, 18–29 (2015)
38. Fung, F.M., et al.: Applying a virtual reality platform in environmental chemistry education to conduct a field trip to an overseas site. J. Chem. Educ. **96**(2), 382–386 (2019)
39. Wang, C.Y., et al.: A review of research on technology-assisted school science laboratories. Educ. Technol. Soc. **17**(2), 307–320 (2014)
40. Lee, E.A.-L., Wong, K.W.: Learning with desktop virtual reality: low spatial ability learners are more positively affected. Comput. Educ. **79**, 49–58 (2014)
41. Smits, M., Staal, J.B., van Goor, H.: Could virtual reality play a role in the rehabilitation after covid-19 infection? BMJ Open Sport Exerc. Med. **6**(1), e000943 (2020)
42. Anthony, K., Nagel, D.A.: Therapy Online: A Practical Guide. SAGE Publications Ltd. (2013)
43. Pompeo-Fargnoli, A., Lapa, A., Pellegrino, C.: Telemental Health and student veterans: a practice perspective through voices from the field. J. Technol. Hum. Serv. **38**(3), 271–287 (2019)
44. Luo, Z., et al.: Gamification of upper limb virtual rehabilitation in post stroke elderly using SilverTune- a multi-sensory tactile musical assistive system. In: 2021 IEEE 7th International Conference on Virtual Reality (ICVR) (2021)
45. Lin, H.-T., Li, Y.-I., Hu, W.-P., Huang, C.-C., Du, Y.-C.: A scoping review of the efficacy of virtual reality and exergaming on patients of musculoskeletal system disorder. J. Clin. Med. **8**(6), 791 (2019)
46. Wang, S., et al.: Augmented reality as a telemedicine platform for remote procedural training. Sensors **17**(10), 2294 (2017)
47. Li, J.-H.: The application of virtual reality and augmented reality technologies in biofeedback. Adapt. Med. **9**(9), 3867–3880 (2017)
48. Park, M.J., Kim, D.J., Lee, U., Na, E.J., Jeon, H.J.: A literature overview of virtual reality (VR) in treatment of psychiatric disorders: recent advances and limitations. Front. Psychiatry **10**, 505 (2019)
49. De Luca, R., et al.: Improving neuropsychiatric symptoms following stroke using virtual reality: a case report. Medicine **98**(19), e15236 (2019)
50. Rutkowski, S.: Management challenges in chronic obstructive pulmonary disease in the COVID-19 pandemic: telehealth and virtual reality. J. Clin. Med. **10**(6), 1261 (2021)
51. Imam, B., et al.: A telehealth intervention using Nintendo Wii fit balance boards and iPads to improve walking in older adults with lower limb amputation (Wii.n.walk): study protocol for a randomized controlled trial. JMIR Res. Protoc. **3**(4), e80 (2014)
52. Levin, M.F., Demers, M.: Motor learning in neurological rehabilitation. Disabil. Rehabil. **43**(24), 1–9 (2020)
53. Bond, W.F., et al.: The use of simulation in emergency medicine: a research agenda. Acad. Emerg. Med. **14**(4), 353–363 (2007)
54. Duarte, M.L., Santos, L.R., Guimarães Júnior, J.B., Peccin, M.S.: Learning anatomy by virtual reality and augmented reality. A scope review. Morphologie **104**(347), 254–266 (2020)
55. Fried, M.P., Uribe, J.I., Sadoughi, B.: The role of virtual reality in surgical training in otorhinolaryngology. Curr. Opin. Otolaryngol. Head Neck Surg. **15**(3), 163–169 (2007)

56. Maresky, H.S., Oikonomou, A., Ali, I., Ditkofsky, N., Pakkal, M., Ballyk, B.: Virtual reality and cardiac anatomy: exploring immersive three-dimensional cardiac imaging, a pilot study in undergraduate medical anatomy education. Clin. Anat. **32**(2), 238–243 (2018)

57. Silva, J.N.A., Southworth, M., Raptis, C., Silva, J.: Emerging applications of virtual reality in cardiovascular medicine. JACC: Basic Transl. Sci. **3**(3), 420–430 (2018)

58. Mallepally, N., Bilal, M., Hernandez-Barco, Y.G., Simons, M., Berzin, T.M., Oxentenko, A.S.: the new virtual reality: how covid-19 will affect the gastroenterology and hepatology fellowship match. Dig. Dis. Sci. **65**(8), 2164–2168 (2020)

59. Uruthiralingam, U., Rea, P.M.: Augmented and virtual reality in anatomical education – a systematic review. In: Rea, P.M. (ed.) Biomedical Visualisation. AEMB, vol. 1235, pp. 89–101. Springer, Cham (2020). https://doi.org/10.1007/978-3-030-37639-0_5

60. Walbron, P., Thomazeau, H., Sirveaux, F.: Virtual reality simulation" in der orthopädie und unfallchirurgie in Frankreich. Unfallchirurg **122**(6), 439–443 (2019)

61. Järvelä, S., Cowley, B., Salminen, M., Jacucci, G., Hamari, J., Ravaja, N.: Augmented virtual reality meditation. ACM Trans. Soc. Comput. **4**(2), 1–19 (2021)

62. Doggett, R., Sander, E.J., Birt, J., Ottley, M., Baumann, O.: Using virtual reality to evaluate the impact of room acoustics on cognitive performance and well-being. Front. Virtual Reality **2**, 20 (2021)

63. Kim, S., Kim, E.: The use of virtual reality in psychiatry: a review. J. Korean Acad. Child Adolesc. Psychiatry **31**(1), 26–32 (2020)

64. Beidel, D.C., et al.: Trauma management therapy with virtual-reality augmented exposure therapy for combat-related PTSD: a randomized controlled trial. J. Anxiety Disord. **61**, 64–74 (2019)

65. Mubin, O., Alnajjar, F., Jishtu, N., Alsinglawi, B., Al Mahmud, A.: Exoskeletons with virtual reality, augmented reality, and gamification for stroke patients' rehabilitation: systematic review. JMIR Rehabil. Assist. Technol. **6**(2), e12010 (2019)

66. Parham, G., et al.: Creating a low-cost virtual reality surgical simulation to increase surgical oncology capacity and capability. Ecancermedicalscience **13**, 910 (2019)

67. Vergara, D., Rubio, M., Lorenzo, M.: On the design of virtual reality learning environments in engineering. Multimodal Technol. Interact. **1**(2), 11 (2017)

68. Norouzi, N., Bölling, L., Bruder, G., Welch, G.: Augmented rotations in virtual reality for users with a reduced range of head movement. J. Rehabil. Assist. Technol. Eng. **6**, 2055668319841309 (2019)

69. Tang, Y.M., Chau, K.Y., Kwok, A.P., Zhu, T., Ma, X.: A systematic review of immersive technology applications for medical practice and education - trends, application areas, recipients, teaching contents, evaluation methods, and performance. Educ. Res. Rev. **35**, 100429 (2022)

70. Zhang, J., Patel, V.L., Johnson, K.A., Smith, J.W.: Designing human-centered distributed information systems. IEEE Intell. Syst. **17**(5), 42–47 (2002)

71. Garrett, B., Taverner, T., Gromala, D., Tao, G., Cordingley, E., Sun, C.: Virtual reality clinical research: promises and challenges. JMIR Serious Games **6**(4), e10839 (2018). https://doi.org/10.2196/10839

72. Xiong, Y., Chen, H.: Status quo of VR technology applied in clinical medicine and reflections. China Med. Educ. Technol. **31**(3), 283–291 (2017)

73. Bohil, C.J., Alicea, B., Biocca, F.A.: Virtual reality in neuroscience research and therapy. Nat. Rev. Neurosci. **12**(12), 752–762 (2011)

74. Rizzo, A.A., Strickland, D., Bouchard, S.: The challenge of using virtual reality in telerehabilitation. Telemed. J. E Health **10**(2), 184–195 (2004)

75. Botella, C., Garcia-Palacios, A., Baños, R.M., Quero, S.: Cybertherapy: advantages, limitations, and ethical issues. PsychNology J. **7**(1), 77–100 (2009)

Find Your ASMR: A Perceptual Retrieval Interface for Autonomous Sensory Meridian Response Videos

Qi Zhou, Jiahao Weng, and Haoran Xie[(✉)]

Japan Advanced Institute of Science and Technology, Ishikawa 9231292, Japan
xie@jaist.ac.jp

Abstract. Autonomous sensory meridian response (ASMR) is a type of video contents designed to help people relax and feel comfortable. Users usually retrieve ASMR contents from various video websites using only keywords. However, it is challenging to examine satisfactory contents to reflect users' needs for ASMR videos using keywords or content-based retrieval. To solve this issue, we propose a perceptual video retrieval system for ASMR videos and provide a novel retrieval user interface that allows users to retrieve content according to watching purpose and anticipated expectations, such as excitement, calmness, stress and sadness. An ASMR video perception dataset is constructed with annotations on affective responses after watching the videos. To verify the proposed video retrieval system, a user study is conducted showing that users can retrieve satisfactory ASMR contents easily and efficiently compared to conventional keywords-based retrieval systems.

Keywords: ASMR · Video retrieval · User interface · User perception

1 Introduction

Autonomous sensory meridian response (ASMR) is a type of video content that has become popular in recent years due to the pervasive influence of social medias, such as YouTube and TikTok. Especially for young people, ASMR has changed their life styles with the daily use of applications for relaxing and sleeping. As reported in the previous studies, ASMR videos can bring users the sensation phenomenon called tingles [1,7]. This sensation is mainly felt at the back of the users' heads and is accompanied by a sense of pleasure and relaxation. However, examining satisfactory ASMR videos from conventional retrieval interfaces remains a challenging issue.

As shown in Fig. 1, the titles of ASMR videos usually describe a simple and personal introduction to the video content and have difficulty describing videos for special retrieval purposes, such as relaxation and looking for companionship and attention. The video frames of ASMR videos are usually produced with the action sounds and spoken voices. Classifying videos with multi-modal information is a complicated issue. Therefore, conventional keywords-based and content-based video retrieval approaches may fail for ASMR videos. In such cases, the

© Springer Nature Switzerland AG 2022
V. G. Duffy et al. (Eds.): HCII 2022, LNCS 13521, pp. 215–225, 2022.
https://doi.org/10.1007/978-3-031-17902-0_16

216   Q. Zhou et al.

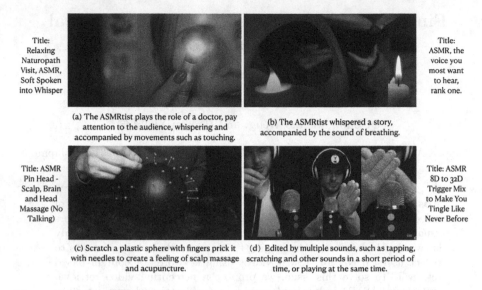

Fig. 1. Finding satisfactory ASMR videos using only the keywords in the video titles is difficult. (a)–(d) indicate the four different categories of ASMR videos used in this work.

users may want to relax but continuously switch ASMR videos because they are dissatisfied with the retrieved results. They wasted time and become unable to relax.

To solve these issues, we propose a novel perceptual video retrieval interface for ASMR videos. In the proposed system, an ASMR video dataset from online sources was constructed. Then, the participants were asked to evaluate the perception scores of all the collected videos. We implemented a perceptual video retrieval interface with perception filters. We conducted a comparison study between the proposed system and conventional retrieval interfaces to verify the user experience in the user study.

2 Related Works

ASMR is a sensory phenomenon that includes different triggers in videos, such as whispering, personal attention, crisp sounds and slow movements. This sensory-emotional phenomenon can be felt in listeners' head, neck and shoulders [1]. The sensitivity of the triggers can be measured with a resting-state functional magnetic resonance imaging scan [9]. ASMR videos have been investigated to study the emotional and physiological correlation with responses [7]. Aside from the tingling sensation, ASMR videos have been reported to relate to experiences of social connection and physical intimacy [2]. An online community of video sharing was found to have various ASMR videos created by ASMR artists looking for cultural and scientific legitimacy [8]. In this work, we focus on the video retrieval of ASMR videos.

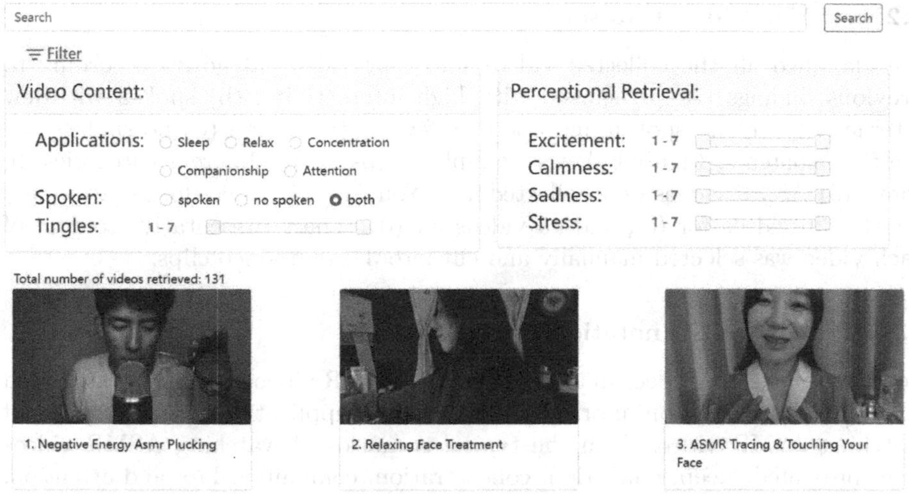

Fig. 2. The proposed perceptual video retrieval interface.

The common approaches for video retrieval are keyword and content-based video indexing and retrieval [10]. A hierarchical retrieval interface was proposed to explore video content through poster-style summarization [12]. A perception-based approach was explored to achieve the desired design using sensation words [4]. A perceptual video summarization and retrieval was proposed to provide a precise representation of video contents [11]. The interaction modalities and parasocial attractions of ASMR videos was annotated for multi-modal video interactions [5]. However, an effective way to explore ASMR videos has been lacking in previous works. To solve this issue, we aimed to achieve perceptual retrieval by annotating the videos in the dataset construction.

3 Retrieval System

3.1 System Overview

The proposed retrieval system provides a perceptual retrieval interface in which users can adjust their perceptual parameters to find satisfactory ASMR videos as shown in Fig. 2. Users can adjust the application purpose of watching ASMR videos, the desired level of tingles, and the perceptual expectations. For the retrieval system, an ASMR video dataset was constructed, and the participants were asked to evaluate the videos for the level of tingles and perceptual expectations. The proposed system was confirmed to be superior in terms of retrieval time cost and the quality of retrieved videos with satisfactory usability scales.

3.2 ASMR Video Dataset

We classified all the collected videos into four video categories according to previous findings [7]: (a) spoken with high interactivity, (b) spoken with low interactivity, (c) no spoken and one or a few contents, and (d) no spoken and multiple contents. Figure 1 shows example videos of the different categories. In total, 131 ASMR videos were collected from YouTube: 41 videos for (a), 29 videos for (b), 36 videos for (c), and 25 videos for (d). The representative content of each video was selected manually and cut into 3–5 min video clips.

3.3 Perceptual Annotation

For all the collected videos in the dataset, the ASMR videos were annotated with the following perception metrics: (a) Anticipated applications: Five purposes of watching ASMR videos from the typical scenarios of watching ASMR videos were presented: sleep, relaxation, concentration, companionship, and attention. (b) Tingles: This refers to the degree of stimulating effect of the ASMR video. (c) Perceptual expectation: This refers to positive effects on human emotions.

According to a previous study [7], the perceptual expectations were divided into four categories, namely excitement, calmness, sadness, and stress, which were used to measure users' perceptual expectations after watching the ASMR video. We adopted these four expressions for the video annotation.

We asked four participants (female graduate students) to join our video annotation. The participants were asked to watch the ASMR videos and annotated them using the aforementioned perception metrics. For each video, the participants were asked to answer the following six questions on a seven-point Likert scale, with 1 indicating strong disagreement and 7 indicating strong agreement.

Q1. Can you feel tingles from this ASMR video?
Q2. Do you feel more excited after watching the video?
Q3. Do you feel calmer after watching the video?
Q4. Do you feel sadder after watching the video?
Q5. Do you feel more stressed after watching the video?
Q6. For which purpose do you think this ASMR video is suitable? (multiple-choice questions).

According to a survey of the participants (works) in advance, all four participants had experience watching ASMR videos. They had different preferences for ASMR, with two of them liking humans speaking in ASMR videos and the others liking ASMR videos without speaking. Moreover, two participants were more satisfied with videos that made people calmer, and the other two were more satisfied with videos that made people more excited. All videos were randomly assigned to the participants according to the four categories (Fig. 1).

3.4 User Interface

As shown in Fig. 2, we designed a novel perceptual video retrieval interface with a perception filter for an advance search. For the filer, we created two sections, namely, the video content section and the perceptional retrieval section, to fulfill the user search scenario. The video content section has three items: applications, spoken, and tingles. Application denotes retrieval for the specific purpose of watching, and spoken denotes searching for videos that have or do not have vocals. Users employ a two-handle slider to select the range of the tingle feature. The perceptional retrieval section has four items: excitement, calmness, stress, and sadness. These items also use a two-handle slider for range selection.

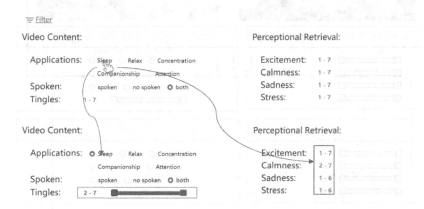

Fig. 3. Workflow of the perceptual filter in the proposed user interface. (Color figure online)

When users chooses one watching application, the system automatically determines the maximum and minimum video perception values in the dataset and changes the corresponding values on the sliders simultaneously, as shown in the red box in Fig. 3. The default states of the sliders are illustrated in Fig. 2, When users change the range of a specific item, the slider can be changed to the activated state, as shown in the blue box in Fig. 3.

4   User Study

4.1   Comparison Study

We conducted a comparative study between the proposed perceptual retrieval interface and two conventional retrieval approaches: keyword-based video retrieval (UI-1) and content-based video retrieval (UI-2). These two user interfaces were implemented for the user study, as shown in Fig. 4. UI-1 denotes a traditional user interface that only has a keyword search, and UI-2 has a combined traditional user interface and the video content section of the proposed system.

All participants were asked to use each of the three video retrieval interfaces to complete three different assigned tasks. Our task was designed based on a specific scene, the content of the video, and the perceptual expectations after

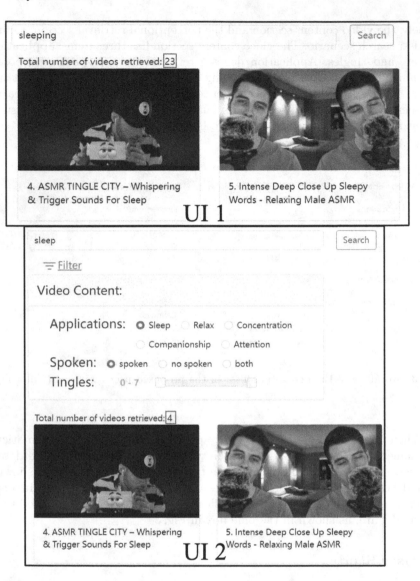

Fig. 4. Conventional video retrieval interfaces used in the comparison study. UI-1 represents keyword-based retrieval, and UI-2 represents content-based retrieval.

watching the video. For example, "You are going to rest and sleep. Please find as many suitable ASMR videos as possible (no spoken, used for relaxation, and can make people calmer or more excited)."

We invited six graduate students (three males and three females), all of whom familiar with ASMR videos, to join the study. The participants were randomly assigned retrieval and permutation tasks. After the participants retrieved the ASMR videos, they were asked to watch them in order, from beginning to end, and confirm whether they were satisfactory. The amount of time the participant took to find the first satisfactory video and the time interval between finding two satisfactory videos were set as the criteria for evaluating the proposed system. The total number of video views and the number of satisfaction videos for each participant were also recorded.

4.2 User Experience Study

We asked six graduate students (two males and four females), all of whom were familiar with ASMR videos, to join the user experience study. They were asked to use the proposed retrieval system to complete two tasks:

(1) Find as many ASMR videos as possible, with constraints of no spoken, and for relaxation and calming applications.
(2) Find satisfactory ASMR videos easily.

After completing each task, the participants watched the retrieved videos for 5–10 min to determine whether they were satisfied with the retrieved results. They were then asked to answer question items from the system usability scale (SUS).

5 Results

5.1 Implementation Details

This system was implemented on Python, and used a Django 3.2.0 web framework. Bootstrap 4.6.1, an open source cascading style sheets (css) framework, was used to render and decorate the website. JavaScript Query 3.6.0 (jQuery), an open-source JavaScript library, was used to implement user interactions. When users chose one watching purpose of the application, we used the asynchronous JavaScript and XML function in jQuery to obtain specific values from the dataset and modify the values in the sliders without refreshing the website.

A two-handle slider (Fig. 3) was designed with a combination of two traditional (only one handle) sliders. The z-index, a css attribute, was used to overlap the two traditional sliders. Then, we declared a function to determine if the two sliders would collide. If the left handle had the same value as the right one, it would collide. In this case, the left handle would not be able to move to the right anymore, and vice versa.

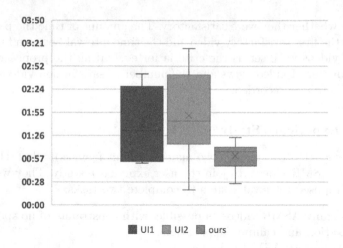

Fig. 5. Amount of time for finding the first satisfactory video.

5.2 Comparison Study

Figure 5 shows that the proposed interface could find satisfactory videos for all participants in the shortest amount of time. Although our interface took more time in the initial parameter setting than a conventional keyword retrieval, more accurate retrieval results were achieved in a significantly shorter amount of time for the participants to find the first satisfactory video. When using the keyword retrieval method, some participants found the first satisfactory video faster because they could quickly locate familiar video content by inputting keywords. The content-based retrieval method (UI2) disregarded the emotional needs of the participants. Thus, compared to the proposed perceptual retrieval system, the variance in the video content distribution was larger, and the participants have a relatively lower probability of quickly finding the first satisfactory video.

As shown in Fig. 6, a short interval was observed between finding two satisfying videos consecutively when using the proposed interface. The proposed system was verified to retrieve more satisfactory videos, and users had a better experience in finding and switching between satisfactory ASMR videos. The participants revealed that they usually did not watch ASMR videos completely. When bored with the content of an ASMR video, they would look for other videos and switch between them until they find satisfactory video content. Therefore, we consider that the interval between closing one video and finding another satisfactory one is an important indicator when evaluating a retrieval system, as a short interval can reduce the energy loss caused by switching between videos and significantly increase the comfort of system users. One of the participants commented the following about the proposed retrieval system was: "I feel that the retrieved videos were very new and that most of them were very interesting. I can quickly find the next satisfactory video."

As shown in Fig. 7, the proposed system can retrieve the highest ratio of satisfactory videos relative to the total number of viewed videos. The partic-

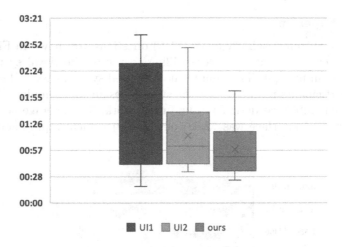

Fig. 6. Time intervals between finding two satisfactory videos.

ipants indicated that the proposed retrieval method increased the diversity of video types retrieved. According to one of the participants, "I usually use a few keywords I know to search for ASMR videos, In this way, I can find videos that meet my preferences. However, after a period, the videos retrieved using these keywords will have no new content, and most of them I have already seen. However, your retrieval method is not limited to specific video content, and it can find many videos with unexpected new content."

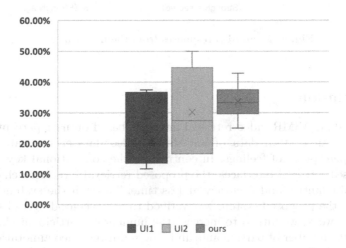

Fig. 7. Ratio of satisfactory videos to total viewed videos.

5.3 User Experience

The results of System Usability Scale (SUS) questions are shown in Fig. 8. Five participants reported that they were willing to use our retrieval system regularly confident in using it. They found the proposed system easy to learn. However, four participants reported that the system design was complex. We intend to improve our interface design in our future work. The average score of the proposed retrieval interface was 72.08 (out of 100), which implies good overall usability.

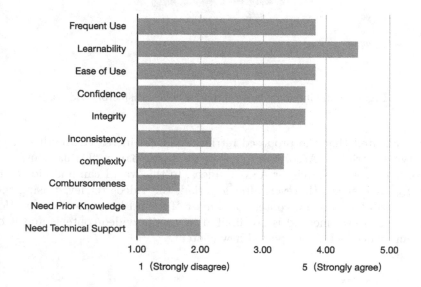

Fig. 8. Mean SUS responses from the user study.

6   Conclusion

We proposed an ASMR video retrieval interface based on user perceptions. We collected the annotation data of an ASMR video dataset for watching purposes and perception of feelings. In contrast to the conventional keyword- and content-based retrieval interfaces, the proposed retrieval interface achieved better retrieval quantity and accuracy at less time. Through the system usability experiment, the proposed system was verified to achieve good overall usability.

In future work, we intend to increase the number of participants in the user study and the number of participants and videos during video annotation. Using a deep supervised learning approach for the estimation of perceptual metrics of an unknown ASMR video using the annotation dataset is a promising topic. The proposed interface design can be improved for simplicity of use. We also plan to examine the use of a perception-driven interface for other daily activities, such as taking selfies [3] and animation design [6].

Acknowledgement. The authors thank the anonymous reviewers for their valuable comments. This project has been partially funded by JAIST Research Grant and JSPS KAKENHI grant JP20K19845, Japan.

References

1. Barratt, E.L., Davis, N.J.: Autonomous sensory meridian response (ASMR): a flow-like mental state. PeerJ **3**, e851 (2015)
2. Bartolome, A., Ha, N.B., Niu, S.: Investigating multimodal interactions and parasocial attractiveness in YouTube ASMR videos. In: Companion Publication of the 2021 Conference on Computer Supported Cooperative Work and Social Computing, CSCW 2021, p. 14–18. Association for Computing Machinery, New York (2021). https://doi.org/10.1145/3462204.3481763
3. Fang, N., Xie, H., Igarashi, T.: Selfie guidance system in good head postures. In: ACM International Conference on Intelligent User Interfaces Workshops (2018)
4. Fujita, Y., Xie, H., Miyata, K.: Perceptual font manifold from generative model. In: 2019 Nicograph International (NicoInt), pp. 41–48 (2019). https://doi.org/10.1109/NICOInt.2019.00016
5. Niu, S., Manon, H.S., Bartolome, A., Ha, N.B., Veazey, K.: Close-up and whispering: an understanding of multimodal and parasocial interactions in YouTube ASMR videos. In: CHI Conference on Human Factors in Computing Systems, CHI 2022. Association for Computing Machinery, New York (2022). https://doi.org/10.1145/3491102.3517563
6. Peng, Y., Zhao, C., Huang, Z., Fukusato, T., Xie, H., Miyata, K.: Two-stage motion editing interface for character animation. In: The ACM SIGGRAPH/Eurographics Symposium on Computer Animation, SCA 2021. Association for Computing Machinery, New York (2021). https://doi.org/10.1145/3475946.3480960
7. Poerio, G.L., Blakey, E., Hostler, T.J., Veltri, T.: More than a feeling: autonomous sensory meridian response (ASMR) is characterized by reliable changes in affect and physiology. PloS One **13**(6), e0196645 (2018)
8. Smith, N., Snider, A.M.: ASMR, affect and digitally-mediated intimacy. Emot. Space Soc. **30**, 41–48 (2019). https://doi.org/10.1016/j.emospa.2018.11.002. https://www.sciencedirect.com/science/article/pii/S1755458617301494
9. Smith, S.D., Fredborg, B.K., Kornelsen, J.: Functional connectivity associated with five different categories of autonomous sensory meridian response (ASMR) triggers. Conscious. Cogn. **85**, 103021 (2020). https://doi.org/10.1016/j.concog.2020.103021. https://www.sciencedirect.com/science/article/pii/S105381002030088X
10. Spolaôr, N., Lee, H.D., Takaki, W.S.R., Ensina, L.A., Coy, C.S.R., Wu, F.C.: A systematic review on content-based video retrieval. Eng. Appl. Artif. Intell. **90**, 103557 (2020). https://doi.org/10.1016/j.engappai.2020.103557. https://www.sciencedirect.com/science/article/pii/S0952197620300488
11. Thomas, S.S., Gupta, S., Subramanian, V.K.: Context driven optimized perceptual video summarization and retrieval. IEEE Trans. Circuits Syst. Video Technol. **29**(10), 3132–3145 (2019). https://doi.org/10.1109/TCSVT.2018.2873185
12. Weng, J., Zhang, C., Yang, X., Xie, H.: Hierarchical visual interface for educational video retrieval and summarization. In: International Workshop on Advanced Imaging Technology (IWAIT 2022), vol. 12177, pp. 693–698. International Society for Optics and Photonics, SPIE (2022). https://doi.org/10.1117/12.2626092

Universal Access and Active Aging

Digital Mahjong System: Towards Precise Cognitive Assessment with IoT Technologies

Ning An[1,2,3,4], Enze Hu[1,3], Yanrui Guo[5], Jiaoyun Yang[1,3,4,6(✉)], Rhoda Au[7,8], and Huitong Ding[7]

[1] School of Computer Science and Information Engineering, Hefei University of Technology, Hefei, China
jiaoyun@hfut.edu.cn

[2] Anhui Province Key Laboratory of Affective Computing and Advanced Intelligent Machine, Hefei University of Technology, Hefei, China

[3] National Smart Eldercare International S&T Cooperation Base, Hefei University of Technology, Hefei, China

[4] Intelligent Interconnected Systems Laboratory of Anhui Province, Hefei University of Technology, Hefei, China

[5] Shenzhen Corecloud Innovation Technology Co., Ltd., Shenzhen, China

[6] Key Laboratory of Knowledge Engineering with Big Data of Ministry of Education, Hefei University of Technology, Hefei, China

[7] Department of Anatomy and Neurobiology, Neurology and Framingham Heart Study, Boston University School of Medicine, Boston, USA

[8] Department of Epidemiology, Boston University School of Public Health, Boston, USA

Abstract. To the best of our knowledge, this paper is the first to apply IoT technologies to transform the popular Mahjong game into a Digital Mahjong System (DMS) for digitally performing cognitive assessments. People have started exploring digital cognitive assessment tools for better objectivity and simplification. However, most of these tools are not friendly for older adults. This paper aims to address this issue by integrating IoT technologies with Mahjong to make cognitive assessment simpler and more engaging for older adults. DMS has the following features: 1) integrating motion tracking devices into Mahjong tiles and transferring them into Digital Mahjong Tiles (DMTs), which can precisely capture their moving trajectory during the assessment, 2) using a Near Field Communication reader to configure DMT's primary data, 3) supporting Over-The-Air Device Firmware Update that can be done remotely via Bluetooth, and 4) developing a charging base that can charge 16 DMTs simultaneously using Qi wireless charging standard. With further testing, the DMS has the potential to become a digital platform to implement and test various cognitive assessment tools integrating Mahjong elements.

Keywords: Digital Mahjong System · Digital Mahjong Tile · Cognitive assessment · IoT · OTA DFU · Wireless charging

V. G. Duffy et al. (Eds.): HCII 2022, LNCS 13521, pp. 229–241, 2022.
https://doi.org/10.1007/978-3-031-17902-0_17

1 Introduction

Many older adults experience cognitive decline. Mild Cognitive Impairment (MCI) is a stage in which cognitive decline does not affect essential functions of daily life [1]. It may also be an early symptom of a neurodegenerative disorder, such as Alzheimer's disease (AD) [2, 3]. When tied to progressive dementia, these symptoms can be irreversible and progress to severity levels that significantly impact an older adult to function independently in their home. With increasing evidence that modifiable risk factors can slow down and even potentially prevent the onset of dementia/AD, early detection of cognitive deterioration, particularly at the preclinical stages of MCI, when interventions may be most effective, is critical [4]. Therefore, an efficient and accurate cognitive assessment method is needed to assess the cognitive level of older adults.

Many traditional cognitive assessments are performed using pen and paper and manually scored by a trained examiner [5–10]. Although this approach has been standard, the assessment is usually subjective and time-intensive to administer. The test stimuli are often educationally and culturally biased. Further, older adults may experience the assessment process as tedious and burdensome.

While population aging and digital technology expansion are two megatrends that have persisted recently, the challenge is integrating them for mutual benefits [11]. Digital technologies provide an opportunity to alter cognitive assessment methods and solve some of the longstanding bias problems. Compared with traditional cognitive assessment methods, digital cognitive assessment can provide test content that is simpler and more interesting for older adults [12–18]. However, some older adults find using technology difficult. Thus, creating digital assessment tools that are more user-friendly for older adults is warranted.

The Internet of Things (IoT) has been a transformative force since the 21st century [19]. IoT technology makes it possible for various sensors, actuators, or other devices to connect to the Internet [20]. There are several successful cases of IoT technology applications in cognitive assessment. For example, some research groups have integrated pressure and gravity sensors into pens, allowing older adults to use these digital pens to complete cognitive assessment tests [21]. Moreover, the system extracts the characteristic values from the sensors' raw data and translates them into cognitive and other brain-related measures. The physician can then interpret these extracted values to determine the cognitive status of older adults. Other research groups have integrated pressure sensors into floor tiles, allowing older adults to perform cognitive tests by stepping on these tiles and determining the cognitive level from the digitally-derived scores [22]. A study demonstrated that the digital Clock Drawing Test using a digital ballpoint pen and smart paper could be an effective cognitive assessment tool [23].

The above research efforts have started exploring IoT technology for developing digital cognitive assessment tools. The primary issue with current digital cognitive assessment technologies is their inability to be used by older people properly. They also require the assessment subject to come to the testing site, which is challenging for older individuals with restricted physical mobility.

To enable cognitive assessments to be carried out quickly, anytime, and anywhere, we leveraged the popularity of the Mahjong game and paired it with IoT technologies to develop a more user-friendly cognitive assessment method for older adults. Mahjong, a traditional Chinese game, has spread throughout China, Eastern, and Southeastern Asia and has become popular in Western countries [24]. Previous research has demonstrated that playing Mahjong has cognitive and other health benefits [25, 26]. Therefore, one can use the system developed in this paper as an integrated platform for cognitive assessment. This platform can further facilitate designing and validating clinical assessment protocols. Figure 1 shows an application scenario of the digital Mahjong tiles.

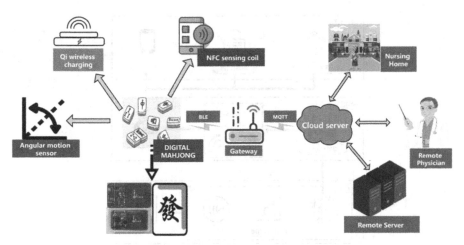

Fig. 1. Application scenario of digital Mahjong tiles

2   Digital Mahjong System

2.1   Network Architecture

The network architecture of the Digital Mahjong System (DMS) comprises sensing, transmission, and remote application layer (Fig. 2).

The sensing layer consists of a motion tracking device, a microcontroller unit (MCU), and a Near Field Communication (NFC) coil. The ICM-20689, as the motion tracking device, combines a 3-axis gyroscope and a 3-axis accelerometer, which can calculate the angle and speed of each Digital Mahjong Tile (DMT) along the X, Y, and Z-axis in real-time. Finally, the MCU calculates the coordinate points of the Mahjong tile in space and sends them to the gateway. The DMS supports NFC, i.e., a user can use an NFC reader to configure the DMS according to actual scenarios hence improving its flexibility.

The transmission layer consists of a gateway and a cloud server. The gateway is compatible with various wireless protocols such as Bluetooth, LoRa, and 3G/4G networks. The gateway is responsible for receiving and adjusting the data sent by the DMS and then sending the data to the cloud server using the MQTT protocol. The cloud server is responsible for receiving and storing the data that the gateway has processed. Authorized users can view these data anytime and anywhere later.

The remote application layer provides direct connectivity with patient monitoring systems in clinical care settings such as hospitals. For example, when an older adult uses the DMS at home or in a nursing home, the physician can remotely examine this older adult's recorded data, including the movement of DMTs, thinking time, and more. With other physiological evaluation information on file, the physician can quickly conduct an initial screening of this older adult.

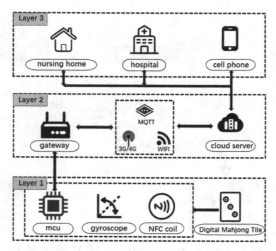

Fig. 2. The network architecture of digital Mahjong

2.2 Highly Integrated "Sandwich" Structure Design

The DMT in this paper uses an authentic 43.8 mm × 33 mm × 22 mm size Mahjong that is typically sold in the market to dig and fabricate the mold. We use nRF52832 as the microcontroller unit (MCU), and inside the Mahjong tile, we also integrated the NFC coil, battery, motion tracking devices, and wireless charging coil. To maximize the endurance of each DMT, we set the default Mahjong mode into a deep sleep. When older adults move the DMT, the signal generated by the system interruption will allow the DMT to switch from deep sleep mode to high-performance work mode.

To protect the DMT from heavy usage, we have left a wall thickness of 3 mm for each DMT (Fig. 3) during the mold opening process. Therefore, the actual space left for the embedded module is only about 16.3 cm³ (37.8 mm × 27 mm × 16 mm), similar to the size of a matchbox. We changed the traditional circuit board design ideas, the flat design, into a "sandwich" three-dimensional design to fit this small interior space. Assuming that the control and calculation layers are layer 1, layer 2, and layer 3 are the battery and wireless charging layers.

The back cover of the DMT is glued to the shell using chloroprene adhesive, which is extremely sticky. Still, after being heated for about 15 s, the stickiness decreases significantly, making it possible to replace the lithium battery inside the Mahjong tile.

The typical lifetime of a lithium battery is 5–6 years and should not need replacing before then.

The following sections will detail the three layers in the "sandwich" structure.

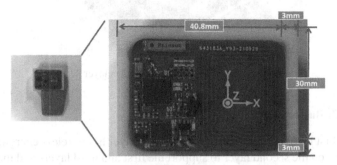

Fig. 3. 3 mm thick wall of DMT

2.3 Layer 1: Control and Calculation Layer

This layer consists of the MCU, data sensing and collecting device, and NFC coil to collect and send data. For the MCU, we choose the Nordic's nRF52832 chip with the following characteristics 1) support for Bluetooth 5.0, which is faster, has lower power consumption, and higher bandwidth than previous generations of Bluetooth [27, 28], 2) support of NFC and OTA DFU functions, and 3) low price, which is suitable for large-scale deployment.

To accurately collect the moving angle, speed, acceleration, and additional DMT data, we used the ICM-20689 as the motion tracking device. When ICM-20689 is not in use for a long time, it will automatically enter sleep mode. Sleep mode significantly reduces electric energy consumption. Any interruption can wake the DMT in sleep mode.

DMT may require unique configurations for different scenarios. For example, when simulating a scenario when an older individual plays Mahjong with the DMS, we need to know which DMT she gets at what time. By coding them continuously from 001 to 144, we distinguish DMTs with the same design and color. In a professional cognitive assessment environment, we must give each DMT a real Mahjong name, such as "Red Dragon." We integrate the NFC coil in the DMT so that one can conveniently complete the configuration using an NFC reader or smartphone. NFC is mature short-range communication technology, expanding RFID [29]. Devices with NFC can exchange data when they are close to each other. We only need to place layer 1 with the NFC coil close to the NFC reader to configure the DMT. Our tests confirm that its magnetic field would interfere with Bluetooth data transmission when a DMT is working. After many adjustments, we discovered that interference could be minimal when the center of the NFC coil is 25 mm away from the center of nRF52832. Therefore, we divided the first layer into two parts. 50% of the space belongs to the NFC coil, and the other 50% was integrated into other modules, as shown in Fig. 4. In the cognitive assessment process, the older adult moves one DMT at a time by design, so we only need to consider the internal interference of DMTs, not the interference between DMTs.

Fig. 4. Control and calculation layer

2.4   Layer 2: Battery Layer

Because the first layer has NFC coils and the third layer has wireless charging coils, we put the battery on the second layer to support the first and third layers and make the first and third layers as close to the shell of DMT as possible, which can improve the success rate of NFC configuration and the efficiency of wireless charging.

The battery model we chose was the 334060-lithium battery (Fig. 5). This battery has a capacity of 1200 mAh, which is more significant than other lithium batteries of the same size. The outside of the battery wraps the aluminum foil, the passivation layer, and thermoplastic resin film, which can effectively isolate heat and protect the battery.

The life of this lithium battery was only reduced by 10% after 800 times of charging, which means there will be no need to replace the battery for many years, saving both human and material resources.

Fig. 5. Structural diagram of battery layer

2.5   Layer 3: Wireless Charging Layer

Since the battery is in the middle of the DMT, replacing the battery is inconvenient as covers are bonded with chloroprene adhesive. Thus, we decided to adopt wireless charging to solve the problem of battery replacement. Wireless charging is a contactless protocol for transmitting electrical energy, and it breaks the situation that electric energy transmission can only rely on the direct contact transmission of wires.

There are three significant industrial alliances committed to developing wireless charging technology and standard formulation: Alliance for Wireless Power (A4WP), Power Matters Alliance (PMA), and Wireless Power Consortium (WPC) [30]. The Qi standard is a wireless charging standard developed by WPC in 2010, and it adopts mainstream electromagnetic induction charging technology [31]. Its stability has been verified in many device deployments and has become one of the most mature wireless charging protocols. Since there are 144 DMT in each DMS, we chose to use the Qi wireless charging standard to save cost and ensure the stability of system operation.

The Qi wireless charging standard principle is to transfer energy through coil coupling. A coil is set at the transmitting and receiving end, respectively. The transmitting end is connected with a high-frequency alternating signal to generate an electromagnetic signal. The receiving end converts the received electromagnetic signal into current through the coil. The current provides power to the equipment after rectification, voltage stabilization, and other circuits are processed. The wireless charging layer has a pure copper receiving coil whose output end directly connects to the input end of the battery's charging IC. When the DMT is near the sending end, the current will be transmitted to the battery through the receiving coil to complete charging.

3   DMS Functions

The DMT has a kinematics sensor, NFC coil, wireless charging coil, and wireless transmission module. Its focus is on sensing, calculating, and transmitting various kinematic indicators of DMT, including the angle, speed, and acceleration. The key features and innovative ideas of the DMS are as follows.

3.1   DMT Movement, Error, or Malfunction

When an older adult moves the DMT, the computing unit will first receive the original data transmitted from the ICM-20689 and calculate the spatial coordinate points of the DMT. Second, the DMT will send these coordinate points to the gateway by Bluetooth, and finally, the gateway will upload the result to the cloud server. Testing revealed that the coordinate point was not accurate due to data drift. DMS uses the following methods to solve this problem. First, DMS solves the angular velocity collected by ICM-20689 through the direction cosine algorithm. Then DMS treats the attitude angle error caused by ICM-20689's dynamic drift as a time-varying signal. By utilizing the state equation and observation equation of attitude angle drift error and the Kalman filter algorithm, DMS estimates attitude angle drift error. Finally, DMS can correct the ICM-20689 dynamic drift error. Figure 6 illustrates the trajectory of a moving DMT. With further clinical validation, the DMS could be used to evaluate the participants' cognitive state by capturing and analyzing their circled movements, similar to performing the clock drawing test using a digital pen.

Sometimes, DMTs can suddenly shut down, a rare but severe error. This error may be caused by insufficient battery power and too long calculation time. Detecting an error in DMT selection during a task is potentially different because there are 144 tiles in a typical Mahjong set. Further, DMT malfunction could also lead to incorrect interpretation of data. We propose a solution based on NFC and DFU mode to address this error detection challenge.

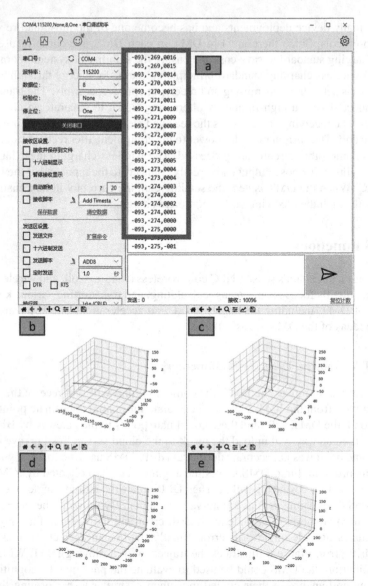

Fig. 6. a) DMT coordinates when moving, b) the trajectory of DMT moving horizontally, c) the trajectory of DMT moving vertically, d) the trajectory of DMT being picked up and put down, e) the trajectory of DMT moving irregularly

As shown in Fig. 7, the NFC coil is adjacent to the back cover of DMT. We can configure DMT if the back cover is close to the NFC reader. Using NFC, we can observe five parameters through software: ID, Name, FVN, Power, and State. The following are the details of these five parameters:

ID. Each DMT has a unique ID to distinguish it from the others. The ID number ranges from 001 to 144.

Name. Name the DMT. We can quickly identify the DMT moved in error from the repeated DMT with ID.

FVN (Firmware version number). We can check the current Mahjong firmware version number to determine if any DMT needs an upgrade. The format of the firmware version number is 0.1.0, 0.2.1.

Power. We can check the remaining battery electric quantity to determine if any DMT needs a recharge. The format of the remaining battery is 1%, 50%, and 100%.

Status. Displays whether the DMS is operating normally. If it is working correctly, "running" shows; otherwise, "error" shows.

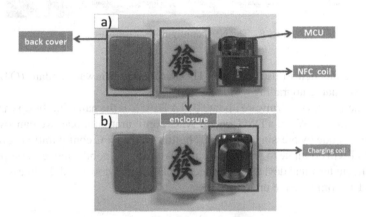

Fig. 7. a) The enclosure, back cover of Mahjong, and composition of the control layer, b) the charging coil composed of pure copper

Example: By checking the data in the remote server, we found that the DMT with ID number 10 had an obvious fault. Then we checked it was the "Red Dragon" DMT by checking the "Name" parameter. There are four "Red Dragon" DMTs in a DMS, so we can first separate the four "Red Dragon" ones from the 144 DMTs by checking their "Name". Finally, we can place these four DMTs on top of the NFC reader, check their own "status" parameters (Fig. 8) and find the faulty DMT

In addition, when more than one older adult uses DMS for cognitive assessment simultaneously, DMS can use the NFC function to determine which older adult moves which DMT. For example, before the cognitive assessment starts, NFC readers can be deployed in front of older adults and coded accordingly, such as 1, 2, 3, and 4. When an older adult moves a DMT near her body, the NFC reader will read this DMT and record it.

It is critical to find a suitable firmware upgrade method for the DMS. Limited by the structure of DMT, it is challenging to upgrade digital Mahjong through the wiring.

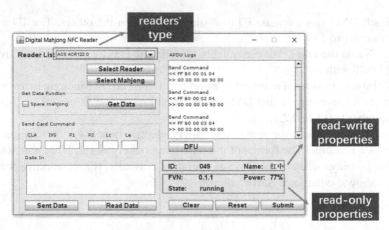

Fig. 8. The NFC configuration software

Therefore, we decided to use the Over-The-Air device firmware update (OTA DFU) technology to enable upgrading.

Over-The-Air device firmware update (OTA DFU), as the name implies, is a wireless upgrade technology. When a DMT enters NFC configuration mode, we can switch the DMT to DFU mode by pressing the "DFU" button on the NFC configuration software so that the DMT will continue to send broadcasts. We can use mobile phones, computers, or other intelligent terminal devices to connect the DMT and download the latest firmware to the DMT to complete the upgrade.

3.2 Wireless Charging and Automatic Sleep Mode

We developed a wireless charging base for the DMS to save charging time, and it can charge 16 DMTs simultaneously (Fig. 9). The charging base comprises a charging coil, led, and plastic shell. LEDs can display the charging status of each DMT. For example, when the power of the DMT is 30%, the charging base LED will light up as red; when the power is 31%–69%, the LED light is yellow; when the power is 70% or above, the LED light is blue.

We have integrated charging IC into the DMT to improve the charging efficiency and protect the battery. The charging IC can control the charging current and voltage of the wireless charging base. The charging IC can control the charging current and voltage of the wireless charging base at any time, regardless of whether the power of the wireless charging base is on. When the battery of a DMT becomes full, the charging IC instantly cuts off the charging current to protect the battery, as Fig. 10 shows. When the voltmeters of both batteries reach the maximum, the current will immediately drop to 0 to protect the battery.

We also set up an automatic sleep mode. When DMT is idle for 90 s, it will automatically switch from working mode to sleep mode to extend the endurance of DMT.

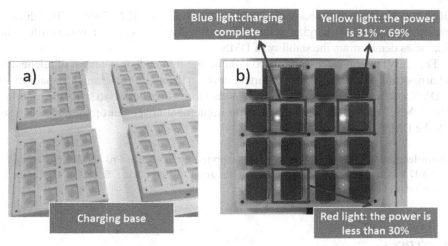

Fig. 9. a) The charging base, which can charge 16 Mahjong tiles simultaneously, b) the working conditions of the charging base

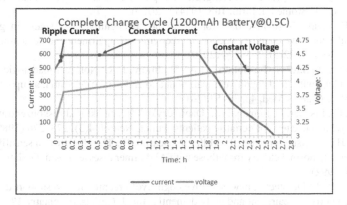

Fig. 10. Complete charge cycle of DMT

It takes about 4 h to charge the battery fully, and because of the auto-sleep mode, the maximum standby time of a DMT is 170 h. Recharging is only needed every three months to preserve battery life when unused.

4   Conclusion

To the best of our knowledge, this paper is the first to apply IoT technologies to transform the popular Mahjong game into a Digital Mahjong System (DMS) for digitally performing cognitive assessments. The DMS implements three significant technical features to lay the groundwork for this innovation. The first is implementing the "sandwich" type three-layer three-dimensional circuit integration to ensure stable operations. The next one is tracking DMT movement trajectory by integrating a high-performance MCU (nRF52832) and a high-precision motion tracking device (ICM-20689). The third is developing a wireless charging solution for easy charge and better battery life. The initial tests demonstrate the stability of DMS.

The COVID-19 pandemic has shed light on the tremendous potential of telehealth. To harness this potential, we plan to further develop the remote assessment capability of the DMS, particularly on the cloud side. Another immediate task is to study the usability of the DMS. These tasks will prepare us to implement novel neuropsychological tests with the DMS.

Acknowledgment. This work was partially supported by the Anhui Provincial Key Technologies R&D Program (2022h11020015) and the Program of Introducing Talents of Discipline to Universities (111 Program) (B14025).

References

1. Gauthier, S., et al.: Mild cognitive impairment. The Lancet **367**(9518), 1262–1270 (2006)
2. An, N., Ding, H., Yang, J., Au, R., Ang, T.F.: Deep ensemble learning for Alzheimer's disease classification. J. Biomed. Inform. **105**, 103411 (2020)
3. Poptsi, E., et al.: Normative data for the montreal cognitive assessment in greek older adults with subjective cognitive decline, mild cognitive impairment and dementia. J. Geriatr. Psychiatry Neurol. **32**(5), 265–274 (2019)
4. Rodakowski, J., Saghafi, E., Butters, M.A., Skidmore, E.R.: Non-pharmacological interventions for adults with mild cognitive impairment and early stage dementia: an updated scoping review. Mol. Aspects Med. **43**, 38–53 (2015)
5. Gatterer, G., Fischer, P., Simanyi, M., Danielczyk, W.: The akt ("alterskonzentrations-test") a new psychometric test for geriatric patients. Funct. Neurol. **4**(3), 273–276 (1989)
6. Tuokko, H., Hadjistavropoulos, T., Miller, J., Beattie, B.: The clock test: a sensitive measure to differentiate normal elderly from those with Alzheimer disease. J. Am. Geriatr. Soc. **40**(6), 579–584 (1992)
7. Kalbe, E., et al.: Demtect: a new, sensitive cognitive screening test to support the diagnosis of mild cognitive impairment and early dementia. Int. J. Geriatr. Psychiatry **19**(2), 136–143 (2004)
8. Folstein, M.F., Folstein, S.E., McHugh, P.R.: "Mini-mental state": a practical method for grading the cognitive state of patients for the clinician. J. Psychiatr. Res. **12**(3), 189–198 (1975)
9. Duley, J.F., Wilkins, J.W., Hamby, S.L., Hopkins, D.G., Burwell, R.D., Barry, N.S.: Explicit scoring criteria for the rey-osterrieth and taylor complex figures. Clin. Neuropsychol. **7**(1), 29–38 (1993)
10. Reitan, R.M.: Trail making test results for normal and brain-damaged children. Percept. Mot. Skills **33**(2), 575–581 (1971)
11. Kleinman, A., et al.: Social technology: An interdisciplinary approach to improving care for older adults. Front. Public Health **9**, 729149 (2021)
12. Lee, K., Jeong, D., Schindler, R.C., Short, E.J.: Sig-blocks: tangible game technology for automated cognitive assessment. Comput. Hum. Behav. **65**, 163–175 (2016)
13. Hafiz, P., et al.: The internet-based cognitive assessment tool: system design and feasibility study. JMIR Formative Res. **3**(3), e13898 (2019)

14. Gielis, K., et al.: Dissecting digital card games to yield digital biomarkers for the assessment of mild cognitive impairment: methodological approach and exploratory study. JMIR Serious Games **9**(4), e18359 (2021)
15. Seelye, A., et al.: Feasibility of in-home sensor monitoring to detect mild cognitive impairment in aging military veterans: prospective observational study. JMIR Formative Res. **4**(6), e16371 (2020)
16. Groppell, S., et al.: A rapid, mobile neurocognitive screening test to aid in identifying cognitive impairment and dementia (braincheck): cohort study. JMIR Aging **2**(1), e12615 (2019)
17. Hafiz, P., Bardram, J.E.: The ubiquitous cognitive assessment tool for smartwatches: design, implementation, and evaluation study. JMIR Mhealth Uhealth **8**(6), e17506 (2020)
18. Chan, J.Y., et al.: Electronic cognitive screen technology for screening older adults with dementia and mild cognitive impairment in a community setting: development and validation study. J. Med. Internet Res. **22**(12), e17332 (2020)
19. Wu, M., Lu, T.J., Ling, F.Y., Sun, J., Du, H.Y.: Research on the architecture of Internet of things. In: 2010 3rd international conference on advanced computer theory and engineering (ICACTE), vol. 5, pp. V5–484. IEEE (2010)
20. Atzori, L., Iera, A., Morabito, G.: The internet of things: a survey. Comput. Netw. **54**(15), 2787–2805 (2010)
21. Prange, A., Sonntag, D.: Assessing cognitive test performance using automatic digital pen features analysis. In: Proceedings of the 29th ACM Conference on User Modeling, Adaptation and Personalization, pp. 33–43 (2021)
22. Liu, Y.X., Lund, H.H., Wu, L.L.: Playful cognitive training with physical interactive tiles for elderly. In: 2018 international conference on information and communication technology robotics (ICT-ROBOT), pp. 1–4. IEEE (2018)
23. Yuan, J., et al.: Association between the digital clock drawing test and neuropsychological test performance: large community-based prospective cohort (framingham heart study). J. Med. Internet Res. **23**(6), e27407 (2021)
24. Heinz, A.: Mahjong: A Chinese Game and the Making of Modern American Culture. Oxford University Press (2021)
25. Lee, Y.H., Chang, Y.C., Shelley, M., Liu, C.T.: A panel analysis of the mahjong card game and social activity with sleep-related measurements among chinese older adults. Sleep Biol. Rhythms **18**(2), 109–119 (2020)
26. Zhang, H., et al.: Playing Mahjong for 12 weeks improved executive function in elderly people with mild cognitive impairment: A study of implications for TBI-induced cognitive deficits. Front. Neurol. **11**, 178 (2020)
27. Yaakop, M.B., Abd Malik, I.A., Bin Suboh, Z., Ramli, A.F., Abu, M.A.: Bluetooth 5.0 through-put comparison for Internet of thing usability a survey. In: 2017 International Conference on Engineering Technology and Technopreneurship (ICE2T), pp. 1–6. IEEE (2017)
28. Au, E.: Bluetooth 5.0 and beyond [standards]. IEEE Veh. Technol. Mag. **14**(2), 119–120 (2019)
29. Ceipidor, U.B., Medaglia, C., Moroni, A., Orlandi, G., Sposato, S.: Nfc: Integration between rfid and mobile, state of the art and future developments. RFIDays (2008)
30. Shidujaman, M., Samani, H., Arif, M.: Wireless power transmission trends. In: 2014 International Conference on Informatics, Electronics & Vision (ICIEV), pp. 1–6. IEEE (2014)
31. Hui, S.: Planar wireless charging technology for portable electronic products and qi. Proc. IEEE **101**(6), 1290–1301 (2013)

Automatically Labeling Aging Scenarios with a Machine Learning Approach

Ning An[1,2,3,4], Yang Xu[1,3], Qinglin Gao[5], Wenjie Zhu[6(✉)], Aoran Wu[7], and Honglin Chen[8]

[1] School of Computer Science and Information Engineering, Hefei University of Technology, Hefei, China
[2] Key Laboratory of Knowledge Engineering with Big Data of Ministry of Education, Hefei University of Technology, Hefei, China
[3] National Smart Eldercare International S&T Cooperation Base, Hefei University of Technology, Hefei, China
[4] Intelligent Interconnected Systems Laboratory of Anhui Province, Hefei University of Technology, Hefei, China
[5] Shanghai Tianyu Senior Living Service Co., Ltd., Shanghai, China
[6] School of Basic Courses, Bengbu Medical College, Bengbu, China
zwj_2002@sohu.com
[7] Management and Business Department, Skidmore College, Saratoga Springs, NY, USA
[8] Department of Social Sciences, University of Eastern Finland, 70150 Kuopio, Finland

Abstract. Older adults have diversified needs often associated with particular aging scenarios. People started to use aging scenarios to provide better Smart Eldercare services and develop innovative solutions. The problem is how to manage these scenarios effectively. To our best knowledge, this study is the first to develop a model to provide a structured framework of aging scenarios for research and teaching of eldercare services. Labeling aging scenarios can facilitate their collection, classification, and consolidation within this model. This study uses the automatic labeling approach to manage and utilize aging scenarios. Under each class, there are labels with different numbers and smaller granularity to reflect the requirements in each scenario case. Since a scenario case often involves more than one label, properly labeling it becomes a multi-label text classification problem. We extend the multi-label text classification model LSAN for labeling aging scenario cases. For evaluation purposes, we collected 938 scenario cases as the dataset. Experimental results show that our proposed method can achieve an average accuracy of 61.66%, better than other classical methods.

Keywords: Aging scenario · Smart Eldercare · Scenario case · Multi-label text classification · Multi-task

© Springer Nature Switzerland AG 2022
V. G. Duffy et al. (Eds.): HCII 2022, LNCS 13521, pp. 242–260, 2022.
https://doi.org/10.1007/978-3-031-17902-0_18

1 Introduction

1.1 Background

The world's population is aging rapidly, and the proportion of older adults in almost every country is increasing [1]. Population aging brings a heavy burden to families and societies. The traditional eldercare service model has been unable to meet the growing needs of older adults [2]. With the rapid development of big data and artificial intelligence, Smart Eldercare has become an integral part of the eldercare industry. Research has shown that technology has important practical significance for improving the quality of eldercare services and alleviating the pressure of population aging [3].

Although Smart Eldercare technologies have shown great potential, particularly in China, it faces many challenges because it is in the initial development phase [4]. For example, fewer older adults are willing to buy and use Smart Eldercare products. Many of these products have had data security and privacy issues [5], and their effectiveness in real-world settings has yet to satisfy needs. Many Smart Eldercare products failed to fully consider the actual needs, usability, and living habits of older adults.

Some leading cities in China have recently started establishing a requirements list of Smart Eldercare application scenarios to tackle these issues. In April 2020, Shanghai released the first requirements list that included 12 application scenarios [6], and in June 2021, it released the second one with 8 scenarios [7]. Guangzhou [8] and Chengdu [9] followed suit and published their requirements list of Smart Eldercare application scenarios in November 2021 and May 2022, respectively.

Smart Eldercare application scenarios are a subset of aging scenarios that current technologies might or might not be able to address. An aging scenario depicts the context of a set of unique needs of older adults and connects to many cases that put this scenario into real-world perspective.

This study aims to design a multi-label classification method to manage and utilize scenario cases. With the help of multi-category and fine-grained scenario labels, it can provide technical support for personalized recommendation, efficient retrieval, and similar case aggregation. To meet the allocation requirements of different label classes, we adopt a strategy of joint optimization of multiple tasks. We hope this study will increase the awareness of aging scenarios and encourage further work to utilize them automatically.

1.2 Aging Scenario Model

Lawrence Pervin [10] defined a scenario as "In most cases, including a specific place, a specific person, a specific time, and a specific activity." The general public often knows it as a term in theater, film, or television. With the rapid growth of the Internet, people have recognized the importance of the scenario as a conceptual device and started to employ it in various application domains [11–14].

A well-built scenario is invaluable in unpacking history, understanding the current circumstances, and predicting future developments. To the last point, Kahn and Wiener [15] observed in 1967, "The description of the possible future and the way to achieve it constitutes a scenario."

Understanding the behavior and needs of older adults is not trivial. As Nisbett [16] pointed out, "Field theory in physics prompted research showing that situational and contextual factors are often more important in producing behavior than personal dispositions such as traits, abilities, and preferences."

Aging scenarios aim to capture situational and contextual factors of older individuals and associated stakeholders. Constructing and utilizing aging scenarios can help accurately capture the diverse needs of older individuals and provide them with a highly personalized service experience, thereby forming user stickiness and loyalty.

Table 1. List of the detailed descriptions of scenario elements

Scenario elements	Explanation
When	The time of the scenario
Where	The location of the scenario
Who	The main person in the scenario
Whom	The person receives service or action in the scenario
What	What is the behavior of the main person in the scenario
Which	Which method or instrument is used in this scenario
How	How is the process, often illustrated by a scenario case
Why	The reason for the behavior

To our best knowledge, this study is the first to provide a structured framework of aging scenarios for research and teaching of eldercare services by developing a formal model and associated algorithms. We define the elements of the aging scenario as When, Where, Who, Which, Whom, What, Why, and How. Using this model is straightforward to figure out who did what to whom, when and where, using which method or instrument, why, and how the process worked. The proposed aging scenario model also includes novel elements including occurrence frequency (high/ medium/ low), impact depth (deep/ medium/ shallow), influence breadth (wide/ medium/ narrow), and urgency (high/ medium/ low). These elements can be instrumental in capturing the practical information of real aging scenario cases.

Table 1 presents a list of scenario elements in detail. We will use the following scenario case [17] as a running example in this paper, and Table 2 shows the scenario elements in this case.

On December 15, 2020, Aibo second Village, Xinhong Street, Minhang District, Shanghai, launched a cognitive function screening activity for older adults at its community center. This event was part of a local government effort to build a dementia-friendly community. Seventy older adults attended this event, including some oldest old, some older adults living alone, and some disabled older adults in this community. The onsite cognitive evaluators guided them to complete the screening questionnaire and effectively alleviated the pressure on older adults in the screening process. This event helped identify some older adults with a high risk of cognitive decline and made attending older adults better understand the cognitive impairment.

Table 2. List of scenario elements of the cognitive function screening scenario

Scenario elements	Analysis
When	December 15, 2020
Where	The community center of Aibo second Village, Xinhong Street, Minhang District, Shanghai
Who	Cognitive evaluators
Whom	The oldest old, the older adults living alone, and the disabled older adults in the community
What	Cognitive function screening
Which	Screening questionnaire
How	The guidance of cognitive evaluators alleviated the pressure on older adults in the screening process
Why	To build a dementia-friendly community

1.3 Scenario Labels

Since the inception of Web2.0, the traditional classification method was no longer applicable to the enormous number and types of network information. In August 2004, Thomas Vander Wal combined "folks" with "taxonomy" to create "Folksonomy" [18], which became a classification method. It classifies information over WWW by labeling the bookmarks, photos, or other web-based content [19]. Unlike traditional classification approaches, Folksonomy is a process in which users spontaneously identify and share network information with labels. It is a bottom-up social classification generated by non-professionals [20]. The basic idea is to encourage users to select labels according to their ideas for information, with powerful knowledge aggregation and sharing function.

Selecting labels to annotate scenario cases depends on the scenario collector's understanding of the scenario. Each label is a category, and a scenario case can belong to multiple categories. All scenario cases exist on a shared platform, and the same label can aggregate the scenarios of different older adults under the same category.

This paper focuses on the scenario elements closely related to the needs of older adults in the scenario cases. At the same time, considering the labeling difficult, we only extract some of them instead of using all the scenario elements as scenario label classes. The extracted elements are When, Where, Who, and What, representing the differences in requirements in each scenario case. For example, different types of older adults may have different needs for one particular event. Utilizing the requirements list of Smart Eldercare application scenarios in Shanghai, we predefined fine-grained labels under each class. We provided scenario collectors with predefined scenario labels during the scenario collection process and enabled them to create their own scenario labels. After that, we finalized 55 scenario labels with the collector's annotations. Figure 1 presents the second-level classification of scenario labels. In the figure, person-labels, location-labels, time-labels, and event-labels correspond to Who, Where, When, and What, respectively.

Regarding our running example, the cognitive function screening scenario, Fig. 2 shows its related scenario labels.

Fig. 1. The second-level classification of scenario labels

Scenario labels:
Community | The oldest old | Older adults living alone | Disabled older adults | Cognitive impairment | Managing health | Daytime

---

Fig. 2. Labels for the cognitive function screening scenario

2 Related Works

2.1 Multi-label Text Classification

Unlike traditional text classification, multi-label text classification aims to label as relevant as possible for each sample. A simple example is the classification of news topics. A news piece can belong to "finance" and "economic." The form of multi-label annotation can better reflect the semantic information contained in the text and refine the classification granularity. In addition, many practical applications have used this technology, including label recommendation [21], information retrieval [22], and more.

This section reviews the research on multi-label text classification. There are two research methods: traditional machine learning methods and deep learning methods. There are roughly two types of traditional machine learning methods according to solution strategies: problem transformation and algorithm adaptation [23]. The key to problem transformation methods is to fit data to the algorithm [24]. For example, Binary Relevance (BR) method [25] converts multi-label text classification tasks into multiple single-label classification problems. It assumes that labels are independent, completely ignoring the correlations between labels. The Classifier Chains (CC) method [26] transforms the multi-label classification problem into a binary classification problem chain to consider the correlations between labels. However, since the subsequent binary classifiers in the chain build on previous predictions, the computational complexity will be higher when the dataset is large. Compared with problem transformation methods, the philosophy of algorithm adaptation methods is to fit algorithms to data [24], such as ML-KNN [27], ML-DT [28], Rank-SVM [29], and CML [30]. These algorithms can capture first-order or second-order label correlations but are difficult to calculate when considering high-order label correlations.

In recent years, deep learning methods have seen wide application in NLP. Some neural network models have achieved notable progress in multi-label text classification tasks. In 2014, Yoon Kim [31] proposed TextCNN and applied CNN structure to sentence classification tasks. It used the convolution layer to extract the semantic features of sentences and capture the local correlations of texts. Besides, RNN [32], CNN-RNN [33], Attention [34], LSTM [35], and other structures have also made great contributions in feature extraction. However, effectively exploiting the label correlations information is the key to the success of multi-label learning techniques [24]. To this end, researchers have paid tremendous efforts. For example, Yang [36] proposed SGM, which regards the multi-label classification task as a sequence generation problem, and applies the Attention mechanism to consider the contribution of different parts of the text to labels. LSAN [37], proposed by Lin, fuses the semantic information of labels and documents to construct label-specific document representation. Using one-hot vectors to represent true labels ignores the semantic information of labels and their correlation with samples. Therefore, Guo [38] designed LCM to model the distribution of labels. In addition, DXML [39], EXAM [40], GILE [41] are also proposed to capture label correlations. Although they obtained promising results in some cases, the labeling requirements of scenario labels in this paper make them unable to work well. Specifically, the secondary labels under location-labels and time-labels are independent, so we only select the most related label under each class. In contrast, the secondary labels under person-labels and event-labels are relevant, and we select multiple labels under each class.

2.2 Multi-task Learning

Multi-task learning [42] is a paradigm that aims to jointly learn multiple related tasks and improve learning efficiency and prediction accuracy by appropriately sharing parameters between different tasks [43]. Compared with each task being solved separately by its network, multi-task learning demonstrates the advantages of less memory, faster inference speed, and better model generalization ability.

One of the challenges of multi-task learning is the weight optimization of loss for each task. The manual cost of this optimization is prohibitively high as it requires significant labor time from experienced people [44]. If we directly sum up the loss of all tasks, it will cause an imbalance in model optimization. Therefore, we should carefully balance the joint learning of all tasks to avoid a situation where one or more tasks dominate the network weights [45]. There have been many studies in this area. For example, Chen [46] proposed a gradient normalization (GradNorm) algorithm, which automatically balances the training in the multi-task model by dynamically adjusting the gradient size. Like GradNorm, Liu [47] proposed a dynamic weighted average (DWA) method, which adapts the task weights over time by considering the loss change rate of each task. Besides, Kendall [44] proposed an uncertainty weighting method, which weighs multiple loss functions by considering the homoscedastic uncertainty of each task. It can effectively improve the accuracy of each task in multi-task learning.

3   Proposed Method

We introduce our proposed method in detail in this section. First, we give an overview of the model in Sect. 3.1. Second, we detail the model structure for Task-I in Sect. 3.2, which aims at the multi-label classification problem of person-labels and event-labels. Third, we explain the model structures of Task-II and Task-III in Sect. 3.3, which targets the classification of location-labels and time-labels, respectively. Finally, Sect. 3.4 introduces the trade-off and optimization of loss between multiple tasks.

3.1   Overview

First, we define some notations and describe the multi-label text classification task. Let $D = \{d_1, d_2, \ldots, d_m\}$ represent a dataset composed of m scenario cases. Given the label space with l labels $Y = \{y_1, y_2, \ldots, y_l\}$. The task is to assign a subset y in the label space Y to d_i, $d_i \in D$.

Figure 3 shows an overview of our proposed model. The input of the model is the text after preprocessing. Each text comprises a sequence of words. Let $d_i = \{x_1, x_2, \ldots, x_n\}$ denote the ith text, where n is the number of words in this text. We feed the original text into the input encoder and convert them into vectors. Then its output is fed into the Bi-directional Long Short-Term Memory (Bi-LSTM) [48] language model to capture the semantic information of the input sequence in the forward and backward directions.

At time-step t, the forward LSTM layer obtains the information of time-step t and the last time of the input sequence. The backward LSTM layer obtains the information of time-step t and the subsequent time in the input sequence. We get the hidden states of Bi-LSTM at time-step t as follows:

$$\vec{h}_t = \overrightarrow{LSTM}\left(\vec{h}_{t-1}, w_t\right) \tag{1}$$

$$\overleftarrow{h}_t = \overleftarrow{LSTM}(\overleftarrow{h}_{t-1}, w_t) \tag{2}$$

where $w_t \in R^k$ is the embedding vector of the tth word in the input sequence, and k is the dimension of the embedding vector.

To obtain the overall representation of the input sequence, we concatenate the forward and backward word context representations. We represent the whole text as a matrix $H \in R^{2k \times n}$.

$$\overrightarrow{H} = \left(\overrightarrow{h}_1, \overrightarrow{h}_2, \ldots, \overrightarrow{h}_n \right) \tag{3}$$

$$\overleftarrow{H} = \left(\overleftarrow{h}_1, \overleftarrow{h}_2, \ldots, \overleftarrow{h}_n \right) \tag{4}$$

$$H = \left(\overrightarrow{H}, \overleftarrow{H} \right) \tag{5}$$

Each label contains semantic information. Like the text to be classified, we input labels into the input encoder to get the embedding vectors. In this case, matrix $L \in R^{l_1 \times k}$ indicates the embedded vector of the label set, and l_1 is the number of labels for Task-I.

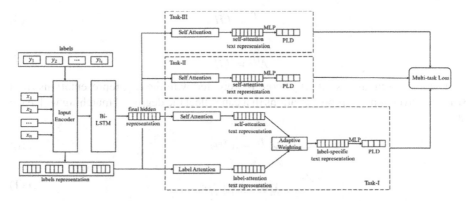

Fig. 3. The overview of our proposed model

3.2 Task-I

Self-Attention. Each sample in the multi-label text classification task is labeled with multiple labels, and each label has its context. However, the features in each sample are not easy to map precisely to the corresponding labels. One approach is to capture the contribution of all words in a sample to each label. We use the self-attention mechanism to obtain the labels' attention score matrix of all words in the text. The attention score matrix $A^{(s)} \in R^{l_1 \times n}$ is as follows:

$$A^{(s)} = softmax(W_2 tanh(W_1 H)) \tag{6}$$

where $W_1 \in R^{d_a \times 2k}$ and $W_2 \in R^{l_1 \times d_a}$ are the self-attention parameters to be trained, and d_a is a hyper-parameter. *tanh* is the hyperbolic tangent nonlinearity activation function [49]. Without an activation function like *tanh*, the output would be a linear combination of inputs, making it meaningless to increase the number of neural network layers.

We perform a weighted calculation on this weight matrix and the hidden layer representation of the input text. By assigning a higher weight to the context most relevant to the label, we obtain textual representation ($M^{(s)} \in R^{l_1 \times 2k}$) that can reflect the degree of contribution to each label:

$$M^{(s)} = A^{(s)} H^T \tag{7}$$

Label-Attention. Self-attention does not consider the semantic information of the labels but only trains according to the text content. Some labels have fewer samples than others, so the learning effect of these labels will be affected to some extent. Furthermore, their related context will differ even if two samples have the same labels. Therefore, it is necessary to use the semantic information of the labels to establish the matching relationship between the text representation and each label. With the label embedding matrix and the text representation of the Bi-LSTM output, we obtain the semantic similarity score between each label and the text through the dot product method:

$$\vec{A}^{(l)} = L \vec{H} \tag{8}$$

$$\overleftarrow{A}^{(l)} = L \overleftarrow{H} \tag{9}$$

The above semantic similarity score is weighted with the text representations from Bi-LSTM to obtain text representations that can reflect the degree of matching with each label:

$$\vec{M}^{(l)} = \vec{A}^{(l)} \vec{H}^T \tag{10}$$

$$\overleftarrow{M}^{(l)} = \overleftarrow{A}^{(l)} \overleftarrow{H}^T \tag{11}$$

$$M^{(l)} = (\vec{M}^{(l)}, \overleftarrow{M}^{(l)}) \tag{12}$$

where $\vec{M}^{(l)} \in R^{l_1 \times k}$ and $\overleftarrow{M}^{(l)} \in R^{l_1 \times k}$ represent the text's forward and backward embedding representations under the label-attention, respectively. $M^{(l)} \in R^{l_1 \times 2k}$ is a complete textual representation that reflects the matching degree of each label.

Adaptive Weighting. $M^{(s)}$ focuses on text information that contributes more to the labeled labels while $M^{(l)}$ focuses on text information that is more semantically related to labels. To fully use these two parts of information, we adopt a fusion strategy to weigh them to construct a comprehensive text representation.

Perform linear transformation on $M^{(s)}$ and $M^{(l)}$, W_3, $W_4 \in R^{2k}$ are the parameters to be trained. Then input the sigmoid function to map them to the 0–1 interval to obtain two weight vectors (λ, $\mu \in R^{l_1}$). Each row of λ and (λ_j, μ_j), respectively, represents the weight of self-attention and label-attention in constructing the text representation when considering the relevance of the jth label to the text.

$$\lambda = sigmoid\left(M^{(s)} W_3\right) \tag{13}$$

$$\mu = sigmoid\left(M^{(l)}W_4\right) \tag{14}$$

The final text representation combines the text representations obtained by self-attention and label-attention. Therefore, we restrict λ_j and μ_j to add up to 1. Based on the fusion strategy, when considering the correlation between the jth label and the text, the text representation is as follows:

$$M_j = \lambda_j M_j^{(s)} + \left(1 - \lambda_j\right)M_j^{(l)} \tag{15}$$

Then, we can concatenate M_j to get the comprehensive-textual representation $M \in R^{l_1 \times 2k}$.

Label Prediction. After obtaining the comprehensive-textual representation, we can build a multi-layer perceptron (MLP) to predict label distribution (PLD). For Task-I, each scenario case can have multiple labels. As a correlation coefficient between 0.8 and 1.0 indicates a strong correlation [50], we set 0.8 as the threshold. When the predicted probability is greater than 0.8, we consider this label is relevant to the scenario case. We define the predicted probability as follows:

$$\hat{y} = sigmoid\left(W_6 f\left(W_5 M^T\right)\right) \tag{16}$$

where $W_5 \in R^{a \times 2k}$ and $W_6 \in R^a$ are the parameters of the fully connected layer and output layer, respectively. The value of a depends on the number of labels for Task-I. f is a nonlinear activation function. The sigmoid function maps the predicted probability to between 0 and 1.

3.3 Task-II and Task-III

Self-Attention. Task-II and Task-III are different from Task-I. In Task-II and Task-III, an input text can only select one fine-grained label from location-labels and time-labels, respectively. The contents corresponding to the labels in these two tasks are relatively stable. Therefore, these two tasks only obtain the high-level features of the text through the self-attention mechanism, which can also reduce the time cost with little compromise of accuracy. According to the attention score matrix, we weigh the text representation. The calculation process is as follows:

$$B^{(s)} = softmax(W_8 tanh(W_7 H)) \tag{17}$$

$$N^{(s)} = B^{(s)} H^T \tag{18}$$

where $W_7 \in R^{d_b \times 2k}$ and $W_8 \in R^{l' \times d_b}$ are the self-attention parameters to be trained. d_b is a hyper-parameter we can set arbitrarily. $N^{(s)} \in R^{l' \times 2k}$ is the text representation after weighting calculation. $l' = l_2$ and $l' = l_3$ represent the number of labels for Task-II and Task-III, respectively. *tanh* is an activation function used to increase the nonlinearity of the neural network model.

Label Prediction. In Task-II and Task-III, a scenario case can only have one scenario label. Therefore, we select the label with the highest predicted probability as the final prediction result. We define the predicted probability as follows:

$$\hat{y} = sigmoid\left(W_{10}f\left(W_9 N^{(s)T}\right)\right) \tag{19}$$

where $W_9 \in R^{b \times 2k}$, $W_{10} \in R^b$ are the parameters of the fully connected layer and output layer, respectively. The value of b depends on the number of labels for the current task.

3.4 Loss Optimization

For Task-I, we use cross-entropy as the loss function. L_1 represents the loss of Task-I:

$$L_1 = -\sum_{i=1}^{m} \sum_{j=1}^{l_1} y_{ij} \log(\hat{y}_{ij}) + \left(1 - y_{ij}\right)\log\left(1 - \hat{y}_{ij}\right) \tag{20}$$

where m is the number of training texts. For the ith text, $y_{ij} \in \{0, 1\}$ indicates the target probability of the jth label, and $\hat{y}_{ij} \in [0, 1]$ is the predicted probability.

Use the label smoothing method [51] when calculating the loss for Task-II and Task-III. The regularization strategy adds noise to the 0–1 probability distribution of the true labels, reducing their weight in calculating the loss function and preventing the model from overfitting. L_2 and L_3 are as follows:

$$L_2 = \sum_{i=1}^{m} \sum_{j=1}^{l_2} L(\hat{y}_{ij}, y'_{ij}) \tag{21}$$

$$L_3 = \sum_{i=1}^{m} \sum_{j=1}^{l_3} L(\hat{y}_{ij}, y'_{ij}) \tag{22}$$

where L is the standard cross-entropy loss, and y'_{ij} indicates the soft labels after smoothing.

We use the uncertainty weighting method [44] proposed by Kendall to optimize the loss of the three tasks. Multiple loss functions are measured by considering the uncertainty of the same variance for each task:

$$L_{total} = \sum_{i=1}^{3} \frac{1}{2\sigma_i^2} L_i + \log\sigma_i \tag{23}$$

where σ_i is the model's observation noise parameter. It captures how much noise the outputs have.

4 Experiment

4.1 The Dataset

Scenario data collection in this study began on October 24, 2021, over 15 days, and 108 undergraduate students from Hefei University of Technology participated in this effort.

Considering the ambiguity of the scenario concept, we first explained the scenario elements and predefined scenario labels to the scenario collectors. To meet the labeling needs of collectors, we allowed collectors to customize labels beyond that scope. Collectors then filled out scenario collection forms describing the life scenarios of older adults around them or on the Internet and news.

The form content includes a complete scenario description and scenario labels associated with the scenario case. The scenario description includes time, location, older adults, events, and more. The scenario labels are represented in a hierarchical structure with two levels, as shown in Fig. 1. There are four classes of first-level scenario labels: person-labels, location-labels, time-labels, and event-labels. We consider only leaf nodes to simplify the problem. The secondary labels under location-labels and time-labels are independent, so collectors can only select one label under each class. Unlike the above, the secondary labels under person-labels and event-labels are relevant, and collectors can select multiple labels under each class. We aim to label all related labels for each scenario case as much as possible.

Finally, we collected 938 scenario cases and identified 55 scenario labels. We use this dataset to train and test our proposed method. The sample distribution of scenario labels is non-uniform and presents a class imbalance challenge. The majority of scenario cases have five or fewer labels. However, only a few scenario labels are used regularly, two of which refer to more than 500 scenario cases, namely "Daytime" and "The self-care older adults." Fig. 4 shows the distribution of scenario labels to scenario cases. Each bar corresponds to a scenario label, and the height represents the number of its scenario cases.

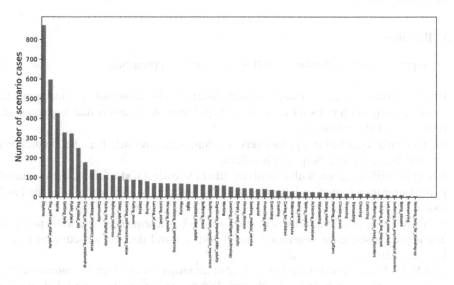

Fig. 4. Sample distribution of each scenario label

Before our work, scenario collectors would manually label scenario cases. This process is costly and time-consuming. Because each scenario case can belong to more than one scenario label, different annotators may have differing ideas on the labels involved in the same scenario case. Reconciling these differences and maintaining consistency between scenario cases is a considerable challenge.

4.2 Evaluation Metrics

Following the settings of previous work, we adopt the micro-F1 score and hamming loss to evaluate the model's performance. In addition, we also report precision and recall for reference. These metrics use the following parameters: True Positives (TP), True Negatives (TN), False Positives (FP), and False Negatives (FN).

$$Precision = \frac{TP}{TP + FP}$$

$$Recall = \frac{TP}{TP + FN}$$

$$F_1 = 2 \times \frac{Precision \times Recall}{Precision + Recall}$$

Micro-F1: the weighted average of precision and recall. Labels with large sample sizes usually have a more significant impact on the final evaluation.

Hamming-loss: the fraction of the wrong labels to the total number of labels. The optimal value is zero, and the upper bound is one. The smaller the value, the better one's classification ability.

4.3 Baselines

We compare our approach with the following baseline approaches:

- BR [25] works by decomposing the multi-label classification task into independent binary classification tasks for each label. Its potential weakness is that it ignores the correlations between labels.
- CC [26] links together binary classifiers in a chain structure such that label predictions become features for subsequent classifiers.
- CNN [31] utilizes layers with convolving filters to extract text features, then inputted to the linear transformation layer to output the probability distribution over the label space.
- SGM [36] views the multi-label classification task as a sequence generation problem and applies a sequence generation model with a novel decoder structure to model label correlations.
- LSAN [37] uses a self-attention and label-attention mechanism to determine the semantic connection between labels and documents for constructing label-specific document representation.

4.4 Parameter Setting

We implement our model in Pytorch and run our experiments on NVIDIA Tesla T4.

Sentence length: We performed length statistics on the preprocessed scenario cases. The CDF diagram is drawn according to the text length statistics, as shown in Fig. 5. The average length of all scenario cases is 195.8 words. If the text length is too long, it will introduce mixed information. On the other hand, if it is too short, the text information will be lost. We conducted length comparison experiments, choosing 400 as the length of the input texts and adopting the strategy of long truncation and short complement.

Embedding layer: Transformer models show outstanding performance on a wide array of NLP tasks. We use the pre-trained language model BERT [52] as the input encoder, where the embedding space size is 768, i.e., k = 768. The hidden size of Bi-LSTM is 300.

Neuron weights: The parameters corresponding to the neuron weights are $d_a = 200$ for W_1 and W_2, $d_b = 256$ for W_7 and W_8.

Optimization: The whole model is trained via Adam [53] with an initial learning_rate = 5e–5, weight_decay = 1e–5 and the batch size is 4.

Training: We trained the model for 40 epochs and chose the best model according to the performance of the validation set. After 1000 batches, if there is no improvement in the effect of the model, the training is ended early.

The parameters of all baseline models are adopted from their original papers. All baselines follow the same data division.

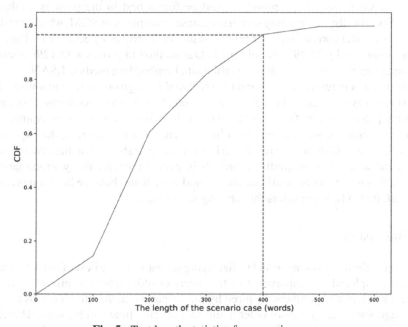

Fig. 5. Text length statistics for scenario cases

4.5 Results and Analysis

In this section, we report the evaluation results of our method and all baselines on the test set. We use the same 10 random seeds to train the proposed model and baselines and calculate the mean. As shown in Table 3, the symbols HL, P, R, and F1 denote hamming loss, micro-precision, micro-recall, and micro-F1, respectively. The symbol + indicates that the higher the value is, the better the model performs. The symbol − indicates the opposite, i.e., the higher the value, the worse the model performs. In each line, we mark the best result in bold.

Table 3. Comparison between our method and all baselines on the aging scenarios dataset

Models	HL(−)	P(+)	R(+)	F1(+)
BR	0.0745	0.3748	**0.7911**	0.5086
CC	**0.0744**	0.3763	0.7906	0.5098
CNN	0.0745	0.8235	0.3484	0.4859
SGM	0.1207	0.4311	0.5075	0.4654
LSAN	0.0792	**0.8410**	0.3355	0.4249
Ours	0.0805	0.6523	0.6061	**0.6166**

Results show that our proposed method performs best in the primary evaluation metrics. Specifically, on the aging scenarios dataset, compared to SGM, which considers capturing the label correlations, our proposed model decreases by 33.31% on hamming loss and improves by 32.49% on micro-F1. Our method improves a 45.12% micro-F1 score on the aging scenarios dataset over the label embedding method LSAN.

The experiment results of CNN and LSAN also show high precision and low recall. In other words, they can predict the high-frequency labels for most scenario cases but cannot accurately predict the low-frequency labels. The low-frequency labels are connected to only a few scenario cases, making them hard to learn. On the contrary, the experiment results of BR and CC show high recall and low precision. It shows that these two methods improve the accuracy by outputting more labels, even if there are many wrong labels in the prediction results. In comparison, our method has a better balance between precision and recall. It also fully considers the labeling requirements.

5   Conclusion

This paper is the first to manage and utilize aging scenarios to the best of our knowledge. Firstly, we explored the importance of the needs of older adults in providing quality eldercare services and products. Inspired by the scenario era, the life scenarios can well show the problems and needs of older adults in a specific time and location. Therefore, analyzing the aging scenarios is one of the ways to obtain their actual needs.

Further, we constructed the scenario model in the field of Smart Eldercare. Considering the generation of personalized needs of older adults, we used part of the scenario elements as scenario label classes. We aim to label relevant labels to scenario cases to facilitate their classification, retrieval, and aggregation. After that, according to the characteristics of the scenario labels, we adopted a strategy of joint optimization of multiple tasks for the multi-label classification of scenario cases. This strategy can alleviate model overfitting and improve generalization ability by parameter sharing. Compared with baseline models, the proposed method can achieve an accuracy of 61.66% and is better than other models.

This study encourages the eldercare practitioners and Smart Eldercare enterprises to focus more on the needs of older adults with aging scenarios. This study also builds the foundation for building an aging scenarios database that stores, shares, and manages scenarios and their cases. In this database, product requirements analysts in the eldercare field can efficiently retrieve and associate related scenario cases through automated scenario annotation in this paper. Furthermore, they can design demand-centric products and services for older adults by analyzing the actual needs in the same category of scenarios.

This study has the following limitations. First, the label distribution of this dataset is unbalanced. Some labels are only associated with a handful of scenario cases. To solve this problem, we can find more related scenario cases in the future. Then these new scenario cases are merged with training data, and we will retrain the model to ameliorate the effects of class imbalance. Second, we chose 400 as the length of the input texts after length comparison experiments. There is room to optimize this process to find the optimized text as input in the future.

In addition, we did not desensitize the currently used dataset. Usually, scenario descriptions include time, location, characters, and other detailed information, and some scenario cases even expose the actual name of older adults. Therefore, it is necessary to desensitize the personal information in the dataset before adding them to an aging scenarios database. We can also take measures to protect the privacy of older adults. For example, let data collectors not use any private information such as real names and concrete addresses of older adults. This operation will prevent the personal data of older adults from being leaked. At the same time, it can improve the trust of older adults in the database and encourage more people to share their life scenarios.

Acknowledgments. This work was partially supported by grants from the Anhui Provincial Key Technologies R&D Program (2022h11020015), the Program of Introducing Talents of Discipline to Universities (111 Program) (B14025), and the Non-profit Central Research Institute Fund of the Chinese Academy of Medical Sciences, Grant No. 2021-JKCS-026 with accordance ethical approval from the funding academy.

References

1. Wang, S.: Spatial patterns and social-economic influential factors of population aging: a global assessment from 1990 to 2010. Soc. Sci. Med. **253**, 112963 (2020)
2. Ying, G., Zonghua, L.: Application and development of smart pension products in China. In: 2020 4th International Seminar on Education, Management and Social Sciences (ISEMSS 2020), pp. 287–291. Atlantis Press (2020)

3. Kleinman, A., et al.: Social technology: an interdisciplinary approach to improving care for older adults. Front. Public Health **9**, 729149 (2021). https://doi.org/10.3389/fpubh.2021.729149
4. Sun, J., Li, W.: How is smart pension possible from the perspective of population aging. In: 7th International Conference on Humanities and Social Science Research (ICHSSR 2021), pp. 345–348. Atlantis Press (2021)
5. Xin, S., Li, J., Wang, Y.: The development of smart pension with benefits and challenges. Tech. Rep., EasyChair (2019)
6. Requirements list of Smart Eldercare application scenarios in Shanghai. https://www.shanghai.gov.cn/nw31406/20200820/0001-31406_1441030.html (2020 version). Accessed 10 June 2022
7. The second requirements list of Smart Eldercare application scenarios in Shanghai. https://mzj.sh.gov.cn/2021bsmz/20210629/6a32755904584d21a7c665a8b86e8ae3.html. Accessed 10 June 2022
8. Requirements list of Smart Eldercare application scenarios in Guangzhou. http://mzj.gz.gov.cn/gkmlpt/content/7/7925/post_7925097.html#346. Accessed 10 June 2022
9. Requirements list of Smart Eldercare application scenarios in Chengdu. http://cd.wenming.cn/wmbb/202205/t20220509_7605909.shtml. Accessed 10 June 2022
10. Meyrowitz, J.: No Sense of Place: The Impact of Electronic Media on Social Behavior. Oxford University Press (1986)
11. Wu, F., Huang, S., Yin, B.: Scenario-based service: new thinking of the design of learning service. e-Educ. Res. **39**, 63–69 (2018)
12. Shi, L., Yang, X., Li, J., Wu, J., Sun, H.: Scenario construction and deduction for railway emergency response decision-making based on network models. Inf. Sci. **588**, 331–349 (2022)
13. Seibert, K., et al.: Application scenarios for artificial intelligence in nursing care: rapid review. J. Med. Internet Res. **23**(11), e26522 (2021)
14. Yifei, Y., Longming, Z.: Application scenarios and enabling technologies of 5g. China Commun. **11**(11), 69–79 (2014)
15. Kahn, H., Wiener, A.J.: The Next Thirty-Three Years: A Framework for Speculation, pp. 705–732. Daedalus (1967)
16. Nisbett, R.E.: Mindware: Tools for Smart Thinking. Farrar, Straus and Giroux (2015)
17. Cognitive function screening in Xinhong Street. http://www.shmh.gov.cn/shmh/sqxx-xhjd/20201216/499154.html. Accessed 24 Feb 2022
18. Sturtz, D.N.: Communal categorization: the folksonomy. INFO622: Content Representation **16** (2004)
19. Shen, K., Wu, L.: Folksonomy as a complex network (2005)
20. Quintarelli, E.F.: Power to the people. In: ISKO Italy-UniMIB Meeting, Milan, June 24, 2005 (2005)
21. Katakis, I., Tsoumakas, G., Vlahavas, I.: Multilabel text classification for automated tag suggestion. In: Proceedings of the ECML/PKDD, vol. 18, p. 5. Citeseer (2008)
22. Yang, Y.: Multilabel classification with meta-level features. In: Proceedings of the 33rd International ACM SIGIR Conference on Research and Development in Information Retrieval, pp. 315–322 (2010)
23. Tsoumakas, G., Katakis, I.: Multi-label classification: an overview. Int. J. Data Warehousing Mining **3**(3), 1–13 (2007)
24. Zhang, M.L., Zhou, Z.H.: A review on multi-label learning algorithms. IEEE Trans. Knowl. Data Eng. **26**(8), 1819–1837 (2013)
25. Boutell, M.R., Luo, J., Shen, X., Brown, C.M.: Learning multi-label scene classification. Pattern Recogn. **37**(9), 1757–1771 (2004)
26. Read, J., Pfahringer, B., Holmes, G., Frank, E.: Classifier chains for multi-label classification. Mach. Learn. **85**(3), 333–359 (2011)

27. Zhang, M.L., Zhou, Z.H.: ML-KNN: a lazy learning approach to multi-label learning. Pattern Recogn. **40**(7), 2038–2048 (2007)
28. Clare, A., King, R.D.: Knowledge discovery in multi-label phenotype data. In: Raedt, L., Siebes, A. (eds.) PKDD 2001. LNCS (LNAI), vol. 2168, pp. 42–53. Springer, Heidelberg (2001). https://doi.org/10.1007/3-540-44794-6_4
29. Elisseeff, A., Weston, J.: A kernel method for multi-labelled classification. Adv. Neural Inf. Process. Syst. **14** (2001)
30. Ghamrawi, N., McCallum, A.: Collective multi-label classification. In: Proceedings of the 14th ACM International Conference on Information and Knowledge Management, pp. 195–200 (2005)
31. Kim, Y.: Convolutional neural networks for sentence classification. In: Proceedings of the 2014 Conference on Empirical Methods in Natural Language Processing (EMNLP), pp. 1746–1751. Association for Computational Linguistics, Doha, Qatar (Oct 2014). https://doi.org/10.3115/v1/D14-1181. https://aclanthology.org/D14-1181
32. Liu, P., Qiu, X., Huang, X.: Recurrent neural network for text classification with multi-task learning (2016)
33. Chen, G., Ye, D., Xing, Z., Chen, J., Cambria, E.: Ensemble application of convolutional and recurrent neural networks for multi-label text categorization. In: 2017 International Joint Conference on Neural Networks (IJCNN), pp. 2377–2383. IEEE (2017)
34. Yang, Z., Yang, D., Dyer, C., He, X., Smola, A., Hovy, E.: Hierarchical attention networks for document classification. In: Proceedings of the 2016 Conference of the North American Chapter of the Association for Computational Linguistics: Human Language Technologies, pp. 1480–1489 (2016)
35. Hochreiter, S., Schmidhuber, J.: Long short-term memory. Neural Comput. **9**(8), 1735–1780 (1997)
36. Yang, P., Sun, X., Li, W., Ma, S., Wu, W., Wang, H.: SGM: sequence generation model for multi-label classification (2018)
37. Xiao, L., Huang, X., Chen, B., Jing, L.: Label-specific document representation for multi-label text classification. In: Proceedings of the 2019 Conference on Empirical Methods in Natural Language Processing and the 9th International Joint Conference on Natural Language Processing (EMNLP-IJCNLP), pp. 466–475 (2019)
38. Guo, B., Han, S., Han, X., Huang, H., Lu, T.: Label confusion learning to enhance text classification models (2020)
39. Zhang, W., Yan, J., Wang, X., Zha, H.: Deep extreme multi-label learning. In: Proceedings of the 2018 ACM on International Conference on Multimedia Retrieval, pp. 100–107 (2018)
40. Du, C., Chen, Z., Feng, F., Zhu, L., Gan, T., Nie, L.: Explicit interaction model towards text classification. In: Proceedings of the AAAI Conference on Artificial Intelligence, vol. 33, pp. 6359–6366 (2019)
41. Pappas, N., Henderson, J.: Gile: a generalized input-label embedding for text classification. Trans. Assoc. Comput. Linguist. **7**, 139–155 (2019)
42. Caruana, R.: Multitask learning. Mach. Learn. **28**(1), 41–75 (1997)
43. Zhang, Y., Yang, Q.: A survey on multi-task learning. IEEE Trans. Knowl. Data Eng. 1 (2021). https://doi.org/10.1109/TKDE.2021.3070203
44. Kendall, A., Gal, Y., Cipolla, R.: Multi-task learning using uncertainty to weigh losses for scene geometry and semantics. In: Proceedings of the IEEE Conference on Computer Vision and Pattern Recognition (CVPR) (2018)
45. Vandenhende, S., Georgoulis, S., Van Gansbeke, W., Proesmans, M., Dai, D., Van Gool, L.: Multi-task learning for dense prediction tasks: a survey. IEEE Trans. Pattern Anal. Mach. Intell. 1 (2021). https://doi.org/10.1109/TPAMI.2021.3054719

46. Chen, Z., Badrinarayanan, V., Lee, C.Y., Rabinovich, A.: GradNorm: gradient normalization for adaptive loss balancing in deep multitask networks. In: Dy, J., Krause, A. (eds.) Proceedings of the 35th International Conference on Machine Learning. Proceedings of Machine Learning Research, vol. 80, pp. 794–803. PMLR (10–15 Jul 2018). https://proceedings.mlr.press/v80/chen18a.html

47. Liu, S., Johns, E., Davison, A.J.: End-to-end multi-task learning with attention. In: Proceedings of the IEEE/CVF Conference on Computer Vision and Pattern Recognition (CVPR) (2019)

48. Zhou, P., Qi, Z., Zheng, S., Xu, J., Bao, H., Xu, B.: Text classification improved by integrating bidirectional LSTM with two-dimensional max pooling. arXiv preprint arXiv:1611.06639 (2016)

49. Kalman, B.L., Kwasny, S.C.: Why tanh: choosing a sigmoidal function. In: Proceedings of the 1992 IJCNN International Joint Conference on Neural Networks, vol. 4, pp. 578–581. IEEE (1992)

50. Moore, D.S., Notz, W.I., Notz, W.: Statistics: Concepts and Controversies. Macmillan (2006)

51. Müller, R., Kornblith, S., Hinton, G.E.: When does label smoothing help? In: Wallach, H., Larochelle, H., Beygelzimer, A., d'Alché-Buc, F., Fox, E., Garnett, R. (eds.) Advances in Neural Information Processing Systems, vol. 32. Curran Associates, Inc. (2019)

52. Devlin, J., Chang, M.W., Lee, K., Toutanova, K.: Bert: pre-training of deep bidirectional transformers for language understanding (2019)

53. Kingma, D.P., Ba, J.: Adam: a method for stochastic optimization. arXiv preprint arXiv:1412.6980 (2014)

Web Accessibility for People with Cognitive Disabilities: A Systematic Literature Review from 2015 to 2021

Mateo Borina, Edi Kalister, and Tihomir Orehovački(✉) ⓘD

Faculty of Informatics, Juraj Dobrila University of Pula, Zagrebačka 30, 52 100 Pula, Croatia
tihomir.orehovacki@unipu.hr

Abstract. Web accessibility refers to the extent to which websites can be consumed by people with disabilities, elderly people, as well as people living in rural areas and developing countries. To make sure that everyone is included and has an equal user experience, developers need to create highly accessible websites. Cognitive disability, which can take various forms, represents an umbrella term that is used when a person has certain limitations in mental functioning and skills such as communication, self-help, and social skills. To determine the degree to which web accessibility for people with cognitive disabilities has been examined in the period from 2015 to 2021, we have carried out a systematic literature review. Reported findings indicate that accessibility of the majority of current websites is very poor but can be improved with a simple design of user interface elements, by providing relevant information in various forms and on the top of the website, and by avoiding distractors of any kind. We also discovered that studies in which people with cognitive disabilities actively participate in the development and evaluation of software solutions meant for enhancing their web experience are rather rare. Drawing on reported findings, limitations of current studies and future work directions are presented and discussed.

Keywords: Systematic literature review · Web · Accessibility · Cognitive disabilities

1 Introduction

Web accessibility denotes the degree to which a website can be used by people with the widest range of characteristics and capabilities [35]. The success of a particular website depends on the extent to which it is usable to all people. Therefore, websites should be designed in such a way that the peculiarities of each potential user are considered. While disability refers to a condition that prevents a person from using a physical or mental part of his/her body fully or with ease, its cognitive aspect (which is by far the most common) is related to the degree to which a person can conduct mental tasks [8]. Cognitive disability can take many forms, including Down syndrome (chromosomal disorder that results in varying degrees of physical and mental retardation), traumatic brain injury

© Springer Nature Switzerland AG 2022
V. G. Duffy et al. (Eds.): HCII 2022, LNCS 13521, pp. 261–276, 2022.
https://doi.org/10.1007/978-3-031-17902-0_19

(a sudden injury that causes damage to the brain), autism (range of conditions characterized by challenges with social skills, repetitive behaviours, speech and nonverbal communication), dementia (group of symptoms affecting person's memory, thinking and social abilities), dyslexia (form of language-based learning disability), attention deficit hyperactivity disorder (person's disability to focus, sit still, and pay attention), dyscalculia (difficulty in learning or comprehending math), amnesia (deficit in learning new information and in retrieval of information from long-term memory), aphasia (impairment or loss of language), alexia (partial or complete inability to read), agraphia (disturbance problems in writing), acalculia (impairment in doing numerical computations), apraxia (skilled movement disorders which cannot be reduced to elementary factors such as impaired comprehension or motor weakness), agnosia (failure of recognition), and neglect (difficulty in reporting, responding, or orienting to information due to an injury), among others [16, 50]. Around 15% of the world population has some form of disability [53]. Although a global estimate for people with cognitive disabilities does not exist, it is reasonable to assume that a considerable portion of one billion people with disability deals with some variety of cognitive disability. With such an extensive and complex structure of cognitive disabilities and their presence in the world of web users, it is important to consider the difficulties persons with such disabilities face.

The objective of this paper is to present and discuss the findings of the systematic review of the literature published in the period from 2015 to 2021 that tackles web accessibility for people with cognitive disabilities. The remainder of the paper is structured as follows. Overview of related work is provided in the next section. The research method is described in the third section. Findings of the systematic literature review are reported in the fourth section. Conclusions are drawn in the last section.

2 Related Work

Although web accessibility guidelines [52] represent authority for designing and developing websites that are usable to all people, they do not address all the problems users with disabilities are facing. To determine those problems, Calvo et al. [13] carried out a study in which seven accessibility experts examined 62 accessibility evaluation reviews. The analysis of the audit revealed that 6% of problems found are not covered by web accessibility guidelines. These problems are as follows: (1) information is hidden visually but not for screen readers or vice versa, (2) common design patterns are not followed properly, (3) wide gaps which separate related content, (4) the use of custom components to adapt interface elements or interaction to requirements of a particular company, (5) size of buttons and text is too small, (6) color contrast ratio between icons and background is too low, and (7) important information is not shown at the top of a website.

Paiva et al. [39] conducted a systematic literature review of 92 papers in the period from 2011 to 2019 to find out how accessibility has been included in the software development process. They in particular discovered that studies were most commonly focused on testing web systems in the domain of government and education. Their findings also indicate that there is a paucity of studies dealing with the human aspects of using interactive systems by people with disabilities. Given that current studies are most commonly addressing visual impairment, the same authors emphasized that future studies should consider other disabilities as well.

Menger et al. [31] explored factors that might act as barriers or facilitators to Internet use by people with aphasia. Since aphasia is a condition that often co-exists with other medical issues, people facing it are commonly digitally excluded individuals because is quite complex for them to access the Internet. According to the same authors, the reason for this does not necessarily have to be just the medical condition of a user but also other concomitant factors (e.g. age, disability, social exclusion) or additional factors at the individual level (e.g. cognitive skills, type and amount of therapy intervention available, personal goals, motivation, support from family, caregivers, and friends). To overcome these barriers, Menger et al. [31] suggested that people with aphasia should be actively involved in research projects dealing with the development of specific technologies as domain experts.

Alzahrani et al. [36] examined to what degree animations on websites affect autistic people. Given that people with autism can be easily distracted by potentially irrelevant elements, the authors emphasized that animations, images, and pop-ups on the website may reduce their efficiency in performing a particular activity or even prevent them to complete the task.

Drawing on a review of 17 papers published in the period between 2005 and 2015, Pagani Britto and Brigante Pizzolato [36] proposed a set of 28 guidelines for designing accessible websites for people with autism. These guidelines are systemized in the following ten categories: visual and textual vocabulary, customization, engagement, redundant representation, multimedia, feedback, affordance, navigability, system status, and interaction with touch screen.

The systematic literature review conducted by Cinquin et al. [15] tackled the accessibility of online e-learning systems for people with cognitive disabilities. As an outcome, they found that current studies most commonly offer design recommendations while only a few of them evaluate the effectiveness of e-learning systems. The authors also discovered that current studies are more focused on particular neuropsychological disorders or syndromes (e.g. ADHD, dyslexia) rather than on impairments of cognitive function (e.g. attention, memory, etc.) and that accessibility standards are poorly and inconsistently used across the studies without a rationale for their employment in the design process.

The aim of the systematic literature review carried out by Bernard et al. [4] was to identify barriers people with mental disorders encounter when interacting with websites as well as facilitation measures that would make websites operable, understandable, perceivable, and robust to a sufficient extent. The authors uncovered that distracting and confusing design, complicated content and website functions, an overabundance of information, high demand for good fine motor skills, and rapid information processing are the most common barriers that are decreasing the experience of using websites for people with mental disorders. To overcome these barriers, the same authors suggested the use of intuitive navigation, correctly functioning features, simple language, explicit, consistent, and easy-to-detect website components, organized content, a flat hierarchical content structure, multimedia formats, and easy-to-operate functions.

Rocheleau et al. [46] reviewed 58 publications to find out the main purpose of Assistive Technologies for Cognition (ATC). Their findings revealed that ATC is commonly used for enhancing or maintaining users' cognitive functioning, reducing the cognitive demands of everyday tasks, informing caregivers about the person's daily well-being and functioning, and supporting independent living.

To improve the usability of websites for people with cognitive disabilities, Blazheska-Tabokovska et al. [7] provided a set of guidelines that need to be considered when creating web content. These guidelines are summarized as follows: (1) navigation needs to be unambiguous and have various options, (2) interaction with interface elements needs to be simple, brief, and without any distractions, (3) text should be short, understandable, and presented in multiple formats while non-literal content should be avoided, and (4) page layout should be consistent while extra material and clutter need to be reduced.

All the aforementioned findings indicate that barriers people with cognitive disabilities are facing when interacting with websites still have not been addressed properly and that there is much room for improvement. To determine the extent of advancement in web accessibility for people with cognitive disabilities in the period from 2015 to 2021, we carried out a systematic literature review whose results are presented and discussed in the following sections.

3   Research Method

A systematic literature review was carried out based on the guidelines proposed by Kitchenham and Charters [29]. The backbone of our study is composed of the following four research questions: (1) how to make it easier for people with cognitive disabilities to use and navigate the web? (2) how accessible is the average website for people with cognitive disabilities? (3) what are unresearched subdomains regarding the accessibility of the web for users with cognitive disabilities? (4) what are the shortcomings of current studies on web use by people with cognitive impairments? The current literature was searched using the following strings:

- ("HCI" OR "human-computer interaction") AND ("web" OR "world wide web" OR "internet") AND ("accessibility" OR "ease of access") AND ("cognitive disabilities" OR "mental disorders" OR "intelligence impairments")
- "human-computer interaction" AND ("web" OR "world wide web" OR "internet") AND "accessibility" AND ("cognitive disabilities" OR "mental disorders" OR "intelligence impairments")
- "HCI" AND "web" AND "accessibility" AND "cognitive disabilities"
- HCI web accessibility cognitive disabilities

The systematic literature review was carried out in the period between November 2021 and January 2022 and included papers from the following databases: Google Scholar, IEEE Xplore, Emerald Insight, Elsevier ScienceDirect, ACM Digital Library, Web of Science, Hindawi, Inderscience, MDPI, SAGE Journals, SpringerLink, and Taylor & Francis. Based on the aforementioned search strings, we identified 5477 records. A summary of the number of records discovered in databases is shown in Table 1.

Table 1. Distribution of identified records by databases.

Source	Number of records
Google Scholar	4150
IEEE Xplore	2
Emerald Insight	38
Elsevier ScienceDirect	92
ACM Digital Library	258
Web of Science	2
Hindawi	1
Inderscience	3
MDPI	0
SAGE Journals	8
SpringerLink	893
Taylor & Francis	30

The selection process was performed in three phases. During the first one, papers were selected based on the connection of their title with the topic of the systematic literature review. As a follow-up, all papers that have met the criterion of the first phase have been downloaded. If it was not possible to find and download the full version of a particular paper, it was excluded from the further selection procedure. In the second phase, the abstract of each paper that passed the purification procedure of the first phase has been read. All papers which were found relevant based on the content of their abstract proceeded to the third phase in which the whole text of every paper has been thoroughly examined. Papers that have met the requirements of all four research questions have been added to the final pool of relevant studies. In all three selection phases, we excluded papers that have not been written in the English language, which have been published in books or as book chapters, and those that turned out to be duplicates.

4 Results

4.1 Identification of Studies

Out of 5477 identified records, the title of only 82 of them was related to the topic of our research and they have been therefore included in the screening step. Five of the screened studies were not retrieved because their full versions could not be found. The remaining 77 studies were assessed for eligibility. Out of them, two duplicate studies were identified, two studies were not written in English, twelve studies were not of a desired and required type of literature, and seventeen of the assessed studies were not in the scope of our study. As an outcome, the systematic literature review resulted in 44 studies that were thoroughly analyzed. A standardized report of the selection process in the form of the PRISMA 2020 flow diagram [38] is presented in Fig. 1.

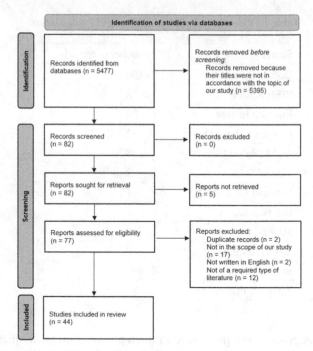

Fig. 1. Flow diagram of the studies selection procedure

4.2 Summary of Findings

The list of reviewed papers consists of twelve quantitative studies [19–22, 24–26, 30, 44, 45, 48, 54], ten qualitative studies [6, 9, 11, 18, 32, 34, 40, 41, 43, 55], five mixed studies [12, 14, 17, 27, 49], nine systematic literature reviews [2, 4, 7, 13, 15, 31, 36, 39, 46], five studies focused on the development of software solutions [3, 10, 23, 47, 48], one study in which both a literature review and qualitative research were carried out [33], one paper in which software solution was proposed and quantitative study was conducted [1], and one paper in which qualitative evaluation of introduced software solution was carried out [5]. The aforementioned indicates that out of 44 studies, there are 20.46% of systematic literature reviews, 15.91% of them are focused on software development, 27.27% of studies include qualitative research methods, 29.55% of studies are quantitative in nature while in 11.36% of them both quantitative and qualitative studies were conducted. The set forth findings are presented in Fig. 2.

Regarding the publication type, 47.73% of papers were published in journals [1, 4, 6, 10, 15, 17, 18, 20, 21, 24–26, 30–32, 34, 39, 44, 49, 54, 55] while 52.27% of them were presented at conferences [2, 3, 5, 7, 9, 11–14, 19, 22, 23, 27, 33, 36, 37, 40, 41, 43, 45–48].

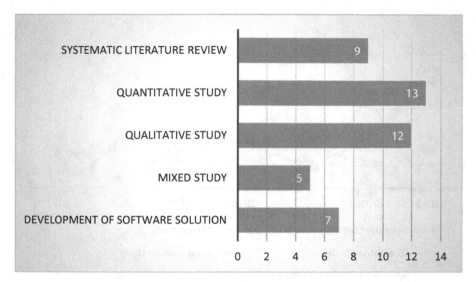

Fig. 2. Distribution of studies per category

Papers that are included in this systematic literature review were mainly published in different journals and conference proceedings. The most popular journals in that respect are Universal Access in the Information Society and ACM Transactions on Accessible Computing with two papers being published in each of them. When conferences were considered from the perspective of frequency in publishing papers related to the topic of this systematic literature review, we discovered that six papers were presented at International Web for All Conference (W4A) while two papers were included in proceedings of the International Conference on Software Development and Technologies for Enhancing Accessibility and Fighting Info-exclusion (DSAI), the International Conference on Human-Computer Interaction (Interacción), and the International Conference on Universal Access in Human-Computer Interaction (UAHCI).

The number of literature reviews and proposed software solutions ranges up to two per year. The amount of both quantitative and qualitative studies as well as the overall number of papers being published is in a declining trend. The highest number of papers (thirteen) was published in 2015 while the smallest amount (three) of them was published in 2021. Trends in publishing papers on web accessibility for people with cognitive disabilities in the period from 2015 to 2021 are shown in Fig. 3.

Findings on the frequency of publishing papers related to web accessibility of particular types of cognitive disability in the period from 2015 to 2021 are summarized in Fig. 4.

When web accessibility for different cognitive disabilities was tackled, we found that majority of studies (70.45%) is dealing with this topic in general. Autism is the most researched cognitive disability with six published papers followed by dyslexia and impairment in elderly people that were examined in three papers each while aphasia was explored in only one paper in the period from 2015 to 2021.

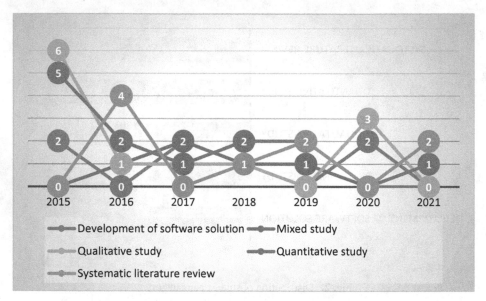

Fig. 3. Distribution of research types by year of publication

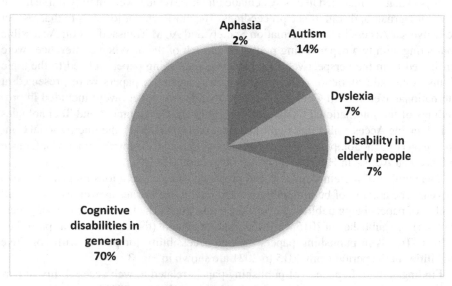

Fig. 4. Distribution of studies per type of research on cognitive disability

4.3 Qualitative and Quantitative Studies

Considering forty-four studies were analyzed in this systematic literature review, there is a lot of theoretical knowledge extracted. To start with, web accessibility is defined as the extent to which all people can use the web in many different contexts [41]. By using the words "all people", it is particularly referred to the elderly and people with disabilities. Contexts of use include both mainstream technologies and the ones which assist people with impairment.

If we look at web accessibility from a legal perspective, a lot of work has already been done [6]. However, there are still challenges that need to be overcome. People with cognitive disabilities are frequently excluded from proper use of the web in different ecosystems. For instance, barriers related to information retrieval, website navigation, file management, and authentication are making online education hard for young adults with intellectual disabilities [11]. To enhance their level of inclusion in that respect, it is important to implement software solutions that mitigate the challenges they are facing with. In addition, a solution that works for users who have different cognitive impairments has not yet been created [54]. This is because every user with a cognitive disability has a variety of individual needs.

Although web content that belongs to governments is required to be equally accessible to everybody, web forms and transactional services are not yet fully there [32]. Different actions can be taken to mitigate these barriers. However, making changes to such systems and improving mentioned aspects requires a lot of effort [18]. Regarding the guidelines for the development of web content, there have been a lot of new recommendations in recent years. Unfortunately, improvements are arriving slowly and implementation of guidelines into the development process is rather difficult. Awareness of accessibility is increasing, but it is not yet at a satisfactory level [37]. The majority of recommendations are directed toward content simplification and the use of certain design choices such as using easy-to-read fonts. Most notable and extensive recommendations are offered by Britto and Pizzolato [36], who systemized existing accessibility guidelines and best practices to design web interfaces appropriate for people with autism. Eraslan et al. [21] carried out an eye-tracking empirical study to evaluate guidelines related to the visual complexity of web pages and the distinguishability of web page elements. They found that people with autism have a higher number of fixations and make more transitions with synthesis tasks. On the other hand, Rello [43] suggested guidelines for typeface and font size that are beneficial for both people with and without dyslexia. Although new guidelines are a positive thing, it is equally important to avoid accessibility errors when creating web content [40] and to provide suitable technologies to improve its readability and understandability [33]. Even though accessibility guidelines are widely available, many web developers do not seem to be aware of them nor their relevance [14].

The web is a pool of information consumed by many users on daily basis. Since the web offers a lot of information in a variety of forms, it is often challenging for people with cognitive disabilities to find exactly what they searched for. People with autism experience many barriers because of different eye tracking scan paths [19] which is why the employment of an eye-tracker for data collection, while they are using websites, is very useful [54]. Users with cognitive disabilities commonly prefer different methods of searching the web [34], which makes it even harder to solve everyone's problem. The most important guidelines that have been offered in that respect are simple design and error corrections. Hu and Feng [26] found that people with cognitive disabilities prefer searching over browsing because less information is required for using search engines than for using hyperlinks. It is a common misconception that the web is rarely used by elderly people while the reality is quite the opposite. Problems that prevent elderly people to use the web effectively are mostly related to a decrease in their cognitive power [24] which is the reason why this group of users also requires content simplification.

4.4 Development of Software Solutions

There are seven papers in which authors introduced software solutions designed to make the web more accessible for users with cognitive disabilities. In 2015 de Avelar et al. [3] developed a browser extension to facilitate the use of the web by people with dyslexia. The extension has a lot of features for changing the appearance of the text which makes web content easier to read. Although the browser extension was perceived as a useful and helpful solution, its makers emphasized that the use of that kind of piece of software can sometimes be tiring. Rupprecht et al. [47] developed a system for generating electronic forms that are accessible to dyslexic users. Its main advantages are support for additional clarification of elements that can be in different types of media, personalization, and modeling the arbitrary state information for a form which all together is enhancing the self-confidence of people with dyslexia. Saggion et al. [48] developed an email client named Kolumba that based on speech technology, text simplification, and text-to-pictographs improves web accessibility for users with intellectual or developmental disabilities. The empirical study on Kolumba evaluation uncovered the wrong choice of synonyms and the unnatural voice of the text-to-speech system as its major drawbacks which were addressed by its authors [48]. Later in 2017, Galiev et al. [23] proposed a combined tangible (Sifteo cubes) and distributed (accessible web form, AWF) user interface in the form of an AWF-Cube prototype that makes navigation through and interaction with a web form easier for cognitively impaired persons. The findings of an empirical study revealed that although the speed of tilting was too fast and the colored semicircles were too small, the AWF-Cube prototype was perceived as easy to use solution by the sample of representative users [23]. In 2018, Adio and Adeyemo [1] designed an interface whose objective was to enhance the user experience of elderly people with cognitive impairment. The results of the performance evaluation indicate that memorability, learnability, utility, effectiveness, and efficiency of the novel interface were perceived as better when compared with the existing interface of a social web application [1]. On the other hand, Bircanin et al. [5] went in a completely different direction with iterative application design. They created an interactive information retrieval research apparatus that enables collecting and examining browsing patterns of non-verbal individuals with severe autism and intellectual disability on a video platform. However, the use of such an apparatus requires long-term engagement and trials because it is hard for cognitively impaired people to stay focused for long periods [5]. Finally, Broccia et al. [10] developed an open and flexible integrated solution for automatic accessibility assessment that enables single page and multi-page evaluation, generating reports in various formats for both web developers and users, and validating the accessibility according to WCAG 2.1 guidelines [52].

4.5 Answers to Research Questions

This section contains answers to research questions that represented the main motivation for conducting a systematic literature review and were raised at the beginning of this paper.

Facilitated use of the Web

The first research question was: "how to make it easier for people with cognitive disabilities to use and navigate the web?"

The analysis of the literature suggests that the answer lies in simple navigation and content. To make navigation easier, both browser and website should be well-designed. This means avoiding any clutter on the pages and making their design simple as possible. The relevant text should be much more noticeable than the background which can be achieved with high contrast [17]. It is also advisable to avoid having too many functionalities on the interface because they would distract a person with disabilities from what (s)he is looking for. There should not be too much information on one screen, and it would be good to discreetly point out links that would help users to deepen their searches.

State of the Art on the Accessibility of the Average Website

The second research question was: "How accessible is the average site for people with cognitive disabilities?"

Findings of a systematic literature review indicate that the accessibility of the majority of current websites is very poor. Namely, websites are not designed for people with cognitive disabilities because they do not use websites regularly [42]. Apart from the variety of advertisements that constantly interfere with the work of even the most focused users, the design of the pages itself is such that numerous distractors give the website a better design, but significantly impair its visibility and usefulness. Also, the multimedia nature of many websites makes them completely unusable for most people with cognitive disabilities.

Unresearched Domains and Open Questions.

One of the most important research questions of our study was: "what are unresearched subdomains regarding web accessibility for users with cognitive disabilities?"

The extant body of knowledge is composed of studies in which authors are offering different solutions to enhance the web experience for people with cognitive disabilities. Although there are papers in which proposed solutions have been evaluated, usually by a small sample of representative users, studies focused on obtaining feedback from people with cognitive difficulties are rather scarce. Empirical studies in which data will be collected with different measuring instruments and examine various facets of usability and user experience for people with cognitive disabilities are necessary. Specific methods, algorithms, and interfaces that would facilitate the evaluation process are also needed.

Shortcomings and Limitations of Existing Research

The last research question in our study was: "what are the shortcomings of current studies on web use by people with cognitive impairments?"

The first shortcoming of current studies in which validation of the introduced solution was carried out is the homogeneity and size of the sample of users [51]. Although people with disabilities represent a minority in a society, to draw sound and generalizable conclusions they should involve a more heterogeneous sample of people with cognitive disabilities concerning their demographics, including age, gender, geographic location, type and severity of impairment (if applicable since some solutions are focused on only one type of cognitive disability), etc. The second shortcoming is that current studies are not tackling all types of cognitive impairment equally. For instance, the researchers are mainly focused on people who suffer from autism and dyslexia while studies dealing with other forms of cognitive disabilities are deficient and this is what should be changed in the future. The fact that it has not been sufficiently researched how people with cognitive disabilities understand the web represents a third drawback of current studies since their perception should serve as a backbone for designing a solution that would enrich their experience in interaction with websites. The last shortcoming of previous studies is that people with cognitive disabilities are not sufficiently involved in the design of solutions that would help them to use the web more effectively. To address this drawback, people with cognitive disabilities should actively participate in every relevant stage of the development process, from collecting requirements to verification and validation of the solution.

4.6 Future Work Directions

Web accessibility for people with cognitive disabilities is quite specific and therefore insufficiently researched in the human-computer interaction field. To fill the gaps that were identified in the current literature, we are proposing the following suggestions for future research efforts:

- Existing web browsers offer a large number of features but people with cognitive disabilities are employing a very limited number of them [3]. It would be therefore interesting to find out which browser functionalities are most commonly used by all people with cognitive disabilities and if some of them are used only by certain groups of people with cognitive difficulties. As a follow-up, a specialized web browser for people with a certain type of cognitive disability could be developed.
- Considering that range of cognitive difficulties is large and complex, it would be very hard to develop a universal algorithm that could cover all types of cognitive impairment. Also, recent studies are suggesting that people with cognitive disabilities should be approached individually [28]. Therefore, future research should focus on developing a smart search algorithm or pattern recognition algorithm that would automatically adapt the websites to the needs of people with certain cognitive disabilities, suggest the results they most commonly searched for in their prior sessions, and provide recommendations on content that is the most similar to those they recently interacted with. An integral part of such an algorithm should also be the evaluation procedure that will be triggered after a certain time or number of uses to collect data on satisfaction with the design and the quality of the information obtained as well as the perceived accessibility of websites.

- The growing popularity of artificial intelligence and machine learning raises the question of their suitability for enhancing web accessibility. Machine learning could be applied to find accessibility issues in web applications. As an outcome of data training, a machine can be taught to act like a person with cognitive disabilities and accordingly used for finding elements in web applications that could cause issues for users with particular impairments.

5 Conclusion

This paper aimed to carry out a systematic literature review on web accessibility for people with cognitive disabilities. To get answers to four research questions, current literature was searched with predefined strings. An initial pool of 5477 records was reduced to 44 papers which were subsequently thoroughly examined. We in particular found that 20.46% of papers were systematic literature reviews, 15.91% of them were focused on the development of specialized software solutions, 29.55% of them employed quantitative research methods, and 52.27% were published in conference proceedings. The majority of papers (70.45%) were dealing with cognitive disabilities in general while autism was the most researched type of cognitive disability. The highest number of papers was published in 2015.

Current literature indicates that accessibility guidelines have not been implemented properly in the design of the majority of current websites. Namely, there are a lot of advertisements on websites that constantly interfere with user activities while the multimedia nature of many pages significantly impairs their visibility and usefulness for people with cognitive disabilities. When designing websites, any kind of clutter should be avoided because people with cognitive disabilities will otherwise have a hard time finding what they are looking for. There should not be too many elements on the user interface and not too much information on one screen. Website designers need also make sure that relevant text is as noticeable as possible and that links that facilitate further search are discreetly pointed out.

Although there are many papers focused on enhancing web experience for people with cognitive difficulties, their feedback and involvement in the studies are uncommon. An additional drawback of current empirical studies is that sample of representative users is commonly composed of a small number of participants who share similar demographic characteristics which makes it difficult to draw sound and generalizable conclusions. Considering all the aforementioned, future studies should involve more heterogonous samples of users and aim to determine how the web is perceived and used by users with cognitive disabilities.

References

1. Adio, M.A., Adeyemo, O.: Development of a usable and accessible interface for the cognitively impaired aged. Int. Res. J. Advanced Eng. Sci. 3(2), 76–82 (2018)
2. Alzahrani, M., Uitdenbogerd, A.L., Spichkova, M.: Human-computer interaction: influences on autistic users. Procedia Comput. Sci. 192, 4691–4700 (2021)

3. de Avelar, L.O., Rezende, G.C., Freire, A.P.: WebHelpDyslexia: a browser extension to adapt web content for people with dyslexia. Procedia Comput. Sci. **67**, 150–159 (2015)
4. Bernard, R., Sabariego, C., Cieza, A.: Barriers and facilitation measures related to people with mental disorders when using the web: a systematic review. J. Med. Internet Res. **18**(6), 157–175 (2016)
5. Bircanin, F., Sitbon, L., Favre, B., Brereton, M.: Designing an IIR research apparatus with users with severe intellectual disability. In: Proceedings of the 2020 Conference on Human Information Interaction and Retrieval, pp. 412–416. ACM, Vancouver (2020)
6. Blanck, P.: eQuality: web accessibility by people with cognitive disabilities. Inclusion **3**(2), 75–91 (2015)
7. Blazheska-Tabakovska, N., Savoska, S., Ristevski, B., Jolevski, I., Gruevski, D.: Web content accessibility for people with cognitive disabilities. In: 9th International Conference on Applied Internet and Information Technologies, pp. 70–74. University of Novi Sad, Technical Faculty "Mihajlo Pupin", Zrenjanin (2019)
8. Braddock, D., Rizzolo, M.C., Thompson, M., Bell, R.: Emerging technologies and cognitive disability. J. Spec. Educ. Technol. **19**(4), 49–56 (2004)
9. Brito, E., Dias, G.P.: LMS accessibility for students with disabilities: The experts' opinions. In: 15th Iberian Conference on Information Systems and Technologies, pp.1–5. IEEE, Seville (2020)
10. Broccia, G., Manca, M., Paternò, F., Pulina, F.: Flexible automatic support for web accessibility validation. In: Proceedings of the ACM on Human-Computer Interaction 4 (EICS), pp. 1–24 (2020)
11. Buehler, E., Easley, W., Poole, A., Hurst, A.: Accessibility barriers to online education for young adults with intellectual disabilities. In: Proceedings of the 13th International Web for All Conference, pp. 1–10. ACM, Montreal (2016)
12. Cadzow, A.: Impact of cognitive learning disorders on accessing online resources. In: Antona, M., Stephanidis, C. (eds.) UAHCI 2017. LNCS, vol. 10279, pp. 363–381. Springer, Cham (2017). https://doi.org/10.1007/978-3-319-58700-4_30
13. Calvo, R., Seyedarabi, F., Savva, A.: Beyond web content accessibility guidelines: Expert Accessibility Reviews. In: Proceedings of the 7th International Conference on Software Development and Technologies for Enhancing Accessibility and Fighting Info-exclusion, pp. 77–84. ACM, Vila Real (2016)
14. Cao, S., Loiacono, E.: Perceptions of web accessibility guidelines by student website and app developers. In: 17th Annual Pre-ICIS Workshop on HCI Research in MIS Sponsored by AIS SIGHCI, AIS, San Francisco (2018)
15. Cinquin, P.-A., Guittonb, P., Sauzéon, H.: Online e-learning and cognitive disabilities: a systematic review. Comput. Educ. **130**, 152–167 (2019)
16. Cognitive Disability: Information on Intellectual Disabilities. https://www.disabled-world.com/disability/types/cognitive/. Accessed 22 May 2022
17. Cormier, M., Moffatt, K., Cohen, R., Mann, R.: Purely vision-based segmentation of web pages for assistive technology. Comput. Vis. Image Underst. **148**, 46–66 (2016)
18. Dinc, E.: Web-based education and accessibility. Int. J. Technol. Educ. Sci. **1**(1), 29–35 (2017)
19. Eraslan, S., Yaneva, V., Yesilada, Y., Harper, S.: Do web users with autism experience barriers when searching for information within web pages? In: Proceedings of the 14th International Web for All Conference, pp. 1–4. ACM, Perth (2017)
20. Eraslan, S., Yaneva, V., Yesilada, Y., Harper, S.: Web users with autism: eye tracking evidence for differences. Behav. Inf. Technol. **38**(7), 678–700 (2019)
21. Eraslan, S., Yesilada, Y., Yaneva, V., Ha, L.A.: Keep it simple! an eye-tracking study for exploring complexity and distinguishability of web pages for people with autism. Univ. Access Inf. Soc. **20**(1), 69–84 (2021)

22. Erazo, M., Zimmermann, G.: Design and evaluation of a simplified online banking inter-face for people with cognitive disabilities. In: Proceedings of the 17th International ACM SIGACCESS Conference on Computers & Accessibility, pp. 309–310. ACM, Lisbon (2015)
23. Galiev, R., Rupprecht, D., Bomsdorf, B.: Towards tangible and distributed UI for cognitively impaired people. In: Antona, M., Stephanidis, C. (eds) Universal Access in Human–Computer Interaction. Human and Technological Environments. Lecture Notes in Computer Science 10279, pp. 283–300. Springer, Vancouver (2017). https://doi.org/10.1007/978-3-319-58703-5_21
24. Haesner, M., Steinert, A., O'Sullivan, J.L., Steinhagen-Thiessen, E.: Evaluating an accessible web interface for older adults – the impact of mild cognitive impairment (MCI). J. Assist. Technol. 9(4), 219–232 (2015)
25. Hong, S.G., Trimi, S., Kim, D.W., Hyun, J.H.: A Delphi study of factors hindering web accessibility for persons with disabilities. J. Comput. Inf. Syst. 55(4), 28–34 (2015)
26. Hu, R., Feng, J.H.: Investigating information search by people with cognitive disabilities. ACM Trans. Accessible Computing 7(1), 1–30, 1 (2015)
27. James, A., Draffan, E.A., Wald, M.: Designing web-apps for all: how do we include those with cognitive disabilities? Studies in Health Technol. Informatics 242, 665–668 (2017)
28. Juvino De Araújo, E.C., Andrade, W.L.: A systematic literature review on teaching pro-gramming to people with cognitive disabilities. In: IEEE Frontiers in Education Conference, pp.1–8. IEEE, Lincoln (2021)
29. Kitchenham, B., Charters, S.: Guidelines for performing systematic literature reviews in software engineering, Version 2.3. Department of Computer Science, University of Durham, Durham. Tech. Rep. EBSE-2007–01 (2007)
30. de Lara, S.M.A., de Mattos Fortes, R.P., Russo, C.M., Freire, A.P.: A study on the acceptance of website interaction aids by older adults. Universal Access in the Information Society 15(3), 445–460 (2016)
31. Menger, F., Morris, J., Salis, C.: Aphasia in an Internet age: wider perspectives on digital inclusion. Aphasiology 30(2–3), 112–132 (2016)
32. Moreno, L., Martínez, P., Muguerza, J., Abascal, J.: Support resource based on standards for accessible e-Government transactional services. Computer Standards & Interfaces 58, 146–157 (2018)
33. Moreno, L., Martínez, P., Segura-Bedmar, I., Revert, R.: Exploring language technologies to provide support to WCAG 2.0 and E2R guidelines. In: Proceedings of the XVI International Conference on Human Computer Interaction (Interacción '15), pp. 1–8. ACM, Vilanova i la Geltru (2015)
34. Nour, R.: Web searching by individuals with cognitive disabilities. ACM SIGACCESS Accessibility and Computing 111, 19–25 (2015)
35. Orehovački, T., Babić, S.: Identifying the relevance of quality dimensions contributing to universal access of social Web applications for collaborative writing on mobile devices: an empirical study. Univ. Access Inf. Soc. 17(3), 453–473 (2017)
36. Pagani Britto, T.C., Brigante Pizzolato, E.: Towards web accessibility guidelines of interaction and interface design for people with autism spectrum disorder. In: 9th International Conference on Advances in Computer-Human Interactions, pp. 138–144. IARIA, Venice (2016)
37. Pagani Britto Pichiliani, T.C., Brigante Pizzolato, E.: A survey on the awareness of Brazil-ian web development community about cognitive accessibility. In: Proceedings of the 18th Brazilian Symposium on Human Factors in Computing Systems, pp. 1–11. ACM, Vitória Espírito Santo (2019)
38. Page, M.J., et al.: The PRISMA 2020 statement: an updated guideline for reporting systematic reviews. BMJ, London. Tech. Rep. 372: n71 (2021)
39. Paiva, D.M.B., Freire, A.P., de Mattos Fortes, R.P.: Accessibility and software engineering processes: a systematic literature review. J. Systems Software 171, 110819 (2021)

40. Pascual, A., Ribera, M., Granollers, T.: Empathic communication of accessibility barriers in Web 2.0 editing. In: Proceedings of the 12th International Web for All Conference, pp. 1–8. ACM, Florence (2015)
41. Petrie, H., Savva, A., Power, C.: Towards a unified definition of web accessibility. In: Proceedings of the 12th International Web for All Conference, pp. 1–13. ACM, Florence (2015)
42. Reid, B.E.: Internet architecture and disability. Indiana Law J. **95**(2), 591–648 (2020)
43. Rello, L.: Dyslexia and web accessibility: synergies and challenges. In: Proceedings of the 12th International Web for All Conference, pp. 1–4. ACM, Florence (2015)
44. Rello, L., Baeza-Yates, R.: The effect of font type on screen readability by people with dyslexia. ACM Trans. Accessible Computing **8**(4), 1–33 (2016)
45. Rocha, T., Bessa, M., Magalhães, L., Cabral, L.: Performing universal tasks on the Web: interaction with digital content by people with intellectual disabilities. In: Proceedings of the XVI International Conference on Human Computer Interaction (Interacción '15), pp. 1–7. ACM, Vilanova i la Geltru (2015)
46. Rocheleau, J.N., Cobigo, V., Chalghoumi, H.: Recognizing everyday information technologies as assistive technologies for persons with cognitive disabilities. In: Miesenberger, K., Kouroupetroglou, G. (eds.) ICCHP 2018. LNCS, vol. 10896, pp. 504–508. Springer, Cham (2018). https://doi.org/10.1007/978-3-319-94277-3_78
47. Rupprecht, D., Etzold, J., Bomsdorf, B.: Model-based development of accessible, personalized web forms for icf-based assessment. In: Proceedings of the 7th ACM SIGCHI Symposium on Engineering Interactive Computing Systems, pp. 120–125. ACM, Duisburg (2015)
48. Saggion, H., Ferrés, D., Sevens, L., Schuurman, I., Ripollés, M., Rodríguez, O.: Able to read my mail: an accessible e-mail client with assistive technology. In: Proceedings of the 14th International Web for All Conference, pp. 1–4. ACM, Perth (2017)
49. Schmutz, S., Sonderegger, A., Sauer, J.: Easy-to-read language in disability-friendly web sites: Effects on nondisabled users. Appl. Ergon. **74**, 97–106 (2019)
50. Stuss, D.T.: Cognitive impairment. In: Aminoff, M.J., Daroff, R.B. (eds.): Encyclopedia of the Neurological Sciences, pp. 737–740. Academic Press, Amsterdam (2003)
51. Vereenooghe, L.: Participation of people with disabilities in web-based research. Web-Based Research in Psychology **229**(4), 257–259 (2021)
52. Web Content Accessibility Guidelines (WCAG) 2.1. https://www.w3.org/TR/WCAG21/. Accessed 22 May 2022
53. World report on Disability, World Health Organization (WHO), Geneva, Switzerland. https://apps.who.int/iris/rest/bitstreams/53067/retrieve. Accessed 19 May 2022
54. Yaneva, V.: Autism and the web: using web-searching tasks to detect autism and improve web accessibility. ACM SIGACCESS Accessibility and Computing **121**, 1–8 (2018)
55. Yusril, A.N.: E-Accessibility analysis in user experience for people with disabilities. Indonesian J. Disability Studies **7**(1), 106–109 (2020)

TACTILE – A Mixed Reality Solution for Staying Active and Socially Included

Elisabeth Broneder[1(✉)], Christoph Weiß[1], Emanuel Sandner[1], Stephanie Puck[2], Monika Puck[2], Gustavo Fernández Domínguez[1], and Birgit Unger-Hrdlicka[3]

[1] AIT Austrian Institute of Technology, Vienna, Austria
elisabeth.broneder@ait.ac.at
[2] GTA GedächtnistrainingsAkademie E.U, Salzburg, Austria
office@gedaechtnistraining.at
[3] Myneva Austria GmbH, Vienna, Austria

Abstract. Seniors are often affected by a decline in physical and mental abilities, resulting in social isolation, anxiety, and frailty. They often live alone, spatially separated from family members and friends, who cannot visit them regularly. Moreover, seniors often suffer from physical ailments. Thus, they cannot go outside anymore on their own and feel even more isolated or depressed. Various studies show that playing board games and doing physical exercises keep the mind and body trained and thus have the potential to prevent loneliness and diseases. Therefore, we developed TACTILE – a mixed-reality (MR) solution that connects seniors with family members and friends even when apart. The TACTILE system offers two basic functionalities: (i) board games that can be played with a remote partner and, (ii) physical exercises that are done together with a virtual avatar. While using the system, users can also talk to each other when playing games and interact with the virtual avatar that accompanies the physical exercises. Such interaction strengthens the intuitiveness of the system and the social component even more. Three prototype versions were evaluated within three end-user workshops and a final prototype during long-lasting field trials in two test countries: Austria and the Netherlands. This paper describes the status of the TACTILE system, its components, the strong end-user involvement, and the results and findings from the field trials where the final prototype has been tested for an extended period by 64 end-users in their home and life setting.

Keywords: Mixed reality · Seniors · Social interaction · Physical training · Staying fit

1 Introduction and State of the Art

Elderly people are frequently affected by a decline of mental and physical abilities, which results in anxiety, frailty, and reclusiveness. The risk of developing dementia grows with declining mental and physical abilities. Previous studies show that the combination of cognitive and physical training has a positive effect on slowing down mental and physical decline[1–4]. The combination of physical and cognitive activity induces cognitive

© Springer Nature Switzerland AG 2022
V. G. Duffy et al. (Eds.): HCII 2022, LNCS 13521, pp. 277–291, 2022.
https://doi.org/10.1007/978-3-031-17902-0_20

gains [3, 5]. When an individual trains an individualized task at an appropriate level of challenge, learning is maximized [6]. Emotional well-being and social interaction are important factors for health and improving quality of life [7, 8].

Augmented Reality (AR), Virtual Reality (VR) and Mixed Reality (MR) technologies offer novel opportunities that allow users to perform physical and cognitive exercises in a fun and interactive way. There are some existing solutions that support seniors in staying active and socially included using VR or AR but not MR. Rehabilitation Gaming System (RGS)[1] was a project aimed to develop and validate a VR tool for the rehabilitation of elderly people after suffering brain damage from a stroke. The authors conducted a pilot-controlled trial selecting a representative sample of patients with chronic stroke [9]. After receiving a daily training of 30 min for six weeks, patients were asked to solve individual cognitive tasks (e.g., word search puzzle or draw specific figures). A specialist assessed the patients' responses using the Consolidated Standards of Reporting Trials (CONSORT) statement[2]. The system was exhaustively evaluated by real patients [9–11] and is commercialised by EODYNE Systems[3]. Rendever[4] offers a virtual reality platform that allows people to share experiences or stories and deepen social interaction between them in a defined group setting. The system aims to overcome social isolation through reminiscence therapy (e.g., visit the childhood home), family bonding (e.g., go to a family vacation), and travel (e.g., climb a mountain). Huang and Lee [12] investigated the effects of a VR software on cognitive function and balance in elderly people with mild cognitive impairment (MCI). Although the response and acceptance by the patients was positive, the authors remarked the difficulty to generalize the results of the study due to the limited number of participants [12]. Tuena et al. [13] provided an overview of current research of VR systems oriented to elderly people evaluating feasibility and usability regarding healthy aging and age-related clinical conditions. The authors reported a good usability and acceptance between the participants. Further research regarding further VR and AR applications for the elderly target group can be found in [14–18]. MR-based solutions have various supporting potentials but are not widely used, especially not in the target group of older adults. Existing solutions mainly aim to entertain, but there is no communication or possibility to play together with a real person especially combined with a training aspect.

TACTILE[5] aims to connect seniors with their family and friends and support their social interaction. TACTILE's novelty is the use of MR that makes the remote partner virtually present focusing on communication and interaction with their loved ones. The MR software is specifically designed and developed for elderly people to interact in a natural way (Fig. 1). Users can play board games and do physical training exercises. When playing board games, they can interact with the real game pieces and game board while seeing the game figures of the remote partner projected onto their own game board. To increase the social aspect of gaming, a VoIP connection is established during the game. During the physical trainings, users are accompanied by a virtual avatar that

---

[1] http://www.aal-europe.eu/projects/rgs.

[2] http://www.consort-statement.org/

[3] https://www.eodyne.com/

[4] https://rendever.com/

[5] http://mytactile.eu/

Fig. 1. End-users testing the system. Left: Training with the virtual avatar; Right: Playing Ludo

guides them through the exercises. Users can place the virtual avatar inside their real-world surroundings (e.g., in the middle of the living room) and the avatar encourages and accompanies the user in a joint training session. Physiotherapists or skilled residential caretakers can adapt the training to the individual needs via a web interface. Advantages are twofold: (i) addressing potential physical limitations of the user, and (ii) avoiding frustration using generalized training plans because one single training plan cannot fit all users properly. Previous prototypes of the TACTILE system were evaluated and positive results by end-users were reported [19, 20]. Recommendations from the users' feedback were considered in the further developments of the current prototype. This paper extends previous work [19, 20], where we had introduced the TACTILE system, the corresponding User-Centred Design (UCD) process and presented the results and findings of the first and second end-user workshops. Since then, we have incorporated the feedback from the user workshops and provided a final prototype that not only fits the end-users' needs but also brings them joy in their everyday life. This paper complements the aforementioned work by describing the strong end-user involvement, and the results and findings from the field trials where the final prototype has been tested for an extended period by 64 end-users in their home and life settings.

The paper is organised as follows: Sect. 2 focuses on the technical description of the TACTILE system consisting of the MR application and the web-based backend portal that manages users and their individual physical exercises and training plans. We also describe the system's extensibility (i.e., how additional cognitive games and physical exercises can be easily added) and we describe how we implemented logging mechanisms for enabling remote support for secondary end-users to detect possible misuse during the field trials. Section 3 focuses on the final design, accessibility, and usability improvements gained in the second and third user workshop and the corresponding UCD approach. Besides, a description on how the feedback has been incorporated towards the final prototype is given. Section 4 summarises the field study design, the methodology used for testing the prototype (including advantages and limitations), the several-week long-lasting user involvement, and the results gained from this final field trial. This section also describes how the set-up in the user's home has been prepared and carried out, i.e., how users found their way with the system when using it on their own. Section 5 concludes the paper with an outlook toward the market perspectives and about possibilities to foster the TACTILE concept utilizing new, upcoming, and more affordable devices.

2 The TACTILE System

The TACTILE system consists of a frontend and a backend. The frontend is a mixed reality application, which allows the user to play common board games with remote opponents and train together with a virtual avatar at the user's home. The backend provides a web-portal for account management and exercise setup by secondary end-user such as formal and informal caregivers.

2.1 Mixed Reality Application

The MR application was developed for and tested on the Magic Leap One[6] (ML1) mixed reality glasses. The field trial ready prototype provides two board games – Ludo and Halma – as well as 14 physical exercises.

Board Games. The idea of playing board games in the TACTILE system is to allow traditional gameplay with a remote partner. The player is wearing the ML1 and uses a physical game board and physical game pieces. The glasses display the opponent's game pieces virtually at the correct location on the physical game board. The local players use real game pieces and move them by hand, experiencing the tactile feedback they are used to while playing board games. This provides an intuitive user interaction.

The detection of the game pieces on the board is done in two steps: In the first step the physical game board is detected via computer vision algorithms and AprilTag[7] markers. Four markers are applied to the board to allow for users looking at different parts of the board while still being able to detect it (see Fig. 2). Via the marker detection the game board's position and orientation within the real environment can be derived.

The second step is the game piece detection. Using the well-known geometry of the possible positions (game fields) on the game board, the game piece detection determines if a game piece is present at one of these positions. If a game piece is detected, the MR glasses display it on the correct position at the other player's game board. To inform users of the complete state of the game, not only the opponent's pieces are projected on the board, but also the player's own game pieces are projected to visualize that the detection has been correct. Brightly coloured game pieces are used to enable robust game piece detection. Color-coded game pieces would allow for the detection of different types of game-pieces (as in Checkers or Chess), however the currently implemented games only use one type of game pieces. To avoid occlusions that can happen especially when the board is viewed from low angles, hindering the efficiency of computer vision algorithms, flat Checkers pieces are used in all games. Changing light conditions, which could affect colour-based detection algorithms, are mitigated through continuous white-balancing on the white parts of the markers. A sanity check algorithm also checks if detections can be correct based on the game played and discards them otherwise.

---

[6] https://www.magicleap.com/magic-leap-1.

[7] https://april.eecs.umich.edu/software/apriltag.

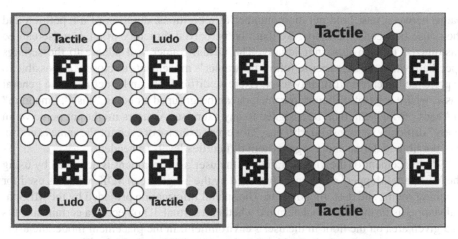

Fig. 2. Ludo and Halma game boards with attached markers

To allow a similar level of a social experience as in classic board gameplay, users can communicate via a Voice over IP (VoIP) connection from the moment they decide to play a game until the end of the game. When playing dice-based board games such as Ludo, the players can use a virtual dice, visible to both users, to mitigate distrust of unseen dice rolls of the opponent.

The TACTILE system uses a modular and a simple configuration system that would allow for quick additions to the games provided in the system (e.g., Nine Man Morris, Chutes and Ladders, Checkers).

Physical Exercises. The TACTILE app provides end users the means to stay physically fit by doing physical exercises together with a virtual trainer. The used MR technology allows the user to place the virtual avatar inside their home environment. The final TACTILE prototype includes 8 distinct exercises to activate and strengthen upper and lower body parts as well as exercises to improve balance and coordination. Some of those 8 exercises were animated in a standing and sitting stance to ensure maximum flexibility with regards to user requirements and to consider potential physical impairments. Thus, a total of 14 distinct exercise animations were created. The training capabilities of the TACTILE system are easily extensible, as the avatar animations are provided in the BVH format[8] and are thus loaded dynamically during the app's start-up phase. This process allows for adding new or removing or modifying existing animations through the backend system, described in Sect. 2.2. The exercise animations together with the training configuration are stored locally on the ML device, which allows the usage of the training system in an offline setting, when no internet connection is available. If an internet connection is available, an automatic update mechanism ensures that the latest exercise animations and training configuration are fetched from the backend system and the local exercises are updated. The training configuration is used to define the exercises and their difficulty levels individually for each user, such as number of sets,

---

[8] https://www.cs.cityu.edu.hk/~howard/Teaching/CS4185-5185-2007-SemA/Group12/BVH.html.

pause between sets, hold duration, number of repetitions, duration of a repetition and the pause between repetitions. By that, the perceived difficulty of an exercise can be customized to each user individually. The virtual trainer will adhere to the settings specified, while the user tries to follow the trainer's movements as closely as possible to experience the chosen difficulty level. Exercise difficulties can be defined on a general basis, where a set of difficulty parameters can be grouped as being "easy", "medium" or "hard", which can then be assigned to any exercise. As users might not perceive an "easy" difficulty setting similarly "easy" for every exercise or even for the same exercise, it is possible to define and assign custom difficulties levels as needed.

The placement of the virtual trainer in the user's environment is achieved by using the MLSpatialMapper[9] component provided by the Magic Leap SDK, which is used for scanning rooms and detecting objects. The spatial information provided by the MLSpatialMapper is further used to determine whether a virtual 3D object of a certain size fits in a given area on the floor in the user's environment. In the placement mode, the users see the avatar in front of them through the Magic Leap (ML) with a minimum distance of 2 m. The avatar is moved by turning the head, i.e., by looking around in the room. A color indicator on the avatar's clothes informs the user whether the current position is suitable for the virtual trainer. A suitable position is found when the avatar is not obstructed by objects in the room like furniture or when being too close to a wall. Once the trainer's clothes turn green, the avatar can be placed at that position. Otherwise, the clothes would show red. This concept is shown in Fig. 3.

 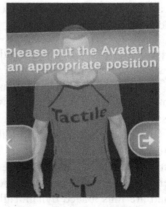

Fig. 3. The placement of the virtual trainer, showing a valid position (left image with green outfit) and in an invalid position (right image with red outfit)

Once the virtual trainer is put in place, the user can choose to do a predefined training session containing multiple exercises (which are configured by physiotherapists or skilled residential caretakers through the web interface) or select one specific exercise from a list. During the exercises, the avatar acts as a trainer and shows the exercise while the end-users are free to follow the movements at their own pace. After each exercise the

---

[9] https://www.magicleap.com/en-us/privacy/spatial-mapping-overview-and-detail-options.

user is asked to give feedback about the exercise e.g., stating whether it was too hard, too easy or just right. Likewise, once the whole training session is finished, the uses are asked to give feedback on whether they liked it. This feedback is saved in the backend system and shown in the web interface. Based on the given feedback, the associated caretaker can adjust the exercise and training intensity for the user. Figure 4 depicts a female and male virtual trainer, showing different exercises and using virtual props like chairs and tables.

Fig. 4. The virtual training: male and female avatars, displayed through the MR glasses, showing different exercises in sitting and standing stances.

Since users in TACTILE's target group do not usually have special training equipment at home, none of the exercises require any. However, household items like chairs and tables are included into the training plan and used instead. The avatar lets users know whenever such an item is needed for the upcoming exercise. Using furniture can help the seniors to safely perform exercises, for example by holding onto the backrest of a chair to keep the balance.

2.2 Web Portal

The backend portal was created for the secondary users (e.g., relatives, caregivers) to manage the settings for the primary users. It allows to create and adapt training plans, assign exercises and manage difficulty levels. To be able to do this adequately, the secondary users can see the feedback on exercise levels given by the primary users via the web portal. Furthermore, the backend portal allows monitoring the use of the TACTILE system through a timeline.

Further, the MR application automatically transmits game and exercise data and log information to the backend. The backend provides the possibility to customize a user's account, for example providing them with a nickname and a profile picture that other users can see, when looking for a partner to play a board game with. In the timeline the use of the system is visualized alongside the user's feedback on the actions. This together with the logging information of the system, facilitates finding out if users struggle with the complexity of the system or might need help. The logging information was also incorporated for technical partners to give technical support to the secondary end-users during the field trials if needed.

The most important feature of the portal is the setup of training plans which the secondary users can manage for the primary end-users according to their needs. Exercises can be selected along with the number of repetitions and sets and thus difficulty levels can be adapted. A selection of these exercises makes up a training plan, which is then downloaded by the mixed reality application and can be performed by the primary end-user.

3   Design and Development Methodology

Within the TACTILE project a user-centred design process took place. The development phase was accompanied by three end-user workshops where users could test the current state of development. Within the first workshop that took place in October 2019, different user interfaces and interaction methods as well as avatar designs and first physical exercises were tested. The results can be found in [19]. In the second user workshop that took place in March 2020, the end-users tested the second prototype, that included the board game "Ludo" as well as the first 8 training exercises. Results from the second workshop are described in [20]. In the 3rd workshop in Q4 2020 the users tested the 3rd prototype consisting of 14 physical exercises and two board games – Ludo and Halma. The feedback from the 3rd workshop was incorporated into the final prototype. The following Sects. 3.1 and 3.2 describe this process. The final prototype was tested in 4 field trial rounds at the end-users' homes (see Sect. 4).

3.1   Board Games

The selection of the implemented board games started with a user survey on ranking the users' favourite board games. Taking in consideration not only the answers of the users, but also the technical feasibility of the games, the consortium chose Ludo and Halma. The main problem during the second and third user workshops was, that the tracking of the game figures was sometimes too slow. This happened mainly if game figures were not in the field of view of the Magic Leap's RGB camera. Thus, we implemented hints to notify users when the game board or the game figures are not seen by the glasses. When playing Ludo, the users wished for a possibility to see the opponent's dice rolls and to choose a game figure colour as the implemented concept had fixed colours for the local and the remote player. Therefore, a virtual dice has been implemented that can be thrown by pressing a button of the Magic Leap controller. The virtual dice of the user and the opponent is projected on the real game board of the user. So, each user can see his/her own dice as well as the dice of the other player. When playing Halma, the users wanted to see how the other player moved from position A to position B. Thus, a virtual tracer was implemented, which visualizes the path the game figure took. Figure 5 shows the virtual dice projected onto the Ludo game board and the virtual path in Halma.

3.2   Physical Exercises

For the selection of the physical exercises a literature research was conducted. A good overview on exercises according to strength, coordination and balance was found in

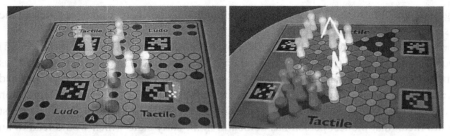

Fig. 5. Left: Virtual dice of player and opponent; Right: The yellow path shows which way the game figure took for the game move (Color figure online)

[21]. Another bundle of exercises that can have an impact on the cognitive and physical abilities are taken from [22] and [23]. The exercises were chosen in two steps: First, the literature research findings were discussed with a physiotherapist, an occupational therapist and an ergo therapist, who chose the exercises with the highest benefit. Then, from these exercises the ones with a clearly visible range of motion chosen so that they can be effectively shown by the virtual trainer in the MR glasses.

Using the selected exercises from the literature as a template, the exercise animations were created.

User feedback regarding the physical exercises was gathered in 3 user workshops. In the third user workshop the biggest challenge for the seniors was to place the avatar in the room. The avatar was sometimes stuck in the floor or moving the avatar with the controller was not convenient. These issues were resolved in the final prototype by adapting the algorithms to find the floor and by placing the avatar by moving the user's head rather than the hand controller. A minimum distance between the user and the avatar was added and the algorithms became more tolerant concerning the distance to walls and furniture. Apart from this, the feedback regarding the training's user interface (e.g., hiding the interface during an exercise) was incorporated into the developments towards the final prototype. Further, the refinement of animations to reduce collisions and clipping between the virtual trainer and the props (chair, table) was realized.

Finally, the loading time of the TACTILE app was reduced by introducing an exercise animation caching mechanism to store a copy of each exercise on the ML device after it was downloaded from the TACTILE backend.

4 Results

In this section the field trials that took place in the last months of the TACTILE project are described in detail. For testing the final prototype of the system 4 rounds of testing periods took place. In the first 3 rounds, only primary users tested the system. In the last round seniors (primary users) had the possibility to test the system together with a relative (secondary end-user). Each period lasted 5 weeks and included 8 test-users in Austria and 8 test-users in the Netherlands. Due to personal reasons of end-users (e.g., illness) one person in Austria and 4 persons in the Netherlands did not complete the field trial. Further, in Austria 5 primary users decided to also participate in the last field trial together with relatives, whereas in the Netherlands only newly recruited users tested the system together with their relatives.

At the end of the field trials, the data of 46 primary (N-AUT = 21, N-NL = 25) and 8 secondary users (N-AUT = 5, N-NL = 3) was analysed. In order to participate as primary end user, participants had to be 65 + years old. Further, every test person had to do the Montreal Cognitive Assessment (MoCA) [24] and the Geriatric Depression Scale (GDS) [25] to test exclusion criteria. A score of 23 or lower in the MoCA test would mean that the test person has dementia in an early state which would lead to an exclusion of the test person. In GDS a value of 10 or higher was the cut off score to exclude a person because of a major depression.

75% of the participants in the field trials also participated at least in one of the three conducted user-workshops. The other 25% were recruited because some test users dropped out during the workshop phase for reasons like e.g., illness or having less time because of a care situation in the partnership.

In May 2021 the field trails started with the briefing of the first test users in their homes. The users were informed about the conditions of their participation and had to sign the informed consent before testing the exclusion criteria.

After passing the questionnaires, the components of the TACILE system (MR glasses, router, etc.) have been explained to the users. The whole system was set up together with a representative of the end-user organisation. The participants had to start the TACTILE app and were guided through the system. The participants did a training session with the avatar together with a supervisor of the end-user organization to get to know the system. After finishing the setup and answering the participant's questions, the supervisor asked the participant to play a board game and do a training at least twice a week. It was recommended to make appointments with other participants via telephone or to use a fixed weekly timeslot.

The participants were informed that they will receive a five-minutes phone call once a week for feedback and questions as well as an invitation to a round table in the third test week to discuss their experiences together with other test-users.

After the field trials, the standard questionnaires UEQ-S (User Experience Questionnaire – Short version) and SUS (System usability scale) were filled in and open interview questions were answered by the end-users.

For questions and technical support, the test-users had the possibility to call a representative of the end-user organisation or write an e-mail.

The Austrian sample included N = 21 primary users (15 female, 6 male) and 5 couples of a primary (4 female, 1 male) and a secondary user (4 female, 1 male). The 21 primary users in Austria were on average 74,75 years old (standard deviation 7,07). The 23 (15 female, 8 male) primary users in the Netherlands were on average 80,21 years old (standard deviation 6,76). The living condition of the test-users has been very different in Austria and the Netherlands. In Austria, all 21 test-users were living independently at home. In the Netherlands 4 persons lived at home independently, 10 persons visited a day care facility and 11 people lived permanently in a care institution.

4.1 Qualitative Results

The statements users gave in the phone calls, round tables and final interviews are summarized in the following section. It must be stated, that for primary users it was hard to distinguish between the ML1 and the TACTILE app. For them, it was one system.

38% of the test-users claimed that they would like to continue to use the system after the project. Most users that claimed that they do not want to continue using the system, said that they feel fit and independent and thus do not have the need to use TACTILE in their daily life. However, 95% of the test users would recommend TACTILE to persons who are feeling alone and have a small number of social contacts.

Hardware

In terms of hardware 18 of the 21 Austrian test users reported that the Magic Leap became uncomfortably hot after some time, so they avoided to use the glasses for too long. Further, the users were sometimes overwhelmed with the cables that came with the Magic Leap. The users wished for a manual to have a better understanding about the cables (e.g., loading cable for the controller) and would wish for a smaller device.

Boardgames

As mentioned before, TACTILE provides 2 board games that can be played together with a remote player. This should provide social inclusion. 77,7% of the users claimed that they felt socially connected to the other player. 71% of the test persons claimed that besides having fun during the game, they enjoyed the IP telephony. Regarding problems, the users reported that sometimes game pieces disappeared or were seen at the wrong position. This occurred especially for users that needed glasses in daily life. Further, a problem for the users was to arrange an appointment with another player because they often had other plans. Due to the low number of participants (N = 8) in each trial it was unlikely to find another player online if no appointment had been scheduled. Apart from this, one participant with color blindness had problems because of the red and green game figures. Thus, the colors of the game figures should be changed to blue and yellow in the future. When the users were asked what they would wish for in the future to be integrated into the system, three main points came up: (a) the possibility to schedule appointments, (b) more challenging games, and (c) the update of the game pieces should be faster.

Physical Trainings

Apart from the board games, TACTILE offers 14 physical exercises that can be adapted to physical restrictions of the end-users. Regarding the physical exercises, 42,8% of the users did not like the training exercises, since they had the feeling that the exercises were designed to help seniors to stay fit when suffering from a certain amount of immobility. Further, the duration of breaks between the sets was too long for them, since the exercises were too easy from them. They would wish for more advanced exercises with higher difficulty levels that they can adjust by themselves. Regarding technical difficulties, they claimed that it was sometimes hard to position the avatar in the room.

4.2   Quantitative Data

After the field trials each user filled out the UEQ-S (User Experience Questionnaire) and the SUS (System Usability Scale) questionnaire. In this section the results are described.

UEQ-S – User Experience Questionnaire Short Version
The UEQ-S [26] measures classical usability and user experience aspects. It contains eight items that refer to two dimensions. The pragmatic quality reflects the terms of usability, whereas the hedonic quality shows the feeling and perception of the user.

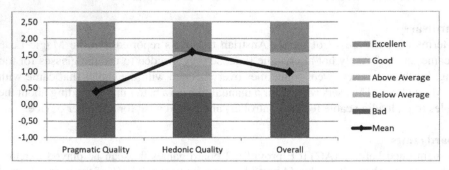

Fig. 6. Results of the UEQ

Figure 6 shows the outcome of the UEQ-S. The hedonic quality is rated excellent in the range of the best 10%, but the pragmatic quality is rated bad – so just 25% of the results could be worse. In total this leads to a result that is slightly above the average.

SUS – System Usability Scale
Similar results as in the UEQ can be seen for the SUS [27]. The questionnaire consists of 10 questions that are rated within a five-rating-scale from "strongly agree" to "strongly disagree". The cut off value of this questionnaire is 68. A score of 68 and higher shows that the usability of the system is better than the average. The results in the SUS reflect the results of the UEQ. The usability is rated below the average from more than 75% of the participants (see Fig. 7 Left).

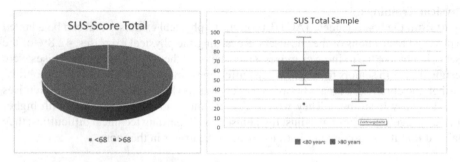

Fig. 7. Left: Results of the SUS; Right: SUS usability ratings corresponding to age

The right diagram of Fig. 7 shows that there is a difference in rating the usability corresponding to age. Primary users aged under 80 years rated the system more positively than higher aged users. This could also be a matter of familiarity with new technology.

5 Summary and Outlook

This work highlights the goals, the technical prototype, and the results of the field trials of the TACTILE project. The paper presents the benefits of our MR solution. Section 4 shows the qualitative and quantitative results. The qualitative results show that most of the end-users enjoyed the solution, but the training exercises were too easy for them. The major problems were the placement of the avatar and the device's RGB camera's limited field of view resulting in missed detections of game pieces not in view. Furthermore, the complexity of the hardware (multiple chargers, number of cables, bulkiness, heat retention) reduced the comfort of the system. The quantitative results show that the hedonic quality stayed the same compared to the results of the second user workshop [20], whereas the pragmatic quality was reduced. This can be explained by higher expectations on the system in comparison to the second workshop and the decrease of the novelty factor of the system as most end-users that participated in the field trials already knew the system from the workshops.

Regarding market perspective, it can be stated that current MR glasses are still too expensive for the private market. However, it is assumed that future MR glasses, released within the next years, will become more affordable. This can be already seen with the Nreal Light MR glasses[10], which, at almost the size of sunglasses, are less bulky and are powered by the connected smart phone, thus reducing the need for extra chargers.

Acknowledgment. The project TACTILE is co-funded by the AAL Joint Programme (AAL-2018–5-143CP) and the following National Authorities and R&D programs in Austria, Switzerland, and the Netherlands: FFG, Schweizer Eidgenossenschaft, ZonMw.

References

1. Cohen, G., Perlstein, S., Chapline, J., Kelly, J., Firth, K., Simmens, S.: The impact of professionally conducted cultural programs on the physical health, mental health, and social functioning of older adults. Gerontologist **46**(6), 726–734 (2006). https://doi.org/10.1093/geront/46.6.726
2. Verghese, J., Lipton, R., Katz, M., Hall, C.: Leisure activities and the risk of dementia in the elderly. Massachusetts Medical Society (2003)
3. Gheysen, F., et al.: Physical activity to improve cognition in older adults: can physical activity programs enriched with cognitive challenges enhance the effects? a systematic review and meta-analysis. Int. J. Behavioral Nutrition and Physical Activity **15**(63) (2018). https://doi.org/10.1186/s12966-018-0697-x
4. Ingold, M., Tulliani, N., Chan, C.C.H., Liu, K.P.Y.: Cognitive function of older adults engaging in physical activity. BMC Geriatrics **20**(229) (2020). https://doi.org/10.1186/s12877-020-01620-w

---

[10] https://www.nreal.ai/light/

5. Guo, W., Zang, M., Klich, S., Kawczynski, A., Smoter, M., Wang, B.: Effect of combined physical and cognitive interventions on executive functions in older adults: a meta-analysis of outcomes. Int. J. Environ. Res. Public Health 17, 6166 (2020). https://doi.org/10.3390/ije rph17176166

6. Guadagnoli, M.A., Lee, T.D.: Challenge point: a framework for conceptualizing the effects of various practice conditions in motor learning. J. Motion Behavior 36(2), 212–224 (2004)

7. Pawlaczyk, M., et al.: Quality of life of the elderly residents of nursing homes and patients of the psychogeriatric day ward. J. Medical Science 86(1), 36–41 (2017)

8. Pinkas, J., Gujski, M., Humeniuk, E., Raczkiewicz, D., Bejga, P., Owoc, A., Bojar, I.: State of health and quality of life of women at advanced age. Medical Science Monitor 22(3095), 105 (2016)

9. Maier, M., Rubio Ballester, B., Bañuelos, N.L., Oller, E.D., Verschure, P.F.: Adaptive conjunctive cognitive training (ACCT) in virtual reality for chronic stroke patients: a randomized controlled pilot trial. J. Neuro Eng. Rehabilitation 17(1), 1–20 (2020)

10. Maier, M., Rubio Ballester, B., Duff, A., Duarte Oller, E., Verschure, P.F.: Effect of specific over nonspecific VR-based rehabilitation on poststroke motor recovery: a systematic meta-analysis, Neurorehabilitation and Neural Repair 33(2), 112–129 (2019)

11. Rubio Ballester, B., Ward, N.S., Brander, F., Maier, M., Kelly, K., Verschure, P.F.: Relationship between intensity and recovery in post-stroke rehabilitation: a retrospective analysis. J. Neurology, Neurosurgery Psychiatry (2021). https://doi.org/10.1136/jnnp-2021-326948

12. Hwang, J., Lee, S.: The effect of virtual reality program on the cognitive function and balance of the people with mild cognitive impairment. J. Phys. Ther. Sci. 29(8), 1283–1286 (2017)

13. C. Tuena, E. et al.: Usability issues of clinical and research applications of virtual reality in older people: a systematic review. Front. Hum. Neurosci. 14, 93 (2020). https://doi.org/10.3389/fnhum.2020.00093

14. Freeman, D., et al.: Virtual reality in the assessment, understanding, and treatment of mental health disorders. Psychol. Med. 47(14), 2393–2400 (2017)

15. Dey, A., Billinghurst, M., Lindeman, R.W., Swan, J.: A systematic review of 10 years of augmented reality usability studies: 2005 to 2014. Front. Rob. AI 5, 37 (2018)

16. Cao, S.: Virtual reality applications in rehabilitation. In: Kurosu, M. (ed.) HCI 2016. LNCS, vol. 9731, pp. 3–10. Springer, Cham (2016). https://doi.org/10.1007/978-3-319-39510-4_1

17. Kwon, J.U., Lee, E.S., Ahn, S.C.: Projector-camera based remote assistance system for the elderly: design issues and implementation. In: System Integration (SII), 2016 IEEE/SICE International Symposium on, IEEE, pp. 230–235 (2016)

18. Lo Bianco, M., Pedell, S., Renda, G.: A health industry perspective on augmented reality as a communication tool in elderly fall prevention. In: Proceedings of the International Symposium on Interactive Technology and Ageing Populations, ACM, pp. 1—11 (2016)

19. Broneder, E., et al.: TACTILE – A novel mixed reality system for training & social interaction. In: 22nd International Conference on. Human-Computer Interaction HCII 2020, Copenhagen, Denmark (2020)

20. Broneder, E., et al.: TACTILE – a mixed reality-based system for cognitive and physical training. In: Ahram, T., Taiar, R. (eds.) IHIET 2021. LNNS, vol. 319, pp. 752–759. Springer, Cham (2022). https://doi.org/10.1007/978-3-030-85540-6_95

21. Rainer, H.: Sturzprophylaxe im Seniorenalter. http://sport1.uibk.ac.at/lehre/lehrbeauftragte/Huber%20Reinhard/Sturzprophylaxe%20im%20Seniorenalter%20gesamt.pdf Accessed 20 May 2019

22. Lindenberg-Kaiser, M.: Bewegungselemente für Gedächtnistrainingsstunden". Bundesverband für Gedächtnistraining (2011)

23. Zelf oefenen na een beroerte (CVA): https://www.kcrutrecht.nl/wp-content/uploads/2018/09/Snel-in-beweging-Oefengids-beroerte.pdf

24. Nasreddine, Z.S., Phillips, N.A., Bédirian, V., Charbonneau, S., Whitehead, V., Collin, I., et al.: The montreal cognitive assessment, MoCA: a brief screening tool for mild cognitive impairment. J. Am. Geriatr. Soc. **53**, 695–699 (2005). https://doi.org/10.1111/j.1532-5415.2005.53221.x

25. Yesavage, J.A., Brink, T.L.: Development and validation of a geriatric depression screening scale: a preliminary report. J. Psychiatr. Res. **39**, 37–39 (1983). https://doi.org/10.1016/0022-3956(82)90033-4

26. Schrepp, M., Hinderks, A., Thomaschewski, J.: Design and evaluation of a short version of the user experience questionnaire (UEQ-S). In: IJIMAI **4**(6), 103–108 (2017)

27. Matthias, R.: Quantitative usablility-analysen mit der system usability scale (SUS). In: Seibert Media Weblog (2011). Accessed 12 May 2022

Multisensory Experience for People with Hearing Loss: A Preliminary Study Using Haptic Interfaces to Sense Music

Diana Carvalho[1,2](✉) [iD], João Barroso[1,2] [iD], and Tânia Rocha[1,2] [iD]

[1] UTAD - University of Trás-Os-Montes E Alto Douro, Quinta de Prados,
5001-801 Vila Real, Portugal
{dianac,Jbarroso,trocha}@utad.pt
[2] INESC TEC, Rua Dr. Roberto Frias, 4200-465 Porto, Portugal

Abstract. In this paper, we describe a preliminary study on a multisensory music experience for people with hearing loss. Our main goal is to provide a music event through visual and tactile stimuli, granting a multisensory experience using haptic interfaces and taking advantage of visual feedback, vibrations and pressure to induce feelings. In this context, a mobile application was developed, allowing the user to interact with recorded audio samples that exploit vibrations to trigger emotions, such as fear, adrenaline, anxiety, suspense, drama, adventure, or even more complex moods like when dancing and relaxing. We thus describe our methodology (design, implementation and user assessment) for a preliminary study of a music experience based on a user-centered design approach. Indeed, we gathered promising results as the experience was considered effective and satisfying. We also uncovered some development issues to be addressed in future work, having to do with the use of specific hardware for providing a fully immersive experience.

Keywords: Multimedia · Multisensory experience · Haptic interfaces · Interaction design · Audio · Mobile applications · Hearing loss · Digital inclusion

1 Introduction

In recent years, interactive computer-based systems have become tools for communication, collaboration and social interaction amongst diverse user population with different abilities, skills, disorders, requirements and preferences in a variety of contexts of use [1]. Indeed, the development and implementation of new systems and methodologies should assure a more user-friendly approach and become a motivational/behavioral solution that aggregates multiple advantages regarding different fields of interest (e.g., rehabilitation of patients) [2]. As such, the needs of the users are becoming increasingly important and digital environments should be accessible and usable by anyone, anytime, anywhere.

Digital inclusion is considered a Human Right, as digital environments provide an unlimited number of services, products and benefits for personal, professional and social contexts. The term "user interfaces for all", firstly coined by Stephanidis et al. in the late 90's [3–5], represents an effort to overcome known accessibility and usability challenges

V. G. Duffy et al. (Eds.): HCII 2022, LNCS 13521, pp. 292–306, 2022.
https://doi.org/10.1007/978-3-031-17902-0_21

and should be conceived as a new perspective on HCI. However, "one solution does not fit All", as there are specific target-populations not able to handle digital environments similarly, mainly due to cognitive or physical setbacks. In this perspective, our top research goal is to provide a user-centered solution for one main audience – people with disabilities – to accomplish specific tasks.

With this goal in mind, we followed a new approach and explored a new area of interest in our research: provide people with hearing loss with a multisensory music experience, through visual and tactile stimuli. Specifically in this study, we present the audio samples recorded, the mobile application developed and the contexts of use.

Indeed, our first step was to analyze previous studies, in which authors use sound as a mean to convey information. Furthermore, after recording some audio samples, we tested them in order to understand which type of emotion could be transmitted to a person with impairments of the auditory system. Hence our focus on haptic interfaces and its capacity to cause vibrations as the mean to provide the user with important feedback. Indeed, the proposal of our preliminary investigation is to create a mobile application, thus providing portability, that allows testing of some audio samples with the multisensory goal in mind. Our ultimate ambition is to be able to convey specific basic emotions, such as fear, adrenaline, anxiety; and even cause more complex feelings like the ones affiliated with the act of dancing or relaxing. Likewise, we developed audio samples to evoke moods of Suspense, Drama and Adventure.

Finally, we pursued a user-centered design methodology and invited a smartphone user with hearing loss to be part of our development process, thus providing valuable feedback regarding the accessibility and usability of the solution presented.

The paper is structured as follow: first, we present a background analysis with a brief statistical context and characterization of hearing loss as a disability. We deepen the concept of inclusive sound experience through vibrations and introduce studies of sound as an inclusive content, i.e., studies that use sound as a mean to convey information in different areas. After presenting a brief overview regarding haptic interfaces and their benefits, we discuss the basis on the theory of emotions, thus underlying our choices for this preliminary study. We then introduce our multisensory experience and describe: the methodology and context of use; the mobile application developed; the audio samples recorded; the results of the assessment and the discussion regarding the initial user evaluation. Finally, we present the main conclusions and point out future work.

2 Theoretical Framework

2.1 Statistical Context and Characterization of Hearing Loss

The World Health Organization (WHO) estimates over 5% of the world's population has hearing loss (approximately 466 million people). By 2030, there will be nearly 630 million people with hearing loss; and by 2050, the number can rise to over 900 million. Furthermore, nearly 1 out of 3 people over 65 years old and up to 5 out of every 1000 babies are affected by hearing loss [6].

When we talk about hearing disabilities, we must consider four levels of severity: mild, moderate, severe or profound; that can affect one ear or both, leading to difficulties in "hearing conversational speech or loud sounds" [7]. Furthermore, there are four established types of hearing disabilities: conductive hearing loss, sensorineural hearing loss, mixed hearing loss (contains elements of both conductive and sensorineural hearing loss) and central auditory loss [7].

Another relevant aspect worth mentioning are the different expressions used when referring to people with limits in the auditory system. A person is considered to have "hearing loss" if he or she is not able to hear "as well as someone with normal hearing" – hearing thresholds of 25 dB or higher in both ears. Specifically, the diagnosis of people with hearing loss is based on [6]:

- Adults (15 years and older) hearing more than 40 decibels (dB) in the better hearing ear;
- Children (0 – 14 years of age) hearing more than 30 dB in the better hearing ear.

Another expression commonly used is "hard of hearing" and it refers to people with hearing loss ranging from mild to severe. This group "usually communicates through spoken language and can benefit from hearing aids, cochlear implants, and other assistive devices, as well as captioning" [7].

On the other hand, "deaf people" is an expression regularly used in the literature and refers to people who have profound hearing loss, i.e., very little or no hearing. In these cases, sign language is used to communicate [7].

WHO describes three main areas of impact for people with hearing loss [7]. First, the functional impact: the individual's ability to communicate with others is compromised, as the "spoken language development is often delayed in children with unaddressed hearing loss". This affects, clearly, the students' learning experience. Second, the social and emotional impact: people with hearing disabilities can feel, or even be, excluded from the most basic communications, leading to feelings of alienation, frustration and social isolation, since it is through the process of communication that we relate to each other, developing our identity. This situation is particularly common among older people with hearing loss. Third, the economic impact: "WHO estimates that unaddressed hearing loss poses an annual global cost of US$ 750 billion. This includes health sector costs (excluding the cost of hearing devices), costs of educational support, loss of productivity, and societal costs" [7].

Regarding communication, not all have the same skills: some individuals communicate using oral language and/or writing and lip-reading, others use sign language, and some are bilingual that use both forms of communication [8–10]. The development of communication skills involves various factors, such as: the family profile, which determines the way a child is raised and has contact with sign language; the social context, i.e., the education inclusion policies specific to each country; and the type of deafness and the psychological affectations that may result from the disability [7, 8].

Lastly, WHO has asserted the importance of sign language as well, stating that "family members, medical professionals, teachers and employers should be encouraged to learn signs/sign language in order to facilitate communication with deaf people" [6].

2.2   What is Sound?

Sound is defined as air vibrations that the ear can pick up on and convert into electrical signals, which are then interpreted by the brain. The hearing sense is not the only one able to provide this experience: touch can provide a similar experience. With low-frequency vibrations, the ear becomes ineffective and the remaining sensory areas of the body begin to take on more control over the audio capture. For some reason, we tend to make a distinction between hearing a sound and feeling a vibration, but, in fact, they may be the same. In this context, Holmes affirmed "deafness could not mean that you cannot hear, only that there is something wrong with your biological auditory system. Even someone who is deaf can still hear and/or feel sounds" [11].

Namely, sound is a mechanical wave that propagates longitudinally in physical materials. The speed of sound varies with the density of the material in which it propagates, so the denser the medium, the faster the sound. Indeed, sound waves are classified as: sound – mechanical waves produced by a source that emits human audible frequencies, ranging from 20 Hz to 20 000 Hz; infrasound – mechanical waves where the frequency is less than 20 Hz and cannot be heard by humans (notwithstanding the fact that there are some animals that make and hear sounds at these frequencies); and ultrasound – mechanical waves that have a frequency higher than 20,000 Hz, which means they cannot be heard by humans, either.

As Friedner and Helmreich stated in their study, "the frequency spectrum where hearing and deaf scholars have recently been meeting in order to unsettle the earcentrism of sound studies and the visually centered epistemology of much Deaf studies" is infrasound or vibration lower than 20 Hz [9].

Goodman has even gone further and proposed the notion of "unsound", referring to the infrasonic and the ultrasonic as zones at "the fuzzy periphery of auditory perception, where sound is inaudible but still produces neuro effects or physiological resonances" [12].

Therefore, these authors motivate the use of "sound as a vibration of a certain frequency in a physical material rather than centering vibrations in a hearing ear. Sound plays, thus, a role in experiences where people with hearing impairment can benefit" [12].

2.3   A Brief Note on Haptic Interfaces

Haptic technology refers to the sense of touch, taking advantage of vibrations and / or forces being applied to the user's body. This designation contemplates data acquisition and object manipulation by the means of the user's touch, considered as manual interaction with environments that can be real or virtual [13]. Indeed, studies show that tangible user interfaces may even influence the speed and accuracy of specific age groups when completing basic tasks, as content insertion or manipulation, whether they are children or older adults [14, 15].

These sensorial interfaces should adjust to other interaction paradigms and allow a more intuitive use of the systems multimodally, considering several input / output mechanisms in order to create synergies amongst them [16, 17].

Haptic computing is a field of rapid progress and development. There is a multiplicity of disciplines it can embrace, such as biomechanics, neurosciences, mathematics, software engineering, rehabilitation, product design, among others [13].

This technology is, thus, studied within the scope of people with disabilities, as visual or hearing impairments [18, 19], since the touch is more intimately related to the users' emotions than any other natural interaction paradigm [20].

2.4 The Theory of Emotions

It is relevant to state that emotions and feelings are often used interchangeably, but they do not refer to the same thing. Indeed, emotions come first, then feelings follow with our bodies' release of specific chemicals, in response to our interpretation of a specific trigger. Then moods grow from a combination of feelings. Indeed, there are different types of emotions that can influence how we live and interact with others [21].

Throughout the years, researchers have tried to identify the different types of emotions that people can experience. Distinct theories have emerged to help categorize and explain the emotions that people feel.

During the late 1970s, Eckman identified the six basic emotions universally experienced in all human cultures: happiness, sadness, disgust, fear, surprise, and anger [22]. He named them the Big-Six emotions and theorized that not all expressions are the result of culture. Instead, they express universal emotions and are therefore biological. Later, he extended this list of basic emotions to include such things as pride, relief, shame, guilt, embarrassment and excitement.

On the other hand, psychologist Robert Plutchik introduced the "wheel of emotions". Much like the color wheel, he grouped emotions into common areas illustrated with colors, and defended emotions can be combined to form different feelings, much like colors can be mixed to create other shades [23, 24]. He proposed eight primary bipolar emotions: joy versus sadness; anger versus fear; trust versus disgust; and surprise versus anticipation.

Since then, other theories have emerged, focusing on what emotions make up the core of the human experience. A more recent study suggests that there are at least 27 distinct emotions, all of which are highly interconnected [25]. Thus, rather than being entirely distinct, people experience these emotions along a gradient: complex, sometimes mixed emotions, are a merge of basic ones (e.g., basic emotions like joy or trust can be combined to create love).

2.5 Technological Breakthroughs for People with Hearing Loss

The technological breakthroughs for people with hearing loss have been prominent and the use of technology to provide musical experiences is a recurrent practice for people with central auditory loss, sensorineural or mixed hearing loss [9].

The following studies present technological solutions for this specific target by promoting visual or tactile stimuli in order to provide a musical experience in different forms, whether through sound, vibrations or visual displays. In point of fact, several researches defend the use of vibrations and tactile stimuli, as it can allow the transmission of support information in daily lives activities for people with hearing loss.

Ohtsuka et al. presented a body-braille tool as an information transmission support tool for the deaf-blind using vibrations. They used a vibration speaker to improve readability and obtained a correct answer rate of 85%, even with participants with no experience with a two-point Body-Braille system [26].

Manaf and Sulaiman created a mobile application for scenarios involving fire, which integrated vibration sensing and non-speech visualization to notify hearing impaired students in a controlled situation. Specifically in this study, it was proven that integration of vibration detection increased the level of alertness of the hearing impaired during a fire notification occurrence, and that signals can be an effective tip-off with the visualization of alert images [10].

Yao et al. presented a pair of shoes designed to allow vibrotactile sensing and fulfil the dancing entertainment demand of the hearing-impaired dancers [27]. Overall, it seems that the cerebral response to vibrations reaches a speed and a response identical to the capture of sounds or images. This evolutionary mechanism allows people with deprivation of a sense to adapt and compensate using other senses. Some authors report that deaf people have the sensation of vibration in the part of the brain that other people use to hear [27]. These findings suggest that deaf people receiving vibrations have similar emotions to other people when they listen to music.

The study of Mazzoni and Bryan-Kinns (DATA) explored a glove as a "portable, hands-free, wearable haptic device that maps the emotions evoked by the music in a movie into vibrations." In this study, authors did not test the solution with people with hearing loss. Overall, results indicated "people are able to associate emotional states to vibrotactile stimuli played at different frequencies and intensities". Specifically, "combination of low intensity and low frequency would induce in participants a low sense of arousal and a low sense of valence, whereas vibrations at high intensity combined with high frequency communicated to people a high sense of valence and a high sense of arousal" [28].

Petry et al. presented MuSS-Bits (Music Sensory Substitution Bits), an ad-hoc wearable solution that enables deaf people to explore sound from various audio sources (instruments, digital devices or environmental sounds) and receive real-time feedback [29]. The authors also presented a literature review of existing music sensory substitution systems and affirmed that the HCI community explored assistive technology using visual [30–32] and vibrotactile [33–35] sensory substitution systems to bridge the feedback loop gap for musical activities.

Tranchant et al. tested seven individuals with hearing loss and compared performances of 14 individuals with no hearing impairments in order to investigate beat synchronization to vibrotactile electronic dance music in hearing and deaf people. In the experiment, the first group used a vibration stimulus and the second one the auditory stimulus (no vibration). Results showed there was no difference in performance between the two groups and most participants were able to precisely time the bounces to the vibrations. On the other hand, the hearing group showed a higher performance regarding the auditory condition when compared to the vibrotactile condition. Also, they observed that accurate tactile-motor synchronization in a dance-like context occurs regardless of auditory experience, though auditory-motor synchronization is of superior quality [36].

In the research by Trivedi et al., an affordable wearable haptic device for people with hearing disabilities to experience music was developed. The prototype consisted of Vibrotactile sleeves with bone conduction speakers, providing sensory input of vibrations via the bone conduction speakers. The development process was based on subjects' surveys and feedback on different assistive technologies. For assessment, the authors developed a visualization system that gives visual clues that represent the given musical notes. User testing results showed that this system can be used to provide a musical experience to people with hearing impairments [37].

Furthermore, the visual stimulus is another sense effectively promoted in the development of adapted or universal technological solutions for this specific target. In previous studies, different solutions were described to provide inclusive and autonomous interaction. For example:

Sridhar et al. presented the relationship between pixel colors and sound type, or illumination pattern and sound type, exists for one-pixel-displays among deaf and hearing persons. Results suggested patterns might be more intuitive when compared to pixel colors; and the position and size of the one-pixel-display seems to depend on the personal preferences and should, therefore, be customizable. They also pointed a preference to two of Harrison's patterns identified in the study: the Staircase Blink pattern for alarm sounds and the Blink Slow pattern for notification sounds [38].

MyCarMobile [39] is a travel assistance android mobile application for deaf people, and was a solution presented to manage the deaf people's serious communication problems, where the use of smartphones has been explored as a solution to break communication barriers and enhance their communication, providing access to basic services. In this APP, authors explored the usage of iconographic interfaces in smartphones as a solution for providing further autonomy to deaf people, by applying a model for asynchronous and non-verbal communication through iconography. This solution allowed travel assistance services without involving audio, using an iconographic interface to report road accidents. The authors used a user-centered design approach on the development of the prototype and performed usability tests with eleven deaf users, in order to validate the mobile application. They stated good performance and satisfaction levels of the users that interacted with the application.

3 Multisensory Music Experience

Music is an important part of our daily life. We listen to the radio, enjoy concerts or make music. This high exposure to music makes even children experts in music-listening [11]. In musicmaking activities, this expertise enables humans to compare the created with the intended sound and completes the feedback-loop for music-making (play, listen, evaluate, adjust). However, this is a challenging task for a deaf individual (deaf, deafened or hard of hearing) interested in learning to play an instrument [29]. While those systems are well studied and deliver accurate musical information in real-time, often the input possibilities (sound sources) and portability are limited or pre-defined.

Wearable electronics, such as smartwatches, mobile phones and MUVIB [10] could provide pervasive access to sound through vibrations [29], thus demonstrating that music can be capable of conveying emotions [28].

In this framework, and as previously explained, it is thought that people with hearing loss can feel music through vibrations, as they are processed on the same side of the brain where auditory people can hear. Therefore, with the application presented, we intend to produce vibrations through samples so that users can feel emotions transmitted by music, just like with people without hearing problems.

3.1 Methodology

Following a user-centered design methodology, we prepared eight audio samples through vibrations (low frequencies). These were meant to test if we could convey specific basic emotions, such as: fear, adrenaline, anxiety; as well as incite more complex feelings related to suspense, drama or adventure. Likewise, we developed audio samples to evoke moods associated with the act of dancing or simply relaxing. We decided on these feelings / moods following the assumptions of previous researchers that introduced the complexity of emotions, as explained in the previous section.

For this preliminary study, each audio sample was created with virtual instruments and audio manipulation, and developed with a fundamental frequency, ranging from 20 Hz to 250 Hz. Likewise, we took under consideration the audio speed and repetition, depending on the feeling we wished to stimulate. The sound samples were digitally created, with virtual instruments and audio manipulation, using LOGIC X [40] and Ableton Live [41].

Specifically, the fundamental frequencies used for the different audio samples were: 64–67 Hz, for fear; 74 Hz, for drama; 50 Hz, for anxiety; 108 Hz, for the relaxing mood; 90 Hz, for the dancing mood; 55 Hz, for adrenaline; 61Hz, for suspense; and 39 Hz, for adventure.

Regarding the sound experience, and to achieve a fully inclusive sound experience, we considered two experimental test scenarios, each with different devices for the haptic response. Firstly, the user must be in a controlled room and have speakers that can reproduce the full frequency range. They can use a portable computer or a mobile device. For the first, a wood table or other physical material capable of resonating frequencies must be available. Hands are used to feel vibrations or (for an optimized experience) a sub-woofer, where users can put their feet against in order to feel the vibrations. The second scenario takes advantage of a mobile application (and smartphone) with an audio system and Bluetooth, like JBL or BOOSE, to achieve an autonomous and portable sound experience closer to the daily reality. Through this software, the user's request is sent to the speakers, or other audio system chosen, and the chosen audio sample is played.

Next, we present the application development and test the audio samples.

3.2 Interface Design

The application was designed with the aim of transmitting emotions to users with hearing loss, through vibrations. Specifically, it was created to be ease-of-use and intuitive for all users, thus following a user-centered design methodology.

To handle the application, users should read the instructions to understand its purpose and options; and then, start navigating.

Fig. 1. Application's main screen

Fig. 2. Application's main menu

After loading the main screen (Fig. 1), the main menu appears, presenting three options: Instructions, Who are we?, Start the experience (Fig. 2). In the "Instructions" section, the application provided information regarding the experience (materials used and scenarios) and the different sound samples. The procedures of the experiment were also described (e.g., how and when to put the hands closer to the haptic device in order to feel the vibrations). Regarding the "Who are we?" section, the bedrock of our study was explained. On the other hand, in the "Start the Experience" section, users could choose from eight sound samples, each representing an emotion / mood. Figure 3 shows the first four sound samples' menu. After selecting the intended sound sample, the user could sense the corresponding vibration.

Fig. 3. Application's sound menu

3.3   Preliminary User Evaluation

We performed a preliminary assessment session with one user in order to understand their first impression and feedback, and also discover sample problems, if any. Our goal was always to improve the sound experience for people with hearing loss. Next, we describe the assessment carried out in our early study.

Indeed, with the aim of developing an interface capable of helping deaf people, we understand that its validation in a real context of use was important. We did not intend to carry out a profound study on the interface and the overall multisensory experience during this stage, but did acknowledge the value of having a target user participating in the assessment of the interface and its implementation. With a participatory design approach in mind, we invited a user with moderate hearing loss to take part in the entire development process and, thus, better understand and meet our target's needs. The user was 38 years old, with experience using mobile systems and tactile/haptic interaction on a daily basis, due to their use of a smartphone with those capabilities every day for the last ten years. Naturally, the participant gave their signed consent.

The user testing was performed in a controlled environment, but not in a completely isolated room. Both the mobile device (Fig. 4) with the application and the computer (Fig. 5) were provided to the participant, and they were asked to randomly navigate through the application, encouraging an autonomous interaction. It was, however, mandatory to go through all the options provided. Therefore, the participant needed to test the three menu options described in the previous section ("Who are we?", "Instructions", "Start the experiment"). When navigating through the audio samples, each time the user selected a sample and sensed it, they were asked to describe the emotion felt for evaluation purposes, i.e., give feedback about which emotion the audio sample transmitted – ultimately, the goal was to verify if there was any correlation between the emotion selected and the one felt.

Fig. 4. Participant exploring the application in the mobile device

Fig. 5. Participant exploring the application in the computer

The results were promising. The participant was pleased to enroll in this experience and recognized the importance of the studies on digital accessibility, emphasizing, nonetheless, some aspects that needed improvement.

In detail, some of the samples were not able to correspond to the emotions that the user felt, due to our choice to try and recreate complex emotions, and even moods, in this preliminary stage. Basic emotions, such as anxiety and fear were correctly discovered / felt. However, complex moods, like dancing or relaxing were somehow difficult to explain, and thus difficult to be perceived. Namely, the participant revealed that they could not perceive some samples, as well as not being able to interpret a sample that had three sounds including the fundamental frequency. This situation could be due to the room conditions, as it was not completely isolated.

Another feedback given was that the application was well-designed and very easy to interact with. Also, text and images were easy to understand. The participant could test all the options without difficulties or errors during interaction.

Overall, the participant was excited about the multisensory experience and considered it to be an important step for digital inclusion of people with hearing loss.

4 Conclusions and Future Work

With this introductory study, it was possible to have a glance at understanding how people with hearing loss can feel emotions through vibrations. During this preliminary experience, we set two scenarios for user testing and retrieved feedback from it. Much more work must still be conducted with regards to the fidelity of the samples, but we considered this first approach an important step towards the study of inclusive solutions for people with hearing constraints.

Overall, we verified that some emotions initially determined on the audio samples did not correspond to the emotions reported by the participant. Indeed, this early study shows that simple emotions are easier to translate than complex moods. However, we obtained promising results, as the experience was considered effective and satisfactory.

We are aware of the embryonic nature of our study. Consequently, as future work we feel ready to initiate a methodical strategy for user evaluation with multiple participants, thus validating our approach. We also intend to proceed with the production of other samples and provide a different multisensory experience environment, e.g., project a full immersive sound experience resorting to different sensory stimuli.

Acknowledgments. This work is a result of the project INOV@UTAD, POCI-01–0247-FEDER-049337, financed by FEEI and supported by FEDER, through the Competitiveness and Internationalization Operational Program. Furthermore, we thank all people who directly or indirectly helped in this study, particularly to José Vieira, João Faiões e Tiago Teixeira.

References

1. Stephanidis, C.: User interfaces for all: new perspectives into human-computer interaction. In: Stephanidis, C. (ed.) User Interfaces for All - Concepts, Methods, and Tools, p. 760. Lawrence Erlbaum Associates, Mahwah, NJ (2001)
2. Reis, A., et al.: Developing a system for post-stroke rehabilitation: an exergames approach. In: Antona, M., Stephanidis, C. (eds.) UAHCI 2016. LNCS, vol. 9739, pp. 403–413. Springer, Cham (2016). https://doi.org/10.1007/978-3-319-40238-3_39
3. Constantine, S., Pier, L.E.: 'Connecting' to the information society: a European perspective. Technology and Disability 10(1). IOS Press, pp. 21–44, Jan. 01, 1999. (2015). http://content.iospress.com/articles/technology-and-disability/tad00013
4. Stephanidis, C., Salvendy, G.: Toward an information society for all: an international research and development agenda. Int. J. Human-Computer Interaction 10(2), 107–134 (1998). https://doi.org/10.1207/s15327590ijhc1002_2

5. Stephanidis, C., et al.: Toward an information society for all: HCI challenges and R&D recommendations. Int. J. Human-Computer Interaction **11**(1), 1–28 (1999). https://doi.org/10.1207/s15327590ijhc1101_1

6. World Health Organization (WHO): Deafness and hearing loss. https://www.who.int/en/newsroom/fact-sheets/detail/deafness-and-hearing-loss Accessed 8 Jan 2022

7. World Health Organization (WHO): International Classification of Diseases (ICD). https://www.who.int/standards/classifications/classification-of-diseases Accessed 8 Jan 2022

8. Martins, P., Rodrigues, H., Rocha, T., Francisco, M., Morgado, L.: Accessible options for deaf people in e-learning platforms: technology solutions for sign language translation. Procedia Computer Sci. **67**, 263–272 (2015). https://doi.org/10.1016/J.PROCS.2015.09.270

9. Friedner, M., Helmreich, S.: Sound Studies Meets Deaf Studies. **7**(1), 72–86 (2015). https://doi.org/10.2752/174589312X13173255802120

10. Manaf, M.B.A., Sulaiman, S.B.: Integrating vibration sensing and non-speech visualization to notify hearing impaired students on fire in a controlled situation. In: 2015 International Symposium on Mathematical Sciences and Computing Research, iSMSC 2015 - Proceedings, pp. 36–41 (2016). https://doi.org/10.1109/ISMSC.2015.7594024

11. Holmes, J.A.: Expert listening beyond the limits of hearing: music and deafness. J. Am. Musicol. Soc. **70**(1), 171–220 (2017). https://doi.org/10.1525/JAMS.2017.70.1.171

12. Goodman, S.: Sonic Warfare : Sound, Affect, and the Ecology of Fear. MIT Press (2010)

13. Srinivasan, M.A., Basdogan, C.: Haptics in virtual environments: taxonomy, research status, and challenges. Comput. Graph. **21**(4), 393–404 (1997). https://doi.org/10.1016/S0097-8493(97)00030-7

14. Carvalho, D., Bessa, M., Magalhães, L., Carrapatoso, E.: Age Group Differences in Performance Using Diverse Input Modalities: Insertion Task Evaluation (2016)

15. Carvalho, D., Bessa, M., Magalhães, L.: Different interaction paradigms for different user groups: an evaluation regarding content selection. In: Proceedings of the XV International Conference on Human Computer Interaction – Interaccion'14, p. 40 (2014). https://doi.org/10.1145/2662253.2662293

16. Hale, K.S., Stanney, K.M.: Deriving haptic design guidelines from human physiological, psychophysical, and neurological foundations. IEEE Comput. Graphics Appl. **24**(2), 33–39 (2004). https://doi.org/10.1109/MCG.2004.1274059

17. Khan, M., Sulaiman, S., Said, M.D.A., Tahir, M.: Exploring the quantitative and qualitative measures for haptic systems. In: *2010 International Symposium on Information Technology*, pp. 31–36 (2010). https://doi.org/10.1109/ITSIM.2010.5561305

18. Li, Y., Johnson, S., Nam, C.: Haptically enhanced user interface to support science learning of visually impaired. In: Jacko, J.A. (ed.) HCI 2011. LNCS, vol. 6764, pp. 68–76. Springer, Heidelberg (2011). https://doi.org/10.1007/978-3-642-21619-0_10

19. Johnson, S., Li, Y., Nam, C.S., Yamaguchi, T.: Analyzing user behavior within a haptic system. In: Jacko, J.A. (ed.) HCI 2011. LNCS, vol. 6762, pp. 62–70. Springer, Heidelberg (2011). https://doi.org/10.1007/978-3-642-21605-3_7

20. Ichiyanagi, Y., Cooper, E.W., Kryssanov, V.V., Ogawa, H.: A haptic emotional model for audio system interface. In: Jacko, J.A. (ed.) HCI 2011. LNCS, vol. 6763, pp. 535–542. Springer, Heidelberg (2011). https://doi.org/10.1007/978-3-642-21616-9_60

21. Freedman, J.: At the Heart of Leadership: How To Get Results with Emotional Intelligence. 3rd edition. Six Seconds (2012)

22. Ekman, P., Freisen, W., Ancoli, S.: Facial signs of emotional experience. J. Personality Social Psychology **39**(6), 1125–1134 (1980). https://doi.org/10.1037/h0077722

23. Plutchik, R.: A general psychoevolutionary theory of emotion. Theories of Emotion, pp. 3–33 (1980). https://doi.org/10.1016/B978-0-12-558701-3.50007-7

24. Imbir, K.K.: Psychoevolutionary Theory of Emotion (Plutchik). In: Encyclopedia of Personality and Individual Differences, Springer International Publishing, Cham, pp. 1–9 (2017). https://doi.org/10.1007/978-3-319-28099-8_547-1

25. Cowen, A.S., Keltner, D.: Self-report captures 27 distinct categories of emotion bridged by continuous gradients. Proc. Natl. Acad. Sci. U.S.A. **114**(38), E7900–E7909 (2017). https://doi.org/10.1073/PNAS.1702247114/-/DCSUPPLEMENTAL

26. Ohtsuka, S., Chiba, H., Sasaki, N., Harakawa, T.: Alternative vibration presentation methods for the two-point Body-Braille system. In: 2016 IEEE 5th Global Conference on Consumer Electronics, GCCE 2016 (2016). https://doi.org/10.1109/GCCE.2016.7800451

27. Yao, L., Shi, Y., Chi, H., Ji, X., Ying, F.: Music-touch shoes: vibrotactile interface for hearing impaired dancers. p. 276 (2010). https://doi.org/10.1145/1709886.1709944

28. Mazzoni, A., Bryan-Kinns, N.: How does it feel like? An exploratory study of a prototype system to convey emotion through haptic wearable devices | IEEE Conference Publication | IEEE Xplore. In: 7th International Conference on Intelligent Technologies for Interactive Entertainment (INTETAIN), pp. 64–68 (2015)

29. Petry, B., Illandara, T., Forero, J.P., Nanayakkara, S.: Ad-hoc access to musical sound for deaf individuals. In: ASSETS 2016 - Proceedings of the 18th International ACM SIGACCESS Conference on Computers and Accessibility, pp. 285–286 (2016). https://doi.org/10.1145/2982142.2982213

30. Fourney, D.W., Fels, D.I.: Creating access to music through visualization. In: 2009 IEEE Toronto International Conference Science and Technology for Humanity (TIC-STH), pp. 939–944 (2009). https://doi.org/10.1109/TIC-STH.2009.5444364

31. Mori, J., Fels, D.I.: Seeing the music can animated lyrics provide access to the emotional content in music for people who are deaf or hard of hearing?, In: 2009 IEEE Toronto International Conference Science and Technology for Humanity (TIC-STH), pp. 951–956 (2009). https://doi.org/10.1109/TIC-STH.2009.5444362

32. Zhou, X., et al.: Cortical speech processing in postlingually deaf adult cochlear implant users, as revealed by functional near-infrared spectroscopy. Trends in Hearing, vol. 22, p. 233121651878685 (2018). https://doi.org/10.1177/2331216518786850

33. Karam, M., Russo, F.A., Fels, D.I.: Designing the model human cochlea: an ambient cross-modal audio-tactile display. IEEE Trans. Haptics **2**(3), 160–169 (2009). https://doi.org/10.1109/TOH.2009.32

34. Nanayakkara, S., Wyse, L., Taylor, E.A.: The haptic chair as a speech training aid for the deaf. In: Proceedings of the 24th Australian Computer-Human Interaction Conference on - OzCHI '12, pp. 405–410 (2012). https://doi.org/10.1145/2414536.2414600

35. Flores, G., Kurniawan, S., Manduchi, R., Martinson, E., Morales, L.M., Sisbot, E.A.: Vibrotactile guidance for wayfinding of blind walkers. IEEE Trans. Haptics **8**(3), 306–317 (2015). https://doi.org/10.1109/TOH.2015.2409980

36. Tranchant, P., Shiell, M.M., Giordano, M., Nadeau, A., Peretz, I., Zatorre, R.J.: Feeling the beat: Bouncing synchronization to vibrotactile music in hearing and early deaf people. Frontiers in Neuroscience **11**, 507 (2017). https://doi.org/10.3389/FNINS.2017.00507/BIBTEX

37. Trivedi, U., Alqasemi, R., Dubey, R.: Wearable musical haptic sleeves for people with hearing impairment. In: Proceedings of the 12th ACM International Conference on PErvasive Technologies Related to Assistive Environments, pp. 146–151 (2019). https://doi.org/10.1145/3316782.3316796

38. Sridhar, P.K., Petry, B., Pakianathan, P.V.S., Kartolo, A.S., Nanayakkara, S.: Towards one-pixel-displays for sound information visualization. In: Proceedings of the 28th Australian Conference on Computer-Human Interaction - OzCHI '16, pp. 91–95 (2016). https://doi.org/10.1145/3010915.3010980

39. Rocha, T., Paredes, H., Soares, D., Fonseca, B., Barroso, J.: MyCarMobile: a travel assistance emergency mobile app for deaf people. In: Bernhaupt, R., Dalvi, G., Joshi, A., Balkrishan, D.K., O'Neill, J., Winckler, M. (eds.) INTERACT 2017. LNCS, vol. 10513, pp. 56–65. Springer, Cham (2017). https://doi.org/10.1007/978-3-319-67744-6_4
40. Logic Pro - Apple. https://www.apple.com/logic-pro/ Accessed 8 Jan 2022
41. Music production with Live and Push | Ableton. https://www.ableton.com/ Accessed 8 Jan 2022

From Requirements to Prototyping: Proposal and Evaluation of an Artifact to Support Interface Design in the Context of Autism

Áurea Hiléia da Silva Melo[1]([🖂]), Ana Carolina Oran[2],
Jonathas Silva dos Santos[1], Sergio Cleger Tamayo[1], Davi Viana[3], Luis Rivero[3],
and Raimundo da Silva Barreto[2]

[1] Universidade do Estado do Amazonas (UEA/EST), Manaus, Brazil
`asmelo@uea.edu.br`
[2] Universidade Federal do Amazonas (UFAM), Manaus, Brazil
`{ana.oran,rbarreto}@icomp.ufam.edu.br`
[3] Universidade Federal do Maranhão (UFMA), São Luis, Brazil
`{davi.viana,luis.rivero}@ufma.br`

Abstract. Developing appropriate user interfaces is crucial for a positive user experience, as some users may require that the interaction supports specific interface elements for them. However, developing adequate interfaces for autistic users is not easy, as software development teams may not know how to design a user interface from the collected requirements. This paper presents a specific artifact, called Table of Requirements and Constraints, or simply TRC, to support interface design from requirements identification to prototype development of applications for the autism domain. Also, we identified quality attributes and defined a process to refine the requirements into user interface design ideas. We evaluated our proposal in an interface project development with industry practitioners to gather data on its feasibility. The obtained results indicate that these practitioners found that the artifacts guide the development team by defining an interface while providing opportunities for improvement in the requirements registration template to improve its use. With this work, we intend to support the professionals from the requirements identifications until the prototyping stage by developing and integrating these artifacts.

Keywords: ASD · Autism Spectrum Disorder · Interface design · Software requirements

1 Introduction

There are several techniques to help engineers gather requirements. In the requirements gathering phase, analysts obtain software functionality from customers and users. In addition, they also identify information about business

© Springer Nature Switzerland AG 2022
V. G. Duffy et al. (Eds.): HCII 2022, LNCS 13521, pp. 307–321, 2022.
https://doi.org/10.1007/978-3-031-17902-0_22

rules and usability characteristics [14]. Among the various types of existing requirements and their main elicitation techniques, there are graphical interface requirements, which present software demands related to interface components and information presentation [5,13].

For a good interface design, it is necessary to ensure that the client's request has been replicated both in the prototyping and in the software product. Therefore, an accurate description and presentation of these requirements are fundamental so that the development team can interpret and carry out a consistent implementation. And when the software user has a disorder, such as Autism Spectrum Disorder (ASD), the choice of technique and the appropriate presentation of the requirements becomes even more important, to adapt to their usability and accessibility needs [2]. People with ASD have several limitations in communication, social interaction, and behavior [1]. In addition, there are other autistic users' characteristics to be taken in software development, such as verifying whether it is verbal or non-verbal, whether it is high or low functioning, age, etc. Such characteristics and limitations are, in most cases, not known by the software development team. Due to this, it is necessary to use specific techniques to elucidate the requirements of this type of software. However, techniques and works are scarce in the literature for gathering software requirements for autistic people.

In this context, this article presents an artifact called Requirements and Constraints Table (TRC), which aims to aggregate and represent interface requirements for software designed for low-functioning autistic people. Due to its ability to combine requirements and constraints with the representation of interface components, TRC strongly contributes to mapping requirements into interface elements, significantly helping with the prototyping activity.

It is important to emphasize that the context of autism is because TRC is part of ProAut, which is a process to support the prototyping of application interfaces aimed at autistic people, the result of a doctoral thesis. ProAut includes activities and artifacts that also meet the needs of low-functioning autistics.

2   Context and Related Work

Requirements Engineering [14] is the name given to the set of activities related to the discovery, analysis, specification, and maintenance of a system's requirements. The term engineering reinforces that these activities must be performed systematically, throughout the life cycle of a system, and, whenever possible, using well-defined techniques [16]. Several techniques are used for requirements elicitation, including interviews with stakeholders, application of questionnaires, reading documents and forms from the organization hiring the system, conducting workshops with users, implementing prototypes, and analyzing usage scenarios [16]. In this way, requirements gathering activity has always been a challenging task because changing or incompletely defining requirements is one of the main challenges and can contribute to failure or failure of the software project [6,12].

In the universe of existing software requirements, this work falls into the context of user interface requirements, which is the key to application usability. Interface requirements, generally, include non-functional aspects for content presentation, application navigation, and user assistance. And due to the extensive framework of requirements elicitation techniques for a graphical interface, it is crucial to focus on how these requirements are presented to developers to facilitate understanding and, consequently, build a software interface in the right way [13].

Based on this context, Hadar's work [10] proposes a methodological approach for integrating accessibility requirements in descriptive language-based user interface (UIDL) development. The proposed strategy involves integrating accessibility requirements in the first versions of the application requirements. The approach automatically generates the interface design. However, this work does not present a clear description of which components are used in the assembly of the graphical interface, unlike TRC, which for each requirement already presents the recommendation of interface elements. Specifically for the public with ASD, Tahir et al. [15] created the Autistic Users Requirements Engineering (AURE), which is a methodology for collecting requirements from autistic users composed of 9 stages that go from requirements gathering through the creation of mind maps and documentation, and ending with evaluation. Although the authors present a methodology to help requirements engineers in requirement elicitation with autistic users, no technique adapted to the autism context was introduced, and no form of requirements presentation to support specific software design for the autistic audience.

Cabral [2] presents a set of requirements elicitation techniques based on the adaptation of existing approaches, allowing the software engineer to include the autistic child in the process, and bring a more realistic view of the requirements needed to direct the development of the application. The author proposes several techniques, such as interviews and brainstorming, to extract necessary information from the child, from expressions or gestures, replacing the need for dialogue commonly used in these techniques with other types of audiences. The differential of our proposal to Cabral's work, among others, is that we promote a mapping of the requirements into interface elements, which will help in more efficient and effective prototyping. Another point to highlight is the challenge when dealing with low-functioning autistic people.

3   Table of Requirements and Constraints (TRC)

The TRC is an artifact in the form of a table belonging to ProAut [7]. ProAut has four stages based on Design Thinking (DT) [18], namely Immersion, Analysis, Ideation and Prototyping. Activities of the ProAut include artifacts that are used since requirements elicitation [4], through the generation of empathy with autistic people [8–10] to the TRC for prototyping. In the context of ProAut, the TRC is an artifact used from the analysis phase to prototyping, based on the requirements collected in the Immersion phase. The goal of TRC is to provide a macro but specific view to designers, to guide them accurately and quickly in prototyping an interface.

3.1 TRC Conception

The TRC arose from the need to contemplate the requirements for prototype development of applications for autistic people in a broad and generalized way. Our inspiration to TRC was the Product Backlog List of the Scrum Methodology, which presents a product's functional and non-functional requirements. However, we wanted an artifact that would record both the requirements and its form of interface representation.

The TRC was initially designed in two tables: Summary and Detailing Tables. The Summary Table consisted of three columns: the element identification (ID), the element description, and the type. The Breakdown Table had four columns, namely: *(i)* Requirement Identifier (ID); *(ii)* Requirement, to give a brief description of the requirement; *(iii)* Detailing for specifying the requirement; and *(iv)* Persons, to indicate who would interact with the requirement. This first version of TRC, called simply TRC1, was evaluated by three focus groups, with a total of nine industry professionals that worked in application developing/design.

3.2 Method

A focus group generates valuable research data by facilitating discussion and interaction among its members, who come together to discuss and evaluate a specific topic [11]. This research method is perfect when the aim is to elicit people's understanding, opinions and views and explore how they might be elaborated in a social context [17]. "Face-to-face" discussions allow for more spontaneous responses and can provide a sense of belonging, helping participants feel safe to share information [18]. The method used to conduct the focus group followed the procedure presented by Wong [18] which includes the following: planning the research questions, developing the discussion guide, planning and executing participant recruitment, setting the location, planning the data collection and analysis, and ending with reporting the findings. We detail each of these items as follow:

- **Research questions** - The goal of the focus group was to evaluate and validate each element of TRC1 composition (in this case, the columns);
- **Discussion guide** - We began the discussions with an explanation of the purpose of the focus group, on the context of TRC in ProAut and in the topic of autism. Then, we presented TRC1, its elements, purpose, and the proposed recommendation of using it in each process step. We invited participants to ask questions and give feedback about the TRC1 elements (in this case, the columns) during and after the presentation. Some questions that guided the discussion were: Do any of you disagree with the function of the components of TRC1? Is there anything that should be considered and that was not addressed?

- **Recruitment of participants** - We invited a total of 17 industry profession-als, but only ten agreed to contribute, and of these, only nine participated. We contacted them by telephone and text message app since they had already participated in other studies. Due to the difficulties of reconciling the partic-ipants' schedules, we divided them into three focus groups according to their abilities. Thus, we had a group with three requirements engineers, a group with two developers, and a group with four designers. None of them had expe-rience with autistic applications or even familiarity with the topic of autism. Five of them (78%) had more than four years of professional experience;
- **Location definition** - Due to the Coronavirus pandemic, all sessions were held via the Google Meet platform. We had three meetings with each group and an average duration of 1 h 30 min.
- **Data collect** - After presenting the group's goals, we asked permission to record the meeting. Next, we read the Informed Consent Form (ICF) and asked if everyone agreed with it, to which we obtained unanimity. Everyone agreed, so we recorded the session using the Google Meet Platform's resources. We also took notes during the discussions.
- **Analysis and Results** - As a result of evaluating the elements of TRC1 in the focus groups, we obtained that 100% of participants of all groups did not agree with the two-part composition of TRC1. The main argument was that more and more people are looking for simple techniques and artifacts that make tasks less laborious and more productive. Another issue was that five of the nine participants pointed out the PERSONAS column as unnecessary since we used personas when drawing interface ideas for the requirements in the brainstorming session. Furthermore, Some participants also suggested that TRC should have some column about the context of autism, as none of the current columns reflected this. Thus, we analyzed all suggestions, and we redefined the TRC in a single table with six columns, namely: Id, Type, Requirement, Requirement Item, Description of Requirement Interactivity, and Interactive Features.

3.3 Final Version of TRC

To reduce interpretation bias in creating the artifact by a single researcher, we presented the modified TRC to a new focus group. This group was composed of four specialists in software development: a designer and three requirements engineers. They were industry professionals with a minimum of 8 years of experi-ence. Only one of them participated in evaluating the first version of TRC. The procedures followed were the same as those defined for the focus groups in the TRC1 evaluation.

We summarized the result of the evaluation of this group of specialists in the following: (i) renaming of the columns **Description of Required Interac-tivity** and **Interactive Resources**, to **Specification of Required Item** and **Main Interface Elements** respectively; (ii) insertion of two columns: **Com-plementary Interface Elements** and **Notes**. The first is to supplement the information in the *Main Elements* column, and the second is to register extra information that may be needed (including the autism context). The contents of these two columns should be aligned with the guidelines for supporting the interface design of autism applications. Thus, we highlight to TRC users that for including aspects related to the autism theme, they have consulted specific guidelines for application interface projects for autistic people.

Therefore, the second version of the TRC was left with eight columns, as follows:

- **ID** - to identify the requirement/constraint;
- **Type** - to define whether it is a requirement (RQ) or a constraint (RT)
- **Requirement** - to describe the requirement or the constraint;
- **Requirement Item** - to represent a sub-item of the requirement, since a unique requirement can originate several requirement items;
- **Requirement Item Specification** - to describe the Requirement Item in more detail. This detailing can include aspects such as navigability, types of buttons, messages, among others;
- **Main interface elements** - for reference to the elements that constituted the main idea of the requirement. They are the main focus points for those who will use the system. In other words, they are the elements that will contextualize the scope of the application. Some example content for this column could be: the format of the central figure of the interface (if in a drawing or photo), if using voice, what would be the tone of voice, if there would be an option to increase/decrease volume and muting. It is worth pointing out that the content of this TRC column is primordial since, to fill it out, the development team must consider the essential information to meet the needs of autistic users;
- **Complementary elements of the interface** - correspond, as the name implies, to any element that should be part of the interface, but in a more discrete way. For example, the color of the background and the color of buttons; and finally
- **Notes** - any extra information that is necessary to register.

Figure 1 presents a view of the TRC with its respective columns. For space reasons, the figure illustrates only one example of the TRC resulting from the experimental study described in Sect. 4, containing two constraints and only one requirement.

3.4 Filling the TRC

Considering that one of ProAut's focuses is low-functioning autistic people, the use of its artifacts requires, whenever possible, the participation of those responsible in general, or specialists in the care of autistic people, such as speech therapists, psychologists, among others, or even the customer himself. Therefore, They become responsible for "giving voice" to the low functioning autistic since most have communication limits, such as echolalic language (repeating what was said outside the context of the conversation).

ID	Type	Requirement	Requirement Items	Requirement Item Specification	Main interface elements	Complementary interface elements	Notes
CT01	RC	It should not have indications of days and times, as they are difficult for autistics to understand	See requirement RQ01 for details	-	-	-	-
CT02	RC	Do not use long texts or figures of speech in the interface	Can't have small print		-	-	-
RQ05	RQ	Child mark the activities you have already performed	When children indicate that they have already performed the activity, receive reinforcement. e.g., applause, congratulations	"1. The child will be able to see the activities of the day (possibly in list form). 2. Each activity will have a button that will indicate if the activity has been completed. 3. When marking an activity as done, the selected virtual assistant should appear for the child clapping and saying, "Congratulations! You got it." 4. Parents will have access to success/failure information for activities that were or were not carried out. 6. When the activity ends, the child can express his emotion: happiness or anger."		-	
			Being able to unmark an activity performed if you have marked it incorrectly	1.An activity marked as completed may be unmarked as the child may mark it by mistake.			

Legend:

ID - requirement/constraint identifier;

Type - defines whether it is a requirement (RQ) or a constraint (CT);

Requirement - a brief description of the requirement or constraint;

Requirement item - represents a sub-item of the requirement;

Requirement item specification - describes in more detail the requirement item;

Main interface elements - refers to the elements that constitute the main idea of the requirement;

Complementary interface elements - corresponds to any element that should be part of the interface, but in a more discrete way; and, finally

Notes - any extra information that it is necessary to register.

Fig. 1. A view of TRC resulting from the experimental study. (Color figure online)

The artifacts produced in the first stage of ProAut (Immersion) are three canvas [7]. The first canvas consolidates the information obtained in the interview with caregivers. The second summarizes the information resulting from the interviews with autism specialists. The third consolidates the information obtained in the interview with the application requester(client). The customer can be a parent, an expert, a teacher, or another person interested in the software product. All these canvas serve as inputs to start using TRC in the next step (Analysis).

The Analysis phase (second step) consists of triangulating the data contained in the Canvas for filling in columns 1 to 4 of the TRC. It is important to note that the Analysis stage also includes two more artifacts aimed exclusively at generating empathy between the developers/designers and the autistic: EmpathyAut [8], and PersonAut [9]. Each of these artifacts has specific and exclusive sections for the characterization of the autistic individual. In the next step (Ideation), the team conducts a brainstorming session. The three artifacts resulting from the analysis phase are used in this brainstorming: TRC, EmpathyAut (Empathy Map), and Personas. Then, each requirement must be discussed to promote ideas for its representation in the interface. In addition, the team should have relevant guidelines for designing application interfaces for autistic people so that the interfaces are as suited as possible to the needs of these individuals.

The selected ideas fill in columns 5 to 8 of the TRC. Finally, the designer will be able to build the prototype, having in single document information about requirements, restrictions, and elements to be considered and included in the prototype's interfaces.

4 Experimental Study

4.1 Participants

We conducted an experimental study with a team of five members, composed of industry professionals, and most of them with more than three years of experience. The team consisted of a requirements engineer, two designers, and two developers. None of them had experience with autistic applications. We emphasize that the study consisted of the complete experimentation of the stages and artifacts ProAut. However, in this article, we deal only with the experiment on the use of TRC.

4.2 Context of Application

Apps that teach compliance with daily routines are familiar. However, many autistic people have difficulty dealing with routine changes. The client requested an App to teach routine breaking, preparing the child to perform activities outside their daily routine, for example, going to the dentist. Thus, the App will help the child become familiar with the event so that when the day comes to perform it, he will be more prepared, avoiding or minimizing possible stress crises.

4.3   Study Execution

We developed the study from the following steps:

(i) *Training* - We conducted training on the Google Meet platform for approximately 2 h. The objective was to present the phases of ProAut and the use and filling of the artifacts. In this training, we provide the team with a supporting document and the artifacts in editable mode. The document information explained the conduction step-by-step of the process, the description, and guidance for using and filling in both the TRC and the other artifacts. We emphasize that at each start of a new stage, we performed the corresponding training;

(ii) *Immersion* - the team conducted an immersion in the autism theme, seeking information about the main characteristics of an autistic person, as well as existing applications in the context of routine teaching and routine breaking for these children. The team collected requirements by interviewing a mother of a 6-year-old male low-functioning non-verbal autistic child, an occupational therapist as an autism specialist, and the applicant of the application who, despite his role as a client, was the father of an 11-year-old low-functioning, verbal-echolalic autistic girl. After the interviews, the team filled out the output artifacts of this stage (canvas);

(iii) *Analysis* - at this stage, the team initiated the use of the TRC. They triangulated the data from the requirements elicitation and filled in the columns pertinent to this stage. The TRC resulting has five constraints and ten requirements with 34 requirement items. For space reasons, it is not possible to present this TRC entirely.

(iv) *Ideation* - In this stage, the team performed brainstorming, brain drawing and made the requirements specifications according to the procedures for filling out the TRC;

(v) *Prototyping* - Based on the final TRC, the team's designers developed the prototyping of the application's screens. Finally, through an electronic questionnaire, the team performed a quantitative evaluation regarding the use of each artifact, through perceived ease of use and usefulness, based on the TAM [3], and a qualitative evaluation.

The complete execution of the study took approximately three months, of which one only was for the Analysis and Ideation phases. Such phases required six meetings to fill the TRC fully. Due to the coronavirus pandemic, we used the Google Meet platform to hold all meetings. In each meeting, one participant played the role of leader and was responsible for scheduling and recording the meetings. To define the interface elements, each member represented the requirement, photographed it, and sent it to a WhatsApp group explicitly created for exchanging messages between the participants. The leader would project the photo sent, and everyone would make suggestions. Although everyone participated with suggestions and opinions, only the leader was responsible for completing the TRC.

4.4   Results Achieved

Figure 1 shows the TRC produced from the study performed. The team colored the constraint lines pink and the requirement lines yellow to make it easier to see. We emphasize that, for space reasons, the photos produced by the study team are presented in columns 6 and 7 but refer only to column 6.

In the conception of the TRC, we defined filling in text form of the Main Elements and Complementary Elements columns. However, we realized that it was a mistake because the team pointed out the difficulty of filling columns 6 (Main Interface Elements) and 7 (Complementary Interface Elements) in textual form during the study. Faced with this difficulty, we allowed filling in the graphic form of columns 6 and 7. Figure 1 shows one of the drafts that represent the defined requirements, specifically **requirement item**: *When the child indicates that he has already performed the activity, receive reinforcement. For example, applause, congratulations*, and the **requirement specification**: *When marking an activity as complete, the selected virtual assistant should appear to the child clapping and saying Congratulations! You did it!* Figure 2 presents the interfaces referring to these drafts of requirement RQ05.

To evaluate the TRC, the team answered an online questionnaire. This questionnaire was of three parts: the first one included the characterization of the respondents; the second one with questions to evaluate artifacts based on the Technology Acceptance Model (TAM) [4], and the third part addressed qualitative questions with open-ended questions.

Fig. 2. Example of one of the prototype screens resulting from the experimental study.

As for the quantitative evaluation, the Figs. 3 and 4 present, respectively, the graphs resulting from the evaluation of the TRC regarding the perception of ease and the perception of usefulness by the study participants. We can see that the TRC had a very positive evaluation in both aspects.

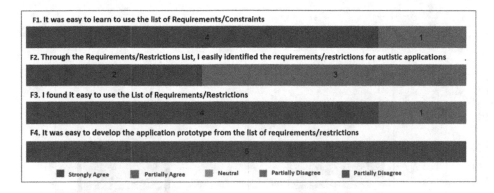

Fig. 3. Evaluation of perceived easy of use of TRC.

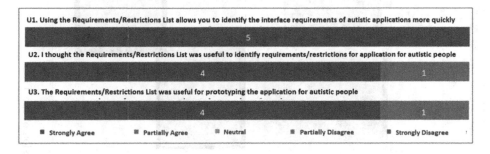

Fig. 4. Evaluation of perceived of usefulness of TRC.

Figure 6 presents the questions that comprised the qualitative assessment (identified by the letter **Q** before the numeral), as well as the most relevant responses from the participants. The letter **P** before the digit indicates the participant-for example, P1 for participant 1, P2 for participant 2, and so on.

As seen in Fig. 6 in the answers to questions Q2, Q4 and Q7, the participants reinforced the difficulty of filling in the columns *Main Interface Elements* and *Complementary Interface Elements*. Therefore, the participants P1 and P6 pointed out this difficulty in Q2; by participants P1, P5, and P6 in Q4; and finally, participants P1 and P5 in Q7. This problem highlighted during the study, and added to the evaluation comments, led us to update the base document and insert this topic in training to future users of the TRC or other studies.

Still concerning the filling out of the columns Main Interface Elements and Complementary Interface Elements, we observed that in Q6, two participants commented that they thought there was no need for these two columns. Even with the small number of evaluators of the TRC, we decided to accept the suggestion, keeping in mind that the final TRC, resulting from the study, has ten requirements and 32 requirement items, and none of them had complimentary elements defined. Thus, we unified the two columns into one and named it *Interface Elements*. We also renamed the column *Requirement Specification* to just *Detail*.

1.ID	2.Type	3.Requirement/Constraint	4.Requirement/Constraint Items	5. Requirement Item Specification	6. Interface Suggestions for Requirement	7.Guidelines/Notes
CT01	CT	It should not have indications of days and times, as they are difficult for autistics to understand	See requirement RQ01 for details			-
CT02	CT	Do not use long texts or figures of speech in the interface	Can't have small print			-
CT04	CT	It should not have a gamification system	It should not have scores It should not have an evolution of phases			
RT01	RT	Separate the different times of the day into shifts (morning, afternoon and night)	indicate the morning with a figure of a sun indicate the afternoon with a picture of a setting sun. indicate the night period with a moon Audible callsign for each shift (e.g. Good morning! Good afternoon! Good night!)	* When entering the day's schedule, activities will be separated by shift and in the chronological sequence in which they should occur. * If you are accessing the application in the morning, have a soft voice saying, "Good morning!" If it is the afternoon, "Good afternoon" and in the evening "Good evening!" * Each turn must be indicated by its corresponding figure (Sun for morning / Sun setting for afternoon / Moon for the night) * User will be able to click on each shift to discover its activities * Assigned the action of clicking the turn, an audible greeting according to the turn * The shift indicator may contain colors that refer to the selected period. Yellow for the morning, orange for the afternoon, blue for night. * Must have the option to view future days in the schedule.		
RT04	RT	It should have an option to set up the activity schedule for a given day	Separate activities by category: School / Home / Therapy / New (Routine Break)? Novelty = activities that leave the child's routine. Think of a word that brings a positive connotation to the routine break In the access mode for those responsible, indicate the day and time of the activity. Parents must be able to change the schedule for a given day The child can filter activities by shift and category Must be able to copy the schedule from one day to another / Register recurring events Activities must be separated by shift and arranged in chronological order.	1. RESPONSIBLE MODE: you must be able to configure the start and end of the activity (date and time), if the activity is recurring and if you want to configure the reminder time. It would help if you also informed the activity category (home, school, health, others) and whether it is a routine or special activity. The added activity must be shown in chronological order in the schedule. 2. USER MODE WITH TEA: The interface has less detail in this model. It only informs the activity shift (morning, afternoon, or night), the category, and a brief description. In this case, the new activity must be presented at the end of the activities of the selected shift. * Only the responsible person can delete an activity.		The activity can be seen in a diary on the scheduled day when saving.

Fig. 5. Final version of the TRC.

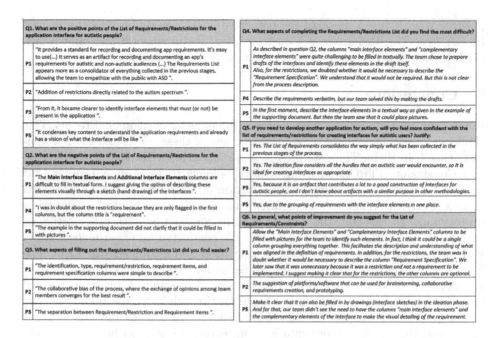

Q1. What are the positive points of the List of Requirements/Restrictions for the application interface for autistic people?		Q4. What aspects of completing the Requirements/Restrictions List did you find the most difficult?	
P1	"It provides a standard for recording and documenting app requirements. It's easy to use(...) It serves as an artifact for recording and documenting an app's requirements for autistic and non-autistic audiences (...) The Requirements List appears more as a consolidator of everything collected in the previous stages, allowing the team to empathize with the public with ASD ".	P1	As described in question Q2, the columns "main interface elements" and "complementary interface elements" were quite challenging to be filled in textually. The team chose to prepare drafts of the interfaces and identify these elements in the draft itself. Also, for the restrictions, we doubted whether it would be necessary to describe the "Requirement Specification". We understand that it would not be required. But this is not clear from the process description.
P2	"Addition of restrictions directly related to the autism spectrum ".	P4	Describe the requirements verbatim, but our team solved this by making the drafts.
P3	"From it, it became clearer to identify interface elements that must (or not) be present in the application ".	P5	In the first moment, describe the interface elements in a textual way as given in the example of the supporting document. But then the team saw that it could place pictures.
P5	"It condenses key content to understand the application requirements and already has a vision of what the interface will be like ".	Q5. If you need to develop another application for autism, will you feel more confident with the list of requirements/restrictions for creating interfaces for autistic users? Justify:	
Q2. What are the negative points of the List of Requirements/Restrictions for the application interface for autistic people?		P1	Yes. The List of Requirements consolidates the way simply what has been collected in the previous stages of the process.
P1	"The Main Interface Elements and Additional Interface Elements columns are difficult to fill in textual form. I suggest giving the option of describing these elements visually through a sketch (hand drawing) of the interfaces ".	P2	Yes. The ideation flow considers all the hurdles that an autistic user would encounter, so it is ideal for creating interfaces as appropriate.
P4	"I was in doubt about the restrictions because they are only flagged in the first columns, but the column title is "requirement".	P3	Yes, because it is an artifact that contributes a lot to a good construction of interfaces for autistic people, and I don't know about artifacts with a similar purpose in other methodologies.
P5	"The example in the supporting document did not clarify that it could be filled in with pictures ".	P5	Yes, due to the grouping of requirements with the interface elements in one place.
Q3. What aspects of filling out the Requirements/Restrictions List did you find easier?		Q6. In general, what points of improvement do you suggest for the List of Requirements/Constraints?	
P1	"The identification, type, requirement/restriction, requirement items, and requirement specification columns were simple to describe ".	P1	Allow the "Main Interface Elements" and "Complementary Interface Elements" columns to be filled with pictures for the team to identify such elements. In fact, I think it could be a single column grouping everything together. This facilitates the description and understanding of what was aligned in the definition of requirements. In addition, for the restrictions, the team was in doubt whether it would be necessary to describe the column "Requirement Specification". We later saw that it was unnecessary because it was a restriction and not a requirement to be implemented. I suggest making it clear that for the restrictions, the other columns are optional.
P2	"The collaborative bias of the process, where the exchange of opinions among team members converges for the best result ".	P2	The suggestion of platforms/software that can be used for brainstorming, collaborative requirements creation, and prototyping.
P3	"The separation between Requirement/Restriction and Requirement items ".	P5	Make it clear that it can also be filled in by drawings (interface sketches) in the ideation phase. And for that, our team didn't see the need to have the columns "main interface elements" and the complementary elements of the interface to make the visual detailing of the requirement.

Fig. 6. Part of the result of the qualitative evaluation

Constraints refer to conditions, observations, and details mapped from the recommendations/guidelines or interviews with parents and autism specialists in the Immersion phase. The result of the evaluation also showed that although the TRC contemplates requirements and restrictions and has a column called *Type* to differentiate a requirement from a restriction, the restriction is not referenced in the other columns of the TRC, confusing the TRC user about how to handle restrictions. Based on this, we added the word constraint in columns 3 and 4. Thus, the columns named *Requirement* and *Requirement Item* are now named *Requirement/Restriction* and *Requirement Item/ Constraint* respectively. In addition, we have also updated the base document and training guide with information about the description of restrictions in columns 1 to 4 only.

To make the base document less complex, we decided to include in the TRC header, besides the title of each column, a number indicating their order, to facilitate reference in the text and future studies. The last aspect of the evaluation concerns question Q7, in which participant P2 suggested using platforms/software for brainstorming. However, we decided not to address this aspect in TRC, leaving it up to the professional or group of professionals who will use it to seek the best means of performing brainstorming.

The final TRC version was made from the study's results, with the suggestions for improvement and the relevance of comments from those who used it. In general, we observed that the TRC served to assist software development teams in mapping requirements for interface generation and prototyping in a positive way. Figure 5 presents the definitive TRC containing six columns: (i) Id, (ii) Type, (iii) Requirement/Constraint, (iv) Requirement/Constraint Items, (v) Interface Suggestions for Requirement, and (vi) Guidelines/Notes.

5 Conclusions

Developing apps for autistic audiences is a challenge for development teams. This challenge consists mainly of the unpreparedness of these teams and the few artifacts that help them. Thus, we present an artifact called Table of Requirements and Constraints (TRC). Such an artifact belongs to ProAut, a process that aims to support the prototyping of application interfaces for autistic users. TRC includes activities ranging from requirements specification to interface design or prototyping. To this end, the TRC is used in conjunction with other artifacts, such as the Empathy Map and Personas. We conducted an experimental study with a team of industry professionals who used and evaluated the TRC. The TRC was defined based on focus group discussions and validated by experts in Requirements Engineering and Interface Design. The result of this study showed that the artifact is very promising. Therefore, through TRC, we intend to make the designer's task easier and faster. With TRC, he will already have the requirements and their proper representations since the information in the TRC will already be ready to be created.

We hope that the artifact can contribute positively to teams that develop applications for people with ASD. In the following steps, we intend to carry out other studies to validate the improvements suggested by the team in this experimental study and thus make the TRC an instrumental artifact for mapping requirements in interfaces.

Acknowledgments. This research was partially funded by the brazilian Coordination for the Improvement of Higher Education Personnel (CAPES). The authors' thank the Universidade do Estado do Amazonas (UEA) for their support. The results were published through the research and development activities of the project ACADEMIA STEM, sponsored by Samsung Electronics of Amazonia Ltda., with the support of SUFRAMA under the terms of Federal Law No. 8.387/1991.

References

1. American Psychiatric Association, et al.: Diagnostic and statistical manual of mental disorders: DSM-5 (2013)
2. Cabral, L.N., et al.: Análise de técnicas para elicitação de requisitos de softwares gamificados para crianças com autismo (2021)
3. Chuttur, M.Y.: Overview of the technology acceptance model: origins, developments and future directions. Work. Pap. Inf. Syst. **9**(37), 9–37 (2009)
4. Davis, F.D.: Perceived usefulness, perceived ease of use, and user acceptance of information technology. MIS Q. **13**, 319–340 (1989)
5. Hadar, I., Soffer, P., Kenzi, K.: The role of domain knowledge in requirements elicitation via interviews: an exploratory study. Requir. Eng. **19**(2), 143–159 (2012). https://doi.org/10.1007/s00766-012-0163-2

6. Kulk, G., Verhoef, C.: Quantifying requirements volatility effects. Sci. Comput. Program. **72**(3), 136–175 (2008)

7. Melo, A., Oran, A., dos Santos, J., Rivero, L., Barreto, R.: Requirements elicitation in the context of software for low-functioning autistic people: An initial proposal of specific supporting artifacts. In: Brazilian Symposium on Software Engineering, pp. 291–296 (2021)

8. Melo, A.H.d.S., Rivero, L., dos Santos, J.S., Barreto, R.d.S.: EmpathyAut: an empathy map for people with autism. In: IHC 2020. Association for Computing Machinery, New York (2020). https://doi.org/10.1145/3424953.3426650

9. Melo, A.H.d.S., Rivero, L., dos Santos, J.S., Barreto, R.d.S.: PersonAut: a personas model for people with autism spectrum disorder. In: Proceedings of the 19th Brazilian Symposium on Human Factors in Computing Systems, IHC 2020. Association for Computing Machinery, New York (2020). https://doi.org/10.1145/3424953.3426651

10. Miñón, R., Moreno, L., Martínez, P., Abascal, J.: An approach to the integration of accessibility requirements into a user interface development method. Sci. Comput. Program. **86**, 58–73 (2014)

11. Onwuegbuzie, A.J., Dickinson, W.B., Leech, N.L., Zoran, A.G.: A qualitative framework for collecting and analyzing data in focus group research. Int. J. Qual. Methods **8**(3), 1–21 (2009)

12. Pitts, M.G., Browne, G.J.: Improving requirements elicitation: an empirical investigation of procedural prompts. Inf. Syst. J. **17**(1), 89–110 (2007)

13. Schmidt, R.F.: Software requirements definition. In: Schmidt, R.F. (ed.) Software Engineering, Chap. 17 , pp. 291–303. Morgan Kaufmann, Boston (2013). https://doi.org/10.1016/B978-0-12-407768-3.00017-3. https://www.sciencedirect.com/science/article/pii/B9780124077683000173

14. Sommerville, I.: Software Engineering, 9th edn. (2011). ISBN-10 137035152, 18

15. Tahir, M.N., Khan, S., Raza, A.: Challenges in requirements engineering for mobile applications for disabled-autism. J. Ind. Intell. Inf. **1**(4) (2013)

16. Valente, M.T.: Engenharia de software moderna (livro digital) (2020)

17. Wilkinson, S.: Focus group methodology: a review. Int. J. Soc. Res. Methodol. **1**(3), 181–203 (1998)

18. Wong, L.P.: Focus group discussion: a tool for health and medical research. Singap. Med. J. **49**(3), 256–260 (2008)

Older Adults Use of Technology for Decision-Making: A Systematic Literature Review

Elisabeth Dubois[1], DeeDee Bennett Marie Gayle[1]([✉]), Xiaojun Yuan[1],
Pallavi Khurana[2], and Thora Knight[1]

[1] College of Emergency Preparedness, Homeland Security and Cybersecurity,
University at Albany, State University of New York, Albany, USA
dmbennett@albany.edu
[2] Department of Communication, Social Science, University at Albany,
State University of New York, Albany, USA

Abstract. Older adults face barriers in using technology to make decisions. With the ongoing global pandemic, this issue has become more important than before due to our initial reliance on technology and social distancing policies. This has emphasized the critical need to understand better how older adults use technology to make timely decisions. This review outlines how we address this gap, determines how older adults use technology, and identifies barriers to making decisions. Using a three-stage PRISMA review framework, a total of 335 articles were found across four highly regarded databases (ACM Digital, IEEE Digital Library, PubMed, and Web of Science), resulting in a final sample of 10 articles. From these 10 articles, the review presents three emergent themes: (a) the use of technology for health decision-making is predominant; b) while technologies for decision-making are positively received, access and usability present challenges; and c) there is limited focus on older adults' use of technology in the context of decision-making across all life choices. These findings highlight the importance of older adults' use of technology to engage in a digitized world to help them make decisions as they age. This review identified specific research gaps in terms of older adults' use of technologies in decision-making. Some future research directions are discussed at the end.

Keywords: Aging and individual differences · Gerontology · Technology use · Judgment and decision-making

1 Introduction

Currently, 1.4 billion people worldwide are aged 60 years and over, with the pace of population aging expected to grow to one-sixth of the population by 2030 [1]. The increasing aging population makes it necessary to consider individual and environmental approaches to limit loss, aid in decision-making abilities, and ensure success among older adults. As people age, they may experience a myriad of cognitive, physical, and/

© Springer Nature Switzerland AG 2022
V. G. Duffy et al. (Eds.): HCII 2022, LNCS 13521, pp. 322–333, 2022.
https://doi.org/10.1007/978-3-031-17902-0_23

or perceptual declines, which may limit their ability to make decisions [2]. These changes are often not linear nor constant. Instead, they can relate to an individual's physical and social environment, which can vary depending on the family one was born into, sex, ethnicity, mobility, and social support, which can lead to inequalities in health.

The impact of globalization and technological advancements influence the lives of older adults in a variety of ways [1]. As the dependency on technology expands, especially in the wake of the COVID-19 pandemic, older adults must adopt and use technology. Increasingly, technologies have been used throughout life, from assisting individuals with work, education, and daily living, to streamlining government and organizational services, to delivering lifesaving healthcare measures and emergency response [3–5]. The technologies adopted to make decisions across life segments include communication devices, video conference systems, personal health trackers, telehealth services, specialized equipment to aid in a particular job or a task, or technologies to assist daily living activities. Such technologies are adopted differently by sub-populations due to a variety of factors. In particular, older adults' reliance on technology is affected by common cognitive or physical barriers, digital illiteracy, or general wariness regarding technological innovation that comes with age [6, 7]. These barriers may limit the use of technology and thus the ability to make decisions in a society that is heavily reliant on technology.

Decision-making, be it social, academic, occupational, or medical, is a necessary aspect of life. However, older adults are faced with a greater risk of illness and disease, social isolation, or economic constraints, thereby emphasizing the need for technology that supports decision-making [8]. With the expansion of technology to aid in decision-making, it is necessary to understand how older adults approach decisions via technology and the general success of such endeavors. To date, a few systematic reviews have focused on how older adults use technology for decision-making [9]. This signifies there are critical knowledge gaps about the ways older adults use technology for decision-making. These gaps must be addressed to create better communication techniques and enhance decision-making capabilities in circumstances where a decision could affect the economic or social state, health outcomes, or general wellbeing of older adults.

Therefore, this systematic review seeks to investigate academic research on how older adults use technology to make decisions. This study addresses the gaps in literature and presents future research directions. The specific aims of this study are: (1) to identify existing works on older adults and the use of technology for decision-making; and (2) to collect evidence for ways technology can be utilized to improve decision-making in daily life.

This study conducts a systematic literature review to examine the types of research conducted since 2016 on older adults' use of technology for decision-making. The decision to begin the search in 2016 is that it can provide context pre-pandemic, where beginning in 2020 there was a significant global reliance on technology. The results, discussion, and conclusion follow.

2 Background

Technology use since 2016 has increased among all age groups. Several researchers have investigated the use of technology and its connection to well-being. While there has been a slight negative impact on the well-being of adolescents, a higher correlation was found between the use of information and communication technology (ICT) and the well-being of older adults aged 80 and older [10]. In a 12-month randomized field trial by Czaja [11], older adults who used the Personal Reminder Information and Social Management System (specifically designed for older adults) were found to have enhanced social connectivity and reduced loneliness, as well as increased technology self-efficacy. Similarly, older adults' use of social technologies was found to increase well-being, result in better self-rated health, fewer chronic illnesses, and depressive symptoms [12]. Conversely, some research explains that the use of ICT was associated with more psychological distress and less sense of community when used by older adults who are also lonely [13].

Previous studies have investigated technology use by older adults finding that the more popular activities included the use of social technologies such as mobile phones, social networking (e.g., emailing), and surfing the Internet [12, 14, 15]. There was also evidence that demographic differences might be predictors of use, with educated, married, younger white men leading in technology use among older adults [15]. Barriers to technology use by older adults have included lack of knowledge, negative attitudes, and age-related changes such as vision and hearing loss and fine motor difficulties [14]. Since the pandemic, there is evidence that older adults have faced some exclusion in the use of digital tools [16, 17].

Older adults are more frequently faced with medical decision-making because of the increased use of healthcare services than younger adults [18, 19]. The use of technology such as the Internet has been related to better healthcare and financial decision-making among older adults [20]. Older adults use the Internet to seek health information that assists them in making informed decisions [20, 21]. As mentioned in the introduction, the pandemic also forced an increase in the use of various technologies by older adults to assist in decision-making.

Information and communication technologies such as telemonitoring and telemedicine increase older adults' awareness of their health conditions and thereby enables them to take appropriate action when needed [22]. Older adults use technology to attain knowledge, and it helps them make their life simple [23].

3 Methods

In this systematic literature review, we conducted a comprehensive, exhaustive search of the literature and synthesized the results to answer the research question [24]. According to Xiao and Watson, systematic reviews are conducted in an unbiased, reproducible way to identify gaps to improve academic research and practice [24]. The following outlines the search strategies, record selection, and eligibility criteria used in this study.

The search strategy utilized in this review ensured we identified a range of academic studies from highly-regarded electronic databases. We performed three rounds of systematic searches in four databases, ACM Digital, IEEE Digital Library, PubMed, and Web of

Science. First, we searched predetermined keywords in the selected databases. Next, we screened the titles and abstracts of the records using predetermined inclusion/exclusion criteria. Lastly, we screened the full text of the remaining articles to ensure that they met the same inclusion/exclusion criteria.

On April 11, 2021, we searched using the string [elderly OR "older adults"] AND [decision-making OR "decision making"] AND [technology] in each of the selected databases limiting results to those published between 2016–2021. From there, articles were included in Stage 1 if the combination of the three search terms were in the title, keywords, or abstract, and/or corresponding metadata. In ACM Digital, 63 results were found searching Title, Abstract, and Keywords. In IEEE Digital Library, 65 results were found searching All Metadata (i.e., title, abstract, and indexing terms). In PubMed, 76 results were found searching Mesh Terms. In Web of Science, 183 results were found searching Topic (i.e., title, abstract, and keywords). A total of 297 non-duplicate results were found, 90 duplicates were omitted.

To ensure that this review contained all relevant academic studies to date, another search was run on October 20, 2021, in each of the databases to extract any additional literature published between April 2021 and October 2021. This secondary search resulted in an additional 38 results. Therefore, 335 non-duplicate results advanced to stage two of screening.

Next, all the authors independently screened approximately 1/5 of the titles and abstracts of the 335 articles. The initial exclusion criteria included determination of the study type, population sampled, study design, publication status, and language. Five reviewers examined the titles and abstracts. Using the exclusion criteria (listed in more detail below), we removed 234 articles that did not meet one or more of the set criteria based on the abstracts and titles. After removing the 234 articles, 101 remained for full-text review.

Third, we screened the full text of the remaining 101 articles and eliminated 91 articles using the same exclusion criteria. The screening led to the inclusion of 10 studies for review in this paper. Following the PRISMA guidelines for reporting systematic reviews, we summarize the selection process in Fig. 1.

3.1 Eligibility Criteria

The eligibility criteria for inclusion in this review were based on six items, 1) the type of study, 2) the population sampled, 3) the study design, 4) the publication status, 5) the language, and 6) the year of publication. Records that intentionally focus on older adults and the use of technology for decision-making were included in this review. Decision-making is thought of as a reasoning process based on the assumptions of values, preferences, and beliefs of the decision-maker. Technology refers to communication devices, video conference systems, personal health trackers, telehealth services, specialized equipment to aid in a particular job or a task, or technologies to assist in daily living activities.

   *Articles excluded in both the first and second screening using 5 reviewers.

The population of interest in this study is elderly or older adults. This paper utilizes measures and indicators of population aging of the United Nations and most researchers, which are based on a person's chronological age, defining older persons as those aged 60 or 65 years or over [25]. In solely focusing on these participants, we are making sure to

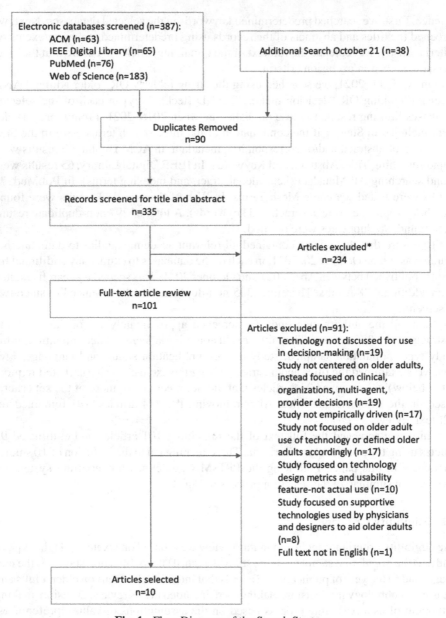

Fig. 1. Flow Diagram of the Search Strategy

provide vital understanding to academics and practitioners about a subsection of socially vulnerable populations, such as adolescents, racial and ethnic minorities, people with disabilities, and others facing barriers to technology use for decision-making [3, 5]. We do recognize in limiting studies to those that study older adults aged 60 or over, we may be missing studies that include this age range but define older adults at lower ages.

We included only empirical studies that used data to synthesize the empirically vali-dated evidence, although conceptual findings were used to capture scholarly insights about older adults' use of technology for decision making. Additionally, we only included peer-reviewed journal articles and conference papers. Furthermore, we only selected English written records in accordance with common practice, given the difficulties in translating and reproducing the review [26].

Finally, we selected records between 2016 and 2021. The year 2016 was chosen as the starting point, given the growth and changes in technology. Technology research changes due to the emergence of novel and new approaches to technology and decision-making regularly, so anything older than 2016 may not account for the drastic changes brought forth by artificial intelligence (AI) or social media. Furthermore, the social distancing and stay-at-home policies implemented globally in 2020 contributed to an increase use of technology across all demographics.

4 Results

The findings of the 10 articles are summarized below (See Table 1). The number of publications was consistent, although it increased each year between 2016 and 2021.

Table 1. Summary of the Final Review Articles

Year	Author	Participants	Method	Country	Tech	Sector
2021	Soubutts et al	4 primary users, 2 additional household residents (including 3 older adults), and 9 service providers	interviews and focus groups	UK	Stairlift	Lifestyle, Health
2021	Povey et al	26 surgeons, 30 patients between 68–72 years old	semi-structured interviews	UK	three-dimensional imaging	Health
2021	Segkouli et al	One Case study of Aging at Work	the framework was applied and tested in the use case of an EU-funded project, Aging @ Work	Europe	SmartFrameWorK	Workplace, Health
2018	Angelova et al	507 telecare service users (with a majority of the sample aged 60 +)	statistical analysis, decision trees	England	Telecare	Health
2018	Bozan & Gewald	46 participants aged 65 +	survey	USA	health goal tracking software	Health

(continued)

Table 1. (*continued*)

Year	Author	Participants	Method	Country	Tech	Sector
2021	Caldeira et al	17 participants aged 65 +	interviews	USA	technologies for managing chronic conditions	Health
2020	Eng et al	371 cancer survivors, 58 of which were older adults aged 65 +	cross-sectional survey	USA	internet and social media use	Health
2020	Holden et al	23 primary care patients aged 60 + that use anticholinergic medications	task-based usability testing of Brain Buddy	USA	Brain Buddy, consumer-facing mHealth technology for medication safety	Health
2019	Jaana, Sherrard, & Paré	23 patients aged 60 + with chronic heart failure	Longitudinal study/ survey	Canada	telehealth monitoring	Health
2017	Richards	Two local crafting groups (Discardia and a local senior center lap quilting group)	8 h of observation of crafting groups, technology design for crafters, and 2 h of beta testing	USA	Tech-enabled crafts and systems	Lifestyle

Of the studies that include individual participants, over 700 older adults use technology for health and well-being [27–34]. The participants in the studies were older adults aged 60 +. All but two of the studies had sample sizes below 50 participants (ranging from 1 to 46). The two studies had sample sizes of 504 and 371 with mixed aged participants. Most of the articles (60%) used qualitative research to test their theory-informed hypotheses. A majority of the studies were thus small sample size utilizing qualitative methods, with few using larger datasets.

Most of the articles (90%) focused on the use of technologies for decision-making in the health care sector, including one focused on a case study on aging-at-work. As shown in Table 1, most of the studies (70%) emphasize the importance of telemonitoring and Internet use in influencing the life decisions of older adults, especially regarding their health and wellness. Though most of the studies focused on a variety of health solutions, such as telehealth, mhealth, and other health technologies, other technologies were included, as well. The studies tested the outcome of whether one had a willingness to adopt technology to aid in decision making, with limited focus on how they use the technologies to make decisions. Furthermore, 90% of articles involve holistic or collaborative uses of technology to help older adults make health decisions. One study specifically investigated technology outside of healthcare, focused on a variety of mainstream technologies used by older adults and the other for educational or skill development [35]. There was limited literature on decision-making outside of health and wellness (one article), signifying a gap and area for future research.

According to Jaana et al. [34], older adults use telemonitoring services for self-care and self-management. Senior patients with heart failure were found to be more confident in assessing their symptoms, taking actions to alleviate these symptoms, and analyzing the effectiveness of their actions.Richard [35] found older adults to be open to technology and were interested in customized technological functionalities. "For example, one quilter asked if one of their current projects could be made interactive by playing a tune when pressing different quilt squares, a possible task using a LilyPad buzzer" [32, p. 170]. Similarly, Bozan and Gewal [30] noted that older adults use self-management apps to set health goals and receive feedback from physicians on their goal progression. While most studies indicated a general trust in technology, at least one showed that older adults are less likely to trust online health information than younger adults [32].

While all the articles discussed digital technologies, three of them presented new technologies to aid in life choices [33, 35, 36]. A majority of the studies discussed smart devices, software, and technology use [30–34], and two of the studies focused on mobility or lifestyle enhancement technologies [27, 35]. Only one study focused on work or employment for older adults [36]. Many of these studies reported positive outcomes when older adults used technology for decision-making, including significant improvements in decision confidence, greater efficiency in decisions, increase employability, and improvement in wellness (or life) skills. Despite examples of positive outcomes, some of the studies noted that technology may have negatively affected decision confidence. Reported challenges that older adults face when using technology for decision-making included access, ease of use, management, functionality, digital literacy, perceived usefulness, and perceived security. At the forefront of these challenges were access, ease of use, and digital literacy.

The studies were conducted around the world, with most in North America (60%) and 50% of the total articles from the United States. The other region represented was Europe (40%), with thirty percent of articles focused on the UK. This limits the knowledge learned from other regions and developing countries.

5 Discussion

This paper reports a systematic review using the PRISMA framework. A total of 335 articles were found across four highly regarded databases (ACM Digital, IEEE Digital Library, PubMed, and Web of Science). The three-stage PRISMA resulted in a final sample of 10 articles.

From these 10 articles, the review presents three emergent themes: (a) studies primarily focus on the use of technology for health decision-making, b) while technologies for decision-making are positively received, access and usability present challenges to older adults, and c) there is limited focus on older adults' use of technology in the context of decision making across all life choices including daily activities like grocery shopping, work, and accessing government services.

Noticeable among the included articles is that 60% were published during the COVID-19 pandemic, this may indicate a growing interest in the use of technology for decision-making, given the reliance on technology during that time [1, 3, 5]. These findings highlight the importance of older adults' using technology to engage in a digitized world to help their decision-making as they age.

Given these studies were conducted in North America and the United States, it raises concerns about whether older adults in developing countries receive opportunities to use technologies to make their decisions in their daily lives and if so, are their needs being explored. It also presents challenges for researchers to delve into the research to see if there are ways to help older adults all over the world.

It can also be observed that a majority of the articles (90%) are focused on the health sector. It might be worth examining if health is the only sector that older adults need to make decisions in or whether researchers' perspective is that it is the only sector that older adults need to make decisions. Previous studies indicate that technologies were used in various sectors to make decisions during COVID, indicating that older adults might need to use technologies in sectors other than health [4, 5]. Therefore, if the latter is the case, much work needs to be carried out to investigate other sectors in which older adults can use technologies to improve decision-making.

Among the ten articles, respective technologies were offered to older adults for their use. Obviously, the number of technologies identified in this review is quite limited. It limits our knowledge in comprehensively understanding the use of technologies in older adults' decision-making processes. More research is needed to identify and develop innovative technologies for older adults' decision-making.

In Segkouli et al., the ethics of digitized workplaces for older adults were investigated [36]. Specifically, ethical aspects have been identified in alignment with smart, personalized, and adaptive ICT solutions. Human values, including "sense of control, trust, sense of freedom and ownership" were considered. With the development of artificial intelligence and other advanced technologies, and the interest in using advanced technologies to assist older adults in their everyday life, the ethical aspects of technologies should receive enough attention in future research endeavors.

This systematic review has its limitations. The selection of our initial search terms was not exhaustive. Because we use "technology" as our search term, we may have missed other terms that researchers used as synonyms or more specific technologies that were used to analyze decision-making. Additionally, there is the potential for selection bias, whereby a researcher unintentionally chooses articles that support their own belief. To reduce the potential for this bias, five coders were used. Despite these limitations, this systematic review is valuable as it has identified existing work and research gaps on older adults' decision-making using technologies.

6 Conclusion

This review indicates there is a great demand for understanding how older adults use technology to make timely decisions in their daily lives. In particular, this review identified a huge knowledge gap in the area relevant to older adults' decision-making using technologies. In future work, we will focus on identifying additional technologies that can contribute to improving the life qualities of older adults and examining other sectors that may contribute to this goal. Future research in this area should consider studying the use of technology in fields other than health, such as for work and socializing. Additionally, studies in other regions beyond North America and Europe would add to the broader understanding of the technology used by older adults in various cultures and in developing countries.

References

1. World Health Organization: Ageing and health (2021). https://www.who.int/news-room/fact-sheets/detail/ageing-and-health. Accessed 19 Oct 2021
2. Dyer, C.B., Regev, M., Burnett, J., Festa, N., Cloyd, B.: SWiFT: a rapid triage tool for vulnerable older adults in disaster situations. Disaster Med Public Health Prep **2**, S45–S50 (2008). https://doi.org/10.1097/DMP.0b013e3181647b81
3. Dubois, E., Bright, D., Laforce, S.: Educating minoritized students in the united states during COVID-19: how technology can be both the problem and the solution. IT Prof **23**, 12–18 (2021). https://doi.org/10.1109/MITP.2021.3062765
4. Dubois, E., et al.: Socially vulnerable populations adoption of technology to address lifestyle changes amid COVID-19 in the US. Data Inf. Manag. 100001 (2022). https://doi.org/10.1016/j.dim.2022.100001
5. Bennett Gayle, D., Yuan, X., Knight, T.: The coronavirus pandemic: accessible technology for education, employment, and livelihoods. Assist. Technol. 0, 1–8 (2021). https://doi.org/10.1080/10400435.2021.1980836
6. McSweeney-Feld, M.H.: Assistive technology and older adults in disasters: implications for emergency management. Disaster Med Public Health Prep **11**, 135–139 (2017). https://doi.org/10.1017/dmp.2016.160
7. Schreurs, K., Quan-Haase, A., Martin, K.: Problematizing the Digital Literacy Paradox in the Context of Older Adults' ICT Use: Aging, Media Discourse, and Self-Determination (2017). https://doi.org/10.22230/CJC.2017V42N2A3130
8. Denburg, N.L., et al.: Poor decision making among older adults is related to elevated levels of neuroticism. Ann. Behav. Med. Publ. Soc. Behav. Med. **37**, 164–172 (2009). https://doi.org/10.1007/s12160-009-9094-7
9. Astell, A.J., McGrath, C., Dove, E.: 'That's for old so and so's!': does identity influence older adults' technology adoption decisions? Ageing Soc. **40**, 1550–1576 (2020). https://doi.org/10.1017/S0144686X19000230
10. Sims, T., Reed, A.E., Carr, D.C.: Information and communication technology use is related to higher well-being among the oldest-old. J. Gerontol. B Psychol. Sci. Soc. Sci. **72**, 761–770 (2017). https://doi.org/10.1093/geronb/gbw130
11. Czaja, S.J., Boot, W.R., Charness, N., Rogers, W.A., Sharit, J.: Improving social support for older adults through technology: findings from the prism randomized controlled trial. Gerontologist **58**, 467–477 (2018). https://doi.org/10.1093/geront/gnw249
12. Chopik, W.J.: The benefits of social technology use among older adults are mediated by reduced loneliness. Cyberpsychology Behav. Soc. Netw. **19**, 551–556 (2016). https://doi.org/10.1089/cyber.2016.0151
13. Fang, Y., Chau, A.K.C., Fung, H.H., Woo, J.: Loneliness shapes the relationship between information and communications technology use and psychological adjustment among older adults. Gerontology **65**, 198–206 (2019). https://doi.org/10.1159/000495461
14. Gitlow, L.: Technology use by older adults and barriers to using technology. Phys. Occup. Ther. Geriatr. **32**, 271–280 (2014). https://doi.org/10.3109/02703181.2014.946640
15. Gell, N.M., Rosenberg, D.E., Demiris, G., LaCroix, A.Z., Patel, K.V.: Patterns of technology use among older adults with and without disabilities. The Gerontologist **55**, 412–421 (2015). https://doi.org/10.1093/geront/gnt166
16. Seifert, A.: The digital exclusion of older adults during the COVID-19 pandemic. J. Gerontol. Soc. Work. **63**, 674–676 (2020). https://doi.org/10.1080/01634372.2020.1764687
17. Haase, K.R., Cosco, T., Kervin, L., Riadi, I., O'Connell, M.E.: Older adults' experiences with using technology for socialization during the COVID-19 pandemic: cross-sectional survey study. JMIR Aging **4**, e28010 (2021). https://doi.org/10.2196/28010

18. Taha, J., Sharit, J., Czaja, S.: Use of and satisfaction with sources of health information among older Internet users and nonusers. Gerontologist **49**, 663–673 (2009). https://doi.org/10.1093/geront/gnp058
19. Xie, B.: Older adults' health information wants in the internet age: implications for patient-provider relationships. J. Health Commun. **14**, 510–524 (2009). https://doi.org/10.1080/10810730903089614
20. James, B.D., Boyle, P.A., Yu, L., Bennett, D.A.: Internet use and decision making in community-based older adults. Front Psychol. **4**, 605 (2013). https://doi.org/10.3389/fpsyg.2013.00605
21. Hall, A.K., Bernhardt, J.M., Dodd, V.: Older adults' use of online and offline sources of health information and constructs of reliance and self-efficacy for medical decision making. J. Health Commun. **20**, 751–758 (2015). https://doi.org/10.1080/10810730.2015.1018603
22. Vollenbroek-Hutten, M., et al.: Possibilities of ICT-supported services in the clinical management of older adults. Aging Clin. Exp. Res. **29**(1), 49–57 (2017). https://doi.org/10.1007/s40520-016-0711-6
23. Fausset, C., Harley, L., Farmer, S., Fain, W.B.: Older adults' perceptions and use of technology: a novel approach. In: HCI (2013)
24. Xiao, Y., Watson, M.: Guidance on conducting a systematic literature review. J. Plan Educ. Res. **39**, 93–112 (2019). https://doi.org/10.1177/0739456X17723971
25. United Nations Department of Economic and Social Affairs, Population Division. World Population Ageing, 2019 Highlights (2019)
26. Wilson, S.J., Lipsey, M.W., Derzon, J.H.: The effects of school-based intervention programs on aggressive behavior: a meta-analysis. J. Consult Clin. Psychol. **71**, 136–149 (2003). https://doi.org/10.1037/0022-006X.71.1.136
27. Soubutts, E., Ayobi, A., Eardley, R., Cater, K., O'Kane, A.A.: Aging in place together: the journey towards adoption and acceptance of stairlifts in multi-resident homes. Proc. ACM Hum-Comput Interact **5**, 320:1–320:26 (2021) . https://doi.org/10.1145/3476061
28. Povey, M., Powell, S., Howes, N., Vimalachandran, D., Sutton, P.: Evaluating the potential utility of three-dimensional printed models in preoperative planning and patient consent in gastrointestinal cancer surgery. Ann. R. Coll. Surg. Engl. **103**, 615–620 (2021). https://doi.org/10.1308/rcsann.2020.7102
29. Angelova, M., Ellman, J., Gibson, H., Oman, P., Rajasegarar, S., Zhu, Y.: User activity pattern analysis in telecare data. IEEE Access **6**, 33306–33317 (2018). https://doi.org/10.1109/ACCESS.2018.2847294
30. Bozan, K., Gewald, H.: How can technology enhance elderly adherence to self-managed treatment plan? In: Shakshuki, E., Yasar, A. (ed): 9th International Conference On Emerging Ubiquitous Systems And Pervasive Networks (Euspn-2018) / 8th International Conference On Current And Future Trends Of Information And Communication Technologies In Healthcare (ICTH-2018). pp. 472–477 (2018)
31. Caldeira, C., Gui, X., Reynolds, T.L., Bietz, M., Chen, Y.: Managing healthcare conflicts when living with multiple chronic conditions. Int. J. Hum-Comput. Stud. **145**, 102494 (2021). https://doi.org/10.1016/j.ijhcs.2020.102494
32. Eng, L., et al.: Age differences in patterns and confidence of using internet and social media for cancer-care among cancer survivors. J. Geriatr. Oncol. **11**, 1011–1019 (2020). https://doi.org/10.1016/j.jgo.2020.02.011
33. Holden, R.J., et al.: Usability and feasibility of consumer-facing technology to reduce unsafe medication use by older adults. Res. Soc. Adm. Pharm. **16**, 54–61 (2020). https://doi.org/10.1016/j.sapharm.2019.02.011
34. Jaana, M., Sherrard, H., Paré, G.: A prospective evaluation of telemonitoring use by seniors with chronic heart failure: adoption, self-care, and empowerment. Health Informatics J. **25**, 1800–1814 (2019). https://doi.org/10.1177/1460458218799458

35. Richards, O.K.: Exploring the empowerment of older adult creative groups using maker technology. In: Proceedings of the 2017 CHI Conference Extended Abstracts on Human Factors in Computing Systems. Association for Computing Machinery, New York, NY, USA, pp. 166–171 (2017)
36. Segkouli, S., Giakoumis, D., Votis, K., Triantafyllidis, A., Paliokas, I., Tzovaras, D.: Smart Workplaces for older adults: coping 'ethically' with technology pervasiveness. Univers. Access Inf. Soc. (2021). https://doi.org/10.1007/s10209-021-00829-9

Inclusive Technical Terms for the Deaf

Paula Escudeiro[✉] 🆔, Nuno Escudeiro 🆔, and Márcia Campos Gouveia 🆔

Games, Interaction and Learning Technologies R&D Center, Instituto Superior de Engenharia do Porto, Rua Dr. António Bernardino de Almeida, 431, Porto, Portugal
{pmo,nfe,magia}@isep.ipp.pt

Abstract. Understanding the meaning of technical terms is essential when using technical and scientific documentation, whether directed to education, research, or labour. In education settings, there is a need to provide clear definitions of terms, to use a glossary explaining the meaning of each technical term when introducing a new topic, and to align terminology and communication channels to the abilities of the target audience. It is exactly at this last point that equity and inclusion issues originate. If we provide definitions or explanations of new concepts using spoken languages in writing, as we commonly do, we leave apart all those who cannot fluently read them. Deaf people cannot read fluently. Sign languages and spoken languages are distinct languages, each one on its own. Sign and spoken languages in the same country use distinct channels, different phonology and morphology, different grammar and arise from different cultures. When we force deaf students to study via written/spoken languages, we are placing them at a clear disadvantage and seriously compromising equity. Inclusive education is about assuring that all students have the conditions and the resources they need to succeed; this does not happen when we force students to study using a language they do not master. There is a need for a tool that can introduce and explain to deaf students technical and scientific concepts from specific areas of knowledge in sign language. TechWhiz is a glossary of scientific and technic concepts, described in sign language, aiming to assist deaf students in gaining access to education in their first language and enhance their learning achievements.

Keywords: Sign language · Scientific glossary

1 Introduction

Deaf students, who use sign language to communicate, continuously experience difficulties in educational settings. "Users of sign languages are often forced to use a language in which they have reduced competence simply because documentation in their preferred format is not available" [1]. Unable to be accompanied by sign interpreters, communication between teachers and students is not always effective, jeopardizing the learning process [2]. This ineffective communication relates to the shortage of information and lack of availability of sign language, thus making it so important to improve access to information and educational content in sign language [3].

Sign and written/spoken languages have different features, creating a deep gap between them, and making it quite difficult for deaf individuals to read/understand written languages [4].

© Springer Nature Switzerland AG 2022
V. G. Duffy et al. (Eds.): HCII 2022, LNCS 13521, pp. 334–344, 2022.
https://doi.org/10.1007/978-3-031-17902-0_24

"Communication barriers are constantly present and arise naturally due to the use of different languages. Different forms and channels of communication by the deaf community, the blind community, and the rest of the students and teachers often lead to the loss of information. Although some deaf can read text fluently, they are a minority" [5].

In fact, sign languages are the only languages deaf individuals can learn effortlessly. Sign languages are the deaf's first language [6]. As any other student, deaf students have the right to access information and education in their first language.

The number of deaf students attending higher education has been steadily rising [3] which demands new methods allowing the deaf to have easy access to educational content and technical terminology like a dictionary prepared to deliver explanations of technical terminology in any study field, in any students' first language.

1.1 TechWhiz: An Inclusive Approach for the Deaf

A key issue for European Higher Education is the access to equal opportunities and educational and social inclusion of disabled people. Numerous efforts are now being made to improve education, by the means of inclusion. To address existing and future challenges, it is necessary to develop new tools to enhance educational settings and the learning experience. Those tools can lead to new opportunities for educational and social inclusion [7].

Focusing on accessibility and educational inclusion is crucial for the Deaf community. The development of assistive tools that enhance access to information and educational content in deaf students' first language – sign language – is of extreme importance for the fulfillment of their learning experience. For those reasons, dictionaries are being made available for the learning of basic signs and specific terms of different areas, i.e., engineering or psychology, for instance [6].

The TechWhiz project begins to help deaf students overcome constraints in the understanding of educational specific terminology. The expected results correspond to the components that integrate into the TechWhiz platform. These are an online dictionary, mainly directed to deaf students, that can be searched to find explanations of technical and scientific terms in any of the four sign languages of the partnership; a gloss loader, mainly directed to teachers and interpreters, that will be used to edit explanations and to add new terms/concepts and their explanations to the online dictionary; a tool to configure signs and store the corresponding 3D animations into the TechWhiz avatar database allowing to use other sign languages besides the four base ones (the sign languages from the partner countries) and to add new signs into the avatar vocabulary in any sign language; a staff training course and the online tutorial to teach how to use and fully explore the TechWhiz platform. The online tutorial will be directly accessible from each one of the platform components to provide instructions for the use of each one of its functionalities.

Accessibility and improving deaf students' experiences in every environment where they don't have the possibility of being accompanied by a sign interpreter is the primary goal of this project, and this scientific glossary can prove to be very helpful towards that, by reducing communication barriers between students and teachers, through an assistive tool of sign language translation/explanation.

By reducing communication and education barriers, which have "a significant impact in the academic, personal, and professional development of deaf (…) students" [5], the TechWhiz project is a means towards equity. The enhancement of the learning experience can encourage more deaf students to enroll in higher education and promote professional and social competencies in those already engaged.

2 Methodology

The TechWhiz project aims to enhance access to education in every student's first language, by supporting common teaching explanations in the languages that deaf students do master. Its purpose is to be educational and inclusive since it is developed towards accessibility and educational inclusion of students with disabilities. The TechWhiz project methodology and its outcomes will enhance and value inclusiveness and education while assisting and enhancing higher education students learning experience.

2.1 Concept

Technical terms are an essential part of all technical and scientific documentation, whether directed to education, research, or labor. Each study field typically uses a vocabulary that relays a variety of specialized concepts through technical language. These special terms convey concentrated meanings that have been built up over significant periods of study of a field. The value of a specialized set of terms lies in the way each term condenses a mass of information into a single word. Technical terminology is often thought of as a shorthand, a way of gaining great depth and accuracy of meaning with the economy of words. However, technical terms can also lead to a great density of prose that is difficult to understand.

There is a need to provide clear definitions of unfamiliar terms, to use a glossary explaining the meaning of each technical term when introducing a new topic, and to match terminology and communication channels to the target audience's abilities. It is exactly at this last point that equity and inclusion come into the scene. If we provide these explanations, as we currently do, using spoken languages we leave aside all those who cannot fluently understand them.

Deaf people cannot read fluently. Sign languages and spoken languages are distinct [2]. They have different channels, different phonology, different morphology, different grammar and arise from different cultures [6]. One cannot expect that a deaf person used to communicate via sign language can understand written languages as well as we cannot expect that a person used to communicate in written/spoken languages can understand sign language [2].

So, when we force deaf students to study via spoken languages, we are putting them at a clear disadvantage and seriously compromising equity. Inclusive education is about assuring that all students have the conditions and the resources they need to succeed; this does not happen when we force students to study using a language they do not master. The lexicon of sign language is more reduced than that of spoken language.

This difference is particularly notorious in technical vocabulary that is usually used only by those directly involved or with an interest in a specific scientific area. Common fields of study, such as engineering or geography, lack signs representing specific lexica like nanotechnology or tropical rain belt. This is a tough barrier for deaf students who face serious difficulties to understand new technical concepts all along their academic path.

There is a need for a tool that can introduce and explain technical or scientific concepts from specific areas of knowledge to deaf students in sign language through a dynamic process enabling the co-creation - by experts in the field and sign language experts - of glossaries addressing specific needs [8].

TechWhiz aims to assist deaf students in gaining equal access to education and enhance their learning experience. TechWhiz addresses a concrete need faced by deaf students and teachers; they need to understand and explain, unknown technical concepts to students who don't master spoken languages. This need was noticed on several occasions by researchers when discussing with deaf teachers the challenges faced by deaf students in education.

The solution to developing by the TechWhiz project is innovative, in the sense that there is no similar solution available for schools, teachers, and students, and is grounded on the technology and previous results in the field of automatic translation of sign languages [1].

The TechWhiz platform will advance inclusive higher education by tearing down the barriers that deaf students face when coming across unknown technical or scientific concepts. Such concepts require an explanation to be provided to promote a swift takeover of new knowledge. When a sign language interpreter is not available to provide these explanations using a language the deaf student can understand, students get blocked in their learning process. Progressing studies under such circumstances demands significant time to disclose the meaning of unknown concepts hampering students' intents and motivation.

TechWhiz will develop a semi-automatic glossary able to provide explanations of technical terms/concepts in any sign language. The glossary/dictionary will be deployed through an online platform offering all the functionalities required to have it accessed by deaf students looking for explanations as well as teachers willing to update the dictionary with new terms and explanations. The sign language dictionaries already available online do not provide explanations; instead, they represent the sign language signs corresponding to spoken language words. Most of them, not to say all, are exclusively dependent on pre-recorded video clips which is a rather static approach that does not escalate well. None of the dictionaries available online can explain words/terms that have not been previously uploaded into the system.

The TechWhiz glossary/dictionary is based on artificial intelligence, web scrapping, and 3D animation technologies that, merged, generate a solution that overcomes all these handicaps.

The foundations of TechWhiz rely on VirtualSign, a computer system for the translation between spoken and sign languages, a research result developed by the R&D GILT-Games Interaction and Learning Technology Unit [3]. TechWhiz will use the VirtualSign 3D avatar and its translation infrastructure to provide explanations in sign language. The results of I-ACE, another R&D GILT Unit project, allow us to have a glossary available in any national sign language. In summary, TechWhiz will build on top of the automatic translation between spoken language and sign language provided by VirtualSign – in particular the 3D avatar and the translation infrastructure – and the translation model by I-ACE enabling the translation to any sign language [5]. Building on top of these previous achievements is crucial to developing the TechWhiz platform.

2.2 Objectives

The TechWhiz project aims to assist deaf students in gaining access to education in their first language thus enhancing their learning experience. To address this goal, we will develop an online semi-automatic platform to create and search a glossary providing explanations of technical or scientific terms in sign language.

TechWhiz aims to promote equity in education by providing access to explanations of technical and scientific concepts for deaf students in their mother language. Although the project results are aiming for higher education, they will be designed, deployed, and disseminated to be publicly available for anyone interested in using the TechWhiz platform regardless of its study field and level of education. By the end of the project, the TechWhiz platform will be available to all those who might be interested in using it.

A tutorial will be publicly available so any interested person can learn how to use and tailor the TechWhiz platform to specific areas, to address specific needs of a person, a group of persons, a school, a company, or any other type of organization.

The design and the validation of the project results – the TechWhiz platform and all its components – will be assured to verify its applicability in all fields of education and training and not exclusively higher education although this is our main target. Tech-Whiz brings in a direct and valuable contribution to advance inclusion and equity in the education and training of deaf communities.

Thus, the main objective of the TechWhiz project is to enhance inclusion and diversity in all fields of education, training, youth, and sport. To do that, the specific objectives are:

- Develop an online semi-automatic platform to dynamically create, maintain and search a glossary providing explanations of technical or scientific terms in sign language.
- Deploy a version of the glossary for the study fields of Information Technologies and Electrical Engineering in Portuguese, German, Slovenian, and Greek sign languages.
- Setup a course to introduce new users to the TechWhiz platform and its correct usage.

2.3 Implementation

The TechWhiz platform will be an application available on the web and accessible to the public to search for technical or scientific terms grouped per study field and subject. The platform will provide explanations of terms in the user sign language. Portugal, Germany, Slovenia, Greece, and Cyprus sign languages' will be available.

As a proof of concept, we will use the platform to create a glossary covering concepts from the subjects of Databases, Big Data, Artificial Intelligence, Blockchain, and Virtual

Reality, framed by the study field of Information Technologies. We expect to load 50 technical explanations with an estimated lexicon of about 500 signs that have to be loaded in each national sign language. The sign language explanations loaded into the platform will finally be certified by experts.

The translation and production of sign language will be performed using the VirtualSign technology. VirtualSign is a research result developed at the R&D GILT Unit for automatic translation between spoken and sign language pairs [9]. The first stage of the project will be devoted to developing the TechWhiz platform. During the first phase, we will analyze and design the platform, its components, and their integration with the VirtualSign technology. This will be also the time to design the verification and validation procedures, the quality scenario, and the test cases.

We will develop the platform following an iterative and incremental methodology confined by four releases. At the end of each release, we will have a subset of the functionalities implemented and being validated by end-users. This agile approach allows integrating independent feedback throughout all the development cycle assuring a final product under end-users needs and expectations. In the meanwhile, we will develop a video tutorial, to integrate into the online platform as a quick reference guide, and a course to teach new users how to use the platform, to introduce participants to the functionalities and added value of TechWhiz.

3 Development

The TechWhiz platform (Fig. 1) integrates three components: the Dictionary, the Gloss Loader, and the Studio. The TechWhiz Dictionary is an online glossary of technical terms explained in the sign language of the user. The dictionary is editable by registered users so teachers and sign language experts can create specific terms' explanations and glossaries to meet specific needs in an open freeway. If the user searches for a term that is not yet available in the dictionary, an automatic explanation will be generated using artificial intelligence and web scraping technologies.

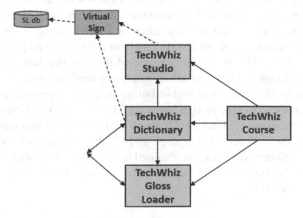

Fig. 1. TechWhiz architecture.

The Dictionary is the core project result and the one that satisfies in its own the project goal. However, the explanations available at the Dictionary require the other two components which are the tools that support the creation and maintenance of the glossaries and the sign language explanations available for search at the Dictionary.

The TechWhiz Gloss Loader allows experts from the technical fields to upload explanations in spoken language and sign language experts to load the corresponding sign language gloss (a gloss is a sequence of words from a spoken language that represent the signs in a sign language sentence). The Gloss Loader is a crucial component for a dynamic live dictionary since it will make the glossaries editable and maintainable by registered users.

The TechWhiz Studio is a tool allowing sign language experts to create and load new sign animations in a specific sign language. This component links TechWhiz to the VirtualSign 3D avatar that will produce the sign language explanations. When a new explanation includes new signs, they will be configured at the Studio by sign language experts and, after being validated, they will become available for all. The Gloss Loader and the Studio empower experts to co-create glossaries for specific fields of knowledge.

These three components, Dictionary, Gloss Loader, and Studio, constitute the Tech-Whiz platform that will bring a fresh push to the inclusion of deaf students in higher education as well as at any other level of education. The TechWhiz course and the online video tutorial will assist newcomers to start exploring the TechWhiz platform and will promote multiplier effects and the sustainability of the platform beyond the funding period.

3.1 TechWhiz Dictionary

The TechWhiz Dictionary is the core output of the project. This is an online glossary where deaf students in higher education or other levels of education can search for terms and find their explanations provided in their own sign language by a 3D avatar.

There are no tools that might provide explanations of technical terms that have no corresponding sign in the students' national sign language or convey new technical or scientific meanings unknown to the students. When faced with such cases, deaf students, who cannot read fluently text in spoken languages, are blocked in their learning process. To proceed they will have to wait until a teacher, or a sign language interpreter explains the concept. These solutions are not always handy or affordable and place deaf students at a clear disadvantage. This is a notorious case of inequity that has a serious negative impact on the ambitions and learning achievements of deaf students.

Currently, there are no tools available online that might provide explanations of technical or scientific concepts in sign language. The TechWhiz Dictionary brings in the following innovations: (1) it uses a 3D avatar and the VirtualSign translation model [9] to provide explanations in sign language and (2) the explanations for terms not yet available in the dictionary database are obtained in real-time using artificial intelligence and web scraping techniques. This way, the student will always have an explanation provided by the platform.

Deaf students will be empowered for an independent study process being able to understand new concepts anywhere and at any time regardless of the availability of a teacher or a sign language interpreter to assist them. A unique solution to promote equity in the education of deaf students.

By the end of the project, we will support the sign languages of Portugal, Germany, Slovenia, Greece, and Cyprus. A pilot glossary for Information and Communication Technologies will be set up as a proof of concept. Other sign languages can be added to the dictionary since the sign language 3D avatar used by TechWhiz is based on VirtualSign, a sign language translation technology that supports multiple sign languages and dialects. Existing glossaries can be updated, and new glossaries can be added on a continuous and dynamic process available to users registered in the platform and assigned to the role of Editor. This functionality will allow to address new specific subjects and enlarge its reach and its added value to the deaf communities and education in general regardless of its level and study field [8, 10].

3.2 TechWhiz Gloss Loader

The TechWhiz Gloss Loader is a component of the TechWhiz platform that will be used to upload explanations in a non-automatic (manual) fashion. Through the Gloss Loader, registered users, namely teachers and sign language interpreters, can submit explanations for existing terms or submit new terms and their explanations. Sign language gloss is a written representation of a sign language sentence, using spoken language words as labels for each sign. When signing the corresponding sign, we have the sentence expressed in sign language. To use VirtualSign we need to generate or acquire the gloss corresponding to the explanation. Then, the avatar signs sequentially each term in the gloss to produce sign language [10].

The TechWhiz Gloss Loader is a fundamental component of the TechWhiz platform. It is essential to allow for updates of existing glossaries as well as the creation of new glossaries. Although we may use VirtualSign to generate gloss from spoken language, the gloss provided by sign language experts will be more effective. The Gloss Loader will allow improving the explanations provided in sign language whenever required.

It will be possible to submit manual (non-automatic) explanations in several formats: plain-spoken language in text format, sign language gloss in text format, or sign language in video format. Having an online tool available for registered users to upload explanations simplifies the interaction between teachers and students through the platform and promotes multiplier effects.

The flexible way to provide explanations to existing terms or new terms, either in spoken language, sign language gloss, or sign language, in text or video, makes the glossary a very dynamic tool easily adaptable to new ideas and innovative didactic activities.

3.3 TechWhiz Studio

The TechWhiz Studio is a component of the TechWhiz platform through which sign language experts like teachers and sign language interpreters will be able to configure the 3D sign animations that are needed to produce the sign language explanations. This will be a simplified version of the VirtualSign configuration tool currently in use. The 3D animation database is a live resource that must evolve to give support to new glossaries and new term explanations. The animation database must store all the signs required for each explanation in each available sign language. When new glossaries are created for new subjects, some of the signs from the sign language lexicon for that specific subject might not be available in the database and have to be configured; this is the purpose of the TechWhiz Studio.

The VirtualSign platform for automatic translation of sign languages already has a configuration tool in use. The TechWhiz Studio will be a new version of this configurator with a simpler lightweight user interface. It will allow the continuous update of the sign language vocabulary available to generate technical terms explanations and open the door for the integration of new sign languages.

The TechWhiz platform has the potential to be extended for use in other countries, thanks to the TechWhiz Studio.

3.4 TechWhiz Course

The TechWhiz Course and the online tutorial provide the required information to start using and taking advantage of the TechWhiz platform for educational activities or any other usage scenario where the explanation of terms in sign language can be an asset.

Although the TechWhiz platform and each one of its components will be designed with a core concern on user-friendliness and simplicity of use, this course will provide a comprehensive view of the purpose, the features, the procedures, and the use cases of this tool. The online tutorial provides the information details on each feature of the platform that will be available on the fly to clarify any issues the user may face while using the platform. The online tutorial is planned to save newcomers time when they start using the platform.

The TechWhiz course and the online tutorial complement the TechWhiz platform with the required resources to place the platform to the service of society in an autonomous way. Those interested in using and benefiting from the TechWhiz platform will find in this course and the online tutorial all the information, the practice, and the guidelines they might need.

Any person interested in using the TechWhiz platform will be able to understand its purpose, architecture, operational procedures, and features through the course. Course modules will be designed to be as autonomous and independent from each other as possible to assure that trainees will only be required to attend the specific modules addressing their current needs. Certification will have this possibility into account; course units will be certified independently.

The course will be available to the public through Moodle or a similar learning management system. A lightweight version will also be available online, embedded in the TechWhiz platform, as a tutorial to provide clear and straightforward information on the use of the platform features and operation procedures. The course and the online tutorial will be available in English, Portuguese, German, Slovenian, and Greek.

4 Evaluation

The approach to assessing the performance of the TechWhiz platform is adapted to each one of its components. The Dictionary is the core outcome of the project and the one that will be used by the end-users, i.e., mainly deaf students willing to understand the meaning of a given technical term in their sign language. The assessment of this component will be based on its added value as perceived by the end-users who will have the chance to like/dislike the explanations provided by the TechWhiz Dictionary. This feedback will be also of high relevance to improve the learning algorithm of the automatic explanation process; in fact, the web-scrapping and the artificial intelligence components of the TechWhiz Dictionary that are gathering explanations on the web will rely on the quality of each explanation, computed from the number of likes/dislikes it gets over time.

The Gloss Loader and the Studio are the backstage tools allowing experts to manually improve or create new entries in the available glossaries or to generate new glossaries for new study fields/topics. These two components will be assessed from two distinct points of view: the content will be evaluated by the frequency of updates while the functionality will be evaluated through periodic surveys to the experts using the platform to maintain its glossaries using the Gloss Loader and the Studio.

To assess the course, we will rely on questionnaires that the participants in the pilot course editions will be asked to fill in.

5 Conclusions

Deaf students face several challenges in their learning experience in higher education as well as other levels of education. The educational system is often unprepared to welcome and assist deaf students. The fact that students in higher education must deal with technical and scientific specific terminology generates a need for an assistive tool capable of explaining the meaning of such terms in students' first language, let it be a spoken or a sign language.

The TechWhiz Dictionary is an online tool generating and providing explanations of technical terms in sign language. This is an innovative feature not currently available to deaf students unless they have permanent access to sign language interpreters or sign language interpretation online services. Both these alternatives are expensive and not always available. It is not feasible to rely on such solutions because they will not be available whenever they might be needed during the academic path of a student. TechWhiz is a unique assistive technology solution that will overcome these blocking factors bringing equity to higher education while placing deaf students in an educational environment where they meet the resources they need to succeed.

TechWhiz is a step forward in the digitalization of higher education services relying on Information and Communication Technologies and Artificial Intelligence to offer access to explanations of technical and scientific concepts in sign language anywhere and at any time they might be needed. It is a dynamic access point to create, search, explore and benefit from technical glossaries for specific technical fields.

Acknowledgments. This work is being developed at the research group GILT – Games, Interaction and Learning Technologies from the Polytechnic Institute of Porto, with the support of FEDER – Fundo Europeu de Desenvolvimento Regional through the Sistema de Incentivos à Investigação e Desenvolvimento Tecnológico – I&D Empresas, under the frame of Portugal 2020, project number POCI-01-0247-FEDER-069949 and the Erasmus+ Programme, European Education and Culture Executive Agency, through project InSign - Advancing inclusive education through International Sign, project number 2019-1-DE01-KA203-004964, and ATHENA – Advanced Technology Higher Education Network Alliance, project number 101004096 EAC-A02–2019.

References

1. Morrissey, S., Way, A.: An example-based approach to translating sign language. In: Second Workshop on Example-based Machine Translation, Phuket (2005)
2. Oliveira, T., Escudeiro, N., Escudeiro, P., Rocha, E., Barbosa, F.M.: The virtualSign channel for the communication between deaf and hearing users. In: IEEE Revista Iberoamericana de Technologias del Aprendizaje, pp. 188–195 (2019)
3. Escudeiro, P., et al.: Virtual sign translator. In: International Conference on Computer, Networks and Communication Engineering, Beijing (2013)
4. Escudeiro, P., et al.: Virtual sign – a real time bidirectional translator of portuguese sign language. In: Procedia Computer Science, pp. 252–262 (2015)
5. Ulisses, J.P.P.S., Oliveira, T., Escudeiro,. P.M., Escudeiro, N.F.: ACE assisted communication for education: architecture to support blind. In: IEEE Global Engineering Education Conference, Santa Cruz de Tenerife (2018)
6. Wheatley, M., Pabsch, A.: Sign language legislation in the european union. European Union of the Deaf, Brussels (2012)
7. Verma, G.K.: Education and social integration for all: challenges and responses. In: Approaches to educational and social inclusion: International perspectives on theory, policy and key challenges, London, Routledge, pp. 9-21 (2017)
8. Escudeiro, P., Escudeiro, N., Norberto, M., Lopes, J., Soares, F.: Digital assisted communication. In: 13th International Conference on Web Information Systems and Technologies, Porto (2017)
9. Escudeiro, P., Escudeiro, N., Reis, R., Barbosa, M., Bidarra, J., Gouveia, B.: Automatic sign language translator model. Adv. Sci. Lett. **4**, 400–407 (2011)
10. Oliveira, T., Escudeiro, P.M., Escudeiro, N.F., Rocha, E.: Automatic sign language translation to improve communication. In: IEEE Global Engineering Education Conference, Dubai (2019)

Guidelines for the Development of Common Ground-Based Relational Agents for Elderly

Thiago Gama[(⊠)], Andressa Ferreira, and Francisco Oliveira

Ceará State University, Fortaleza, CE 60714-903, Brazil
{thiago.dias,andressa.magda}@aluno.uece.br,
fran.oliveira@uece.br

Abstract. The elderly population grows worldwide while the size of families decreases. In addition, there is the figure of caregivers of the elderly, who play a crucial role in preserving these older adults' health and reducing their loneliness. However, in the not-too-distant future, the availability of this professional in the market may become scarce to meet the growing demand arising from the aging of the world population. Therefore, it is necessary to build systems that promote healthy aging. Social agents embedded in devices like Alexa can be a significant weapon in this scenario. However, the development of such agents is still in its infancy, and there are few guidelines to guide new projects. This work investigated the construction of an agent based on the common ground theory as a conversation starter, which proved to be effective in producing meaningful dialogues. The text reports this experience and presents a series of guidelines for future developers.

Keyword: Guidelines · Relational agent · Common ground · Elderly · Wizard of Oz experiment

1 Introduction

According to the World Health Organization (WHO), the number of people over the age of 60 will reach 2 billion by 2050. With data from the Ministry of Health, Brazil, in 2016, had the fifth-largest elderly population in the world. However, the forecast is that by 2030, the number of older people will exceed the total number of children between zero and 14 years old. Thus, numbers show us that there will be a higher percentage of older adults in our population with advancing age. Therefore, we need to pay attention to adapting and understanding more and more about longevity. This high proportion, as already mentioned, is due to the high fertility observed in the 1950s and 1960s and to the drop in birth and mortality rates with benefits for all population groups.

The proportion of older people living alone in Brazil is increasing. This puts pressure on the health system due to falls, mental health problems, among other reasons. The profession of caregivers for the elderly also emerged due to this.

Older adults who decide to live alone or with caregivers or nurses are likely to develop depression, according to National Institute on Aging [20]. In addition to this disease, high expenses with health plans, medicines, caregivers, and accessibility infrastructure

© Springer Nature Switzerland AG 2022
V. G. Duffy et al. (Eds.): HCII 2022, LNCS 13521, pp. 345–365, 2022.
https://doi.org/10.1007/978-3-031-17902-0_25

suitable for the elderly, constitute obstacles for middle and low-income families. The more a retiree who, in addition to losing income, has higher expenses with medicines and health plans, etc. It appears that a viable option for these patients is their empowerment.

At the same time, people are increasingly communicating through the most diverse mobile devices, such as smartphones, tablets, and notebooks. Moreover, with the emergence of communication applications (WhatsApp, Telegram, Signal, among others) increasingly sophisticated, accessible, and secure, their popularity is also noticeable in this segment.

Chatbots are simple chat programs, while conversational agents are chatbots enhanced with machine learning. They can identify linguistic and context variations and thus better understand user inputs. However, these systems do not guarantee a long-term engagement with the user, as explained in Campbell [6]. Finally, the relational agent is a conversational agent with humanized traits (see Sect. 4.5), which determines a long-term engagement for the application that has this resource. In the case of this work, the aim is to prototype an application to achieve a long-term engagement with elderly users using, for this purpose, the common ground technique.

According to Clark [9], common ground is information shared by two or more people. Technically, it's the sum of your mutual knowledge, mutual beliefs, and mutual assumptions. To find common ground between the parties, participants must look for positive, neutral, or negative signs of recognition, often subtle and subject to misunderstanding. This seeks to solve a complex problem of chatbots, which is that they do not have any common ground with the elderly, which makes the whole process of acceptance and engagement of the elderly with technology difficult.

In this sense, these relational agents could help older people by offering them medical instructions and guidance to change unhealthy habits (physically or mentally). However, the definition of a practical technological and communicational approach to influence positive behavior change is a result. These individuals are anyone's guess in the context of chatbots.

There are still no published works that present guidelines to the developers of relational agents aimed at the elderly public. Therefore, it is expected that this research will address the construction and evaluation of this type of chatbot, and, in the end, these guidelines will be produced. This will be possible for future researchers and developers to take advantage of this theoretical-experimental framework designed to guide their decision-making in projects involving this specific scenario.

When embedded in smart speakers, these dialogue systems represent a promise for the HCI area that, for some reasons, deserves to be investigated. Among these reasons, we can highlight:

1. Improvement of the significance of the conversations carried out; and
2. Increased user engagement with the application compared to the engagement found between users and trivial chatbots.

Thus, this work aims, finally, to devise guidelines for the elaboration of chatbot dialog flows aimed at the elderly public based on the results observed from the intervention, the Wizard of Oz experiment, adopted in this work. But unfortunately, there is also the fact that no one has tested these conversational agents with older adults from different social classes in Brazil.

Subsequent sections of the work are organized as follows. In Sect. 2, the related works are presented, mainly considering the common ground technique used to establish an initial understanding between the interlocutors, thus facilitating user engagement with the prototyped application. In Sect. 3, the methodology used in this study is discussed in Sect. 4, the topics (process, modeling of the guardian relational agent, common ground questionnaire, interaction architecture, conversation techniques, conversation scripts, participants, and technologies) about the Wizard of Oz experiment's realization. Section 5 presents the results obtained from the investigation, with the following topics: problems identified and proposed guidelines. Finally, in Sect. 6, the conclusion of the results produced in this work is briefly described.

1.1 Objectives

As a general objective, it is intended to investigate the process of building a relational agent, embedded in a smart speaker, aimed at the elderly public, mainly regarding the lack of engagement and, in the end, to produce guidelines for future researchers, developers, and companies of software.

Based on the general objective presented above, the specific objectives of the proposed work are listed below:

1. Design a data collection instrument (questionnaire) that will support the construction of a database of dialogues based on common ground with older people and apply the questionnaire with people who surround the elderly to assist in the creation of a database of common ground with older adults, to create a dialogue bank based on data from older adults to form the initial common ground; and
2. Implement the Wizard of Oz concept, which will serve to talk to the elderly, create a history of conversations, the corpus, and carry out the Wizard of Oz experiment with the research subjects following the interaction methodology to evaluate the impact of the interaction quality of the common ground database.

2   Related Works

Studies [2, 3, 8, 15, 19, 23, 24] e [25] were selected through debates and discussions held between the involved in the production of this research and as a way of expanding the number of studies reviewed here, a second inclusion of studies through the backward snowballing method was carried out in the selected studies collected, to verify the methodology used in these works to base the method proposed in this work. This systematic review activity was dealt with in detail in Gama et al. [13].

In Clark and Brennan [7], the notion of common ground was developed as a concept that refers to the theory where mutual knowledge, common beliefs, and shared assumptions that the authors believe are essential for successful communication. Although, according to Adler and Rodman [1], successful communication occurs when the meaning of the statement is negotiated, several factors can create negative and positive impressions of a speaker: accent, choice of words, speech rate, tone voice, etc. Therefore, common ground is a technique people use to facilitate interpersonal relationships.

According to Clark [9], common ground is information sharing. In this book, it is said that the idea lies behind three contributions:

3. Participants in a conversation work together against a background of shared information;
4. As the conversation proceeds, participants accumulate shared information by adding it to each iteration; and
5. Speakers design their utterances so that their addresses can readily identify what should be added to the conversation at common points.

The basic principles of the common ground theory are based on the foundations of eye-to-eye communication, that is, face to face, which is the primary form of communication and happens intuitively between human beings. At the same time, the symbologies used in writing are more complex processes requiring the knowledge of the writer and reader to understand the symbols used to represent the spoken content. Moreover, some gestures and expressions provide information complexly in addition to writing.

According to Geison [14], the Wizard of Oz experiment can be used for virtually any interface. Still, it is particularly effective for prototyping AI-based experiments because the range of system responses is almost impossible to replicate with prototyping tools. In addition, the cost of building a system to test a concept is prohibitive.

A Wizard of Oz session works like this: the researcher is in a room with a participant talking to a device that looks like a smart speaker or voice-enabled product. Another research team member controls the device's responses in another environment, as shown in Fig. 1 referred to in Geison [14]. No actual programming is involved – just a person behind the curtain pulling the levers like the Wizard of Oz.

Fig. 1. How the Wizard of Oz method works.

3 Methodology

Based on the information presented above, the steps of the methodology used in this study are described below:

1. Modeling the Guardian application architecture;
2. Send this project to the research ethics committee together with another student linked to this research, since the experiment with human beings cannot be carried out without the approval of the ethics committee[1];
3. Construction of one or more anamnesis questionnaires to collect data from the participants of the experiment, based on the purpose of the application (mental health);
4. Validate anamnesis questionnaire with one or more health experts;
5. Collect data with a significant sample;
6. Enable the Wizard of Oz experiment using Alexa installed on smart speakers;
7. Validate the solution;
8. Prepare the dialogue/script flows to use certified content;
9. Test the entire apparatus together[2];
10. Recruit research subjects;
11. Collect data from the anamnesis questionnaire with close people and relatives of the elderly participants in the experiment;
12. Process the anamnesis questionnaire data obtained from the research subjects;
13. Perform the Wizard of Oz Experiment;
14. Collect Alexa data after the participant has it in their home for four days to be then sanitized and transported to the home of the next elderly participant in the experiment. Regarding this step, the researcher who plays the role of Wizard of Oz must be fully available for any scheduled (or unscheduled) interaction time with the experiment participant. However, the interaction is limited to one session per day.
15. Organize and analyze the collected data using statistical methods; and
16. Based on the experiment's findings, establish guidelines for the development of relational agents aimed at the elderly public for software developers and companies aimed at the older adults.

4 Conducting the Wizard of Oz Experiment

4.1 Process

Each elderly participant in the research received the prototype of the Guardian application installed on the Echo Dot smart speaker device at their home, during which they were

---

[1] This research is duly registered on Plataforma Brasil (national and unified database of research involving human beings) under the number CAAE 46437621.7.0000.5534.

[2] "Drop In" functionality of the Alexa app, audio recording application to record the days of the experiment with each participant, scripts of the dialogue flows and the researcher's performance during the experiment sessions Wizard of Oz.

trained to use it. It was explained how the conversation would occur and the times and days that the elderly should be in the environment.

Data collection was carried out with some selected older people who agreed to participate in the experiment proposed in this work. In the experiment in question, an individual simulates the artificial intelligence of the prototyped relational agent application through a technique known as the Wizard of Oz. In this experiment, the user believes he is talking to an artificial intelligence, but he is talking to a person. The objective of this experiment is to obtain information about usability, feeling, and, mainly, the engagement of the participants in the conversations carried out.

A questionnaire was designed to collect data from the elderly to form a database of the participants in the experiment. Furthermore, an application was used to convert the researcher's text into voice so that, in this way, he can play the role of the Wizard of Oz in the intended experiment, to give the older person the impression that he is talking to an artificial intelligence, and, finally, a superficial analysis of the dialogues carried out, consolidated in a corpus, was carried out during the Wizard of Oz experiment with each of the seven participants.

It was created by the author of this work, who plays the role of the Wizard of Oz in the intended experiment, a questionnaire based on an anamnesis interview about the mental and physical health of the elderly with people in his social circle. This work consists of creating a prototype of an application for health supplied with user information (application of the common ground theory).

Seven participants (elderly) were recruited, and to build the common ground of each elder, a person close to each research subject provided data on the elder to be transformed into dialogue flows of the prototype relational agent, by the condition of intervention in the intention to compose the sample of the Wizard of Oz experiment, according to what is suggested by Nielsen [21].

To carry out this experiment, the inclusion and exclusion criteria of the participants are mentioned below:

- **Inclusion criteria:** research subject must be 60 years of age or older; and
- **Exclusion criteria:** there are no exclusion criteria for the intended experiment, thus aiming to cover all characteristics (conditions, diseases, or disabilities) found in this specific audience, thus making this experiment as inclusive as possible.

These research subjects were recruited through a research assistant, considering that the primary author could not have contact or prior information about the experiment participant in order not to bias the conversations between the Wizard of Oz (this role was fulfilled) by the author of this work) and the older adult, who contacted people close to him, offering them the opportunity to participate in this experiment. These participants were reached only by the research assistant, a role performed by another researcher involved in the work that is not the Wizard of Oz since the Wizard of Oz cannot interact with these individuals in order not to be influenced to the point of basing their interactions with these individuals from information and impressions not obtained directly by the questionnaire that was applied to collect a wide variety of information about these selected elderly. The participants were not compensated for their time. They voluntarily made themselves available to collaborate in this stage of the work.

Then, this information was stored in a spreadsheet that served to support the dialogues aimed at the elderly by the Wizard of Oz, who used the Guardian application. Finally, this actor used TTS software and a pre-scripted script to run this simulation conceived for the Wizard of Oz to guide what subjects should be addressed on the day of the experiment in question. In all, four days of the experiment were used for each participant recruited.

The interactions between the older person and the Guardian relational agent were predefined by the participant one day before the Wizard of Oz experiment session took place during the scheduled period. After each session of the Wizard of Oz experiment, the recording of the conversation was heard. Finally, an analysis of the conversation was carried out to support the elaboration of new dialogue flows used in the subsequent conversations with the participant in question.

Candidates were contacted by phone or in person. The study was explained to them by the lead researcher, and a recruitment meeting was scheduled. After the participant was selected, a research assistant went to each participant's home to install and configure the smart speaker at the beginning of the experiment.

At first, consent was obtained. Then, a research assistant configured the Echo Dot device with the developed Skill installed. Next, participants completed a profile questionnaire. Next, it was shown how to interact with the system that makes use of the Wizard of Oz technique (an experiment in which a human actor pretends to be an intelligent relational agent), and, finally, the sessions of the Wizard of Oz experiment were conducted with the recruited participants.

The research subjects' participation data were recorded at the end of the Wizard of Oz experiment sessions. The smart speaker was collected and sanitized to be reused by the following experiment participant until seven individuals who participated in the intended experiment were added.

The interaction history was documented in log files to consolidate a corpus of all communications carried out through a recorder during conversations, keeping track of participants' actions in the developed system. Participants were instructed to interact only once a day with the smart speaker.

As actors of the objectified experiment, we have the following profiles:

- Wizard of Oz represented by the lead author of this study, who was in charge of talking to the elderly to achieve long-term engagement with the application user; and
- Experiment participants must be familiar with technologies such as smartphones, social networks[3], and smart speakers.

The environment where the experiment took place was the experiment participant's house, preferably in a room that the older person feels comfortable with, that has an outlet to power the smart speaker and a good internet connection. The Wizard of Oz experiment sessions took place at pre-established times determined by the participant.

---

[3] For example, Facebook - which is usually more used by elderly users, since this social network stores the birthdays of the grandchildren of older people.

Regarding the division of the groups in this work, the participants were divided between the "protocol validation" and "data collection" groups, since, as this research encompasses an experiment not yet fully mapped in the reviewed literature, we chose to if by selecting only the first participant as a component of the "protocol validation" group, to discover practical approaches to maintain the engagement between the research subject and the Guardian (simulated using the Wizard of Oz technique), so that the from these evidenced findings apply these with the participants included in the "data collection" group.

In short, while the biggest concern of those involved in this study in the interaction with the "protocol validation" group is practical learning, the biggest problem of those involved in the interaction with the "data collection" group is, in fact, the establishment of significant conversations (combining the lessons learned with the other group and the knowledge and techniques found in the specialized literature) and, with that, the verification of a positive engagement between the user of the application and the relational agent Guardian.

4.2 Common Ground Questionnaire

The data collection questionnaire for this work was prepared, as can be seen in Gama, Ferreira, and Oliveira [11], it was applied by the research assistant, a role occupied by a member of this work who was willing to collaborate with this work, with a person from the experiment participant's social circle.

The data collection questionnaire was applied to a person present in the social circle of the elderly (family member, friend, neighbor, etc.). Therefore, this questionnaire should be shared online with people close to the elderly. This stage of the work aims to collect initial data that could help discover the participant's essential characteristics and tastes of the experiment to support the formulation of engaging dialogues (using the common ground technique) that the prototype of the Guardian app would later use.

The interviewees' data about the experiment participants were inserted into the questionnaire. Thus, these are the variables of characterization of the research:

- Personal and social;
- Habits and lifestyle;
- Health; and
- Interpersonal.

4.3 Interaction Architecture

Regarding the architecture of interaction, which takes place through conversation, four conversational flows were established through which predefined dialogues can flow or pass through to increase the chances of the conversation being engaging for the research subjects. The four flows created, with their respective durations in the conversation, are shown in Table 1. The third flow is directly derived from the answers to the common ground questionnaire passed to the experiment participants.

Table 1. Types of dialogue flow used to elaborate the scripts for the Wizard of Oz experiment.

Flow	Conversation topic	Interaction duration
F1	Cordiality	Very short
F2	News	Moderate
F3	Miscellaneous subjects	Long
F4	Coaching	Short
F5	Features	Moderate

4.4 Conversation Techniques

Based on Riker [22], the following techniques and steps were adopted to maintain an interesting conversation with the participants of the intended experiment. Since Technique 1 (T1), nicknamed "the sinking stone", was inspired by the concepts established in the common ground theory, while Technique 2 (T2), active listening, is based entirely on the individual's interpersonal skills, Wizard of Oz, which aims to engage the interlocutor.

- **T1:** a metaphor to skip the surface part of a conversation and engage your interlocutor through emotion. To apply Technique 1, it is necessary to follow the steps listed below:

    1. Be knowledgeable about the other person, what they like, what they do or have done, something they said or mentioned. Keep the hook personal, but not too personal – this is where common ground theory enters the conversation.

    2. Ask about an emotion related to the fact. For example, there are dialogues "Do you like this subject?" and "What are the biggest challenges for those who deal with this subject normally?".

    3. Understand why that emotion arose. For example, we have the dialogues "Why is he so interesting to you?" and "Oh, I figured this issue would work the other way. What made you learn so much about him?"

- **T2:** active listening is when your attention is dedicated to what the person is saying, not just looking for a break to express your own opinion. An example of using active listening is shown below:

    1. In active listening, the listener emits the vocalization "Hm" or the dialogue "I understand".

Based on these techniques and steps, it is intended to maintain an engaging and fluid conversation with the older adult, always open to the emergence of new topics during the speech.

As subjects that will be discussed during the dialogues, always considering the profile of each participant involved in the experiment, the following are presented: family, friends, TV program, cinema, theater, concerts, exhibitions, outdoor programs, bars, and restaurants, reading books, accessing the internet, dancing, traveling, resting, gardening, cooking, handicrafts, painting, football team, sports, physical activities, habits, lifestyle, and health.

4.5 Conversation Scripts

Regarding the elaboration of the dialogue flows for the days of the experiment, based on the information obtained in the questionnaire, found in Gama, Ferreira, and Oliveira [11], the dialogue flows were produced, which is, during each session of the Wizard of Oz experiment, accompanied by the questionnaire proposed to, in this way, supply the common ground (unique for each participant) of humanization, to increase the research subject's engagement with the conversational agent of this work, Lady Laura, a name dedicated to the music of the singer Roberto Carlos[4] who shows a particular welcome by most of the elderly who participated in the experiment.

A parallel script was created with dialogue flows that could supply the conversation if the experiment participant tried to get to know Lady Laura better. The members of this work gave the name to the relational agent prototyped through the Wizard of Oz experiment. Therefore, it was decided to create a character for Lady Laura, her tastes, thoughts, and characteristics. This information can be checked at the Gama, Ferreira, and Oliveira [12]. The technique used in this study is the Wizard of Oz experiment. On that occasion, a TTS conversion API was used so that the author could impersonate the relational agent nicknamed "Lady Laura", a name inspired by the famous song by Brazilian singer Roberto Carlos that was released in 1978. It is a song well known by older adults. Therefore, it was decided to name the relational agent "Lady Laura" to bring the proposed application closer to her target audience.

4.6 Participants

Division of Groups. As a requirement for implementing conversations with research subjects for the Wizard of Oz experiment, Table 2 shows the seven research subjects (RS's) that will be part of the intended experiment. The other participants not selected in the sample did not participate in the proposed experiment due, respectively, to the reasons: death, travel, withdrawal, and excess of the number of participants necessary to carry out the intended investigation.

In Table 2, it is also possible to see that the participants of the experiment were divided into two groups: "protocol validation" and "data collection", in which the research subjects placed in the "protocol validation" group would serve as a practice for the conversational techniques adopted in Sect. 4.4. In contrast, the "data collection" group participants would evaluate the strategies adopted or developed by the researchers of this work in the protocol validation phase of the Wizard of Oz experiment.

---

[4] Brazilian singer, songwriter, and entrepreneur. Known in Brazil and Latin America as "King", Roberto Carlos began his career in the early 1960s.

Table 2. Duration of the Wizard of Oz experiment with selected participants.

ID	Group	Days	Duration	Total duration
RS1	Protocol validation	19/07/2021	44 min 52 s	2 h 21 min 6 s
		20/07/2021	29 min 56 s	
		22/07/2021	33 min 55 s	
		23/07/2021	32 min 23 s	
RS2	Data collect	26/07/2021	25 min 47 s	2 h 27 min 12 s
		27/07/2021	42 min 9 s	
		28/07/2021	44 min 11 s	
		29/07/2021	35 min 5 s	
RS3	Data collect	23/08/2021	33 min 57 s	2 h 31 min 40 s
		24/08/2021	34 min 8 s	
		25/08/2021	49 min 50 s	
		26/08/2021	33 min 45 s	
RS4	Data collect	23/08/2021	31 min 53 s	2 h 31 min 56 s
		25/08/2021	36 min 46 s	
		26/08/2021	42 min 47 s	
		27/08/2021	40 min 30 s	
RS5	Data collect	02/09/2021	36 min 32 s	2 h 36 min 28 s
		03/09/2021	38 min 47 s	
		04/09/2021	44 min 53 s	
		11/09/2021	36 min 16 s	
RS6	Data collect	07/09/2021	21 min 39 s	2 h 29 min 38 s
		08/09/2021	42 min 38 s	
		09/09/2021	42 min 49 s	
		10/09/2021	42 min 32 s	
RS7	Data collect	13/09/2021	39 min 28 s	2h 45 min 37 s
		14/09/2021	42 min 14 s	
		15/09/2021	33 min 15 s	
		16/09/2021	50 min 40 s	

Participants Profile. Based on DISC methodologies Marston [18] and on Ned Herrmann's HBDI (Herrmann Brain Dominance Instrument), which was validated in Bunderson [5], some consultancies developed a test that is already being applied in companies to identify the profile of each professional. The test consists of 25 questions that are presented to the candidate. Each question has four words arranged in a vertical alphabetical list A, B, C, D, which the individual has seven seconds to choose or mark only one of them. In total, there are 25 questions. In the end, the letter that was marked the most times, revealing the person's profile as follows: eagle, wolf, dolphin, and shark are counted. As a result, the following results are obtained:

- **Wolf:** is the administrator. Always attentive to planning, punctuality, and control. Detailed, conservative, organized, predictable, loyal, with difficulty adapting to changes, and responsible for carrying out the agreement are still characteristics.
- **Eagle:** is the visionary. A person who likes to do things differently. Some of the main characteristics of this person are curiosity, creativity, intuition, flexibility, the search for freedom, vision of the future, and innovation.
- **Dolphin:** is the communicator. He is a person who likes to work in a team and interact with other people. This profile is characterized by the need to be socially accepted, put happiness above results, be recognized by their team, and enjoy working in a harmonious environment.
- **Shark:** is the executor. This one is characterized by people who search for results, a sense of urgency, impulsiveness, practicality, focus on the future, and commitment to goals.

In some tests, the dolphin figure is exchanged for the cat. This test aims to draw an individual profile from a behavioral map that indicates each person's brain dominance and how these preferences determine the behaviors and values that motivate all people [17].

A questionnaire that could be applied to identify the profiles of the participants of the experiment carried out can be seen in Weizenmann [26]. In this way, each questionnaire will be answered, pretending to be each research subject, to classify the experiment's participants. Each profile will be related to assessing the engagement they answered at the end of the Wizard of Oz experiment. After analyzing the recordings of the conversations and the data collected through the questionnaires sent to people close to the older person, the profiles of the participants of the experiment carried out are consolidated in Table 3, where the profiles are classified and ordered according to the predominance of the characteristics of individuals.

Table 3. Profiles of the research subjects of the Wizard of Oz experiment.

RS	Profile	Justification
RS1	1. Dolphin 2. Wolf 3. Eagle 4. Shark	RS1 is a calm, friendly and polite participant, in addition to being a very active, organized, and hardworking housewife
RS2	1. Eagle 2. Shark 3. Wolf 4. Dolphin	RS2 is a highly erudite and well-informed participant, has higher education, and is very hardworking, but he is not close to his children

(continued)

Table 3. (*continued*)

RS	Profile	Justification
RS3	1. Dolphin 2. Eagle 3. Wolf 4. Tubarão	RS3 is a friendly, kind, and super friendly participant. She loves her pets (her birds and cats) and enjoys being with her friends and knitting
RS4	1. Wolf 2. Shark 3. Dolphin 4. Eagle	RS4 is a very active and hardworking participant, is well connected to local and national political issues, and is very close to his family members
RS5	1. Dolphin 2. Shark 3. Wolf 4. Eagle	RS5 is a participant who is always thinking about her family, a person with a fighting nature, and very polite and aware of current social and political issues
RS6	1. Eagle 2. Dolphin 3. Wolf 4. Shark	RS6 is a participant who was once a distinguished worker. Today he is a well-informed person with a well-established opinion on various topics and is always available to help his family members, and loves to cook
RS7	1. Dolphin 2. Wolf 3. Eagle 4. Shark	RS7 is a simple, friendly, polite, and humane participant. She does gardening and has considerable knowledge in this practice. She is religious and a housewife dedicated to the house and her family and who sings very well

4.7 Technologies

Software Used. As a requirement for the implementation of conversations with research subjects for the Wizard of Oz experiment, it is exposed in Table 3 the seven participants (RS's) who will be part of the intended experiment. The other participants not selected in the sample did not participate in the proposed experiment due, respectively, to the reasons: death, travel, withdrawal, and an excess number of participants necessary to carry out the intended investigation.

Amazon Alexa, or simply Alexa, according to Kelly [16], is a virtual assistant technology developed by Amazon, first used in the Amazon Echo smart speaker and the Echo Dot, Echo Studio, and Amazon speakers. Tap designed by Amazon Lab126. It can voice interaction, play music, create to-do lists, set alarms, stream podcasts, play audiobooks, and provide weather, traffic, sports, and other real-time information such as news.

A study was carried out on the software that could prototype the relational agent, and the Cloud Text-to-Speech API was found, the text-to-speech converter from Google, which was developed with AI technologies. The main features of this API are custom voice (beta version), WaveNet voices, voice adjustment, and compatibility with text and SSML, among others. To build the corpus of the experiment with the smart speaker, a recorder was used to record the conversations between the relational agent, operated by the Wizard of Oz, and the participant of the experiment.

Alexa can also control various smart devices using itself as a home automation system. Users can extend Alexa's features by installing Skills, which are additional features developed by third-party vendors, in other settings that are more commonly called apps, such as weather programs and audio features. It uses NLU, speech recognition, and other simple AI to accomplish these tasks. Among the Alexa Echo Dot models used in the Wizard of Oz experiment.

Echo Dot 2 and Echo Dot 3 devices were used. The first model mentioned it was used on the researcher's side, playing the role of the Wizard of Oz, while the second was installed and configured on the participant's side of the experiment. This decision was made because, due to the superior quality of the speakers of the latest model of the Echo Dot device, it would be more opportune to leave this device with those with weaker hearing, which, in this case, were the research subjects.

The "Drop In" functionality was used for communication between Echo Dots, which serves to start an instant conversation between devices or Alexa contacts. When a "Drop In" is received, the Echo Dot's light indicator flashes green, and the user is automatically connected to their contact. However, to "Drop In" to contact a different Amazon account, the user and their contact must first grant "Drop In" permissions to each other. Without this permission, the user cannot "Drop In" in the Alexa app and cannot specify which user contact devices can use the "Drop In" feature.

Sounds Used. The names, followed by their applications, of the pre-recorded tracks in MP3 format used in the Wizard of Oz experiment are presented below:

1. **Heart beating:** used when Lady Laura says something exciting to the experiment participant;
2. **Musical tracks:** the musical tracks played during the sessions were all from YouTube videos, which was the video streaming platform used to find and play the participants' favorite songs in the experiment in real-time. This change brought convenience to the Wizard of Oz, already in charge of listening to the recordings of the sessions to prepare the scripts for the following sessions with each research subject;
3. **Applause:** used when the participant spoke of an incredible feat of his own, even if it happened many years ago; and
4. **Laugh:** used when the research subject said something funny. I can say that, by far, this was the most played audio track during all sessions of the Wizard of Oz experiment with all participants because, in addition to having this purpose, it was observed that when the audio of Lady's laughter Laura was reproduced, there was a great chance that the older adult would laugh with the relational agent, which increased the participant's engagement with the prototyped application.

These tracks, which were used to make up for the absence of the emojis feature, are often used in instant messaging applications and social networks to show emotions and reactions to certain content or posts.

The laugh recording was essential throughout the experiment as it was observed that when Lady Laura laughed, the participants often laughed along with her, thus demonstrating that there was an emotional connection between the prototyped realtor and the participants of the experiment, which resulted in a positive impact on user engagement with the application.

5 Results

5.1 Problems Identified

Findings and difficulties observed during this intervention will be synthesized and converted into guidelines for software companies and developers of relational agents in Sect. 5.2, which specifically deals with the design of guidelines for the development of relational agents aimed at the elderly public, which is the final and main objective of this academic work.

The problems observed during the realization of the Wizard of Oz experiment, which can be a harbinger of the difficulties to be faced, in fact, in the course of developing a relational agent aimed at the elderly, are presented below.

- The methodology for applying the data collection instrument (questionnaire) is poorly designed, allowing the collection of dubious or false information, often derived from the lack of knowledge that the interviewee has about the elderly.
- Unavailability or instability of the Cloud Text-to-Speech API used in the text-to-speech conversion, causing crashes during text-to-speech conversion or audio playback, forcing the Wizard of Oz to reload the website page multiple times to send a message to the participant, negatively affecting the user's engagement with the application.
- Difficulty finding: software artifacts made by developers who have previous experience with senior-accessible software projects; records that report failed decisions from last software projects to provide the required level of accessibility for older people; and online training courses that teach how to incorporate accessibility into chatbots designed for the elderly.
- Difficulty knowing: At what points, before and after development, users need to be involved.
- Internet connection instability, either on the user side or on the application/Wizard of Oz side.
- The limitation of conversations produced before the Wizard of Oz experiment session led to the elaboration in real-time of new dialogue flows from the newly acquired information about the older adult to prolong the duration of the conversation.
- The relational agent at times interrupted the older person's speech.
- Absence of method for building the script of dialog flows. Older people sometimes did not understand the questions asked of them.
- Absence of a broad notion of the environment where the experiment participant finds himself resulted in communication failures identified after reviewing the recorded conversations.

- Absence of a multidisciplinary team of professionals (psychology, social communication, health, etc.) for the elaboration or validation of dialogue flow scripts and the lack of a creative team to create the personality of the relational agent.
- Lack, non-existence, or unavailability of legal requirements, national or international standards. Difficulty following relevant specific standards when planning user engagement.
- Limitation of engagement features to put in voice user interfaces.
- Difficulty in keeping the user's attention and gaining the trust of the research subject.

5.2 Proposed Guidelines

Developing accessible software is a complex process – and companies meet the requirements defined in the standards and guidelines set by governments and specific agencies. Some guidelines for developers of relational agents for seniors are presented below. They can help make project decisions so that the products and services developed are more inclusive, considering that the elderly, in many cases, are people with limited digital literacy. The categories (C's) of the proposed guidelines are presented below:

- **C1.** Data collect;
- **C2.** Software engineering;
- **C3.** Software testing;
- **C4.** Computer network;
- **C5.** Communication;
- **C6.** Human resources;
- **C7.** Standardization;
- **C8.** Human-computer interaction;
- **C9.** Attention;
- **C10.** Understanding; and
- **C11.** Trust.

Many guidelines need to be followed for a relational agent conversation to be successful. Any non-compliance with these guidelines can lead to the interruption of the conversation, which exposes, in many cases, a poorly designed user experience. Understanding how and why talks fail can help conversational agent designers design better conversational experiences. Creating conversational happy path scenarios is not tricky. What is problematic is putting alternate path scenarios in mind.

So why do conversations fail? What do users say that takes the conversation off the happy path? There are several reasons why. To understand this, we need to delve deeper into the guidelines on what makes conversations between seniors and relational agents successful, presented in Table 4. Below are the guidelines (G's) developed:

Table 4. Proposed guidelines.

ID	C	Description
G1	C1	The common ground questionnaire prepared proved to help generate meaningful dialogues around the health of the elderly. Therefore, it is recommended to adopt this strategy, always observing the application objectives
G2	C1	To create the data collection instrument, it is suggested to look for a multidisciplinary professional (for example, areas indicated for the context of the application described in this work: design, psychology, health, social communication, etc.) to create the data collection instrument
G3	C2	Searching for certified content and adapting it to the dialogues is advisable
G4	C2	The Wizard of Oz experiment used to prototype the relational agent Guardian through dialogues based on the responses to the common ground construction instrument proved to be efficient. Therefore, relational agent designers should use techniques to build corpora that automatically generate meaningful dialogs
G5	C2	With the corpora formed through the Wizard of Oz experiment sessions, there is material to train mathematical models to generate meaningful dialogues automatically
G6	C3	A second group of users, who satisfy the chatbot's user profile, can be used for summative evaluation (qualitatively and quantitatively). There is also the opportunity to adjust the mathematical model underlying this generation
G7	C4	The dialog generation engine needs to have the speed of response to maintain the fluidity of the conversation. Human-to-human interaction is very sensitive to delays. Any delay from any source will have a very negative impact on the experience and engagement
G8	C9	It is suggested that the chatbot practice active listening to maintain conversation engagement
G9	C5	It is suggested that the relational agent knows how to recognize: his turn in the conversation to not interrupt the user's speech and the environment in which the experiment participant is to avoid communication failures
G10	C5	It is recommended to design the relational agent to inform, either through visual or audible stimuli, the user that the application is receiving or processing their input to avoid communication problems
G11	C5	It is recommended that the communication channels not present noise to be considered appropriate for an engaging conversation
G12	C6	It is suggested to form a multidisciplinary team to collaborate in creating the methodology of elaboration of scripts of dialogue flows and the personality (humanization) of the relational agent
G13	C6	When carrying out the Wizard of Oz experiment, the individual who plays the role of Wizard of Oz is accompanied by another person who can assist him in producing meaningful dialogues in real-time if the prototype application has as purpose the engagement of the experiment participant

(*continued*)

Table 4. (*continued*)

ID	C	Description
G14	C7	It is suggested to consider legal requirements, such as national and international standards, in developing the relational agent aimed at the elderly public
G15	C8	Depending on the subject, it is recommended to have voice user interface engagement features, such as sound effects, reactions, and voice intonation. For example, if the subject is sad, the voice generated must also promote empathy
G16	C8	To facilitate understanding the messages from the relational agent by the elderly, it is advisable to simplify and repeat the dialog flows
G17	C10	The agent must introduce himself to the first dialog. It makes its limitations and qualities clear to the user and, mainly, demonstrates its usefulness in the user's daily life
G18	C11	Strategies should be defined during the design of the relational agent to build trust with the user to ensure their long-term engagement

Above, 18 guidelines were proposed to make the interactions of relational agents successful with older adults who need to be part of a project to develop relational agents aimed at this audience and which, in particular, can serve to increase long-term engagement. However, if these guidelines are followed, they carry the potential to resolve difficulties about the design of relational agents for the elderly in a context favorable to the elderly.

6 Conclusion

As lessons learned for carrying out meaningful conversations with the participants of the experiment, we have the following considerations: being polite all the time; being present in the conversation practicing active listening; let the conversation flow naturally; not paying attention to thoughts unrelated to the discussion that may arise during the conversation; better to err on the side of caution; focus on the experiences of the experiment participant; not delve into the details of the conversation; not comparing experiences, that is, not exposing personal opinions; if a topic is not known, it is possible to research on the internet; not give advice too often to the other person; avoid being repetitive; and be objective.

The creation of the common ground questionnaire, found in Gama, Ferreira, and Oliveira [11], was one of the main contributions of this research since it provided the common ground used during the Wizard of Oz experiment. Moreover, it was observed that it worked very well for the beginning of conversations with the participants during the investigation carried out, which is one of the remarkable findings of this work. Therefore, it is expected that other scholars in relational agents will use this questionnaire.

The common ground emerged as an initial opportunity to generate meaningful dialogues. After this initial generation, the common ground produced by the instrument was dispensed with, as the dialogue itself deepened the common ground. The problem observed in the work Ferreira et al. [10] seems to have been the absence of initial common ground, and, in this regard, the questionnaire developed was handy. First, however, the questionnaire was applied to identify the participant's profile found in Weizenmann [26] in this work.

Using the Wizard of Oz technique, the experiment achieved a satisfactory subjective engagement, based on the content of the recorded conversations, with all seven older adults who participated in the investigation.

Section 5.2, based on the experiment detailed in Sect. 4, provides significant and current insights into developing guidelines around relational agents for older people in context. It provides indicators for activities and actions relevant to different stakeholders, particularly software developers and companies. A fundamental theme that permeates this work is "long-term engagement".

It is believed that the list of guidelines shown in Table 4 can help software developers and companies to anticipate obstacles that can lead to interruptions in the conversation of elderly users due to lack of interest, accessibility, etc. Based on the guidelines formulated in this research, it is expected that the projected relational agent will provide a better conversation experience and that it is configured to anticipate the difficulties pointed out in Sect. 5.1 to be prepared with strategies to recover the user's interest so that it gets back on track for the conversation.

This study presents a framework of guidelines that can immerse the user in a more engaging conversation with a relational voice agent embedded in a smart speaker. It is hoped that the guidelines conceived in this work consider the limitations of the target audience presented in Campbell [6].

All documentation and source code produced in this work was publicly available on the GitHub software repositories platform at the URL https://github.com/thiagoddcqg/guardiaoprojeto.

6.1 Future Works

Part of the assumption of this study is that the intended Guardian application would be more valuable the more isolated the older person was. Still, to reach this conclusion, another study involving demonstrably lonely older adults would have to integrate the sample of individuals, and, preferably, it is expected that this software is implemented.

To alleviate depression and loneliness, it is proposed in the successor implementation work to this study, an application that presents itself as a user's friend. This idealized application will provide the elderly user with means to maintain a long-term engagement with an artificial intelligence programmed to meet the affective demands of someone who needs someone else to listen to their problems and who can influence positive changes in the day to day of its user, according to the information presented in Bickmore, Schulman, and Yin [4].

References

1. Adler, R., Rodman, G.: Comunicação humana. LTC, Rio de Janeiro (2003)

2. Bickmore, T., Caruso, L., Clough-Gorr, K.: Acceptance and usability of a relational agent interface by urban older adults. In: Extended Abstracts on Human Factors in Computing Systems, CHI 2005 (2005)
3. Bickmore, T., Cassell, J.: Social dialongue with embodied conversational agents. In: van Kuppevelt, J.C.J., Dybkjær, L., Bernsen, N.O. (eds.) Advances in Natural Multimodal Dialogue Systems. Text, Speech and Language Technology, vol. 30, pp. 23–54. Springer, Dordrecht (2005). https://doi.org/10.1007/1-4020-3933-6_2
4. Bickmore, T., Schulman, D., Yin, L.: Maintaining engagement in long-term interventions with relational agents. Appl. Artif. Intell. **24**, 648–666 (2010)
5. Bunderson, C.: The validity of the Herrmann Brain dominance instrument. Creat. Brain, 337–379 (1989)
6. Campbell, O.: Designing For The Elderly: Ways Older People Use Digital Technology Differently. https://www.smashingmagazine.com/2015/02/designing-digital-technology-for-the-elderly. Accessed 02 Nov 2021
7. Clark, H., Brennan, S.: Grounding in communication (1991)
8. Clark, H., et al.: What makes a good conversation? Challenges in designing truly conversational agents. In: Proceedings of the 2019 CHI Conference on Human Factors in Computing Systems, pp. 1–12 (2019)
9. Clark, H.: Arenas of language use (1992)
10. Ferreira, A., Oliveira, F., Damasceno, A., Cortés, M.: Conversational agents for the elderly, the guardian platform. In: Anais do XI Computer on the Beach - COTB 2020 (2020)
11. Gama, T., Ferreira, A., Oliveira, F.: Common ground questionnaire (2022). https://drive.goo gle.com/file/d/1PGqqTpQ0a0XBXlqZjhRxaeDIJK2bwJ_X
12. Gama, T., Ferreira, A., Oliveira, F.: Script of the humanized dialogues of the Wizard of Oz experiment (2022). https://drive.google.com/file/d/1zpVlGsWbmqILiDH3XbSFAh3moe YsGqzo
13. Gama, T., Gama, V., Silva, B., Oliveira, F.: Revisão Integrativa da Literatura de Engajamento com Pessoas Idosas Utilizando Agentes Conversacionais. II Congresso Brasileiro Interdisciplinar de Ciência e Tecnologia (2021)
14. Geison, C.: What in the UX is "Wizard of Oz Testing"? AnswerLab. https://www.answerlab. com/insights/wizard-of-oz-testing. Accessed 23 Feb 2020
15. Gilmartin, E., et al.: Social talk: making conversation with people and machine. In: Proceedings of the 1st ACM SIGCHI International Workshop on Investigating Social Interactions with Artificial Agents, pp. 31–32 (2017)
16. Kelly, S.: Growing up with Alexa: A child's relationship with Amazon's voice assistant. https://edition.cnn.com/2018/10/16/tech/alexa-child-development/index.html. Accessed 8 Sept 2021
17. Marques, J.: Análise de comportamento – teste de perfil comportamental. https://www. ibccoaching.com.br/portal/comportamento/analise-comportamento-teste-perfil-comportam ental/. Accessed 19 Jan 2022
18. Marston, W.: Emotions of normal people. Kegan Paul, Trench, Trubner & Co. Ltd., Londres (1928)
19. Moore, R.K.: Is spoken language all-or-nothing? Implications for future speech-based human-machine interaction. In: Jokinen, K., Wilcock, G. (eds.) Dialogues with Social Robots. LNEE, vol. 427, pp. 281–291. Springer, Singapore (2017). https://doi.org/10.1007/978-981-10-2585-3_22
20. National Institute on Aging: Social isolation, loneliness in older people pose health risks. Natl Inst Aging (2019)
21. Nielsen, J.: Usability inspection methods. In: Conference Companion on Human Factors in Computing Systems - CHI 1994 (1994)

22. Riker, R.: How to Connect with People Easily and Improve any Relationship. https://www.thesocialwinner.com/how-to-connect-with-people/. Accessed 20 June 2021
23. Sabelli, A., Kanda, T., Hagita, N.: A conversational robot in an elderly care center: an ethnographic study. In: 2011 6th ACM/IEEE International Conference on Human-Robot Interaction, pp. 37–44 (2011)
24. Spillane, B., et al.: Introducing adele: a personalized intelligent companion. In: 1st ACM SIGCHI International Workshop on Investigating Social Interactions with Artificial Agents, pp. 43–44 (2017)
25. Tapus, A., Maja, M., Scassellatti, B.: The grand challenges in socially assistive robotics. IEEE Robot. Autom. Mag. (2007)
26. Weizenmann, S.: Avaliação de instrumentos e métodos de análise de perfil profissional em estudantes de um centro universitário (2017)

Automatic Life Event Tree Generation for Older Adults

Fang Gui[1,2,3], Xi Wu[1,2,3], Min Hu[1,4,5], and Jiaoyun Yang[1,2,3(✉)]

[1] School of Computer Science and Information Engineering,
Hefei University of Technology, Hefei, China
jiaoyun@hfut.edu.cn
[2] Key Laboratory of Knowledge Engineering with Big Data of Ministry of Education,
Hefei University of Technology, Hefei, China
[3] National Smart Eldercare International S&T Cooperation Base,
Hefei University of Technology, Hefei, China
[4] Laboratory of Affective Computing and Advanced Intelligent Machine,
Hefei University of Technology, Hefei, China
[5] Intelligent Interconnected Systems Laboratory of Anhui Province,
Hefei University of Technology, Hefei, China

Abstract. Studies have shown that learning personal stories could help provide individualized eldercare services. However, personal stories are often disordered because of the scattered collection, including informal interviews or daily interactions, which brings difficulties in acquiring valuable information quickly. One solution to this problem is to extract events from personal stories and automatically organize them in chronological order. Events extracted by current methods from social media or news corpus are mainly organized in a linear structure. These works usually focus on the event time and ignore the consistency of event contents when organizing events. This paper aims to organize events into a tree structure based on an event network, with stem nodes representing key event topics and branch nodes representing detailed events. Social workers or caregivers can clarify the life experience of the older adults quickly through the event tree and have a preliminary understanding of them. The experiments show that the event tree generated by our method has a better performance in consistency than current event organization methods. A survey study shows that our method achieves the highest logical coherence for the event tree branches compared with other algorithms.

Keyword: Personal stories · Eldercare · Event tree

1 Introduction

Some medical workers or caregivers have used personal life story work as an intervention for older adults in nursing homes and older adults who have a cognitive disorder [18]. Learning these life stories can improve family caregivers' insight and judgment of the needs and demands of older adults [17]. It is a basis for individualized care, assists in

V. G. Duffy et al. (Eds.): HCII 2022, LNCS 13521, pp. 366–377, 2022.
https://doi.org/10.1007/978-3-031-17902-0_26

transitions between different care environments, and helps to develop improved relationships between older adults and family caregivers [24]. Besides, older adults can learn about who they are and make meaningful connections with society [23].

Life stories create an opportunity for older adults to tell others about their past experiences and then use these life stories to benefit them in their present situation [12, 18, 19]. They usually tell their life stories in informal interviews or daily communication. Such interactions with older adults are generally short and frequent, resulting in scattered fragments. Besides, older adults just talk about what comes into their minds for each interaction, resulting in disordered and redundant personal life stories. It can be a daunting task for caregivers to manually organize these life stories chronologically. What's more, it's hard to unearth helpful information for eldercare from these redundant and random life stories.

Using artificial intelligence to automatically extract key information from these stories and reorganize them can be an effective way to solve this problem [1]. Therefore, this paper proposes an automatic event tree generation framework, which organizes the events of an older adult into a tree structure to show the logical relationship between events. It can help caregivers quickly clarify the life experience of older adults and get a basic perception of them.

Motivating Example. Figure 1 illustrates an event tree generated by our method to show the story of Wu. $T_1 \cdots T_5$ are stem nodes representing event topics in the event tree. The edges connecting T_1 node to T_5 node forms the trunk of the event tree, which denotes the core experience in Wu's life. $E_1 \cdots E_{12}$ are branch nodes representing the detailed events under different event topics. Each branch denotes the evolution of events under a certain topic. For example, the T_1 stem node represents Wu's education experience. Path $E_1 \rightarrow E_2$ describes Wu's different events during his primary and secondary school, which are chronologically arranged. We can quickly sort out Wu's personal life stories from the event tree. Before generating the tree, these events $E_1 \cdots E_{12}$ are scattered across different documents. It is no doubt that modeling the evolutionary connections

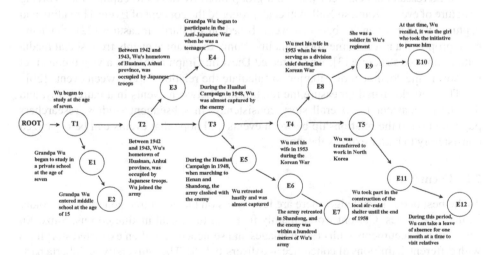

Fig. 1. An event tree example to show the story of Mr. Wu

between events into an event tree structure can help people learn the primary information quickly.

Some attempts have been tried to extract events and organize them in timeline structures or graph structures by linking events with their timestamps [21] or connections [20]. These works focus on measuring and modeling the relationship between events in pairs. However, they ignore the consistency of the whole story. Most biographical events do not follow a simple storyline. Compared with other structures, the tree structure is a more effective way to represent biographical events [12]. At present, the tree structure is mainly used in breaking news corpus to organize events, and few works focus on generating event trees for older adults' personal life stories. Against this backdrop, this paper proposes an automatic event tree generation method based on an event network – EventNET for older adults' personal life stories. The experimental results demonstrate the EventNET method can organize personal life stories into a logical tree structure with better event consistency compared with other methods. These event trees generated by our approach can help caregivers have a preliminary understanding of older adults and provide personalized services.

2   Related Work

2.1   Event Organization

Current event organization work mostly focuses on social media corpus. Chen Lin et al. generated event storylines from microblogs [11]. It is a pioneer work in developing storylines from social media. Jiwei Li et al. studied the problem of reconstructing users' life history based on their Twitter stream and proposed an unsupervised framework that creates a chronological list of individuals' important events (PIE) [10]. The disadvantage is that when users frequently post content about a specific keyword, the algorithm will identify such events as public events and ignore them.

Some researchers extract events and group them by topics to capture the evolving structure of events. Ramesh Nallapati et al. proposed the concept of Event Threading and captured the dependencies between events based on similarity measures [22]. Yi Chang et al. proposed a novel framework Timeline-Sumy to organize events from social media with a timeline structure [3]. And Directed Dicyclic Graph (DAG) is a visual construct by scoring the document distribution to calculate the relationship between events [26].

These works usually measure the relationship between events in a paired way, and they don't consider the overall story consistency. In subsequent studies, researchers pay attention to the relationship between events and hope that events can be organized consistently to better express the story.

2.2   Event Tree

To the best of our knowledge, there are few works on the event tree generation for older adults' life stories. Current works mainly focus on the social medial corpus. Shize Xu summarized documents with crucial images and sentences and then extracted storylines with different definitions of coherence and diversity [25]. The University of Alberta partnered with the Tencent platform, clustered documents with a 2-layer clustering approach based on both keyword graphs and document graphs, and then organized the events in the document as an event tree [15]. Directed edges in the tree indicate a temporal evolution or a logical connection of events. The tree structure can show the development of topics and perform the evolution of events under each topic through the tree's branches. Simon Gottschalk et al. presented a multilingual event-centric temporal knowledge graph – EventKG and verified its effectiveness in generating a biographical timeline [7]. This paper automatically organizes the older adults' personal stories to create an event tree based on an event network, which is a variant of the event logic graph and is essential for building event trees. Liu Ting first proposed the event logic graph [6]. The event logic graph is a theory logic knowledge base with events as nodes and relationships between events as edges. The event network can better describe the relationship between events based on event elements and event texts.

3   Method

This section describes the overall framework of the method. Figure 2 shows the method flow chart.

- Extract events: We improve the open domain event extraction method ODEE to fulfill the event extraction task [16].
- Build an event network: Calculate the similarity between events. Build an event network based on event relationships.
- Cluster the events: Cluster the events with a strong relationship in the event network.
- Generate the event tree: Topics and topic paths generate the trunk of the event tree. Events and event paths create branches of the event tree.

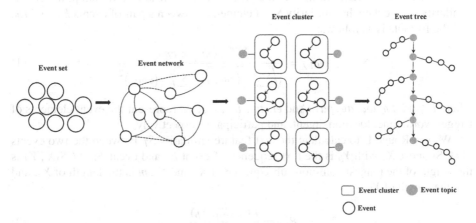

Fig. 2. Framework for the event tree generation

3.1 Event Extraction

We have improved the open domain event extraction method ODEE proposed by Xiao Liu et al. to fulfill the event extraction task. ODEE is an event extraction method suitable for extracting unconstrained type events [16]. The key to event extraction is event detection, which defines a template for matching events. First, we use LTP [4] to extract verbs and gerunds from 15% of the samples as trigger words and manually correct the extracted trigger words. Then we manually classify the events to form the initial seed template types and calculate the similarity of all samples of the initial seed templates according to semantic similarity. Events with high similarity to the seed template will be added to the same template.

The elements of an event may exist in different documents, resulting in numerous referential expressions for the same event element. Therefore, coreference resolution of entities is required. We mainly deal with the named entity types of name elements and location elements. When processing the words, referential terms have the lowest priority, and the non-referential words with higher accuracy have higher priority to be recognized as named entities. Then, we adopt the principle of the statistical majority to replace other entities with the entity with the highest occurrence frequency to achieve the coreference resolution of entities [9].

3.2 Building an Event Network

The event network represents the relationships between event entities, including event entities and edges connecting event entities. The process of building the event network is as follows:

Firstly, the representation of event entity features is the basis of building the event network. We express each event entity feature as a binary vector $E = (em, et)$. et is the sequence of event elements. E_T is the event text. Then, we calculate the correlation according to the similarity of the event elements and text features. We adopt the cosine similarity to calculate the similarity S_E of elements between a pair of events E_a and E_b, and the formula is as follows:

$$S(em_a, em_b) = \frac{\sum_{i=1}^{n} em_{a_i} \times em_{b_i}}{\sqrt{\sum_{i=1}^{n} (em_{a_i})^2} \sqrt{\sum_{i=1}^{n} (em_{b_i})^2}} \tag{1}$$

where $i \in \{ei, tm, loc, ag, pa\}$. And ei, tm, loc, ag, pa represent the event elements of trigger word, time, location, agent, and participant, respectively.

We use Rouge-L to calculate the text feature similarity S_T between the two events [14]. Suppose X_a with Y_b is the text sequence of event E_a and event E_b. $LCS(X, Y)$ is the length of the longest common subsequence of X_a and Y_b. m is the length of X_a, and n is the length of Y_b.

$$R_{lcs} = \frac{LCS(X_a, Y_b)}{m} \tag{2}$$

$$P_{lcs} = \frac{LCS(X_a, Y_b)}{n} \tag{3}$$

$$S_T = \frac{(1 + \beta^2) R_{lcs} P_{lcs}}{R_{lcs} + \beta^2 P_{lcs}} \tag{4}$$

Finally, the correlation φ_E of a pair of events can be calculated by using the Euclidean distance of the weighted coefficient as follows:

$$\varphi_E = \sqrt{\omega_1 S_E{}^2 + \omega_2 S_T{}^2} \qquad (5)$$

Judge the relationship between events according to φ_E. After an experimental comparison of combinations of different thresholds, we set event relationship thresholds (0.11, 0.63, 0.88) and divide the relationship between events into congruent, strong, weak, and uncorrelation. If the relationship between the events is higher than 0.88, merge the two events into one event in the event network. If the relationship between events is between 0.63 and 0.88, establish a strong correlation between the two events in the event network. If the relationship between events is between 0.11 and 0.63, establish a weak correlation between the two events. If the relationship between events is lower than 0.11, we do not specify a correlation between the two events.

Event fusion is an indispensable step in constructing an event network. There may be many redundant events due to the diversity of data sources and the richness of language expression. Therefore, event fusion is needed to remove redundancy to improve data quality and application value. In the event network, we combine the elements of the two events if they are a strong correlation.

We approach conflict resolution based on majority-rule voting or the credibility of the data source. The data sources in this paper are actual data from interviews with older adults. To ignore the credibility of data sources, we only calculate the credibility of event elements and select those with high credibility as the final event elements. In general, the more times the event elements of the same event appear, the greater the credibility. Therefore, the voting mechanism of the minority subordinate to the majority is adopted. When the element's granularity of the same element is different, the higher the granularity of the event element, the higher the credibility of the event element.

3.3 Event Tree Construction

We construct the event tree based on the event network, which is mainly divided into five steps:

Event Clustering. In the event network, we set a topic threshold. When the similarity between events exceeds the topic threshold, we consider events to describe the same topic and cluster these events into one event cluster. To detect the event cluster, we utilize the betweenness centrality score of edges to measure the strength of each edge in the event cluster. An edge's betweenness score is the number of shortest paths between all pairs of nodes that pass through it [13]. An edge between two events is expected to achieve a high betweenness score. The iterative splitting process will stop until the number of nodes in each subcluster is smaller than a predefined threshold of 0.5, or the maximum betweenness score of all edges in the subcluster is smaller than a threshold that depends on the subcluster's size.

Event Rearrangement. The event rearrangement in the event topic needs to consider three factors, which are the event time t_E, the location pi_E of the event in the original text and the correlation φ_E between the events.

Assume that an event node N_{E_i} is given, find the next node $N_{E_{i+1}}$ from the remaining nodes whose event node is closest to the connection of the node N_{E_i}. The event correlation function is as follows:

$$EventRelationship(N_{E_a}, N_{E_b}) = Time(t_{E_a}, t_{E_b}) \times Position(pi_{E_a}, pi_{E_b}) \times \varphi_E(N_{E_a}, N_{E_b})$$

(6)

$Time(t_{E_a}, t_{E_b})$ is used to calculate the timestamp gap between the two events. We convert t_{E_a} to the Epoch Timestamp of the system and then calculate it, as shown below:

$$Time(t_{E_a}, t_{E_b}) = \begin{cases} e^{Timestamp(t_{E_a}) - Timestamp(t_{E_b})} & t_{E_a} < t_{E_b} \\ 0 & otherwise \end{cases}$$

(7)

If the timestamp t_{E_b} is less than the timestamp t_{E_a}, then N_{E_b} should be sorted after N_{E_a} in time, and return the time difference between the them, otherwise, N_{E_b} should not be sorted after N_{E_a}, and return 0.

$Position(pi_{E_a}, pi_{E_b})$ is used to calculate the difference between the positions of two events in the original document. This function returns a valid value only if both events are in the same document.

$$Position(pi_{E_a}, pi_{E_b}) = \begin{cases} e^{pi_{E_a} - pi_{E_b}} & pi_{E_a} < pi_{E_b} \\ 0 & otherwise \end{cases}$$

(8)

If pi_{E_a} is less than pi_{E_b} and both are in the same document, then E_b should be sorted after E_a in the text position, and return the location difference between the them, otherwise E_b should not be sorted after E_a, and return 0.

When sorting the events in one topic, the first step is to find the first event node from the event cluster. We assume that the earliest event of the time element is the first event node under the topic. The earliest event of the time element is the first event node under the topic. Next, we extend the branch of the event topic. The last event node of the current branch is N_{E_i}. Calculate $EventRelationship(N_{E_i}, N_{E_j})$ in the alternate events in turn. When $EventRelationship(N_{E_i}, N_{E_j})$ is the largest, N_{E_j} is the next event node $N_{E_{i+1}}$ of the event node N_{E_i}. This loop continues until the alternate events of the event topic are empty. You can see the detail in the text pseudo-code. All the directed edges from one event node to another are the event paths.

Topic Summarization Extraction. In our previous research on generation timelines based on life stories, we proposed an effective method to extract summaries from life stories -- the ALBERT Based Text Extraction Network (ABTE-NET). We adopt the ABTE-NET method to extract the summary and show it on the event node [1].

Topic Rearrangement. We arrange the topic summarizations in the event tree according to the time element order of the first event in the topic. The topic path is all the directed edges from one topic node to another.

Event Tree Construction: Topics and topic paths generate the trunk of the event tree. Events and event paths create branches of the event tree.

ALGORITHM 1: Event node sorting algorithm (Sort)

Input: A collection of event nodes: $G = \{E_i\}$
Output: The sorted collection of event nodes $G_s = \{E_{s_i}\}$
$t_{N_0} \leftarrow$ Node with a timestamp of 0
$L \leftarrow$ NIL
while not reach the end of G do
    $M \leftarrow$ NIL
    $i \leftarrow$ Index of event
    if $\text{TimeDiff}(t_{N_0}, E_i) < \text{TimeDiff}(t_{N_0}, L)$ then
        $L \leftarrow E_i$
    end if
end While
while $G \neq \emptyset$ do
    $M \leftarrow$ NIL
    while not reach the end of G do
        $i \leftarrow$ Index of event
        if $\text{EventRelationship}(L, E_i) < \text{EventRelationship}(L, M)$ then
            $M \leftarrow E_i$
        end if
    end while
    $L \leftarrow M$
    $G \leftarrow \{E_i | E_i \neq M\}$
    $G_s \leftarrow G_s + M$
end while

3.4 Baseline

Story Forest [12]: Story Forest is a collection of online schemes that automatically group streaming documents into events and connect them in growing trees to produce developing stories.

EventKG [8]: EventKG is a multilingual event-centric temporal knowledge graph and demonstrates the effectiveness of the biographical timeline generation based on the EventKG.

LDA + Temporal Ordering (LDA+ TO) [5]: We build an LDA topic model over the datasets and temporally order the events into a timeline chain as a baseline model. This method exemplifies the naive approach to solving the timeline structure summarization problem.

3.5 Evaluation

We evaluate the coherence between event nodes in the same event topic. We evaluate the consistency of the events by calculating the coherent score of events. The coherent score of the event topic is the average similarity of all events in the event topic according to the topic path [2]. σ_i represents the event node.

$$CS(\sigma_1, \sigma_2, \ldots, \sigma_k) = \frac{1}{|k-1|} \sum_{i=1}^{|k-1|} Sim(\sigma_i, \sigma_{i+1}) \qquad (9)$$

As can be seen from Table 1, the coherent score of EventNET is 32.32%, 19.81%, and 10.28% higher than that of the baseline method LDA + Temporal Ordering, Story Forest, and EventKG, respectively. This shows that EventNET performs well on the coherence between event nodes from the Older Adults' Life Stories dataset. This is because the core idea of the Coherent Score is to calculate the average similarity between all the elements of two events. EventNET focuses on improving the accuracy of event similarity calculation through features, including word vector features of texts, lexical features, grammatical features and semantic features of event elements, etc. The algorithm combines the time and location of the event in the original document and the correlation strength of the events to determine the location of the event node in the event topic branch. This approach rationalizes the event nodes and makes the event tree structure coherent.

Table 1. The coherent score evaluates the event tree structure

Method	Coherent score
LDA+ TO	42.13%
Story Forest	54.64%
EventKG	64.17%
EventNET	74.45%

In addition to the above experiments, we do a human evaluation to measure the quality assessment of the event tree. We invite 12 graduate students from the Gerontechnology Lab of the Hefei University of Technology to participate in the survey to evaluate the event tree quality. All 12 participants have participated in projects related to eldercare. We use LDA+ TO, Story Forest, EventKG, and EventNET to organize older adults' life stories and create four kinds of event trees. In this study, participants need to evaluate four different event trees of 16 older adults.

We designed the following questionnaire based on the questions posed by Bang Liu et al. in their study to evaluate event trees [15]. We compare the output story structures given by different algorithms on the logical coherence of paths and the overall understandability of different story structures. Participants evaluate the quality of the event tree with the following two questions.

Question 1: Do you agree that the paths are logically coherent for each event tree structure given by different algorithms? Based on a seven-point Likert scale, we set 1 to strongly disagree, 2 to disagree, 3 to partially disagree, 4 to not sure, 5 to partially agree, 6 to agree, and 7 to strongly agree.

Question 2: For each event tree structure given by different algorithms, do you agree that the event tree can help you quickly develop a preliminary understanding of older adults? Based on a seven-point Likert scale, we set 1 to strongly disagree, 2 to disagree,

3 to partially disagree, 4 to not sure, 5 to partially agree, 6 to agree, and 7 to strongly agree.

For path coherence, Table 2 shows the proportion that holds the same attitude regarding whether each path is logically coherent under different algorithms. EventNET gives significantly more coherent paths: the average path consistency score is 5.17 for the EventNET and is 0.39, 1.48, and 0.79, respectively, better than LDA+ Temporal Ordering, Story Forest, and EventKG. In addition, the path of the event trees generated by the EventNET method has the lowest standard deviation score for logical coherence. This result shows that the logical consistency of the event trees generated by the EventNET is more stable.

Table 2. Percentage of the path consistency score

Method	1 (%)	2 (%)	3 (%)	4 (%)	5 (%)	6 (%)	7 (%)	M	SD
LDA+ TO	0.76	5.99	10.61	18.46	32.51	24.79	6.89	4.78	1.32
Story Forest	8.57	8.73	7.35	62.76	7.23	4.34	1.03	3.68	1.20
EventKG	2.04	4.34	6.35	51.24	17.43	14.29	4.31	4.38	1.19
EventNET	0.12	0.71	4.27	30.73	18.88	31.87	13.43	5.17	1.18

Table 3 shows the overall understandability of different story structures. The evaluators can better understand the older adults through the event tree generated by EventNET. The LDA+ Temporal Ordering has an average score of 4.66 and a standard deviation of 1.17. The Story Forest has an average score of 4.36 and a standard deviation of 1.16. The EventKG has an average score of 3.17 and a standard deviation of 1.55. EventNET has an average score of 5.50 and a standard deviation of 1.06. The results show that EventNET performs the best in mean and standard deviation.

Table 3. Percentage of the event tree comprehension score

Method	1 (%)	2 (%)	3 (%)	4 (%)	5 (%)	6 (%)	7 (%)	M	SD
LDA+ TO	1.56	6.77	11.98	27.08	39.06	13.02	0.52	4.66	1.17
Story Forest	17.19	20.83	18.23	25.52	9.38	7.29	1.56	4.36	1.16
EventKG	0.52	2.60	12.50	28.65	30.73	20.83	4.17	3.17	1.55
EventNET	0.00	1.04	2.60	10.94	34.90	31.77	18.75	5.50	1.06

4 Discussion

"Life story" is a way to review an older adult's life events by working with them or their families. The stories are recorded and used to help care for them. We explore the importance of the personal life stories of old adults for eldercare services. However, personal life stories are often disorganized and influenced by scattered interactions. Therefore, automatically organize personal life stories to generate event trees is an effective way to reduce the work pressure of caregivers. And event trees can help caregivers better understand the older adults. This study automatically organizes the older adults' personal stories to generate an event tree based on the event network. Experiments show that EventNET has a good performance.

The life event trees solve the disorganization of life stories, reducing the cognitive load and helping caregivers form a preliminary understanding of the older adult quickly. Besides, as the event tree is a kind of formatted text, it is easy for computers to process. In the future, we will develop smart eldercare application by using the event trees of older adults' life stories to analyze the older adults' needs, developing socially assistive robots for older adults, and recommending personalized eldercare services.

5 Limitations

Understanding is a big term and fully understanding an older adult is a daunting challenge. Life event trees which simplify older adults' life stories, may hinder some detailed information that can be learned about older adults, leading to confirmation bias. While this is one limitation of life event trees, they can still give caregivers and older adults a good start and help caregivers establish a more positive relationship with older adults. And as the number of old adults' life stories increases, the hiding of such information will gradually decrease.

Acknowledgment. This work was partially supported by the National Natural Science Foundation of China (No. 62072153), the Anhui Provincial Key Technologies R&D Program (2022h11020015), the Program of Introducing Talents of Discipline to Universities (111 Program) (B14025).

References

1. An, N., Gui, F., Jin, L.Q., Ming, H., Yang, J.Y.: Towards better understanding older adults: a biography brief timeline extraction approach. Int. J. Hum. Comput. Interact. (in Press)
2. Ansah, J., Liu, L., Kang, W., Kwashie, S., Li, J., Li, J.: A graph is worth a thousand words: telling event stories using timeline summarization graphs. In: The World Wide Web Conference, pp. 2565–2571 (2019)
3. Chang, Y., Tang, J., Yin, D., Yamada, M., Liu, Y.: Timeline summarization from social media with life cycle models. In: IJCAI, pp. 3698–3704 (2016)
4. Che, W., Feng, Y., Qin, L., Liu, T.: N-LTP: a open-source neural chinese language technology platform with pretrained models. arXiv preprint arXiv:2009.11616 (2020)
5. Chen, L.C.: An effective lda-based time topic model to improve blog search performance. Inf. Process. Manag. **53**(6), 1299–1319 (2017)
6. Ding, X., Li, Z., Liu, T., Liao, K.: Elg: an event logic graph. arXiv preprint arXiv:1907.08015 (2019)
7. Gottschalk, S., Demidova, E.: EventKG: a multilingual event-centric temporal knowledge graph. In: Gangemi, A., et al. (eds.) ESWC 2018. LNCS, vol. 10843, pp. 272–287. Springer, Cham (2018). https://doi.org/10.1007/978-3-319-93417-4_18

8. Gottschalk, S., Demidova, E.: EventKG+TL: creating cross-lingual timelines from an event-centric knowledge graph. In: Gangemi, A. et al. (eds.) ESWC 2018. LNCS, vol. 11155, pp. 164–169. Springer, Cham (2018). https://doi.org/10.1007/978-3-319-98192-5_31

9. Kantor, B., Globerson, A.: Coreference resolution with entity equalization. In: Proceedings of the 57th Annual Meeting of the Association for Computational Linguistics, pp. 673–677 (2019)

10. Li, J., Cardie, C.: Timeline generation: tracking individuals on Twitter. In: Proceedings of the 23rd International Conference on World Wide Web, pp. 643–652 (2014)

11. Lin, C., Lin, C., Li, J., Wang, D., Chen, Y., Li, T.: Generating event storylines from microblogs. In: Proceedings of the 21st ACM International Conference on Information and Knowledge Management, pp. 175–184 (2012)

12. Little, B.: Forgotten lives: exploring the history of learning disability (1998)

13. Liu, B., Han, F.X., Niu, D., Kong, L., Lai, K., Xu, Y.: Story forest: extracting events and telling stories from breaking news. ACM Trans. Knowl. Discov. Data (TKDD) 14(3), 1–28 (2020)

14. Lin, C.Y.: ROUGE: a package for automatic evaluation of summaries. In: Text Summarization Branches Out, pp. 74–81 (2004)

15. Liu, B., Niu, D., Lai, K., Kong, L., Xu, Y.: Growing story forest online from massive breaking news. In: Proceedings of the 2017 ACM on Conference on Information and Knowledge Management, pp. 777–785 (2017)

16. Liu, X., Huang, H., Zhang, Y.: Open domain event extraction using neural latent variable models. arXiv preprint arXiv:1906.06947 (2019)

17. Lun, M.W.A.: The effectiveness of a life story program on stress reduction among chinese american family caregivers of older adults. Educ. Gerontol. 45(5), 334–340 (2019)

18. McKeown, J., Clarke, A., Ingleton, C., Ryan, T., Repper, J.: The use of life story work with people with dementia to enhance person-centred care. Int. J. Older People Nurs. 5(2), 148–158 (2010)

19. McKeown, J., Clarke, A., Repper, J.: Life story work in health and social care: systematic literature review. J. Adv. Nurs. 55(2), 237–247 (2006)

20. Mei, Q., Zhai, C.: Discovering evolutionary theme patterns from text: an exploration of temporal text mining. In: Proceedings of the Eleventh ACM SIGKDD International Conference on Knowledge Discovery in Data Mining, pp. 198–207 (2005)

21. Minard, A.L.M., et al.: Semeval-2015 task 4: timeline: cross-document event ordering. In: 9th International Workshop on Semantic Evaluation (SemEval 2015), pp. 778–786 (2015)

22. Nallapati, R., Feng, A., Peng, F., Allan, J.: Event threading within news topics. In: Proceedings of the Thirteenth ACM International Conference on Information and Knowledge Management, pp. 446–453 (2004)

23. Phoenix, C., Sparkes, A.C.: Being fred: Big stories, small stories and the accomplishment of a positive ageing identity. Qual. Res. 9(2), 219–236 (2009)

24. Webster, J.D., Bohlmeijer, E.T., Westerhof, G.J.: Mapping the future of reminiscence: a conceptual guide for research and practice. Res. Aging 32(4), 527–564 (2010)

25. Xu, S., Wang, S., Zhang, Y.: Summarizing complex events: a cross-modal solution of storylines extraction and reconstruction. In: Proceedings of the 2013 Conference on Empirical Methods in Natural Language Processing, pp. 1281–1291 (2013)

26. Yang, C.C., Shi, X., Wei, C.P.: Discovering event evolution graphs from news corpora. IEEE Trans. Syst. Man Cybern. Part A Syst. Hum. 39(4), 850–863 (2009)

Eliciting and Prioritizing Services
for Accessible Information
For Residential Real Estate Transactions

Jo E. Hannay[2]([✉]) [ID], Kristin S. Fuglerud[1] [ID], and Bjarte M. Østvold[1] [ID]

[1] Norwegian Computing Center, Pb. 114 Blindern, 0314 Oslo, Norway
`{kristin.skeide.fuglerud,bjarte}@nr.no`
[2] Center for Effective Digitalization of the Public Sector, Simula Metropolitan,
Pb. 4 St. Olavs Plass, 0130 Oslo, Norway
`johannay@simula.no`

Abstract. A number of initiatives are underway for digitalizing real estate transaction processes. Public and private sector bodies are working to automate information retrieval and processing of the financial, ordinance and fiscal aspects of such transactions. Other initiatives, such as ours, are targeted toward helping stakeholders directly involved in selling and buying real estate. We present the results from a set of group sessions, where the focus was on improving the presentation of salient information to sellers and buyers of property. Based on an earlier conceptualization of perceived information difficulties, we elicited user stories for facilitating a better generation, provision and consumption of relevant information for the residential real estate transaction process. A total of ten services were aggregated from the user stories. We then asked a set of stakeholders to rate the effect of the services on functional objectives; i.e., on how they will affect the transaction process. We asked stakeholders at the managerial level to rate the functional objectives on strategic objectives. Combining the two sets of ratings, one obtains a rating of perceived benefit for the services, which can help in prioritizing which services to start developing first. In the outset, real estate transactions involve stakeholders with opposing interests. We conclude that multi-stakeholder group sessions can help generate services that serve these conflicting interests on a common ground.

Keywords: Real estate transactions · Technical conditions information · Service design · Stakeholder journey · Benefit estimation

1 Introduction

In the wake of the rush for digitalization, where information is becoming ever more available, one is left with several challenges [16,17,25–27]. Two such challenges have received particular attention: information protection as expressed through legislation such as the General Data Protection Regulation (GDPR),[1]

---

[1] https://gdpr.eu/.

© Springer Nature Switzerland AG 2022
V. G. Duffy et al. (Eds.): HCII 2022, LNCS 13521, pp. 378–395, 2022.
https://doi.org/10.1007/978-3-031-17902-0_27

and information accessibility as expressed in, e.g., the Web Content Accessibility Guidelines (WCAG).[2] These two important issues pertain to getting information out to everyone in a secure manner. Upon these basic features, however, other complex issues arise. Processes in the public space increasingly utilize and rely on the availability of information [17], and obligations are put on the public to provide, compile and consume information from several sources to make, and act upon, informed decisions [13,14,17,18].

We study the increased demands for human information processing in residential real estate transactions. National legislation holds the property seller and buyer – both of which are usually lay persons – responsible according to the relevant information before the fact, with less opportunity to claim ignorance, or to claim on additional information, after the fact. This places added strain on stakeholders in an already stressful situation that involves a large private investment under an often undue time pressure. Our investigation concerns digital services to help stakeholders with their information processing in residential real estate transactions.

The process of selling and buying real estate is complex and involves information from several sources that may not be coordinated. It can be severely challenging for the stakeholders involved to retrieve and distil the information that is most relevant. Sellers must use this information to make decisions on when to sell, at what asking price and on what to fix in the case there are faults on the property. Buyers must choose between properties on offer, make decisions on how much to bid and have situational awareness on any refurbishments that may be needed. Decisions made must be sustainable in the sense that they are perceived to be valid by all parties after the transaction is completed so as to avoid conflicts and claims in the aftermath.

Responsibilities for the technical condition of a property under sale are becoming clearer cut, with less opportunity to sell real estate *as is*. Examples are the move in the U.K. from *caveat emptor* – where that the seller is not legally required to disclose known or unknown defects, and it is up to the buyer to investigate – to including real estate transactions under the Consumer Protection Against Unfair Trading Regulations[3] and the much stricter information requirements imposed on both the seller and buyer in recent Norwegian legislation.[4] Sellers have a greater obligation to document flaws and adhere to building regulations, and buyers are required to see to it that they are informed. On both sides, there are waning possibilities to claim ignorance. Various innovative digital solutions are being developed to meet the needs for heightened awareness of the attributes of real estate. Examples are Opendoor in the US and Solgt.no in Norway which both operate in the iBuying segment, where the idea is to facilitate home buying directly from sellers without involving a real estate agent.It is important that solutions address the actual needs of stakeholders and that the solutions are accessible to all parts of the public. While it may appear that

---

[2] https://www.w3.org/WAI/standards-guidelines/wcag/.

[3] https://www.legislation.gov.uk/uksi/2008/1277/contents/made.

[4] https://lovdata.no/dokument/LTI/forskrift/2021-06-08-1850.

successful innovation happens by unintended fluke, data suggests that this is only the case for an exceptional minority,[5] while the vast majority of innovations would benefit from analyses of stakeholder needs. For the presentation of real estate information that may have implications, both legal and otherwise, for those who give and posses this information, the development of information services has to be deliberate.

2   Background

To facilitate the deliberate design of information services, we suggested a stakeholder journey framework for innovations [11] based on Halvorsrud et al. [7]. In an earlier study, we used the framework to elicit a high-level journey with possible technology touch points in a real estate transaction process (Fig. 1).

As seen in the figure, the analysis was conducted for five groups of stakeholders, from bottom to top: the residential real estate buyer, the estate agent, the seller, the technical condition assessor and the insurance company providing latent defects cover, an insurance policy that protects the seller against claims from the buyer after the real estate transaction has taken place. Following [7], orange touchpoints are initiated by a service consumer, while blue touchpoints are initiated by a service provider. Solid arrows indicate state sharing between touchpoints. Dark-green touchpoints are adoption points for *innovators*, and light-green touchpoints are adoption points for *early adopters* [21]. Dashed arrows indicate adoption transfers from innovators to early adopters. Touchpoints with the gears symbol signify the type of services relevant to our discussion; namely, those to be provided by a company offering property transaction services. Touchpoints with text indicate existing services widely in use today. The white index cards indicate user stories describing how a particular stakeholder uses a service at a touchpoint.

In Fig. 1, the only touchpoint for the assessor is the technical condition report. The technical condition report is a central document in the Norwegian real estate transaction protocol. It is written by a certified assessor before a home is put on the market. The assessor surveys the home and writes an assessment of the technical condition in a semi-structured format, based on a standard [23]. For each part of the building, the report contains the following: a technical condition grade (TG) being an ordinal scale ranging from TG0 (best) to TG3 (worst) or exceptionally TGIU (not investigated). A TG0 signifies pristine conditions for a building part not more than 5 years old, while a TG1 signifies an intact building part older than 5 years. A TG2 should be given when there is an observable flaw, or likely grounds (e.g., age or unfortunate circumstances) for expecting a flaw if not observable, that needs attention in due course, while a TG3 signifies an acute need for attention to a flaw. In the case of TG2 and TG3, a textual explanation of probable cause and necessary measures to attend to the flaw is expected. In practice, reports may contain technical terms that buyers and sellers have problems understanding. Also, the actual building parts that appear in reports

---

[5] https://www.cbinsights.com/research/venture-capital-funnel-2/.

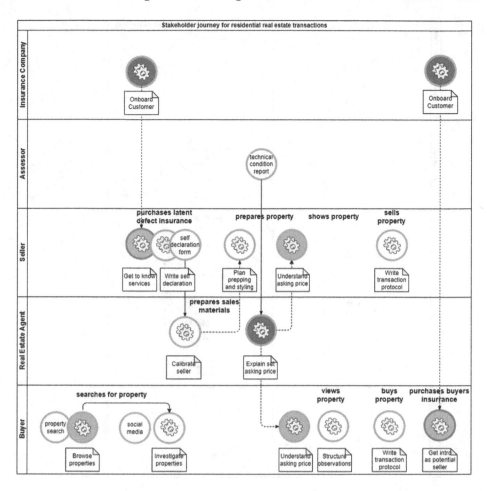

Fig. 1. Planned stakeholder journey, adapted from [11].

and the organization of reports vary and are, to some degree, at the discretion of the assessor.

The technical conditions report is shown as a touchpoint, because real estate assessors use digital editing tools to generate technical condition reports. The analysis so far only considers the technical condition report as an information source to the touchpoint in the Estate Agent swim lane with the user story "Explain set asking price", which reads as follows:

> Explain set asking price: As an estate agent, I can get a seller to understand the rationale for my suggestion for asking price by using a service to show the technical condition of the property.

That touchpoint indicates a desire to make it easier for non-experts to grasp the technical condition of a residential property, and also to make it easier to compare

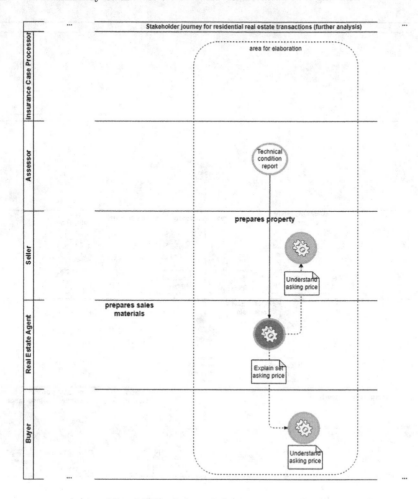

Fig. 2. The focus of the current studies.

the technical condition of different properties. Moreover, several comments in the previous workshops were related to managing expectations about price, as expressed in the following user stories:

Understand asking price: As a seller of a property, I can understand how the asking price is rooted in facts by using a service to show me how the technical conditions report affects the price in relation to other comparable properties.

Understand asking price: As a potential buyer of a property, I can understand how the asking price is rooted in facts by using a service to show me how the technical conditions report affects the price in relation to other comparable properties.

In the current study, we set out to elaborate on the technical condition report touchpoint and the touchpoints with the three user stories above, as indicated by the "area for further elaboration" frame in Fig. 2. In other words, we set out to understand how these touchpoints should function in more detail and what functionality the associated services should provide.

As a foundation for the current study, we conducted a survey [12] to uncover issues concerning the technical condition report from the point of view of the five groups of stakeholders above. From the content analysis of the survey, we developed the conceptual model in Fig. 3. The model shows the two themes of *Form* and *Content* for the technical condition report as what needs to be addressed concretely for producing better reports. Alongside to the right is the *Assessment* theme that calls for increasing the competence of those who produce the reports. Overarching the technical conditions report and the assessment theme is the theme of *Coordination* which calls for explicating and delineating the roles of various documents that are involved in a real estate transaction process and seeing to it that information is coordinated across those documents. Cross-cutting all of this is the theme of *Standardization*, which calls for the systemic oversight on the part of relevant regulatory and advisory bodies to provide ample support in the form of mandatory standards to ensure improvement in all the other themes.

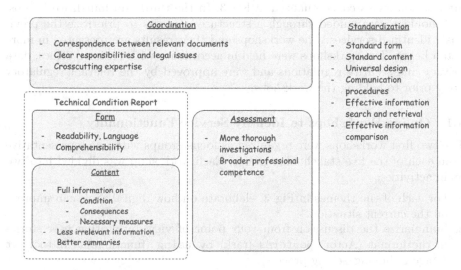

Fig. 3. Presentation of themes for the first two group sessions.

3 Method

Research suggest that stakeholder and user involvement during the systems development process are essential for system success [3, 22]. Workshops are widely used to involve stakeholders, traditionally conducted in a shared physical setting, giving the participants the possibility of getting to know each other and to participate in exercises and discussions to explore a subject or a design. It is also recommended to use clearly defined artefacts for gathering information, and user stories are one of the most frequently used artefacts [22].

Due to the COVID-19 pandemic, researchers have needed to resort to online media to involve stakeholders in research and development activities. In the mean time, people's familiarity and use of video conferencing systems have increased. Recent research indicates that the quality of workshops need not be compromised, and may even be improved, when moving from face-to-face to online environments, if carefully planned for [15].

We conducted four online workshops. The first two workshops were held online due to COVID-19 restrictions. We chose to conduct the remaining workshop online also, even though the restrictions at this time had ceased, since we had positive experiences with the online workshops and because it was easier to get participants to attend online. The aim of the first two workshops was to involve various stakeholders in identifying service functionality to improve on the information issues conceptualized in Fig. 3. In the third and fourth workshops, stakeholders were guided through a structured process to prioritize the previously identified services. The workshops and their results are presented in more detail below. The workshops were held in accordance with national ethics, data privacy and security regulations and were approved by the relevant regulatory body prior to holding the workshops.

3.1 Online Workshops to Identify Service Functionality

The two first workshops were organized as focus groups with one representative from each of the five stakeholder groups. Each work shop was divided into two main activities:

1. For each of the themes in Fig. 3, elaborate on how digital tools can improve on the current situation.
2. Summarize the discussion from your point of view by writing user stories in the format ⟨Actor⟩ `performs` ⟨task⟩ `by` `using` ⟨functionality in tool⟩ `at` ⟨stage in buying/selling process⟩.

The conceptual model in Fig. 3 was presented to participants as an introduction and also functioned as the theme guide for the discussion in the first activity. For the second activity, the participants entered their suggestions in a shared online spreadsheet with column names indicating the various parts of the user story format above. The participants of the two focus groups wrote a total of 52 user stories, several of which expressed similar ideas. To distill the essence of the user stories, we content analysed the `performs` ⟨task⟩ part of the user stories to define services. This resulted in the ten services presented in the next section.

3.2   Elicited Services

Each of the following ten services are presented in Tables 1, 2, 3, 4, 5, 6, 7, 8, 9 and 10 in terms of their constituent user stories, preceded by a high-level description of the service.

On-site access to information   enables assessors and buyers to use portable devices to access information about the dwelling on-site, either to write (assessor) or read (buyer).

Table 1. Service functionality for "On-site access to information".

Actor	Task	Service functionality	Stage in process
Assessor	Write digital report	Use handheld device	On inspection
Buyer	Read listings and reports on site	Download listings and reports to handheld device (via QR code)	At a viewing

Search and share information   enables a stakeholder to locate technical condition reports or other documents based on search queries (buyer, estate agent, seller) or upload documents for other stakeholders to access (all stakeholders).

Table 2. Service functionality for "Search and share information".

Actor	Task	Service functionality	Stage in process
Buyer	Easily find reports to comply with obligation to examine	Search for reports on device	When looking for new residence
Estate agent	Make historical reports accessible	Compile historical reports	When preparing documents
Seller	Compare various assessors	View previous reports from various assessors, with explanations of assessor conclusions	Before ordering an assessor
Estate agent	Prepare sales assignment	Retrieve relevant info from technical condition report to sales documentation, avoiding changes to wording that can confuse or mislead the buyer	When preparing sales documents
Estate agent	Share documents better	Share joint information with stakeholders persistently	When working with the technical condition report
Estate agent	Can upload the sales documentation to a shared platform to save time for all	Store documentation in one place without having to download from various sites	When posting the ad
Assessor	Collect relevant information about the property	Collect information on shared platform for seller, assessor and estate agent	During the process
Buyer	Access all sales documentation readily and rapidly	Use a one-click search bar where one can enter the address of the home of interest	Before, during and after a viewing

Readable documents provides the non-professional stakeholder with explanatory information to help them understand terms or questions in documents or forms that they are to fill in. It also assists the assessor, a professional stakeholder, in writing the technical condition report by both suggesting text and changes to text and by checking the presence of specific topics.

Table 3. Service functionality for "Readable documents".

Actor	Task	Service functionality	Stage in process
Buyer	Understand documents	Search within documents, or get explanation of technical words or phrases	Upon reading technical condition report or a digital sales prospectus
Seller	Understand questions in the self-declaration form	Get information on what the items in the self-declaration form mean	Upon filling in the self-declaration form digitally
Assessor	Ensure the readability of technical condition reports	Get fixed phrases for specific symptoms or deviations and get alternatives to difficult words	When preparing the report

Assist report preparation helps the assessor with preparing the technical conditions report by giving guidance on assessment and tips on information to include or leave out, as well as generating a summary and ensuring consistent treatment of legal issues with the estate agent.

Table 4. Service functionality for "Assist report preparation".

Actor	Task	Service functionality	Stage in process
Assessor	Ensure completeness of technical condition report	Get building-part specific hints on what to comment on	When preparing the report
Assessor, Estate agent	Uncover illegalities; e.g., related to rooms for rent within a home	Ensure that potential legal issues are discussed across stakeholders	When preparing the documentation
Assessor	Understand how building parts should be assessed	Get guidance on the assessment to the relevant issue in the report	When writing the report
Assessor	Improve the provided information	Include images of problem areas and their locations on the floor plan	During and after the inspection
Assessor	Avoid irrelevant information in technical condition reports	Get notification when the provided information is not related to deviations	When writing the report
Assessor	Make a technical condition report summary	Collect critical technical condition scores and other relevant information automatically and include in summary	When writing the report

Costs provides the buyer with cost overviews for future maintenance and also how to make insurance claims related to the property transaction.

Table 5. Service functionality for "Costs".

Actor	Task	Service functionality	Stage in process
Buyer	Get an explanation of the cost of necessary improvements based on technical conditions	(This is mandatory in new technical condition reports since January 2022)	When reading a report
Buyer	Get information about future maintenance and costs	View a prioritized list of items	When reading a report
Buyer	Get an explanation of the latent defects insurance cover	Search the insurance policy, get an explanation of its role and of how to make a claim	At the time of, or after, the transaction

Check documents assists the estate agent in accessibility and completeness of the provided information and consistency with other documents, when preparing the material for the future sale.

Table 6. Service functionality for "Check documents".

Actor	Task	Service functionality	Stage in process
Estate agent	Get accessibility guidance	Receive hints on information accessibility; e.g., picking the right formats, providing meta-information on images.	Before publishing the online advertisement
Estate agent	Check the completeness of information	Follow a checklist of questions ensuring that all relevant information is included	When preparing the sales prospectus
Estate agent	Detect document conflicts	Get a list of conflicts between documents, e.g., between the technical condition report and the sales prospectus	Before publishing the online advertisement

Summary of technical conditions summarizes the technical conditions for the buyer.

Table 7. Service functionality for "Summary of technical conditions".

Actor	Task	Service functionality	Stage in process
Buyer	Get a summary impression of the technical conditions to help decide whether to go to a viewing	See an overview of the technical condition of the dwelling; e.g., using colours	Before attending a viewing
Buyer	Get an overview of deviations of the dwelling	(This is mandatory in new technical condition reports since January 2022)	When reading a report

Compare dwellings lets buyers compare documents pertaining to different dwellings.

Table 8. Service functionality for "Compare dwellings".

Actor	Task	Service functionality	Stage in process
Buyer	Compare technical condition reports or sales prospectuses on a portable device	Compare documents on the same website as the search for dwellings is done; e.g., compare documents page by page	Before or after a viewing

Check legal issues and vagueness lets the real estate agent check the drawings and legal issues of the property during preparations for the sales prospectus. Also, the assessor is warned about potential issues with rooms in the technical condition report.

Table 9. Service functionality for "Check legal issues and vagueness".

Actor	Task	Service functionality	Stage in process
Estate agent	Detect deviations in drawings	Check for deviations between text and drawings such as the floor plan	When writing the sales prospectus
Estate agent	Fill out checklists related to technical conditions, regulations and legal issues	Receive checklists and send the results to the assessor, on a platform open to other stakeholders	After the sales prospectus is drafted (and before the technical condition report is available)
Assessor	Avoid vague assessments and unclear status of rooms	Get a list of legal questions on rooms, e.g., is a basement room approved as a regular bedroom with an escape route?	When writing the report

Standardization assists stakeholders with producing uniform documents that has standardized contents or structure.

Table 10. Service functionality for "Standardization".

Actor	Task	Service functionality	Stage in process
Assessor	Generate an assessment following a standardized list of building parts	Follow a checklist that standardizes which building parts that must be checked and included in the report	When writing the report
Estate agent	Ensure the consistency of documentation	Be presented with a fixed structure of document types	Before writing documents

3.3 Online Workshops to Prioritize Services

Priority workshops have been introduced as a participatory design technique [4], where the main idea is to support user participation in the design process to make it more transparent and to address contextual issues, conflicts of interest and quality of use. Rationality in the sense of explicit rules and rule-based structure of the decision process is emphasized. Various techniques of user involvement in prioritizing activities have been explored further [22].

As a part of the grounds for service providers prioritizing which services should be developed in what order, it can be useful to understand how services contribute to stated objectives and goals that the service provider must relate to. In this particular case, the service provider is a startup company running a research-based innovation project, whose *functional* objectives include:

- Improve the stakeholders' level of understanding of a property's technical condition – meaning that stakeholders understand the technical condition of various building parts, the severity of faults and damages, their necessary repairs and the immediacy of those repairs.
- Increase buyers' and sellers' levels of trust and confidence in the property transaction process – meaning that the stakeholders trust the available information, trust the other stakeholders and have confidence in their own competence to act in the process.
- Increase the accessibility and usability of the property transaction process – meaning that stakeholders find the tasks, and their dependencies in the process, well-defined and transparent through accessible and usable tool support.

Functional objectives pertain to services' effects on business and personal processes. We asked a group of three stakeholders representing buyers, sellers and assessors to assess the magnitude of effect that they foresee the services will have on each objective. They conducted this assessment by assigning *benefit points* [9] from 1 to 10 to each service, for each objective, in group sessions, where stakeholders with various perspectives on benefit iteratively arrive at consensus.

Table 11. Experts' assessments of the effect of services on functional objectives, with geometric means, unweighted and weighted.

Service	Functional objective				Weighted geometric mean
	Improve understanding	Increase trust and confidence	Increase accessibility and usability	Geometric mean	
On-site access to information	8	8	7	7.65	7.61
Search and share information	9	9	7	8.28	8.20
Readable documents	7	7	7	7.00	7.00
Assist report preparation	9	8	6	7.56	7.52
Costs	7	10	8	8.24	8.02
Check documents	5	5	5	5.00	5.00
Summary of technical conditions	6	6	6	6.00	6.00
Compare dwellings	9	9	9	9.00	9.00
Check legal issues and vagueness	8	10	9	8.96	8.82
Standardization	9	9	9	9.00	9.00
Total	77	81	73		

Table 11 shows the stakeholder group's ratings of the relative effect that the services have on each of the functional objectives. For example, the service **Search and share information** is one of four services rated highest on the functional objective **Improve understanding**, while **Check documents** was rated as having the lowest effect on that objective. All services were assessed on each functional objective in this manner. For each service (row), the geometric mean then aggregates the rankings across functional objectives by multiplying the rating for that functional objective and taking the cubic root (since there are three functional objectives). For example, for **On-site access to information**, the geometric mean is $(8*8*7)^{1/3} = 7.65$. More generally; the geometric mean g(s) for ratings of service s on m functional objectives is

$$g(s) = (\prod_{j=1}^{m} r_{s,j})^{1/m}$$

where $r_{s,j}$ is the rating of s on objective j. The geometric means are displayed in the unweighted geometric mean column in Table 11. It is appears that **Legal issues and vagueness** has the highest total rating. We will regard weighted geometric means shortly.

We use the geometric mean rather than the arithmetical mean commonly used to aggregate ratings, because the geometric mean is insensitive to ratings on different scales and to totals being unequal [24]. In our case, the three functional objectives have different underlying metrics, even though the effects on them are all rated on a 1–10 scale. The totals for each objective are not the same, since assessors were not required to keep track of the total. A common fix for the arithmetic mean is to normalize ratings to get equal totals; however this can lead to differences in rankings [24], and raises the question as to whether unequal totals may signify actual perceived differences in obtainable effects, or whether differences are an artefact of the rating exercise [8].

Objectives can be declared at various levels [8,10,11]. Functional effects can, in turn, give effects on objectives that pertain to more strategic goals. Lower-level objectives can thus be rated on how much they contribute to higher-level objectives. We asked a stakeholder group consisting of representatives for business management at the service provider to rate each functional objective on each of the following higher-level *business* and *societal* objectives stated for the innovation project:

- Increase the customer base, which is the business objective of increasing the number of users of the company's service portfolio.
- Reduce the number of buyer-seller conflicts, which is the societal objective of avoiding the substantial number of conflicts arising today due to dissatisfaction in the aftermath of residential real estate transactions.
- Reduce the number of unfounded insurance claims, which is the business/societal objective of avoiding claims based on a poor understanding of the technical conditions under which the residential real estate was sold.

Table 12 shows how this stakeholder group rated the functional objectives on each business/societal objective on a scale from 1 to 10. For example, the group assessed Increase accessibility and usability and Increase trust and confidence as, respectively, least and most influential on the business objective Increase customer base. All functional objectives were assessed on each business/societal objective in this manner. For each functional objective (row), the geometric mean aggregates the rankings across business/societal objectives. For example, for Improve understanding, the geometric mean is $(8 * 10 * 9)^{1/3} = 8.96$. Formally, the geometric mean $g(f)$ of ratings for functional objective f on k business/societal objectives is

$$g(f) = (\prod_{i=1}^{k} r_{f,i})^{1/k}$$

where $r_{f,i}$ is the rating of f on objective i.

Table 12. Experts' assessments of the impact of functional objectives on business/societal objectives, with geometric mean.

Functional objective	Business/Societal objective			Geometric mean
	Increase the customer base	Reduce the number of buyer-seller conflicts	Reduce the number of unfounded insurance claims	
Improve understanding	8	10	9	8.96
Increase trust and confidence	7	5	5	5.59
Increase accessibility and usability	10	8	8	8.62
Total	25	23	22	23.17

We see that functional objectives have different worth when assessed on higher-level objectives. We can now use that fact to compute a *weighted mean* for the effect of services:

$$gw(s) = (\prod_{j=1}^{m} r_{s,j}^{g(j)})^{1/\sum_{j=1}^{m} g(j)}$$

For arithmetic means, weights are expressed by multiplicative factors. Analogously, weights in a multiplicative mean are given as exponents. Here, the exponents are the corresponding geometric means for the functional objectives. For example, the weighted geometric mean for On-site access to information is

$$(8^{8.96} * 8^{5.59} * 7^{8.62})^{1/23.17} = 7.61$$

The weighted geometric mean for each service is then given in the rightmost column of Table 11. In this particular case, the ordering of services according to the unweighted and weighted geometric means is identical, but this may not necessarily be the case in general.

According to the stakeholders' assessments of benefit, the innovation project should prioritize work on the Compare dwellings and Standardization services, followed by Check legal issues and vagueness. The Check documents service is seen as the least beneficial according to the given criteria.

4   Discussion

The highest rated services were Compare dwellings, Standardization and Check legal issues and vagueness. The overarching theme of these services can be said to be standardized, correct and consistent information. The lowest rated services were Check documents, Summary of technical conditions and Readable documents. The overarching theme of these services is more about accessibility and usability. The reason for this prioritization may be that more emphasis is placed on the information content being unambiguous and correct than on it being user-friendly. This should be seen in connection with the fact that, for the buyer and seller in particular, buying and selling a home is a question of large sums of money and the associated risks. It is interesting to note that the assessment at the strategic level rates the functional objective Increase accessibility and usability at the highest mark on the business objective Increase the customer base, while the services that might effectuate that functional objective are rated low by the stakeholders that constitute part of that customer base. This should be a point for further investigation. None of the participants had disabilities, and one could speculate that had the stakeholder representatives been sampled more broadly, the ratings might have shown a different picture. On the other hand, it is conceivable that even for persons with a greater need for accessible and usable services, the requirement for unambiguous and consistent information will be more important than accessibility, in the light of the economic aspects. By law, the services must comply with the Norwegian Web Accessibility Directive (which refers to WCAG). This means that one might assume that services will have a minimum level of accessibility. It is not clear, however, if participants were aware of this fact and whether that awareness had any influence on the rating.

Physical meetings may be advantageous for plenary discussions and social aspects of communication such as body language. Digital workshops may facilitate an opportunity to combine discussions with a more intense focus and greater discipline when performing individual tasks. The success of an online workshop may also depend upon the tools and artefacts that are used, and the goal of the workshop. In our case the online worksheet where participants individually could enter user stories seemed to be understood intuitively and all participants contributed with a number of stories. Depending on the remote environment, it may give an opportunity for working with individual tasks without disturbances and too much awareness of other people in the room, as may be the case in physical workshops. Moreover, the main goal of the workshop was to elicit information and to form consensus around services and the participants did not have a personal relationship. If, on the other side, it had been important to form or strengthen social bonds or gain certain interpersonal benefits, a physical workshop might have been a more appropriate method. Then the benefits of being physically next to each other might be crucial as opposed to, merely a positive side effect for most people.

In the two rating workshops, we asked stakeholders to rate the effectiveness of services and functional objectives on scales from 1 to 10. The geometric mean relies on this scale being a ratio variable; that is, the variable has equidistant intervals (so that addition and subtraction are meaningful) and a zero point (so that multiplication and division are meaningful). The assumption is then that raters perceive that giving a '4' means "twice as much" as giving a '2', and that two items that are rated '3' and '2', respectively, together have equal effect as another item rated '5', etc. It is often more suitable to ask respondents to rank items instead of rating them, since this involves ordering items without any consideration of magnitudes. This is conceptually a different exercise and results in assessments on an ordinal variable, where intervals are not known to be equidistant. We could have asked stakeholders to rank services and functional objectives rather than to rate them. To generate an aggregate ranking is more complicated than computing a geometric or arithmetic mean, but various methods have been suggested [1,2]. The main reason for us to use ratings, rather than rankings, is that a ratio variable lends itself to being incorporated into a benefit/cost index for further considerations of prioritization [8].

5   Conclusion

In many ways, the present real estate transaction process, with its hectic time line and inferior information quality, is designed for *co-destruction* [5,20]. Recent measures to improve this situation places added information requirements and judicial pressure on citizens and may not lead to intended effects. This study aims to develop services that foster *co-production* [6]; which in our context is the trustful and confident collaboration using information services to achieve sustainable transactions. Co-production is hard enough when the collaborating parties ostensibly have the same goal, as in, e.g., public health services [19].

When there are conflicting or opposing interests, such as in public legislative services (tax, customs, etc. – the vast sums involved in tax evasion bears witness of opposing interests) and in real estate transaction (the seller strives for as high a price as possible, while the buyer wants as low a price as possible) service consumers and service providers will struggle in the outset to co-produce a viable result. We propose that multi-stakeholder sessions with systematic service design and benefits evaluations, that explicitly addresses divergence problems in service production, may contribute to the design of services or tools to support better co-production in challenging contexts.

Acknowledgements. This research is funded by the Norwegian Research Council under project number 296256 *Smart Real Estate Transactions*.

References

1. Ahn, B.S., Park, K.S.: Comparing methods for multiattribute decision making with ordinal weights. Comput. Oper. Res. **35**(5), 1660–1670 (2008). Part Special Issue: Algorithms and Computational Methods in Feasibility and Infeasibility
2. Ataei, Y., Mahmoudi, A., Feylizadeh, M.R., Li, D.F.: Ordinal priority approach (OPA) in multiple attribute decision-making. Appl. Soft Comput. **86**, 105893 (2020)
3. Bano, M., Zowghi, D.: A systematic review on the relationship between user involvement and system success. Inf. Softw. Technol. **58**, 148–169 (2015). https://doi.org/10.1016/j.infsof.2014.06.011
4. Braa, K.: Priority workshops: springboard for user participation in redesign activities. In: Proceedings of Conference on Organizational Computing Systems, COCS 1995, pp. 258–267. Association for Computing Machinery, New York, August 1995. https://doi.org/10.1145/224019.224047
5. Engen, M., Fransson, M., Quist, J., Skålén, P.: Continuing the development of the public service logic: a study of value co-destruction in public services. Public Manag. Rev. **23**(6), 886–905 (2021). https://doi.org/10.1080/14719037.2020.1720354
6. Fugini, M., Bracci, E., Sicilia, M. (eds.): Co-production in the Public Sector: Experiences and Challenges. Springer, Cham (2016). https://doi.org/10.1007/978-3-319-30558-5
7. Halvorsrud, R., Kvale, K., Følstad, A.: Improving service quality through customer journey analysis. J. Serv. Theory Pract. **26**(6), 840–867 (2016)
8. Hannay, J.E.: Benefit/Cost-Driven Software Development with Benefit Points and Size Points. Springer, Cham (2021). https://doi.org/10.1007/978-3-030-74218-8
9. Hannay, J.E., Benestad, H.C., Strand, K.: Benefit points–the best part of the story. IEEE Softw. **34**(3), 73–85 (2017)
10. Hannay, J.E., Gjørven, E.: Leveraging network-centric strategic goals in capabilities. J. Mil. Stud. **10**(1), 90–104 (2021)
11. Hannay, J.E., Fuglerud, K.S., Østvold, B.M.: Stakeholder journey analysis for innovation. In: Antona, M., Stephanidis, C. (eds.) HCII 2020. LNCS, vol. 12189, pp. 370–389. Springer, Cham (2020). https://doi.org/10.1007/978-3-030-49108-6_27

12. Hannay, J.E., Fuglerud, K.S., Østvold, B.M.: Stakeholder perceptions on requirements for accessible technical condition information in residential real estate transactions. In: Antona, M., Stephanidis, C. (eds.) Universal Access in Human-Computer Interaction (UAHCI): Novel Design Approaches and Technologies. LNCS, vol. 13308, pp. 1–18. Springer, Cham (2022). https://doi.org/10.1007/978-3-031-05028-2_16

13. Haustein, E., Lorson, P.C.: Co-creation and co-production in municipal risk governance - a case study of citizen participation in a German city. Public Manag. Rev. 1–28 (2021). https://doi.org/10.1080/14719037.2021.1972704

14. Herd, P., Moynihan, D.P.: Administrative Burden: Policymaking by Other Means. Russell Sage Foundation (2018). http://www.jstor.org/stable/10.7758/9781610448789

15. Kennedy, A., Cosgrave, C., Macdonald, J., Gunn, K., Dietrich, T., Brumby, S.: Translating co-design from face-to-face to online: an Australian primary producer project conducted during COVID-19. Int. J. Environ. Res. Public Health **18**, 4147 (2021). https://doi.org/10.3390/ijerph18084147

16. Larsson, K.K.: Digitization or equality: when government automation covers some, but not all citizens. Gov. Inf. Q. **38**(1), 101547 (2021). https://doi.org/10.1016/j.giq.2020.101547.https://www.sciencedirect.com/science/article/pii/S0740624X20303269

17. Larsson, K.K., Skjølsvik, T.: Making sense of the digital co-production of welfare services: using digital technology to simplify or tailor the co-production of services. Public Manag. Rev. 1–18 (2021). https://doi.org/10.1080/14719037.2021.2010402

18. Mäkinen, M.: Digital empowerment as a process for enhancing citizens' participation. E-Learn. Digit. Media **3**(3), 381–395 (2006). https://doi.org/10.2304/elea.2006.3.3.381

19. Palumbo, R., Manna, R.: What if things go wrong in co-producing health services? Exploring the implementation problems of health care co-production. Policy Soc. **37**(3), 368–385 (2018). https://doi.org/10.1080/14494035.2018.1411872

20. Plé, L.: Why do we need research on value co-destruction? J. Creating Value **3**(2), 162–169 (2017). https://doi.org/10.1177/2394964317726451

21. Rogers, E.M.: Diffusion of Innovations, 5th edn. Free Press, New York (2003)

22. Schön, E.M., Thomaschewski, J., Escalona, M.J.: Agile requirements engineering: a systematic literature review. Comput. Stand. Interfaces **49**, 79–91 (2017). https://doi.org/10.1016/j.csi.2016.08.011

23. Norge, S.: Teknisk tilstandsanalyse ved omsetning av bolig. Technical report, Standard Norge (2018). NS3600:2018 (no)

24. Tofallis, C.: Add or multiply? A tutorial on ranking and choosing with multiple criteria. INFORMS Trans. Educ. **14**(3), 109–119 (2014)

25. van Deursen, A.J.A.M., van Dijk, J.A.G.M.: The first-level digital divide shifts from inequalities in physical access to inequalities in material access. New Media Soc. **21**(2), 354–375 (2019). https://doi.org/10.1177/1461444818797082. pMID: 30886536

26. Widlak, A., Peeters, R.: Administrative errors and the burden of correction and consequence: how information technology exacerbates the consequences of bureaucratic mistakes for citizens. Int. J. Electron. Gov. **12**(1), 40–56 (2020)

27. Zouridis, S., van Eck, M., Bovens, M.: Automated discretion. In: Evans, T., Hupe, P. (eds.) Discretion and the Quest for Controlled Freedom, chap. 20, pp. 313–329. Palgrave Macmillan (2020)

A Study of the Challenges of Eye Tracking Systems and Gaze Interaction for Individuals with Motor Disabilities

Lida Huang[1] , Chaomei Xu[2], Thomas Westin[1(✉)] , Jerome Dupire[3],
Florian Le Lièvre[4], and Xueting Shi[5]

[1] Department of Computer and Systems Sciences,
Stockholm University, Stockholm, Sweden
thomasw@dsv.su.se
[2] Department of Physical Geography, Stockholm University, Stockholm, Sweden
[3] Conservatoire national des arts et métiers, Paris, France
jerome.dupire@cnam.fr
[4] CapGame, Paris, France
florian@capgame.fr
[5] Nanning College of Technology, Nanning, People's Republic of China

Abstract. Eye tracking systems are crucial methods by which motor disabled people can interact with computers. Previous research in this field has identified various accessibility affecting eye tracking technologies and applications. However, there is limited research into first-hand user experiences among individuals with motor disabilities. This study aims to examine the actual challenges with eye tracking systems and the gaze interaction faced by motor disabled people. A survey was conducted among people with motor disabilities who used eye trackers for computer interactions. It reveals the current issues from their first-hand experiences in three areas: eye tracking program, gaze interaction, and accessible applications. A knowledge graph arising from the survey delineates the connections among the eye tracking usability issues. The survey's results also indicate practical strategies for future improvements in eye trackers.

Keywords: Eye tracking · Gaze interaction · Challenges · User experiences

1 Introduction

Eye tracking is a technique monitoring the point of gaze or eye movements [1], enabling computers to be operated using gaze control [2–4]. It provides a crucial means of access to human computer interaction for motor disabled people [1,2,4,5]. However, existing eye tracking technologies demonstrate various problems connected with target selection [6–8,11], user interfaces [9,10], and eye tracking accuracy [9,11], alongside the accessibility of eye tracking applications

© Springer Nature Switzerland AG 2022
V. G. Duffy et al. (Eds.): HCII 2022, LNCS 13521, pp. 396–411, 2022.
https://doi.org/10.1007/978-3-031-17902-0_28

[10]. There is limited existing research on gaze-control usability and its related challenges for motor disabled people in practical scenarios. Moreover, individuals with motor disabilities are a minority group in society and therefore less available to participate in surveys. Consequently, the real-life challenges of eye tracking systems and gaze interaction for motor disabled people have to date remained largely unknown. Thus, the research question is what actual challenges with eye tracking systems and gaze interaction are faced by motor disabled people? This paper therefore aims to answer the research question and address this lack of knowledge. This was undertaken by conducting a survey among individuals with motor disabilities who used eye trackers to interact with computers. It then examined their user experiences across multiple aspects, including the eye tracking program, calibration, gaze interaction, and accessible applications. The accessibility of computer games and computer graphics were a particular point of investigation.

The contributions of this paper are twofold. Firstly, it examines first-hand user experiences among motor disabled people, revealing existing challenges of eye tracking technologies and filling the knowledge gap of eye tracking accessibility in real-life scenarios. In addition, it summarizes the reported issues of eye tracking systems and gaze interaction with a knowledge graph, and explicates some practical strategies for improving eye tracking technologies in the future.

2 Related Work

Existing gaze interaction systems have identified several major challenges in previous research, as follows:

2.1 Target Selection and the Midas-Touch Problem

Target selection [6–8] by gaze can be accomplished by fixing on the target for a predefined interval, i.e., the dwell-based approach. However, this approach is likely to cause inadvertent selection as it is impossible to distinguish between intentional and unintentional fixation. This problem is referred to as the Midas-Touch problem [5,11,13]. The current approaches to reduce the Midas-Touch problem are dynamic adjustment of the dwell time by letter prediction for gaze typing [12], and utilizing multi-modals for selection, e.g. combining voice input [14,15], head movement [14], and foot pedalling [15]. However, these multiple modalities are not accessible for people with severe motor disabilities such as lack of speech or physical movement.

2.2 Creative Tasks for Eye Tracking Systems

Previous research has proposed many gaze-control for computer interaction such as typing [12,16,17], desktop controls [18,19], and gaming [20,21]. In terms of creative tasks, drawing by gaze-control was explored by early research a decade ago [22–27]. However, gaze-control drawing proved to be problematic as the continuous gaze signals cannot distinguish between drawing and simply viewing [26]. Neither of these aforementioned studies reported usability evaluation. Yet there are few attempts at using gaze to control design works other than drawing [9]. User experiences and challenges when accessing current creative applications remain unknown.

2.3   Gaze-Based Interfaces

Huang and Westin [10] found that eye tracking fidelity and user interface design significantly affect the ease of gaze-control. In their playtests, losing control of gaze led to game crashes and hindered the game experiences. They also found that some current eye tracking games' user interfaces fail to consider Fitts' law for gaze-control [28]: that is to say, the button sizes are too small for gaze-based selection. As computer interfaces are usually configured for mouse and keyboard, there are limited details as to how popular applications are accessible for gaze interaction among motor disabled people.

Above all, current usability studies in eye tracking technologies generally focus on a specific problem. However, the view and user experiences in eye tracking systems and gaze interaction in daily life scenarios from motor disabled people have been less researched. Therefore, this study will go further into eye tracking challenges based on the aforementioned areas. Moreover, it will focus on a systematic examination of all the possible eye tracking scenarios based on a user paradigm structure (Sect. 3.1).

3   Methodology

3.1   Method

A survey (N = 33) was conducted among motor disabled people to reveal the challenges of using eye tracking technologies. Three major usability stages were uncovered under a usability paradigm structure: starting the eye tracking program[1]; entering applications; and interacting with the gaze-control program (Fig. 1). Accordingly, three aspects of the gaze-control challenges were associated with each stage: the accessibility of the eye tracking program, gaze interaction, and the accessibility of eye tracking applications. The questionnaire was designed with questions in a five-point Likert Scale [29] depicting the difficulty levels or the degrees of agreements. and descriptive analysis.

3.2   Participants and Utilities

We implemented the survey in Sweden, France, and China with the 33 participants (Sweden = 8, France = 7, China = 18) who were motor disabled or severely disabled and depend on eye trackers in their daily lives. Specifically, the

---

[1] This paper uses eye tracking program to indicate the eye tracking drivers and eye tracking setting systems, so that to distinguish it from eye tracking applications.

participants from Sweden were recruited via Tobii, while those from France were recruited via Capgame, and those from China were recruited via the Disabled Persons' Federation of Guangxi and Hubei province. All of the participants were experienced in using eye trackers (Table 1).

The survey was either conducted online with confidential links to the participants internally regarding the Covid-19 pandemic or conducted physically in the participants' living place after receiving their permission. In order to protect privacy and ensure confidentiality during the survey, we excluded personal information in the questionnaire (including but not limited to names, genders, and physical conditions).

Table 1. Participants' experiences in using eye trackers

	1–2 years	3–4 years	More than 4 years
Sweden	3	2	3
France	1	4	2
China	12	5	1

Figure 2 shows five types of eye trackers used by the participants. To order the proportion from high to low, these included the Tobii 5, PCEye series, Tobii 4C, 7Invensum and the Tobii Dynavox i series. In total, up to 65% of participants used Tobii products.

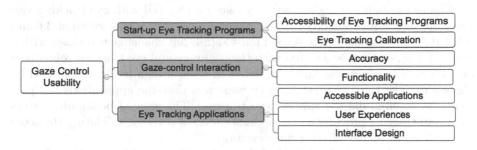

Fig. 1. Gaze-control usability paradigm structure

4 Results

4.1 Start-Up Eye Tracking Programs

63% of the participants considered eye tracking calibration to be difficult. Significant problems included the following: (1) Cannot completely configure the eye trackers by themselves because of their specific disability; (2) Adding and organizing pictograms and various functions was complicated; (3) The need for

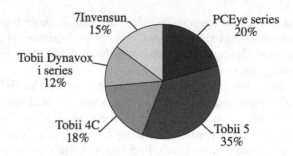

Fig. 2. The eye trackers used by the participants

frequent recalibration; (4) Cannot recalibrate because of the hidden layers of the program, for example, opening the re-calibration window when eye tracking is inaccurate; (5) Low efficiency and failure to recalibrate on many occasions.

4.2   Gaze Interaction

Figure 3 shows five types of gaze interaction, all of which were investigated providing drag-and-drop, with a high score of 3.36. Drag-and-drop was regarded as the most difficult interaction type by participants. The other four types of gaze interaction were similar at the moderate to difficult level. Clicking and target selection represents a similar difficulty level to scrolling. Precise clicking and selection proved to be slightly more difficult than typing and scrolling, whereas switching between different tools/windows has the lowest difficulty.

Figure 4 reveals the highest severity issues associated with eye tracking systems was lack of functionality supporting gaze-control; this was scored at 3.6 and labeled "high difficulty". The second most significant challenge was close, with a score of 3.48, and was associated with the accuracy and eye tracking robustness of the systems, which was also considered to be at a high level as measured by the scales. The third greatest severity issue was that the applications the participants required did not support eye tracking. The issue of positioning errors when eye tracking provides a low-moderate level of severity, validating the score in Fig. 3 (e) as precise clicking and selection.

Additionally, Fig. 5 shows 85% of the participants consider it extremely necessary to customize user interfaces for the purpose of eye tracking.

4.3   Eye Tracking Application

Difficulties were associated with using five types of eye tracking applications. In Fig. 6, drawing (computer graphics software) obtained a significantly high score of 4.58, while the scores provided by other applications were much less. Additional applications were identified on the scale as falling between low and moderate. In the case of these applications, web browsers were labeled as moderately difficult. The third most difficult application is computer games, which

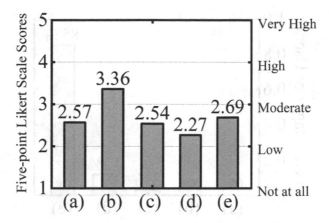

Fig. 3. Difficulties when conducting these interactions: (a) Clicking and target selection (e.g., typing on the on-screen keyboard); (b) Drag-and-drop; (c) Scrolling up and down; (d) Switching between different tools/windows; (e) Precise clicking and selection. A higher score indicates higher difficulty.

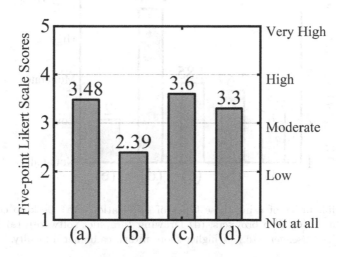

Fig. 4. The severity of the issues associated with eye tracking systems: (a) Serious inaccuracy: the cursor (mouse) loses control; (b) Minor inaccuracy: position errors when tracking the eyes; (c) Not sufficiently functional to replace mouse and keyboard control; (d) Many applications that I need do not support eye tracking. A higher score indicates higher severity.

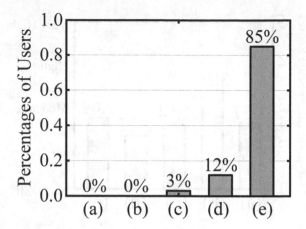

Fig. 5. The necessity to have customized user interfaces for eye tracking: (a) No necessity; (b) A little; (c) A moderate amount; (d) A large amount; (e) Extremely necessary.

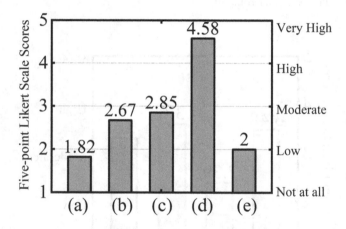

Fig. 6. The difficulties of using these types of applications: (a) Desktop control; (b) Computer games; (c) Web browsers; (d) Drawing (graphics software); (e) Document editing (Word, Messenger, etc.). A higher score indicates higher difficulty.

were also classified at the moderate difficult level. Notably, the difficulty posed by desktop control was the lowest of the five types at only 1.82, close to being considered "not difficult at all".

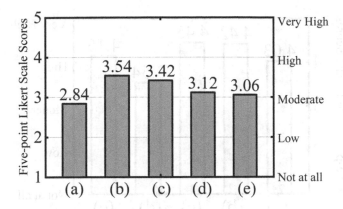

Fig. 7. The levels of the factors that hinder the game experience while playing: (a) Fidelity or accuracy of the gaze-control is not enough; (b) Few games can be played by gaze-control only; (c) Game design is too difficult for gaze-control; (d) Inappropriate game interface for gaze-control; (e) Precise selection. A higher score indicates higher severity.

The probable challenges arising from gaze-control games were investigated in detail. Figure 7 shows five factors with relatively similar scores, i.e., between moderate (2.84) and high (3.54). The effect factor with the highest score reveals few games can be played using gaze-control only. The factor "game design is too difficult for gaze-control" is the second most significant issue with a high score. Inappropriate game interface and the difficulties with precise selection are other two negative factors that result in scores that are slightly higher than moderate. Finally, insufficient fidelity or accuracy of gaze-control is considered moderate.

To explore the existing challenges associated with computer graphics software further, five challenges were examined in the context of drawing. Figure 8 shows all five issues associated with gaze-control drawing achieve significantly high scores (almost above 4), signifying "very high difficulties". Meanwhile, "to control the shape precisely" and "gazing precisely and drawing details" obtain the highest score of about 4.5. "Too many steps when performing tasks" and "the difficulty in switching between tools" also result in relatively high scores. The drawing application is not designed for gaze-control, and receives the lowest score from among the five challenges, despite still having a high level of difficulty (3.54) compared to the other gaze-control applications (Fig. 4, Fig. 6 and Fig. 7).

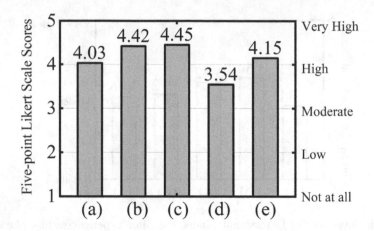

Fig. 8. The level of the challenges when drawing with eye tracking: (a) Too many steps performing tasks; (b) It is difficult to gaze precisely and draw details; (c) It is difficult to control precisely what shape I want to draw; (d) Drawing application is not designed for gaze-control; (e) It is difficult to switch between drawing functions. A higher score indicates a higher degree of agreement.

Figure 9 reveals that 39% of participants did not use drawing applications. Among the remaining participants, Photoshop was the most widely-used application. In total, 18% of the participants used Inkscape or Windows Paint, which was second only to Photoshop. The proportion of participants using Illustrator, Windows Paint3D and ArtRage were similar, namely 9%.

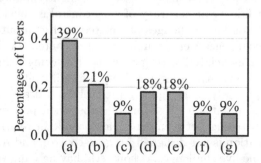

Fig. 9. The graphics applications used among motor disabled people: (a) Do not use drawing applications; (b) Photoshop; (c) Illustrator; (d) Inkscape; (e) Windows Paint; (f) Windows Paint3D; (g) ArtRage.

5   Discussion

The data provided by the participants in this study reveals Tobii as the most popular eye tracker manufacturer. This may be because Tobii has developed economically portable eye trackers and made them sufficiently affordable for motor disabled people to use daily. The other eye tracker producers, for example, SMI, Ergoneers, Pupil Labs, and iMotion typically produce wearable eye trackers and research eye trackers that are more costly.

The questionnaire portion of the survey reveals several challenges associated with eye tracking systems. The problematic areas linked to eye tracking usability are described below.

5.1 Issues with the Eye Tracking Program

The eye tracking program is not sufficiently accessible for disabled people to customize independently. This is due to the multiple hierarchical layers and hidden elements present in the eye tracking program's interface. Furthermore, recalibration is a significant issue of concern in eye tracking programs. Specifically, when eye tracking is inaccurate, it is rather difficult to open the calibration from the second or higher hierarchical menu. Additionally, on many occasions failure occurs during the recalibration process, exposing a lack of accuracy in the eye tracking program.

The issues arising as a consequence of the eye tracking program were rarely mentioned in previous eye tracking research. This was because the majority of the eye tracking research was conducted after the calibration process and affirms that the eye tracking configuration was appropriate. However, the eye tracking program is a crucial component informing the daily usage of the eye tracker. If it does not support unimodal gaze-control or independent manipulation by the user, this makes it inconvenient for severely disabled people who rely on unimodal gaze-control.

Moreover, the most significant issue is that hierarchical layers accompanying recalibration challenges were not reported in existing eye tracking studies, to the best of this authors' knowledge. It is strongly recommended that the calibration process be activated by a straightforward and fast command and located within the first layer on the eye tracking program interface. The eye tracking program interface should also avoid complex hierarchical layers for the purpose of operational efficiency.

5.2 Issues Associated with Gaze Interaction

Among the forms of gaze interaction (i.e., click and target selection, drag-and-drop, scrolling up and down, and switching windows), drag-and-drop was found to represent the biggest challenge for disabled people. It carries a difficulty weighting that is significantly greater than other forms of interaction. Drag-and-drop requires real-time output from gaze trajectories. It means the bias of gaze locations will immediately show on screen and cannot be corrected in the same way as dwell click. Thus, it is most likely to trigger the Midas-Touch problem [5, 11, 13]. Furthermore, the system inaccuracies (as will be discussed below) create a bias in gaze locations, consequently reducing the control potential of drag-and-drop. To the best of our knowledge, there is scant opportunity to conceptualize the drag-and-drop command precisely in current eye tracking research. In contrast, numerous studies exist detailing technical improvements to other forms of interaction identified in gaze interaction research, especially clicking and target selection [6–8,11–13]. Moreover, dwell-click [7,11,30,31] as the major command for gaze-control, is compatible with mouse clicking for the most part, while drag-and-drop has to be activated by clicking on a functional menu [32] to simulate a "drag-and-drop" action in the eye tracking program.

There are three main issues associated with gaze interaction. First, eye tracking systems were determined to have relatively serious inaccuracies. The cursor often lost control during interactions according to user feedbacks. This may be due to many reasons. For example, inaccuracies in the eye tracking program (Sect. 5.1) can produce errors when controlling the cursor. Huang and Westin [10] noted that changes in head posture and body position are likely to cause eye tracking failure. Furthermore, eye tracking applications can produce serious inaccuracies because of inappropriate interface design [10] and system bugs when connected with the API (Application Programming Interface) in the eye trackers. The eye trackers also have inherent errors originating from the hardware and eye tracking algorithm [31,33].

Second, the functions supporting eye tracking systems were relatively limited such that the mouse and keyboard control could not be replaced by the eye tracker and unimodal gaze-control completely. Similar to the issues observed with eye tracking programs, eye tracking does not support unimodal gaze-control or self-control, rather it impedes accessibility among severely disabled users. Additionally, there many of the applications used failed to support eye tracking.

Nearly all the participants found it extremely necessary to provide gaze-adaptive interfaces, and heavily underlined the importance of both gaze-adaptive and customized interface. This clarifies that the user interfaces available with current applications are not adequately compatible with gaze interaction. Notably, interfaces for gaze-control adapted to the current eye tracking accuracy are expected to maintain sparse elements with at least 94px [28]. However, some user interfaces, e.g., gaze-control games fail to observe this rule [10]. The following recommendations are proposed: firstly, design applications for unimodal gaze-control accuracy, which are limited by natural eye behaviours [34] and current eye tracking technology. Secondly, there is a need to enable retrofit the most commonly used applications designed for mouse and keyboard interaction with interface plug-ins to increase their accessibility to people with severe motor disabilities.

5.3   Issues of Eye Tracking Applications

This study categorized gaze-control applications into several genres: desktop control, document editing and typing, computer graphics and computer games. The comparison between the difficulties associated with the applications reveals that drawing by applying gaze interaction is particularly challenging, while the other applications were relatively straightforward to use. It can further be inferred that similar creative applications (e.g., CAD, 3Ds Max) would prove challenging for motor disabled users. Existing gaze-control drawing research [22–27] only focuses on drawing straight lines and producing preset geometric patterns like circles and squares. The results in these studies proved a lack of fidelity and flexibility, and a big gap to free-hand drawing. Approaches to conducting creative tasks via eye tracking system have been explored in recent years [9]. However, this study evaluated applications that rely on dwell-click for the gaze-control, leaving the interactive obstacles when operating drag-and-click unsolved. Thus, computer graphics application have remarkable scope for improvement.

When this study examined the specific challenges associated with gaze-control drawing (Fig. 8), it was indicated that precision is the most significant problem, including the ability to control the brush and fixate at the pixel-level. Since conducting computer graphics has high demand in terms of fidelity and precision when drawing, the limit of eye tracking accuracy and precision [31, 33] make drawing via gaze-control extremely difficult. Notably, lack of accuracy and precision is also a factor affecting level of difficulty when conducting drag-and-drop mouse action via gaze-control (Fig. 3). Therefore, it is rather difficult for gaze-control to emulating free-hand drawing on screen as this activity completely depends on drag-and-drop.

The participants also stated that switching between different drawing functions in graphics software is troublesome. This is probably due to the compiled interface and complicated drawing commands integrated into graphics software. Specifically, when this study examined the graphics software used by motor disabled people, it found no gaze-based drawing software available in the marketplace. The participants who used it to draw applied Photoshop, Inkscape and Windows Paint as the most frequently used graphics software. However, such software was developed for mouse and keyboard interaction, thus has no gaze-based interfaces or assistive function supporting eye tracking. For example, it is impossible to conduct free-hand drawing on canvas, either using marquee, lasso, and eraser, as all of these are executed by drag-and-click. Professional drawing software also has pixel-level icon sizes that are significantly smaller than tolerance for gaze-control accuracy (97 px) [28]. Hence, it is vital to explore drawing systems accessible for gaze interaction.

In contrast, other applications have achieved sophisticated eye tracking techniques and good accessibility for gaze interaction, especially in the context of desktop control. These sophisticated applications take advantage of mainstream eye tracking research, such as target selection [6–8], typing [12, 16, 17], and gaze-controlled game design [20, 21].

In terms of computer games, accessibility to eye tracking utilities is good. Figure 7 shows that the issues associated with eye tracking accuracy, precision and interface only affect gaze-control games moderately. The slightly remarkable finding is the lack of game genres applying gaze interaction. Real-time games remains a challenge, especially for unimodal gaze control, with similar demands of precision and accuracy, limited time for interaction and added challenges of game events that can disturb gaze control. Conclusively, it is recommended that additional gaze-control modes be sought to enable gameplay.

5.4   The Knowledge Graph of the Eye Tracking Issues

Finally, the connection between the eye tracking issues mentioned above is delineated in the knowledge graph (Fig. 10). This also implies a correlation with these three aspects throughout the usage of eye tracking systems (i.e., eye tracking program, gaze interaction, and accessible applications). It is shown here that the issues associated with accessibility and accuracy are the most significant of all the impact factors discussed herein. On one hand, the accessibility of contemporary eye tracking systems and gaze interaction necessitates urgent improvements in many areas, including the interaction modes, functionality, interface design. On the other hand, accuracy problems affect the usability of many eye tracking systems, including calibration (recalibration), gaze-control drawing, and gaze-control games.

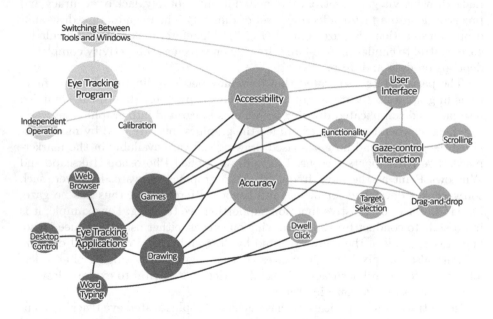

Fig. 10. Knowledge graph of the eye tracking issues. A bigger size of the dot indicates the issue is more influential and correlative to the others.

6   Conclusion and Further Research

This study has conducted a survey of the first-hand user experiences of disabled people utilizing eye tracking systems for human-computer interaction, and has systematically investigated the challenges they encounter. These challenges were identified and evaluated in three narrative stages following the gaze-control usability paradigm structure. The results reveal five major gaze-control challenges, while a knowledge graph delineates the connection between various eye tracking usability issues.

In detail, the challenges uncovered by this study associated with eye tracking systems and gaze interaction are: (1) Independent operation and system configuration for motor disabled people; (2) Tracking and estimating of the eyes in accuracy and precision; (3) Dual input interaction such as click-and-drag; (4) Accessing the gaze-adaptive user interface designed for the tolerance of eye tracking accuracy; (5) Accessing available graphics applications for gaze interaction and enabling gaze-control drawing; and (6) Accessing the diversity of game genres, which are available for eye-tracking-supported game design and gaze interaction. The conclusion of this study provides valuable information about the first-hand user experiences of motor disabled people and provides guidance on the focus of future eye tracking research.

In view of the aforementioned uncovered challenges, our planned future research will be twofold. Firstly, we will seek solutions to produce more accessible eye tracking systems, especially targeting computer graphics and related gaze-control mode, which was revealed to be the most challenging area for computer interaction. Secondly, we will aim to focus on severely motor disabled users and continuously update the usability study with the latest eye tracking technologies.

References

1. Bissoli, A., Lavino-Junior, D., Sime, M., Encarnação, L., Bastos-Filho, T.: A human-machine interface based on eye tracking for controlling and monitoring a smart home using the Internet of Things. Sensors **19**(4), 859 (2019). https://doi.org/10.3390/s19040859
2. Cecotti, H.: A multimodal gaze-controlled virtual keyboard. IEEE Trans. Hum. Mach. Syst. **46**(4), 601–606 (2016). https://doi.org/10.1109/THMS.2016.2537749
3. Lewis, T., Pereira, T., Almeida, D.: Smart scrolling based on eye tracking. IJCA **80**(10), 34–37 (2013). https://doi.org/10.5120/13898-1858
4. Frutos-Pascual, M., Garcia-Zapirain, B.: Assessing visual attention using eye tracking sensors in intelligent cognitive therapies based on serious games. Sensors **15**(5), 11092–11117 (2015). https://doi.org/10.3390/s150511092
5. Hyönä, J., Radach, R., Deubel, H.: The Mind's Eye: Cognitive and Applied Aspects of Eye Movement Research, 1st edn., North-Holland, Amsterdam, Boston (2003)
6. Mollenbach, E., Stefansson, T., Hansen, J.P.: All eyes on the monitor: gaze based interaction in zoomable, multi-scaled information-spaces. In: 13th International Conference on Intelligent User Interfaces, Gran Canaria, Spain, pp. 373–376 (2008). https://doi.org/10.1145/1378773.1378833
7. Qian, Y.Y., Teather, R.J.: The eyes don't have it: an empirical comparison of head-based and eye-based selection in virtual reality. In: 5th Symposium on Spatial User Interaction, Brighton, United Kingdom, pp. 91–98 (2017). https://doi.org/10.1145/3131277.3132182
8. Skovsgaard, H., Mateo, J.C., Flach, J.M., Hansen, J.P.: Small-target selection with gaze alone. In: 2010 Symposium on Eye-Tracking Research & Applications, Austin, Texas, p. 145 (2010). https://doi.org/10.1145/1743666.1743702
9. Creed, C., Frutos-Pascual, M., Williams, I.: Multimodal gaze interaction for creative design. In: 2020 CHI Conference on Human Factors in Computing Systems, Honolulu HI, USA, pp. 1–13 (2020). https://doi.org/10.1145/3313831.3376196

10. Huang, L., Westin, T.: A study on gaze-control - game accessibility among novice players and motor disabled people. In: 17th International Conference on Computers Helping People with Special Needs, Lecco, Italy, pp. 205–216 (2020). https://doi.org/10.1007/978-3-030-58796-3_25

11. Jacob, R.J.K.: The use of eye movements in human-computer interaction techniques: what you look at is what you get. ACM Trans. Inf. Syst. **9**(2), 152–169 (1991). https://doi.org/10.1145/123078.128728

12. Mott, M.E., Williams, S., Wobbrock, J.O., Morris, M.R.: Improving dwell-based gaze typing with dynamic, cascading dwell times. In: 2017 CHI Conference on Human Factors in Computing Systems, Denver Colorado, USA, pp. 2558–2570 (2017). https://doi.org/10.1145/3025453.3025517

13. Murata, A., Karwowski, W.: Automatic lock of cursor movement: implications for an efficient eye-gaze input method for drag and menu selection. IEEE Trans. Hum. Mach. Syst. **49**(3), 259–267 (2019). https://doi.org/10.1109/THMS.2018.2884737

14. Kurauchi, A., Feng, W., Morimoto, C., Betke, M.: HMAGIC: head movement and gaze input cascaded pointing. In: 8th ACM International Conference on PErvasive Technologies Related to Assistive Environments, Corfu, Greece pp. 1–4. Association for Computing Machinery (2015). https://doi.org/10.1145/2769493.2769550

15. Klamka, K., Siegel, A., Vogt, S., Göbel, F., Stellmach, S., Dachselt, R.: Look & pedal: hands-free navigation in zoomable information spaces through gaze-supported foot input. In: 2015 ACM on International Conference on Multimodal Interaction, Seattle Washington, USA, pp. 123–130 (2015). https://doi.org/10.1145/2818346.2820751

16. Urbina, M.H., Huckauf, A.: Alternatives to single character entry and dwell time selection on eye typing. In: 2010 Symposium on Eye-Tracking Research & Applications, Austin, Texas, p. 315 (2010). https://doi.org/10.1145/1743666.1743738

17. Kurauchi, A., Feng, W., Joshi, A., Morimoto, C., Betke, M.: EyeSwipe: dwell-free text entry using gaze paths. In: 2016 CHI Conference on Human Factors in Computing Systems, San Jose California, USA, pp. 1952–1956 (2016). https://doi.org/10.1145/2858036.2858335

18. Hyrskykari, A., Istance, H., Vickers, S.: Gaze gestures or dwell-based interaction? In: Symposium on Eye Tracking Research and Applications, Santa Barbara, California, pp. 229–232 (2012). https://doi.org/10.1145/2168556.2168602

19. Istance, H., Bates, R., Hyrskykari, A., Vickers, S.: Snap clutch, a moded approach to solving the Midas touch problem. In: Symposium on Eye Tracking Research & Application, Savannah Georgia, USA, pp. 221–228 (2008). https://doi.org/10.1145/1344471.1344523

20. Hornof, A.J., Cavender, A.: EyeDraw: enabling children with severe motor impairments to draw with their eyes. In: SIGCHI Conference on Human Factors in Computing Systems, Portland Oregon, USA, pp. 161–170 (2005). https://doi.org/10.1145/1054972.1054995

21. Hornof, A., Cavender, A., Hoselton, R.: EyeDraw: a system for drawing pictures with eye movements. In: Extended Abstracts of the 2004 Conference on Human Factors in Computing Systems, Atlanta Georgia, USA, pp. 86–93 (2004). https://doi.org/10.1145/1029014.1028647

22. Hornof, A., Cavender, A., Hoselton, R.: EyeDraw: a system for drawing pictures with the eyes. In: Extended Abstracts of the 2004 Conference on Human Factors in Computing Systems, Vienna, Austria, pp. 1251–1254 (2004). https://doi.org/10.1145/985921.986036

23. Heikkilä, H.: Tools for a gaze-controlled drawing application – comparing gaze gestures against dwell buttons. In: Kotzé, P., Marsden, G., Lindgaard, G., Wesson, J., Winckler, M. (eds.) INTERACT 2013. LNCS, vol. 8118, pp. 187–201. Springer, Heidelberg (2013). https://doi.org/10.1007/978-3-642-40480-1_12

24. Gips, J., Olivieri, P.: EagleEyes: an eye control system for persons with disabilities. In: 11th International Conference on Technology and Persons with Disabilities, Los Angeles, California, p. 15 (1996)

25. Heikkilä, H.: EyeSketch: a drawing application for gaze control. In: 2013 Conference on Eye Tracking, Cape Town, South Africa, pp. 71–74 (2013). https://doi.org/10.1145/2509315.2509332

26. Biedert, R., Buscher, G., Dengel, A.: The eyeBook - using eye tracking to enhance the reading experience. Informatik Spektrum 33(3), 272–281 (2010). https://doi.org/10.1007/s00287-009-0381-2

27. Turner, J., Iqbal, S., Dumais, S.: Understanding gaze and scrolling strategies in text consumption tasks. In: 2015 ACM International Joint Conference on Pervasive and Ubiquitous Computing and 2015 ACM International Symposium on Wearable Computers, Osaka, Japan, pp. 829–838 (2015). https://doi.org/10.1145/2800835.2804331

28. Hansen, J.P., Rajanna, V., MacKenzie, I.S., Bækgaard, P.: A fitts' law study of click and dwell interaction by gaze, head and mouse with a head-mounted display. In: Workshop on Communication by Gaze Interaction - COGAIN 2018, Warsaw, Poland, pp. 1–5 (2018). https://doi.org/10.1145/3206343.3206344

29. Likert, R.: A technique for the measurement of attitudes. Archives of Psychology (1932)

30. Majaranta, P., Bulling, A.: Advances in Physiological Computing, 1st edn. Springer, London (2014). https://doi.org/10.1007/978-1-4471-6392-3

31. Feit, A.M., et al.: Toward everyday gaze input: accuracy and precision of eye tracking and implications for design. In: 2017 CHI Conference on Human Factors in Computing Systems, Denver Colorado, USA, pp. 1118–1130 (2017). https://doi.org/10.1145/3025453.3025599

32. Menges, R., Kumar, C., Staab, S.: Improving user experience of eye tracking-based interaction: introspecting and adapting interfaces. ACM Trans. Comput. Hum. Interact. 26(6), 1–46 (2019). https://doi.org/10.1145/3338844

33. Kasprowski, P., Harezlak, K., Niezabitowski, M.: Eye movement tracking as a new promising modality for human computer interaction. In: 17th International Carpathian Control Conference, High Tatras, Slovakia, pp. 314–318. IEEE (2016). https://doi.org/10.1109/CarpathianCC.2016.7501115

34. Hayhoe, M., Ballard, D.: Eye movements in natural behavior. Trends Cogn. Sci. 9(4), 188–194 (2005). https://doi.org/10.1016/j.tics.2005.02.009

How Late Middle-Aged People Experience and Deal with Frustration During Online Shopping

Tongtong Jin[1] [iD], Weiwei Zhang[2] [iD], and Yun Wang[1,2]([✉])

[1] Beihang University, Beijing, China
{jintt,wang_yun}@buaa.edu.cn
[2] Tsinghua University, Beijing, China
zww19@mails.tsinghua.edu.cn

Abstract. People aged 55–65 are going through a special period in their life. Many of them don't feel old or identify themselves as older adults in terms of their appearance and daily behavior, but they still face conditions of early physical aging and are a relatively underserved population in the digital age. In this paper, we studied 15 late middle-aged people to understand their behaviors when facing frustrations during online shopping. Their verbal response and physical activity behavior were encoded based on grounded theory. The results show that, when shopping online, late middle-aged users frequently encounter frustrations that affect their emotional state, and they usually lack immediate and convenient help. Finally, four design strategies were suggested in this paper to help reduce the number of frustrations and improve the recovery from the frustration of the late middle-aged users. Furthermore, in the study of adaptive aging, behavior coding can provide useful insights to help designers understand the characteristics of users.

Keywords: Late middle-aged people · User frustration · Online shopping · User experience

1 Introduction

World Health Organization (WHO) considers that people become older adults when they reach 60 or 65 years old [1], which is widely accepted in most elderly-related studies. In China, the Law of the People's Republic of China on Protection of the Rights and Interests of the Elderly defines people over the age of 60 as older adults.[1] In the meantime, the earliest common retirement age for adults with working ability is 55.[2] Existing studies have paid less attention to people between the ages of 55 and 65. At present, there is no unified term to define this group.

---

[1] See Law of the People's Republic of China on Protection of the Rights and Interests of the Elderly, effective on August 29, 1996, amended on August 27, 2009, July 01, 2013, further amended on December 29, 2018.

[2] Interim Measures for the retirement of state functionaries, effective on January 1, 1956.

© Springer Nature Switzerland AG 2022
V. G. Duffy et al. (Eds.): HCII 2022, LNCS 13521, pp. 412–422, 2022.
https://doi.org/10.1007/978-3-031-17902-0_29

In China, the majority of people aged 55–65 have just retired from work and returned to a more family-centric life. They are the primary user group of smartphones over the age of 55 [2] and spend a significant amount of time daily on different online platforms such as social chat, video-sharing and online shopping. Despite the fact that many of them don't identify themselves as older adults, they still face conditions of early aging, therefore cannot be simply classified as general "middle-aged people". The continuous expansion of late middle-aged users indicates that they are becoming an important online user group in the future.

2 Related Work

2.1 The Late Middle-Aged Group

Some researchers in China have already begun to study users aged 55–65 when using smart products [3, 4] or online platforms [5]. The user habits of electronic products will persist for some time in the future when users get older [3], the behaviors of people in this age group reflect the characteristics of future old adults. This paper adopts the definition of people aged 55–65 in previous studies and identifies them as the late middle-aged group. Neither their self-perception nor the public's impression of them makes them feel "old" in terms of their appearance and behavior, this may cause them to become anxious about how well they can use their smartphones. The current neglect of technology acceptance of the late middle-aged people is more likely to lead them to anxiety and to lose self-confidence in the future [4]. In such a context, it becomes an important proposition for researchers and designers to pay more attention to late middle-aged users, understand their anxiety when using smart products, and develop new design strategies to improve their acceptance and adaptability to new technologies.

2.2 User Frustration

In the field of psychology, Freud (1921) defines that frustration occurs when the people's goal is disturbed by inhibition conditions, caused by external reasons such as physical environment, social or legal obstacles and internal reasons such as lack of knowledge and skills [6]. It relates not only to failed actions but also to failed expectations [7]. The importance of the goal to the individual, and the intensity of one's desire to achieve the goal, affect the intensity of one's response to task interruption [8]. In the field of HCI, researchers found that even if the computer system was operating in a correct state, unexpected situations could still cause user frustration, such as pop-up ads and viruses [9]. The user felt mood-changing and low satisfaction when experiencing unexpected frustrations [10]. In conclusion, "frustrations" and "user frustrations" refer to a dynamic emotional state that is constantly associated with the fluency of users' tasks. Frustrations lead to users' negative emotions, which may result in their inability to complete the task. For the late middle-aged group, it is important to understand their feelings and emotions, as well as efficiency and proficiency in using smart products.

2.3   Perceived Self-efficacy and Technology Acceptance

Late middle-aged people are generally healthy, and they seek positive feedback to confirm their confidence or belief in their ability to achieve specific goals, which refers to their perceived self-efficacy [11]. People with high perceived self-efficacy will be more positive and confident in dealing with various problems [11, 12]. Unlike older adults over 65, late middle-aged users' actual performance may contradict their high demand of perceived self-efficacy, which will lead to anxious or depressive emotions, and affect their self-confidence and willingness to learn [13], resulting in more task failure or abandonment.

Technophobia refers to fear, dislike or discomfort caused by using modern technologies and complex technical devices (especially computers) [14] and is common to older adults. Depressive emotions not only affect users' interaction with the computer but also reduce their learning motivation, social activity and technology acceptance [15]. Excessive technology anxiety may limit their benefits from new technologies [14]. Fisk (2020) believes that the benefits of technology should be emphasized to increase users' perceived usefulness of smart products. It is important to let users know that errors are a normal part of the learning process and will not damage the equipment [16].

Adaptive aging design should focus on creating low-frustration experiences with user-friendly guidance, minimizing the negative impact of frustrations, in order to improve perceived self-efficacy and technology acceptance of late middle-aged users.

Based on the above research, we mainly focus on the following research questions:

RQ1: What kind of frustrations do late-middle-aged users experience during online shopping?
RQ2: What is their emotional state when experiencing frustration?
RQ3: How do they solve these frustrations?

3   Method

In this study, we conducted face-to-face semi-structured interviews and observations of late-middle-aged users of online shopping platforms. Each participant was fully aware of the process of the interview and accompanied by 1–2 researchers. The data during the experiment were only used for academic analysis and did not involve any privacy infringement purposes.

3.1   Participant

15 participants aged 55–65 (59.8 on average) from China's first-tier cities were recruited through various channels, including online forums and older adults' activity centers. They are all frequent computer users in their jobs and have more than 7 years of experience in using smartphones. Among them, 12 have retired and 3 have been reemployed after retirement. They were all familiar with online shopping and had at least one online shopping experience during the week. In terms of health condition, they all had myopia or presbyopia, and chronic diseases such as hypertension.

3.2 Platform Selection

Based on a pre-test questionnaire, we identified two online shopping platforms (A, C) that the participants used almost on a daily basis, therefore a different platform (B) was chosen for our study. It was used by all participants but was not the most familiar one for them. This choice helped us to observe the participants' behaviors more accurately excluding their differences in proficiency and memory. The two most common smartphone was chosen to eliminate the interference factors caused by unfamiliarity.

3.3 Procedure

After a brief ice-breaking and introduction to the interview, all participants were invited to go through the following steps:

1. Introduction of the purpose, and process of the interview and the user test to participants. Participants were then asked to sign the informed consent.
2. A brief discussion of the current online shopping scenario, habits, most familiar platforms, frequently encountered problems and degree of trust of the platform. If possible, we hope the participants can show us their previous online shopping orders on their smartphones.
3. Participants were asked to use platform B to buy paper towels and their behavior was recorded.
4. Participants were then asked to apply for a refund, and their behavior was recorded;

After the tests, a more flexible interview was conducted focusing on the user behaviors observed by researchers during the experiment.

To prevent the impact of external factors during the experiment, researchers and participants communicated the time and place of the interview respectively. The overall process lasted a minimum of 40 min and was adapted to the expressive needs of the participants. All of their behaviors and conversations were recorded for subsequent data analysis. If participants could not complete the task, they would be encouraged to try again. If they needed help, we would give them some assistance or hints.

3.4 Analysis Based on Grounded Theory

After the interviews, researchers transcribed, analyzed and coded each video and screen recording based on a unified definition of user frustration. Language and activity behaviors were both encoded aiming to form a more comprehensive observation of user's status when encountering frustration. We focused especially on the moments when users expressed negative emotions. The activity behavior coding clearly showed the user's fluency and hesitation at each step, ensuring that no detailed information was overlooked. Our coding principles are listed below in Table 1.

Each stress, complaint, confusion, doubt and other emotion expressed by the participant that hampered the smoothness of the task was documented as one frustration. The same situation might be recorded differently depending on the scenario. For example, if the participant couldn't find the refund button on the current page, it would be marked as one frustration; if the participant failed to find the button on the wrong page, it would

Table 1. Online shopping frustration behavior code

Behavior types	Behavior descriptions	Expressions
Language behavior	Stress	Negative about their behaviors
	Complaint	Dissatisfaction with the current interface
Activity behaviors	Confusion	1. Hands hesitate and dare not click; 2. Check the interface back and forth, unable to determine the target options and interaction mode;
	Doubt	1. Unable to determine the current state and stop the operation; 2. Continuous invalid operation because the target couldn't be found; 3. Unexpected information after operation; 4. Difficult to see the key information; 5. Icon clicking;
	Hesitation	1. Their hands hesitate and don't know where to click 2. Slide up and down without clicking on the target
	Dissatisfied	1. Stop the operation when they are not satisfied with the information. For example, the refund reason set by the system; 2. Dissatisfied with complex system information

be registered as different frustrations; if the participant realized quickly the error of their search path and returned to the right page, it would not be marked as frustration.

A member of the research team read the documents of each interview independently and coded the data based on grounded theory. MAXQDA was used for coding annotation to form primary, secondary and tertiary codes [17]. Through open coding, a total of 502 codes were generated. Then three researchers discussed, compared and coordinated the location and definition of each code many times. An initial code framework was established, which integrates the behaviors of late middle-aged users during online shopping, including frustrations during online shopping, the emotional impact of frustrations, ways to solve frustrations. Then we discussed the internal relationship between these topics, as shown in Fig. 1.

4 Findings

4.1 Frustration is Common

The minimum number of operations to complete the task is 10–14 steps, and the average number of operations of participants is 17.46. 26% (n = 4) participants met the simplest operation path, 13% (n = 2) users took 27 steps, and 40% (n = 6) users took more than 20 steps. Through coding and sorting, it can be seen that each user encountered 5 frustrations on average and 11 frustrations at most.

Almost half of the situations of difficulty in finding the required functions in the user tests were caused by participants' inability to "see". Late middle-aged people are experiencing a decline in physical function, especially in visual search ability [18]. Even

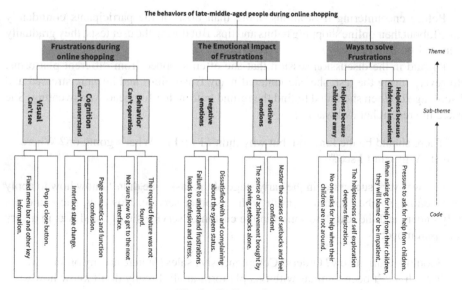

Fig. 1. Coding scheme

though they are familiar with online shopping, they still spend a lot of time searching repeatedly, and may still be unable to locate the information they need.

4.2   The Emotional Impact of Frustrations

When facing frustrations, participants eventually completed the task on their own, but the journey was quite bumpy. Each frustration had an impact on their emotional state and overall experience. Participants may encounter frustrations at almost any stage of online shopping, and their moods were always negative when frustrations occurred. VA model was adopted to descript participants' detailed emotional status in Fig. 2. The most common frustration-related emotions are stress, hesitation and discouragement. Some skilled users also felt dissatisfied and complain about the platform.

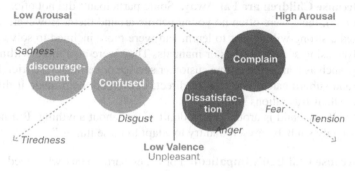

Fig. 2. The emotional impact of frustrations

Before encountering frustrations, more than 80% of the participants confidently talked about their online shopping habits and tips. But during the user tests, they gradually seem to lose confidence.

P4 said in the discussion session that she often shopped from different platforms. However, during the test, she encountered many frustrations and became stressed and discouraged. When she failed to find the refund button, her forehead was sweating. She asked the researcher awkwardly:

"There should be the function, but why didn't I find it? What's going on? Where is it? Why can't I see?"

P11 was very successful in the early stage of the task. She didn't know how to apply for a refund, so she chose to consult with customer service. However, she could not fully understand the text description in the customer service's reply, and was in a very confused mood:

"Should I return it now? Orders? Comprehensive sales? Where are my orders? My God, I haven't been familiar with this platform at all. I really don't know how to find this refund."

Some skilled participants who were very confident in their abilities would also express a stronger emotional response such as dissatisfaction or complaint when they encountered situations that did not meet their expectations.

4.3   Participants Are Helpless When Encountering Frustrations

During the interview stage, we asked about the participants' views on smartphones and online platforms. P3 and P11 made it clear that they were not particularly interested in intelligent gadgets. The remaining 12 participants showed high learning enthusiasm and wiliness to keep up. They want to learn from other people especially younger family members why frustration happened and how to solve it in order to avoid it in the future. However, we found that no matter these 12 participants' living situations with their children is, they were generally helpless.

Helpless Because Children are Far Away.   Some participants did not often meet their children (n = 6), there were often no young people around them. However, these people expressed a strong willingness to learn, and were more inclined to solve problems by themselves using search engines or manuals. They were also more willing to seek remote help, such as contacting online customer service or calling close friends, former colleagues and subordinates. The lack of direct, convenient help made it difficult for them to solve their frustrations smoothly.

P1, P15: "If my child is around me, I don't worry about anything. But now she is abroad. I can only study by myself and try to adapt to these things."

Helpless Because Children's Impatient.   For other participants who lived with their children (n = 7), and their all wished that they could be guided with more patience. Even though they could easily reach out to their children when encountering frustrations, their proficiency was worse than the ones who lived without their children. 70% of them said they didn't want to ask their children for help because they might be blamed. Younger family members may not provide timely and appropriate help. Late middle-aged users might bear great psychological pressure when they had to ask for help.

P7 "Sometimes when I ask my son, he is impatient and operates too quickly. I haven't caught anything yet, but several steps have passed. I just hope he can teach me patiently. Otherwise, I still can't remember next time. And he will ask me why I can't remember."

P4, P12, P14 "My daughter is busy and I'm embarrassed to ask her. She may not have much time. Moreover, young people speak too fast but we understand slowly."

5 Discussion

5.1 Causes of Frustrations

After the age of 60, there is a significant decline in cognitive capacities, such as the ability to receive and process information [19]. In particular, the declining anti-interference ability in the information processing stage makes it difficult for users to find their desired items in time in complex interfaces. And the reduction of their working memory capacity results in heavy cognitive load and difficulty to retain a variety of information. The degradation of these physical functions will accompany the late middle-aged group for a long time. However, the better they understand the causes of their frustrations, the more effectively they can solve the problem.

In the tests, 27% of the participants had no basic understanding of the refund function. About 73% of the participants got stuck in the test because the system feedback was not clear to them. A single frustration may not severe enough to disrupt the whole task but still affect users' emotions and overall experience. The following three categories of causes were identified in this study.

Can't see refers to the failure to obtain vital information visually on the interface. Even if the participants know and can clearly describe the correct operation, they were still less sensitive to the visual change of interface state.

Can't understand refers to the confusion of unclear semantic description, incomplete understanding of icons or unclear status prompts.

Can't operation refers to the frustration of not knowing where to click or not daring to click, etc.The majority of them were in a state of aimless wandering, unsure of where to go next.

5.2 Design Implications

Based on our findings, we develop a number of design implications to address salient issues in the frustrations of the late middle-aged user when shopping online (as shown in Fig. 3). We believe that these strategies could also benefit a certain level of other user groups as well.

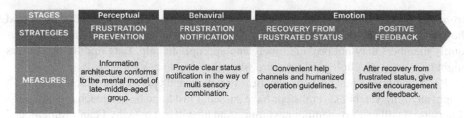

Fig. 3. Design implications

Frustration Prevention: Develop an Age-Friendly Information Structure. The normal aging process will affect the way late middle-aged people use smart products. The information architecture design should adhere to their mental models [20], such as shallow and broad structure with fewer layers, less frequent page switching and clearer semantic descriptions. The button and font size of key features should be emphasized visually.

Frustration Notification: Provide a More Visible Reminder of Frustrations. The primary cause of frustration for older users when using smart devices is the declination of sensory sensitivity and memory capacity, which means the interface should be more enhanced in terms of user perception. System status changes should be displayed more clearly to help users be aware of what's going on. Multi-sensory (audio, haptic etc.) feedback could be used to reduce the visual cognitive load of late middle-aged users.

Recovering from Frustrating Status: Convenient Help Channel and Humanized Operation Guidelines. Although late middle-aged users usually could complete the daily tasks on their own, sometimes they still need to seek help. More and more studies have proved that IVA, as a long-term social partner and exercise coach for seniors, is a feasible way to provide social support [21, 22]. An AI agent can measure the frustration met by the user's behavior such as the number of repeated actions, so as to provide user-friendly step-by-step guidance. It can also record the steps that users most easily forget and provide customized help in time, and assist users to recover from frustrations stress-free [23].

Positive Feedback: Giving Praise after Recovering from Frustrated Status. At the end of the experiment, we asked participants about the use of the "filtering" function in online shopping. 73% of users (n = 11) admitted that they did not know this function and eagerly turned to researchers to learn more. After successfully using this function, every participant was excited.

P4 "I especially like being with young people! I can learn new things, and I feel like I am getting younger."

P9 "Wow! This is very useful. Really good! The next time I buy something I can use this function."

Frustration and confusion in the process of learning are better than boredom [24]. We found frustration could also strengthen the understanding of interface knowledge and let users test their skill, which might give them a sense of achievement. In our study, almost all late middle-aged users had a strong willingness to learn. Positive feedback and appropriate encouragement are vital for them to confirm their perceived self-efficiency and learn better from their mistakes.

6 Conclusion

6.1 Summary and Key Findings

Through the interview and observation, we studied 15 late middle-aged users to understand their behavior when encountering frustrations during online shopping, the emotional impact of frustrations, ways to solve frustrations. User's language and activity behavior were encoded and analyzed based on the grounded theory, which lead us to several insights on the causes of frustrations, emotional characteristics and problem-solving methods of late middle-aged users.

We found that people aged 55–65 generally have a high sense of perceived self-efficacy, and the frustration they encounter when using smart products may cause them to have negative emotions such as doubts, confusion and complaints. Due to their deteriorating eyesight, gradually slowing response and the lack of convenient help, the process of their recovery from encountered frustration is often not smooth, which then continues to have a negative emotional impact on them. Based on the findings, we also proposed design implications aiming to reduce user frustrations, help users recover from frustrations and provide them emotional support.

6.2 Limitations and Future Work

Frustration does not consequentially interrupt users' ongoing tasks but has an intermittent negative effect on the user experience. In this study, the participants were not diverse enough, most of them were highly educated in first-tier cities, and the gender balance was insufficient. And we have not studied the emotional impact on later operations of frustration on late middle-aged users.

In the future, we will enrich the study with a thorough selection of qualitative and quantitative methodologies and continue to study how to help people aged 55–65 reduce the impact of frustrations when using smart products or online platforms.

References

1. Definition of an older or elderly person. World Health Organization (2010)
2. Ma, Q., Chan, A.H.S., Chen, K.: Personal and other factors affecting acceptance of smartphone technology by older Chinese adults. Appl. Ergon. **54**, 62–71 (2016). https://doi.org/10.1016/j.apergo.2015.11.015
3. Men, D., Wang, M.: An empirical study on the elderly visual pleasure experience design elements based on perceptual cognitive characteristics measure and analysis. In: Gao, Q., Zhou, J. (eds.) HCII 2021. LNCS, vol. 12786, pp. 183–202. Springer, Cham (2021). https://doi.org/10.1007/978-3-030-78108-8_14
4. Xi, Z.: Research on user experience design of early elder people using smart phone, Ph.D. thesis. Guangdong University of Technology, China (2021). (in Chinese). https://doi.org/10.27029/d.cnki.ggdgu.2021.000010
5. Xu, B.Q.: A study on the usability of Internet shopping mobile terminal interface for middle-aged and elderly people combined with cognitive characteristics. Master. thesis. Jiangsu University (2020). (in Chinese). https://doi.org/10.27170/d.cnki.gjsuu.2020.000516

6. Freud, S.: Types of onset of neurosis. In: The Standard Edition of the Complete Psychological Works of Sigmund Freud, Volume XII (1911–1913): The Case of Schreber, Papers on Technique and Other Works, pp. 227–238 (1958)

7. Dollard, J.: Frustration and aggression. J. Nerv. Ment. Dis. **92**(3), 408 (1940). https://doi.org/10.1097/00005053-194009000-00045

8. Locke, E., Latham, G.: A theory of goal setting & task performance. Acad. Manag. Rev. **16** (1991). https://doi.org/10.2307/258875

9. Ceaparu, I., Lazar, J., Bessiere, K., Robinson, J., Shneiderman, B.: Determining causes and severity of end-user frustration. Int. J. Hum. Comput. Interact. **17**, 333–356 (2004). https://doi.org/10.1207/s15327590ijhc1703_3

10. Murrell, A.J., Sprinkle, J.: The impact of negative attitudes toward computers on employees' satisfaction and commitment within a small company. Comput. Hum. Behav. **9**, 57–63 (1993). https://doi.org/10.1016/0747-5632(93)90021-j

11. Bandura, A.: Self-efficacy: toward a unifying theory of behavioral change. Psychol. Rev. **84**, 191 (1977). https://doi.org/10.1037/0033-295X.84.2.191

12. Moore, E.J.: Using self-efficacy in teaching self-care to the elderly. Holist. Nurs. Pract. **4**, 22–29 (1990). https://doi.org/10.1097/00004650-199002000-00006

13. González, A., Ramírez, M.P., Viadel, V.: Attitudes of the elderly toward information and communications technologies. Educ. Gerontol. **38**, 585–594 (2012). https://doi.org/10.1080/03601277.2011.595314

14. Osiceanu, M.-E.: Psychological implications of modern technologies: "technofobia" versus "technophilia." Procedia Soc. Behav. Sci. **180**, 1137–1144 (2015). https://doi.org/10.1016/j.sbspro.2015.02.229

15. Klein, J., Moon, Y., Picard, R.W.: This computer responds to user frustration. Interact. Comput. **14**, 119–140 (2002). https://doi.org/10.1016/S0953-5438(01)00053-4.

16. Fisk, A.D., Czaja, S.J., Rogers, W.A., Charness, N., Sharit, J.: Designing for Older Adults: Principles and Creative Human Factors Approaches. CRC Press, Boca Raton (2020)

17. Strauss, A., Corbin, J.M.: Basics of Qualitative Research: Grounded Theory Procedures and Techniques. Sage Publications, Inc., Thousand Oaks (1990). https://doi.org/10.2307/328955

18. Potter, L.M., Grealy, M.A., Elliott, M.A., Andrés, P.: Aging and performance on an everyday-based visual search task. Acta Physiol. **140**, 208–217 (2012). https://doi.org/10.1016/j.actpsy.2012.05.001

19. Cerella, J.: Information processing rates in the elderly. Psychol. Bull. **98**, 67 (1985). https://doi.org/10.1037/0033-2909.98.1.67

20. Zaphiris, P.: Age differences and the depth-breadth tradeoff in hierarchical online information systems. Wayne State University (2002). https://doi.org/10.1007/3-540-36572-9_2

21. Bickmore, T.W., et al.: A randomized controlled trial of an automated exercise coach for older adults. J. Am. Geriatr. Soc. **61**, 1676–1683 (2013). https://doi.org/10.1111/jgs.12449

22. Vardoulakis, L.P., Ring, L., Barry, B., Sidner, C.L., Bickmore, T.: Designing relational agents as long term social companions for older adults. In: Nakano, Y., Neff, M., Paiva, A., Walker, M. (eds.) IVA 2012. LNCS (LNAI), vol. 7502, pp. 289–302. Springer, Heidelberg (2012). https://doi.org/10.1007/978-3-642-33197-8_30

23. Jaksic, N., Branco, P., Stephenson, P., Encarnaçao, L.M.: The effectiveness of social agents in reducing user frustration. In: Extended Abstracts on Human Factors in Computing Systems, CHI 2006, pp. 917–922 (2006). https://doi.org/10.1145/1125451.1125629

24. Baker, R.S.J.d., D'Mello, S.K., Rodrigo, Ma.M.T., Graesser, A.C.: Better to be frustrated than bored: the incidence, persistence, and impact of learners' cognitive-affective states during interactions with three different computer-based learning environments. Int. J. Hum. Comput. Stud. **68**, 223–241 (2010). https://doi.org/10.1016/j.ijhcs.2009.12.003

The Usability of Training Apps for Older Adults – A Heuristic Evaluation

Amrat Kaur and Weiqin Chen[✉]

Oslo Metropolitan University, POB 4, St. Olavsplass, 0130 Oslo, Norway
weiche@oslomet.no

Abstract. The literature has shown that normal ageing is associated with a decline in sensory, perceptual, motor, and cognitive abilities. Physical activities and cognitive training are considered beneficial for maintaining functional abilities and enabling healthy ageing. Recent years have seen an increase of mobile apps for physical and cognitive exercises. However, few studies have investigated the usability of these apps, particularly for older users, to identify in detail the usability challenges older users face when using these apps. In this paper we present a heuristic evaluation of 10 training apps including five for physical training and five for cognitive training. The results show that all the training apps have usability issues. In order to provide apps with high level of usability for older users, apps designers and developers should take into account usability principles and the characteristics and needs of this user group.

Keywords: Usability · Older adults · Training apps · Heuristic evaluation · Physical and cognitive training

1 Background

Ageing is associated with reduced physical and cognitive capacity and a growing risk of disease. Healthy ageing is the process of developing and maintaining the functional ability that enables wellbeing in older age. Several systematic literature reviews and meta-analysis [1–3] have shown the benefits of physical and cognitive training, separately or combined, on healthy ageing.

Mobile technology opens the possibility for providing medical and public health support with mobile devices such as smart phones, tablets, smart watches, and other wireless devices. Mobile health apps for older adults offer promising solutions to manage health issues associated with the aging society and growth of older population. There is an increasing number of smartphone-based apps for physical exercise and cognitive training in the market. Some are developed for younger users and recommended to older adults, while others are developed specially for older adults. Although these apps may be beneficial for the wellbeing of this user group, they can also pose challenges. Poorly designed training apps with low usability could not only discourage older users from using them, but also be potentially harmful for older users.

© Springer Nature Switzerland AG 2022
V. G. Duffy et al. (Eds.): HCII 2022, LNCS 13521, pp. 423–439, 2022.
https://doi.org/10.1007/978-3-031-17902-0_30

Previous studies that investigate the usability of training apps for older adults mostly focus on one particular app [4, 5] and use quantitative measurements to evaluate usability, which often do not provide details of the usability challenges older users face when using the app. The study presented in this paper aims to fill this gap by focusing on the detailed usability challenges posed by cognitive and physical training apps for older users.

2   Related Work

A number of studies have investigated the usability of diverse mHealth apps for older adults, such as apps for medication management [6, 7], diabetes self-management [7], and managing heart failure [8].

Concerning training apps for older adults, Daly and colleagues [4] conducted a pilot study with 20 participants focusing on feasibility, usability and enjoyment of a commercial physical exercise app for older adults living independently in the community. The usability of the app (called "Physitrack") was measured by the System Usability Scale [9]. Pfister and colleagues [5] conducted a mixed methods study on the usability and acceptance of an exercise app (called "Fit") with 20 participants including 10 therapists and 10 adults with mean age 57 years old. In addition to collecting System Usability Scale scores, this study has also measured task completion rate and collected errors and comments made by participants. The data reflected the usability challenges of the app for the participants. Acknowledging the limitation of the study method, the authors of this study commented that combining their study results with other usability methods such as heuristic evaluation or cognitive walkthrough [10] would strengthen their results. A similar study [11] used heuristic evaluation to investigate whether two popular fitness apps Nike+ and RunKeeper were able to accommodate the needs of older users. The study found that small target sizes, insufficient contrast and reduced font sizes are some of the common usability issues that hinder older adults from using these apps. This study concluded that the two fitness apps were not ready to accommodate the needs of older users.

3   Methods

In the study presented in this paper we adopted a heuristic evaluation method to identify usability challenges that training apps pose to older users. A carefully selected group of physical and cognitive training apps (five in each category) for iOS was evaluated based on Jacob Nielsen's 10 usability heuristics[1].

It is difficult to find commercial apps developed specially for older adults. Therefore, we have selected apps that developed mainly for younger users but are recommended to older adults by either health organizations and authorities or ageing-related fora. The five physical exercise apps are: 7 min Workout, C25K 5K Trainer, Daily yoga, MapMyWalk, and Yoga studio. The five cognitive training apps are: CogniFit, Elevate, Lumosity, NeuroNation, and Peak. A free version of each app is downloaded from App Store to iPhone with iOS version 12.5.1.

---

[1] 10 Usability Heuristics for User Interface Design.

In each app, a list of representative pages was selected according to a set of criteria such as essential functions and variety of page types. These selected pages are then evaluated using the usability heuristics. A rating scale is used in the evaluation: 0-not applicable or cannot be evaluated, 1-not comply, 2-partially comply, 3-comply. Along with each rating, a description is provided to explain the rating and screenshots are taken to support the description and rating. In cases of unclear rating, both researchers have discussed and come to an agreement.

4 A Brief Introduction of Selected Apps and Pages

4.1 Cognitive Training Apps

All the cognitive training apps offers a variety of features related to brain training activities. Some of the features can only be accessed in the paid version or after the user has carried out a pre-defined number of training activities. The training in cognitive apps is presented as games.

CogniFit (Version 4.2.12). The interface of CogniFit includes five main pages: 1) gives information on today's games and training sessions, 2) shows overview of results, 3) shows statistics and next goals, 4) shows all games, and 5) shows profile and settings. Users are allowed to play 4 to 40 games every day.

Elevate (Version 5.40.0). The interface of Elevate has five main pages: 1) gives information on today's games, 2) shows statistics of results from playing games, 3) shows overall games and statistics, 4) shows notifications, and 5) gives information about achieved goals and settings. Users are allowed to play 3 games every day.

Lumosity (Version 9.84). The interface of Lumosity contains five main pages: 1) gives information on today's game, 2) shows all games, 3) shows statistics and training history, 4) provides insight into game progress reports, and 5) shows settings. Users are allowed to play 3 games every day.

NeuroNation (Version 3.5.76). The interface of NeuroNation has five main pages: 1) gives information on today's games and training sessions, 2) shows extra physical exercises such as stretching which can help with brain training, 3) shows information about Premiums/paid version, 4) shows overview and statistics of results and achievement of goals, and 5) shows settings.

Peak (Version 5.19.0). In the free version, some of the features require users to see a promotional video to get access. The interface of Peak contains four main pages: 1) gives information on today's games, 2) provides an overview of all games, 3) shows the statistics of results from playing the games, and 4) gives information about achieved goals and settings. Users are allowed to play 2–3 different games once every day and have access to 2–3 new games every day. If users want to play these games again, they must first see a promotional video.

For all five cognitive training apps, the following common features have been selected for evaluation: choosing a game, starting a game, pausing/restarting a game, and quitting a game. In addition, some common pages in each app were evaluated, including the overview page of all games, the main pages for each game where users start game and see information/introduction/statistics about the game, and the pages where users play the games.

4.2 Physical Training Apps

Due to the diversity of the physical training apps, it is difficult to identify common pages in all apps. However, most of the apps have features such as choosing/starting/pausing/quitting a workout/an exercise. These are selected for evaluation. In addition, we have selected some specific pages and features in each app. These are presented in the following sections.

7 min Workout (Version 4.4.9). This app contains three main pages: 1) allows users to choose a workout and start training. Settings for the whole app is also included in this page such as music and favorite exercises. For each workout, users can see which exercises are included and the information about these exercises. 2) allows users to make their own workout by choosing and adding different exercises. 3) shows users' progress over time and allows users to register their weights.

The pages selected for evaluation include the first page where users choose workout, start training and the exercise pages. The features evaluated in these pages include choosing an exercise, seeing an overview of exercises in a workout, and getting information about exercises, turning on/off music, starting an exercise, pausing the exercise, going back and forth between exercises, setting music and voice guidance, and going to full screen.

C25K 5K Trainer (Version 5.1.0). This app has one main page. From this page, users can go to settings, turn on/off dark mode, choose workout, and start workout.

The pages selected for evaluation include the page where users choose and start workout and the page where a workout starts. The features evaluated in these pages are: turn on/off dark mode, choose a workout, start a workout, pause a workout, and continue, change music setting and go back and forth between exercises in a workout.

Daily Yoga (Version 7.49.00). This app has five main pages: 1) gives an overview of a training plan, completed workout and favorites. 2) gives an overview of all workouts. 3) only shows for paid users. 4) allows users to communicate with other users and sharing photos and workouts. 5) allows users to edit profiles and change settings.

The pages selected for evaluation include the pages where users choose and start workout and the page when a workout starts. The features evaluated in these pages are: choose a workout, start a workout, pause a workout, quit a workout, turn on/off music, go back and forth between exercises in a workout, change music setting and voice guidance, and go to full screen mode.

MapMyWalk (Version 21.8.0). This app contains five main pages: 1) allows users to explore the app, find friends and see information about their own training. 2) allows users to make challenges with friends and gives an overview of existing challenges. 3) provides users with choices of activities and changing settings. In this page, users can also connect via Bluetooth to other devices that measure pulse, speed, calories, etc. 4) allows users to set up goals and training plans and shows an overview of completed and future goals. 5) shows diverse additional information and features such as profile, setting, privacy, help, friends, goals and workout routines.

The pages selected for evaluation include the pages where users choose and start a workout and change settings related to the workout. The features evaluated in these pages include: choose a workout, start a workout, pause a workout, quit a workout, change setting for Voice Feedback, set up Delay Start Timer, see notifications, get information about upgrade, and connect to other devices via Bluetooth.

Yoga Studio (Version 4.3.45). This app has five main pages: 1) shows downloaded Yoga poses for use without network connection and allows users to change settings. 2) shows all Yoga blocks users can choose from. Users can make their own blocks by combining a set of poses. 3) shows all Yoga poses where users can browse and search. Yoga poses are described with text and image describing the exercise step-by-step. 4) allows users to plan their own training. 5) shows achieved goals and badges.

The pages selected for evaluation include the pages where users choose and see information about Yoga poses and make their own Yoga blocks. The features evaluated in these pages are: search and choose Yoga poses, choose among blocks, and see/add favorites.

5   Result

In this section we will first present an overview of the evaluation results (Table 1 and 2), followed by a more detailed description of the challenges and issues categorized based on the usability heuristics.

As shown in Table 1, all 10 apps were evaluated either Comply or Partially Comply to all heuristics expect for 7 min Workout and Yoga Studio. Seven apps had more partial complies than full complies across all heuristics. CogniFit fully complies to only one heuristic, while C25K fully complies to six heuristics. Table 2 shows that all heuristics were found to be either complied or partially complied except for Heuristic 9: Help users recognize, diagnose, and recover from errors. Six heuristics received more partial complies than full complies across all apps. Heuristic 3: User control and freedom and Heuristic 4: Consistency and standards received one fully comply each, while Heuristic 2: Match between system and the real world received eight fully complies.

Table 1. Evaluation results of all 10 apps (how many heuristics each app complies, partially complies, does not comply and heuristics that are not applicable or cannot be evaluated).

Apps		Comply	Partially comply	Not comply	Not applicable or cannot be evaluated
Cognitive	CogniFit	1	9	0	0
	Elevate	4	6	0	0
	Lumosity	4	6	0	0
	NeuroNation	3	7	0	0
	Peak	2	8	0	0
Physical	7 min workout	4	5	0	1
	C25K	6	4	0	0
	Daily yoga	5	5	0	0
	MapMyWalk	5	5	0	0
	Yoga studio	4	5	0	1

Table 2. Evaluation results of all 10 training apps categorized by usability heuristics (for each heuristic, how many apps comply, partially comply, do not comply and the heuristic is not applicable or cannot be evaluated).

Usability heuristics	Comply	Partially comply	Not comply	Not applicable or cannot be evaluated
1. Visibility of system status	2	8	0	
2. Match between system and the real world	8	2	0	
3. User control and freedom	1	9	0	
4. Consistency and standards	1	9	0	
5. Error prevention	2	8	0	
6. Recognition rather than recall	2	8	0	
7. Flexibility and efficiency of use	4	6	0	
8. Aesthetic and minimalist design	7	3	0	

(*continued*)

Table 2. (*continued*)

Usability heuristics	Comply	Partially comply	Not comply	Not applicable or cannot be evaluated
9. Help users recognize, diagnose, and recover from errors	5	3	0	2
10. Help and documentation	6	4	0	

5.1 Evaluation Results Categorized by Heuristics

In the following sections we will provide details of the evaluation results of the apps categorized based on the usability heuristics.

Heuristic 1: Visibility of System Status. This heuristic concerns keeping users informed by showing system status and feedback in a timely and appropriate manner. Except for NeuroNation and Daily Yoga, we have found system status visibility issues in all the other apps evaluated. For example, in CogniFit and Elevate, warning sounds are missing when a game starts or finishes. In Lumosity, users do not get immediate feedback that it is a locked game when they try to open one. Instead, the main page for the game opens with a button which users must press to unlock with Premium. In Peak users of the free version are required to see a promotional video when they want to play a game again. However, Peak does not inform users that the video is a promotional video. In 7 min Workout's full screen mode it is not clear for users where to tap in order to pause a workout. In C25K voice feedback announces workout start/stop, but this voice does not announce pause and resume. A similar issue was also found in MapMyWalk. In Yoga Studio, a user can choose a photo for the Yoga block s/he has created. However, there is no indication (e.g. by using a check box) on which photo the user has chosen.

Heuristic 2: Match Between System and the Real World. This heuristic concerns using familiar concepts, symbols, and terms and presenting information in natural and logical order to users. Except for CogniFit and Yoga Studio, all the other evaluated apps have satisfied this heuristic. In CogniFit some of the terms such as *inhibition* and *shifting* under Trained Skills in the game introduction may be difficult for users to understand. Yoga Studio provides descriptions of poses. Most of the descriptions are easy to understand, especially with the additional images of the poses. However, some pose descriptions refer to other pose names which users may not be familiar with. It would be helpful if it provides a link to the other pose descriptions or tooltips explaining the pose names.

Heuristic 3: User Control and Freedom. This heuristic concerns providing users with possibilities for going back, undoing, or canceling their action, thus allowing users to have a feeling of control and freedom and avoid frustration. Except for Yoga Studio, none of the other apps evaluated fully satisfy this heuristic. In CogniFit, users can neither skip over instruction, go back and forth between pages in the introduction, nor have they an option to restart a game. In Elevate, when a user pauses a game, a page shows up with options of *Resume, Restart, Menu,* and *Game Instructions.* The *Menu* option is in fact the possibility to quit the game and go back to the main menu. But this is not clear to users. In Lumosity, if a user chooses to see the introduction before playing a game, the game starts automatically after the introduction. If the user wants to see the introduction again, s/he must pause the game first, then choose *How to play* in the next page. In NeuroNation, after a user has paused a game, s/he must first quit the game and start it again since there is no restart option. In Peak, users must see all the steps in the introduction of a game. They are not allowed to go back and forth between steps. In 7 min Workout it is not possible to pause the animation showing how to carry out the exercise. A similar issue was found in Daily Yoga where users are not allowed to pause instruction videos. In C25K when users start a workout, the app shows some tips. Users can tap anywhere to close tips. However, if users choose *Never Show Again,* it is not possible to find these tips again (Fig. 1a). In MapMyWalk, when users press the *Shoe* icon (connecting to other devices with Bluetooth), if the Bluetooth is not turned on, a message pops up giving users two options (Fig. 1b). Users can press *OK* to continue with turning on Bluetooth. If users choose *Not Now,* a page shows up anyway asking users to either connecting to Bluetooth or learning more about Bluetooth connection and auto-sync.

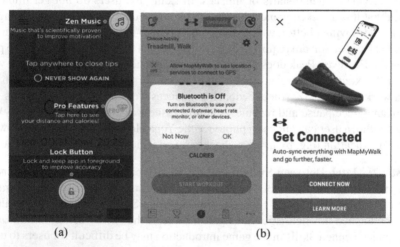

(a)   (b)

Fig. 1. Screenshots illustrating a lack of user control and freedom. (a) In C25K it is not possible for users to find the tips if they choose *Never Show Again.* (b) In MapMyWalk *Not Now* does not stop the app from asking users for Bluetooth connection.

Heuristic 4. Consistency and Standards. This heuristic concerns maintaining internal and external consistency to improve learnability and reduce cognitive load. In our evaluation, all the apps except for Yoga Studio have consistency issues. In CogniFit, some of the warning sounds are the same for all games (e.g. for starting a game or going to a next level), while other warning sounds (e.g. for a right answer or a wrong answer) are different from game to game. A similar issue was also found in Peak. In C25K the icon that is expected to show the length of workout time does not change when the workout length changes. In Elevate, the *Game Instructions* option has a different design than the other options (Fig. 2a). In Lumosity, instructions can be skipped in two different ways, one using *Skip Tutorial* and the other using a cross icon (Fig. 2b). NeuroNation uses different background colors for different games. However, when a user goes back from a game (with a specific background color) to the main page, the main page's background color becomes the same as the game's background color. This could be confusing for users if they use color to recognize games. Daily Yoga shows an icon in the upper right corner of a page with all training courses. It could be difficult for users to understand that this icon means sorting and filtering training courses (Fig. 2c). In MapMyWalk, the *Shoe* icon means connecting to other devices via Bluetooth. A Bluetooth icon would be easier to understand for users. 7 min Workout uses two different icons in different pages for music setting.

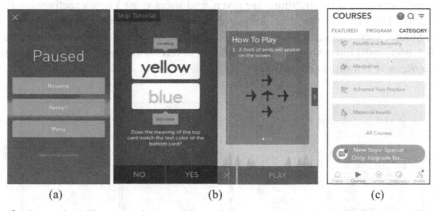

(a)   (b)   (c)

Fig. 2. Screenshots illustrating issues with consistency and standards. (a) Options have different design in Elevate. (b) Different ways to skip an instruction in Lumosity. (c) Icon for sorting and filtering (upper right corner) in Daily Yoga.

Heuristic 5: Error Prevention. This heuristic concerns eliminating error-prone conditions and asking users to confirm before they commit to an action that can cause an error. Except for 7 min Workout and C25K, all the other apps have issues in error prevention. Elevate, Lumosity, Peak, and NeuroNation do not require confirmation or inform users about the exercise is not saved when they press the *Quit/Exit* exercise button or *Pause* button for going back to the main page. CogniFit informs users that if they exit from a game their progress will not be saved. Users are expected to read this information, because when they click on *Exit*, there is not confirmation. In Lumosity, if a user wishes to see instructions again while s/he is playing a game, the game restarts automatically after the instructions finish and the progress data is not saved. The user is not warned about this beforehand, neither is the user required to confirm the see instructions action. In Daily Yoga, users can delete search history by pressing *Clear* without any confirmation or warning. In MapMyWalk, when users press *Learn More* they are taken to an external website for developers. Users are not informed or warned about the external website, nor are they required to confirm. This could be confusing for users. In Yoga Studio, when users delete a Yoga pose from Favorites or from a Yoga block they are not required to confirm.

Heuristic 6: Recognition Rather Than Recall. This heuristic concerns minimizing users' memory load and reducing the information users have to remember by making elements, actions and options visible and easily recognizable. Except for 7 min Workout and MapMyWalk, challenges with this heuristic were found in all the other apps. In CogniFit, Elevate, Lumosity, NeuroNation, and Peak, users have to remember that they need to first pause the game in order to see instructions. In NeuroNation, users also have to remember to swipe up in order to see more information about a game because there is no indication (e.g. a scroll bar) on the page that the users can swipe up (Fig. 3a). In C25K, free version users have to remember which functions are only for paid users and which are available in the free version. In Daily Yoga, when users try to search for courses/poses/users no suggestions are given, and users must know exactly what they search for. This requires that users know for example the name of courses or poses. In Yoga Studio, users can see a list of blocks or favorites. In order to delete one item from the list, users must remember to swipe from right to left on the item in order to make the *Delete/Remove* button visible (Fig. 3b).

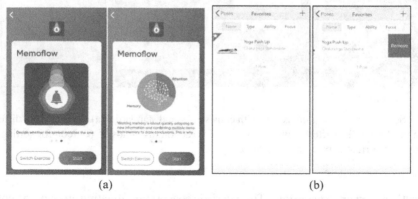

(a)   (b)

Fig. 3. Screenshots illustrating issues with recognition. (a) No visible possibility to scroll down in NeuroNation. (b) No visible *Remove* option in Yoga Studio before swiping.

Heuristic 7: Flexibility and Efficiency of Use. This heuristic concerns flexibility and efficiency of user actions by providing shortcuts, allowing users to customize and tailoring content and functions for individual users. Daily Yoga, C25K, Elevate, and Lumosity were found to comply to this heuristic. In CogniFit, NeuroNation, and Peak users do not have possibility to go back and forth or choose to see only one specific step in the instructions. In 7 min Workout, it is not possible to search. If users wish to find a specific workout, they have to browse through all the workouts. In Yoga Studio, users also need to browse when grouping poses and blocks according to categories. A filtering option will likely make this more efficient. In MapMyWalk, if a user wishes to move some stats from *Not Shown During Workout* to *Shown During Workout* or vice versa, s/he needs to press the icon on the right side, then hold and move the item up or down. There are no other options for users who are not able to perform this drag-and-drop gesture (Fig. 4).

Fig. 4. In MapMyWalk moving item must use drag-and-drop gesture.

Heuristic 8: Aesthetic and Minimalist Design. This heuristic concerns keeping content and visual design of a user interface focused on the essentials and avoiding distracting users with unnecessary elements. Except for 7 min Workout, CogniFit, and NeuroNation, all the other apps satisfy this heuristic. In CogniFit, the backgrounds for the game names are images of the games, which could make the names difficult to read. This also makes the interface seem crowded (Fig. 5a). The same issue is found in 7 min Workout where the backgrounds for workouts/exercises are images (Fig. 5b). In NeuroNation, when choosing an exercise, a user can see the progress levels from Newcomer to Expert. The "er" at the end of Newcomer is put in the next line (Fig. 5c) due to issues in the layout design.

Heuristic 9: Help Users Recognize, Diagnose, and Recover From Errors. This heuristic concerns communicating error messages to users in a clear and understandable manner and providing guidance to recover from errors. C25K, CogniFit, Elevate, MapMyWalk and NeuroNation satisfy this heuristic. In Daily Yoga, if a user using a free version chooses a PRO-workout (not a free workout) by mistake, instead of informing the user that this is a paid workout, it shows *Try for Free* with *Time limited* in small font size. When the user presses *Try for Free*, a warning pops out telling the user about starting a 7-day free demo to get access to the workout (Fig. 6). Such feedback can be confusing for users. Similar issue was found in Lumosity and Peak when users try to open a locked game (not a free game).

Heuristic 10: Help and Documentation. This heuristic concerns providing easily accessible documentation for users. 7 min Workout, C25K, Daily Yoga, Lumosity, MapMyWalk and Yoga Studio satisfy this heuristic. All 10 apps provide some instructions

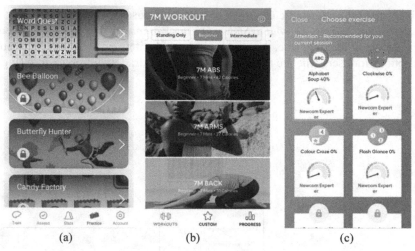

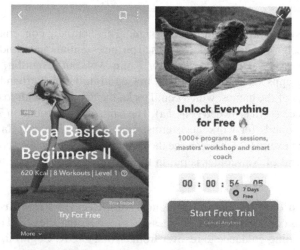

Fig. 5. Screenshots illustrating issues with Aesthetic and minimalist design. (a) Backgrounds for game names in CogniFit. (b) Backgrounds for workout types in 7 min Workout. (c) Word breaking in NeuroNation's layout design.

Fig. 6. Pages shown after a free-version user chooses a non-free workout in Daily Yoga.

for users in the beginning of a game or workout with diverse level of details from video instructions (e.g. Daily Yoga), step-by-step textual instructions with images (e.g. Yoga Studio), to simple and brief instructions in text form (e.g. C25K). When a user has spent a long time on a task, Elevate provides just-in-time help to guide the user to complete the task. While playing a game, users in Peak can press the *Question Mark* icon to access instructions. In CogniFit, at the beginning of a game, the app provides a step-by-step instruction/simulation on how to play, but the instruction cannot be seen again during the game. If users pause the game and choose to see instructions, the app shows a brief instruction in text. In Elevate, the information about the icon is difficult to find which shows the data for the game are not registered. In NeuroNation, instructions are given to users while users are playing the game and it is not possible to skip the instructions. In Peak, instructions in text bubbles fly in from left and disappear in the right, while animations are shown to users how to play the game. To follow the instructions requires multitasking skills.

5.2 Summary of the Results

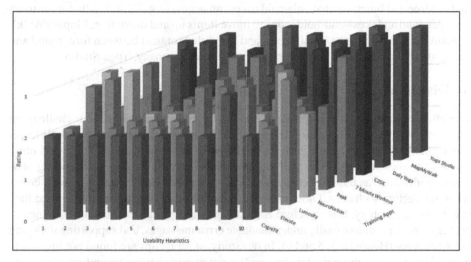

Fig. 7. Overview of evaluation results for all 10 training apps.

Figure 7 shows the overall rating of all apps and all heuristics. The evaluation has shown many good usability practices in the apps, including showing clearly which pages users are in with colors and text (e.g. 7 min Workout, Daily Yoga, CogniFit, Peak) and using warning sounds in combination with text and image as feedback (e.g. C25K, Elevate), using clear and easily understandable languages and familiar images as icons such as moon icon for dark mode, note icon for music settings (e.g. C25K, Daily Yoga, Lumosity, NeuroNation), allowing users to pause/resume/restart games or workouts (C25K, MapMyWalk, Lumosity), and browse, search and group exercises (e.g. Daily Yoga, MapMyWalk, Yoga Studio), consistent use of icons and button layouts (e.g. C25K, Yoga Studio), preventing errors by warnings and confirmations (e.g. C25K, 7 min Workout), providing text together with icons so users do not need to remember the meaning of icons (e.g. C25K, 7 min Workout, Lumosity, Yoga Studio), providing users with possibilities to change settings, making own training plans and Yoga blocks (e.g. 7 min Workout, Yoga Studio), keeping content and visual design focused on essential activities such as choosing and playing games and carrying out exercises (e.g. 7 min Workout, Elevate), giving immediate feedback and suggestions when users make mistakes (e.g.

C25K, 7 min Workout) and providing instructions/help in context right at the moment that the user requires it (e.g. 7 min Workout, Elevate, Peak).

Despite of the good usability practices, the evaluation has also revealed many design issues that do not satisfy the heuristics. In particular, more than half of the apps were found to have usability issues related to heuristics 1, 3, 4, 5, 6, and 7. Some of the main usability issues include not requiring confirmation or informing about progress data is not saved when a user presses the *Quit* exercise button or *Pause* button for going back to main page (e.g. Lumosity, NeuroNation, Elevate), not allowing users to pause, go forward or backward when playing the instruction videos or animations (e.g. 7 min Workout, Daily Yoga, CogniFit), not showing visible scroll bar when users must remember to swipe to see more information (e.g. NeuroNation), not showing differences between functions that are free and functions that only paid users can access (e.g. C25K), difficult for users to understand and press-and-hold icons to move items up and down (e.g. MapMyWalk). In addition, small font size, small icons, and low color contrast between foreground and background were found in several apps (e.g. Elevate, Lumosity, Yoga Studio).

6 Discussion

The effects of ageing on perceptual, motor and cognitive abilities make it challenging for many older adults to use mobile apps [12]. Some older users find the small target size difficult; others find some gestures challenging to perform. In our study and other previous studies such as [11], small target size and specific gesture such as drag-and-drop are identified as usability challenges. Reduced motor skills also cause more errors when interacting with apps. Older users are often afraid of making mistakes when they use digital technology. It is therefore essential that apps for older users are designed to prevent errors, providing easily understandable error messages, and supporting undo and error recovery (Heuristic 3, 5 and 9). In our study, several apps are found not informing users about possible progress data loss and/or not requiring users to confirm when they try to delete information. Such usability issues will enhance the negative experiences of older users with the apps. The decrease in visual perception includes reduced peripheral vision, color vision, contrast detection and dark adaptation [13]. Therefore, many older users found small font size and low contrast difficult. Our study confirms several other studies [11, 14] that apps do not meet older adults' specific visual requirements. Hearing ability declines to 75% for people between 75 and 79 years of age [13] and they are also become more easily distracted by details or noises. In our study, we have found crowded interfaces in some apps (Heuristic 8). Some apps make use of sounds or voice feedback, but lack of consistency (Heuristic 4). Such usability issues will also increase the cognitive load for older users.

Cognitive decline associated with ageing causes the short-term memory to retain fewer items and the working memory to be less efficient. Older adults also have difficulty maintaining attention on more than one aspect at once [15]. Our study shows that some apps do not have a visible scroll possibility and require users to remember to swipe in order to see the complete information (Heuristic 6). Some apps require users to focus on more than one element such as text bubbles flying in while an animation is playing. Some apps use different icons for the same activity and some non-standard icons are found to be difficult to understand (Heuristic 4).

Our findings have not only confirmed the common usability challenges mobile apps pose for older adults such as small target size, small font size, and low contrast, but also revealed some new challenges and good practices that are related to digital literacy of older adults and their technology acceptance. Older users often feel insecure or unconfident about their own ability to use digital technology [16]. Therefore, easily understandable languages, error prevention, multimodal feedback, as well as just-in-time help are important in supporting older users to overcome these challenges. For training apps, in particular, timely, clear, and easily accessible instructions are also crucial for older users to accept and make use of the apps, as shown in our findings.

In the past decade, a few mobile app design guidelines and checklists for older adults have been developed (see [17] for an empirical analysis) which cover an increasingly complex set of usability categories and dimensions. Although these guidelines and checklists need further empirical validation, they can be useful resources for developers when developing mobile apps for older adults. Many of the usability challenges we identified in our study are covered by these guidelines and checklists.

7 Conclusion

This paper presents a heuristic evaluation of 10 training apps for older adults. The results have not only confirmed the findings from previous studies, but also revealed challenges and good practices related to older adults' digital literacy and technology acceptance.

Although we did not use the severity scale in the evaluation, we have identified several severe issues in the apps including the lack of confirmation or feedback about losing progress data when users quit or pause an exercise. Future study should further investigate the usability of training apps for older adults by user testing and evaluating apps on different mobile devices such as Android phones, tablets, and smart watches.

Previous studies have demonstrated that older users are increasingly able to use technology to remain independent, promote a heath lifestyle and improve their quality of life. Decrease in cognitive and physical abilities among older adults can have negative impact on their experienced usability of mobile apps. Training apps developers may overlook a major group of users by failing to provide apps with high level of usability. When recommending training apps to older adults that are not designed especially for them, it is also important to consider the usability aspects and the special needs of this user group.

The universal nature of the 10 usability heuristics by Nielsen allows for its wide application in the evaluation of user interfaces. However, the heuristics have not been created specifically for the design of mobile apps for older adults. Recent years have also seen the efforts in developing heuristics to evaluate mobile apps targeted at older users [18] and in developing mHealth evaluation framework and questionnaires, such as the mHealth App Usability Questionnaire (MAUQ) by [19]. The MOLD-US framework by [20] are specially designed to classify usability barriers of mHealth applications for older adults. Such heuristics, framework, and questionnaires could be considered in future evaluation and analysis of training apps for older adults.

References

1. Daskalopoulou, C., Stubbs, B., Kralj, C., Koukounari, A., Prince, M., Prina, A.M.: Physical activity and healthy ageing: a systematic review and meta-analysis of longitudinal cohort studies. Ageing Res. Rev. **28**, 6–17 (2017)
2. Gavelin, H.M., et al.: Combined physical and cognitive training for older adults with and without cognitive impairment: a systematic review and network meta-analysis of randomized controlled trials. Ageing Res. Rev. **66**, 101232 (2021)
3. Tetlow, A.M., Edwards, J.D.: Systematic literature review and meta-analysis of commercially available computerized cognitive training among older adults. J. Cognit. Enhanc. **1**(4), 559–575 (2017). https://doi.org/10.1007/s41465-017-0051-2
4. Daly, R.M., Gianoudis, J., Hall, T., Mundell, N.L., Maddison, R.: Feasibility, usability, and enjoyment of a home-based exercise program delivered via an exercise app for musculoskeletal health in community-dwelling older adults: short-term prospective pilot study. JMIR Mhealth Uhealth **9**, e21094 (2021)
5. Pfister, P.B., Tobler-Ammann, B., Knols, R.H., de Bruin, E.D., de Bie, R.A.: Usability and acceptance of an interactive tablet-based exercise application: a mixed methods study. Front. Digit. Health **2**, 578281 (2020)
6. Grindrod, K.A., Li, M., Gates, A.: Evaluating user perceptions of mobile medication management applications with older adults: a usability study. JMIR Mhealth Uhealth **2**, e11 (2014)
7. Gao, C., Zhou, L., Liu, Z., Wang, H., Bowers, B.: Mobile application for diabetes self-management in China: do they fit for older adults? Int. J. Med. Inform. **101**, 68–74 (2017)
8. Morey, S.A., Barg-Walkow, L.H., Rogers, W.A.: Managing heart failure on the go: usability issues with MHealth apps for older adults. In: Proceedings of the Human Factors and Ergonomics Society Annual Meeting, vol. 61, pp. 1–5 (2017)
9. Brooke, J.: SUS - a quick and dirty usability scale. In: Jordan, P.W., Thomas, B., We-ermeester, B.A., Mcclelland, A.L. (eds.) Usability Evaluation in Industry. Taylor and Francis, London (1996)
10. Jaspers, M.W.: A comparison of usability methods for testing interactive health technologies: methodological aspects and empirical evidence. Int. J. Med. Inform. **78**, 340–353 (2009)
11. Silva, P.A., Holden, K., Nii, A.: Smartphones, smart seniors, but not-so-smart apps: a heuristic evaluation of fitness apps. In: Schmorrow, D.D., Fidopiastis, C.M. (eds.) AC 2014. LNCS (LNAI), vol. 8534, pp. 347–358. Springer, Cham (2014). https://doi.org/10.1007/978-3-319-07527-3_33
12. Czaja, S.J., Boot, W.R., Charness, N., Rogers, W.A.: Designing for Older Adults: Principles and Creative Human Factors Approaches. CRC Press, Boca Raton (2019)
13. Fozard, J.L.: Vision and hearing in aging. In: Birren, J.E., Schaie, K.W. (eds.) Handbook of the Psychology of Aging, pp. 150–170. Academic Press, New York (1990)
14. Wildenbos, G.A., Jaspers, M.W.M., Schijven, M.P., Dusseljee-Peute, L.W.: Mobile health for older adult patients: using an aging barriers framework to classify usability problems. Int. J. Med. Inform. **124**, 68–77 (2019)
15. Craik, F.I.M.: Ageing memory: ageing memories. In: Rabbitt, P. (ed.) Inside Psychology: A Science Over 50 Years, pp. 73–89. Oxford University Press, UK (2009)
16. Vroman, K.G., Arthanat, S., Lysack, C.: "Who over 65 is online?" Older adults' dispositions toward information communication technology. Comput. Hum. Behav. **43**, 156–166 (2015)
17. Petrovčič, A., Taipale, S., Rogelj, A., Dolničar, V.: Design of mobile phones for older adults: an empirical analysis of design guidelines and checklists for feature phones and smartphones. Int. J. Hum. Comput. Interact. **34**, 251–264 (2018)

18. Silva, P.A., Holden, K., Jordan, P.: Towards a list of heuristics to evaluate smartphone apps targeted at older adults: a study with apps that aim at promoting health and well-being. In: Proceedings of the Annual Hawaii International Conference on System Sciences, pp. 3237–3246 (2015)
19. Zhou, L., Bao, J., Setiawan, A., Saptono, A., Parmanto, B.: The mHealth app usability questionnaire (MAUQ): development and validation study. JMIR Mhealth Uhealth **7**, e11500 (2019)
20. Wildenbos, G.A., Peute, L., Jaspers, M.: Aging barriers influencing mobile health usability for older adults: a literature based framework (MOLD-US). Int. J. Med. Inform. **114**, 66–75 (2018)

A Study on the Development of VR Content for Quantitative Evaluation of Impaired Visuospatial Ability

Fumiya Kinoshita[1(✉)] and Hiroki Takada[2]

[1] Toyama Prefectural University, 5180 Kurokawa, Imizu, Toyama 939-0398, Japan
f.kinoshita@pu-toyama.ac.jp
[2] University of Fukui, 3-9-1 Bunkyo, Fukui 910-8507, Japan

Abstract. To delay cognitive decline, early detection of mild cognitive impairment (MCI) is important. However, early detection of MCI is difficult because it is a condition in which some cognitive functions are impaired but without interfering with daily life. Impaired visuospatial ability, one of the first symptoms of dementia, is a cognitive disorder that causes problems in recognizing the spatial location of objects and the spatial positional relationships of multiple objects. Therefore, quantitative assessment of impaired visuospatial ability would be useful for early detection of MCI. In this study, we developed VR content to quantitatively evaluate user's depth perception ability by using a head-mounted display (HMD) with a gaze measurement function. In this study, we conducted a VR content evaluation experiment developed for the younger group as a preliminary experiment before targeting the MCI patient group. Consequently, it was possible to measure the user's convergence-divergence motion by using pupillary distance.

Keywords: Mild cognitive impairment (MCI) · Head-mounted display (HMD) · VR content · Pupillary distance · Convergence-divergence motion

1 Introduction

To delay cognitive decline, early detection of mild cognitive impairment (MCI), which lies on the borderline between being healthy and having dementia, is important [1]. However, early detection of MCI is difficult because MCI is a condition in which some cognitive functions are impaired but do not interfere with daily life. Objective cognitive function tests are important in the diagnosis of MCI and require multidimensional assessment of many cognitive domains, including memory, language, executive function, visuospatial cognition, and attention [2]. As a cognitive function assessment battery for MCI, the Montreal Cognitive Assessment is considered excellent for detecting MCI and is widely used [3]. However, screening tests based on memory load are effective in detecting amnestic MCI but are not accurate in detecting non-amnestic MCI. As the annual rate of progression from MCI to dementia is not low, being approximately 10% [4], it is important to establish a testing method for the early detection of non-amnestic MCI.

© Springer Nature Switzerland AG 2022
V. G. Duffy et al. (Eds.): HCII 2022, LNCS 13521, pp. 440–450, 2022.
https://doi.org/10.1007/978-3-031-17902-0_31

It is known that early symptoms of Alzheimer's dementia, such as difficulty in drawing figures, getting lost when driving, and inability to drive in a garage, appear even in the absence of visual impairment [5]. These symptoms, called impaired visuospatial ability, are important clinical manifestations for early diagnosis. There are two pathways for visual information processing in the cerebral cortex [6]. The first is the ventral visual pathway, which processes information to identify objects. The ventral visual pathway is a visual pathway that starts in the primary visual cortex, passes through the temporal cortex, and ends in the prefrontal cortex. The other is the dorsal visual pathway, which processes information about the position and depth of objects. The dorsal visual pathway also begins in the primary visual cortex, which is a visual pathway that passes through the parietal cortex to the prefrontal cortex. Visual information from these two pathways converges again in the prefrontal cortex, and visual information processing occurs. In Alzheimer's dementia, in addition to parahippocampal damage, blood flow in the parietal-occipital lobe is known to be reduced from the early stage of the disease [7]. Therefore, reduced blood flow in the parietal-occipital lobes in Alzheimer's dementia affects dorsal visual pathway dysfunction. This is believed to become the responsible lesion, causing clinical symptoms such as "I can understand what the object is, but I cannot understand the spatial information, such as exact location and depth."

Impaired visuospatial ability is a clinical symptom observed not only in Alzheimer's dementia but also in MCI [8]. Therefore, quantitative assessment of impaired visuospatial ability would be useful for early detection of MCI. In this study, we developed VR content that can quantitatively evaluate the depth perception ability of users. The VR content was developed using Unity, and the objects placed on the screen can move freely in the depth direction. The VR contents were presented through a head-mounted display (HMD) with a gaze-measuring function, and the gaze information while gazing at the objects was obtained. In the experiment, we conducted a VR content evaluation experiment developed for the younger group as a preliminary experiment before targeting the MCI patient group. We investigated to what extent the eye information obtained from the HMD can capture the depth change of objects.

2 VR Content Development

Figure 1 shows an example of the VR content developed in this study. This content was developed using Unity, and up to three objects can be displayed in the VR space. The parameters that can be changed are the number of objects, color, size, speed, range, and initial position. The developed VR contents can be presented through an HMD with a gaze measurement function to obtain the gaze information when gazing at an object. In this experiment, we used HTC's Vive Pro Eye VR system as the HMD with a gaze measurement function (Fig. 2). This HMD is equipped with an eye tracker from Tobii Technology, the world's largest eye-tracking company, and is capable of acquiring binocular eye-tracking information with a temporal resolution of 119.5 Hz. The gaze information that can be obtained from the Vive Pro Eye system includes gaze vector, eye position, pupil position, pupil diameter, and eye opening/closing. Examples of the eye information that can be obtained from the Vive Pro Eye system are shown below.

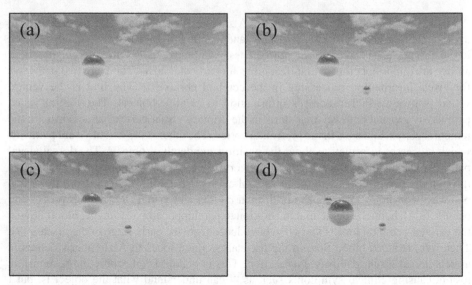

Fig. 1. Examples of the VR content developed: (a) Pattern-1, (b) Pattern-2, (c) Pattern-3, (d) Pattern-4

Vive Pro Eye   coordinate axes   HMD tracking area

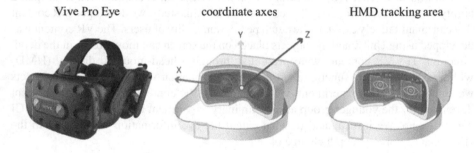

Resolution: 1440 × 1600 pixels per eye (2880 × 1600 pixels combined)

Refresh Rate: 90 Hz,   Field of view: 110 °

Gaze data output frequency: 119.5 Hz,   Accuracy: 0.5 ° –1.1 °

Calibration: 5-point,   Trackable field of view: 110 °

Fig. 2. Main specifications of the Vive Pro Eye VR system [9, 10].

In Tobii's HMD eye trackers, all data describing the coordinates of the 3D space are given in the so-called HMD Coordinate System. The HMD Coordinate System is a millimetric system whose origin is located at a point between the HMD device lenses, at the same distance from the center of each lens. The coordinate axes are oriented as follows: looking from the user's point of view, the x-axis points horizontally to the left side, the y-axis points vertically upward, and the z-axis points (forward) away from the HMD, perpendicular to the HMD tracker lenses.

• Example of a line of sight unit vector

In the Vive Pro Eye system, the gaze direction of the left and right eyes can be obtained as an independent line-of-sight unit vector. Figure 3 shows the movement of a line-of-sight unit vector when the object is periodically moved along the x-axis.

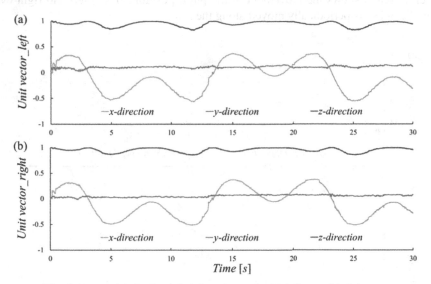

Fig. 3. Example of a line-of-sight unit vector: (a) left eye, (b) right eye.

• Example of eye position

The eye position is the starting point of a line-of-sight unit vector. Figure 4 shows the movement of the eye positions of the left and right eyes when the object is periodically moved along the x-axis. It can be confirmed that the left and right eye movements are linked and that the axes are reversed in the left and right eyes.

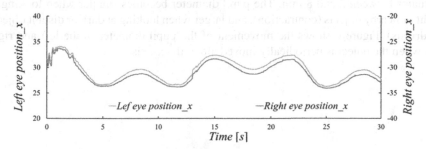

Fig. 4. Example of eye position data in the x-direction.

• Example of pupil position

The pupil position is the position of the left and right eyes in the HMD tracking area. The HMD Tracking Area is a normalized 2D coordinate system with its origin (0, 0) in the upper right corner (from the wearer's point of view), and (1, 1) in the lower left corner. Figure 5 shows the movement of the pupil positions of the left and right eyes when the object is periodically moved along the x-axis.

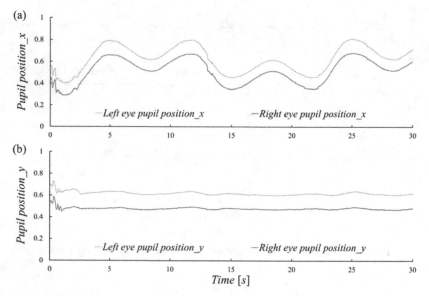

Fig. 5. Example of pupil position: (a) x-direction, (b) y-direction.

• Example of pupil diameter

The pupil diameter can be obtained for each eye. In general, the pupil diameter fluctuates between 2 and 8 mm. The pupil diameter becomes smaller when looking at bright or nearby objects (contraction), and larger when looking at dark or distant objects (mydriasis). Figure 6 shows the movement of the pupil diameter in the left and right eyes when the object is periodically moved along the x-axis.

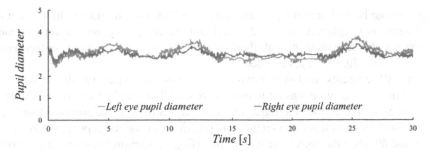

Fig. 6. Example of pupil diameter variation with time.

3   Experimental Methods

In this experiment, we conducted a VR content evaluation experiment developed in this study for a group of young people. The participants were 14 healthy young men and women (21.79 ± 1.26 years). We comprehensively explained the experiment to the participants and obtained their written consent beforehand. This experiment was conducted after obtaining approval from the Ethics Committee of Toyama Prefectural University (R3-1).

The experiment was conducted in a resting sedentary posture. After attaching the HMD to the participant, we always calibrated the Vive Pro Eye system. Afterward, we tested the wearing comfort of the HMD and the video display. After attaching the HMD to the participants, all participants were given the following instructions before the Vive Pro experiment: "always gaze at the object displayed in the center of the screen" and "do

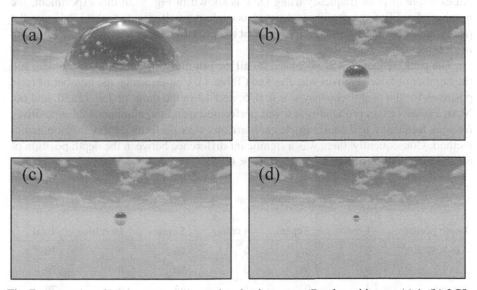

Fig. 7. Examples of VR contents with varying depth patterns. Depth positions at (a) 1, (b) 3.75, (c) 7.5, and (d) 15.

not move your head during the gaze measurement." In this experiment, to account for the influence of eyeglasses, we asked participants wearing eyeglasses to remove them and perform the measurement with their naked eyes. Subjects wearing contact lenses were measured with their eyes unaided.

In the VR contents used in this experiment, only one object was displayed in the center of the screen, and it was set to move periodically from the background direction to the foreground direction at a frequency of five times in 30 s. We prepared four depth patterns for the VR contents, and set the front position to 1 and the depth positions to 7.5, 15, 30, and 60 when the object size was set to 1 (Fig. 7). Measurements were performed five times for each subject. To take into account the order effect, the order of experiments for each depth pattern was randomized.

4 Results

In this experiment, we focused on the pupillary distance between the left and right eyes as an index of depth perception during object gazing. The pupillary distance fluctuates with convergence-divergence motion and can be calculated with the Vive Pro Eye system by calculating the Euclidean distance from the time-series data of the eye positions of the left and right eyes. Figure 8 shows an example of the time-series data of the pupillary distance during object gazing for the same subject. It was confirmed that the divergence motion tended to decrease as the depth position became farther.

In this experiment, the position of the peak frequency was calculated as a representative value using the discrete Fourier transform (DFT). The intervals where blinks were observed in the time-series data were considered as missing values from 0.05 s before and after the blink, and interpolation was performed using linear interpolation. An example of peak frequency using DFT is shown in Fig. 9. In this experiment, the number of oscillations per 30 s is denoted as cycle per half minute (cphm), taken as the peak frequency unit. It can be confirmed that the peak frequency was detected at 5 cphm in all typical time-series data.

The peak frequency was calculated for all the pupillary distance time-series data and the number of false positives was checked (Table 1). Consequently, the number of false positives for the peak frequency was 0, 0, 5, and 12 in the order of 7.5, 15, 30, and 60. Next, Fisher's exact probability test was performed using the number of false positives for peak frequency, and then multiple comparisons were performed using the Bonferroni method. Consequently, there was a significant difference between the depth position of 60 and the depth position of 7.5 and 15 ($p < 0.05$).

Table 1. Detection position of peak frequency of pupillary distance.

Depth position	1 cphm	3 cphm	4 cphm	5 cphm	10 cphm	Total
1 to 7.5	0	0	0	**70**	0	**70**
1 to 15	0	0	0	**70**	0	**70**
1 to 30	4	0	1	**65**	0	**70**
1 to 60	8	1	0	**58**	3	**70**

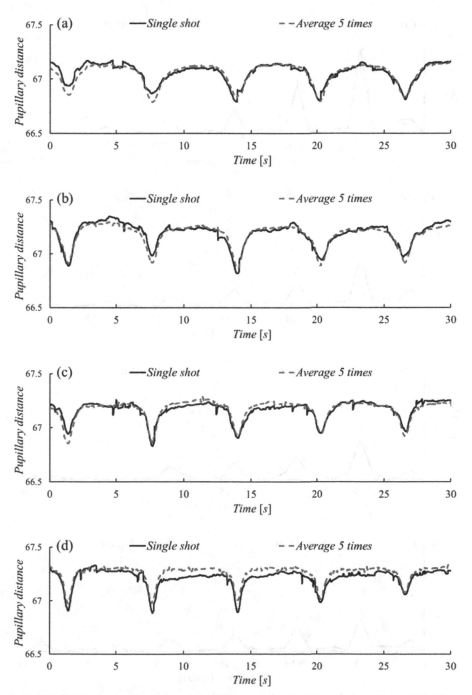

Fig. 8. Example of pupillary distance for the same subject. Depth position at (a) 1 to 7.5, (b) 1 to 15, (c) 1 to 30, and (d) 1 to 60.

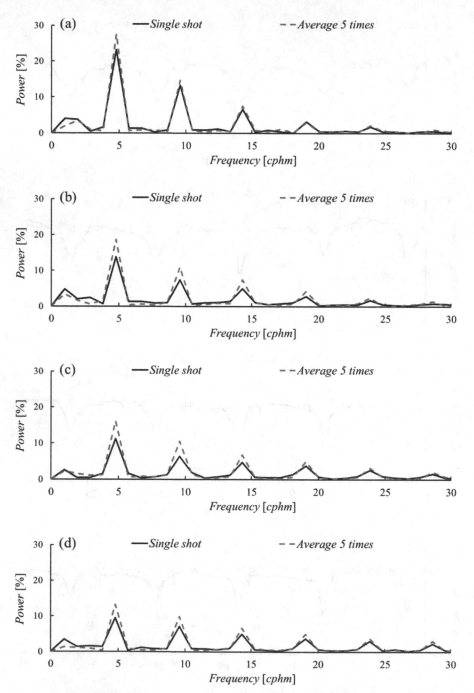

Fig. 9. Example of peak frequency for the same subject. Depth position at (a) 1 to 7.5, (b) 1 to 15, (c) 1 to 30, and (d) 1 to 60.

5 Discussion

In this study, we developed VR content that can quantitatively evaluate the depth perception ability of users and conducted a VR content evaluation experiment on a group of healthy young people. In this study, the temporal change in pupillary distance associated with the congestion-distraction motion was used as an index for depth comprehension. Therefore, we considered the possibility that the pupillary distance value would not change if the depth position was too far away. Therefore, in this experiment, we used four types of VR contents with different depths to examine the characteristics of the pupillary distance time-series data. As a result, the number of false positives at the peak frequency was 0, 0, 5, and 12, in order of depth position from 7.5, 15, 30, and 60. When the depth position was close, the spatial position of the object was correctly captured, but the number of false positives increased as the depth position moved away. A previous study that focused on convergence angle and pupillary distance reported that when the pupillary distance was 65 mm, the limit of spatial and distance understanding based on convergence angle was approximately 2 m [11]. Therefore, the present experiment, which uses the pupillary distance as an index of depth perception, may also have a limit of approximately 2 m for space comprehension based on congestion-opening movements. Conversely, in the time series where false positives occurred, it was confirmed that the change in pupillary distance associated with the congestion-divergence motion was not performed correctly. This may have been due to the speed at which the objects displayed in the VR content moved. In this experiment, the period of the objects moving was always set as constant, so the speed of the objects increased relatively as the depth position moved away. Therefore, the objects move faster when the depth is 60 than when the depth is 7.5. This increase in movement speed may have prevented the object from capturing the space correctly. Therefore, it is necessary to examine the movement speed of objects in the future. In addition, by measuring healthy elderly people and MCI patients, we will examine whether the VR contents developed in this study are effective for the early detection of MCI.

References

1. Dementia Diagnosis and Treatment Guideline Planning Committee (supervised by the Japanese Society of Neurology): 2017 Dementia Diagnosis and Treatment Guidelines, Igaku Shoin, Tokyo (2017). (in Japanese)
2. Petersen, R.C., Smith, G.E., Waring, S.C., Ivnik, R.J., Tangalos, E.G., Kokmen, E.: Mild cognitive impairment: clinical characterization and outcome. Arch. Neurol. 56(3), 303–308 (1999)
3. Suzuki, H., Yasunaga, M., Naganuma, T., Fujiwara, Y.: Validation of the Japanese version of the Montreal cognitive assessment to evaluate the time course changes of cognitive function: a longitudinal study with Mild cognitive impairment and early-stage Alzheimer's disease. Jpn. J. Geriatr. Psychiatry 22(2), 211–218 (2011). (in Japanese)
4. Nakashima, K., Shimohama, T., Tomimoto, H., Mimura, M., Arai, T.: Handbook of Dementia Care, 2nd edn. Igaku Shoin, Tokyo (2021). (in Japanese)
5. Mendez, M.F., Cummings, J.L.: Dementia: A Clinical Approach. Butterworth-Heinemann, Boston (2003)

6. Goodale, M.A., Milner, A.D.: Separate visual pathways for perception and action. Trends. Neurosci. **15**, 20–25 (1992)
7. Thiyagesh, S.N., et al.: The neural basis of visuospatial perception in Alzheimer's disease and healthy elderly comparison subjects: an fMRI study. Psychiatry Res. Neuroimaging **172**(2), 109–116 (2009)
8. Petersen, R.C.: Mild cognitive impairment as a diagnostic entity. J. Intern. Med. **256**(3), 183–194 (2004)
9. Vive Pro Eye Homepage. https://www.vive.com/us/. Accessed 22 Feb 2022
10. TobiiHomepage. https://developer.tobiipro.com/commonconcepts/coordinatesystems.html. Accessed 22 Feb 2022
11. Foley, J.M., Richards, W.: Effects of voluntary eye movement and convergence on the binocular appreciation of depth. Percept. Psychophys. **11**(6), 423–427 (1972)

Does the Proteus Effect with Elderly Simulation Kit Improve Empathy Enhancement to the Elderly?

Kentaro Kotani[✉], Haru Yamazaki, Yudai Sakata, Takafumi Asao, and Satoshi Suzuki

Kansai University, Osaka 564-8680, Japan
kotani@kansai-u.ac.jp

Abstract. The purpose of this study was to construct an experience system using an elderly avatar that produces the Proteus effect, which promotes empathy for the elderly and to evaluate whether the system can improve empathy for the elderly compared to conventional methods. In this experiment, the following three conditions were evaluated for the between-participants experiment: (1) young avatars and a kit for simulating the elderly, (2) elderly avatars and no kit for simulating the elderly, and (3) elderly avatars and a kit for simulating the elderly. The participants were asked to answer a questionnaire to measure their empathy for the elderly and evaluate the difficulty of their movements, which was used in the conventional simulated experience of the elderly, before moving on to the experiment in the virtual space. In the virtual space, it was confirmed that the participants' movements matched those of the avatar and asked them to perform the task for 20 min to generate sense of embodiment. The results showed no change in empathy toward the elderly in the condition using the conventional experience kit. However, empathy toward the elderly increased significantly using the elderly avatar and no experience kit. In conclusion, it was revealed that the simulated experience of the elderly using the Proteus effect proposed in this study may be sufficiently valuable in terms of effectiveness. However, for the system to be used in various fields, there is still room for improvement, such as understanding the decline of physical functions and reproducing the vision of cataract patients using VR.

Keywords: Proteus effect · Empathy · Elderly simulation kit

1 Introduction

The development and design of barrier-free and universal design products require an understanding of the physical functions and psychological changes of the elderly and empathy for them. However, it is difficult for young people to recognize and understand the issues when the elderly enjoys products and services [1]. A method to promote young people's understanding of changes in the physical functions and psychological changes of the elderly is to use a simulated elderly experience kit (elderly simulation kit) [2–7]. In the method using the simulated elderly simulation kit, participants simulate the physical functions of older adults who have declined due to aging, such as hunchback,

© Springer Nature Switzerland AG 2022
V. G. Duffy et al. (Eds.): HCII 2022, LNCS 13521, pp. 451–461, 2022.
https://doi.org/10.1007/978-3-031-17902-0_32

limited range of motion of lower limb joints, and visual and auditory characteristics, using supporters and weights [2].

However, there are reports that these simulated experiences of the elderly can help people understand the physical functions of the elderly that have declined due to aging, whereas they cannot promote empathy for the elderly [8–11]. Conventional simulated experience programs for the elderly are conducted using a method that allows participants to experience various functions of the elderly by physically applying loads and restrictions to their bodies using an elderly simulation kit [9]. In other words, by experiencing the difficulties of movement and behavior in a state of reduced physical function compared to one's current physical function, one can deepen one's understanding of the elderly with similar physical function. However, this understanding of an older adult is indirect and does not directly change one's perception of the elderly. Kurihara et al. [8] stated that actual older adults take a long time to adjust to the decline in their physical functions, and it is difficult for young people to experience precisely the same quality of difficulties as the elderly by wearing the kit and experiencing these programs. Lee et al. [11] also reported that the elderly simulation kit increased participants' understanding of age-related functional decline and vision problems but did not increase their empathy for the elderly.

In this study, we focused on the Proteus effect to improve the understanding of empathy and positive dignity for the elderly. The Proteus effect is an effect in which the attractiveness of the avatar's appearance, which moves in synchronization with one's body movements in the virtual space, changes the attitude and behavior of the operator [12]. In the first study of the Proteus effect, participants who used attractive avatars in virtual space became more intimate with opposite-sex collaborators in self-disclosure and interpersonal distance tasks than those who used unattractive avatars [12]. The Proteus effect has been reported to affect the user's behavior and cognitive functions, and perceptual abilities by reflecting the impressions given by the avatar's appearance on oneself [13–15]. Peck et al. [16] and Banakou et al. [17] have shown that the experience of a white person controlling a black avatar in a virtual environment can reduce the latent racist prejudice against blacks held by whites. In an experiment in which non-human avatars were made to feel embodied in a coral reef avatar, it was reported that the participants' awareness of environmental conservation and maintenance increased after participating in the experiment [18]. Although some previous studies using VR have reproduced the yellowing of vision due to cataracts and the lack of vision due to glaucoma, however, as far as we know, no study mentions the details of the simulated experience of the elderly using avatars.

Therefore, this study aimed to construct an experience system using an elderly avatar that produces the Proteus effect, which promotes empathy for the elderly. In addition, we evaluated whether it is possible to improve empathy for the elderly compared to conventional methods.

2 Methods

2.1 Participants

Fifteen male university students between the ages of 21 and 24 cooperated as participants in this experiment. The participants in the experiment were divided into three groups of five people each. The first group consisted of those who were presented with a youth avatar and wore the elderly simulation kit, the second group consisted of those who were only presented with an elderly avatar, and the third group consisted of those who were presented with an elderly avatar and wore the elderly simulation kit.

2.2 Experimental Setup

The experimental environment in the real space is shown in Fig. 1, and the experimental environment in the virtual space is shown in Fig. 2, respectively. The virtual space was created using Unity as the platform. Vive Pro, a head-mounted display (HTC, 2880 × 1600 resolution, 90 Hz refresh rate, 110-degree viewing angle), presented visual information to the participants. Perception Neuron (NOITOM, latency 20 ms, tracking at 17 points: hands, feet, wrists, knees, shoulders, hips, and head) was used to acquire the positional information of the body parts of the participants.

Fig. 1. Experimental environment in real space

Fig. 2. Experimental environment in virtual space

Figure 3 shows the elderly simulation kit (SANWA Elderly Simulation Materials Standard Set PLUS3 110-058) used in this experiment. Each part of this device simulates the decline of physical functions due to aging. The cataract-simulating parts, which were originally included in the elderly simulation kit, were not used this time because they interfered with the HMD.

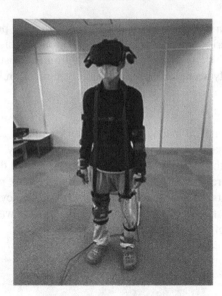

Fig. 3. Elderly simulation kit

2.3   Experimental Procedure

First, we explained the purpose of the experiment, the contents of the experiment, the experimental apparatus, the experimental environment, the experimental procedure, the approximate time required for the experiment, the number of task types, and the questionnaire to be filled out in order for the participants to understand the details of the experiment. We also explained that they could tell the experimenter what they thought and felt during the experiment, even if it was in the middle of the experiment. After that, the participants were asked to answer two types of questionnaires. One was a questionnaire to evaluate the difficulty of daily activities, and the other was a questionnaire to measure empathy toward the elderly. After answering the questionnaire, the participants were fitted with the motion capture system and the elderly simulation kit. We calibrated the head-mounted display so that the front of the display matched the orientation of the participants.

At the start of the experiment, the participants stood in a room in the virtual space that was visible through the head-mounted display and performed the actions instructed by the experimenter. The experimental environment in the virtual space was set to be slightly smaller than that in the real space so that the participants would not collide with walls or objects in reality unless they collided with walls in the virtual space. The constant monitoring of the experimenter ensured the safety of the participants in the experiment.

After the calibration was completed, the experimental environment in the virtual space was projected on the head-mounted display. We asked the participants to look around and move their bodies lightly to confirm that the head-mounted display and motion capture work properly. The first step was to ask the participants to look around and move their bodies lightly to confirm that the head-mounted display and motion capture were working correctly. Once the participants had confirmed the movements, they were asked to perform a designated task to confirm that the movements of themselves and the avatar matched to generate a sense of embodiment for the avatar. The first task was to raise one hand and check its appearance using the subjective perception of the participant and a mirror set up in the virtual space. Next, the participants looked down at their torso and put one foot in front of the other. Then, the participants were asked to perform the following actions: leaning forward, crouching on the spot, moving back and forth, tilting the body back and forth, and moving the body to check the synchronization of the movements. After that, the participants walked around the virtual space to find an object that the experimenter instructed them to find. The experiment was terminated after the participants had completed a battery of the performance in the virtual space for 20 min.

After the task was completed, Sense of Embodiment (SoE) questionnaires were collected from the participants. This questionnaire was designed to determine the degree of sense of embodiment generated by the use of avatars throughout the experiment. In order to confirm the change from the questionnaire before the experiment, the participants were asked to answer the questionnaire again to evaluate their difficulty in daily life and to measure their empathy for the elderly. The entire experiment took about 40 min, including the collection of answers to the questionnaires.

2.4 Data Analysis

The two independent variables in this experiment were the avatars' appearance (young and elderly) and whether or not the avatar was wearing an elderly simulation kit. In this study, we experimented with three of the four conditions with combinations of independent variables:

1. Young avatars with an elderly simulation kit for the elderly
2. Elderly avatars without an elderly simulation kit for the elderly
3. Elderly avatars with an elderly simulation kit for the elderly

Figure 4 shows avatars used in the study.

The experimental design was a between-participants design. The dependent variables were 1) difficulty score, 2) sympathy score, and 3) Sense of Embodiment score.

The difficulty of movement score is part of the "Instant Senior Program" developed by the government of Ontario, Canada, and approved by the Japan Well-Aging Association [8]. For each of the 26 questions, participants were asked to rate their level of difficulty in the activities of the elderly on a scale of 0 to 100 (%), with 100 (%) being their current level. The difference in the scores before and after the experiment was treated as the dependent variable.

The questionnaire score to measure empathy for the elderly was taken from "Creation of a shortened version of the Japanese version of the Fraboni ageism scale (FSA)" [19]. The score consisted of 14 questions, each of which was answered on a 7-point Likert scale ranging from "I do not agree at all (+1)" to "I agree very much (+7)". The difference in scores before and after the experiment was treated as the dependent variable. The lower the total score, the less ageism and more sympathy the participants had for the elderly.

Fig. 4. Elderly avatar and Young avatar used in the experiment

The Sense of Embodiment score was taken from "Avatar Embodiment: A Standardized Questionnaire" [20]. Sixteen questions were used in the original paper cited by Franco et al. In this experiment, the number of questions was adjusted to 15 because it was recommended to adjust the number of questions according to the content of the experiment [20]. The higher the score, the more SoE was generated for the avatar. This score was obtained after the end of the experimental trials.

In this experiment, a total of 15 participants were assigned, 5 for each experimental condition, and the difficulty in movement scores, empathy scores, and SoE scores were obtained in one trial. The experimental data were statistically processed using the statistical analysis package R, version 3.5.2.

3 Results

Figure 5 shows whether the mean empathy score for the elderly in each condition changed before or after the task. The results of the analysis using Wilcoxon's signed rank sum test (significance level 5%) showed that empathy for the elderly increased significantly after the task only in condition 2 ($V = 87$, $p = 0.0636$ for condition 1, $V = 196.5$, $p = 0.007948$ for condition 2, and $V = 416.5$, $p = 0.6944$ for condition 3).

Figure 6 shows the changes in the difficulty ratings of the body movements before and after the task in each condition. The difference between the two conditions was analyzed using Wilcoxon's signed rank-sum test, and it was found that only in condition 3, the post-task rating was significantly higher than the pre-task rating ($V = 1678.5$, $p = 0.4044$ for condition 1, $V = 2616.5$, $p = 0.05885$ for condition 2, and $V = 2821$, $p = 0.001617$ for condition 3, respectively).

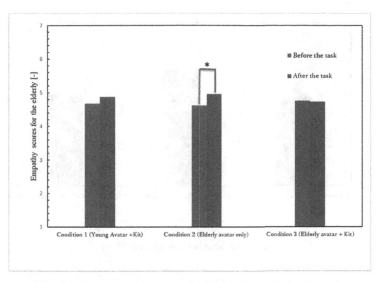

Fig. 5. Mean empathy scores obtained before and after the task

Figure 7 shows the SoE scores for each experimental condition. A one-way analysis of variance (5% level of significance) was conducted on the SoE scores for each condition. The results showed that there was no significant difference between the SoE scores in the three conditions $(F(2,12) = 3.208, p = 0.059)$.

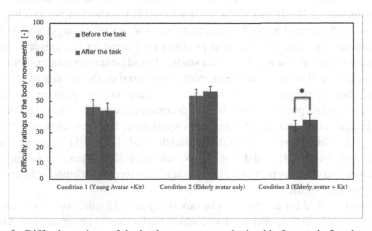

Fig. 6. Difficulty ratings of the body movements obtained before and after the task

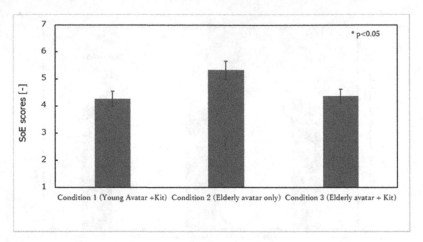

Fig. 7. SoE scores for each condition

4 Discussion

4.1 Effectiveness as a Simulated Experience for the Elderly that Promotes Empathy for the Elderly

The results of this experiment and previous studies are shown in Table 1. Since most conventional studies using simulated elderly people have been conducted with nursing and medical students, the Jefferson Scale of Empathy (JSE) has been used as the evaluation questionnaire [21]. In this study, we used the FSA instead of the JSE because our objective was not limited to medical students but was set up to target a wide range of people, such as engineers who develop products that consider the universal design. A direct comparison of this study with other studies based on questionnaire scores was not clearly appropriate. Therefore, we made inferences based on the amount of score change before and after the program experience, program duration, and program content.

Based on the data presented in Table 1, a comparison was made based on the amount of score change before and after the program experience. The score change in the present study was 4.8, while it was 8.2 in Gholamzadeh et al. [22], 0.31 in Jeong and Kwon [23], 5.9 in Ferri et al. [24], and 2.7 in Van Winkle et al. [25]. Thus, the amount of score change before and after the program experience in this study was found to be comparable to that of previous studies.

The time required for the program in this study was 15 min, which was about 1/10 of the time required in the previous study, which had a shorter program time. This result indicates that the time required was less than 1/10 of the time required in the previous study, and the same level of effectiveness was achieved.

4.2 Factors Affecting the Difficulty Ratings of the Body Movements

We expected that the difficulty ratings of the body movements would decrease after the experiment in conditions 1 and 3, in which the participants were physically restrained by the elderly simulation kit, compared to condition 2, in which they were not physically restrained. However, the results in Fig. 6 indicated that the difficulty ratings increased after the experiment in condition 1, whereas they decreased before and after the experiment in conditions 2 and 3. In a previous study [8], the items for which the movement difficulty score decreased significantly were items related to vision, such as "seeing," "color discrimination," and "reading public information boards," and items involving large body movements, such as "overall movement" and "arm bending". In this experiment, goggles with visual impairment, which are used in conventional simulated experiences of the elderly, were not used because of the HMD. Therefore, there was no difference in the vision-related conditions in any experimental conditions. In condition 3, most of the items in which the movement difficulty score decreased significantly were physical movement items such as "bending the arm," "stretching the arm," and "getting up from a chair". These detailed conditions suggest that the difference between experimental conditions 1 and 3, i.e., the difference in avatars (young and elderly), affected the evaluation of physical movements.

Table 1. Literature reporting empathy scores compared with current study

Article	Participants	Time to complete the program (hrs)	Task items in the program	Questionnaire used to evaluate empathy scores (number of items)	Empathy score before attending the program	Empathy score after attending the program
This study	Male university students	0.25	Light work in virtual space to experience the Proteus effect	Fraboni scale of ageism (14)	64.6 ± 12.7	69.4 ± 10.5
Gholamzadeh et al. [22]	Nursing students	8	Lectures, workshops and role-playing	JSE-HPS(20)	77.8 ± 10.7	86.0 ± 7.3
Jeong and Kwon [23]	Nursing students	2.5	Use of elderly simulation kit	Behavior toward the elderly (17)	58.0 ± 4.93	58.31 ± 5.3
Ferri et al. [24]	Nursing students	7	Meeting with expert and patients, seminar	JSE-HPS(20)	115.9 ± 10.1	121.8 ± 10.0
Van Winkle et al. [25]	Pharmacy students	3	Participation in role-playing on the subject of aging	JSE-HPS(20)	110.5 ± 12.2	113.2 ± 13.5

5 Conclusion

In this study, experiments were conducted using motion capture to synchronize avatars' movements placed in a virtual space. The task assigned in the experiment was selected based on previous studies that reported the involvement of the Proteus effect. The results showed that empathy toward the elderly significantly increased only in the condition in which the elderly avatars were used without the elderly simulation kit. The SoE for the avatars was also highest in the condition in which the elderly avatars were used without the elderly simulation kit. The fact that empathy for the elderly was higher than in the conventional experience with the kit revealed the possibility that the Proteus effect may be sufficiently valuable for simulating the elderly.

There is room for improvement to ensure that the system can be used in various settings without problems with the Proteus Effect. For example, understanding the decline in physical functions and reproducing the vision of a cataract patient using VR are practical issues to be considered for improvement effects. In addition, a medium- to a long-term evaluation of the effects of the Proteus Effect is required for the proposed system to be widely used. Therefore, future research should include improvements to the simulated experience of the elderly, such as changing the appearance of the avatar and reproducing the vision of the elderly, as well as evaluating the persistence of the Proteus effect overtime after the program experience.

References

1. Zavlanou, C., Lanitis, A.: Virtual reality-based simulation of age-related visual deficiencies: implementation and evaluation in the design process. In: Ahram, T., Taiar, R., Colson, S., Choplin, A. (eds.) IHIET 2019. AISC, vol. 1018, pp. 262–267. Springer, Cham (2020). https://doi.org/10.1007/978-3-030-25629-6_41
2. Okamoto, N., Takada, D., Izumi, K.: Awareness though experience and observation in the elderly simulated for freshman in department of nursing. Bull. Teikyo Univ. Sci. **9**, 139–145 (2013)
3. Zavlanou, C., Lanitis, A.: An age simulated virtual environment for improving elderly wellbeing. In: Kyriacou, E., Christofides, S., Pattichis, C.S. (eds.) XIV Mediterranean Conference on Medical and Biological Engineering and Computing 2016. IP, vol. 57, pp. 885–890. Springer, Cham (2016). https://doi.org/10.1007/978-3-319-32703-7_173
4. Tsao, H.H., Lei, X., Rau, P.: Design, development, and evaluation of a virtual aging simulation system. Educ. Gerontol. **46**(6), 317–330 (2020)
5. Nagata, H.: Long-term effect of the elderly simulation program. J. Jpn. Acad. Health Sci. **4**(1), 38–46 (2001)
6. Kurihara, T., et al.: The significance of elderly–simulation program for students in allied health and medicine - as analyzed from their changing views of the elderly-. J. Jpn. Acad. Health Sci. **7**(3), 194–199 (2004)
7. Kurokochi, K., Mase, Y.: Learning and awareness through the elderly simulation experience in elementary and junior high school students. Kanagawa Univ. Hum. Serv. **17**(1), 103–112 (2020)
8. Kurihara, T., et al.: The significance of elderly-simulation program for students in allied health and medicine - as analyzed from their changing views of the elderly-. J. Jpn. Acad. Health Sci. **7**(3), 194–199 (2004)

9. Kobayashi, Y., Takadaya, K., Yamagishi, H., Takizawa, T.: Influence on the gait of wearing equipment for the experience of the aged. Yamanashi Nurs. J. **1**, 33–36 (2002)
10. Aiba, T., Yamamura, E., Itakura, I.: A descriptive study examining the changes of nursing students' perceptions toward the elderly via virtual reality. Seirei Christopher Univ. Nurs. **11**, 119–126 (2003)
11. Lee, K., Han, A., Kim, T.H.: Effectiveness of simulation-based empathy enhancement program for caregivers (SEE-C) evaluated by older adults receiving care. Int. J. Environ. Res. Public Health **18**(15), 7802 (2021)
12. Yee, N., Bailenson, J.: The Proteus effect: the effect of transformed self-representation on behavior. Hum. Commun. Res. **33**(3), 271–290 (2007)
13. Kilteni, K., Bergstrom, I., Slater, M.: Drumming in immersive virtual reality: the body shapes the way we play. IEEE Trans. Vis. Comput. Graph. **19**(4), 597–605 (2013)
14. Banakou, D., Groten, R., Slater, M.: Illusory ownership of a virtual child body causes overestimation of object sizes and implicit attitude changes. Proc. Natl. Acad. Sci. **110**(31), 12846–12851 (2013)
15. Banakou, D., Kishore, S., Slater, M.: Virtually being Einstein results in an improvement in cognitive task performance and a decrease in age bias. Front. Psychol. **9**, 917 (2018)
16. Peck, T.C., Seinfeld, S., Aglioti, S.M., Slater, M.: Putting yourself in the skin of a black avatar reduces implicit racial bias. Conscious. Cogn. **22**(3), 779–787 (2013)
17. Banakou, D., Hanumanthu, P.D., Slater, M.: Virtual embodiment of white people in a black virtual body leads to a sustained reduction in their implicit racial bias. Front. Hum. Neurosci. **10**, 601 (2016)
18. Ahn, S.J., Bostick, J., Ogle, E., Nowak, K.L., McGillicuddy, K.T., Bailenson, J.N.: Experiencing nature: embodying animals in immersive virtual environments increases inclusion of nature in self and involvement with nature. J. Comput.-Mediat. Commun. **21**(6), 399–419 (2016)
19. Fraboni, M., Saltstone, R., Hughes, S.: The Fraboni Scale of Ageism (FSA): an attempt at a more precise measure of ageism. Can. J. Aging **9**(1), 56–66 (1990)
20. Peck, TC., Gonzalez-Franco, M.: Avatar embodiment. A standardized questionnaire. Front. Virtual Real. **1**, 44 (2021)
21. Kataoka, H.: On Empathy and medicine (focusing on the empathy scale). Jpn. J. Intern. Med. **101**(7), 2103–2107 (2012)
22. Gholamzadeh, S., Khastavaneh, M., Khademian, Z., Ghadakpour, S.: The effects of empathy skills training on nursing students' empathy and attitudes toward elderly people. BMC Med. Educ. **18**(1), 1–7 (2018)
23. Jeong, H., Kwon, H.: Long-term effects of an aging suit experience on nursing college students. Nurse Educ. Pract. **50**, 102923 (2021)
24. Ferri, P., Rovesti, S., Padula, M.S., D'Amico, R., Di Lorenzo, R.: Effect of expert-patient teaching on empathy in nursing students: a randomized controlled trial. Psychol. Res. Behav. Manag. **12**, 457 (2019)
25. Van Winkle, L.J., Fjortoft, N., Hojat, M.: Impact of a workshop about aging on the empathy scores of pharmacy and medical students. Am. J. Pharm. Educ. **76**(1) (2012)

Empirical Studies Aimed at Understanding Conversational Recommender Systems and Accessibility Aspects

Lucas Padilha Modesto de Araujo$^{(\boxtimes)}$, Cynthya Letícia Teles de Oliveira ,
Kamila Rios da Hora Rodrigues , and Marcelo Garcia Manzato

University of São Paulo, São Carlos, Brazil
{padilha.lucas,cynthya}@usp.br, {kamila.rios,mmanzato}@icmc.usp.br

Abstract. Conversational systems allow communication by voice, touch, and text between system and user through interactive interfaces. They also allow users to carry out tasks such as shopping, answering emails, and with few interactions, the user reaches the goal. The industry usually disregards the limitations of the elderly public when designing conversational systems. Such users may have problems with dexterity, vision, and hearing, impacting their interactions with the system and, consequently, requiring applications accessible to their cognitive and physical characteristics. The goal of this work was to propose a set of functional and non-functional accessibility requirements for the development of conversational systems for elderly. A first set of requirements were gathered through the Wizard of Oz technique, applied with eleven participants. For this, a conversational system, named Bob, was designed to recommend YouTube videos to the user. Recommendations were made according to the user's needs and preferences, adapting visual and auditory resources through the interface. After the trials, the results showed that, especially for the elderly population, conversational systems can also play the role of a friend or virtual company, with adaptable and adaptive accessibility and interaction settings.

Keywords: Human-centered computing · Empirical studies in HCI · Conversational recommender systems · Accessibility · Elderly

1 Introduction

The expressive amount of applications available has brought challenges to the design of accessible applications. The audience that uses the applications can be diverse, and therefore each one has their perceptions, needs, and interests. Elderly people, for example, who were not born immersed in technological languages need to migrate to a different reality from which they are used to. In addition, they have needs which are different from those usually faced by people

V. G. Duffy et al. (Eds.): HCII 2022, LNCS 13521, pp. 462–478, 2022.
https://doi.org/10.1007/978-3-031-17902-0_33

born with the use of technologies, such as young people and non-elderly people. This fact, consequently, brings the necessity of research on accessibility and usability in the technological context.

In the case of the elderly people, often, efforts to create solutions and tools that help are limited to visual aspects such as customizing contrast, adjusting font size on print screens, and easy pressing application buttons. But, there are other problems that are associated with usability, such as the inability to understand the procedures that make up the use of the proper tools for accessibility [3]. In other words, there is a problem to facilitate access to the different parameters offered by a solution regarding its usability, otherwise users may give up on using an application because they do not know how to configure it according to their needs and preferences. Providing accessibility means removing barriers that prevent people with disabilities from participating in substantial activities, including the use of services, products and information [24]. Conversational systems must meet this premise, in addition to considering usability requirements and being intuitive for users, especially for the elderly with low literacy or with difficulties and disabilities.

Conversational systems are designed to carry out a variety of tasks in order to simulate dialogues and interactions with humans. There are architectures capable of bringing relevant information in a conversational environment, such as Frequently Asked Questions Systems (known as FAQ's), which encompass frequently asked questions of a system based on a probabilistic model [1]. However, this strategy is not very relevant in the context of Natural Language Processing (NLP), as the user is not able to express their request or ask about other issues that are not frequent and related to the FAQ proposal.

Proposed in 1964, ELIZA was the first conversational system that simulated dialogues based on natural language [32]. The system proposed a conversation between the user and a psychologist, in which ELIZA was the psychologist and the user was the patient. Its success was determined by characteristics similar to human feelings. With the flow of conversation, the system could not maintain a coherent dialogue, but it was still a historic landmark for the study of conversational systems.

Currently, virtual assistants have become popular with the development of mobile devices such as smartphones and tablets. They consist of software that interacts with the user through audio and text interactions. Popular agents such as *Siri (Apple)*, *Google Assistant (Google)* and *Alexa (Amazon)*, support a variety of solutions, such as turning on lamps, closing curtains, turning on the television and other electronics in order to facilitate everyday tasks. They also offer other functionalities, such as providing weather information, opening applications, sending messages, among others.

In particular, such applications also offer content recommendations according to users' requirements, such as suggestions for restaurants near their location and tourist attractions. Even though agents have become increasingly efficient and useful for performing essential and non-essential tasks, the benefit generated by them cannot be restricted to the average audience only. Rather, there is untapped potential for using these agents in the support needed for different groups of users with disabilities or difficulties, such as the elderly audience.

In this sense, this work aims to analyze a sample of the target audience and collect interaction and accessibility requirements to build an adaptable (by the user) and adaptive (by the system) conversational system that recommends content according to the user's interests. For this, studies were carried out with users using the Wizard of Oz technique[1], and the data were analyzed, resulting in a set of requirements to guide the development of conversational systems.

This paper is structured as follows: Sect. 2 presents the related works, Sect. 3 provides information on the preliminary case study conducted, Sect. 4 presents the methodology used in this work, in Sect. 5 the results obtained with the research are highlighted, Sect. 7 contains the discussion, and Sect. 8 contains the final considerations and future work.

2   Related Works

This work considered three distinct themes for the identification of related works. The first is related to the conversational interface that considers topics of accessibility and usability, the second considers conversational recommender systems and, finally, the third considers participatory design.

Ryu et al. [27] consider human psychological aspects in his work, and uses a chatbot to relate and contribute to the mental health of elderly people. In this sense, the research proposes a conversational system based on buttons to make interactions. Button-based systems make it easy for the chatbot to successfully identify what the user's interaction intentions are, but limit interactions as users may have other preferences related to the use of buttons, audio, text, or other forms of input. Considering that works's Ryu et al. [27] is a conversational system for the elderly, the results obtained in the case study we did with the chatbot Bob, suggests more types of interactions, which were not attributed to Ryu et al. [27]. Because it is limited to this type of interaction, content recommendations are not entirely accessible either.

Valtolina and Hu [31], in turn, using strategies to improve the quality of life of the elderly, considers a chatbot that enables a connection between family members and doctors. It is also able to remind users of their appointments and medications, which for the elderly is promising. In addition, a proposal contributes to factors related to loneliness and contextualizes the experiences lived during a COVID-19 pandemic. Therefore, even though this is a preliminary work, it considers the current aspects of the elderly's daily life, but it was not considered that the elderly may need and/or prefer the means of interaction

Georgieva [12] raises questions about digital inclusion and how it affects the daily lives of the elderly population. This work considers a sample of first generation and second generation elderly people, to make a comparison between

---

[1] Term was invented by John Falk ("Jeff") Kelley, around 1980, during the development of his dissertation at Johns Hopkins University. More details: http://www.musicman.net/oz.html.

issues of digital inclusion, thus it is concluded that first generation elderly people believe that technologies fail when they need it most, besides also showing that others elderly people believe that technology makes things better. The author brings these data to a discussion involving the behavior of chatbots. Additionally, natural language processing would be an important factor for the tasks of a chatbot that supports the dynamics and behaviors of elderly users, as they can assist in complex tasks involving financial risk issues, such as banking services per application. Although natural language processing helps the elderly to communicate with the system, there is still a gap on how chatbots should behave and be built for this specific audience, as there are language, physical and cognitive limitations that are characteristic of the decline of human functions in relation to the natural aging process.

The work of Furini et al. [11] considers a problem still open in relation to accessibility, which refers to the profile of each user, in a way that a child interacts differently from an adult, who, in turn, interacts differently from elderly. With the results obtained in this work, accent personalization strategies and regionalism are shown to be a promising strategy regarding the user's experience in relation to their profile.

Pradhan, Mehta and Findlater [23], on the other hand, consider the approach through voice commands that serves many people with disabilities. Thus, people with reduced mobility can carry out tasks such as closing doors, turning on the TV, while the visually impaired also benefit from questions such as "How is the weather today?". So, with just one accessibility feature, the user can carry out everyday functions. Even though conversational agents have evolved to be more accessible, researchers are still trying to understand the behavior of average users in this type of system. The interactions of users with specific needs also need to be researched, so, considering conversational solutions, this work shows some results that address the need to go beyond the voice resources available on the market, or even its evolution in different contexts of user.

Yu, Shen and Jin [33] bring a conversational recommendation system, in which the user can evaluate content recommendations by visual resources. Grasch, Felfernig and Reinfrank [13], in turn, feature a conversational recommendation system, which supports voice interactions, but its recommendations are limited to textual mode. Although they are two systems that enable different types of interaction, they are similar in using hybrid dialogue strategies. Hybrid strategies enable greater accessibility in terms of interaction, so Ikemoto et al. [18] combined natural language models with structured elements based on forms, using visual resources for their responses to the user, although they did not propose voice or text interactions.

The domain of a conversational application is a widely discussed topic in the literature, and it should be task-oriented, considering precise and short interactions, in order to allow people to communicate more easily and find what they want with few messages [15]. From the consulted literature, it was evidenced that some applications use hybrid interaction approaches for content recommendation. However, they are still restricted to a few accessibility features.

Therefore, this paper explores conversational systems from another aspect, which is to include accessibility features in applications for users with multiple difficulties, such as the elderly.

In isolation, each system considers issues that evolve conversational systems, but considering the elderly audience and their needs, more information and resources are needed for the use of a conversational system.

The importance of participatory design is due to the objectives it seeks, which are: to give voice to "invisible" people in the context in which they are inserted; perform actual tasks in places familiar to the user in their real context; mutual learning with the participants, in search of an intersection; use of tools that effectively, in practical, concrete and specific situations, help the participant; alternative visions about technology that can generate equality in any environment, and; democratic practices learned in the form of equality practices or models [20]. However, Schlomann et al. [29] point out in their study that elderly people, especially with cognitive deficits, are neglected by Voice Assistant developers, thus showing the need for participatory design. The authors recommend these users' high level of involvement in research on trade assistants, in order to identify the best ways to introduce the use of these assistants, their benefits, limitations, and possible risks to the elderly.

The next section describes more aspects of the elderly audience and their interaction with technologies.

3   Elderly and Technology

A Brazilian Institute of Geography and Statistics (IBGE, in Portuguese) study [8] on the use of Internet, television and cell phones in Brazil made it possible to verify the increase in Internet use by 8 age groups. The study showed that two groups had the same growth rate (6.7%) and were the ones that increased the most between the years 2018 and 2019, one of them being the elderly population. This shows that the use of the Internet by the elderly population is growing, and the software that meets their needs must support the demand. In fact, the digital inclusion of the elderly is something recent, and has benefits such as reducing isolation, increasing autonomy and independence, as well as improving health [16]. Making content, such as videos, accessible is part of the task of digitally including elderly people [25, 26].

Youtube® is the most accessed video platform in the world [7]. Users access *Youtube*® in search of entertainment and information on various subjects. It is a platform for easy dissemination of opinion-forming content. Videos made available often have subtitles and other accessibility features available for use. To enable them, it is necessary to interact with the layout to identify what the buttons mean and how to customize their content in order to improve the user experience. In a few steps it is possible to configure the player of the video and watch the personalized content. However, the availability of resources does not mean that the user will be able to reach the goal of using them, because when it comes to users with low literacy, or elderly people who are not used to technologies, they have difficulty accessing, identifying and activate the features [30].

Elderly people find it difficult to see, understand texts and symbols and remember instructions, which is an issue related to sensory, motor and cognitive [10] problems, inherent to age, which make it difficult to use smartphones. The ability to handle smartphones is also related to how accessible are the systems that comprise it. In fact, older people tend to write more slowly and can also make mistakes when using buttons by pressing more than one button at a time. Therefore, larger buttons can contribute to increase the chance of the user to interact according to their expectations [17]. Customizing buttons can be useful and makes the system accessible for some people, but when considering the elderly audience, the interface design needs to be done in a personalized way, for each individual [19], considering not only an interaction mechanism, but also assigning others that support the needs of each user.

Considering these limitations with the use of buttons, conversational systems exempt the user from dealing with customization only through buttons, which is the solution employed by *Youtube*®. It is possible to customize the use according to the needs of each individual, whether by text, voice, buttons, forms or some visual aid. This way, the interface design is adjusted in advance so that the content personalization interactions are done in a satisfactory way from the beginning of the conversation.

Based on the preliminary case study of the *Youtube*® platform reported in this paper, the goal of this search group is to develop a conversational video recommendation system, which uses different types of inputs and considers the customization of the parameters of the recommended video. Initially, the system aims to integrate with the *Youtube*® platform, but it can be adapted to any other streaming service that has accessibility features and a programming interface.

4 Preliminary Case Study

In this paper, the results of the first phase of the development of the accessible conversational system will be described. This first phase corresponds to the collection of requirements related to interaction and accessibility. For this, a study was carried out with users in order to understand what needs and particularities would be necessary for the system. In the next subsections, the study methodology is presented in detail.

4.1 Participants

The case study had eleven voluntary participants, five men and six women, aged between 62 and 73 years, attending a digital literacy course. Of these, two have visual difficulties and therefore need, in addition to eyeglasses and a device configured with large fonts, the aid of a magnifying glass. One of them was color blind. Some participants reported having hearing problems, one of them using a hearing aid.

Participants were selected using a non-probabilistic sampling technique known as convenience sampling. In this type of sampling, participants are selected according to availability, location and interest in participating in the research [9]. For the selection of participants, the profile of the application's target audience and the group for which there was approval by the Research Ethics Committee, CAAE number: 57875016.3.0000.5390, was also taken into account.

4.2 Procedures and Methods

The study aimed to collect information that would allow collecting requirements for the construction of a chatbot capable of making recommendations for *YouTube*® videos to users. The procedure of the conducted study consisted of simulating a dialogue between the chatbot and the user, applying the Wizard of Oz technique [6]. In this technique, the user's interaction with the system is simulated, when, in fact, there is a person performing the activities that simulate the interaction. Sometimes, as in this case, acting in such a way that the user believes that the system is fully functional. That said, the participation of two researchers was necessary in the application of the test, one being responsible for observing the interaction between the user and the bot represented by the other researcher. It is noteworthy that at all times the participants believed they were interacting with a functional chatbot.

To carry out the study, the two applicators of the study and one participant at a time met, through the *Google Meet*® platform, through which the participant shared the screen of the device he was using, either smartphone or computer. For the simulation of interaction with the chatbot, called Bob, an account was used in the *Whatsapp*® messaging application, in the Web version, in which one of the applicators, simulating the bot, started the conversation with the user. The chatbot introduced itself saying: *"Hi! I'm Bob and I'm here to help you find YouTube videos you might like. What's your name? Tell me a little about yourself"*. After the participant's response, the following question was sent: *"Nice name! <participant's name>, I know you like movies. What movie genre do you like best?"*. Then, the researcher that simulated the bot brought to the conversation a video related to the participant's response, and asked if the participant liked the recommendation. The next two questions were about the participant's favorite singer and travel destination. Similarly to the first question, the researcher representing Bob searched for videos in *Youtube*® referring to the participant's preferences, so that the participant believed that he/she was receiving personalized recommendations. A simulation with a user of this study is illustrated in Fig. 1 and it contains screenshots of the real interaction between the user and the simulator. Some details, such as name, have been hidden to ensure user privacy.

Based on the responses, the researcher responsible for the dialog would look for videos on *YouTube*® and send them to the user, who would reply whether he/she liked the recommendation made by the bot or not. After this step, the bot asked the user some questions, related to some accessibility issues of *Whatsapp*®, such as preference for chatting via text or audio, and *YouTube*®, such as the preference by the use of subtitles, playback speed and video resolution.

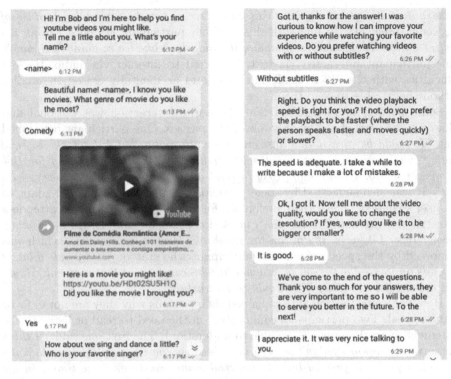

Fig. 1. Example of a snippet of dialogue between participant and Bob.

After the study was carried out by *Whatsapp*®, a unstructured interview was started with each participant, in order to reinforce some statements that they had made previously or so that they could go deeper into any answer that they might have answered very briefly, leaving applicants with doubts.

5 Results

This section presents the results of our preliminary case study. They are based on a qualitative assessment carried out from the analysis of the participants' discourse on the studies conducted, from which categories of meaning emerged that highlight important points about the use and interaction with Bob and are presented below.

5.1 Audio and/or Text Interaction

During the study, the participant was free to choose the way they wanted to interact with Bob (audio or text), but all of Bob's answers were sent by text. One participant with vision problems, even though he chose to interact via text, commented: *"[...], even with the people I talk to, it's usually always via audio, because then it's quick. Typing takes a long time, I make a mistake, because of my vision problem".* In line with this, another participant stated: *"I think it's perfect that he could answer by audio, it would look like we're doing here now".* This participant interacted via text, but tried to interact via audio. He had difficulties with the *Whatsapp®* interface, and accidentally erased the audios without being able to send them.

Some participants suggested that the audio interaction was optional and allowed to be carried out by only one of the parties. One participant mentioned that *"It would be nice if Bob answered me with audio, but I don't like to send audio."* while another participant said: *"I don't think it's interesting for Bob to answer audio, I think more easy to send audio, but I prefer it answers with text".* It was also suggested by some participants that the bot should adapt to the user's context or ask their preference for interaction. One of the attendees said: *"As for interacting via audio, I think it depends on context, if I'm 'cooking' I won't type. Likewise, if I'm 'on the notebook' I won't send audio",* which was reinforced by the speech of another participant who stated: *"It depends a lot, it depends on where the person is, whether he/she can hear at that moment. Maybe if it asked before sending it, it would be interesting".*

However, some participants explained their reasons why they are not in favor of the appeal. Two participants commented on the need to read or listen to the statement more than once to be able to understand. The first one said: *"I think answering by audio wouldn't be very nice, because the voice will deliver that it's a robot, I prefer it just by text. I also read some questions three times, in the audio it wouldn't be much nice to keep repeating.",* which was in line with the opinion of another participant: *"I already had an experience with audio (with another application), I didn't clearly understand what it was asking, you know? At my age it is common to have hearing problems, so depending on the phoneme it can be bad to understand, until you understand it has already said some other things. So I think I might have the choice 'do you want audio or written?"'* In particular, this case can be solved by customizing the way of interacting with Bob.

5.2   Subtitles, Playback Speed and Video Resolution

Participants were unanimous regarding the subtitles of the *YouTube®* videos. Everyone said they only use it when the video's audio is not in Portuguese, as one participant mentioned: *"I only use subtitles if I don't speak the language".* Only one participant mentioned that he sometimes prefers to slow down the video playback speed a little, and that he does this when the pronunciation is fast or the speaker has an accent, and there are no subtitles available.

As for the resolution, everyone said it was good, but that it could start with a better resolution whenever available and compatible with the user's Internet speed.

5.3   Use of Emojis and Stickers

The use of emojis and stickers was associated with reinforcing the message or feeling the user wants to convey, as one participant mentioned: *"I love talking using stickers and gifs, I laugh. I would love for it to talk to me like that"*. In this study, Bob only responded with text, without emojis.

However, a negative point was noted regarding the lack of consensus for the interpretation of emojis. *"I use a lot of emoji and stickers, I think it's really cool, but I don't think it's interesting for Bob to answer me like that, because like... I know what I mean, but I don't know what the other person means"*. When asked if he used emojis when chatting through *Whatsapp*, one participant said: *"Sometimes there are things I don't use because I don't know what it means, it can lead to misinterpretations"*, showing the need for *chatbot* customization options.

5.4   Friend or Virtual Assistant

Among the elderly participants, the idea of a virtual friend was cited a lot, as in *"Oh, I'd rather talk to Bob than stay there* [on YouTube®]... *Because I'm going to talk to bot, it'll answer me ... Even if it's virtual, even if I can't see it, answering what I ask is already something very important. You have no idea at this moment (of the pandemic) what it's like."*, and in *"Bob is working with a very wide range of options it seems, that's why it looks like a friend, because it seems to talk about everything. Bob talks about movies, singing, traveling and such, it seems like a friend who can talk about any subject"*.

5.5   Use of Buttons

Three participants showed interest in using the buttons with quick answers, for example, "yes", "no", "like it" and "did not like it", as we can see in: *"I think it would be interesting to use buttons, the more it facilitates interaction, I think it's interesting."*, and in *"I would definitely use buttons, you look at the options, identify what you want, then it goes faster, sometimes it even expresses better because sometimes we want to say something and can't express it, right?"*.

5.6   Information Verification

Currently, a lot of information reaches users through messaging apps and social networks. There is, therefore, a difficulty for the elderly public to determine if the information is true or false, especially if it comes from a source they believe to be reliable. In this sense, there is also the problem of authenticity verification, for example, when purchasing a product or service. One participant reports: *"Another thing would be for Bob to help me know what is true, for example, now I want to take a course but I don't know who will teach, Bob could help me know if he is trustworthy"*.

5.7   Return on Response Time

In cases where Bob was slow to respond, there was a certain feeling of frustration in the user. One of the participants suggested: *"Would you be able to put a 'Wait' message, so that it informs you that it is processing the information? The person might wonder what happened due to the bot's response time"*. This issue can be resolved with a message to the user that Bob is still verifying the order and asking the user to wait.

5.8   Accents and Regionalisms

Conducting the study online allowed for participants from all regions of Brazil. Thus, it could be noted that the participant could feel more comfortable in the conversation if Bob used regional terms, as well as being able to understand these terms when used by the user. This can be seen in the speeches of the participants, as in *"Bob writes very well, but these (regional) expressions would make Bob more natural."*, and in *"Bob needs to understand accents (in this case of voice interaction) and regionalisms, it has to know who it is 'speaking with. From Pará, to Rio Grande do Sul, to the northeast, it changes a lot"*. To resolve this issue, a solution will be developed based on informal text mining approaches and heterogeneous data classification (considering the informal text and the geographic information where the text was written), so the sentences can be validated by the classifier and later, used in synthetic voice tools. Thus, each user could instantiate a textual set according to the linguistic variations of their region.

5.9   Classification of Requirements

The study allowed classifying the aforementioned categories into functional and non-functional requirements of the proposed conversational system. For classification and understanding of non-functional requirements, the set of software quality metrics ISO/IEC [22] was used. Tables 1 and 2 illustrate the requirements collected with the study.

Table 1. Functional requirements.

Functional requirements	Description
Using buttons and forms	The system must provide use of buttons and forms
Audio interaction	The system must offer voice interactions
Text interaction	The system must offer text interactions
Use of emojis and stickers	The system must offer interactions by emojis and stickers
Accents and Regionalism	The system must be customized for each person with regard to accents and local slang

Table 2. Non-functional requirements.

Non-functional requirements	Description
Usability (button size)	The system must contain larger buttons compared to the popular patterns [5]
Adaptability (customizable contents)	The system must contain custom interface and configurable
Performance (Response Time)	The system should reply the user with a time less than 5 s [2]
Performance against memory	The system must provide the conversation history whenever requested, without prior storage on the user's device
Maintainability	The system must be implemented by modules [14]
Interoperability	The system must work on the most used platforms by the target audience
Usability	The system must be self-explanatory [28]
Availability	The system must persist the modules independently
Accessibility	The system must be responsive
Accessibility	The system must be adaptive (by user) and adaptive (by system)

To deal with non-functional requirements, software quality metrics that referred to the results obtained during the user testing phase were considered. Thus, for system usability, two requirements were raised: to have a self-explanatory system, allowing users to understand how to use the system and if the user is confused, the system must clearly guide him/her on how to proceed; and consider button sizes, as it is one of the factors found in the case study that will impact not only functionality but also implementation issues.

Regarding adaptability, as this paper presents questions of user preference and/or needs, the system must have a customizable and configurable interface, that is, for each user with different preferences, the system must support the demands related to interaction factors.

Considering the performance of conversational systems for the elderly, two factors were found: the first with regard to memory, which should not store user content and information on the device the user is using; another regarding the response time, something that was also found through the case study carried out in this research.

As the functionalities are diverse, the systems must be implemented by modules and this is a maintainability requirement, since in case of failure of some interaction functionality, developers will be able to deal with it without impeding other functionalities, thus, it also stands out as a requirement availability, since the user will be able to take advantage of others and will not be frustrated by not being able to reach their final objective.

This system should work on conversational platforms that are most used in the world, taking advantage of the fact that users already use it to talk to other people and facilitating access without having to install new applications, which is a requirement for system interoperability.

Regarding accessibility, the system must be configurable to support the elderly audience and their interaction preferences, in addition to being responsive.

To classify the degree of relevance of each requirement, the definitions high, medium and low [21] were used. Regarding the functional requirements, all are of high relevance, except the use of 'emojis and stickers', 'accents and regionalism', which were classified as low relevance. Non-functional requirements were rated as high relevance, except 'performance against memory' which was rated as medium relevance.

6   Pilot Evaluation

Some features were implemented in the Bob chatbot and then a 1-user test was performed. The pilot test was intended to find possible coding problems and new proposals, in addition to considering a restaurant recommendation domain. The participant's profile is configured as non-elderly and their specialties are related to psychology. The evaluation was carried out in a controlled environment and had the participation of two applicators, one of them was in person mode, accompanying the user and coordinating the test, the other was in remote mode, following the test and also observing the system logs. After the test, the user answered the SAM (Self-Assessment Manikin) questionnaire, an instrument that uses images for personal affective assessment in the domains of pleasure, arousal and dominance, after exposure to a stimulus [4], in this case, referring to the use of the chatbot. The results allowed verifying problems in the implementation, such as: increasing the flow of conversations, giving users more options for paths, recommending more restaurants, especially if the user doesn't like the recommendation, and providing filtering options by types of food.

New tests are been carried out with a larger sample of users and also with new application domains, such as recommendation of establishments and news.

7   Discussion

The analysis of the requirements presented in Sect. 5.9 allowed the research team to verify important aspects in the construction of the chatbot. One of the points observed was the existence of greater agreement on preferences or needs for interaction and accessibility among the elderly. For this reason, the points discussed take into account this population and their suggestions.

It was observed that users would like there to be voice interaction by at least one of the parties, but it was a consensus that the audios sent by Bob should be short. However, in the participants' speeches, it was noted that the user's context needs to be analyzed, either with Bob asking, at the beginning of the conversation, which type of interaction is preferred, either allowing personalization with a kind of user profile, or doing this adaptation automatically. Customizing according to user preferences and needs can also include Bob's use of emojis and stickers, as not all users would like to use them.

The interest of elderly users in a virtual friend was also noted. The statements of some elderly participants showed that they sometimes experience moments of solitude. Having a companionship, even in a virtual form, that can maintain a dialogue, or even help you with some tasks, such as searching online. Another functionality in this case would be for Bob to make a call or send a message via *Whatsapp*® itself to an emergency user contact, simply by means of a voice command or by touching a button.

The idea of having Bob as a facilitator also extends to the verification of news, which usually arrives by *Whatsapp*® and in large volumes, that the elderly, in particular, cannot or do not know whether it came from a reliable source and if it is true. Thus, Bob would check the news and certify the users, preventing them from propagating fake news.

After conducting the studies and analyzing the results, it was possible to conclude that several features can be added to Bob, making it more than a conversational recommendation system. Customizing Bob to meet the user's needs proves to be a necessary viable solution, allowing the user to manually configure the system preferences (adaptable), or this custom configuration to be done automatically by the system (adaptative).

Many issues brought up in this discussion are directly related to Natural Language Processing techniques, another idea that emerged during the study, is to extract behavioral patterns and identify possible depressive users through these techniques. Thus, Bob could check if the users are having depressive episodes and recommend content that helps them in this regard.

8   Final Remarks

This work presented a study carried out to raise interaction and accessibility requirements for the construction of a conversational recommendation system aimed at the elderly audience.

With the studies carried out, it was possible to verify the preferences and needs for interaction and accessibility for the elderly. The use of resources, such as buttons with quick responses and voice interaction, proved to be important, but especially when the user is allowed to use it according to their will. Therefore, it is interesting to build a chatbot with an adaptive and adaptable interface, to improve user interaction with the system interface, as well as use the accessibility features according to their needs.

At first there were expectations regarding user interactions and what would be possible to collect to understand and build an adaptive and adaptable conversational system, but only after the study was it possible to sustain the ideas and obtain others that are significant in the user experience. A future work is to expand the language training of the conversational system, from the point of view of natural language processing and also of regional aspects, considering that users are more attracted by the accents and customs of their regions.

Another important future work will be the recommendation of videos through a recommendation system that filters out fake content. Note that the elderly audience is more likely to believe in untrue content, unconsciously disseminating this information on social networks. Thus, the support of a fake news verification system will be of great relevance.

Adapting the system to different domains can also be a future work, so, in addition to recommending personalized content, users will be able to interact with the bot for other entertainment activities, such as sustaining a dialogue to talk about everyday life.

It is also intended to carry out a new stage of studies using Whatsapp, with 36 volunteers, arranged in 3 groups. One group is interacting with the conversational agent by voice, and the second group is doing the interactions by text. The third group could use both types of interactions, by audio or text. The choice of which users would go to a given group was made randomly, except for users who had some disability that made it impossible to interact with a given group, so it was transferred to another. At the end of each test, two researchers are interviewing the volunteer, and they are answering a questionnaire. It has a similar methodology to the first, however, with Bob working and being adaptable, dispensing with the role of the Wizard of Oz. At this stage, we want to check if the accessibility issues implemented in Bob are practical and easy to configure.

Finally, regarding the current state of the area of accessible conversational recommendation systems and, considering the lack of conversational corpora for applications, an innovative contribution of this work is the construction of an annotated *corpus* that can be used by others researchers, since this was not found in the literature.

Acknowledgments. The authors would like to thank the financial support from Brazilian agencies: CNPq, CAPES and FAPESP. We would also like to thank the participants in the preliminary case study and the pilot evaluation.

References

1. Abo Khamis, M., Ngo, H.Q., Rudra, A.: FAQ: questions asked frequently. In: Proceedings of the 35th ACM SIGMOD-SIGACT-SIGAI Symposium on Principles of Database Systems, pp. 13–28 (2016)
2. Ahmadvand, A., et al.: Emory IrisBot: an open-domain conversational bot for personalized information access. In: Alexa Prize Proceedings (2018)
3. Akatsu, H., Miki, H.: Usability research for the elderly people. Oki Tech. Rev. (Special Issue Hum. Friendly Technol.) **71**(3), 54–57 (2004)
4. Bradley, M.M., Lang, P.J.: Measuring emotion: the self-assessment manikin and the semantic differential. J. Behav. Ther. Exp. Psychiatry **25**(1), 49–59 (1994)
5. Cunha, B.C., Rodrigues, K.R., Pimentel, M.D.G.C.: Synthesizing guidelines for facilitating elderly-smartphone interaction. In: Proceedings of the 25th Brazillian Symposium on Multimedia and the Web, pp. 37–44 (2019)

6. Dahlbäck, N., Jönsson, A., Ahrenberg, L.: Wizard of OZ studies: why and how. In: Proceedings of the 1st International Conference on Intelligent User Interfaces, IUI 1993, pp. 193–200. ACM, New York (1993). https://doi.org/10.1145/169891. 169968
7. Demir, M., Taken, K., Eryilmaz, R., Aslan, R., Ertas, K.: Youtube as a health information source: COVID-19 and andrology. Med. Bull. Haseki/Haseki Tip Bulteni 59(2) (2021)
8. Educa, I.: Uso de internet, televisão e celular no brasil (2019)
9. Etikan, I., Musa, S.A., Alkassim, R.S.: Comparison of convenience sampling and purposive sampling. Am. J. Theor. Appl. Stat. 5(1), 1–4 (2016)
10. Fisk, A.D., Czaja, S.J., Rogers, W.A., Charness, N., Sharit, J.: Designing for Older Adults: Principles and Creative Human Factors Approaches. CRC Press, Boca Raton (2020)
11. Furini, M., Mirri, S., Montangero, M., Prandi, C.: Do conversational interfaces kill web accessibility? In: 2020 IEEE 17th Annual Consumer Communications & Networking Conference (CCNC), pp. 1–6. IEEE (2020)
12. Georgieva, L.: Digital inclusion and the elderly: the case of online banking. In: Proceedings of the LREC 2018 Workshop "Improving Social Inclusion using NLP: Tools, Methods and Resources" (ISI-NLP 2), vol. 7, pp. 8–12 (2018)
13. Grasch, P., Felfernig, A., Reinfrank, F.: Recomment: towards critiquing-based recommendation with speech interaction. In: Proceedings of the 7th ACM Conference on Recommender Systems, pp. 157–164 (2013)
14. Hayes, J.H., Zhao, L.: Maintainability prediction: a regression analysis of measures of evolving systems. In: 21st IEEE International Conference on Software Maintenance (ICSM 2005), pp. 601–604. IEEE (2005)
15. Hill, J., Ford, W.R., Farreras, I.G.: Real conversations with artificial intelligence: a comparison between human-human online conversations and human-chatbot conversations. Comput. Hum. Behav. 49, 245–250 (2015)
16. Holgersson, J., Söderström, E., Rose, J.: Digital inclusion for elderly citizens for a sustainable society (2019)
17. Iancu, I., Iancu, B.: Designing mobile technology for elderly. A theoretical overview. Technol. Forecast. Soc. Change 155, 119977 (2020)
18. Ikemoto, Y., Asawavetvutt, V., Kuwabara, K., Huang, H.H.: Tuning a conversation strategy for interactive recommendations in a chatbot setting. J. Inf. Telecommun. 3(2), 180–195 (2019)
19. Lim, C.-K.: The implementation of 3D printing in customized interactive design for elderly welfare technology. In: Stephanidis, C. (ed.) HCI 2014. CCIS, vol. 435, pp. 299–303. Springer, Cham (2014). https://doi.org/10.1007/978-3-319-07854-0_53
20. Luck, R.: What is it that makes participation in design participatory design? Des. Stud. 59, 1–8 (2018)
21. Marçal, E.K., et al.: Auditoria da qualidade de um software de contabilidade. Gestão Regionalidade 23(66) (2007)
22. Morais, R., Costa, A.L., Góes, W.M., Somera, S.C.: Aplicação de métricas de software em um modelo de avaliação de qualidade para sistemas de informação de saúde: um estudo de factibilidade em um hospital público universitário (2013)
23. Pradhan, A., Mehta, K., Findlater, L.: "Accessibility came by accident" use of voice-controlled intelligent personal assistants by people with disabilities. In: Proceedings of the 2018 CHI Conference on Human Factors in Computing Systems, pp. 1–13 (2018)
24. Rocha, J.A.P., Duarte, A.B.S.: Diretrizes de acessibilidade web: um estudo comparativo entre as wcag 2.0 e o e-mag 3.0. Inclusão Soc. 5(2) (2012)

25. Rodrigues, K., Zaine, I., Orlandi, B., da Graça Pimentel, M.: Ensinando configurações do smartphone e aplicações sociais para o público 60+ por meio de aulas semanais e intervenções remotas. In: Anais do XII Workshop sobre Aspectos da Interação Humano-Computador para a Web Social, pp. 25–32. SBC, Porto Alegre (2021). https://doi.org/10.5753/waihcws.2021.17541. https://sol.sbc.org.br/index.php/waihcws/article/view/17541

26. Rodrigues, K.R., Onuki, L.A., Assunção, D.M., Junior, S.G., Pimentel, M.G.: Possibilities for the digital literacy of the older people in times of social distancing. In: Proceedings of the 19th Brazilian Symposium on Human Factors in Computing Systems, pp. 1–6 (2020)

27. Ryu, H., Kim, S., Kim, D., Han, S., Lee, K., Kang, Y.: Simple and steady interactions win the healthy mentality: designing a chatbot service for the elderly. Proc. ACM Hum.-Comput. Interact. 4(CSCW2), 1–25 (2020)

28. dos Santos, V.C.: Agentes inteligentes na educação a distância: uso de sistemas tutores inteligentes como auxiliares no estabelecimento da comunicação dialógica. LínguaTec 3(2) (2018)

29. Schlomann, A., et al.: Potential and pitfalls of digital voice assistants in older adults with and without intellectual disabilities: relevance of participatory design elements and ecologically valid field studies. Front. Psychol. 12 (2021)

30. Silveira, M.M.D., Portuguez, M.W., Pasqualotti, A., Colussi, E.L., et al.: Envelhecimento e inclusão digital: Significado, sentimentos e conflitos. Geriatr. Gerontol. Aging 8(3), 178–184 (2014)

31. Valtolina, S., Hu, L.: Charlie: a chatbot to improve the elderly quality of life and to make them more active to fight their sense of loneliness. In: CHItaly 2021: 14th Biannual Conference of the Italian SIGCHI Chapter. pp. 1–5 (2021)

32. Weizenbaum, J.: Eliza-a computer program for the study of natural language communication between man and machine. Commun. ACM 9(1), 36–45 (1966). https://doi.org/10.1145/365153.365168

33. Yu, T., Shen, Y., Jin, H.: A visual dialog augmented interactive recommender system. In: Proceedings of the 25th ACM SIGKDD International Conference on Knowledge Discovery & Data Mining, pp. 157–165 (2019)

Comparative Analysis of Accessibility Testing Tools and Their Limitations in RIAs

Obianuju Okafor$^{(\boxtimes)}$ (ID), Wajdi Aljedaani (ID), and Stephanie Ludi (ID)

Department of Computer Science and Engineering, University of North Texas,
Denton, TX, USA
{obianujuokafor,wajdialjedaani,stephaieludi}@unt.edu

Abstract. Accessibility is a required quality for websites today, and several tools exist to test for this quality. These tools are highly advantageous, but sadly they also have some limitations. A particular set of challenges they face is in the evaluation of Rich Internet Applications (RIAs). In this paper, we carry out an experiment to compare and analyze different accessibility testing tools as they evaluate 10 educational websites. We judged these tools based on their error detection, guideline coverage, speed, similarity to one another, and their relative performance when evaluating RIAs. The experiment findings revealed the strength and limitations of each tool. The results of this experiment also exposed that there are many guidelines and success criteria that accessibility testing tools are not able to cover, and that some evaluation tools are similar to each other in terms of the results they produce. Lastly, this experiment highlights a discrepancy in the behavior of the tools when evaluating RIAs compared to when evaluating static websites, although some more than others. This experiment has some limitations which we presented. As a future work, we intend to work with an expert to determine the accuracy of the results produced from the experiment. We also intend to delve deeper into the limitations of these tools and come up with possible solutions.

Keywords: Accessibility · Accessibility evaluation tools · Online education · Web Content Accessibility Guideline

1 Introduction

Web accessibility is the quality of a web application or website that determines how it can be used by people with the widest possible range of capabilities [14]. The more accessible a website is, the more diverse the people who can use it are, including people with disabilities like blindness, deafness, etc. Providing equal access to online services is required by law in many countries, particularly their government, educational institute websites, and learning management systems [11]. Regardless of the law, it is important for every website to be accessible to everyone to avoid excluding anyone.

© Springer Nature Switzerland AG 2022
V. G. Duffy et al. (Eds.): HCII 2022, LNCS 13521, pp. 479–500, 2022.
https://doi.org/10.1007/978-3-031-17902-0_34

As beneficial as accessibility is, websites today are either partially or entirely inaccessible [13]. According to the 2020 Web Accessibility Annual Report, 98% of websites in the United States are not accessible [7]. This is could be due to a number of reasons, such as web developers not having sufficient knowledge concerning accessibility and how to achieve it in websites [18], and there not being an efficient way to test for accessibility compliance. For a website to be considered accessible, it has to meet the requirements of accessibility guidelines [14], such as the Web Content Accessibility Guidelines (WCAG)[1], Section 806[2], BITV[3], ADA[4], etc.

There are three ways to test websites for conformance to an accessibility guideline: manually, automatically, or combining both methods [16]. In manual evaluation, tests are carried out by humans using the guidelines as a rule book. The automated testing approach involves the use of software tools with no human intervention. The last method of testing combines the features of the other two, testing is done partly by software tools and partly by humans, e.g., SAMBA [4].

In this paper, we focus on the automatic approach of testing, which involves the use of software tools. This method of testing for accessibility has several advantages [8]. A particular benefit it has is that it is an easy and efficient method for developers who do not have expertise inaccessibility to ensure their websites comply with accessibility guidelines. This approach also has several limitations. One challenge they face is in evaluating Rich Internet Applications (RIAs) [29]. In this context, the goal of this paper is to compare and analyze several accessibility evaluation tools in terms of error detection, guideline coverage, speed, correctness, tool similarity, and their relative performance with respect to RIAs.

The paper makes the following contributions:

- This paper conducts a comparative analysis of four existing accessibility evaluation tools. We provide experimental results highlighting each tool's weaknesses and strengths.
- This paper also presents the limitations these tools have regarding testing for accessibility in RIAs.
- We expect that our findings will provide researchers and developers with an overview of which tools are suitable for the evaluation of static and dynamic websites. It will also help them get a better understanding of accessibility.
- Our findings also highlight the remaining opportunities and research directions for better design of tools that evaluate RIAs.

The rest of this paper is organized as follows. We present background information in Sect. 2. In Sect. 3, discusses the other research that has been carried out relating to this research topic. We explain the approach we took when carrying out the experiment in Sect. 4. In Sect. 5, we present the results of this experiment and discuss them. In Sect. 5.1 presents the limitation of our study. We conclude and discuss some future works in Sect. 6.

---

[1] https://www.w3.org/WAI/standards-guidelines/wcag/.
[2] https://www.section508.gov/.
[3] https://www.accessi.org/bitv.
[4] https://www.access-board.gov/ada/.

2 Background

This section presents background information on the research problem. It first gives an overview of the Web Content Accessibility Guidelines (WCAG), then it discusses the existing tools used to automatically check for compliance to these guidelines and highlights some of their limitations. Finally, it talks about RIAs and the challenges they pose to accessibility evaluation tools.

2.1 Web Content Accessibility Guidelines (WCAG)

WCAG was created by the World Wide Web Consortium (W3C)[5]. The goal for creating WCAG is to provide a single standard for the creation of accessible web content that meets the needs of individuals, organizations, and governments globally [28]. The WCAG standards are grouped into four principles: perceivable, operable, understandable, and robust. Under these four principles, there are a total of 12–13 guidelines, depending on the version. Each guideline contains testable success criteria, which are associated with different levels of conformance: A (lowest), AA, and AAA (highest). The success criteria are what determines conformance to WCAG. In Table 1 we present the four principles and their respective guidelines, along with the number of success criteria in each guideline.

There are several versions of WCAG, but in this paper, we will be focusing on versions WCAG 2.0[6] and WCAG 2.1[7]. WCAG 2.0 was published in December 2008 and adopted in October 2012 by the International Organization of Standardization (ISO) as ISO an standard [28]. WCAG 2.1 was published in June 2018 [28]. WCAG 2.0 has a total of 61 success criteria, while WCAG 2.1 has a total of 78 success criteria. WCAG 2.1 extends WCAG 2.0, therefore all success criteria from 2.0 are included in 2.1, but there are 17 additional success criteria in WCAG 2.1 that are not in WCAG 2.0. This means that a website that meets WCAG 2.1 also meets the requirements of WCAG 2.0 [28].

2.2 Accessibility Evaluation Tools

Accessibility evaluation tools are websites, web applications, or desktop applications that help developers determine if web contents meet accessibility guidelines [3]. These tools verify compliance by testing for each success criteria of a guideline. Figure 1 shows the website of the AChecker tool, one of the tools used in this experiment. Table 2 gives some examples of these tools and their features.

The use of evaluation tools has several benefits [8]. It is a fast and easy way to obtain information on the accessibility level of a website and it is affordable in terms of evaluating large numbers of web pages [23]. However, as beneficial

---

[5] https://www.w3.org/.
[6] https://www.w3.org/TR/WCAG20/.
[7] https://www.w3.org/TR/WCAG21/.

Table 1. Organization of WCAG 2.0 and WCAG 2.1

Principles	Guidelines	Number of success criteria	
		WCAG 2.0	WCAG 2.1
Perceivable	1.1 Text Alternatives	1	1
	1.2 Time-based Media	9	9
	1.3 Adaptable	3	6
	1.4. Distinguishable	9	13
Operable	2.1. Keyboard Accessible	3	4
	2.2. Enough Time	5	6
	2.3. Seizures and Physical Reactions	2	3
	2.4. Navigable	10	10
	2.5. Input Modalities	–	6
Understandable	3.1. Readable	6	6
	3.2. Predictable	5	5
	3.3. Input Assistance	6	6
Robust	4.1. Compatible	2	3
	Total	**61**	**78**

as these tools are, there are still drawbacks to using them. Apart from the fact that they are not able to check for all guidelines [21,22], and that they are not accurate, i.e., may produce false negatives or positives [1,23], they also face challenges when evaluating RIAs [29].

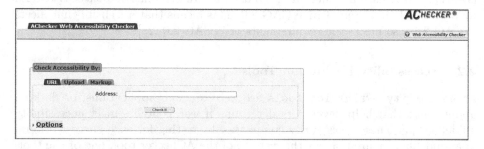

Fig. 1. Interface of the AChecker tool, via AChecker's website (https://achecker.achecks.ca/checker/index.php)

2.3 Rich Internet Applications (RIAs)

According to the author in [6], Rich Internet Applications are web applications or websites aimed to provide users with a similar desktop experience. RIAs are dynamic in nature and offer a richer and more interactive environment compared to traditional websites [29]. This is due to the use of a new set of technologies, such as DHTML, XML-HTTPRequest, DOM Events, etc. It was later discovered that these new technologies and capabilities introduce new sets of accessibility challenges to the Web [12]. Accessibility evaluation tools are not able to evaluate the dynamically generated contents that constitute RIAs [29]. These tools possess limited crawling capabilities and are only able to analyze static HTML content, therefore, DOM elements often go unnoticed [29].

To address the accessibility challenges posed by RIAs, the Web Accessibility Initiative (WAI) created a new specification called the Accessible Rich Internet Applications ARIA [31]. This specification stipulates how to make web pages, particularly dynamic content, more accessible [30]. Sadly, the majority of the existing accessibility evaluation tools are not able to evaluate websites using the ARIA specification.

3 Related Work

This section highlights several prior works that profoundly influenced our approach. We divided the related work into three sections: comparison of accessibility evaluation tools, accessibility evaluation for educational websites, and accessibility in Rich Internet Applications.

3.1 Comparing Accessibility Evaluation Tools

Previous studies have performed comparisons of accessibility evaluation tools. In the study by Christian et al. [20], conducted a comparative analysis of the performance of online accessibility evaluation tools. They compared six tools and found that the best tools were AChecker and TAW, with AChecker being the better tool of the two. They also proposed the classification of accessibility tools according to their usage and functionality. The research conducted in [1] compared five accessibility evaluation tools. In this study, faults were intentionally injected into web pages and then tested to investigate how the tools can detect injected faults. Their results showed that the tools do not discover all accessibility faults in web pages and that they produce inaccurate results.

Vigo et al. [24], performed an empirical investigation on six tools to show their capabilities in terms of coverage, completeness, and correctness regarding WCAG 2.0 conformance. They performed their investigation by using the semi-automated method of testing, and they combined the results of the tools LIFT and Bobby with human evaluation. They deduced that relying on automated tests alone has negative effects and could lead to unwanted consequences.

3.2 Accessibility Evaluation for Educational Websites

Several studies have conducted an experiment to evaluate educational websites. For example, Abdullah Alsaeedi [2] evaluated six Saudi universities' websites by using two tools, WAVE and Siteimprove. The author proposed a novel framework to compare the performance of the tools. Another study [9] analyzed 44 higher education websites in India. Their analysis was performed with two tools, TAW and aXe, and the results showed that TAw identified more issues than aXE. A more recent study [5] performed a systematic review of empirical studies on educational websites for web accessibility. The study identified 25 studies. The authors' recommendation is to improve the automatic evaluation tools.

3.3 Accessibility in Rich Internet Applications

In the third category are studies relating to RIAs and how to make them accessible. The first study we examined was by Watanabe et al. [29]. They describe an approach for testing accessibility requirements in RIAs that involves the use of acceptance tests. They also implemented a tool that automatically runs test cases and considers assistive technology user scenarios to raise accessible design flaws. Another study relating to RIAs was done by Linaje et al. [12]. They combined two methods from previous works, the RUX-Method and SAW, to provide accessibility features to Rich Internet Applications. To combine these two techniques, they used ontoRUX, an ontology based on WAI-ARIA. The result of this is a process that makes Web applications with RIA features accessible [12].

Our study is similar to all 3 categories of related work. We compare 4 accessibility tools to identify how they perform in terms of error detection, guideline coverage, speed, and similarity to one another, just like some of the studies in the first category. Furthermore, like the studies in the second category, we used the tools to evaluate computer science educational websites. Some of the websites we will be evaluating are RIAs, akin to the studies in the 3rd category. Our study differs from the others because we used the tools to evaluate both static websites and RIAs, and we have analyzed the tools' relative performance when evaluating the two types of websites.

4 Experiment

This experiment was carried out to compare web accessibility evaluation tools and analyze their performance in terms of error detection, guideline coverage, speed, tool similarity, and relative performance when evaluating RIAs.

In this study, we aim to address the following research questions:

- RQ1: Which tool is able to detect the most errors?
- RQ2: How is the coverage of the tools in terms of WCAG 2.0 or WCAG 2.1 guidelines?
- RQ3: How fast are the tools when evaluating websites for accessibility?
- RQ4: Which tools produce the most similar results?
- RQ5: What is the relative performance of the tools when evaluating Rich Internet Applications?

To achieve our research goals, we followed four main steps:

4.1 Tool Selection

We conducted research to determine what are the existing accessibility evaluation tools. We found several articles on some of the best tools being used to evaluate websites for accessibility [10,15,17,19,25]. We selected four of some of the most recommended tools. They are AChecker[8], FAE[9], TAW[10], and WAVE[11].

The tools which we chose have in common their ability to test web pages against the WCAG 2.0 or WCAG 2.1 guideline, they are free, web-based, and can evaluate websites using their URL. Some of the tools also evaluate websites using their source code, or by uploading their code files. Table 2 gives more information on each of the selected tools.

Table 2. Accessibility evaluation tools and their features

Tool	Guideline	License	Deployment	Report format
AChecker	BITV 1.0 (Level 2), Section 508, Stanca Act, WCAG 1.0 (A, AA, AAA), WCAG 2.0 (A, AA, AAA)	Free, Commercial	Website, Desktop Application	HTML
FAE	WCAG 2.1 (A, AA, AAA), ARIA	Free	Website	HTML, Email, CSV
TAW	WCAG 2.0 (A, AA, AAA)	Free	Website, Desktop Application	HTML, Email
WAVE	WCAG 2.1 (A, AA)	Free, Commercial	Website, Browser extension	HTML

4.2 Website Selection

In this experiment, we evaluate two categories of websites, static and dynamic websites (RIAs). In this context, static websites are websites in which the content of each page does not change, while dynamic websites are websites whose contents are generated dynamically.

We selected the websites in the context of computer science (CS) education. They are websites that can be used to learn different CS concepts. To find websites for the study, we did a Google search for websites that offer CS tutorials, and we found a total of 52 websites. We selected 10 out of 52, 5 static websites and 5 dynamic websites. We made sure to choose the websites that do not require a login, as that can affect the tools' ability to evaluate them. Table 3 shows the selected static websites and their URLs, and Table 4 shows the selected dynamic websites and their URLs.

---

[8] https://achecker.achecks.ca/checker/index.php.
[9] https://fae.disability.illinois.edu/.
[10] https://www.tawdis.net/resumen.
[11] https://wave.webaim.org/.

Table 3. Static websites and their URL

Website	URL
Geeksforgreek	https://www.geeksforgeeks.org/
w3schools	https://www.w3schools.com/
KD Nuggets	https://www.kdnuggets.com/tutorials/index.html
Guru99	https://www.guru99.com/
TutorialPoint	https://www.tutorialspoint.com/

Table 4. Dynamic websites and their URL

Website	URL
Snap	https://snap.berkeley.edu/snapsource/snap.html
Blockly	https://blockly-demo.appspot.com/static/demos/code/index.html
Code.org	https://studio.code.org/s/dance-2019/lessons/1/levels/1
Vidcode	https://www.vidcode.com/project/intro
Make Code	https://makecode.microbit.org/#editor

4.3 Experimental Procedure

During the experiment, the 4 selected tools (see Table 2) were applied to the 10 selected websites(see Tables 3 and 4). Thus, for every website, we carried out 4 tests, leading to a total number of 40 tests that were carried out in this experiment. Only a single page of each website was evaluated, often times this was the home page.

For all tools except WAVE, we configured the settings to ensure that they were evaluating websites using the proper guideline and conformance level. In Achecker, we selected **WCAG 2.0** as the guideline, and level **AAA** as the conformance level. TAW did not have the option to select a guideline, but we were able to select conformance level **AAA**. FAE had the most options to choose from. We could choose the ruleset (guideline), depth of evaluation, number of pages to be evaluated, etc. We selected the guideline **HTML4 Legacy Technique**, which entails the WCAG 2.0 guideline levels A, AA, and AAA, as well as HTML4, HTML5, and ARIA techniques. We selected the depth as **Top-level page only**, and the number of pages as **5**. Since we selected **Top-level page only**, only a single page was evaluated. WAVE was the only tool that did not provide options to choose from. It was built to evaluate websites using WCAG 2.1 and conformance levels A and AA only.

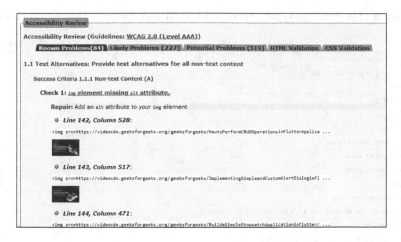

Fig. 2. Evaluation report generated by the AChecker tool (https://achecker.achecks. ca/checker/index.php)

To evaluate a website, the URL of the selected website was entered into each tool. Before starting each evaluation, we started a timer, and once the evaluation was done, we stopped the timer and recorded the time taken. After each test, we were presented with an evaluation report showing the total number of errors found, error description, which success criteria failure caused the error, a suggestion on how to fix the error, other potential errors, etc. The 40 tests that were carried out in the experiment produced 40 evaluation reports.

We observed that all tools did not produce results in the same format. Some tools' evaluation report was displayed on the screen as HTML content (see Fig. 2), while the evaluation report was sent through email in some cases. Additionally, some tools reported their errors according to HTML elements on the screen, e.g., images, links, forms, etc., while some tools categorized the results according to the guidelines failed. Due to this, we had to extract the data from each report and organize it in a uniform format. We created an excel sheet. For each test conducted, we entered into the excel sheet, evaluation time, total number of errors found, error details, success criteria failed, as well as any comments we had. We analyzed the data and wrote down our findings. We present the tables, diagrams, results, and discussion in the next section.

5   Result and Discussion

In this section, we present the results of the experiment. We also further discuss these results. The result of this experiment is divided into five sections, with each section addressing the research questions RQ1, RQ2, RQ3, RQ4, and RQ5, respectively.

488   O. Okafor et al.

Table 5. The different types of errors detected and the tools that found them.

Error	WAVE	Achecker	FAE	TAW
Image missing alternative text	Y	Y	Y	Y
Input element is missing form label	Y	Y	Y	Y
Empty link	Y	Y	Y	Y
Empty heading	Y	N	N	Y
Empty button	Y	N	Y	N
Contrast errors	Y	Y	Y	N
Web page well-formedness	N	N	N	Y
b (bold) element used	N	Y	N	N
i (italic) element used	N	Y	N	N
Font used	N	Y	N	N
Incorrect Header nesting	N	Y	Y	Y
Two headers of the same level with no content in between	N	N	N	Y
No h1 element in the document	N	N	Y	Y
Data cells does not use headers or ID attribute	N	Y	Y	N
Data table with both row and column headers does not use scope to identify cell	N	Y	N	N
Data table elements used in layout tables	N	N	N	Y
id attribute is not unique	N	Y	N	N
Form with no standard submission method	N	N	Y	Y
Frames without title	N	N	N	Y
Links with same link text but different destinations	N	N	N	Y
Consecutive text and image links to the same resource	N	N	N	Y
The language of the document is not identified or is invalid	Y	Y	Y	Y
Elements with event handlers must have roles	N	N	Y	N
Presence of empty lists	N	N	N	Y
Use of device-dependent event handlers	N	N	Y	Y
ARIA values must be valid	N	N	Y	N
Broken ARIA menu	Y	N	N	N
Use of labels to modify the presentation	N	N	N	Y
Widget labels must be descriptive	N	N	Y	N
Widgets must have label	N	N	Y	N
Label must reference control	N	N	Y	N
Role must have parent	N	N	Y	N
iframe must have accessible name	N	N	Y	N
Selection form control without grouping	N	N	N	Y
"div" elements that simulate paragraphs	N	N	N	Y
Total	**8**	**12**	**18**	**19**

RQ1: Which tool is able to detect the most errors?

At the end of each website evaluation, an evaluation report was generated. Part of the things shown in this report is the total number of errors found and the error description (see Fig. 2). In this section, we present the different types of errors found by each tool and the total number of errors reported in each website per tool.

Result. After compiling the results, we observed that there are 35 types of errors that were detected by the tools. Table 5 is a list of errors found across all websites by all tools. The most commonly reported error was *'Missing form label'*, it was found as an error in all 10 websites. The next most common error reported was *'Image missing alternative text'* and *'Empty link'*. They were both found in 70% of websites.

Table 6. Total number of errors detected per tool in each static website

Website	WAVE	AChecker	FAE	TAW
Geeksforgeeks	129	83	211	164
KDNuggets	8	54	7	35
W3School	26	48	–	91
Guru99	30	203	69	102
TutorialPoint	71	121	34	35
Average	52.8	101.8	80.25	85.4

Table 7. Total number of errors detected per tool in each dynamic website

Website	WAVE	AChecker	FAE	TAW
Snap	2	2	3	4
Code.org	26	14	8	68
MakeCode	2	0	2	2
Blockly	4	0	22	18
Vidcode	13	4	23	34
Average	9.4	4	11.6	25.2

No tool was able to detect all 35 errors. However, some tools detected more types of errors than others. TAW was able to detect the most type of errors. It found 19 different types of error out of 35, across all 10 websites. TAW could detect several errors that the others could not e.g. *'Web page well-formedness'*, *'Frames without title'*, etc. However, all tools except TAW were able to detect *'Contrast errors'*. TAW is closely followed by FAE, which was able to detect 18 types of errors. The next tool on the rank is Achecker. Although it could detect only 12 out of 35 errors, it is the only tool that reports text errors such as the *'Fonts used'*, *'i (italic) element used'*, and *'b (bold) element used'*. The tool that detected the least types of errors is WAVE. It detected just 8 out of 35 types of error. The only error it could detect that others could not was *'broken ARIA menu'*.

Regarding the number of errors found in each website, Tables 6 and 7 show the number of errors each tool detected in static and dynamic websites, respectively. The total number of errors reported is derived from the different types of errors found in a website multiplied by the number of elements that cause these errors. Some tools found more types of errors than the others, while for each type of error, some tools found more violating elements. All of this contributed to the difference in the number of errors reported by each tool.

Looking at Table 6, we can see that on average, Achecker reported the highest number of errors in static websites, with a mean of 101.8. It is followed by TAW, with a mean of 85.4. FAE had a mean of 80.25, making it the 3rd in this category. FAE might have had a higher mean, but it was not able to evaluate the website *'W3school'*. WAVE had the lowest average of 52.8, which is almost half the average of Achecker. In the dynamic website category (see Table 7), TAW had the highest mean of 25.2, while Achecker had the lowest mean of 4. The average of WAVE and FAE was 9.4 and 11.6, respectively.

Discussion. Although Achecker had the highest average for the number of errors in static websites, we can deduce that TAW performed the best in terms of error detection. It detected the most types of errors. It had the highest average number of errors in dynamic websites and the second highest average number of errors in static websites. TAW and Achecker's performance in terms of detecting a higher number of errors in static and dynamic websites than WAVE and FAE, was unexpected. TAW and Achecker both check against WCAG 2.0, which has fewer guidelines to violate than WCAG 2.1, which WAVE and FAE check against.

While going through the results of each tool, we observed that TAW and Achecker evaluation reports sometimes had errors that were duplicates. TAW and Achecker categorize errors by success criteria (see Fig. 2), hence, they often had errors that were repeated in the report, as one error could violate multiple success criteria. In contrast, WAVE and FAE grouped errors according to the elements that cause them, e.g., images, forms, etc., hence the errors were never repeated. Additionally, in the event that all tools detected a particular error in a website, TAW and Achecker often reported a higher number of violating elements than FAE and WAVE. All of these could be the reason Achecker and TAW had higher number of errors compared to WAVE and FAE. WAVE's low numbers could also be due to the fact that it could only check for conformance levels A and AA, while the other tools could check up to conformance level AAA.

As the tools often reported different numbers for the number of errors found in a website, it is hard to determine which tool produced the most accurate result. Some tools may have reported non-existing or trivial problems (false positives) or they might have missed true problems (false negatives). We will need to work with an accessibility expert to determine which tool has the most accurate results.

RQ2: How is the coverage of the tools in terms of WCAG 2.0 or WCAG 2.1 guidelines?
When evaluating a website, the tools check for adherence to the success criteria of the WCAG 2.0 guideline, in the case of Achecker and TAW, or the WCAG 2.1 guideline, in the case of WAVE and FAE. In this section, we analyze the tools in terms of their coverage of the WCAG 2.0 or WCAG 2.1 guideline.

Result. Table 8 shows which guidelines and success criteria failure at least one of the tools was able to detect across all websites. You can find the full list of guidelines and success criteria for WCAG 2.0 in [26], and for WCAG 2.1 in [27]. The green tick signifies (√)that the tool was able to detect those success criteria in at least one of the 10 websites. If a tool never detected a success criteria failure in any website, a red (×) is shown. Table 9 shows how many success criteria failures were detected in static and dynamic websites.

Looking at Table 8, we can see that there were only 9 out of 13 possible guidelines failures that were detected. The following guidelines were never covered by

Table 8. Table showing the coverage of the tools in terms of WCAG 2.0 and WCAG 2.1

Principle	Guideline	Success Criteria	WAVE	Achecker	FAE	TAW
Perceivable	**1.1**	1.1.1 Non-text Content (A)	✓	✓	✓	✓
	1.3	1.3.1 Info and Relationships (A)	✓	✓	✓	✓
		1.4.1 Use of Color (A)	×	×	✓	×
		1.4.3 Contrast (Minimum) (AA)	✓	✓	✓	×
	1.4	1.4.4 Resize text (AA)	×	✓	×	×
		1.4.6 Contrast (Enhanced) (AAA)	×	✓	✓	×
Operable	**2.1**	2.1.1 Keyboard (A)	✓	×	×	×
		2.1.3 Keyboard (No Exception) (AAA)	×	×	×	✓
		2.4.1 Bypass Blocks (A)	✓	×	✓	×
		2.4.4 Link Purpose (A)	✓	✓	✓	✓
	2.4	2.4.6 Headings and Labels (AA)	✓	✓	✓	×
		2.4.9-Link Purpose (Link Only) (AAA)	×	×	✓	✓
		2.4.10-Section Headings (AAA)	×	×	✓	✓
Understandable	**3.1**	3.1.1 Language of Page (A)	✓	✓	✓	✓
		3.2.2 On input (A)	×	×	✓	✓
	3.2	3.2.3 Consistent Navigation (AA)	×	×	✓	×
		3.2.4 Consistent Identification (AA)	×	×	✓	×
	3.3	3.3.2 Labels or Instructions (A)	✓	✓	✓	✓
		4.1.1-Parsing (A)	✓	✓	×	✓
Robust	**4.0**	4.1.2 Name, Role, Value (A)	×	×	✓	✓
Total	9	20	10	10	16	11

Table 9. Total number of success criteria detected in static and dynamic websites

	WAVE	Achecker	FAE	TAW
Static websites	7	9	12	10
Dynamic websites	9	5	16	10

any of the tools: 1.2, 2.2, 2.3, 2.5. Because some of the tools check for WCAG 2.1, there are 78 possible success criteria that could be detected. However, only 20 success criteria was covered. All of the success criteria detected can be found in both WCAG 2.0 and WCAG 2.1 guidelines. Additionally, over half of the success criteria failures reported had conformance level **A**.

FAE had the highest overall guideline coverage and the highest coverage in both static and dynamic websites. It detected 12 success criteria failures in static websites, while it detected 16 success criteria failures in dynamic websites. It is followed by TAW, which detected 11 different success criteria failures in total. It detected 10 success criteria failures in both static and dynamic websites. Achecker and Wave were both able to detect 10 types of success criteria failures, however, WAVE detected a higher number of success criteria failures in dynamic websites compared to Achecker. It found 9 success criteria failures while Achecker found 5. Achecker reported a higher number of success criteria failures in static websites compared to WAVE. It detected 9 success criteria violations while WAVE detected 7.

Discussion. Given that TAW performed best in terms of error detection, one would expect that it will also have the highest coverage in terms of guidelines. However, that was not the case. FAE had the most coverage instead. FAE's performance could be due to the fact that it uses a combination of techniques and guidelines when evaluating websites, e.g., WCAG 2.1, ARIA, HTML4, and HTML5 specifications. In addition, it performed almost as well as TAW in terms of detecting the most type of errors. Its ability to detect different types of error and its use of several techniques, might have led to it being able to detect the most success criteria violations.

WAVE's low guideline coverage in static websites was expected, as it is the only tool out of the four that does not reach level AAA of conformance. Thus, there are more guidelines it can not check for. For instance, looking at Table 8, 1.4.6, 2.1.3, 2.4.9, 2.4.10 are level AAA success criteria, and they were never detected by WAVE. Likewise, Achecker's low guideline coverage in dynamic websites did not come as a surprise as out of all tools, it found the least number of errors in dynamic websites.

Overall, all tools had below average guideline coverage. There were many guidelines and success criteria that were never covered by any of the tools. This could mean that these websites did not fail those guidelines. It could also mean that the tools are not able to detect those guidelines and success criteria violations. However, the latter is probably the case, as it has been said that most existing tools are only able to detect about 30% of the WCAG guidelines [21,22], and that 70% of guidelines have to be checked manually. The number of success criteria detected in this experiment was 20, which is about 26% of 78, and about 33% of 61. This supports the claims stated in [21,22]. To get a more comprehensive evaluation, there is a need for human evaluation.

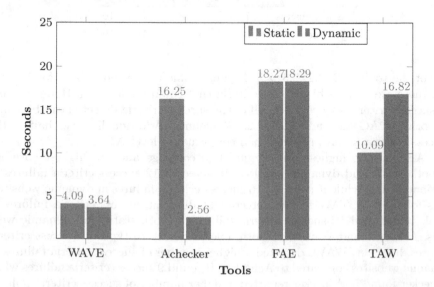

Fig. 3. Average time taken by each tool to evaluate the chosen page of each website

RQ3: How fast are the tools when evaluating websites for accessibility?

Before beginning each evaluation, we started the timer, and at the end, we stopped it and recorded the time. The time recorded is how fast the tool evaluated a single page of a website. In this section, we present the average time taken by each tool in seconds.

Result. We grouped the evaluation time into two, one for static websites and another for dynamic websites. For each tool, we calculated the average time in these two groups. Figure 3 is a bar chart showing the average time taken by each tool to evaluate a single page of a static or dynamic website. The blue bar represents the average time for static websites, and the red bar represents the average time for dynamic websites.

Looking at the figure, you can see that the tool that took the least time when evaluating static websites is WAVE, with an average time of 4.09 s. In the dynamic website category, Achecker took the least time with an average time of 2.56 s. The tool that took the most time in both dynamic and static websites is FAE, with an average time of 18.27 s in static websites and 18.29 s in dynamic websites. Additionally, the average time spent by FAE in both static and dynamic websites exceeded the time spent by all other tools in both categories.

Furthermore, from the figure, you can see that, except in the case of FAE and TAW, all other tools spent more time evaluating static websites than they did when evaluating dynamic websites. FAE took almost the same time when evaluating dynamic and static websites. It had an average time of 18.27 s when evaluating static websites, and when evaluating dynamic websites it had an average of 18.29 s. TAW took more time evaluating dynamic websites than it did evaluating static websites. When evaluating dynamic websites, the tool had an average time of 14.32 s, while it had an average time of 10.59 s when evaluating static websites.

Discussion. We observed that there is a relationship between the time it takes for the tool to evaluate a website, with the number and types of errors a tool detected, and its guideline coverage. For instance, WAVE had the least average time in the static website category. In turn, it was reported earlier that on average, WAVE detected the least number of errors and had the lowest guideline coverage in static websites. Additionally, WAVE detected the least types of errors. Similarly, the tool Achecker had the least time of 2.67 s in dynamic websites while also having the least average number of errors and the lowest guideline coverage in dynamic websites. This further reinforces the notion that the less time it takes for the tool to evaluate websites, the less error and success criteria it detects.

On the other hand, FAE took the longest time when evaluating both static and dynamic websites. This could be due to several reasons, one of which is the reason stated prior, that the more errors and guidelines a tool can detect, the longer it takes for it to evaluate a website. This reason still holds in this case as FAE had the highest coverage overall, and it detected the second most types of errors, after TAW. Another possible reason is that in addition to WCAG 2.1

success criteria, FAE also uses HTML4, HTML5, and ARIA accessibility techniques. Hence, it had more criteria to check for than the other tools. Additionally, after FAE finishes evaluating a website, it takes extra time to save the result before presenting it. The other tools displayed the result immediately after evaluation.

Table 10. Total number of times a tool reported the same error in a website with another tool

	WAVE	Achecker	FAE	TAW
WAVE	0	18	24	23
Achecker	18	0	18	21
FAE	24	18	0	23
TAW	23	21	23	0

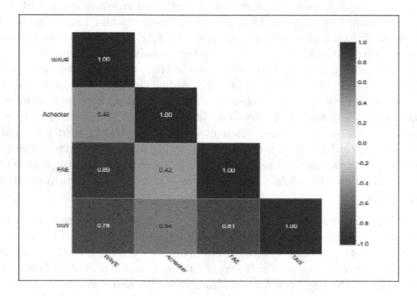

Fig. 4. Correlation matrix comparing the total number of errors found in each website per tool

RQ4: Which tools produce the most similar results?

In this subsection, we compare the tools to see which ones act the most similar. The tools can be similar to each other in the following ways: the closeness in value of the total number of errors they reported for a particular website, and if they found the same errors in a website.

Result. Table 10 shows how similar tools are in terms of the total number of times they detected the same error in a website for all 10 websites. This values in the table were calculated as follows: if two tools, say FAE and TAW, both detected the error *'image missing alternative text'* in the website *'Snap'*, a point is given to their pair. If two tools never detect the same error in any website, their pair will have 0 points. Figure 4 is a correlation matrix comparing the total number of errors reported by each tool for each website. The correlation matrix was created using a combination of Table 6 and Table 7.

From Fig. 4 and Table 10, it can be seen that the tool most similar to Wave is FAE, and vice versa. FAE and WAVE had a correlation coefficient of 0.89, which was the highest overall. In addition, the total number of times they reported the same error on a website was the highest. They reported the same error 24 times across all 10 websites. WAVE and FAE both had the least similarity with Achecker. WAVE and Achecker had a correlation coefficient of 0.46, while FAE and Achecker had a correlation coefficient of 0.42. WAVE and FAE both detected the same errors in a website with Achecker 18 times.

In contrast, the relationship between Achecker and TAW is not as symmetrical as the one WAVE has with FAE. Achecker had the highest correlation coefficient with TAW, which was 0.54. It also had the most similarity with TAW in terms of the total number of times it detected the same error in a website. They were able to detect the same errors in a website 21 times. On the other hand, TAW was most similar to FAE. They had a correlation coefficient of 0.81, and they detected the same errors in a website 23 times.

Discussion. WAVE is most similar to FAE, and vice versa. They both check against the WCAG 2.1 guideline, and this could be the reason they are most similar. Likewise, Achecker and TAW check against the same guideline, hence why Achecker had more similarity with TAW. However, the reverse is not the case between TAW and Achecker, TAW is more similar to FAE. This could be due to the fact that TAW and FAE were able to detect more types of error compared to Achecker and WAVE, hence there is a higher probability for them to detect the same error in a website.

We observed that all tools had the least similarity with Achecker. This could be attributed to the fact that Achecker had one of the lowest coverage in terms of types of errors and success criteria, compared to TAW and FAE, hence why TAW had more similarities to FAE, and not Achecker when they both checked against the WCAG 2.0 guideline. Another reason could be that Achecker produced results that were not congruent with the ones produced by the other tools.

Although there are some tools that are similar and comparable to one another, no two tools are identical. It is interesting that even tools that evaluate websites using the same guidelines and conformance level, do not produce identical results. The tools often show disparities in the types and number of errors detected in a website, and the number of elements that cause these errors. More investigation is needed to determine why this is so.

RQ5: What is the relative performance of the tools when evaluating Rich Internet Applications?

One of the reasons for selecting websites in two categories, one for static websites and the other for dynamic websites, was to observe the performance of the tools when evaluating static websites versus when evaluating dynamic websites. In this section, we compare how the tools behaved when evaluating static websites relative to how they behaved when evaluating dynamic websites.

Result. Earlier, we presented Tables 6 and 7, which shows the total number of errors reported in static websites and dynamic websites, respectively. We also presented Fig. 3, which shows the average time taken by the tools in static and dynamic websites, and Table 9, which shows the total number of success criteria failures detected in both static and dynamic websites.

Comparing Tables 6 and 7, we can see that when evaluating static websites, most of the tools reported a higher number of errors and a higher average for the number of errors compared to when evaluating dynamic websites. For instance, the maximum number of errors detected in static websites is 211, while the maximum number of errors detected in dynamic websites is 68. Also, the maximum average of the number of errors detected in static websites was 101.8, while the maximum average in dynamic websites was 25.2. Additionally, in dynamic websites, over 50% of the time the total number of errors reported was less than 5.

A common error that was found in dynamic websites but was never found in static websites, was the error *'The language of the document is not identified or is invalid'*. This error was reported in 80% of dynamic websites and was not reported in any static website. Additionally, text errors such as the *'Fonts used'*, *'i (italic) element used'*, and *'b (bold) element used'* was found in 4 out of 5 static websites, while it was only detected in 1 out of 5 dynamic websites.

Looking at Fig. 3, you can also see that when evaluating dynamic websites versus when evaluating static websites, there is often a difference in time taken. On average, WAVE and Achecker took more time evaluating static websites than they did when evaluating dynamic websites, while FAE and TAW took more time to evaluate dynamic websites. Although, in the case of FAE, the time difference between the two categories was minuscule. The biggest disparity in time can be seen in the tool Achecker, when evaluating static websites, it had an average time of 16.25 s, while in dynamic websites, it had an average time of 2.56 s. It had over an 80% decrease in time when evaluating dynamic websites.

TAW showed the least variation in terms of the number of errors and the number of success criteria failures reported when evaluating static versus when evaluating dynamic websites. Out of all tools, the number of errors TAW reported in dynamic websites was closest to the number of errors reported in dynamic websites. Additionally, TAW detected the same number of success criteria in both static and dynamic websites. FAE showed the least variation with regard to the time taken when evaluating static websites compared to when evaluating dynamic websites. The difference in time was 20 ms, which was the least difference across all tools.

Achecker behaved the most differently when evaluating dynamic websites. It had the lowest average total number of errors in the dynamic website category, while it had the highest average total number of errors in the static website category. In addition, it was the only tool that detected no errors in 2 out of 5 dynamic websites. Additionally, there was a substantial difference in the average time it took to evaluate dynamic websites versus the time it took to evaluate static websites. The average time it took to evaluate dynamic websites was over 80% less than the time it took to evaluate static websites. There was also almost a 50% decrease in the number of success criteria failures detected in dynamic websites compared to the success criteria it detects in static websites.

Discussion. From the results above, we can see that most tools acted differently when evaluating dynamic websites compared to when evaluating static websites. The biggest difference in behavior can be seen in the total number of errors the tools reported in static websites compared to the ones reported in dynamic websites. This disparity could be due to the dynamic websites used in this experiment being more accessible than the static websites used. Alternatively, it could be that the tools are not able to evaluate dynamic web content [29]. In almost all of the dynamic websites, the error *'The language of the document is not identified or is invalid'* was reported. The fact that the language used in dynamic websites does not seem to be supported could be part of the reason the tools were not able to evaluate their contents.

Achecker showed the most disparity in the results it produced for static websites in comparison to the results it produced for dynamic sites. It had a relatively good performance in terms of error detection and guideline coverage in static websites, while it performed poorly in those aspects in dynamic websites. Furthermore, the time it took to analyze static websites was significantly greater than the time it used to analyze dynamic websites. Going by our theory that states that the longer it takes for a tool to evaluate websites, the more types of errors it can detect, we can say that Achecker was only able to detect a few errors in dynamic websites. Achecker's struggle when evaluating dynamic websites compared to when evaluating static websites could be due to the fact that it was built to evaluate static websites and not dynamic websites.

FAE is the only tool that uses the Accessible Rich Internet Applications (ARIA) guideline when evaluating websites. As we mentioned earlier, ARIA is used to provide accessibility to RIAs [31]. This could be the reason it had less discrepancy when evaluating static websites versus dynamic websites, compared to some of the other tools. TAW performed equally well, given that it does not use ARIA when evaluating websites. However, it does use HTML, CSS, and Javascript technologies, which might have helped its performance.

5.1 Limitations

While carrying out this research study, we had several limitations. Firstly, we are not experts on web accessibility, thus, we are not able to ascertain the accuracy and precision of the results presented by each tool. Although, for each error reported in a website, we checked to make sure it was valid. Another limitation we faced was the heterogeneity of the tools. They did not all check against the same guideline. In addition, the format in which they reported their results were different. This made it very difficult to compare them. Lastly, it was hard to categorize websites as static or dynamic. A lot of websites have some attributes of both. However, we tried our best to select the websites that best fit the respective categories.

6   Conclusion and Future Work

Providing accessibility to websites today has become a necessity, but sadly most websites are still not accessible. A particular type of website that poses the most challenges in regard to accessibility, are Rich Internet Applications (RIAs). Most tools are not able to evaluate RIAs due to the technologies they comprise of [12,29].

This paper presents a comparative analysis of four accessibility evaluation tools in terms of error detection, guideline coverage, speed, similarity to one another, and their relative performance when evaluating RIAs. The results of the experiment exposed the strengths and weaknesses of the tools. TAW was the tool that was able to detect the most errors. On average, WAVE was the fastest when evaluating web pages. FAE had the most guideline coverage. Additionally, the study revealed that tools are only able to cover a small fraction of the WCAG 2.0 or WCAG 2.1 guidelines and that some tools are similar to each other. Most importantly, the results showed that the tools behave differently when evaluating Rich Internet Applications versus when evaluating traditional static websites, especially the tool Achecker.

We expect our findings will provide researchers and developers with an overview of which tools are available and suitable for automatic accessibility evaluation of static and dynamic websites, their capabilities, and limitations. Through exploring the efficacy and limitations of the existing tools, developers can get a better understanding of accessibility and can thus, design websites that meet accessibility standards and tools for evaluating them. This research also highlights the remaining opportunities and research directions for better design of tools that evaluate dynamic content.

This study has some limitations which we have discussed. As a future work, we intend to work with an accessibility expert to determine the accuracy of the results produced in this experiment. Furthermore, we also plan to delve deeper into some of the issues associated with accessibility evaluation tools, to determine the root causes and come up with a viable solution.

References

1. Al-Ahmad, A., Ahmaro, I.Y., Mustafa, M.: Comparison between web accessibility evaluation tools, January 2013. https://www.researchgate.net/publication/279181298
2. Alsaeedi, A.: Comparing web accessibility evaluation tools and evaluating the accessibility of webpages: proposed frameworks. Information 11(1), 40 (2020)
3. Baazeem, I.S., Al-Khalifa, H.S.: Advancements in web accessibility evaluation methods: how far are we? In: Proceedings of the 17th International Conference on Information Integration and Web-based Applications & Services. iiWAS 2015, 11–13 December 2015. ACM Press, New York. https://doi.org/10.1145/2837185.2843850

4. Brajnik, G., Lomuscio, R.: Samba: a semi-automatic method for measuring barriers of accessibility. In: Proceedings of the 9th International ACM SIGACCESS Conference on Computers and Accessibility, Assets 2007, October 15–17 2007, pp. 43–50. ACM Press, New York. https://doi.org/10.1145/1296843.1296853

5. Campoverde-Molina, M., Lujan-Mora, S., Garcia, L.V.: Empirical studies on web accessibility of educational websites: a systematic literature review. IEEE Access **8**, 91676–91700 (2020)

6. Fortes, R.P., Antonelli, H.L., de Lima Salgado, A.: Accessibility and usability evaluation of rich internet applications. In: Proceedings of the 22nd Brazilian Symposium on Multimedia and the Web, Webmedia 2016, 08–11 November 2016, pp. 7–8. ACM Press, New York. https://doi.org/10.1145/2976796.2988221

7. Human Network Contributor: Websites fail to comply with accessibility for people with disabilities. November 2020. https://isemag.com/2020/11/telecom-98-percent-of-websites-fail-to-comply-with-accessibility-requirements-for-people-with-disabilities/

8. Investis Digital: Accessibility testing - manual or automated? January 2020. https://www.investisdigital.com/blog/web-design-and-development/accessibility-testing-manual-or-automated. Accessed 23 Oct 2021

9. Ismail, A., Kuppusamy, K.: Web accessibility investigation and identification of major issues of higher education websites with statistical measures: a case study of college websites. J. King Saud Univ. Comput. Inf. Sci. (2019)

10. Kumar, A.: 5 free must have web accessibility testing tools - leader in offshore accessibility testing — section 508 compliance — wcag conformance — barrierbreak, October 2021. https://www.barrierbreak.com/5-free-must-have-web-accessibility-testing-tools/

11. Law Office of Lainey Feingold: Digital accessibility laws around the globe, May 2013. https://www.lflegal.com/2013/05/gaad-legal/. Accessed 23 Oct 2021

12. Linaje, M., Lozano-Tello, A., Perez-Toledano, M.A., Preciado, J.C., Rodriguez-Echeverria, R., Sanchez-Figueroa, F.: Providing ria user interfaces with accessibility properties. J. Symb. Comput. **46**, 207–217 (2011). https://doi.org/10.1016/j.jsc.2010.08.008

13. Lopes, R., Gomes, D., Carriço, L.: Web not for all: A large scale study of web accessibility. In: Proceedings of the 2010 International Cross Disciplinary Conference on Web Accessibility (W4A). W4A 2010. Association for Computing Machinery, New York (2010). https://doi.org/10.1145/1805986.1806001. https://doi.org/10.1145/1805986.1806001

14. Mankoff, J., Fait, H., Tran, T.: Is your web page accessible?: a comparative study of methods for assessing web page accessibility for the blind. In: In Proceedings of the SIGCHI Conference on Human Factors in Computing Systems, CHI 2005, pp. 41–50. ACM Press, New York (2005)

15. Misfud, J.: 8 free web-based website accessibility evaluation tools - usability geek. https://usabilitygeek.com/10-free-web-based-web-site-accessibility-evaluation-tools/

16. Mucha, J.M.: Combination of automatic and manual testing for web accessibility. Master's thesis, Grimstad, Norway (2018). Accessed 05 Aug 2019

17. Neova Tech Solutions: 7 web accessibility testing tools you should know, April 2020. https://www.neovasolutions.com/2020/04/08/7-web-accessibility-testing-tools-you-should-know/. Accessed 03 Mar 2022

18. Smith, S.: Website accessibility standards should be higher to help disabled people - vox, May 2019. https://www.vox.com/the-goods/2019/2/5/18210912/websites-ada-compliance-lawsuits. Accessed 04 Mar 2022

19. Software Testing Help: Top 20 accessibility testing tools for web applications, Feb 2022. https://www.softwaretestinghelp.com/accessibility-testing-tools/. Accessed 03 Mar 2022

20. Timbi-Sisalima, C., Amor, C.I.M., Tortosa, S.O., Hilera, J.R., Aguado-Delgado, J.: Comparative analysis of online web accessibility evaluation tools. In: Proceedings of the 25th International Conference on Information Systems Development, ISD 2016, pp. 562–573. University of Economics, ACM Press, New York (2016)

21. Usablenet: Quick guide to manual accessibility testing and why it's important, June 2018. https://blog.usablenet.com/quick-guide-to-manual-accessibility-testing-and-why-its-important. Accessed 02 Mar 2022

22. Usablenet: Automated wcag testing is not enough for web accessibility ada compliance [blog], July 2020. https://blog.usablenet.com/automated-wcag-testing-is-not-enough-for-web-accessibility-ada-compliance. Accessed 02 Mar 2022

23. Vigo, M., Brajnik, G.: Automatic web accessibility metrics: where we are and where we can go. Interact. Comput. **23**, 137–155 (2011). https://doi.org/10.1016/j.intcom.2011.01.001

24. Vigo, M., Brown, J., Conway, V.: Benchmarking web accessibility evaluation tools: measuring the harm of sole reliance on automated tests. In: Proceedings of the 10th International Cross-Disciplinary Conference on Web Accessibility, w4A 2013, pp. 1–10. ACM Press, New York (2013). https://doi.org/10.1145/2461121.2461124

25. W3C: Web accessibility evaluation tools list. https://www.w3.org/WAI/ER/tools/

26. W3C: Web content accessibility guidelines (wcag) 2.0, December 2008. https://www.w3.org/TR/WCAG20/. Accessed 04 Mar 2022

27. W3C: Web content accessibility guidelines (wcag) 2.1, June 2018. https://www.w3.org/TR/WCAG21/. Accessed 04 2022

28. W3C Web Accessibility Initiative (WAI): Wcag 2 overview, July 2005. https://www.w3.org/WAI/standards-guidelines/wcag/. Accessed 04 Mar 2022

29. Watanabe, W.M., Fortes, R.P.M., Dias, A.L.: Using acceptance tests to validate accessibility requirements in ria. In: Proceedings of the International Cross-Disciplinary Conference on Web Accessibility, W4A 2012, 16–17 April 2012. ACM Press, New York. https://doi.org/10.1145/2207016.2207022

30. World Wide Web Consortium: Wai-aria, January 2016. https://www.w3.org/WAI/standards-guidelines/aria/. Accessed 24 Aug 2019

31. World Wide Web Consortium: Accessible rich internet applications (wai-aria) 1.1. https://www.w3.org/TR/wai-aria/. Accessed 05 Sept 2019

Camera Mouse: Sound-Based Activation as a New Approach to Click Generation

Phoenix Pagan[✉], Hanvit Choi, and John Magee

Department of Computer Science, Clark University, Worcester, MA 01610, USA
{ppagan,hachoi,jmagee}@clarku.edu

Abstract. In the rapid development of HCI technology, mouse-replacement interfaces have innovated the user interaction experience with graphical user interfaces, specifically for those with neuromuscular diseases. By employing click actuation modalities that do not require a mouse for performing the tasks of pointing and clicking, the individuals are provided with a solution for effective interaction with computers. We present an alternative click actuation modality called "sound-click recognition" for the users of Camera Mouse, a mouse-replacement interface that tracks user motion. Using the sound-click recognition feature, users can generate a left click of the mouse based on the volume of the sound they generate. Furthermore, we present the findings of the evaluation of Camera Mouse while employing two input methods including sound-click recognition and dwell-time selection to analyze the user performance with each approach through side-by-side comparison. The metrics used to measure performance are generated by the GoFitts evaluation tool and are movement time(ms), throughput(bits/s), error rate (%), and target re-entries.

Keywords: Accessibility · Sound recognition · Click actuation · Neuro-muscular diseases

1 Introduction

Camera Mouse is a computer-vision-based program that works as a mouse-replacement interface, providing computer access to people with motor disabilities that hinder the ability to use a mouse [1]. This program helps the user control the mouse pointer in two fragments. The system first tracks the user's motion through a webcam to translate it into the movement of the mouse pointer on the screen, allowing the user to "point". Subsequently, the user can "click," or select the target element the cursor is placed on.

By default, the Camera Mouse supports the dwell-time click activation method which is to maintain the cursor located at the target region for a certain period of time [6], after which a left mouse click is actuated. The other feature that the interface supports is the muscle contraction method using a sensor called ClickerAID [6]. This feature lets the users choose a preferred muscle group

© Springer Nature Switzerland AG 2022
V. G. Duffy et al. (Eds.): HCII 2022, LNCS 13521, pp. 501–509, 2022.
https://doi.org/10.1007/978-3-031-17902-0_35

such as brow muscle and detects a sudden contraction of the muscle to actuate the clicks [4].

Despite the convenience that the dwell-time selection and the muscle contraction feature provide, there have been reported issues during the use of the methods, including the "Midas Touch" problem, or generating inadvertent clicks of target elements [2], and the difficulty of selecting small target elements [4]. In an attempt to address these issues while using the Camera Mouse, we present an add-on feature of the program, namely "sound-click recognition."

Sound-click recognition uses the sound the user makes, such as "click" or other vocal commands, to generate clicks when the noise exceeds a certain threshold. The method, therefore, does not require the tracking of muscle movement or the positioning of the cursor for a certain period, possibly lowering the risk of producing unintentional clicks that arise when only using the dwell-time feature by only actuating the clicks exactly at the moment the user's vocal command is input.

This paper includes the ways in which the sound-click recognition method is evaluated, an explanation about the experimental tool used for evaluation, a discussion on the results of the experiment, and ways to improve the technology in the future.

2   Experiment

2.1   Tools and Apparatus

We used an HP Laptop 15-ef0xxx with a 15-inch screen, and by default, the computer's resolution was set to 1366 by 768. The sound-clicking tool was created using Python's pyaudio library. The sound-clicking tool operates by actuating a click when the subject generates a noise above a volume threshold which is set prior to the experiment.

To perform a preliminary evaluation on the mouse selection method, we followed the conventions in previous Camera Mouse studies to use an interactive tool called FittsTaskTwo which is part of the application GoFitts containing different Fitts' law applications [7]. FittsTaskTwo software was developed specifically for evaluating the user performance of pointing devices or interaction modalities on computers [7]. By gathering and saving the performance data and implementing 1-D or 2-D Fitt's law tasks, the software outputs files for analysis [7].

Using the software begins with setting up the parameters in which the current evaluation is performed. The software can be configured to use different target sizes and different distances between each target [4]. Under the 2D setting, the parameters considered include target amplitudes referring to the diameter of the circular layout, and target widths referring to the diameter of each of the target circles [7]. The units for both parameters are pixels [7].

Once the parameters are determined, the user begins performing a sequence of trials by positioning the mouse pointer on the highlighted target region and clicking on it to move to the next target region [4,7]. For 2D layouts, the high-lighted target region moves from a circle on one side to the circle on the direct opposite side upon each clicking, the process of which continues until each circle of the layout has been selected once, and the first target has been highlighted and selected again [7]. At the end of the sequence, the software displays "Sequence Summary" of the performance results for the sequence [7].

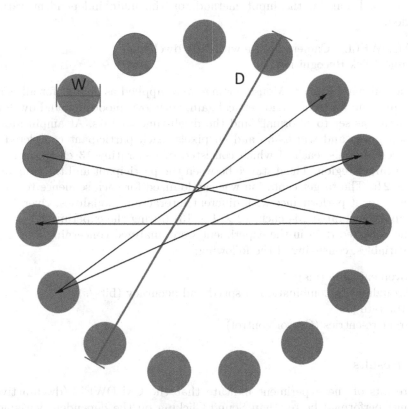

Fig. 1. The testing layout of FittsTask2D interface with the arrows displaying the pattern of which the highlighted target region changes. W refers to the width of each target region and D refers to the amplitude, or the diameter of the target circle layout.

2.2 Participants

Ten participants of six male-identifying individuals and four female-identifying individuals were involved in the experiment to evaluate the two mouse selection methods using the evaluation tool FittsTaskTwo(2D) [3]. Considering the number of participants, we employed a within-subjects study design to measure data from each participant. Thus, the participants were divided into two groups of five individuals, denoted as Group 1 and Group 2.

2.3   Procedure

Using FittsTaskTwo(2D), each participant's performance on sound-click recognition and dwell-time selection was recorded. The participants in Group 1 evaluated the dwell-time selection method first, followed by the sound-click recognition method, while the participants in Group 2 evaluated the sound-click recognition method first, followed by the dwell-time selection.

The conditions in the input method, or the main independent variable, included:

- CM_DWELL - Camera Mouse with 1.0 s dwell time
- Sound-Click Recognition

The following Camera Mouse settings were applied as default for all participants: medium horizontal and vertical gain, very low smoothing, and dwell-time click area was set to "Normal" and the dwell-time to 1.0 s. At amplitudes 300 and 600 pixels and widths 50 and 80 pixels, each participant completed four sequences of trials, each of which consisted of generating 13 clicks on a blue-colored target region. The distance between the participant and the camera was kept at 2 ft. The target condition was randomized for each sequence to analyze the participant performance with different interaction modalities. Overall, each participant generated 104 clicks ($2 \times 4 \times 13$) during the experiment.

The collected data in the experiment were analyzed concerning four dependent variables, consisting of the following:

- Movement time (ms)
- Throughput, a combination of speed and accuracy (bits/s)
- Error rate (%)
- Target re-entries (Cursor control)

2.4   Results

The results of the experiment indicate that the CM_DWELL(dwell-activated clicking) performed better than Sound-Clicking on the dependent variables of throughput and error rate. The throughput for CM_DWELL compared to Sound-Clicking was 48.46% greater, with throughput of 1.143 bits/s and .589 bits/s, respectively. The difference between the two was statistically significant as well with $p < 0.01$.

The mean error rate for Sound-Clicking was 6.73% higher than the mean error rate for CM_DWELL. During sessions using Sound-Clicking, the mean error rate was 18.08%, which is relatively larger than the mean error rate recorded for CM_DWELL at 11.35%. The difference was statistically significant with $p < .01$.

We found that although the mean movement time(ms) for Sound-Clicking at 2766.93 ms was 2.79% faster than the mean movement time for CM_DWELL at 2846.43 ms, the difference was not significant($p > .05$).

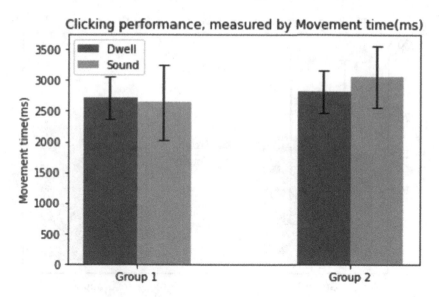

Fig. 2. Mean movement time in milliseconds

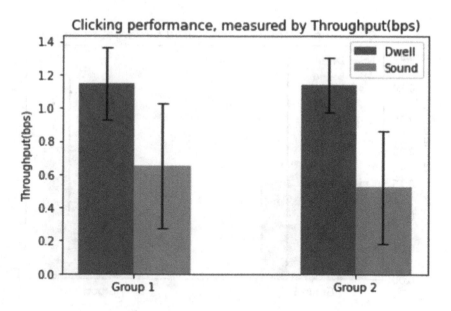

Fig. 3. Mean throughput in bits/s

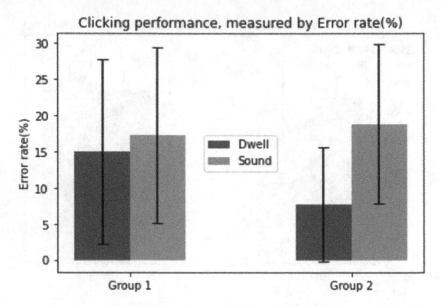

Fig. 4. Mean error rate in %

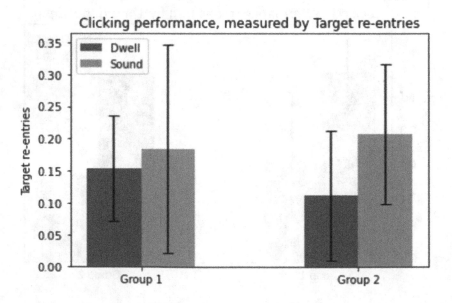

Fig. 5. Mean target re-entries

For the final dependent variable, target re-entries, CM_DWELL was the favorable choice. Sound-Clicking averaged 0.20 re-entries/trial while CM_DWELL averaged 0.13 re-entries/trial. In other words, Sound-Click averaged 47.83% more target re-entries/trial than CM_DWELL. Furthermore, the difference was statistically significant with $p < .05$.

While CM_DWELL outperformed Sound-Clicking on most of the dependent variables, the performance of each individual study participant varied widely. As shown in Fig. 4, there was a high variance in error rate across all groups, while Fig. 3 and Fig. 5 demonstrate that during Sound-Clicking trials there was a generally more varied performance in terms of throughput and target re-entries relative to study participants' more consistent performance with the CM_DWELL.

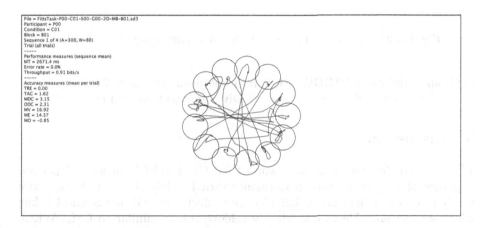

File = FittsTask-P00-C01-S00-G00-2D-MB-B01.sd3
Participant = P00
Condition = C01
Block = B01
Sequence 1 of 4 (A=300, W=80)
Trial (all trials)

Performance measures (sequence mean)
MT = 2671.4 ms
Error rate = 0.0%
Throughput = 0.91 bits/s

Accuracy measures (mean per trial)
TRE = 0.00
TAC = 1.62
MDC = 3.15
ODC = 2.31
MV = 16.92
ME = 14.37
MO = -0.85

Fig. 6. FittsTask2D tracing for a study participant using CM_DWELL

An advantage of the Sound-Clicking tool is that it allows users more direct control over when and where they click. Figure 6 demonstrates that when utilizing CM_DWELL, the cursor tends to have more motion within the target. While the FittTask2D test provided large clicking targets, having more control would be an advantage in real-life use. Figure 7, the tracing data for Sound-Clicking shows that the study participant spent less time looking at each target, although it is important to note the higher target re-entries/trial statistic which is indicative of difficulties with target acquisition.

The within-subjects aspect of the study, where we divided the ten participants into two groups, demonstrated that having study participants use CM_DWELL first and then Sound-Clicking or the opposite, where study participants used Sound-Clicking then CM_DWELL, had a statistically significant impact on the mean movement time. We found that study participants in Group 2 performed better on mean movement time while using Sound-Clicking than participants in Group 1; 3056.18 ms vs. 2636.68 ms, respectively. The difference was statistically significant ($p < .05$). Additionally, we found that study participants in Group 2 using CM_DWELL performed better than study participants

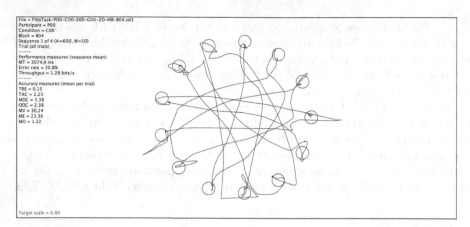

File = FittsTask-P00–C00–S00–G00–2D–MB–804.sd3
Participant = P00
Condition = C00
Block = 804
Sequence 1 of 4 (A=600, W=50)
Trial (all trials)

Performance measures (sequence mean)
MT = 3074.9 ms
Error rate = 30.8%
Throughput = 1.29 bits/s

Accuracy measures (mean per trial)
TRE = 0.15
TAC = 2.23
MDC = 3.38
ODC = 2.38
MV = 30.24
ME = 23.36
MO = 1.22

Target scale = 0.80

Fig. 7. FittsTask2D tracing for a study participant using Sound-Clicking

in Group 1 also using CM_DWELL in terms of mean error rate; 7.69% vs. 15.0%, respectively. The difference was statistically significant, as well ($p < .05$).

3   Discussion

While Sound-Clicking performed worse than CM_DWELL on most dependent variables, study participants' performance varied widely. Some subjects, particularly in Group 1, had great difficulty with effectively utilizing Sound-Clicking while others were able to consistently achieve results similar to CM_DWELL. A criticism of the Sound-Clicking approach raised by study participants was that the volume-activated clicking would inadvertently activate when coughing, sneezing, or yawning. Additionally, loud background noises would occasionally interfere with the Sound-Clicking tool causing further errors. Participants appreciated that Sound-Clicking offered more direct control over their clicking actions than CM_DWELL; this was an area where that we identified key improvements that could be made to improve the Sound-Clicking tool's performance.

By adding the functionality to Sound-Clicking that allows it to have a preset "keyword" that activates clicking, we believe that the issue of accidental mis-clicks can be resolved. An obstacle to this approach is the additional technical complexity that such an improvement would require, namely, the need for using machine-learning techniques that require large amounts of training data to be accurate. By using pre-trained sound recognition models offered by cloud providers such as AWS or Microsoft Azure, this hurdle may be overcome, but at the cost of increased technical complexity and reliance on an external vendor. An approach that would manage both the issue of a lack of training data and a reliance on external solutions would be using open-source repositories of data such as Kaggle.com; while creating an accurate sound-recognition tool would be a challenge, having high-quality data would make it easier to train an effective Sound-Clicking tool.

4   Conclusion

The empirical evidence from our experiments demonstrated that Sound-Clicking underperformed CM_DWELL on the four dependent variables of movement time (ms), throughput, a combination of speed and accuracy (bits/s), error rate (%), and target re-entries (cursor control). That said, with optimizations in the Sound-Clicking tool's audio recognition capability, we hypothesize it could improve its performance on the FittTask2D test. Furthermore, a longer-term study where participants use Sound-Clicking or CM_DWELL during their daily computer use could yield an understanding about Sound-Clicking's real-world viability.

As stated in the discussion section, a major potential issue with the Sound-Clicking tool is that the user may register unwanted sounds into the system, which may cause the system to generate unintentional clicks. We hypothesized that a more advanced sound-recognition system that takes advantage of machine learning's sound recognition capabilities could resolve this. However, this would also need further consideration for those with neuro-muscular diseases that make creating consistent sounds challenging. In addition, the issue of low performance of the system during initial clicks due to lack of user voice data must be addressed accordingly. Using open-source repositories of audio data could address this problem.

Acknowledgements. The undergraduate authors would like to acknowledge and appreciate Clark University's Department of Computer Science for providing guidance and necessary resources for this research project. NSF support for this project is also acknowledged and greatly appreciated (#IIS-1551590).

References

1. Camera Mouse, January 2018. http://www.cameramouse.org
2. Jacob, R.J.K.: What you look at is what you get: eye movement-based interaction techniques. In: Proceedings of the SIGCHI Conference on Human Factors in Computing Systems (CHI 1990), pp. 11–18. ACM (1990)
3. MacKenzie, I.S.: Human-Computer Interaction: An Empirical Research Perspective. Elsevier, New Delhi (2013). 291 pages
4. Magee, J., Felzer, T., MacKenzie, I.S.: Camera mouse + ClickerAID: dwell vs. single-muscle click actuation in mouse-replacement interfaces. In: Antona, M., Stephanidis, C. (eds.) UAHCI 2015. LNCS, vol. 9175, pp. 74–84. Springer, Cham (2015). https://doi.org/10.1007/978-3-319-20678-3_8
5. Missimer, E., Betke, M.: Blink and wink detection for mouse pointer control. In: The 3rd ACM International Conference on Pervasive Technologies Related to Assistive Environments (PETRA 2010), Pythagorion, Samos, Greece, pp. 1–8 (2010)
6. Zuniga, R., Magee, J.: Camera mouse: dwell vs. computer vision-based intentional click activation. In: Antona, M., Stephanidis, C. (eds.) UAHCI 2017. LNCS, vol. 10278, pp. 455–464. Springer, Cham (2017). https://doi.org/10.1007/978-3-319-58703-5_34
7. GoFitts. http://www.yorku.ca/mack/FittsLawSoftware/doc/index.html?GoFitts.html. Accessed 4 March 2022

Photo Analysis for Characterizing Food-Related Behavior and Photo Elicitation to Set-Up a Mixed Reality Environment for Social Eating Among Older Adults Living at Home

Helene Christine Reinbach[1] (ID), Thomas Bjørner[2](✉) (ID), Thomas Skov[1], and Dannie Michael Korsgaard[2]

[1] Food Science, Copenhagen University, Copenhagen, Denmark
[2] Architecture, Design and Media Technology, Aalborg University, Copenhagen, Denmark
tbj@create.aau.dk

Abstract. To be more successful in preventing malnutrition for older adults living at home, there is a need for better methods to characterize their food behavior, as well as there is a need for health-supporting technologies focusing more on individualized contextual preferences. This study reveals how photos can be used to characterize older adults' food-related behavior and preferences, and how photo elicitation can be used to design an eating environment in mixed reality for older solitary adults. This study is based on a sample of 22 older adults, who took in total 153 pictures of their meals, and a workshop using photo elicitation with 16 older adults in a community center. The findings revealed how photos can be used as a self-monitoring process to create meaningful and rich in-depth information on food-related behavior of older adults living at home. Photo elicitation can be used as a supplement to characterize older adults' food-related behavior and preferences in a mixed reality environment. Further, we outline both advantages and limitations of using photo elicitation in a context of human-computer interaction.

Keywords: Photo elicitation · Malnutrition · Older adults · Mixed reality

1 Introduction

In an aging world where malnutrition and lifestyle diseases (e.g., cardiovascular disease, type 2 diabetes) are general problems, the focus is often directed towards obesity, healthy diet and physical activity to promote healthy aging. There are also major challenges among older adults with malnourishment due inappropriate food behavior and preferences. These challenges are well covered and monitored in institutionalized settings [1, 2], but there are still missing methods to capture the food behavior and preferences among older adults living at home, as well as to include impacts for preventing malnourishment in this target group. It is well known how older adults who live at home are at relatively risk of malnutrition [3]. Is it also with strong evidence how malnourishment among older adults increases the risk of morbidity, mortality, delayed wound healing

© Springer Nature Switzerland AG 2022
V. G. Duffy et al. (Eds.): HCII 2022, LNCS 13521, pp. 510–523, 2022.
https://doi.org/10.1007/978-3-031-17902-0_36

[4, 5], and raises societal costs [6]. The food intake of older adults is influenced by a wide range of individual factors (e.g., preferences, appetite, acute illness, oral issues, mood, dysphagia, confusion, isolation) and structural issues (e.g., meal context, mealtimes, difficulty accessing food and beverage packaging, variety, sensory properties) [7]. Further, risk of malnutrition is closely connected to functional capacity, well-being, and social factors [1, 3, 7]. Thus, early identification and treatment of nutrition problems can improve outcomes and quality of life for older adults [4]. Various technologies in human-computer interaction perspectives are increasingly being used as facilitators to help reduce malnutrition issues among older adults [8–11]. Although both public health scientists and foodservice providers address malnutrition and unhealthy lifestyle practices, evidence suggests that the current strategies to change eating behaviors and address chronic diseases are not achieving the desired effects [12]. More focus could, therefore, be directed toward developing more tailored health interventions that are relevant and meaningful for older adults to promote and support healthy aging, adequate food intake, and independent living as long as possible.

There are two objectives in this study: 1. To characterize older adults' food-related behavior and preferences by a proposed approach using photos taken by the older adults. 2. To use photo elicitation to design an eating environment in mixed reality for older solitary adults.

2 Previous Research

There is common agreement about the importance to have appropriate tools for assessing food intake to investigate the effects of health initiatives targeting malnutrition among older adults [1, 7, 12]. Traditional dietary assessment methods (e.g., weighed food record, 24-h dietary recall, dietary record (DR) food frequency questionnaire [FFQ], food diaries) can provide detailed information on eating frequencies, energy intake, and nutritional value. However, they rely on self-reporting with a relatively high subjective information [13], and are, therefore, prone to recall bias [14]. Traditional dietary assessment methods can be combined with home visits and individual discussions to support the older adults in registering their daily food intakes [14, 15]. This approach is quite labor-intensive, and supplementary methods that more meaningful for the older adults and that provide knowledge on food-related behavior are needed. Visual methods such as photo analysis and photo elicitation have been suggested as innovative research tools to strengthen self-reported measures of dietary intake in underserved groups. Such tools work by revealing personal knowledge and perceptions [12], portion sizes, and behaviors (e.g., shopping, preparation, eating) within cultural and social contexts [12]. In previous research, visual methods have helped with the challenges of quantifying the dietary intakes of children, and to investigate children's food preferences [13, 16].

Photo elicitation uses photos often in conjunction with interviews to guide the interview, stimulate memory, or instigate conversations about a particular subject. Photo elicitation is used across disciplines and has successfully provided a broader understanding of complex meal experiences in a hospital context [17], as well as used broadly in human-computer interaction contexts when involving sensitive topics, vulnerable participants, or when developing early-stage design ideas [18–22]. Studies have used photo elicitation as a research tool, but there is missing more research on how photos can be used to measure the eating behaviors of older adults, and how photo elicitation can be used to design technology solutions for older solitary adults as within a virtual reality or mixed reality environment, providing the opportunity for older adults to eat together, while being apart [33].

3 Methods

3.1 Participants

Through community center leisure activities for older adults and an advertisement in a senior's magazine, a quota sampling technique was used to recruit older adults. Seven participants withdrew from the study and the final sample included 22 older adults (11 men and 11 women), both singles (11 participants), and members of couples. Participants with major cognitive impairments or major physical disabilities were excluded from the study. The 22 participants were aged = 65 years (74.2 M/ ± 7.9 SD) living at home. 18.2% of the participants were obese (BMI ≥ 30), 31.8% were overweight (BMI ≥ 25), 45.5% were at normal weight (BMI 18.50–24.99), and 4.5% were underweight (BMI < 25). Informed consent was obtained before the study was initiated. The participants were informed they had the right to withdraw from the study at any time and that all data would be anonymized with ID numbers. The participants' personal information was kept in encrypted databases separate from the other information used in the study. We applied special ethical considerations, following the ICC/ESOMAR International Code [23] and a specific checklist for research-related data processing. This study obtained ethical approval from Aalborg University (ID 2020-020-00433) based on an ethical review. The review has assessed the ethical aspects of the project's objectives, design, methodology, and potential impact. The protocol was assessed against the guidelines for good scientific practice, and the Danish code of conduct for research integrity.

3.2 Procedure

The participants (n = 22) filled out a qualitative food diary. They took pictures of their meals over six days to provide a deeper understanding of their food-related behavior in the context of their everyday lives. We handed-out digital cameras to the participants. Instructions on how to fill out the diary and use the digital camera were given before these items were handed out. Face-to-face, semi-structured, in-depth interviews were then conducted. After the interviews, the subjects filled out a questionnaire about their meal habits and health status. In the diary, each older adult described his or her daily meals and meal experiences and answered a "today's question" related to the social environment (e.g., number of close contacts), meal context, and attitudes toward meal consumption.

The semi-structured interview guide included 20 questions focused on four predetermined themes: meal experiences and food preferences, everyday life, skills and desires, and future solutions for optimal meal service. The interviews were conducted face-to-face, and permission to record was sought before all interviews. After the interviews, the older adults were asked to fill out a questionnaire consisting of ten questions, which focused on their meal habits, general well-being, and functioning - including health status and physical limitations.

The photo analysis (based on the pictures taken by the older adults) was a sub element in the decision to provide an augmented virtuality solution with the aim to prevent malnourishment among older adults. The purpose was to facilitate remote social eating for solitary older adults, as people tend to eat more when socializing [30].

3.3 Data Analysis

Of the 22 participants, nineteen older adults took between 0 and 39 pictures (mean = 12) each, amounting to 253 pictures, whereas three participants did not use the camera.

153 pictures captured the meals. Excluded photos were duplicates (n = 37), photos of the cooking processes and ingredients (n = 27), the kitchen (n = 22), and other contextual or sensitive content (n = 17), e.g. of family, friends, or nursing staff. The 153 meal pictures included in the content analysis were coded in NVivo 10 (QSR International Pty Ltd., 2012) for 11 predetermined meal characteristics within four different themes (Table 1).

Table 1. Coding scheme for meal photo analysis

Sensory properties	1: Color: one, two, or multicolored meal 2: Variety: Number of food items
Nutritional properties	3: Energy density: low, medium, high
	4: Among (kJ) for breakfast, lunch, dinner (low, medium, high)
	5: Protein E%: low, medium, high
	6: Plate model: Y-shape, O-shape, Ø-shape, or unit sizes
Gastronomic properties	7: Traditional Danish or Exotic
	8: Diet type: Animal based, plant based, or animal + plant based
	9: Temperature: Hot or cold meal
Physical environment	10: Décor: Enhanced or not enhanced

The analysis of the photos was made with experts in food science, based on standardized nutritional national (Danish) and international values. Meals were classified based on the time of consumption as breakfast (morning), lunch (noon), or dinner (evening). Consumptions in between those meals, such as fruits, salads, desserts (e.g., cakes, porridge), or bread with cheese, were classified as snacks. The amounts of individual food items (g) in each photo were estimated from tables of weights [24]. The estimated amounts of food (g) were entered into an Excel spreadsheet and converted to energy per meal (kJ), protein, carbohydrates, and fat content (kJ, %E). The energy density of the meals (kJ/g) using standard nutritional values from the Danish Food Composition Databank, Frida 2 (2017). Nordic Nutrition Recommendations (NNR) (Nordic Council of Ministers, 2014) were used to classify the nutritional properties (e.g., Protein E%, kJ) as medium (equivalent to NNR), low (equivalent to the 10th percentile of Danish survey samples), or high (equivalent to the 90th percentiles of Danish survey samples).

The meal photos were further classified into different plate models (Y-, O-, Ø-shaped) or unit sizes depending on the distribution and shape of the food items (Fig. 1).

Fig. 1. Photos classified into different plate models (Y-, Ø, O, and unit sized-shaped)

The Y-plate model, suggests that one-fifth of the main meal should include meat, fish, eggs, or cheese, two-fifths vegetables or fruits, and two-fifths potatoes, bread, rice, or pasta. A meal service dinner exemplifies the Y-plate (Fig. 1, upper left) with pork, mushroom sauce, potatoes, and cauliflower. Other plate models identified within the meal pictures were the Ø-shape, a 50–50% distribution of meat and vegetables/rice/pasta. The Ø-plate (Fig. 1, upper right) is exemplified by a dinner cooked at home with pork chops, raw vegetables, fruits, and raisins. The O-shape is a homogeneous fluent mass (e.g., stews, yogurt, porridge, oats with milk), and the O-plate (Fig. 1, lower left) is exemplified by a photo of a home-cooked breakfast with yogurt, an apple, and raisins. The unit-sized plate consists of individual unit sizes or separated elements, often smaller pieces (e.g., open sandwiches, eggs, fruits). In Fig. 1 (lower right), it is exemplified by a photo of a home-cooked lunch, including rye bread, cheese and celery, pickled herring with eggs, and liver pâté with pickled cucumber.

It was necessary to combine the photo analysis with information from the food diaries to make the best estimations of the meal compositions because of the poor quality of some pictures, including blurred ones or ones that captured only part of the meal (n = 10). There were also lapses in reporting (e.g., taking a picture of only a selected meal, such as dinner, instead of documenting all meals throughout the day) and a lack of stringent guidelines on how and when to take pictures (e.g., before serving, before starting to eat, or during the meal).

3.4 Second Stage: A Workshop

After these first stages (3.1–3.3), we completed a workshop among a group of 16 older adults who were present in a community center. Some of the findings is already reported elsewhere [26, 28]. However, in this paper, we would like to include more emphasis on the use of photo elicitation [18, 20] in the workshop, as used within a human-centered design approach [18, 20, 27]. The participants in the workshop were divided into two focus groups and discussed contextual matters during a meal, including the arrangement of meals with family, friends, or strangers. The framework for this workshop was that a mixed reality set-up could be integrated within social eating. A prototype (within augmented virtuality) was developed to stimulate a discussion about suitable virtual eating environments [26, 28]. A formative evaluation was followed as a central location test, and its purpose was not just to test the usability and performance of an HMD-based eating interface, but also to use photo elicitation as a catalyst for discussions about engaging meal-based virtual environments. The photos (selected by the researchers) included a park, a kitchen, a fireplace lounge, a swimming pool (with a bar), a terrace, an undersea restaurant, an Italian restaurant, and floating mountains (Fig. 2).

Fig. 2. How ID1 and ID4 pair foods within 8 different scenarios, displayed as photos.

The older adults were asked to pair a list of 15 common (traditional) Danish foods with the preferable eating environment (Fig. 2). For example, as in Fig. 2 (left) with placed crispy pork with parsley sauce (in Danish 'stegt flæsk med persillesovs') as preferred to eat in a kitchen environment. The participants could also include an alternative environment, besides the 8 selected scenarios from the researchers. No restrictions where set regarding how many foods could be placed on a single environment, and foods that the participants disliked were placed in a separate pile.

4 Findings

4.1 Analysis of the Meal Photos Taken by the Participants

The content analysis revealed that the photographs were taken from one of three positions: a middle photographic perspective (73%) showing the meal, cutlery, and drinks, a close-up perspective (15%) focusing on the meal, or a distant perspective (12%, n = 18) capturing the dining table. Most of the pictures were produced during dinner (42%, n = 64) and lunch (32%, n = 49), whereas breakfast (19%, n = 29) and snacks (7%, n = 11) accounted for the least documentation. Meals were generally traditional Danish dishes (88%) containing both animal and plant origins (93%) (Table 2). Univariate analysis based on the meal composition revealed that breakfast, lunch, and dinner were of similar energy content, whereas snacks were significantly smaller energy-wise (kJ) than these meals (p < 0.0001) (Table 2). Overall, the lunch and dinner meals were traditional and typically animal-and-plant-based (Table 2); therefore, they were higher in protein and complexity than the breakfast meals. The protein levels were significantly lower in breakfasts and snacks than lunch and dinner meals (p < 0.001).

Table 2. Meal characteristics coded from the content analysis (n = 153 meal pictures)

	Plate model* % (n) p < 0.0001	Colour % (n) p < 0.001	Cuisine % (n) p = 0.21	Diet type % (n) p = 0.01		Temperature % (n) p < 0.0001	Décor** % (n) p = 0.16
Break-fast	Y-shape 0 (0) O-shape 3 (24) Ø-shape 0 (0) Unit sizes 17 (5)	One 38 (11) Two 38 (10) Multi 28 (8)	Trad. 93 (27) Exotic 7 (2)	Animal (0) Plant 3 (1) Anim.+plant 97 (28)		Hot 3 (1) Cold 97 (28)	Enhanced 28 (8) Not enhanced 66 (19) Not allocated 7 (2)
Lunch	Y-shape 10 (5) O-shape 6 (3) Ø-shape 4 (2) Unit sizes 0 (39)	One 10 (5) Two 20 (10) Multi 69 (34)	Trad. 92 (45) Exotic 8 (4)	Animal 4 (2) Plant 4 (2) Anim.+plant 92 (45)		Hot 25 (12) Cold 75 (37)	Enhanced 18 (9) Not enhanced 74 (36) Not allocated 8 (4)
Dinner	Y-shape 7 (24) O-shape 4 (9) Ø-shape 41 (26) Unit sizes 8 (5)	One 14 (9) Two 41 (26) Multi 45 (29)	Trad. 84 (54) Exotic 16 (10)	Animal 2 (1) Plant 2 (1) Anim.+plant 97 (62)		Hot 92 (59) Cold 8 (5)	Enhanced 27 (17) Not enhanced 70 (45) Not allocated 3 (2)
Snack	Y-shape 0 (0) O-shape 45 (5) Ø-shape 0 (0) Unit sizes 55 (6)	One 55 (6) Two 6 (4) Multi 9 (1)	Trad. 73 (8) Exotic 27 (3)	Animal 9 (1) Plant 27 (3) Anim.+plant 64 (7)		Hot 9 (1) Cold 91 (10)	Enhanced 46 (5) Not enhanced 54 (6)
Total	Y-shape 19 (29) O-shape 27 (41) Ø-shape 18 (28) Unit sizes 36 (55)	One 20 (31) Two 33 (50) Multi 47 (72)	Trad. 88 (134) Exotic 12 (19)	Animal 3 (4) Plant 5 (7) Anim.+plant 93 (142)			Enhanced 26 (39) Not enhanced 69 (106) Not allocated 5 (8)

Breakfast. Univariate analysis of meal composition revealed that a majority of the breakfast meals were classified as being a medium portion size; however, only 10% of the breakfasts followed the recommended energy (kJ) content of NNR (Nordic Council of Ministers) (Table 3) [25]. The breakfasts and snacks were characterized as having low to medium protein (48% of the breakfast meals followed the NNR [25] recommendations for protein level) and high carbohydrate content (E%), and they were generally served cold (Table 2). These meals had medium to high energy density (data not shown), which might be explained by using butter and/or cheese for the breakfast meals and sugar for the desserts. Breakfast meals tended to be more plant-based (e.g., fruits, oats) than lunches and dinners; contain white bread and mini portions of milk; have an O-plate shape (Fig. 1), and have one color (Table 2). Interestingly, the weaker older adults seemed to report larger intake (total energy) from breakfast than the healthy older adult group did, which reported eating a traditional Danish breakfast of medium portion size.

Table 3. Nutritional values of the pictured meals

	Energy per meal		Protein	
	% (n)	≥NNR [25] % (n)	% (n)	≥NNR % (n)
Breakfast av	100 (29)	10.3 (3)	100 (29)	48.3 (14)
Low	3.4 (1)	≤700 kJ[d]	20 (6)	
Medium	93.1 (27)	~2000 kJ[a]	60 (18)	
High	3.4 (1)	≥2700 kJ[d]	20 (5)	
Lunch av	100 (49)	12.2 (6)	100 (49)	75.5 (37)
Low	16.3 (8)	≤900 kJ[d]	14.3 (7)	
Medium	77.6 (38)	2500–3000 kJ[a]	28.6 (14)	
High	6.1 (3)	≥3200[d]	57.1(28)	
Dinner av	100 (64)	7.8 (4)	100 (64)	81.3 (52)
Low	65.6 (42)	≤1800 kJ[d]	10.9 (7)	
Medium	31.3(20)	2500–3500 kJ[a]	21.9 (14)	
High	3.1 (2)	≥4900 kJ[d]	67.2 (43)	

[a] NNR [25], % indicate meals that follow recommendations. Protein: Low ≤13 E% [34], Medium = 15–20 E% [25], High ≥19 E% [34], [b]Low (10 percentiles), high (90 percentiles) [34], [d]Low (10 percentiles), high (90 percentiles) [35]

Lunch. Univariate analysis of meal composition revealed that most of the lunch meals were classified as being a medium portion size, 12% of the meals followed the recommended energy content (kJ) whereas approximately 76% of the lunches followed the NNR recommendations [25] for protein level (≥15 E%) (Table 3). Interestingly, lunches were significantly more energy dense than dinner meals (p < 0.0001), and 69% of the lunch meals contained fish (n = 34), whereas 22% contained pork (n = 11). The lunches were typically cold and multicolored (Table 2) and had unit sizes consisting of bread (e.g., rye bread or crisp bread) with pickled herring, canned tuna, ham, eggs, or cheese with different toppings (e.g., olives, basil, fennel, canned beetroot or corn, red onion, or fine vegetables). Furthermore, the lunch meals were typically reported by the healthy older adult group, as opposed to the weaker group of adults, who were more likely to report their dinner, breakfast, and snacks.

Dinner. Univariate analysis of meal composition revealed that most of the dinner meals were classified as being a low portion size, as only 8% of the dinner meals followed the energy (kJ) content recommended by NNR (Table 3) [25]. Approximately 81% of dinners followed the recommendations for protein level (≥15 E%). The dinner meals were generally traditional, hot, and two-colored and followed either the recommended Y model (38%) or the 50–50% distribution (41%) of meat and vegetables. A typical dinner meal included boiled potatoes, a sauce (e.g., brown or hollandaise), coarse vegetables (e.g., legumes or carrots), and some meat (e.g., meatballs or pork) or fish (e.g., cod)

(Fig. 3). Overall, 34% (n = 22) of the dinner meals were pork-based, 27% (n = 17) were fish-based, and 12.5% (n = 8) contained chicken.

4.2 Why a Lower Energy Intake?

The interviews revealed several factors that could explain why the home-living older adults generally had an energy intake lower than recommended by the NNR [25]. A common factor was the social factor, as already strongly supported in the literature [3–5, 29], where social isolation increases the risk of malnourishment. Five older adults reported reduced food intake or reduced energy needs with age or a lack of appetite. Therefore, they preferred to eat smaller portions, divide the meals into two portions, or skip the meat (e.g., from meal service), eat the dinner meal for lunch, or eat a starter or dessert for dinner. Meals were also substituted with crackers, milk, chocolate milk, or crisp bread when the older adults were not feeling hungry. Meal skipping was more commonly mentioned among older adults with a weak health condition. They occasionally skipped breakfast and lunch because of a lack of desire or competing desires (e.g., tiredness vs. hunger, eating to avoid getting up at night). Several older adults acknowledged the importance of food for health reasons and expressed awareness about how much "one needs" or avoiding malnutrition. Some considered breakfast a standard routine or ritual, indicating the importance of having breakfast.

Furthermore, some tried to avoid skipping meals and foods that would upset their stomach (e.g., vegetables and fruits, milk/lactose, pasta, or white bread) or influence their cholesterol level (e.g., chocolate). Several of the healthy older adults reported having changed their diet in a healthier direction to include more vegetables (e.g., fennel), less fat (e.g., lean meat, no mayo or margarine), meat, and more fish. Four older adults mentioned dysfunction (e.g., lack of saliva, false teeth, stomach or gut operations, diabetes) as limiting their ability to eat or maintain weight. Some singles reported difficulties adjusting their shopping and meal sizes for one person and had concerns about food waste, which seemed to affect their motivation to cook. Several older adults experienced a decrease in flavor, taste, or smell perception, whereas others reported being very sensitive to smells. Some older adults mentioned that taste and smell perception, food variety, or the serving and the colors of the foods were important for the meal experience and wished to have more flavors.

4.3 Photo Elicitation Used for an Identification for MR Environment

We used photo elicitation to identify the right environment in the augmented reality. The findings from the photo elicitation provided clear preferences for specific environments [28]. The scenarios are here listed as included with the number of the total number of picked food items within each (photo) scenario: Floating mountains (1), Undersea restaurant (3), swimming pool (5), park (8), not placed (9), restaurant (16), fireplace lounge (18), kitchen (19), terrace (25).

The information gathered through this photo elicitation approach provided valuable insights to understand how older adults perceived complex variables within different meal context in an augmented reality set-up. It has already been addressed in the literature how photo elicitation can facilitate verbalization of thoughts that enables researchers to better comprehend perceptions, barriers, and facilitators of those complex behaviors [31]. The photos as included within the interviews provided not only interesting aspects in where the older adults would like to eat, but also worked as an entry/ice-breaker to talk about something as abstract as mixed reality within this target group. The photos did evoke deeper elements of consciousness than just said words would do. By that, we found the photos not only provided more information, but also different information. That said, it also important to note that the photos can also limit further understandings, as the photos can limit interpretations, as the photo itself gives certain perceptions and connotations, which might be a limitation for other kinds of responses outside the idea that the photos create. Our experience with the used photo elicitation was that it was important to provide the participants with the possibilities of alternative scenarios. After the photo elicitation, the participants tried various scenarios (i.e., the park, and the kitchen) in a prototype of the mixed reality, as already reported elsewhere [26, 28]. The system was based on Oculus Rift CV1 HMD with an Intel Realsense SR300 depth sensor mounted on top of the HMD.

Fig. 3. A participant testing mixed reality, as with a kitchen scenario used in the photo elicitation.

5   Conclusion

The novelty of the current study is how photos can be used as a self-monitoring process to create meaningful and rich in-depth information on food-related behavior of older adults living at home. The photo elicitation can be used as a supplement to characterize older adults' food-related behavior and preferences. By the photo analysis we identified typical meals, food practices, and preferences that can be used for a better understanding of the challenges of maintaining adequate food intake than traditional interviews and dietary assessment methods.

The photo analysis, based on the meal-photos from the elderly revealed how they in general ate traditional Danish meals that followed the national recommendation for protein content (≥ 15 E%). The meals were high in energy density, especially lunches, and low in energy intake (kJ), especially dinners, supporting the fact that the small portions could explain the meals' low energy content. Further, the analysis revealed breakfast is an important meal for older adults, and we can conclude that more variety in lunch and dinner meals might help increase food intake, especially for the weaker older adults.

The conclusion from the workshop was that photo elicitation can be used as early stage design ideas for selecting environments for eating in mixed reality.

5.1 Advantages of Photo Elicitation

This participatory approach strengthened the validity of the study and opened new possibilities for gaining insights into the causes of malnutrition among the elderly. Further, we can outline specific advantages using the participatory approach:

First, the photo elicitation served as an icebreaker and empowered the participants to communicate their lived (meal) experiences, also in the context of talking about something as abstract as mixed reality. The photo elicitations were especially an advantage with older adults as participants. Through dialogue, the participants and researchers could build and explore their understandings to improve the interview's integrity [12] and provide valuable knowledge of the eating behavior and its determinants [12]. Our insights may not be obtained with more traditional verbal interviews, as the method may create awareness of eating behavior and the motivation to it in a more beneficial way (e.g., by eating out of pleasure instead of duty) or by obtaining adequate energy intake by eating according to the Y-plate model.

Secondly, photographic documentation can improve participants' memory and help them overcome recall bias and the difficulties of estimating portion sizes, similar to what Sabinsky et al., [13] has reported as an advantage.

Thirdly, photo elicitation allowed for the collection of more complete data (both quantitatively and qualitatively), compared to more traditional research methods. The older adults documented what they did by taking pictures, rather than only verbalizing or writing what they did. Further, the approach may still be more meaningful, less obtrusive, and less burdensome for older adults than traditional dietary-assessment methods (e.g., 24-h recall, weighed food records, or FFQ). However, this must be investigated further among older adults. Like traditional dietary assessment methods, photo elicitation can be useful for collecting data from a large population.

5.2 Limitations of Photo Elicitation

First, dealing with photo elicitation, based on participants taken the photos, it is important to have very precise instructions of what they should capture, and when they should capture it. In our study we should have been clearer in the instructions. Because of not very clear instructions, most of the older adults did not report all their meals. Approximately 24% of the breakfasts, 43% of the lunches, and 56% of the dinner meals were documented (if meal skipping was not occurring). Thus, a complete dietary assessment of food intake was not obtained.

Second, we agree with what Gomez [32] already have described, with a need to be more clear in the taxonomies, and differentiate more clear within different kinds of visual methods, e.g., photo elicitation, photo stories, and photovoices, to better understand their contributions, limitations and complementarities, as well as their relation to applied visual methods. Visual research methods are also used in HCI, but we also suggest to have clearer taxonomies and differentiations of visual methods when used in human-computer interaction research. There is a need to better understand in which contexts (as within both different users, and technologies) visual methods can be applied (if they should be applied), and how they in the best way can be part of the procedure, and how the visual methods can be analyzed. Especially for the data analysis from the visual methods in a HCI perspective, there is missing much further research. There remains more focus on how to make interpretations of used visual methods, including an improved validity and reliability.

Third, photo elicitation can be used in many ways, but also demands some qualitative skills and competences to apply the method in a successful way. It is important to also include certain procedures as within the qualitative methods, including the awareness that photo elicitation can provide specific images and connotations, and by that limit the (design) ideas or communication. We found it very useful to encourage and provide information that the participants also could provide alternative scenarios/pictures, than already provided.

References

1. Maltais, M., et al.: The effect of exercise and social activity interventions on nutritional status in older adults with dementia living in nursing homes: a randomised controlled trial. J. Nutr. Health Aging **22**(7), 824–828 (2018). https://doi.org/10.1007/s12603-018-1025-5
2. Ge, L., Yap, C.W., Heng, B.H.: Association of nutritional status with physical function and disability in community-dwelling older adults: a longitudinal data analysis. J. Nutr. Gerontol. Geriatr. **39**(2), 131–142 (2020)
3. Boulos, C., Salameh, P., Barberger-Gateau, P.: Social isolation and risk for malnutrition among older people. Geriatr. Gerontol. Int. **17**(2), 286–294 (2016)
4. Agarwal, E., Miller, M., Yaxley, A., Isenring, E.: Malnutrition in the elderly: a narrative review. Maturitas **76**(4), 296–302 (2013)
5. Shatenstein, B., Gauvin, L., Keller, H., Richard, L., Gaudreau, P., Giroux, F., et al.: Baseline determinants of global diet quality in older men and women from the NuAge cohort. J. Nutr. Health Aging **17**(5), 419–425 (2013)
6. Mitchell, H., Porter, J.: The cost-effectiveness of identifying and treating malnutrition in hospitals: a systematic review. J. Hum. Nutr. Diet. **29**(2), 156–164 (2016)
7. Mudge, A.M., Ross, L.J., Young, A.M., Isenring, E.A., Banks, M.D.: Helping understand nutritional gaps in the elderly (HUNGER): a prospective study of patient factors associated with inadequate nutritional intake in older medical inpatients. Clin. Nutr. **30**(3), 320–325 (2011)
8. Oberschmidt, K., Grünloh, C., Tunç, S., van Velsen, L., Nijboer, F.: You can't always get what you want: Streamlining stakeholder interests when designing technology-supported services for Active and Assisted Living. In: 32nd Australian Conference on Human-Computer Interaction, OzCHI 2020, Sydney, NSW, Australia, 2–4 December 2020, pp. 649–660 (2020)

9. Happe, L., Sgraja, M., Hein, A., Diekmann, R.: Iterative development and applicability of a tablet-based e-coach for older adults in rehabilitation units to improve nutrition and physical activity: usability study. JMIR Hum. Factors 9(1), e31823 (2022)
10. Leitão, R., Silva, P.A.: Target and spacing sizes for smartphone user interfaces for older adults: design patterns based on an evaluation with users. In: 19th Conference on Pattern Languages of Programs, Tucson, Arizona, 19–21 October 2012 (2012)
11. Kramer, L.L., Mulder, B.C., van Velsen, L., de Vet, E.: Use and effect of web-based embodied conversational agents for improving eating behavior and decreasing loneliness among community-dwelling older adults: protocol for a randomized controlled trial. JMIR Res. Prot. 10(1), e22186 (2021)
12. Sebastião, E., Gálvez, P.A.E., Bobitt, J., Adamson, B.C., Schwingel, A.: Visual and participatory research techniques: photo-elicitation and its potential to better inform public health about physical activity and eating behavior in underserved populations. J. Public Health 24(1), 3–7 (2016)
13. Sabinsky, M.S., Toft, U., Andersen, K.K., Tetens, I.: Validation of a digital photographic method for assessment of dietary quality of school lunch sandwiches brought from home. Food Nutr. Res. 57(1), 20243 (2013)
14. Shim, J.S., Oh, K., Kim, H.C.: Dietary assessment methods in epidemiologic studies. Epidemiol. Health 36, e2014009 (2014)
15. Engelheart, S., Lammes, E., Akner, G.: Elderly peoples' meals. a comparative study between elderly living in a nursing home and frail, self-managing elderly. J. Nutr. Health Aging 10(2), 96–102 (2006)
16. Alm, S., Olsen, S.O.: Using photo interviews to explore children's food preferences. Int. J. Consum. Stud. 41(3), 274–282 (2017)
17. Justesen, L., Mikkelsen, B.E., Gyimóthy, S.: Understanding hospital meal experiences by means of participant-driven-photo-elicitation. Appetite 75, 30–39 (2014)
18. Van House, N.A.: Interview viz: visualization-assisted photo elicitation. In: CHI 2006 Extended Abstracts on Human Factors in Computing Systems, Montreal, Canada, pp. 1463–1468. ACM (2006)
19. Gautam, A., Shrestha, C., Tatar, D., Harrison, S.: Social photo-elicitation: the use of communal production of meaning to hear a vulnerable population. In: Proceedings of the ACM on Human-Computer Interaction, 2(CSCW), New York, United States, pp. 1–20. ACM (2018)
20. Hall, L., Jones, S., Hall, M., Richardson, J., Hodgson, J.: Inspiring design: the use of photo elicitation and lomography in gaining the child's perspective. In: Proceedings of HCI 2007 the 21st British HCI Group Annual Conference University of Lancaster, UK 21, pp. 1–10 (2007)
21. Carter, S., Mankoff, J.: When participants do the capturing: the role of media in diary studies. In: Proceedings of the SIGCHI Conference on Human Factors in Computing Systems, Portland Oregon USA, pp. 899–908. ACM (2005)
22. Li, Y., Vishwamitra, N., Hu, H., Caine, K.: Towards a taxonomy of content sensitivity and sharing preferences for photos. In: Proceedings of the 2020 CHI Conference on Human Factors in Computing Systems, Honolulu HI USA, pp. 1–14. ACM (2020)
23. ICC/ESOMAR International Code (2016)
24. World Cancer Research Fund: Food, nutrition, physical activity, and the prevention of cancer: a global perspective American Institute for Cancer Research (2007)
25. Nordic Council of Ministers: Nordic nutrition recommendations 2012 integrating nutrition and physical activity Nordic Council of Ministers (2014)
26. Korsgaard, D., Bjørner, T., Sørensen, P.K., Bruun-Pedersen, J.R.: Older adults eating together in a virtual living room: opportunities and limitations of eating in augmented virtuality. In: Proceedings of the 31st European Conference on Cognitive Ergonomics, Belfast, United Kingdom, pp. 168–176. ACM (2019)

27. Steen, M.: Tensions in human-centered design. CoDesign 7(1), 45–60 (2011)
28. Korsgaard, D., Bjørner, T., Nilsson, N.C.: Where would you like to eat? A formative evaluation of mixed-reality solitary meals in virtual environments for older adults with mobility impairments who live alone. Food Res. Int. 117, 30–39 (2019)
29. Bjørner, T., Korsgaard, D., Reinbach, H.C., Perez-Cueto, F.J.: A contextual identification of home-living older adults' positive mealtime practices: a honeycomb model as a framework for joyful aging and the importance of social factors. Appetite 129, 125–134 (2018)
30. de Castro, J.M.: Age-related changes in the social, psychological, and temporal influences on food intake in free-living, healthy, adult humans. J. Gerontol. A Biol. Sci. Med. Sci. 57(6), M368–M377 (2002)
31. Lachal, J., et al.: Qualitative research using photo-elicitation to explore the role of food in family relationships among obese adolescents. Appetite 58, 1099–1105 (2012)
32. Gomez, R.: Photostories. Qual. Quant. Methods Libr. 9(1), 47–63 (2020)
33. Korsgaard, D., Bjørner, T., Bruun-Pedersen, J.R., Sørensen, P.K., Perez-Cueto, F.J.: Eating together while being apart: a pilot study on the effects of mixed-reality conversations and virtual environments on older eaters' solitary meal experience and food intake. In: 2020 IEEE Conference on Virtual Reality and 3D User Interfaces Abstracts and Workshops (VRW), pp. 365–370. IEEE (2020)
34. Pedersen, A.N., et al.: Danskernes kostvaner [Dietary habits in Denmark] 2011–2013 (2015)
35. Christensen, L.M., Kørup, K., Trolle, E., Fagt, S.: Måltidsvaner for Voksne Med Kort Uddannelse 2005–2008 (2013)

Older Adults' Activity on Creative Problem Solving with Modular Robotics

Margarida Romero[✉]

Université Côte d'Azur, Nice, France
Margarida.romero@univ-cotedazur.fr

Abstract. Older adults are challenged in their adoption of new ways of interacting with different type of devices including not only screen-based artifacts but also augmented reality and robotic technologies. The diversity of the devises in relation to the adoption process engage older adults in a creative exploration process when they face new technologies. We analyze the creative problem-solving (CPS) process in the context of modular robotics technologies by focusing on divergent thinking. We first introduce divergent thinking within the scope of creative problem-solving process and then we analyze the results in relation to the three main components of divergent thinking in CPS: fluidity, flexibility, and originality. We evaluate fluidity, flexibility, and originality by engaging 342 participants according to their age. Results shows older adults and children show higher fluidity than adolescents, young adults and adults but also take more time to complete the CPS task.

Keywords: Human-robot interactions · Creative problem solving · Divergent thinking · Modular robotics · Fluidity · Flexibility · Originality

1 Introduction

Within the different stages of lifespan, the way we perceive and interact with our environment evolves not only based on the experience but also on the evolution of the biological capacities of our body which affect all the cognitive functions: from perception to decision making, including attention, memory, and language comprehension. Elders cognitive functions decline, especially among those with lower literacy levels [1]. The continuous emergence of new technologies requires older adults to adapt to a continuous evolution of Human Computer Interaction (HCI) in screen-based technologies [2, 3] but also to Human Robot Interaction (HRI) which shows a high diversity of affordances and technological features. Some of the robots developed for older adults care are human shaped and integrate vocal based interactions like the Nao robotic robot in which the user can engage in turn-taking like in human-to-human interactions [4]. However, other robots are not human-shaped and require a higher level of adoption to interact with them. In this study we focus on the use of the Cubelets modular robots [5] to study divergent thinking (DT) as the idea generation process. We focus on three main components of divergent thinking (DT) in Creative Problem-Solving (CPS): fluidity, flexibility, and originality.

© Springer Nature Switzerland AG 2022
V. G. Duffy et al. (Eds.): HCII 2022, LNCS 13521, pp. 524–533, 2022.
https://doi.org/10.1007/978-3-031-17902-0_37

We observe these three components of DT among elderly engaged in the interactions with this robotic technology when solving an ill-defined problem task named CreaCube [6]. Divergent thinking (TD) refers to the "efficient generation of a variety of ideas to meet a given question or problem" [7]. In this context, CPS is an important competency to explore new robotic technologies, understand their technological affordances and the system features to use them for the intended goal of the user (Fig. 1).

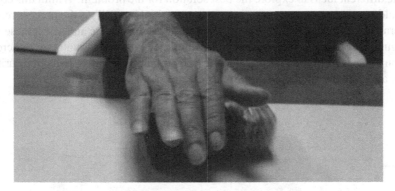

Fig. 1. Older participant exploring the Cubelets during the CreaCube task

The CreaCube tasks is a playful ill-defined problem-solving task [6, 8] which permits to evaluate the three main components of divergent thinking according based on the adaptation of the DT operationalization of Guilford's Alternate Use Test (AUT) [9]. In the CreaCube task fluidity is operationalized as the total number of configurations the participant builds during the activity; fluidity as the total number of different configurations and originality as the configurations that appear in fewer than 5% of the different configurations build by all the subjects within the same age group. Through the CreaCube task we have the possibility to observe the development of new ideas, the evaluation, their inhibition, and their transformation across the CPS process through the

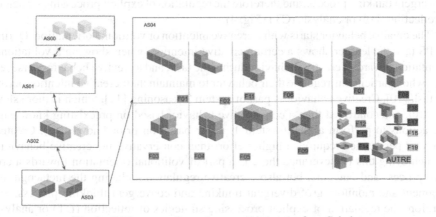

Fig. 2. Different configurations combining the four Cubelets

robotic cubes the subjects manipulate in this ill-defined CPS task mediated by tangible interactive technologies (Fig. 2).

2 Creative Problem Solving in Human Robot Interaction

When engaged in CPS activities such CreaCube, the participants should be able to generate different ideas to explore the best solution for the problem. Within this context, we should consider two main processes. Divergent thinking (DT) is the process required to generate ideas. Convergent thinking (CT) is process to evaluate and select these ideas. The regulation of DT and CT is essential within the CPS task to maintain the creative intention at the start of the task and be able to maintain the creative behavior during all the task allowing the subject to develop its creative perseverance (Fig. 3).

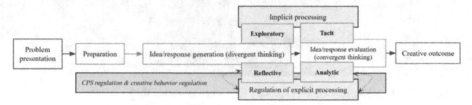

Fig. 3. CPS regulation

The regulation of DT and CT could be considered as a type of meta control or regulatory processes of creative behavior. Creative behavior starts with a creative intention or volitional orientation. During a CPS task the subject shows a certain creative intention, when showing a volitational orientation towards a creative behavior during the task, and a creative behavior perseverance when participants regulate their behavior to maintain their creative intention across the task. For achieving this perseverance there is a part of volitional orientation towards a creative process and outcome, but also a creative regulation including the metacognitive judgment and monitoring of divergent thinking and convergent thinking process, and therefore the regulation of explicit processing strategies of reflection (DT) or analysis (CT) (Fig. 4).

The creative behavior starts with a creative intention or volitional orientation. During a CPS task the learner shows a certain creative intention, when showing a volitational orientation towards a creative behavior during the task, and a creative behavior perseverance when participants regulate their behavior to maintain their creative intention across the task [10]. Creative behavior is part of system 2 reasoning [11], which is more slow, effortful, and controlled than a conservative behavior based on preexisting knowledge and actions to perform a task (system 1, faster based on prior knowledge). Creative behavior persistence requires a higher effort than conservative noncreative behaviors. For achieving this perseverance there is a part of volitional orientation towards a creative process and outcome, but also a creative regulation including the metacognitive judgment and monitoring of divergent thinking and convergent thinking process, and therefore the regulation of explicit processing strategies of reflection (DT) or analysis (CT).

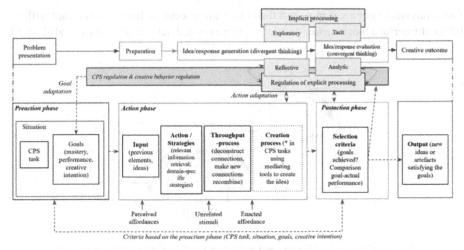

Fig. 4. CPS regulation considering from problem presentation to the creative outcome

We consider the dual-process model of creativity of Augello and colleagues [12] "which takes into account the different interaction mechanisms involving both S1 and S2 systems as well as both the generative and evaluative processes" (p. 7). As shown in Fig. 10, this model considers that some processes are implicit when generating ideas (exploratory process) but also when selecting them (tacit process), but other processes can be regulated explicitly at the divergent thinking stage (reflective process) and the convergent thinking one (analytic process).

3   Creative Problem Solving in Human Robot Interaction

Robots are defined as "an autonomous system existing in the physical world that can detect the environment and take action to achieve the goal" [13]. Munich, Ostrowski and Pirjanian [14] define a robot "as a system that has a number of sensors, processing units (e.g., computer), and actuators". Because of the diversity of robotic technologies, older adults can have difficulties in recognizing robotic features and the way they can interact with them. There is a gap between the metal representation of a robot, often associated to a humanoid robot, and the robotic technologies that could be small and very diversity shaped. Users with no knowledge in robotic technologies does not perceive humanoid robots as robots. When facing robotic solutions such the Cubelets [5], they consider them as electronic toys without considering them as robots [8]. In this context, older adults engaged in ill-defined problem-solving tasks require to develop a creative problem solving (CPS) process. As described previously, CPS engages not only DT and CT, but also a regulatory process across the CPS process to maintain the objective of the task through the exploratory interactions to mind the "execution gap" between the robotic system and the task goal.

The "execution gap" can be represented based on Norman [15] cycles of iteration between the evaluation bridge in which the user analyze the interface display, interprets and evaluated the interface of the means which can be used (screen based interaction if any, physical systems if any) and then enter the execution bridge to interact with the different interface mechanism, develops intentions and actions towards a goal (Fig. 5).

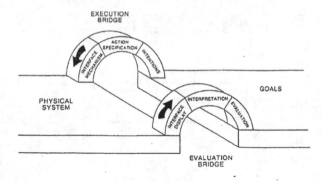

Fig. 5. Cycles of evaluation and execution to close the execution gap [15]

These different cycles of evaluation and execution allows the subject to analyze the different means, which in the case of the CreaCube task are four modular robotic cubes which should be assembled in a configuration permitting to reach to goal to build an "autonomous vehicle that moves from a starting red point to a finish black point". The figure below represents the cycles of interactions through the evaluation and execution bridge described by Norman [15] (Fig. 6).

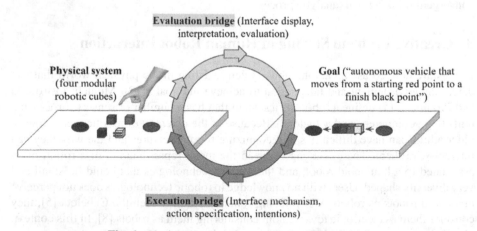

Fig. 6. Closing the execution gap in the CreaCube task

4   CPS as a Disambiguation Process to Cross the 'Execution Gap'

Generating ideas (DT) is not enough in CPS tasks requiring to develop a solution (idea or artifact) to solve a problem. In CPS the subject engages in a problem without knowing in advance the means and actions to be developed to succeed the CPS task. In this context, there is an 'execution gap' between the means made available in the task and the representation of the goal of the task that the subject could potentially achieve [15]. In the context of solving ill-defined problem solving, it may happen that the subject cannot move forward with a top-down approach (goal-driven) and therefore not simply organize himself mentally to achieve the CPS goal. He must then engage in an exploratory behavior aimed at enabling an emerging behavior (which will then be partially developed in a stimulus-driven way), which could provide new information to better understand the way of articulating the means available (in the case of CreaCube task, the robotic cubes) to achieve the goal (build an autonomous vehicle) (Fig. 7).

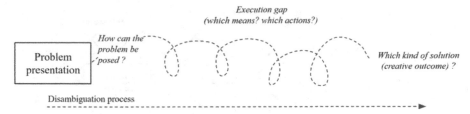

Fig. 7. Execution gap in CPS

CPS tasks have different degrees of ill-definition. Moreover, the ill-definition could concern any of the phases at different degrees. For example, some CPS tasks could be ill-defined in the way the task is defined, requiring a higher effort to finish the problem posing; other CPS tasks could be ill-defined in relation to the creative outcome, or even in the idea generation process (Fig. 8).

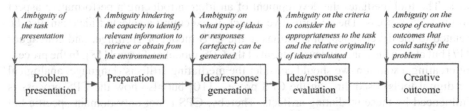

Fig. 8. Degree of ill-definition in different phases of the CPS task

The CPS task engages the subject into a goal. Nevertheless, the CPS task could require a process of disambiguation at the different phases of the task:

- posing the problem to disambiguate the problem task presentation;
- identifying relevant information to disambiguate the information and means required to develop the task;
- disambiguate the type of idea, artifact or other response that could be generated in the specific situation of the task (e.g., materiality of the artifacts);
- disambiguate the criteria to consider the appropriateness to the task and the relative originality of ideas evaluated;

• disambiguate the scope of creative outcomes that could satisfy the problem.

Through the process of CPS, different decisions will engage the subject in advancing from the initial problem space towards a solution space without knowing in advance the path to follow. There are many ways to solve the process (generative path) but also different types of solutions that could satisfy the CPS task requirements (generative outcome). The representation of CPS by Hay and colleagues [16] shows the multiplicity of CPS paths between the problem state and the goal state in the process of 'solution search' (Fig. 9).

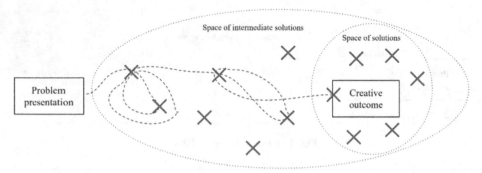

Fig. 9. Solution search process between the problem state and a potential goal state, adapted from Hay [16]

On the CPS process to navigate from the space of intermediate solutions towards one solution within the space of solutions we should consider the mediating artifacts of the task. The tool mediates the development of an idea introducing a performative aspect in the CPS process. The performative aspect of executing a selected idea can also be related to the development of solutions in the CPS model of Treffinger and colleagues [17] but also in the concept development of the CPS model of Tassoul [18]. In the process of creating a solution, we should consider the mediating artifacts (language, analogical or digital tools) used through the CPS process [10] but also how the CPS process is influenced by these mediating artifacts. Thereby, CPS is not only domain-specific but also specific in the way it is mediated by the different tools available for the CPS process [19].

5   Methodology

In this study we analyze CPS based on the analysis of DT components of fluidity, flexibility, and originality through the CreaCube task [6]. We engage 342 participants and analyze the results according to the following age categories: children (7 to 12 years old), adolescents (13 to 18 years old), young adults (19 to 29 years old), adults (30 to 59 years old), older adults (60 to 79 years old).

6 Results

We introduce the results according to the DT scores for each of the three components (fluidity, flexibility, and originality) but also the duration of the task. Despite the duration is not a component on DT the temporal performance is often considered in the analysis of creativity as a factor which can influence the DT process in different ways depending on the task.

In Table 1 we present the results of the three components of DT and the duration of the task (in seconds) according to age during the first activity.

Table 1. DT components according to the age group

Age	N	Fluidity	Flexibility	Originality	Time (seconds)
Children	48	m: 8.3 sd: 8.1	m: 3.6 sd: 2.3	m: 1.1 sd: 1.3	m: 291.1 sd: 220.0
Adolescents	5	m: 3.2 sd: 1.6	m: 2.0 sd: 0.7	m: 0 sd: 0	m: 112.6 sd: 64.7
Young adults	39	m: 4.0 sd: 5.0	m: 1.9 sd: 1.1	m: 0.3 sd: 0.5	m: 139.0 sd: 88.4
Adults	29	m: 3.0 sd: 3.3	m: 2.0 sd: 1.6	m: 0.5 sd: 0.9	m: 119.0 sd: 72.4
Older adults	5	m: 4.4 sd: 3.5	m: 2.2 sd: 0.8	m: 0 sd: 0	m: 220.8 sd: 154.1

Older adults and children show higher fluidity than adolescents, young adults and adults but also take more time. However, children show the highest scores on all three creative components (fluidity, flexibility, and originality) compared to other age categories, but they also engage more time than other age categories.

7 Discussion

As part of this study, we were able to analyze the different components of DT as part of a CPS task. In the study of DT components with the CreaCube task we observe older adults shows higher fluidity than adolescents, young adults and adults but also take more time, but children are clearly those scoring higher in the three DT components.

We can discuss these results considering that children and older adults are less oriented to perform in terms of time, which allows them to engage in a more creative process than adolescents and adults, who have developed the task more quickly and less creatively. These results can be put into perspective with studies that consider the link between activity duration and creativity. The effect of time pressure has differential effects depending on the participants [21]. Within the framework of the CreaCube task, the children do not perceive the task as inducing them any time pressure, but as an opportunity to create creative solutions. These results lead us to consider the importance of engaging adolescents and adult participants in an approach less oriented to temporal performance to support them to be as creative as children and older adults. Further studies will evaluate DT components not only in individual contexts but also in dyads and small groups of participants to understand the effect of collective settings in CPS across the lifespan.

Acknowledgments. This research is developed as part of the Project-ANR CreaMaker project (18-CE38-0001). We would like to thank Eloïse Duhot-Prevot for her valuable contribution to CreaCube platform and Louis Kohler for contribution to the analysis.

References

1. Manly, J.J., Schupf, N., Tang, M.-X., Stern, Y.: Cognitive decline and literacy among ethnically diverse elders. J. Geriatr. Psychiatry Neurol. **18**(4), 213–217 (2005). https://doi.org/10.1177/0891988705281868
2. Ahmad, B., Richardson, I., Beecham, S.: A systematic literature review of social network systems for older adults. In: Felderer, M., Méndez Fernández, D., Turhan, B., Kalinowski, M., Sarro, F., Winkler, D. (eds.) PROFES 2017. LNCS, vol. 10611, pp. 482–496. Springer, Cham (2017). https://doi.org/10.1007/978-3-319-69926-4_38
3. Wagner, S.P.: Robotics and children: science achievement and problem solving. J. Comput. Child. Educ. **9**(2), 149 (1998)
4. Pelikan, H.R., Broth, M.: 'Why that nao?: How humans adapt to a conventional humanoid robot in taking turns-at-talk'. In: Proceedings of the 2016 CHI Conference on Human Factors in Computing Systems, pp. 4921–4932 (2016)
5. Correll, N., Wailes, C., Slaby, S.: A one-hour curriculum to engage middle school students in robotics and computer science using cubelets. In: Ani Hsieh, M., Chirikjian, G. (eds.) Distributed Autonomous Robotic Systems. STAR, vol. 104, pp. 165–176. Springer, Heidelberg (2014). https://doi.org/10.1007/978-3-642-55146-8_12
6. Leroy, A., Romero, M., Cassone, L.: Fluidity, flexibility, and innovation assessment in the Alternative Uses Test and in the CreaCube task. Think. Ski. Creat., submitted
7. Guilford, J., Guilford, J.: Match Problems: Manual of Instructions and Interpretations. Sheridan Psychol. Serv., Orange (1980)
8. Romero, M., David, D., Lille, B.: CreaCube, a playful activity with modular robotics. Presented at the GALA 2018, Palermo, IT (2018)
9. Guilford, J.P.: Creativity: its measurement and development. Source Book Creat. Think., 151–167 (1962)
10. Leroy, A., Romero, M.: Teachers' Creative behaviors in STEAM activities with modular robotics. Front. Educ. **6**, 642147 (2021). https://doi.org/10.3389/feduc.2021.642147
11. Kahneman, D.: Thinking, Fast and Slow. Penguin Books, London (2012)
12. Augello, A., Infantino, I., Pilato, G., Rizzo, R., Vella, F.: Introducing a creative process on a cognitive architecture. Biol. Inspired Cogn. Archit. **6**, 131–139 (2013). https://doi.org/10.1016/j.bica.2013.05.011
13. Matarić, M.J., Arkin, R.C.: The Robotics Primer. MIT Press, Cambridge (2007)
14. Munich, M.E., Ostrowski, J., Pirjanian, P.: ERSP: a software platform and architecture for the service robotics industry. In: 2005 IEEE/RSJ International Conference on Intelligent Robots and Systems (IROS 2005), pp. 460–467 (2005)
15. Norman, D.A.: Affordance, Conventions, and Design. Interactions **6**(3), 38–43 (1999)

16. Hay, L., Duffy, A.H., McTeague, C., Pidgeon, L.M., Vuletic, T., Grealy, M.: A systematic review of protocol studies on conceptual design cognition: design as search and exploration. Des. Sci. **3** (2017)
17. Treffinger, D.J., Isaksen, S.G., Stead-Dorval, K.B.: Creative Problem Solving: An Introduction. Prufrock Press Inc., Waco (2006)
18. Tassoul, M.: Creative facilitation, a Delft approach. VSSD (2005)
19. Sawyer, R.K., et al.: Creativity and Development. Oxford University Press, New York (2003)

Considering Ethics and Privacy Issues in Modern ICT-Tools

Patrick Serafin⬛, Ann Kathrin Wissemann⬛, Hansjürgen Gebhardt$^{(\boxtimes)}$⬛, Christoph Mühlemeyer, Andreas Schäfer, and Karl-Heinz Lang

Institute for Occupational Medicine, Safety and Ergonomics (ASER), Wuppertal, Germany
{serafin,gebhardt}@institut-aser.de

Abstract. This article presents ethics and privacy issues as they were used in the Ageing@Work project. It provides information on identified challenges and summarizes fundamental requirements to deal with ethical, privacy and other related issues. It shows how compliance with ethical and related requirements during and after an ICT-project may be considered. The contribution aims to help beneficiaries to comply with privacy policies and to decide if and for which actions may require external support. It is based on seven basic principles, which have to be considered in the ethical implementation and evaluation of research as well as in modern ICT-tools. This article shows, how these principles originally designed for clinical research may be adapted for ICT-tools, whenever data from individuals are collected and processed. The adaption means to meet the seven basic principles of the General Data Protection Regulation for personal data. Besides the adaption, some examples show how it may be applied in modern ICT-tools.

Keywords: Ethics · Privacy · ICT · Ageing workforce

1 Introduction

The current era is characterized by rapidly evolving technologies that may bring benefits to the development of humanity, but also pose challenges. In particular, this article considers ethical and privacy issues that arise from research on modern ICT-tools with the example of the Ageing@Work project.

The progress in digitalization brings with it the effect that more and more personal data of individuals are stored and digitalized information can be quickly accessed. The abundance of information and its ease of reuse raises expectations to use the data for beneficial purposes and at the same time opens gates for the misuse of potentially sensitive personal data. One example of application is the use of new ICT tools in organizations to improve the health and productivity of ageing workforces. [1] For this primarily well-meaning purpose, employees' personal data, which may include also sensitive health data, may be collected, processed and stored through the use of digital data collection devices. At the same time, this brings risks as the data may be used for tracking, profiling or combining data from different sources that could be used for unknown purposes. Therefore, special attention must be paid to ethical and data protection aspects

V. G. Duffy et al. (Eds.): HCII 2022, LNCS 13521, pp. 534–545, 2022.
https://doi.org/10.1007/978-3-031-17902-0_38

in the development of ICT tools in research projects and in their subsequent use in organizations.

Ageing@Work is a transnational European Union funded HORIZON 2020 research project that aims to develop a series of highly adaptive, personalized ICT tools for the working and living environments of ageing workforces, to allow them to remain healthy, productive and competitive for longer. The developed Ageing@Work toolkit includes productivity enhancement tools, knowledge sharing and collaboration tools, supports an ageing-appropriate workplace design, in terms of ergonomics, process orchestration, task assignments and scheduling and offers incentives for both work-related and life aspects of the ageing worker, through a personalized virtual assistant and reward system [2].

The research of Ageing@Work includes research with humans like interviews, surveys, physical and psychometric tests, observations, monitoring and tracking of activities at work and in private life. The developed ICT solutions capture daily routines and additional data that is collected and processed. These may include age, gender, data on health and lifestyle as well as other data such as workability and physiological, psychometric behavioral and social parameters. Design of these and other solutions of the project is carried out with Ethics by Design and by Default approach. This means that ethical aspects are considered from the very beginning and ethical aspects are included in all evaluation activities. In addition, possibly confidential company data on the workplace's design, work processes and other working conditions are recorded. This results in special requirements for data protection, confidentiality and other ethical aspects like the principle of voluntary participation based on informed consent as well as integrity and dignity of study participants.

This article provides information on identified challenges and summarizes fundamental requirements to deal with ethical, privacy, data protection and other related issues. This includes, among others, how to comply with privacy policies, to obtain ethics approvals or deal with ethical issues involving an Ethics Advisory Board.

2 Ethical Framework in ICT Research

2.1 General Ethical Principles

When implementing Horizon 2020 funded projects, beneficiaries must act in accordance with ethical principles – this includes standards of research integrity – and applicable international EU and national laws. Article 34 of the H2020 - Annotated Model Grant Agreement (AGA) lists the following basic ethical principles that must be followed [3]:

- *"Respecting human dignity and integrity*
- *Ensuring honesty and transparency towards research subjects and notably getting free and informed consent (as well as assent whenever relevant)*
- *Protecting vulnerable persons*
- *Ensuring privacy and confidentiality*
- *Promoting justice and inclusiveness*
- *Minimising harm and maximising benefit*

- *Sharing the benefits with disadvantaged populations, especially if the research is being carried out in developing countries*
- *Maximising animal welfare, in particular by ensuring replacement, reduction and refinement ('3Rs') in animal research*
- *Respecting and protecting the environment and future generations"*

Also to be mentioned in this context are requirements for gender equality (Article 33), avoidance or disclosure of conflicts of interest (Article 35) and confidentiality (Article 36) [3]. Fundamental legal bases include the Charter of Fundamental Rights of the European Union (CFR) [4] and the European Convention on Human Rights (ECHR) [5].

In an article by Emanuel et al. [6] seven basic principles are enumerated, which have to be considered in the ethical implementation and evaluation of research.

1. Value, which means that research must have benefits for science and society as well as for individuals involved.
2. Scientific validity, which means that suitable research methods must be carefully and professionally selected.
3. Fair subject selection, which means that this has to be done in a transparent dependence of the research objectives. Discrimination or privileged treatment of individuals has to be avoided, inclusion and exclusion criteria must be formulated.
4. Favorable risk-benefit ratio, which means that possible risks must be minimized and the intended benefit must clearly outweigh them.
5. Independent review, which means that the intended procedures and the results are transparently described and reviewed by independent bodies.
6. Informed consent, which means that stakeholders must be fully informed of the course of action and the consent or refusal to participate is entirely voluntary.
7. Respect for enrolled subjects, which means that the well-being of the participants is continuously monitored, their privacy is respected and there is the possibility to revoke the participation without negative consequences.

Although these originally refer to clinical research, they were also applied to the studies planned in the Ageing@Work project and adapted to the specific conditions in the development of ICT solutions. The adaption means to meet the seven basic principles of the General Data Protection Regulation (GDPR) for personal data [7]:

1. Personal data must be processed lawfully. The consent to the storage and processing of personal data must be voluntary, specific, unambiguous and based on information. Personal data must be processed fairly and in a manner understandable to the data subject. The principle of transparency assumes that all information is easily accessible and understandable and written in clear and simple language.
2. Personal data must be collected for specified, explicit and legitimate purposes and must not be further processed in a way incompatible with those purposes. Further processing for archiving purposes in scientific research purposes shall not be considered to be incompatible with the initial purposes as long as it is in accordance with Article 89(1) GDPR.

3. Personal data must be adequate, relevant and limited to what is necessary for the purposes of the processing. Personal data should be allowed to be processed only if the purpose of the processing cannot reasonably be achieved by other means.
4. Personal data must be accurate and, where necessary, kept up to date. All reasonable steps shall be taken to ensure that personal data which are inaccurate for the purposes of their processing are erased or rectified without delay.
5. Personal data must be stored in a form which allows data subjects to be identified for no longer than is necessary for the purposes for which they are processed. Exception: Personal data may be retained for longer periods, to the extent that the personal data are used exclusively for scientific and non-commercial purposes in accordance with Article 89(1) GDPR subject to the implementation of appropriate technical and organizational measures required by the GPDR to protect the rights and freedoms of the data subject.
6. Personal data must be processed in a manner which ensures adequate security of personal data, including protection against unauthorized or unlawful processing and against accidental loss, destruction or damage using appropriate technical or organizational measures.
7. The controller shall be responsible for and be able to demonstrate compliance with the above principles and GDPR requirements.

The following sections show how these principles can be applied and which challenges have to be addressed in the research on modern ICT-tools illustrated by the example of Ageing@Work.

2.2   Ethical Issues in Ageing@Work

The principles of research integrity and the resulting Good Research Practices [8] certainly apply to all activities within the framework of the Ageing@Work project. The ethical principles listed in the previous section mainly relate to activities involving human subjects or including collection, processing or sharing personal data, for example in the development of worker and workplace models and orchestration support tools and the Ageing@Work platform integration and validation in industrial organizations. This applies in particular to the development (and application in pilot studies) of the ICT solutions and the Ageing@Work platform.

The aim of adhering to these principles is to derive maximum benefit from research activities and to reduce adverse effects and risks for all stakeholders, but in particular for the research subjects, as far as possible. Adverse effects for the research subjects can be characterized in particular by the following points:

- Physical damages (i.e. injuries)
- Major psychological or emotional harms (i.e. stress or anxiety)
- Economic, social or reputational disadvantages (i.e. loss of job or salary, discrimination, stigmatization or harassment)
- Violation of privacy or misuse/loss of personal data (i.e. non-protection of anonymity, unauthorized transfer of data to third parties or data theft)

The Ageing@Work research involves human participants on a voluntary basis and (sensitive) personal data is collected and processed. In addition, it includes tracking with sensors and observation of the participants. This is the basis for mainly privacy and data protection requirements. Further requirements arise with regard to the recruitment process of the participants and the informed consent. The participation should be absolutely voluntary. However, the participants are employees of the participating organizations, which in turn are involved in the recruitment process, data collection, processing and analysis. This means that the participants are in a relationship of dependence. This results in very special challenges to the recruiting process in order to ensure the voluntariness and avoid adverse consequences of participation. Therefore, the Ethics Summary Report of Ageing@Work recommends an ethics check of the recruiting procedure. Furthermore, it is required, among other things, to describe the nature and extent of data collection, data processing and data dissemination and to carry them out in accordance with international and national law. An Incidental Findings Policy is required too.

The use of new technologies in smart workplaces raises a number of ethical issues that should be considered systematically. This requires a holistic view in the planning and implementation of research projects, ranging from the active participation of the affected target groups to the researchers' handling of the collection, processing and storage of personal data. The use of ICT solutions such as wearable sensors, smart mobile devices and artificial intelligence (AI) must meet ethical requirements such as the protection of the autonomy, freedom and dignity of the data subjects, and appropriate safeguards for data management. This requires a transparent approach to the benefits and risks of using digital technologies [9].

To address these ethical issues, a specific work package "Ethics requirements" has been added to the project plan of Ageing@Work. In order to identify further possible ethics issues, all beneficiaries have participated in a survey on ethical and legal issues. In addition, the activities of the project were analyzed in order to uncover further fields of action. Apart from the points already mentioned above, further possible ethical aspects to be considered were identified. These include, but are not limited to, the prevention of physical (and other) adverse effects on participants, the minimization of risks, the maximization of benefits, the safety and adequacy of the equipment and methods used, and the confidentiality of company information.

3   Managing Ethical Challenges in Ageing@Work

3.1   Ethics by Design

An Ethics/Privacy by Design approach is pursued within the framework of the project. This means that ethical and data protection issues are considered and observed during the planning and implementation phase for the entire duration of the project and beyond. First, an Ethics Advisory Board (EAB) consisting of ethical experts and consortium members was established that supports the project partners in identifying ethical, privacy and related issues. It helps and advises the project partners in ensuring compliance with ethical principles, the rights of study participants and conformity with applicable law in the areas of ethics, data protection and related issues. Before any activity involving research with humans or the collection or processing of personal data, the study design including relevant aspects of data protection must be described in detail. This information is to be send to the EAB of the project before starting the respective activity. Then the EAB can make recommendations on whether and to what extent the planned activities should be carried out. In addition, the board recommends whether an ethics approval by an external ethics committee is advisable.

As Ageing@Work planned activities include research with human participants and the collection and processing of (sensitive) personal data, it may be necessary to obtain the consent of independent ethics committees before starting research. Therefore, an Ethics Checklist (see Fig. 1) was developed to identify ethical issues and to decide whether an ethics approval may be required. In addition, the EAB may be consulted. Moreover, national legislation may require an approval. If such ethics votes are required, they should usually be submitted to an ethics committee from the country/region where the research is being conducted. In the case of transnational multicentre research projects, it may also be advisable to submit an additional vote in the country where the researchers come from [10].

Within the framework of Ageing@Work and other ICT research, the responsible developers must carefully examine whether and if so which of the ICT solutions fall within the scope of Regulation (EU) 2017/745 on medical devices (MDR) [11] and related national or international regulations. Any resulting requirements must be adhered to. According to Art. 2, 1 of the MDR.

"'medical device' means any instrument, apparatus, appliance, software, implant, reagent, material or other article intended by the manufacturer to be used, alone or in combination, for human beings for one or more of the following specific medical purposes:

No.	Question	Yes	No
1.	Does your research involve human participants?		
2.	If yes, are they potentially vulnerable individuals or groups? (e.g. children, students, employees)		
3.	Does your research involve the collection of confidential or sensitive information?		
4.	Does your research involve controversial subject matter? (e.g. sensitive, embarrassing or intrusive topics)		
5.	May your research cause any harm to participants, researchers or others? (e.g. invasive techniques, physical interventions)		
	If all answers above are "No", then no formal ethics approval is required.		
6.	Has the research activity already approval from an ethics committee?		
7.	Is the research activity part of a larger study that has already received approval from an ethics committee?		
	If answer to question 6 or 7 is "Yes" then no further ethics approval is required.		
8.	Have health and safety risks due to the research been considered?		
9.	Are data protection compliance measures taken for any personal data collected by the research?		
	If one of the answers to question 1 – 5 is "Yes" and neither 6 nor 7 is "Yes", then a formal verification of the requirement of an ethics approval is advised under consideration of aspects 8 – 9.		

Fig. 1. Ethics Checklist to identify the need for ethics approval

- *diagnosis, prevention, monitoring, prediction, prognosis, treatment or alleviation of disease,*
- *[...]."*

If this is the case, the efforts made in the project to test the ICT solutions could be understood as 'clinical evaluation' or 'clinical investigation'. If ICT solutions developed and tested within the framework of the project fall within the scope of application of the MDR [11] as well as related national or international regulations, a vote of an ethics committee may also be necessary.

3.2 Risk-Based Approach

The GDPR includes a risk-based approach to data protection and privacy which was applied in the Ageing@Work project. Controllers are obliged to assess the severity and likelihood of risks to the fundamental rights and freedoms of data subjects and, in response to their data processing activities, to take protective measures corresponding to the level of risk. According to GDPR, controllers must perform risk assessments within the framework of DPIA where there are high risks involved in data collection or processing. Therefore, the data protection principles described above must be considered, e.g. data security, data protection by design, fair processing, legitimate interest, purpose limitation.

To standardise the risk assessment procedure in Ageing@Work, the individual steps were explained in more detail. The legislation demands data controllers to ensure a level of security proportionate to the risk involved in collecting and processing of personal data in Ageing@Work. Beneficiaries can comply with this requirement by first identifying the risks, before implementing the appropriate level of technical and organisational measures to mitigate the risks.

There is no clear definition of the term "risk" in the GDPR, but it can be derived for example from the Recital 75. Therein it means that risks to the rights and freedoms of natural persons may result from personal data processing which could lead to physical and (non-)material damage. [7] In particular, the following impacts are highlighted:

- *discrimination;*
- *identity theft or fraud;*
- *financial loss;*
- *damage to the reputation;*
- *loss of confidentiality of personal data protected by professional secrecy;*
- *unauthorised reversal of pseudonymisation;*
- *any other significant economic or social disadvantage;*
- *discrimination in their rights and freedoms;*
- *prevention from exercising control over their personal data;*

Before starting research activities with human participants or the collection of personal data, the planned procedures shall be described in detail in a research/study/experimental protocol. In addition, it must be decided whether a Data

No.	Question	Yes	No
1.	Does the activity involve the systematic monitoring of publicly accessible spaces?		
2.	Are the persons unaware of the collection and processing of their data?		
3.	Does the activity use automated data collection from open sources?		
4.	Does the activity involve the use of new technologies?		
5.	Is there a combination of a person's data from more than one source?		
6.	Is the personal data used for a purpose other than its original intention?		
7.	Would the processing of personal data be perceived as disruptive in this way?		
8.	Might data processing concern specific categories of personal data? (e.g. health)		
9.	Does the data processing involve decisions or assumptions about individuals?		
10.	Would the data subject consider the processed information to be private?		

Fig. 2. Risk assessment checklist to identify the need for DPIA

Protection Impact Assessment (DPIA) is necessary. The need for a DPIA can be derived from the key questions in the Risk Assessment Checklist (see Fig. 2).

In order to decide whether there are high risks, the checklist on risk assessment may be used. It contains risk assessment questions which serve to identify possible risks arising from the planned research activity. If the result does not reveal any risk, no additional measures other than the usual compliance measures need to be taken. If any question is answered with "Yes", a full risk assessment must be carried out.

To ensure security of processing operations, beneficiaries should assess the risks associated with the processing and implement measures to mitigate those risks, e.g. pseudonymisation or encryption. Appropriate measures depend on the context and the specific risks of the processing operations. Those measures should ensure an adequate level of security, including confidentiality, considering the state of the art and costs of implementation in relation to the risks and nature of the personal data to be protected.

The assessment of the data security risk should consider the risks arising from the processing of personal data, such as accidental or unlawful destruction, loss, alteration, unauthorised disclosure or access to personal data transmitted, stored or otherwise processed which may in particular lead to physical, material or non-material damage.

According to Article 35 GDPR, beneficiaries shall carry out an assessment of the impact of the envisaged data processing on the protection of personal data before starting the data collection where it is likely to result in a high risk to the rights and freedoms of natural persons. In general, a DPIA concerns a single data processing operation. A single assessment may address a set of similar processing operations that present similar high risks. The risk assessment shall contain at least [7]:

- *"a systematic description of the envisaged processing operations and the purposes of the processing, including, where applicable, the legitimate interest pursued by the controller,*
- *an assessment of the necessity and proportionality of the processing operations in relation to the purposes,*
- *an assessment of the risks to the rights and freedoms of data subjects,*

● *the measures envisaged to address the risks, including safeguards, security measures and mechanisms to ensure the protection of personal data and to demonstrate compliance [with the GDPR] taking into account the rights and legitimate interests of data subjects and other persons concerned."*

The legislation does not specify the method by which a DPIA is to be conducted, but there are criteria that it must include. Figure 3 shows the general cycle process for carrying out a DPIA. As it is an iterative process, it is likely that each of the phases will be repeated several times before the DPIA can be completed. According to Article 35 GDPR, the controller shall carry out a review to assess if processing is performed in accordance with the data protection impact assessment at least when there is a change of the risk represented by processing operations. In principle, a DPIA should be continuously reviewed and regularly re-evaluated in order to establish good practice.

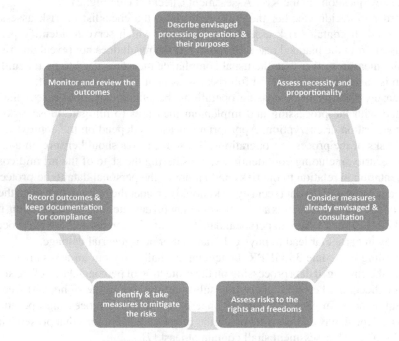

Fig. 3. General iterative process of DPIA

On the basis of the DPIA, appropriate technical and organisational measures must be taken to mitigate risks to the rights and freedoms of individuals. Risk reduction does not mean eliminating the risk, but reducing it as far as possible, considering the desired benefits and the appropriate economic and technological parameters. The DPIA must be well documented and retained as evidence of compliance.

Where the processing operation is carried out by joint controllers, they must clearly define their respective obligations. Their DPIA should set out which party is responsible for the various risk management measures and for protecting the rights and freedoms of the data subjects. This is especially important in the cooperation in transnational research projects like in the context of the Ageing@Work project processing operations.

A DPIA may also be useful for assessing the data protection impact of a technology product, e.g. hardware or software, if it is likely to be used by different data controllers to perform different processing operations. Of course, the data controller using the product remains obliged to perform its own risk assessment in relation to the specific implementation, but this may be communicated by a DPIA created by the product provider [12].

3.3 Processing Sensitive Data

Several of the studies planned within Ageing@Work with different objectives involve human participants. All people that are participating in the pilot activities of the developed ICT solutions take part in a thorough recruitment and informed consent procedure, that will be particularly stringent to ensure that participation is voluntary and no coercion (not even soft or indirect) is exerted. The participants concerned are to be informed about, among other things, the objectives of the project, the persons responsible, the methods used, the data collected, the handling and processing of this data, possible benefits and risks as well as the possibility of withdrawing their participation.

Since the participants are employees of the pilot organizations involved and are therefore in a relationship of dependence, they are to be regarded as vulnerable [10, 13]. This results in special requirements for recruitment and the procedure of informed consent in order to ensure absolute voluntariness and to exclude direct or indirect consequences from participation or non-participation. For example, the companies involved (or their management) should not know which employees participated and which employees did not. It must also be carefully clarified whether and in what form the participating companies (or their management) are given insight into the study results in order to ensure that no conclusions can be drawn about individual employees or small groups of employees. This is particularly true as the project also collects sensible data on health status, lifestyle or work ability. There is thus a risk that knowledge of such data may result in disadvantages (e.g. job loss, discrimination, poorer career opportunities). Appropriate measures must be taken to protect the participants and to eliminate or mitigate such risks. In any event, participants must be fully informed of such risks, should they exist. On the other hand, participants should not receive any special advantages or preferential treatment in relation to their job.

The consent procedures have to be carefully determined and managed by data collection and pilot-specific tasks within Ageing@Work that will manage the trials which will be performed in selected data collection areas. Thus, it requires the enrolment of people voluntarily declaring their consent to participate in each of the data collection process and the pilot use cases. However, the design of the observational study is prepared in collaboration with the EAB of the Ageing@Work consortium, in order to respect privacy and ethical issues implied by the data to be collected and analysed. The consent procedure for all data collection processes and the pilot use case realisation at each of the selected pilot sites can be obtained through a two-stage procedure:

a. Initially the data collection responsible (here pilot trial leader) orally presents the purpose of the study to people that will be involved, carefully describing the level of privacy infringement that the execution of each of the process involves. In the event that someone cannot/does not wish to participate in the presentation, he/she will be excluded from the study. This must not result in any other disadvantages (except non-participation) for the person concerned.

b. Secondly, after a few days, subjects will be required to read and sign an Informed Consent Form (ICF) that will explain in both plain English and in local language what the study/trial leader has already orally explained.

Data should best be collected in anonymous form so that it no longer relates to identifiable individuals. Then the anonymised data is not subject to data protection law but the data collection may still raise significant ethical issues due to the origins of the data or the applied method to obtain the data. If anonymisation is not possible, personal data should be pseudonymised in order to protect the participants' privacy and minimise the risk to their fundamental rights. It works in such a way that an identification code is assigned to all participants so that the different actions of the participants during data collection can be mapped. The relationship between the identification code and the participant is stored separately and securely and is only accessible to defined persons.

Upon completion of the research project, all data from the project pilots and studies that are considered confidential should be discarded. Only the public models and respective datasets described in detail in the Ageing@Work Data Management Plan will be made open.

Acknowledgements. This work has been supported by the EU Horizon 2020 funded project "Smart, Personalized and Adaptive ICT Solutions for Active, Healthy and Productive Ageing with enhanced Workability (Ageing@Work)", under grant agreement no: 826299.

References

1. Wissemann, A.K., Pit, S.W., Serafin, P., Gebhardt, H.: Strategic guidance and technological solutions for human resources management to sustain an aging workforce: review of international standards, research, and use cases. JMIR Hum. Factors **9**(2), e27250 (2022). Advance online publication https://doi.org/10.2196/27250
2. Giakoumis, D., Votis, K., Altsitsiadis, E., Segkouli, S., Paliokas, I., Tzovaras, D.: Smart, personalized and adaptive ICT solutions for active, healthy and productive ageing with enhanced workability. In: PErvasive Technologies Related to Assistive Environments (PETRA), Rhodes, Greece, 5–7 June 2019, pp. 442–447. https://doi.org/10.1145/3316782.3322767
3. European Commission (ed.): H2020 Programme AGA – Annotated Model Grant Agreement, Version 5.1 (2018). https://ec.europa.eu/research/participants/data/ref/h2020/grants_manual/amga/h2020-amga_en.pdf. Accessed 27 May 2022
4. Charter of Fundamental Rights of the European Union (CFR) 2010/C 83/02. https://www.europarl.europa.eu/charter/pdf/text_en.pdf. Accessed 26 May 2022
5. European Convention for the Protection of Human Rights and Fundamental Freedoms, as amended by Protocols Nos. 11 and 14 (ECHR). https://www.echr.coe.int/Documents/Convention_ENG.pdf. Accessed 27 May 2022

6. Emanuel, E.J., Wendler, D., Grady, C.: What makes clinical research ethical? JAMA **283**(20), 2701–2711 (2000). https://doi.org/10.1001/jama.283.20.2701

7. Regulation (EU) 2016/679 of the European Parliament and of the Council of 27 April 2016 on the protection of natural persons with regard to the processing of personal data and on the free movement of such data, and repealing Directive 95/46/EC (General Data Protection Regulation). https://eur-lex.europa.eu/legal-content/EN/TXT/PDF/?uri=CELEX:32016R0679& from=DE. Accessed 27 May 2022

8. All European Academies (ALLEA): The European Code of Conduct for Research Integrity - Revised Edition (2017). ISBN 978-3-00-055767-5. https://www.allea.org/wp-content/ uploads/2017/05/ALLEA-European-Code-of-Conduct-for-Research-Integrity-2017.pdf. Accessed 27 May 2022

9. Segkouli, S., Giakoumis, D., Votis, K., Triantafyllidis, A., Paliokas, I., Tzovaras, D.: Smart workplaces for older adults: coping 'ethically' with technology pervasiveness. Univ. Access Inf. Soc. (2021). https://doi.org/10.1007/s10209-021-00829-9

10. Council for International Organizations of Medical Sciences (CIOMS) (ed.): International Ethical Guidelines for Health-related Research Involving Humans (2016). ISBN 978-929036088-9. https://cioms.ch/wp-content/uploads/2017/01/WEB-CIOMS-Eth icalGuidelines.pdf. Accessed 27 May 2022

11. Regulation (EU) 2017/745 of the European Parliament and of the Council of 5 April 2017 on medical devices, amending Directive 2001/83/EC, Regulation (EC) No 178/2002 and Regulation (EC) No 1223/2009 and repealing Council Directives 90/385/EEC and 93/42/EEC (Text with EEA relevance.) https://eur-lex.europa.eu/legal-content/EN/TXT/PDF/?uri=CELEX: 32017R0745&from=DE. Accessed 27 May 2022

12. Guidelines on Data Protection Impact Assessment (DPIA) and determining whether processing is "likely to result in a high risk" for the purposes of Regulation 2016/679 17/EN WP 248 rev.01. https://ec.europa.eu/newsroom/document.cfm?doc_id=44137. Accessed 27 May 2022

13. European Commission (ed.): Ethics in Social Science and Humanities (2018). http://ec. europa.eu/research/participants/data/ref/h2020/other/hi/h2020_ethics-soc-science-humani ties_en.pdf. Accessed 27 May 2022

User Experience Design of Elderly-Oriented Social Apps Based on Kano Model—The Case of WeChat

Xiaokang Song[✉] ⓘ

Xuzhou Medical University, Xuzhou 221004, Jiangsu, China
sxksxk666@163.com

Abstract. Social applications (apps) are becoming more and more important for the elderly in achieving various purposes and pursuing happiness. However, the design of social applications often ignores the user experience and needs of the elderly. It is necessary to design elderly-oriented social apps. Combined with user interviews, this paper obtained the design elements of elderly-oriented social apps, and designed the Kano questionnaire and importance questionnaire. 297 valid samples were obtained based on offline and online surveys. The Kano Two-Dimensional model is used to classify the design elements, and the priority of relevant elements is determined combined with the importance analysis. The study found that the elderly-oriented social apps should ensure the stable operation and rapid response of the system, shield inserted advertisements, set large fonts, simple interface and collection function. The findings of this paper will provide a theoretical reference for the design, evaluation, and user experience studies of elderly-oriented mobile applications.

Keywords: Elderly-oriented design · Social applications · User experience · Kano model

1 Introduction

Now two significant changes are taking place in society, the elderly population is increasing and the application of digital technology is becoming more and more extensive [1]. According to China's seventh census data in 2021, the elderly population over 60 years old reached 264 million, accounting for 18.7% of the total population. The elderly have become an essential group in society. In addition, the development of digital technology, especially the rise of social media, has changed people's way of life. People can socialize, entertain, work and consume online. Digital applications have become indispensable tools for people. Due to digital inequality, how to improve the well-being of the elderly by the digital technology has also become a topic of concern [2, 3].

Actually, a large number of elderly people have begun to use the Internet. According to the report of CNNIC, as of June 2021, there were 123 million Internet users over the age of 60 in China. Today's older people are richer, healthier and more familiar with the technology. They also use mobile digital technology more frequently for various

© Springer Nature Switzerland AG 2022
V. G. Duffy et al. (Eds.): HCII 2022, LNCS 13521, pp. 546–558, 2022.
https://doi.org/10.1007/978-3-031-17902-0_39

purposes [4]. Some studies found that mobile digital technology has great potential in improving the life quality of the elderly, which provides opportunities to reduce social isolation, promote the implementation of daily tasks, enhance healthy behavior and health level [5].

However, due to the decline of physical function and cognitive ability, the elderly may face more challenges when interacting with mobile applications [6]. In the context of COVID-19, the problem of digital technology use disorder has brought greater inconvenience to the daily life of the elderly. The Chinese government has issued a series of policies to solve this problem, including required to transform the mobile application systems to facilitate the use of the elderly. In addition, most of the current digital products are designed based on the preferences of young people, often ignoring the characteristics and needs of the elderly [2]. Digital technology should embrace the elderly rather than exclude them, so as to improve the well-being of the elderly [3].

In China, WeChat is one of the most commonly used mobile applications for the elderly. It provides users with a wide range of social functions, such as video calls, moments, group chat, comments, red envelopes, etc. Few studies have focused on optimizing the design of social media to improve the user satisfaction of the elderly. This paper combs the social media design elements concerned by the elderly from the perspective of user experience. Then, this paper determines the priority of elderly-oriented social media design elements based on the Kano model. The results will help improve the social media use rate and satisfaction of the elderly.

2 Related Work

2.1 Mobile Applications Design for the Elderly

Due to a series of age-related changes, it is necessary to specially design technologies and applications suitable for the elderly [7]. Chou et al. [8] pointed out that the physiological, psychological and cognitive changes of the elderly make it more difficult for them to learn and use digital technology than young people. In terms of physiology, the sight, hearing, memory and finger flexibility of the elderly have declined, which makes the elderly have some obstacles in interacting with text, charts and buttons in the interface of digital application system [9, 10]. In terms of psychology, the elderly often diffident, fear and anxiety when using mobile applications, resulting in higher attention to the friendliness, security and attractiveness of digital application systems [6, 8]. In terms of cognition, the elderly has poor understanding ability and processing ability of complex tasks, which makes it difficult for the elderly to use the deep-seated navigation, complex icons and multi-step operation tasks of mobile application systems [11].

Some studies have explored the design elements and rules for developing mobile applications for the elderly. In terms of interface design of mobile smart phones, some common navigation, interaction and visual design elements are often mentioned, such as font size, button shape, contrast, menu, navigation convenience, text input, function label, etc. [7, 12]. In addition, the design of mobile games for the elderly has also been concerned by some researchers. Through questionnaires and interviews with the elderly, Cota et al. [2] determined some factors affecting the use of mobile games, including event feedback and reward, game difficulty design, story narration and so on.

Tabak et al. [13] developed a game-based mobile physical coaching application for the elderly using an iterative method. What's more, there are some studies on mobile health application design for the elderly. Wildenbos et al. [11] identified 28 key design factors related to motivation and cognitive impairment in the elderly, based on an aging barriers framework. Kirkscey [14] introduced a method to develop mHealth applications for the elderly, and pointed out that the design process should meet the experience and needs of elderly users.

2.2 Kano Model

Based on Herzberg's two-factor theory [15], Japanese scholar Kano et al. proposed an evaluation model to describe the relationship between product or service quality and user satisfaction, which is called Kano model [16]. Kano model uses questionnaires to investigate users' feelings about quality elements, including forward and reverse questionnaires. The answers include five options: "like", "taking it for granted", "no feeling", "tolerable" and "dislike" [17]. Matzler and Hinterhuber [18] revised the classification standard of two-dimensional quality elements, as shown in Table 1. Researchers can divide elements into five categories according to the element classification table, namely "attractive element (A)", "one-dimensional element (O)", "must-be element (M)", "indifferent element (I)" and "reverse element (R)". In order to determine the priority of a quality element to be improved, Matzler and Hinterhuber [18] put forward two calculation indexes: satisfaction increment index (SII) and dissatisfaction decrement index (DDI). Their calculation formula are as follows:

$$SII = (A + O)/(A + O + M + I) \tag{1}$$

$$DDI = -(O + M)/(A + O + M + I) \tag{2}$$

Table 1. The element classification table of Matzler and Hinterhuber (1998) [18].

An element		Reverse				
		Like (5)	Taking it for granted (4)	No feeling (3)	Tolerable (2)	Dislike (1)
Forward	Like (5)	Q	A	A	A	O
	Taking it for granted (4)	R	I	I	I	M
	No feeling (3)	R	I	I	I	M
	Tolerable (2)	R	I	I	I	M
	Dislike (1)	R	R	R	R	Q

Since Kano model was proposed, it has attracted extensive attention in the fields of quality management and product design. Huang [17] combines Kano model with IPA method to determine the priority of design elements that need to be improved in mHealth applications, so as to improve the quality of health services. Mao et al. [19] analyzed the technical elements needed by the elderly based on the Kano model, and put forward the optimization scheme for the application of elderly-friendly intelligent drug management. Ho and Tzeng [20] use the Kano model to analyze the needs of mobile reading applications for the middle-aged and elderly, which provides a reference for the design of mobile reading applications.

3 Research Design

3.1 Design Elements of Elderly-Oriented Social App

In response to the requirements of the Chinese government, WeChat has launched a special mode for elderly users, named "care mode". Based on the relevant studies of designing for the elderly, this paper summarizes the design elements combined with the elderly's user experience of WeChat care mode. Five elderly people over 60 who have used WeChat care mode were recruited for simple interviews. The contents of satisfaction and dissatisfaction of the elderly were recorded and coded.

Vyas and van der Veer [21] introduce a framework for describing the technology design experience. The three system-related affordances (appearance, interaction and function) are integrated with the four user experiences (aesthetics, emotional, cognitive, and practical). This paper summarizes the design elements of three dimensions: appearance elements, interaction elements, and function elements. The elements and sources are shown in Table 2.

Table 2. Design elements and sources.

Dimensions	No.	Design element item	Sources
Appearance elements	1	The font of main functions and interfaces should be large enough	Li and Luximon [6]
	2	The text and pictures shall be displayed with beautiful effect and no overlap	User interviews
	3	The contrast of text, images and other elements should be obvious enough	User interviews
	4	Simple interface design and comfortable color matching	Chen et al. [22]
Interaction elements	5	Simple registration and personalization setting procedures	Chen et al. [22]
	6	Clickable buttons or components should be large enough and obvious	User interviews
	7	The system should respond quickly and operate stably	Huang [17]

(*continued*)

Table 2. (*continued*)

Dimensions	No.	Design element item	Sources
	8	With help and feedback function	Chen et al. [22]
	9	Set up obvious praise and comment buttons in the moments	User interviews
Function elements	10	There are games for the elderly	Cota et al. [2]
	11	Provide tips and introduction of common functions	Li and Luximon [6]
	12	Advertising plug-ins and induced buttons are prohibited	Xu et al. [23]
	13	There is a user privacy statement	Huang [17]
	14	Provide effective tips or feedbacks when the operations such as moments publishing and red envelope sending are completed	User interviews
	15	Put common functions, such as video call, scanning, etc., in the obvious position	User interviews
	16	It can easily call the camera to record life	User interviews
	17	Simple friend management (such as adding, deleting, searching, etc.)	User interviews
	18	Simple group chat management (such as initiating, saving, no interrupting and exiting)	User interviews
	19	Simple emoticon stickers management (such as sending, adding, forwarding, etc.)	User interviews
	20	Provide collection function	Xu et al. [23]

3.2 Participants and Data Collection

This paper designs a questionnaire based on the elements in Table 2. The questionnaire consists of three parts. The first part is the basic information of the respondents, including gender, age, education, place of residence and health status. The second part is the importance questionnaire, which uses a 5-point Likert scale to measure the respondents' perception of the importance of design elements. The third part is the forward and reverse questionnaire based on the Kano model, which is used to measure the user's perception of a specific design element in two cases, with and without this element.

This paper collects data through two ways: offline collection and online collection through "Wenjuanxing" (http://www.wjx.cn). The respondents recruited in this paper need to meet the following three conditions: (1) be current WeChat users, (2) over 60 years old and (3) has used the "care mode" of WeChat. From December 20, 2021 to January 5, 2022, a total of 312 participants completed the questionnaire, including 297 valid questionnaires, with an effective rate of 95.2%.

Table 3 shows the basic demographic information of participants. Among them, 58.9% of the participants (N = 175) were female and 41.1% (N = 122) were male. Most participants are aged between 60–70 (N = 223, 75.1%), have a junior middle school education level (N = 227, 76.4%), and perceived normal health status (N = 136, 45.8%). 61.3% of the participants (N = 182) were from urban and 38.7% (N = 115) form rural.

Table 3. Demographic information of participants.

Variables	Number	Proportion
Gender		
Female	175	58.9%
Male	122	41.1%
Age		
60–70	223	75.1%
70–80	73	24.6%
Above 80	1	0.3%
Education		
Primary school and below	10	3.4%
Junior middle school	227	76.4%
High school	47	15.8%
College education and above	13	4.4%
Place of residence		
Rural	115	38.7%
Urban	182	61.3%
Health status		
Very poor	2	0.7%
Poor	16	5.4%
Normal	136	45.8%
Good	121	40.7%
Very good	22	7.4%
Note: n = 297		

4 Results

4.1 Results of Reliability and Validity Analysis

Because the questionnaire is constructed on the basis of literature review and user interviews, it is necessary to test the reliability and validity before data analysis. First, this paper uses SPSS statistical software to analyze the reliability of sample data. The Cronbach's alpha values of the importance questionnaire, forward and reverse Kano questionnaires, and each dimension were tested. The results of reliability analysis are shown in Table 4. All alpha values are above 0.7, indicating that the questionnaire and each dimension have a high degree of reliability. Then, in terms of content validity, most of the design elements in this paper come from existing studies, and the expression and classification of each item have been revised with the advice of experts. Therefore, the questionnaire sample of this study meets the standard requirements of reliability and validity.

Table 4. Results of reliability analysis.

Dimensions	Items	Importance questionnaire	Kano questionnaire	
			Forward	Reverse
Appearance	1–4	0.735	0.706	0.737
Interaction	5–9	0.754	0.704	0.781
Function	10–20	0.870	0.816	0.866
Overall	1–20	0.924	0.888	0.924

4.2 Results of Importance Questionnaire Analysis

The importance questionnaire uses the 5-point Likert scale to measure the importance of various elderly-oriented social app design elements perceived by the users. The 1–5 scores of the scale indicate "very unimportant", "unimportant", "general", "important" and "very important" respectively. The mean of the importance scores of each element is shown in Fig. 1. The results show that the important elements of elderly-oriented social app are element 7 (M = 4.69) in the interaction dimension, elements 12 (M = 4.59), 15 (M = 4.15), 18 (M = 4.16) and 20 (M = 3.99) in the function dimension, and elements 1 (M = 4.04) and 4 (M = 4.21) in the appearance dimension. The less important elements are element 8 (M = 3.84) in the interaction dimension, elements 10 (M = 3.33), 11 (M = 3.84), and 16 (M = 3.67) in the function dimension, and elements 2 (M = 3.75) and 3 (M = 3.81) in the appearance dimension. Due to the small difference in importance

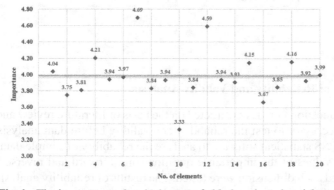

Fig. 1. The importance of each element of elderly-oriented social app.

scores between various elements, this study also needs to combine the results of Kano questionnaire to finally determine the priority of them.

4.3 Results of Kano Two-Dimensional Analysis

Based on the classification table of Matzler and Hinterhuber [18], this paper classifies the 20 design elements of elderly-oriented social apps, and calculates the values of SII and DDI, as shown in Table 5. Calculate the proportion of elements belonging to each Kano category, that is, the membership degree in each category, and classify the elements into the category with the highest membership degree. The results show that design elements 7 and 12 are classified as one-dimensional element (O), design elements 9, 15, 18 and 19 are classified as attractive element (A), design elements 1, 4 and 20 are classified as must-be element (M), and the rest design elements are classified as indifferent element (I).

Table 5. Classification of elderly-oriented social app elements.

No.	Membership of design elements in each category					Classification	SII	DDI
	A (%)	I (%)	M (%)	O (%)	R (%)			
1	3.70	27.95	37.71	29.97	0.67	M	0.34	−0.68
2	24.24	49.83	11.11	14.48	0.34	I	0.39	−0.26
3	24.92	47.81	14.14	13.13	0.00	I	0.38	−0.27
4	13.13	22.22	34.34	30.30	0.00	M	0.43	−0.65
5	21.21	41.75	14.14	22.90	0.00	I	0.44	−0.37
6	22.56	37.04	15.15	24.24	1.01	I	0.47	−0.40
7	17.51	6.40	3.37	72.73	0.00	O	0.90	−0.76
8	21.89	45.79	16.16	16.16	0.00	I	0.38	−0.32
9	46.46	29.63	3.03	20.54	0.34	A	0.67	−0.24
10	21.21	62.96	4.04	6.40	5.39	I	0.29	−0.11
11	22.56	43.77	13.80	19.53	0.34	I	0.42	−0.33
12	20.20	9.43	2.02	68.35	0.00	O	0.89	−0.70
13	12.46	34.68	30.98	21.89	0.00	I	0.34	−0.53
14	18.86	42.09	17.17	21.55	0.34	I	0.41	−0.39
15	52.19	13.13	1.68	33.00	0.00	A	0.85	−0.35
16	22.90	53.20	9.76	13.47	0.67	I	0.37	−0.23
17	26.94	40.07	15.82	17.17	0.00	I	0.44	−0.33
18	53.20	14.48	3.37	28.96	0.00	A	0.82	−0.32
19	53.87	26.94	2.02	17.17	0.00	A	0.71	−0.19
20	13.80	29.29	36.70	20.20	0.00	M	0.34	−0.57

This paper also draws the scatter diagram of each element distribution with satisfaction increment index (SII) as the X axis and dissatisfaction decrement index (DDI) as the Y axis, as shown in Fig. 2. Taking X = 0.5 and Y = −0.5 as the center line, all elements are divided into four quadrants. Elements 7 and 12 in the fourth quadrant can not only significantly improve user satisfaction, but also significantly reduce user dissatisfaction. They are the most important design elements of elderly-oriented social app, such as "care mode of WeChat".

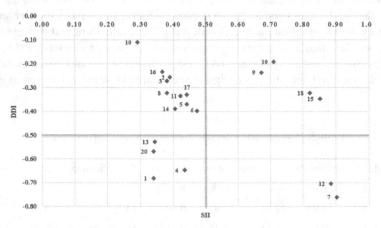

Fig. 2. Distribution of SII and DDI values for each element.

5 Discussion

5.1 Key Findings

Based on user interviews, this study obtained the elderly-oriented social app design elements concerned by users. Then, this study uses the importance questionnaire to determine the importance of each design element in the user experience. Design elements are finally classified into four categories through Kano Two-Dimensional model.

In Kano model, the attribute of one-dimensional element is more sufficient, users will feel higher satisfaction, and the attribute is more insufficient, users will feel higher dissatisfaction. In this study, design elements 7 and 12 are classified as one-dimensional element (O). The elderly regard the rapid response and stable operation of social application system as one-dimensional quality elements. It shows that the elderly users' adoption of social media conforms to the theory of technology acceptance model [24]. The better the usefulness of the system, the higher the satisfaction of users. The elderly users also classify prohibited advertising plug-ins and inducement buttons as one-dimensional elements. Due to the decline of cognitive ability, the elderly users are often not confident in their ability to deal with advertising information [8]. The elderly also believe that irrelevant advertisements or inducement buttons will affect their system operation, and even cause them some losses, such as money loss. Therefore, in the elderly-oriented social app design, we should try our best to ensure the operation performance of the system and the shielding of inserted advertisements, so as to improve the satisfaction of elderly users.

When the attribute of must-be element is sufficient, the user's satisfaction is at an acceptable level and will not be increased, and users will feel dissatisfied when the attribute is insufficient. In this study, design elements 1, 4 and 20 are classified as must-be element (M). The elderly users believe that larger fonts, simple interface design and collection function are must-be elements of elderly-oriented social apps. Consistent with some previous research results, the decline of eyesight, touch and finger flexibility of the elderly makes elderly-oriented products need larger fonts and concise interfaces [19, 20]. Otherwise, it will reduce the elderly's acceptance of the product. Due to the decline of memory, the elderly users often collect some pictures, videos and articles they think are valuable in social media [23]. Therefore, the elderly believe that the collection function is also a must-be element of elderly-oriented social apps. According to Kano model, the elements divided into must-be attributes are the most basic needs of users for products, which should be given priority in product design.

In the Kano model, the attribute of attractive element is the product attribute that the users did not expect, which will make them feel satisfied. If the element is insufficient, it will not have much impact on users' satisfaction. In this study, design elements 9, 15, 18 and 19 are classified as attractive element (A). Chinese elderly users often use moment of WeChat to post information and interact with information published by others [25]. However, in the care mode WeChat, the praise and comment buttons in the moment are folded and hidden under a small button, which is inconvenient for elderly users. Similarly, older users often use video call and scan functions. However, these functions are hidden under some buttons. The elderly must click the button to see these functions, which brings inconvenience to them. Group chat and emoticon sticker are also common functions for the elderly in social apps. The management of chat groups and emoticon stickers generally require multiple steps, which are not easy for the elderly. The findings are consistent with some previous studies. Multi-level navigation and complex operation steps will bring confusion to elderly users [8, 11]. Therefore, set up obvious praise and comment buttons in the moment, put video call and scanning in the obvious position, simple group chat management, and simple emoticon stickers management will be attractive for the elderly.

In the Kano model, whether the attributes of indifference elements are sufficient or not will have no impact on users' satisfaction. In this study, the elderly users classified the information display type, contrast, personalized settings, large click buttons, feedback function, games, function introduction, privacy statement, tips for successful red envelope sending, camera call and friends management as indifferent elements (I). The main reasons are as follows: (1) the elderly often only pay attention to the core and practical attributes of digital application systems, and do not pay attention to the infrequent functions and settings [19]. (2) Elderly users are used to the current WeChat system. They are familiar with the current functional icons, personalized settings, moments sending and red envelope sending. Therefore, they believe that the relevant design elements proposed in this paper are no difference. (3) Many elderly people, especially those who have not experienced higher education, tend to ignore privacy protection when using ICT [26].

Overall, one-dimensional elements and must-be elements are the most priority elements in the design of elderly-oriented social apps. These elements can not only improve the satisfaction of the elderly users, but also have a high degree of importance and can reduce the degree of dissatisfaction. The elderly-oriented social apps should ensure the stable operation and rapid response of the system, shield inserted advertisements, set large fonts, simple interface and collection function. In addition, attractive elements are the secondary elements in the design of elderly-oriented social apps. These elements can effectively attract the elderly users to use elderly-oriented social apps. On the premise of ensuring one-dimensional elements and must-be elements, elderly-oriented social apps should also consider optimizing the display and placement of common functions and buttons, such as praise and comment buttons in the moment, as well as video call and scan functions. It also needs to optimize the steps of group chat and emoticon sticker management. Although indifference elements do not need too much attention, it is worth noting that element 13 "privacy statement" is of high importance and can effectively reduce users' dissatisfaction (DDI $= -0.53$). Therefore, it is also need to pay attention to users' privacy in the design of elderly-oriented social apps.

5.2   Theoretical Implications

This paper enriches the theories related to elderly-oriented social application design. Firstly, from the perspective of user experience, this paper obtains the social media design elements, they like and feel disabled, through interviews with elderly users. Combined with the literature review, we finally get the set of elderly-oriented social application design elements in this paper. Then, this paper uses Kano Two-Dimensional questionnaire and importance questionnaire to determine the priority of these elements. The results of this paper will provide a theoretical reference for the design, evaluation and user experience research of elderly-oriented mobile applications.

5.3   Practical Implications

With the development of digital society, the use of ICT is becoming more and more important for the elderly. They use social media to achieve various purposes and pursue happiness. Therefore, how to design social media apps suitable for the elderly to solve their use barriers has become a problem. This study has some practical implications. For elderly-oriented social app developers, they can optimize the application system based on the findings of this paper, so as to improve the satisfaction of elderly users. For government managers, they can evaluate the existing elderly-oriented social apps based on the findings of this paper, so as to improve the ICT utilization rate of the elderly.

6   Limitations and Future Research

There are some limitations. The survey object of this paper is the elderly who have used WeChat care mode. Although WeChat is the most popular social application in China, there are many other social apps for the elderly. Future research will include a wider range of older social media users. Second, this study only investigates the elderly in the form of text, which may not be conducive to their understanding. In the future, the elderly can be investigated by combining text and graphics. Finally, this study aims at elderly-oriented social applications. In the future, researchers can study the elderly-oriented design of other types of products, such as financial technology applications, eHealth applications, etc.

References

1. Pruchno, R.: Technology and aging: an evolving partnership. Gerontologist **59**(1), 1–5 (2019)
2. Cota, T.T., Ishitani, L., Vieira Jr., N.: Mobile game design for the elderly: a study with focus on the motivation to play. Comput. Hum. Behav. **51**, 96–105 (2015)
3. Mannheim, I., Schwartz, E., Xi, W., et al.: Inclusion of older adults in the research and design of digital technology. Int. J. Environ. Res. Public Health **16**(19), e3718 (2019)
4. Plaza, I., Martín, L., Martin, S., et al.: Mobile applications in an aging society: status and trends. J. Syst. Softw. **84**(11), 1977–1988 (2011)
5. Nam, S., Han, S.H., Gilligan, M.: Internet use and preventive health behaviors among couples in later life: evidence from the health and retirement study. Gerontologist **59**(1), 69–77 (2019)
6. Li, Q., Luximon, Y.: Older adults' use of mobile device: usability challenges while navigating various interfaces. Behav. Inf. Technol. **39**(8), 837–861 (2020)
7. Petrovčič, A., Taipale, S., Rogelj, A., et al.: Design of mobile phones for older adults: an empirical analysis of design guidelines and checklists for feature phones and smartphones. Int. J. Hum.-Comput. Interact. **34**(3), 251–264 (2018)
8. Chou, W.H., Lai, Y.T., Liu, K.H.: User requirements of social media for the elderly: a case study in Taiwan. Behav. Inf. Technol. **32**(9), 920–937 (2013)
9. Holzinger, A., Searle, G., Nischelwitzer, A.: On some aspects of improving mobile applications for the elderly. In: Stephanidis, C. (ed.) UAHCI 2007. LNCS, vol. 4554, pp. 923–932. Springer, Heidelberg (2007). https://doi.org/10.1007/978-3-540-73279-2_103
10. Lepicard, G., Vigouroux, N.: Touch screen user interfaces for older subjects. In: Miesenberger, K., Klaus, J., Zagler, W., Karshmer, A. (eds.) ICCHP 2010. LNCS, vol. 6180, pp. 592–599. Springer, Heidelberg (2010). https://doi.org/10.1007/978-3-642-14100-3_88
11. Wildenbos, G.A., Jaspers, M.W.M., Schijven, M.P., et al.: Mobile health for older adult patients: using an aging barriers framework to classify usability problems. Int. J. Med. Inform. **124**, 68–77 (2019)
12. De Barros, A.C., Leitão, R., Ribeiro, J.: Design and evaluation of a mobile user interface for older adults: navigation, interaction and visual design recommendations. Procedia Comput. Sci. **27**, 369–378 (2014)
13. Tabak, M., De Vette, F., Van Dijk, H., et al.: A game-based physical activity coaching application for older adults: design approach and user experience in daily life. Games Health J. **9**(3), 215–226 (2020)
14. Kirkscey, R.: mHealth apps for older adults: a method for development and user experience design evaluation. J. Tech. Writ. Commun. **51**(2), 199–217 (2021)
15. Herzberg, F., Mausner, B., Snyderman, B.B.: The Motivation to Work. Wiley, New York (1959)
16. Kano, N., Seraku, N., Takahashi, F., et al.: Attractive quality and must-be quality. Hinshitsu (Qual. J. Jpn. Soc. Qual. Control) **14**, 39–48 (1984)
17. Huang, J.C.: Application of Kano model and IPA on improvement of service quality of mobile healthcare. Int. J. Mob. Commun. **16**(2), 227–246 (2018)
18. Matzler, K., Hinterhuber, H.H.: How to make product development projects more successful by integrating Kano's model of customer satisfaction into quality function deployment. Technovation **18**(1), 25–38 (1998)

19. Mao, J., Xie, L., Zhao, Q., et al.: Demand analysis of an intelligent medication administration system for older adults with chronic diseases based on the Kano model. Int. J. Nurs. Sci. **9**(1), 63–70 (2021)
20. Ho, H.H., Tzeng S.Y.: Using the Kano model to analyze the user interface needs of middle-aged and older adults in mobile reading. Comput. Hum. Behav. Rep. **3**, 100074 (2021)
21. Vyas, D., van der Veer, G.C.: APEC: a framework for designing experience. https://www.res earchgate.net/publication/251990033_APEC_A_Framework_for_Designing_Experience. Accessed 28 Dec 2021
22. Chen, J., Zhong, Y., Deng, S.: Empirical research of influencing factors of mobile social networking platform user experience. Inf. Stud. Theory Appl. **39**(1), 95–99 (2016)
23. Xu, Y., Li, Y., Zhu, L.: Design of the elderly smart phone APP user interface based on Kano model. Packag. Eng. **38**(16), 163–167 (2017)
24. King, W.R., He, J.: A meta-analysis of the technology acceptance model. Inf. Manage. **43**(6), 740–755 (2006)
25. Wang, W., Zhuang, X., Shao, P.: Exploring health information sharing behavior of Chinese elderly adults on WeChat. Healthcare **8**(3), e207 (2020)
26. Karlsen, C., Ludvigsen, M.S., Moe, C.E., et al.: Experiences of community-dwelling older adults with the use of telecare in home care services: a qualitative systematic review. JBI Evid. Synth. **15**(12), 2913–2980 (2017)

User Centred Method to Design a Platform to Design Augmentative and Alternative Communication Assistive Technologies

Frédéric Vella[1]([✉]), Flavien Clastres-Babou[1], Nadine Vigouroux[1], Philippe Truillet[1], Charline Calmels[2], Caroline Mercadier[2], Karine Gigaud[2], Margot Issanchou[2], Kristina Gourinovitch[2], and Anne Garaix[2]

[1] IRIT Laboratory, Paul Sabatier University, 118 Route de Narbonne, 31062 Toulouse Cedex 09, France
Frederic.Vella@irit.fr

[2] OPTEO Foundation, 82 Rte de Saint-Mayme, 12850 Onet-le-Château, France

Abstract. We describe a co-design approach to design the online WebSoKeyTo used to design AAC. This co-design was carried out between a team of therapists and a team of human-computer interaction researchers. Our approach begins with the use and evaluation of an existing SoKeyTo AAC design application. This step was essential in the awareness and definition of the needs by the therapists and in the understanding of the poor usability scores of SoKeyTo by the researchers. We then describe the various phases (focus group, brainstorming, prototyping) with the co-design choices retained. An evaluation of WebSoKeyTo is in progress.

Keywords: User centered design · Co-design · AAC · Multi-disabled person

1 Introduction

Assistive technologies for communication and home automation allow people with disabilities to be autonomous and better social participation. However, many of these assistive technologies are abandoned [1] because they do not sufficiently take into account the expression of the needs of these people. In order for these technologies to meet the needs, it is important to involve, in user-centred design approach, occupational therapists and psychologists who can complement or express the needs of people with disabilities as part of their ecosystem [2]. In the field of augmentative alternative communication (AAC), their expertise allows to evaluate the abilities of the disabled person to better select and adapt the AAC. Some AAC sometimes integrate customization functionalities such as the communication board generator [3] or the Yellow Customize application [4], which allows the creation of one's own communication notebook. Currently, occupational therapists and psychologists use these functionalities for adapting and personalizing AAC.

In the framework of a research collaboration between therapists and researchers in human-computer interaction where the AAC were designed by IRIT researchers with

© Springer Nature Switzerland AG 2022
V. G. Duffy et al. (Eds.): HCII 2022, LNCS 13521, pp. 559–571, 2022.
https://doi.org/10.1007/978-3-031-17902-0_40

the SoKeyTo platform [5], the therapists of the OPTEO Foundation expressed their need to possess this tool in order to design and adapt the AACs themselves for people with multiple disabilities.

In this paper, we will first present a state of the art on AAC design platforms and we will situate the SoKeyTo platform in relation to this state of the art. We will then describe the therapists' training approach as well as the tools and results of the therapists' evaluation of the SoKeyTo platform. These evaluation results led us to design the WebSoKeyTo platform. We will then describe the co-design approach implemented (brainstorming, low-fidelity mock-ups, focus-group) as well as the design choices that guided the design of the WebSoKeyTo platform in terms of functionalities for the design of AAC.

2   SoKeyTo Platform and Therapists' Needs

2.1   Description of the SoKeyTo Platform

Sauzin et al. [5] have developed SoKeyTo which is a platform for AAC and home automation control interfaces. With this platform it is possible to design any type of interface (pictogram-based communication interface [6], mathematical input editor [7] and environment control [8]). It includes psychophysical models (Fitts [9], Hick-Hyman [10, 11] and Card [12]) for people with motor impairments that provide indicators of whether the interface is suitable for these people profiles.

SoKeyTo was/is used by researchers in human-computer interaction for the design of augmentative and alternative communication interfaces [13]. A lot of back and forth between therapists and researchers were therefore necessary to design customized AAC. This platform is composed of two components: the editor component and the generation of an executable AAC with a configuration interface (type of interaction, feedback, scanning system parameters, etc.).

The editor component allows to define the morphology and the contents of the AAC buttons, the layout and the structure of the AAC, the visual and audio feedback and the type of associated functions (communication function, running an application, sending a message to be broadcast by a text-to-speech system). It also enables to associate to each button the communication protocol (MQTT: Message Queuing Telemetry Transport, [14], bus IVY [15], https, radio frequency, infrared) needed to interact with the connected objects or devices used by the disabled person.

The player component allows the customization of the AAC and the interface between several input interaction modes (pointing device, eye tracker, joystick, speech recognition, on/off switch). The platform also allows various control modes to be configured (pointing, time delay click, scanning system [16]) according to the abilities of disabled people.

Table 1 gives 4 examples of applications designed by the SoKeyTo platform by researchers in human-computer interaction. The functionalities of SoKeyTo show that it is possible to design several types of input applications, navigation keyboards or even environment control applications accessible to the elderly. Designed and used by researchers, the question is whether this platform is efficient, useful and usable by expert AAC therapists? The ergonomic study carried out on the Bastien and Scapin criteria

Table 1. Application designed with the SoKeyTo platform.

Type of applications	Example of applications
AAC [13]: example of communication page: white background Communication button, yellow background, navigation color	
Text input interface: two illustrations: on the left, an input keyboard designated by the person with a disability herself [17] and on the right, a mathematical input keyboard [7]	
Environment control interface [8]; this interface allows to control a home automation system (light, door, etc.). The SoKeyTo platform made it possible to take into account accessibility rules (maximisation of contrast: black background and white characters)	
Command interface of video games: virtual keyboard of video game controllers	

reveals some limitations: no und-o/redo function, little flexibility in the commands, no alternative commands, little feedback, no error handling.

3 Related Work on AAC Design Platforms

Many AAC systems exist on the market for people with multiple impairments whose communication needs may evolve according to their human environment and abilities.

The analysis of the functionalities of some AAC authoring applications (see Table 2) shows that most of them integrate editing and configuration functions to take into account these evolving needs of AAC. Table 2 lists the main features of these applications and comparatively the missing functionalities of SoKeyTo.

Table 2. Applications in competition with SoKeyTo.

Competing applications	Features	Functions not available in SoKeyTo
EDiTH [16]	Customisable AAC interface; button customization; interface model availability; column scan strategy	Access to the different interfaces through menus
Pictocom [18]	AAC Interface Editor; several interaction modes; integrated home automation extension; execution of software on a computer	Combination of several modes on one button (text, sound, image)
Boardmaker7 [19]	AAC Interface Editor; execution of software on a computer; predefined page templates; several interactions modes	Teaching oriented software; printing of AAC
AraBoard [20]	AAC Interface Editor and Player; customization; on line web application; promote Arasaac symbols [21]	Usable under Android; export of the AAC in pdf
Cboard [3]	AAC Interface Editor; on line web application	Usable under Android; history of pictographic communication in a digital tape; Printing of AAC; Multilingual
Jellow [4]	AAC Interface Editor; on line web application; customization	Extension to uses for the hearing impaired; Multilingual
Proloquo2Go [22]	AAC Interface Editor; predefined page templates; import of pictograms; customization, execution of software on a computer	Usable under Mac Os; creation of a customized synthetic speech; history of pictographic communication in a digital tape

All these platforms integrate an editor and a player. The editing features differ between the applications. Two of them offer the possibility to use page templates [19, 22] and two others offer the possibility to have a band for the communication history [3, 22]. Several platforms [5, 18, 19] allow interfacing with several control modes. The PictoCom platform [18] is the closest to the SoKeyTo platform because it includes the home automation and communication aspect in the AAC. A strong point is the ability of

SoKeyTo to configure several scanning strategies [13] and to allow to associate several communication protocols to a button. This allows a priori to control many connected objects or applications that a person with a disability could use to increase his autonomy. This comparative analysis allows to identify and discuss the interest of having these missing functionalities in the SoKeyTo.

The objective of the article is to describe the process implemented to evaluate the usefulness and usability of SoKeyTo and the co-design of the new Web-SoKeyTo platform.

4 Co-design of the WebSoKeyTo Platform Using a User-Centred Design Method

4.1 Therapists' Needs

The transition from SoKeyTo to WebSoKeyTo is the result of a request from therapists and characteristics analysis of the applications listed in Table 2. Indeed, the researchers designed the AAC based on the needs and specifications of the AAC provided by the therapists. However, this collaboration has shown its limits:

- The design of the AAC was time-consuming, with various back and forth between the two parties (researchers/therapists); these delays had negative consequences: the AAC was no longer suitable for the abilities of the multi-disabled person and/or the new needs were taken into account too late;
- The non-adaptation of AAC during the therapists' sessions: if the therapist wished to make adaptations during the appropriation or use sessions these were not possible.

These two reasons made the therapists wish to have autonomy in the design of AAC and thus to have an increased efficiency in its implementation. The ergonomic tests of Bastien and Scapin [17] and the needs of therapists for AAC tools led us to:

- Firstly, to carry out a user experience of SoKeyTo;
- Secondly, to implement a user-centred design method for the design of WebSoKeyTo accessible to therapists for the design of AAC adapted to the needs of people with disabilities.

4.2 Co-design Tools of the WebSoKeyTo Platform

Co-design uses a collaborative team approach that allows non-designers to become equal members of the design team. Sanders and Stappers [23] defined *"Co-design is a specific instance of co-creation practice that allows users to become part of the design team as 'experts of their experience"*. *"It represents a shift away from design as the task of individual experts towards using the collective creativity of a team with members from different backgrounds and interests"* [24]. We deployed this co-design approach in the design of the WebSoKeyTo platform which has involved two type of therapists (psychologist and occupational therapists) and researchers in human-computer interaction.

Table 3 shows the main stages of this process. In order to measure the contribution of the co-design of WebSoKeyTo, we first conducted an evaluation of the SoKeyTo platform which will constitute a baseline evaluation.

Table 3. Steps of the co-design of WebSoKeyTo.

Platform	Steps	Outcomes
SoKeyTo	Training and trials during two months	Experience in designing AAC
	User experience	UX Value (USE [26] and AttrakDiff [27] and verbatim of open questions
	Focus group	Therapists' needs
WebSoKeyTo	Brainstorming	Functional and ergonomic requirements
	Prototyping	Middle mock-ups and high fidelity prototype
	User experience	UX Value (USE and AttrakDiff)

4.3 Therapist Population

Six therapists (2 occupational therapists and 4 psychologists) were recruited to participate in the user centred approach to co-design WebSoKeyTo. Five therapists had never used another AAC design tool before and one occupational therapist is expert in the use of SoKeyTo.

4.4 Assessment of SoKeyTo

Training of SoKeyTo. Firsly, we trained the therapists to use the SoKeyTo platform by demonstrating all the features in a practical way They were invited to use the SoKeyTo platform for two months: firstly, a scenario imposed by the SoKeyTo platform designers for one month, and then a free scenario for the design of an AAC for a disabled person. These therapists could benefit from the help of the SoKeyTo designers in case of bugs or difficulties of use. At the end of this trial phase of the SoKeyTo platform, we proceeded to the evaluation of the usability of this platform by means of the USE (Usefulness, Satisfaction, and Ease of use) questionnaire [26], the AttrakDiff [27] and open questions (failures, most useful functionality, missing functionality and estimated usefulness). They reported the difficulties in ease of use, low satisfaction with the function mode and average learning and usefulness [28]. The therapists mentioned that the SoKeyTo platform were too computer-oriented and not needs-oriented enough.

User Experience. Figure 1 shows the results of the AttrakDiff questionnaire [27]. We have chosen not to average the results by type of therapist, given the very small sample size. However, we believe that the individual results are of interest to the platform's designers. Indeed, the AttrakDiff questionnaire quantifies both the pragmatic qualities (perceived usefulness and usability) and the hedonic qualities (subjective emotions felt) of a digital system. This measurement of hedonic qualities provides a significant added value when we want to understand how our users feel. The results show that for 4 therapists (two occupational therapists and two psychologists) the results are neutral for both axes $(-1, +1)$. One psychologist $[-0, 2, 4]$ characterizes the hedonic quality of the platform more positively. These results show that satisfaction is minimal and that improvements need to be made. The evaluation of the computer psychologist is in the superfluous zone $(-3, -1)$ for both axes. The use of the SoKeyTo platform has therefore generated dissatisfaction for this user. This evaluation shows that the usability and hedonic qualities must be improved.

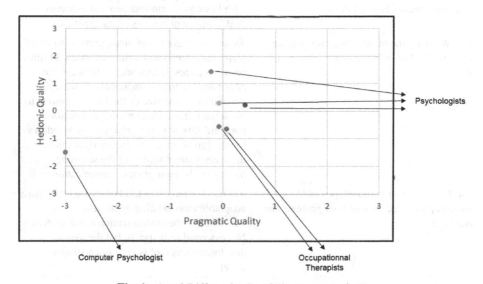

Fig. 1. AttrakDiff results (Portfolio representation).

We complemented this evaluation with 4 open questions in order to identify limitations that would explain the poor scores of the AttrakDiff scale and that could increase usefulness and usability. Table 4 lists the topics of these questions (identified limitations, most useful and missing features, perceived usefulness).

The end of the testing phase highlighted therapists' frustrations with the functional limitations and bugs of the SoKeyTo platform. These limitations were a hindrance to learning and using the platform. Indeed, for question Q2, three of the therapists did not answer because of the lack of use. Four of the six therapists report that the platform will help meet the needs of their patients in designing AAC. The other two therapists have negative opinions of the current state of the platform due to the bugs and functional limitations reported in questions Q1 and Q3 respectively.

The analyses of the SoKeyTo evaluation show the usefulness of such a tool but the need to design a more ergonomic AAC design platform that better meets the needs of therapists.

Table 4. Open questions to therapists.

Questions	Summary of therapists' answers
Q1: Have you encountered any problems in using the SoKeyTo platform? Which ones?	Bugs; lack of visual feedback; lack of un-do/redo; logic problems (management of pictograms and pages; bad logic for accessing the functions of creating and modifying an AAC button); no consideration of the screen resolution for the display of the AAC; complexity in the parameterization of the scanning technique
Q2: What are the existing functionalities used to design interfaces? List them	Link between pages; ability to associate actions with keys; platform-independent execution of AAC; choice of buttons characteristics
Q3: What are the missing features that are essential to design in the new platform? List them	Access to databases of pictograms or pages of pictograms (read and write); overview of links between pages; independence between the editor and runtime components of SoKeyTo; generation of the size of the keys according to the screen resolution; undo/redo function; compatibility with the principles of Windows for the functions accessible by right-click; more ergonomic setting of the scanning; history of the pictogram communication
Q4: Is this platform an indispensable tool for the complete execution of your professional activity?	Yes need to have this kind of tool, as it is more adaptable than existing applications Yes, to meet the customization needs of AACs Not essential as it stands, but the idea of developing this tool is very interesting and novel

Focus Group. A focus group between the six therapists and three researchers in human-computer interaction enabled us to define the priority needs of an AAC design platform. Therapists have taken an active role in making conceptual artifacts via function proposal card and and audio explanations based on their digital experience that express ideas hox they wish to use the WebSoKeyTo platform. These needs are mainly listed in Table 4 (answers Q1 and Q3).

4.5 WebSoKeyTo Design Process

Brainstorming. The people who participated in this brainstorming are 3 seniors and two students in human-machine interaction. One of the participants is the developer of the SoKeyTo application. The objective of this brainstorming was to think about proposing a more ergonomic, attractive and fun interface. The proposals focused on handling interaction techniques (management of zoom in page navigation, proposal for shortcuts and affording icons), visual and sound feedback to be associated with the buttons and the assistance mechanisms to be implemented. These proposals were used for the medium fidelity mock-up.

Medium Fidelity Mock-Ups. The mock-ups were developed based on the results of the design team's brainstorming and the needs expressed and discussed in the focus group by the therapists. We present three interface mock-ups (specification of an AAC button, page navigation, and specification of scanning strategies). The mock-ups were developed with AdobeXD or Balsamiq.

Specification Interface

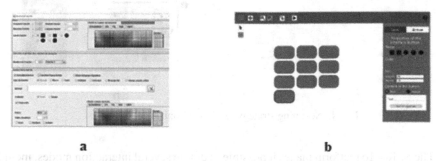

a   **b**

Fig. 2. Specification interface: a. SoKeyto; b. WebSoKeyTo.

In the SoKeyTo, the interface for specifying characteristics (morphological and associated actions) was superimposed on the key design grid (Fig. 2.a). An ergonomic study using the Bastien and Scapin criteria [25] confirmed that the presence of a side panel (Fig. 2.b) was more accessible and allowed feedback on the effects of key creation and modification actions. Work on structuring and naming items was also proposed (morphological characteristics, specification of actions associated with keys). Examples of actions were proposed and completed by the therapists (dependency link, access to applications such as music players, etc.). The therapists validated the mock-up.

Page Navigation

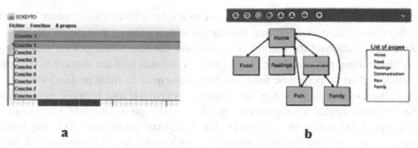

a   **b**

Fig. 3. Page navigation: a. SoKeyTo; b. WebSoKeyTo.

The way of handling pages with SoKeyTo posed a problem: access to pages in list form, no representation of links between pages (Fig. 3.a). The representation in the form of a graph (Fig. 3.b) was proposed to the therapists in order to visualize the dependency links between pages. This visual representation is associated with the list of pages. As the number of pages for a AAC can reach more than 50 pages [13], the question of representation and handling will have to be addressed by evaluating the techniques of Fisheye tree views and lenses for graph visualization [29] and of tree map [30] which consists of dividing the interface into several zones by giving more space to the focus.

Scanning Strategy

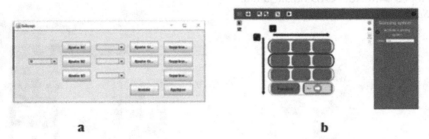

Fig. 4. Scanning strategy: a. SoKeyTo; b. WebSoKeyTo

The SoKeyTo platform makes it possible to define several interaction modes, including the scanning technique [16]. The configuration parameters are the scanning direction (row then column or column then row, the specification of the scanning block, the scanning speed, the associated visual feedbacks, etc.), the scanning speed, the scanning direction and the visual feedbacks. The SoKeyTo specification interface (Fig. 4.a) was found to be very difficult for therapists to understand for specifying scanning strategies via a list of buttons. The mock-up (Fig. 4.b) proposes visual elements to indicate scanning direction (horizontal and vertical arrow) and order (dice symbol 1 and 2). These more affording proposals have been validated to set the scanning order.

5   Discussion of the Co-design Approach

We implemented a co-design approach between a team of human-computer interaction researchers and a team of therapists. We started with a training session on the SoKeyTo platform, which allowed the therapists to discover the functionalities for designing an AAC. This training phase and the two months of use allowed the therapists to identify their needs and to propose new functionalities, essential in their professional activity. However, the evaluation of SoKeyTo's negative pragmatic and hedonic quality scores and the needs expressed highlighted the need: 1) to design a complete, ergonomic tool for designing AAC online and oriented to the therapists' profession; 2) to implement a co-design. Except for the SoKeyTo training, which took place face-to-face, all the co-design activities (1 focus group on needs, two brainstormings on low-fidelity mockups, 3 focus groups following the medium-fidelity models) took place by videoconference due to the sanitary conditions of the COVID. The collaborative work and video-conferencing tools allowed for numerous and fruitful exchanges during the focus group to identify the needs and those to present the mock-ups. Arbitration took place on divergent points of view by majority consensus. This approach will be continued for the functionalities (pictogram editor and access to the page and pictogram databases). Another extension is the creation of importable page templates and page categories between therapists to increase the speed of design of AAC. The WebSoKeyTo application is online and used by therapists to design AACs and a new user experience is planned to qualify the benefits of the redesign of SoKeyTo.

6 Conclusion

Firstly, we performed a state of the art on AAC design platforms and we situated the SoKeyTo platform in relation to this state of the art. Then, we describe a co-design approach to design the online WebSoKeyTo used to design AAC. This co-design was carried out between a team of therapists and a team of human-computer interaction researchers (HCI). Our approach begins with the use and evaluation of an existing SoKeyTo AAC design application. This step was essential in the awareness and definition of the needs by the therapists and in the understanding of the poor usability scores of SoKeyTo by the researchers. Numerous exchanges where both knowledge (AAC profession and HCI) took place during the numerous focus groups and brainstorming to identify the needs and validate the mockups. This co-design approach highlighted that the expression of needs and the solution evolved together as reported by Sanders and Stappers [23]. As a perspective, we plan to: 1) analyze the frequency of use of WebSoKeyTo functions by therapists; 2) measure the design and adjustment time of a AAC, 3) analyze the impact of WebSoKeyTo use on therapists' activities and relationships with caregivers; 4) propose the WebSoKeyTo interface according to the context of action in the next versions through adaptation algorithms that would be deduced from activity logs.

Acknowledgment. This work is partially funded by the ANS (Agence du Numérique en Santé, France) in the framework of Structures 3.0 program.

References

1. Sugawara, A.T., Ramos, V.D., Alfieri, F.M., Battistella, L.: Abandonment of assistive products: assessing abandonment level and factors that impact on it. Disabil. Rehabil. Assist. Technol. **13**(7), 716–723 (2018). https://doi.org/10.1080/17483107.2018.1425748
2. Guffroy, M., Vigouroux, N., Kolski, C., Vella, F., Teutsch, P.: From human-centered design to disabled user & ecosystem centered design in case of assistive interactive systems. Int. J. Sociotech. Knowl. Dev. **9**(4), 28–42 (2017)
3. https://www.cboard.io/fr
4. https://www.jellow.org
5. Sauzin, D., Vella, F., Vigouroux, N.: SoKeyTo: a tool to design universal accessible interfaces (regular paper). In: Ahram, T., Karwowski, W., Marek, T. (eds.) International Conference on Applied Human Factors and Ergonomics (AHFE 2014), Pologne, 19–23 July 2014, pp. 659–670. AHFE International (2014)

6. Vella, F., Sauzin, D., Truillet, Ph., Antoine Vial, A., Vigouroux, N.: Co-design of the medical assistive and transactional technologies system. In: Journées Recherche en Imagerie et Technologies pour la Santé (RITS 2015), Société Française de Génie Biologique et Médical (SFGBM), Dourdan, France, March 2015, pp.122–123 (2015)

7. Vella, F., et al.: Multidisciplinary experience feedback on the use of the HandiMathKey keyboard in a middle school. In: Miesenberger, K., Manduchi, R., Covarrubias Rodriguez, M., Peňáz, P. (eds.) ICCHP 2020. LNCS, vol. 12376, pp. 393–400. Springer, Cham (2020). https://doi.org/10.1007/978-3-030-58796-3_46

8. Bougeois, E., et al.: Post-test perceptions of digital tools by the elderly in an ambient environment. In: Chang, C.K., Chiari, L., Cao, Y., Jin, H., Mokhtari, M., Aloulou, H. (eds.) ICOST 2016. LNCS, vol. 9677, pp. 356–367. Springer, Cham (2016). https://doi.org/10.1007/978-3-319-39601-9_32

9. Fitts, P.M.: The information capacity of the human motor system in controlling the amplitude of the movement. J. Exp. Psychol. 47(1954), 381–391 (1954)

10. Hick, W.E.: On the rate of gain of information. Q. J. Exp. Psychol. 1952, 11–26 (1952)

11. Hyman, R.: Stimulus information as a determinant of reaction time. J. Exp. Psychol. 1953, 188–196 (1953)

12. Card, S.K., English, W.K., Burr, B.J.: Evaluation of mouse, rate-controlled isometric joystick, step keys, and text keys for text selection on a CRT. Ergonomics 21(1978), 601–613 (1978)

13. Calmels, C., Mercadier, C., Vella, F., Serpa, A., Truillet, P., Vigouroux, N.: The ecosystem's involvement in the appropriation phase of assistive technology: choice and adjustment of interaction techniques. In: Antona, M., Stephanidis, C. (eds.) HCII 2021. LNCS, vol. 12768, pp. 21–38. Springer, Cham (2021). https://doi.org/10.1007/978-3-030-78092-0_2

14. van den Bossche, A., et al.: Specifying an MQTT tree for a connected smart home. In: Mokhtari, M., Abdulrazak, B., Aloulou, H. (eds.) ICOST 2018. LNCS, vol. 10898, pp. 236–246. Springer, Cham (2018). https://doi.org/10.1007/978-3-319-94523-1_21

15. Chatty, S.: The Ivy software bus. White Paper (2003). www.tls.cena.fr/products/ivy/documentation/ivy.pdf

16. Ghedira, S., Pino, P., Bourhis, G.: Interaction between a disabled person and a scanning communication aid: towards an automatic adjustment of the scanning rate adapted to the user. In: Miesenberger, K., Klaus, J., Zagler, W., Karshmer, A. (eds.) ICCHP 2008. LNCS, vol. 5105, pp. 1204–1207. Springer, Heidelberg (2008). https://doi.org/10.1007/978-3-540-70540-6_181

17. Vella, F., Vigouroux, N.: Layout keyboard and motor fatigue: first experimental results. AMSE J. Assoc. Adv. Model. Simul. Tech. Enterp. (AMSE) 67, 22–31 (2007)

18. https://www.access-man.com/en/auditrgaa/

19. https://goboardmaker.com/

20. Baldassarri, S., Rubio, J.M., Azpiroz, M.G., Cerezo, E.: AraBoard: a multiplatform alternative and augmentative communication tool. Procedia Compu. Sci. 27, 197–206 (2014). https://doi.org/10.1016/j.procs.2014.02.023

21. https://arasaac.org/

22. Collette, D., Brix, A., Brennan, P., DeRoma, N., Muir, B.C.: Proloquo2Go enhances classroom performance in children with autism spectrum disorder. OTJR Occup. Particip. Health 39(3), 143–150 (2019)

23. Sanders, E.B., Stappers, P.J.: Co-creation and the new landscapes of design. CoDesign 4(1), 5–18 (2008). https://doi.org/10.1080/15710880701875068

24. Steen, M.: Co-design as a process of joint inquiry and imagination. Des. Issues 29(2), 16–28 (2013). https://doi.org/10.1162/DESI_a_00207

25. Bastien, C., Scapin, D.: Ergonomic criteria for the evaluation of human-computer interfaces. Report, INRIA (1993). https://hal.inria.fr/inria-00070012

26. Lund, A.M.: Measuring usability with the USE questionnaire. STC Usability SIG Newsl. **8**, 2 (2001)
27. Hassenzahl, M., Burmester, M., Koller, F.: AttrakDiff: a questionnaire to measure perceived hedonic and pragmatic quality. In: Szwillus, G., Ziegler, J. (eds.) Mensch & Computer, vol. 57, pp. 187–196. Springer, Heifelberg (2003). https://doi.org/10.1007/978-3-322-80058-9_19
28. Clastres-Babou, F., et al.: Participation of stakeholder in the design of a conception application of augmentative and alternative communication. In: Conference ICCHP-AAATE, Lecco, Italy (2022, to appear)
29. Tominski C., et al.: Fisheye tree views and lenses for graph visualization. In: Tenth International Conference on Information Visualisation (IV 2006), July 2006, pp. 17–24 (2006). https://doi.org/10.1109/IV.2006.54
30. Cockburn, A., Karlson, A., Bederson, B.B.: A review of overview+detail, zooming, and focus+context interfaces. ACM Comput. Surv. **41**(1), 2:1–2:31 (2009). https://doi.org/10.1145/1456650.1456652. ISSN: 0360-0300. Accessed 22 Feb 2022

Designing a More Inclusive Healthcare Robot: The Relationship Between Healthcare Robot Tasks and User Capability

Xi Wang[1] and Xiao Dou[2]($\boxtimes$)

[1] Dongguan City University, Dongguan, China
[2] College of Fine Arts, Guangdong Polytechnic Normal University, Guangzhou, China
michelledou007@outlook.com

Abstract. Most previous studies only distinguish users by their age and gender instead of their capability, which can lead to design bias since there are significant differences between users in the healthcare contexts. The aim of this study is to explore the relationship between healthcare robot's tasks and user capability. We have conducted a survey on users with different capabilities about their demands for healthcare robots' functions. The results of One way ANOVA indicated users with different ability impairments have diverse expectations for the functions of health care robots. Moreover, even able-bodied users would expect robots to provide sensory-aid functions. The results can provide insights of creating an inclusive robot that take users with different capability into consideration.

Keywords: Healthcare robot · User capability · Inclusive design · User acceptance · Human-robot interaction

1 Introduction

Social robots have developed rapidly in recent years and are increasingly used in people's daily lives [1–3]. As an important type of social robots, healthcare robots have received more attention because they can help the elderly and disabled people live independently for a longer time and provide them with not just physical but mental, emotional and psychosocial supports [4–6]. Designers of healthcare robot should consider robot tasks in related to user capability [1]. However, the relationship between the tasks of healthcare robot and user capability is unclear. Most previous studies only distinguish users by their age and gender instead of their capability [7, 8], which leads to design bias because there are significant differences between users in the healthcare contexts. For example, young people are normally considered able-bodied, which ignores the fact that some of them may have disabilities (e.g. young people with visual impairment). Clarkson et al. [9] proposed that the inclusive design cube that define user capability by three abilities, namely cognitive, sensory and mobile. Tenneti et al. [10] proposed a range of proxy measures of design-related capabilities. The predictor variables included self-report and performance measures across a variety of capabilities (vision, hearing, dexterity and cognitive function).

© Springer Nature Switzerland AG 2022
V. G. Duffy et al. (Eds.): HCII 2022, LNCS 13521, pp. 572–581, 2022.
https://doi.org/10.1007/978-3-031-17902-0_41

Although studies have proposed a binary relationship framework between product design and user capabilities [11, 12], designing healthcare robots can be more complex than normal products because the performance of robots are affected by both users and their tasks. The aim of this study is to explore the relationship between healthcare robot's tasks and user capability. We have proposed a Human-Robot-Tasks framework which emphasizes that user capability is the key factor to healthcare robots' task. To determine this quantitative relationship, we used questionnaires to collect different users' demands for robots tasks.

2 Literature Review

2.1 Healthcare Robots

Healthcare robotics is defined as a type of robots that aiming to promote and monitor users' health, and prevent further health decline [6]. It has seen a significant growth in recent years [6, 13]. They are expected to benefit a variety of people because they are designed to monitor and maintain users' health and wellbeing. It is reported that physical and cognitive decline can be the main reason that older people are unable to maintain independence and increase their life risks, such as falling down and forgetting to turn off the gas cooker [14]. Studies indicated that healthcare robots can promote active aging by assisting the elderly in health management and encourage them to participant in social life so that the cognitive and physical decline in the elderly can be delayed [15–17]. Moreover, healthcare robots can also assist people with disabilities or partial disabilities (e.g. pregnant women). Healthcare robot and rehabilitation robot are often compared. In fact, there are some overlaps between them based on whether robots are designed to assist or recover users' abilities. Healthcare robots tend to provide assistance to users with impaired abilities in daily life [18], while rehabilitation robots emphasis on helping users recover certain abilities through fixed exercises [19, 20]. Therefore, healthcare robots may be humanoid in design while rehabilitation robots are mostly mechanical in appearance [21]. For example, robotic exoskeleton for the lower limbs is mainly used to help people with lower limb injury, such as knee injury, to restore motor ability.

When there is a serious loss of human capacity, caregivers are usually needed to take care of them. Healthcare robots are promising applications in the context of future human shortage. Health care robots can solve the physiological and functional needs of the elderly, greatly reduce the cost of human resources, so that caregivers can focus on high-quality services. In addition to physical impairment, health care robots can also serve users with psychological, emotional and cognitive supports. Their functional value is not limited to physical assistive devices, but may also provide communication and companionship. According to the CASA paradigm, when computers or robots exhibit certain social cues, people tend to treat them as social entities and apply social norms to them. In previous studies on social robots, a widely accepted design logic is to design the functions and features of robots according to user needs [16, 22–24]. In order to give full play to the value of medical robots, they should be designed according to human needs.

2.2 Inclusive Design in Human-Robot Interaction

Most products, surface and interaction systems are designed for "standard man" because designers usually need to create a portrait of the user so that they can design effectively [25]. However, this may lead to an unfair condition for people with different physical, sensory or cognitive abilities. Particularly, in human-robot interaction, the mainstream user groups are targeted as young people who are usually able-bodied, while the elderly, disabled people and marginalized people have poor interactive experience since most of them are not familiar with robots, computers, even mobile phones. If the interaction design between human and robot cannot be more accessible to those people, technologies can make them more vulnerable.

Inclusive design is a user-centered concept and approach to ensure that products and services address the needs of the widest possible audience, regardless of their age or ability [26]. It is aiming to bridge the design gap between the disabled and able-bodied people. In a study conducted by Mayagoitia et al. [27], they proposed a user-centered design approach to evaluate a stair-climbing. This work emphasis users' emotional perceptions and social context of use as dominated factors. Langdon, Thimbleby [28] have reviewed several papers in terms of inclusive interaction. They claimed that inclusive design will be increasingly important, particularly in the countries with different demographics. Inclusive design relates the capabilities of the population to the design of products by better characterizing the user–product relationship [11, 12]. There are several approaches to evaluating the inclusion of a product or service, including user trial, expert appraisal, exclusion calculations, etc. The User Pyramid developed by Benktzon [29] provided insights of how capability level and design are related. To better match the diversity present within the population, Clarkson [30] have proposed Inclusive Design Cube which is an extension to User Pyamid. The Inclusive Design Cub have three dimensions (i.e. Motor, Sensory and Cognitive). It claims that user capability level are multi-faced and interacted [31]. An example is that some elderly may have mobility despite of the decline in visual and hearing abilities. Tenneti et al. [10] also claim that the understanding the range of user capability measurements can be crucial for design. They have also suggested that a national survey of design-relevant capabilities and creation of a capability database is essential because it enables designers to create more inclusive products for the citizens.

Based on those previous studies, we have proposed a Human-Robot-Tasks framework. It shows that user capability is the primary factor that influence robots' tasks and further affect the design of robots' characteristic. In this study, we have explored the relationship between user capability and healthcare robots' tasks to identify how they can be matched (Fig. 1).

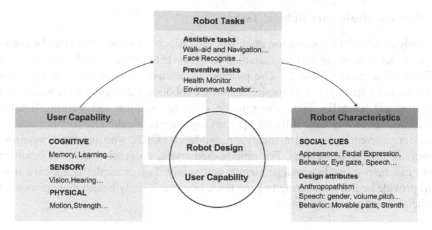

Fig. 1. Human-Robot-Tasks framework

3   Method

3.1   User Groups Based on Inclusive Cube

According to the Inclusive Cube's definition of user capability, we define users as four types of users according to what type of capability impairment they have (Table 1). Each types of user are classified by the capability self-test from Exclusion Calculator Lite v2.1 [9], which includes five items on *Vision, Hearing, Thinking, Dominated and Non-dominated hands* and *Mobility*. The questionnaire o capability self-test have a total of 14 items, and each items have 5 level(1 = very bad; 5 = very good). People who rated their own ability under level 3 will be regarded as having certain ability loss. For people who have *Dominated and Non-dominated hands and Mobile ability* loss are defined as Users with Mobile impairment (MIU). People who have *Vision and Hearing ability* loss are defined as Users with Sensory impairment (SIU). People with *Thinking ability* loss are defined as Users with Cognitive impairment (CIU). People who have little ability impairment are defined as able-bodied users (AU).

Table 1.   Four types of users

Types of users	Description	Example
Users with mobile impairment (MIU)	Having mobility problems or not being able to grab objects	Patients with hemiplegia/ People with leg injuries
Users with sensory impairment (SIU)	Having visual and hearing impairments	People who are color blind or with high myopia
Users with cognitive impairment (CIU)	Having memory and thinking impairments	People with amnesia/ People with Alzheimer's disease
Able-bodied users (AU)	Having no impairments	Healthy people

3.2 Types of Healthcare Robots' Tasks

In a study conducted by Robinson et al. [6], the tasks of healthy robots can be merged into 19 tasks, which are further classified into two categories, namely assistive tasks and preventive tasks (Table 2). The purpose of assitive tasks is to assist users who have losses of capacity. For example, healthcare robots are designed with walking and navigation aid for MIU. They also provide voice recognition and warning functions for SIU who probably have difficulty perceiving sounds. Healthcare robots could also provide cognitive training and medication reminders for CIUs, who may have impairment in memory and concentration. For able-bodied users, preventive tasks of healthcare robots can help users live independently and safely. For example, healthcare robots could provide health monitoring to keep track of a user's daily health management and thus help identify early symptoms.

Table 2. The tasks of healthcare robot

Types		Specific tasks
Assistive tasks	Mobile-aid	Walking and navigation aid
		Fetch and deliver objects
		Cleaning
		Record daily routines
	Sensory-aid	Face recognition
		Reporting unusual situations
		Voice recognition and warning
	Cognitive-aid	Medication reminder
		Cognitive training
		Reminders for daily activities
		Speech and medication
		Information service
Preventive tasks		Companionship
		Entertainment
		Health monitoring
		Fall detection
		Environment detection

3.3 Questionnaire and Measurement

The data of the study is mainly collected through questionnaire (Table 3). The questionnaire contains three sections. The first section is user demographic information which includes users genders and ages. The second section is user capability self-test, based on their self-evaluation on *Vision, Hearing, Thinking, Mobility and Dominated and non-dominated hands*. The third section is the users' demand survey. The 19 tasks are designed as 19 items (Table 2), and a 7-point Likert scale (with 7 being the highest and 1 being the lowest) was used to identify how much user would like the robot to perform this task.

Table 3. Questionnaire

	Questionnaire	Contents
Section 1	User demographic information	Users' gender and age
Section 2	User capability self-test	Vision (5 level) Hearing (5 level) Thinking(5 items) Concentration (5 level) Long-term memory (5 level) Literacy (5 level) Speech comprehension (5 level) Speaking (5 level) Mobility Walking (5 level) Star climbing (5 level) Standing and balancing (5 level) Dominated and Non-dominated hands (4 items * 2) Lifting strength (5 level) Dexterity (5 level) Reaching forward and up (5 level) Reaching down (5 level)
Section 3	Users' demand for healthcare robot's tasks	19 items (Table 2) 7-point Likert scale

3.4 Participants

A total of 49 participants filled out the questionnaire. After removing incomplete questionnaires, 41 valid questionnaires were received (19 men, 22 women; age range 45–88), and the results of the second section indicated that the four types of user capability conditions were covered in this survey.

4 Results and Discussion

4.1 Users' Demand for Healthcare Robots' Tasks

One-way Analysis of Variance (ANOVA) was used to analyze the four types users' demand for healthcare robots' tasks. The result indicates that users with different capability has a significant different demand for *Mobile-Aid tasks* [F (3, 164) = 45.93, p <

0.001], *Sensory-Aid tasks* [F (3, 164) = 24.52, p < 0.05], *Cognitive-Aid tasks* [F (3, 164) = 45.19, p < 0.001] and *Preventive tasks* [F (3, 164) = 8.93, p < 0.05] (Table 4 and Table 5). Specifically, users with mobile impairment (M = 4.84, SD = 0.57) has significant higher demand for robots' mobile-aid tasks. Able-bodied Users(M = 4.48,

Table 4. Results of one-way ANOVA

		Sum of squares	df	Mean square	F	Sig.
Assistive tasks	Mobile-aid	34.23	3	11.41	45.93	0.00
		MIU > CIU, SIU > SIU, AU				
	Sensory-aid	25.44	3	8.48	24.52	0.00
		AU CIU, SIU > MIU				
	Cognitive-aid	27.12	3	9.04	45.15	0.00
		CIU, AU > AU, SIU > MIU				
Preventive tasks		4.40	3	1.47	8.93	0.00
		CIU, MIU > SIU, AU				

Note: MIU = Users with mobile impairment; SIU = Users with sensory impairment; CIU = Users with cognitive impairment; AU = Able-bodied users

Table 5. Results of descriptive analysis

			N	Mean	SD
Assistive tasks	Mobile-aid	MIU	41	4.84	0.57
		SIU	41	3.80	0.51
		CIU	41	3.96	0.47
		AU	41	3.66	0.43
	Sensory-aid	MIU	41	3.50	0.60
		SIU	41	4.24	0.66
		CIU	41	4.45	0.50
		AU	41	4.48	0.58
	Cognitive-aid	MIU	41	3.47	0.43
		SIU	41	4.22	0.47
		CIU	41	4.54	0.49
		AU	41	4.36	0.39
Preventive tasks		MIU	41	4.47	0.35
		SIU	41	4.18	0.38
		CIU	41	4.52	0.41
		AU	41	4.15	0.46

SD = 0.58), Users with cognitive (M = 4.45, SD = 0.50) and sensory (M = 4.24 SD = 0.66) impairment have significantly higher demand for Sensory-Aid tasks. Users with cognitive(M = 4.54, SD = 0.49) impairment and users with no impairment (M = 4.36, SD = 0.39) have significantly significant higher demand for Sensory-Aid tasks. Users with cognitive(M = 4.52 SD = 0.41) and mobile (M = 4.47, SD = 0.46) impairment have significantly higher demand for preventive tasks.

The results of this study indicated that there is a certain relationship between healthcare robots' tasks and user capabilities. From users' perspective, the findings suggested that healthcare robotic is expected to provide diverse functions for users with different capabilities. For MIU, they certainly prefer the robots' mobile-aid functions, such as walking-aid and navigations. For AU, they seem to be paying more attention to the services provided by the healthcare robots than might be expected, especially the sensory-aid tasks. One possible reason is that most AU are people under 40 years old in this study. And sensory-aid tasks include facial recognition, environment detection, etc. These functions may be more interesting and attractive to AU than functions like walking-aid and medical reminder.

4.2 Limitation and Further Research

There are some limitations of the current study. Firstly, in this study, users are defined according to whether their ability is impaired. However, there can be more detailed classification of their ability impairment level. For example, nearsighted or presbyopia users may have visual impairment but wearing glasses does not actually affect their life. According to Inclusive Design Cube [31], future research can set three sampling points on each dimension, which will better establish the relationship between user capability and robots design. Secondly, this study mainly establishes the functional relationship between user capability and robots' tasks, but how this relationship can affect the design of healthcare robot haven't been discussed. Based on this research, future studies can further explore how to design robot's features according to user capabilities and tasks. In this way, the relationship between man and robot and robot tasks can be quantified.

5   Conclusion

The main contribution of this study is to identify the relationship between users with different capability and healthcare robots tasks. The results can provide insights of creating an inclusive robot that take users with different capability into consideration.

References

1. Dou, X., Wu, C.-F.: Are we ready for "Them" now? The relationship between human and humanoid robots. In: Rezaei, N. (ed.) Integrated Science, pp. 377–394. Springer, Cham (2021). https://doi.org/10.1007/978-3-030-65273-9_18
2. Ostrowski, A.K., DiPaola, D., Partridge, E., Park, H.W., Breazeal, C.: Older adults living with social robots: promoting social connectedness in long-term communities. IEEE Robot. Autom. Mag. 26(2), 59–70 (2019)

3. Dou, X., Wu, CF., Wang, X., Niu, J.: User expectations of social robots in different applications: an online user study. In: Stephanidis, C., Kurosu, M., Degen, H., Reinerman-Jones, L. (eds.) HCII 2020. LNCS, vol. 12424, pp. 64–72. Springer, Cham (2020). https://doi.org/10.1007/978-3-030-60117-1_5

4. Kommu, S.S.: Rehabilitation Robotics. BoD–Books on Demand (2007)

5. Looije, R., Neerincx, M.A., Cnossen, F.: Persuasive robotic assistant for health self-management of older adults: design and evaluation of social behaviors. Int. J. Hum. Comput. Stud. **68**, 386–397 (2010). https://doi.org/10.1016/j.ijhcs.2009.08.007

6. Robinson, H., MacDonald, B., Broadbent, E.: The Role of healthcare robots for older people at home: a review. Int. J. Soc. Robot. **6**(4), 575–591 (2014). https://doi.org/10.1007/s12369-014-0242-2

7. Martínez-Miranda, J., Pérez-Espinosa, H., Espinosa-Curiel, I., Avila-George, H., Rodríguez-Jacobo, J.: Age-based differences in preferences and affective reactions towards a robot's personality during interaction. Comput. Hum. Behav. (2018). https://doi.org/10.1016/j.chb.2018.02.039

8. Stanton, C.J., Stevens, C.J.: Don't stare at me: the impact of a humanoid robot's gaze upon trust during a cooperative human–robot visual task. Int. J. Soc. Robot. **9**(5), 745–753 (2017). https://doi.org/10.1007/s12369-017-0422-y

9. Clarkson, P.J., Waller, S., Cardoso, C.C.: Approaches to estimating user exclusion. Appl. Ergon. Hum. Factors Technol. Soc. **46**(B), 304–310 (2015)

10. Tenneti, R., Johnson, D., Goldenberg, L., Parker, R.A., Huppert, F.A.: Towards a capabilities database to inform inclusive design: experimental investigation of effective survey-based predictors of human-product interaction. Appl. Ergon. **43**(4), 713–726 (2012)

11. Persad, U., Langdon, P., Clarkson, P.J.: Inclusive design evaluation and the capability-demand relationship. In: Clarkson, J., Langdon, P., Robinson, P. (eds.) Designing Accessible Technology, pp. 177–188. Springer, London (2006). https://doi.org/10.1007/1-84628-365-5_18

12. Johnson, D., Clarkson, J., Huppert, F.: Capability measurement for inclusive design. J. Eng. Des. **21**(2–3), 275–288 (2010)

13. Heiden, S.M., Holden, R.J., Alder, C.A., Bodke, K., Boustani, M.: Human factors in mental healthcare: a work system analysis of a community-based program for older adults with depression and dementia. Appl. Ergon. (2017). https://doi.org/10.1016/j.apergo.2017.05.002

14. Pearce, A.J., et al.: Robotics to enable older adults to remain living at home. J. Aging Res. (2012)

15. Chang, R.C.S., Lu, H.P., Yang, P.: Stereotypes or golden rules? Exploring likable voice traits of social robots as active aging companions for tech-savvy baby boomers in Taiwan. Comput. Hum. Behav. **84**, 194–210 (2018). https://doi.org/10.1016/j.chb.2018.02.025

16. Tay, B., Jung, Y., Park, T.: When stereotypes meet robots: the double-edge sword of robot gender and personality in human-robot interaction. Comput. Hum. Behav. (2014). https://doi.org/10.1016/j.chb.2014.05.014

17. Broadbent, E., et al.: Robots with display screens: a robot with a more humanlike face display is perceived to have more mind and a better personality. PLoS ONE **8** (2013). https://doi.org/10.1371/journal.pone.0072589

18. Spenko, M., Yu, H., Dubowsky, S.: Robotic personal aids for mobility and monitoring for the elderly. IEEE Trans. Neural Syst. Rehabil. Eng. **14**(3), 344–351 (2006)

19. Lo, A.C., et al.: Robot-assisted therapy for long-term upper-limb impairment after stroke. N. Engl. J. Med. **362**(19), 1772–1783 (2010)

20. Argall, B.D.: Autonomy in rehabilitation robotics: an intersection. Annu. Rev. Control Robot. Auton. Syst. **1**, 441–463 (2018)

21. Riener, R., et al.: A view on VR-enhanced rehabilitation robotics. In: 2006 International Workshop on Virtual Rehabilitation, pp 149–154. IEEE (2006)

22. Dou, X., Wu, C.-F., Lin, K.-C., Gan, S., Tseng, T.-M.: Effects of different types of social robot voices on affective evaluations in different application fields. Int. J. Soc. Robot. **13**(4), 615–628 (2021)
23. Hwang, J., Park, T., Hwang, W.: The effects of overall robot shape on the emotions invoked in users and the perceived personalities of robot. Appl. Ergon. (2013). https://doi.org/10.1016/j.apergo.2012.10.010
24. Savela, N., Turja, T., Oksanen, A.: Social acceptance of robots in different occupational fields: a systematic literature review. Int. J. Soc. Robot. **10**(4), 493–502 (2017). https://doi.org/10.1007/s12369-017-0452-5
25. Abascal, J., Azevedo, L.: Fundamentals of inclusive HCI design. In: Stephanidis, C. (ed.) UAHCI 2007. LNCS, vol. 4554, pp. 3–9. Springer, Heidelberg (2007). https://doi.org/10.1007/978-3-540-73279-2_1
26. Clarkson, P.J., Coleman, R., Keates, S., Lebbon, C.: Inclusive design: design for the whole population (2013)
27. Mayagoitia, R.E., Kitchen, S., Harding, J., King, R., Turner-Smith, A.: User-centred approach to the design and evaluation of a stair-climbing aid. In: Clarkson, J., Langdon, P., Robinson, P. (eds.) Designing Accessible Technology, pp. 127–134. Springer, London (2006). https://doi.org/10.1007/1-84628-365-5_13
28. Langdon, P., Thimbleby, H.: Inclusion and Interaction: Designing Interaction for Inclusive Populations, vol. 22. Oxford University Press, Oxford (2010)
29. Benktzon, M.: Designing for our future selves: the Swedish experience. Appl. Ergon. **24**(1), 19–27 (1993)
30. Clarkson, P.J.: Countering Design Exclusion: An Introduction to Inclusive Design. Springer, London (2004). https://doi.org/10.1007/978-1-4471-0013-3
31. Clarkson, P.J., Coleman, R.: History of inclusive design in the UK. Appl. Ergon. **46**, 235–247 (2015)

An Evaluation of Elderly-Oriented Social Media Apps-From the Perspective of User Satisfaction and Technology Evaluation

Xiaoting Xu[1](✉) [iD] and Xinyue Li[2] [iD]

[1] Nanjing University of Posts and Telecommunications, Nanjing 210023, China
xtxu@njupt.edu.cn
[2] Nanjing University, Nanjing 210023, China

Abstract. In recent years, information technology has been developing rapidly, infiltrating into many aspects of people's life. However, most of the elderly may not enjoy the results of information and intelligence, directly affecting their health, consumption, travel and other daily life. Therefore, in reality, the transformation and construction of elderly-oriented social media is under way, but the status quo and progress is still unclear. Based on the situation, this study is mainly based on the 'The Evaluation System for Elderly-oriented Internet Application and Accessibility Level' and 'The Universal Design Criterion for Elderly-oriented Mobile Internet Application' issued by Ministry of Industry and Information Technology of the People's Republic of China, to evaluate the current three representative elderly-oriented social media versions (WeChat, QQ and Weibo) from two perspectives of user satisfaction and technology evaluation. We had three main findings: (1) The current construction of elderly-oriented social media apps is still a mere formality, and rigid response to standards and norms. (2) The construction of elderly-oriented social media apps lacks the perspective based on the elderly's needs, to carry on the humanization and individuation construction. (3) The existing evaluation system may not be able to take comprehensive evaluation of elderly-oriented social media apps, and which needs further improvement and perfection. This study enriches the relevant theory and provides the reference for guiding the practice development.

Keywords: Social media · Elderly-oriented social media · User satisfaction evaluation · Technology evaluation · Evaluation system

1 Introduction

In recent years, the Internet, big data, artificial intelligence and other information technologies have developed rapidly, which improved to great convenience of people's life. At the same time, with the rapid growth of the aging population, China has entered the aging society. According to the 7th National Census Bulletin issued by National Bureau of Statistics of the People's Republic of China in 2021, the number of people aged 60 and above has exceeded 264 million, accounting for 18.70% of the total population. Compared with 2020, the proportion of people aged 60 and above has increased by 5.44%

V. G. Duffy et al. (Eds.): HCII 2022, LNCS 13521, pp. 582–598, 2022.
https://doi.org/10.1007/978-3-031-17902-0_42

points [1]. Meanwhile, relevant agencies predict that the number of elderly people will exceed 400 million by 2035, accounting for more than 30% of the total population [2]. Therefore, how to help the elderly to enjoy the advantage and benefit brought by the digital era, make them have more sense of gain, happiness, security in the development of information technology, which has become a hot topic of common concern in the academic research and society [3].

Social media as a virtual platform, has broken through the time and space restrictions. It can help users to realize information acquire, communication, and sharing with friends, family members, colleagues and strangers anytime and anywhere, and has a large number of different types of user groups [4]. Relevant study found that using social media can enhance the sense of belonging, happiness and positive emotions of the elderly to a certain extent, thus relieving their loneliness, anxiety and inferiority [5–7]. Statistics show that the elderly users of social media are increasing year by year, but there are also many problems such as wrong operation, bad experience, privacy disclosure, property loss, etc. [8–10]. Based on this, the government attaches great importance to the construction of elderly-oriented social media, in order to effectively enhance experience of elderly users. In 2021, Ministry of Industry and Information Technology of the People's Republic of China issued a notice about the construction of elderly-oriented and accessible internet applications, especially attached two relevant annexes: 'The Evaluation System for Elderly-oriented Internet Application and Accessibility Level' and 'The Universal Design Code for Elderly-oriented Mobile Internet Application' [11]. Therefore, in reality, the construction of relevant elderly-oriented social media began to be paid attention to, resulting in various versions.

In order to effectively understand the current user experience and construction status of social media for aging version, this study taken the above evaluation system as the basis. We selected three representative social media (WeChat, QQ and Weibo) to evaluate their elderly-oriented version. The evaluation method is to carry out operation experiment by recruiting the elderly and use manual evaluation, respectively from the perspective of user satisfaction evaluation and technology evaluation. This study enriches the theoretical research on the evaluation of elderly-oriented social media Apps and guides the development of relevant practice.

2 Literature Review

2.1 Elderly

The criteria for defining elderly adults are different, we can distinguish elderly adults by age, health status, social status, etc. [12]. Among them, defining the elderly adults by age is a common method. The World Health Organization (WHO) has two standards for the classification of the age of the elderly adults. People over 65 years old are defined as the elderly in developed countries, while people over 60 years old are called the elderly in developing countries (especially in the Asia-Pacific region) [13]. At the same time, if a person's health status is closely associated with words such as white hair, wheelchair, age spots, etc., they are often referred to as the elderly. In addition, when a person has grandchildren and becomes a grandparent or has retired, his/her social identity changes and he/she starts to be labeled as an old man/woman [12].

The elderly adults have different physical and psychological performance compared with other groups. In terms of physiology, due to the increase of age, the elderly adults may show delayed action, loss of intelligence and memory, functional degeneration of body organs and so on. About psychology, due to retirement, mobility inconvenience and other reasons, most of the elderly adults appear to be divorced from their social environment. They can't continue to participate in the work, or even lack of contact with the external environment, resulting in loneliness, anxiety, spiritual emptiness and other psychological problems [14]. In addition, due to different education level, cognitive ability, the elderly adults also show an obvious gap with other groups in digital literacy, information literacy, computer literacy and other aspects.

2.2 Social Media

Social media realizes virtual information sharing and is a network platform for information exchange between users, the main form is various websites and apps [15]. In western countries, the representative social media include Facebook, Twitter and Instagram, among which the number of users of Facebook has exceeded 2.5 billion. In China, the representative social media are WeChat, QQ and Weibo, among which the number of users of WeChat also has exceeded 1 billion [16]. With the popularity of the internet, more and more users will use social media.

In social media, users can acquire information, communicate information, share information, etc., which promotes information dissemination and interpersonal communication. Some scholars believed that social media is increasingly being used as a source of information, particularly for health information, about 80% of internet users indicated that they had received health information from social media [17]. Raj et al. conducted research from the perspective of sellers and buyers, and found that social media can promote information exchange, thus improved customer satisfaction to a certain extent [18]. Babajide hold that the information credibility of websites is different, users of social media websites are more willing to share information compared with other websites [19]. However, McLaughlin et al. considered that although social media provided a place for individuals to obtain and share health information, if users shared information about unhealthy behaviors, social media might increase the harm [20]. To sum up, although social media shows certain advantages in information behavior, it should also pay attention to the control of information quality, information source and rumor information when using them.

2.3 The Impact of Social Media on Elderly Users

With the popularity of social media and an emphasis on the health of the elderly adults in reality, scholars are more concerned about the impact of social media use on the elderly adults. The effects included positive and negative results, which involved the health, life, psychology of the elderly adults. About the positive impacts, Parida et al. found that the elderly adults are increasingly using social media sites to obtain health-related information, which is helpful to guide individuals in health management [21]. He et al. selected 1399 elderly adults over 55 years old from 58 cities in China and found that using social media has a positive impact on the health life and social participation of the elderly [22]. Zhao et al. conducted an empirical analysis on 306 elderly people who migrated from rural areas to cities, and verified that using social media promoted the social integration and life satisfaction of the elderly [23]. Zaine et al. hold that social media improved the social connection of the elderly, deepened the existing relationship, and thus avoided social isolation [24]. In addition, scholars also found that social media use has a positive effect on the elderly's self-esteem, self-worth, loneliness and self-disclosure [5, 12].

About the negative impacts, Fitzgerald et al. found that direct social contact was limited during COVID-19, despite increasing social media use and it did not alleviate negative feelings, boredom or depression of elderly adults [25]. Sharifian and Zahodne conducted a empirical analysis, which showed that frequent social media use may aggravate the daily negative emotions of the elderly, thus lead to memory decline [26]. Elliot et al. believed that the improper social media use of the elderly would harm their health and lead to depression and loss of happiness [27]. Therefore, scholars advocate that when paying attention to the positive effects of social media use on the elderly adults, we should attach importance to correct guidance to avoid the adverse consequences caused by excessive and misuse of social media [28].

2.4 Elderly-Oriented Social Media Design

With the increasing number of elderly users of social media, in order to better help the information communication and exchange among the elderly, how to create and design friendly elderly-oriented social media is of great importance. Therefore, some scholars have carried out relevant research on interface design, user experience, evaluation system and other aspects of elderly-oriented social media application. Chang et al. conducted questionnaire survey and interview, and found that when designing elderly user interface of social media, interface design related to physics is easier to implement, but interface design related to cognition is relatively difficult [29]. Pandya and El-Glaly designed screen click way by assistive gestural interactions, the result turned out that Facebook with muti-step single taps TapTag offers a better user experience for elderly in the aspects of learnability, accessibility, and ease of use [30]. Hafez et al. selected Facebook, WhatsApp, Tumblr, Instagram and Twitter as research examples to evaluate their accessibility and usability, the result shows that the current social media applications are not friendly to the elderly users [8].

Therefore, it maybe there aren't enough elderly users or only produce little revenue, designing elderly-oriented social media seems to have been an underappreciated area. In reality, it seems difficult to find a social media that is highly satisfying to the elderly adults. However, with the growing number of elderly people, designing and perfecting social media to meet their physical and emotional needs will take a lot of effort [31].

3 Research Method

3.1 Evaluation Criterion

The evaluation of elderly-oriented social media in this study mainly refers to the Appendix 3 (The Evaluation System for Elderly-oriented Internet Application and

Accessibility Level) issued by Ministry of Industry and Information Technology of the People's Republic of China. This Appendix listed evaluation indexes of elderly-oriented social media App, which are mainly composed of user satisfaction evaluation (40%), technology evaluation (40%) and self-evaluation (20%). Among them, self-evaluation need enterprises and units involved in the transformation to carry out self-evaluation this work is difficult to carry out. Therefore, this study evaluates elderly-oriented social media App from two aspects: user satisfaction evaluation and technology evaluation. The specific evaluation system is shown in Fig. 1:

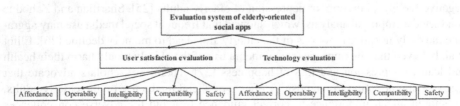

Fig. 1. Evaluation system of elderly-oriented social media App

3.2 Evaluation Process

For user satisfaction evaluation, we acquired the real user experience by recruiting 3 elderly people (P1: Male, 62 years old; P2: Male, 61 years old; P3: Female, 61 years old) to conduct scenario experiments. The recruitment conditions are those who are over 60 years old and can use a smartphone but before have not used the relevant elderly-oriented social media. Before the experiment, the researchers explained the purpose, procedure and precautions of the experiment to the elderly. In the experiment, we required the participants to complete 5 tasks (send a message, send a voice message, view others' moments and click like, change the profile photo, log out and log in again). During the execution of the task, we will arrange a researcher to assist the elderly without interfering, and allow the elderly to think aloud during the process. At the same time, this researcher also need to record screen and audio. Finally, when all the tasks are completed, we will interview the elderly on experience, difficulties and suggestions of elderly-oriented social media App about 20 min. In the experiment, participants used social media Apps installed on iPhone 6S Plus and we pre-established a virtual account for participants to use. All participants were required to use the elderly-oriented versions of WeChat, QQ and Weibo.

For technology evaluation, we will use manual method because there haven't found a good automatic evaluation tool yet. The evaluation standard mainly refers to the Appendix 2 (The Universal Design Code for Elderly-oriented Mobile Internet Application) issued by Ministry of Industry and Information Technology of the People's Republic of China. This appendix involved five design principles about affordance, operability, intelligibility, compatibility and safety, as well as specific criterion and indications. The entire evaluation process will be completed by one teacher and three graduate students.

4 Results

4.1 User Satisfaction Evaluation

After all the experiments were completed, we obtained 9 screen recordings, 9 voice recordings and 9 interview recordings. Through transcription, coding and analysis, we found that the elderly's real experience of elderly-oriented versions of WeChat, QQ and Weibo, which were expressed in four obvious aspects, as follows:

(1) Font and line spacing are larger but inconsistent, preferably the screen can be enlarged.

Through inductive analysis, we found that the most prominent experience of the three elderly people in the process of using elderly-oriented social media versions is that the font and line spacing are obviously larger, which makes the elderly more convenient to view information and operate. For example, a elderly person (P1) mentioned that he can see more clearly in this version compared to the WeChat used before, and even see words without presbyopic glasses. But, not all fonts are the consistent size. The other elderly person (P2) uses elderly-oriented QQ versions to send 'hello' voice which fails to be sent due to short voice time. At this moment, the screen appears an alert that 'message too short', we found by current interface that the fonts size in the red box of Fig. 2 is obviously smaller than other fonts size in the yellow box of Fig. 2. Therefore, this elderly person (P2) expressed that the different fonts size makes him always feel the screen is flashing and sometimes he can't see clearly. Finally, three elderly persons (P1, P2, P3) gave similar proposals, namely, a larger font may affect user experience in the process of using elderly-oriented social media versions. So it would be better for the elderly if social media had a function that the screen can enlarge the font by gestural operation.

Fig. 2. QQ interface of sending voice (Color figure online)

Fig. 3. WeChat interface of clicking like

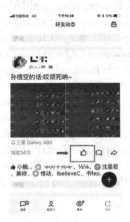

Fig. 4. QQ interface of clicking like

(2) Pictographic signs are convenient to operate, but cannot be used as a substitute for words.

Pictographic signs are convenient to guide users to identify specific functions for operation, which is another prominent experience of the elderly in the experiment process. As we know, due to the limited space on the screen, it is impossible to explain all functions with words and display them on the screen when designing social media. Therefore, the designers used pictographic signs to display functions, which promotes the screen more beautiful and simple, while makes the functions more visual and intuitive. Therefore, the elderly expressed that they could find corresponding functions through pictographic signs, to further help them better complete the operation tasks. For example, a elderly participant (P3) said that 'I didn't know how to send emojis before, but since my grandson told me that the pictographic sign of 'smile face' represents emojis, I can send various emojis freely, which is very good memory'. However, we found a common problem when three elderly people use QQ and Weibo to perform the task of clicking like, that is, although QQ and Weibo all have a pictographic sign of the thumbs at the bottom of user's moments, they did not complete relevant task. However, what is strange is that all three elderly people successfully completed the task of clicking like on WeChat. Therefore, we retrieved the screenshot during the specific operation, and found that the displaying way of clicking like in WeChat was the pictographic sign of 'love heart' with the word of 'zan' on the side (see Fig. 3), while QQ and Weibo only had 'thumbs' without corresponding words (see Fig. 4 and Fig. 5). The elderly people put forward that the some pictographic signs are sometimes not clear and incomprehensible, which also makes us think about the important role of words in the presentation of some functions.

Fig. 5. Weibo interface of clicking like

(3) The elderly-oriented versions may seem easy to use, but may also affect user experience.

The other outstanding experience of the elderly in the execution of tasks is that the imperfect elderly-oriented versions may affect user experience. Two of the outstanding performances are incomplete interface presentation and reduced functionality. The elderly participant (P2) mentioned that the enlarged font made some text barely visible and it is hard to see. As we know, the prominent characteristic of the elderly-oriented social media version is significantly larger font and line spacing, which seems to be convenient for the elderly to use. However, due to the limitation of screen display space, the larger font and line spacing will lead that some words overflows the screen or are only partially displayed. According to the elderly's hint, we found the ID account used in the elderly-oriented version of WeChat, and can see the displayed WeChat ID was obviously incomplete (see Fig. 6). In addition, the elderly person (P2) thought this was

Fig. 6. WeChat interface of ID

Fig. 7. WeChat interface of search

his first time to use Weibo, and he felt the functions were few and boring. Based on this experience, we compared the elderly-oriented version with the normal version, the results did find that the function of the elderly-oriented version becomes very simple. The same situation is also reflected in the elderly-oriented version of WeChat and QQ. We believe that the designers may consider the enlarged font and line spacing will affect function presentation when designing the elderly-oriented version, so they simplified the functions of elderly-oriented social media. However, according to the feedback from the elderly, this seems to have affected the user experience.

(4) The search function on the interface can best realize the navigation for corresponding operation needs, rather than just content search.

Finally, when the elderly performed the two tasks of changing the profile photo and logging in again after logging out, we found a more interesting result about search function in the interface (see Fig. 7). Perhaps because of the increasing difficulty of the task, one elderly participant (P1) asked the graduate student for help, while the other two elderly participants (P2, P3) tried to find an operable interface through the search function in the home page. From the screen recording, we found that the two elderly participants have been inputting the search words of 'change profile photo' and 'log in again' in the search box, but the result is only the content search of the chat frame, and there is no corresponding operation interface. Based on this phenomenon, we have a simple talk with and the elderly, and found that their understanding and demand for search function may be different from other groups. The elderly seem to want to get directly the operation interface by typing keywords into the search box, in this way, it's more helpful and convenient than asking them to find the function themselves.

4.2 Technology Evaluation

This study mainly refers to the Appendix 2 (The Universal Design Code for Elderly-oriented Mobile Internet Application) issued by Ministry of Industry and Information Technology of the People's Republic of China. And we evaluated three elderly-oriented social media versions by manual testing which mainly involving 5 principles, 13 criterion and 25 indications. The final evaluation results are shown in Table 1:

Table 1. Technology evaluation result.

Principle	Criterion	Indication	WeChat	QQ	Weibo
Affordance	Font adjustment	Use a sans serif font	√	√	√
		Font size can be adjusted	√	√	√
		The maximum font on the main screen should not be less than 30dp/pt, and the main information should not be less than 18dp/pt	√	√	√
		Balance mobile application scenarios and display effects	×	×	×
	Line spacing	Paragraph spacing should be at least 1.3 times	√	√	√
		Paragraph spacing is at least 1.3 times greater than line spacing	√	√	√

(*continued*)

Table 1. (*continued*)

Principle	Criterion	Indication	WeChat	QQ	Weibo
		Balance mobile application scenarios and display effects	×	×	×
	Contrast ratio	Contrast ratio is at least 4.5:1	√	√	√
	Color use	Text color is not the only means to distinguish visual elements such as conveying information, indicating actions and prompting responses. Instead, text or voice can be used to directly prompt users that they have entered something wrong, instead of using only color as a prompt	√	√	√
	Verification code	If non-text verification codes (such as jigsaw puzzle or image selection) are not easily understood by the elderly, a voice or text verification code that can be accepted by different types of senses (such as vision and hearing) must be provided	√	√	×
Operability	Component focus size	For major components, the size of the focus area should not be smaller than 48 × 48dp/pt. For other components, the size of the focus area should not be smaller than 44 × 44dp/pt	√	√	√
	Gestures	Feedback should be provided to users on the results of gesture navigation or operation	×	×	×
		Avoid complex gestures that require three or more fingers	√	√	√

(continued)

Table 1. (*continued*)

Principle	Criterion	Indication	WeChat	QQ	Weibo
	Sufficient operating time	Leave enough time for the user to complete the operation. The interface does not change before the user finishes the operation	×	×	√
	Floating window	If a new window is created (including but not limited to pop-ups), a button should be set that makes it easy for the user to close the window	×	×	×
		The close button can only be in the upper left, upper right and bottom of the center, and the minimum click response area should not be less than 44 × 44dp/pt	×	×	×
Intelligibility	Prompt mechanism	When users install mobile applications, they should provide prominent guidance for elderly-oriented settings and common functions of the elderly	×	×	×
		The home page of a mobile app that is embedded with an elderly-oriented version interface should have a prominent entrance to support switching to the elderly-oriented version, or a prominent switching prompt when entering the app for the first time, and a 'zhangbei version' entrance should be provided in 'setting'	×	×	–

(*continued*)

Table 1. (*continued*)

Principle	Criterion	Indication	WeChat	QQ	Weibo
		Mobile apps that have a search function should have 'zhangbei version' as the standard function name, which users can search directly for function, and set aliases such as 'qinqing version', 'guan'ai version' and 'guanhuai version' as search keywords	×	×	×
Compatibility	Assistive technology	Mobile applications should not prohibit or restrict the access and use of auxiliary devices (such as screen reading software) adapted by terminal manufacturers	√	√	√
		When assistive tools are turned on, all functional components in the mobile app work properly: Button can be accessed normally, input box can input normally, multimedia can play normally	√	√	√
		New functional components added to mobile app should also work properly after partial page updates	√	√	√
Safety	Restrictions on advertising plugins and inducement button	Ban advertising plugins	√	√	√
		Ban inducement button	×	×	×
	Ensure the security of elderly users' personal information	Do not process personal information irrelevant to the purpose of processing, in order to protect the personal information security of elderly users	√	√	√

Firstly, about the evaluation result of affordance, we found the font adjustment, linespacing, contrast ratio and color use of three elderly-oriented social media versions all meet the standard design specifications. Font and linespacing are bigger, and the contrast ratio is more obvious. Meanwhile, color is not taken as the only hint. However, there are some differences in the verification code. WeChat and QQ all comply with the design specification, that is, although there is a non-text verification code, the verification can pass in the countdown of 10 s as long as you change the verification mode. This mode is simpler and does not require any other operations. The verification code of Weibo is several numbers sent by mobile phone and the valid time is 60 s, which does not provide the voice or text verification method acceptable to the elderly. Therefore, it may not be friendly for the elderly to find the number from the text message and input it back to Weibo within a limited time.

Secondly, about the evaluation result of operability, we found the component focus sizes of three elderly-oriented social media versions all meet the standard design specifications, and the size of the clickable area meets the requirements. However, the design of the floating windows did not meet the requirements of the standard. Not all new windows appear to be easy to close with the close button in a specific location. In addition, gestures only met partial specifications, meaning that not all action results provide feedback, but avoided complex gestures that require three or more fingers. Finally, for sufficient operating time, WeChat and QQ do not pass the evaluation, while Weibo fits the norm.

Thirdly, about the evaluation result of intelligibility, the prompt mechanism did not meet the standard design specifications. Neither the installation nor the home page of the mobile app provides significant hints or entry for the elderly-oriented version, and in particular, does not include 'zhangbei version' as a standard name. Among them, the elderly-oriented version of WeChat is embedded, which can be found only through WeChat settings, and the corresponding name is 'guanhuai version'. QQ is also embedded, which can only be found in more modes through general use in QQ settings. It is less obvious and a little hidden, and the corresponding name is 'guanhuai model'. The elderly-oriented version of Weibo needs to be downloaded separately, and the corresponding name is 'Weibo dazi version'.

Fourthly, about the evaluation result of compatibility, we found the assistive technology of three elderly-oriented social media versions all meet the standard design specifications. It means that mobile applications should not prohibit or restrict the access and use of other auxiliary devices, and when the auxiliary tool is opened, it does not affect the use of the elderly-oriented version. At the same time, after the partial page is updated, the new function of the elderly-oriented version can be used normally.

Lastly, about the evaluation result of safety, three elderly-oriented social media versions can ensure the security of elderly users' personal information, which all the standard design specifications. Restrictions on advertising plugins and inducement button only partially fit the criteria, though three elderly-oriented social media versions have designs that prohibit advertising plugins. But it may be that the use of some pictographic signs may inductively click a few buttons.

5 Conclusion

The rapid development of internet, big data, artificial intelligence and other information technologies changed people's lifestyle and improved the effect of social governance and services. However, in recent years, with the rapid growth of the number of elderly people, most elderly people cannot enjoy the achievements of informatization and intelligence, which directly affects the daily life of the elderly, such as travel, medical treatment, and consumption. Therefore, the government attaches great importance to the elderly-oriented construction and transformation of applications closely related to the life of the elderly, in order to solve the 'digital divide' problem faced by the elderly, thereby ensuring the fulfillment and happiness of the elderly in their later years. This study is mainly based on the 'The Evaluation System for Elderly-oriented Internet Application and Accessibility Level' and 'The Universal Design Code for Elderly-oriented Mobile Internet Application' issued by Ministry of Industry and Information Technology of the People's Republic of China. And further evaluate three representative elderly-oriented social media (WeChat, QQ, Weibo) from user satisfaction and technology perspectives, so as to clarify the current status and progress of elderly-oriented construction of related social media applications.

Through the combination of scenario experiment and manual evaluation, we have preliminarily obtained the following conclusions:

(1) The construction of elderly-oriented social media is still a mere formality, rigid response to standards and norms. Whether it is from the elderly's real experience or the results of manual evaluation, it can be found that the construction of elderly-oriented social media App pays more attention to the affordance of the interface, mostly the transformation of fonts, line spacing, and contrast, and not enough attention to other design principles.

(2) The construction of elderly-oriented social media lacks an important perspective based on the elderly's needs, to carry on the humanization and individuation construction. Due to the differences in physical, psychological and technical literacy, the elderly have great differences in needs for social media compared with other groups [32]. In the construction of elderly-oriented social media, it is necessary to fully investigate the elderly's needs, and as the basis for construction. However, we found the satisfaction of the elderly is not high on the whole from the whole experience process. Some prominent issues are worthy of our reflection and attention.

(3) The existing evaluation system may not be able to conduct a comprehensive evaluation for related elderly-oriented social media applications, and required further improvement and perfection. The evaluation systems mainly use affordance, operability, intelligibility, compatibility, and safety as the standard principles. However, from the elderly user experience, we should consider some evaluation principle in future such as screen magnification, the combination of pictographic sign and word, the integrity of interface display and functions, and search navigation.

This study enriches the relevant research on elderly-oriented social media a certain extent, especially provides a theoretical basis for the construction and improvement of the evaluation system of elderly-oriented social medias in future. In addition, this study also shows more prominent practical significance. Through this study, we explores the elderly's satisfaction with the elderly-oriented social media version, and understands the current construction situation of the elderly-oriented social media, which has important significance to improve the elderly user satisfaction and guide the transformation of relevant elderly-oriented social media. However, there are some deficiencies. The recruited participants are limited, and who are relatively younger compared with other elderly people. In addition, individual differences are not considered in the evaluation of user satisfaction. Therefore, we should further consider expanding and enriching samples, and pay attention to individual differences, and finally conduct systematic and comprehensive evaluation.

References

1. National Bureau of Statistics of the People's Republic of China. http://www.stats.gov.cn/xxgk/sjfb/zxfb2020/202105/t20210511_1817200.html. Accessed 06 Jan 2022
2. China National Committee on Ageing. http://www.cncaprc.gov.cn/llxw/572.jhtml. Accessed 06 Jan 2022
3. Hardey, M., Loader, B.: The informatization of welfare: older people and the role of digital services. Br. J. Soc. Work. 39(4), 657–669 (2009)
4. Kaplan, A.M., Haenlein, M.: Users of the world, unite! The challenges and opportunities of Social Media. Bus. Horizons 53(1), 59–68 (2010)
5. Xu, X., Zhao, Y., Zhu, Q.: The effect of social media use on older adults' loneliness-the moderating role of self-disclosure. In: Gao, Q., Zhou, J. (eds.) HCII 2020. LNCS, vol. 12209, pp. 131–145. Springer, Cham (2020). https://doi.org/10.1007/978-3-030-50232-4_10
6. Cattan, M., White, M., Bond, J., et al.: Preventing social isolation and loneliness among older people: a systematic review of health promotion interventions. Ageing Soc. 25, 41–67 (2005)
7. Cohen, M.J., Perach, R.: Interventions for alleviating loneliness among older persons: a critical review. Am. J. Health Promot. 29(3), e109–e125 (2015)
8. Hafez, A., Wang, Y.Q., Arfaa, J.: An accessibility evaluation of social media through mobile device for elderly. In: Ahram, T., Falcão, C. (eds.) AHFE 2017. AISC, vol. 607, pp. 179–188. Springer, Cham (2018). https://doi.org/10.1007/978-3-319-60492-3_17
9. Chakraborty, R., Vishik, C., Rao, H.R.: Privacy preserving actions of older adults on social media: exploring the behavior of opting out of information sharing. Decis. Support Syst. 55(4), 948–956 (2013)
10. Meshi, D., Cotten, S.R., Bender, A.R.: Problematic social media use and perceived social isolation in older adults: a cross-sectional study. Gerontology 66(2), 160–168 (2020)
11. Ministry of Industry and Information Technology of the People's Republic of China. https://www.miit.gov.cn/jgsj/xgj/gzdt/art/2021/art_eddf498ded1b44829644bf20d28 c9f6f.html. Accessed 15 Jan 2022
12. Arfaa, J., Wang, Y.K.: An accessibility evaluation of social media websites for elder adults. In: Meiselwitz, G. (ed.) SCSM 2014. LNCS, vol. 8531, pp. 13–24. Springer, Cham (2014). https://doi.org/10.1007/978-3-319-07632-4_2
13. World Health Organization. http://www.jkyl.org.cn/index.php?a=show&c=index&catid=9& id=3628&m=content. Accessed 16 Jan 2022
14. Vally, Z., D'Souza, C.G.: Abstinence from social media use, subjective well-being, stress, and loneliness. Perspect. Psychiatr. Care 55(4), 752–759 (2019)
15. Kaplan, A.M., Haenlein, M.: Users of the world, unite! The challenges and opportunities of Social Media. Bus. Horiz. 53(1), 59–68 (2010)

16. Find Data. https://www.fxbaogao.com/dt?keywords=%E7%A4%BE%E4%BA%A4%E5%
    AA%92%E4%BD%93&order=2. Accessed 16 Jan 2022
17. David, W., Patric, R., Spence, B.V.D.H.: Social media as information source: recency of
    updates and credibility of information. J. Comput. Mediat. Commun. **19**(2), 171–183 (2014)
18. Raj, A., Rebecca, D., Michael, Y.H., et al.: Social media: influencing customer satisfaction
    in B2B sales. Ind. Mark. Manag. **53**, 172–180 (2016)
19. Babajide, O.: Information sharing on social media sites. Comput. Hum. Behav. **29**(6), 2622–
    2631 (2013)
20. McLaughlin, M., Park, M., Sun, Y.: Sharing information promoting unhealthy behavior
    through social media. In: International Conference on Computational Science and Computa-
    tional Intelligence, Las Vegas, NV, USA, pp. 800–803. Institute of Electrical and Electronics
    Engineers Inc. (2015)
21. Parida, V., Mostaghel, R., Oghazi, P.: Factors for elderly use of social media for health-related
    activities. Psychol. Mark. **33**(12), 1134–1141 (2016)
22. He, T., Huang, C.Q., Li, M., et al.: Social participation of the elderly in China: the roles
    of conventional media, digital access and social media engagement. Telematics Inform. **48**,
    101347 (2020)
23. Zhao, L.: The effects of mobile social media use on older migrants' social integration and life
    satisfaction: use types and self-esteem perspective. Soc. Sci. Comput. Rev. https://doi.org/10.
    1177/08944393211042545
24. Zaine, I., Frohlich, D.M., Rodrigues, K.R.D., et al.: Promoting social connection and deepen-
    ing relations among older adults: design and qualitative evaluation of media parcels. J. Med.
    Internet Res. **21**(10), 14112 (2019)
25. Fitzgerald, K., Yue, Z.Y., Wong, J.C.S., et al.: Entertainment and social media use during
    social distancing: examining trait differences in transportability and need for social assurance.
    Psychol. Pop. Media. https://doi.org/10.1037/ppm0000365
26. Sharifian, N., Zahodne, L.B.: Daily associations between social media use and memory
    failures: the mediating role of negative affect. J. Gen. Psychol. **48**(1), 67–83 (2021)
27. Elliot, A.J., Mooney, C.J., Douthit, K.Z., et al.: Predictors of older adults' technology use and
    its relationship to depressive symptoms and well-being. J. Gerontol. Ser. B Psychol. Sci. Soc.
    Sci. **69**, 667–677 (2014)
28. Chris, G., Martin, H., Paul, H.: Community and communication in the third age: the impact
    of internet and cell phone use on attachment to place in later life in England. J. Gerontol. Ser.
    B Psychol. Sci. Soc. Sci. **62**, 276–283 (2007)
29. Chang, J.J., Zahari, N.S.H.B., Chew, Y.H.: The design of social media mobile application
    interface for the elderly. In: IEEE Conference on Open Systems, Langkawi, Malaysia, pp. 104–
    108. Institute of Electrical and Electronics Engineers Inc. (2018)
30. Pandya, S., El-Glaly, Y.N.: TapTag: assistive gestural interactions in social media on touch-
    screens for older adults. In: 20th ACM International Conference on Multimodal Interaction,
    Boulder, CO, USA, pp. 244–252. Association for Computing Machinery (2018)
31. Chou, W.H., Lai, Y.T., Liu, K.H.: Decent digital social media for senior life: a practical
    design approach. In: 3rd IEEE International Conference on Computer Science and Information
    Technology, pp. 249–253. IEEE Computer Society (2010)
32. Hashi, I.: Case management promotion of social media for the elderly who live alone. Prof.
    Case Manag. **21**(2), 82–87 (2016)

Classifying Multigenerational Town Tours and Strolls for a Hyperdiverse Society: Case Studies in an Urban Educational District

Ken-ichiro Yabu[1], Takahiro Miura[1,2]([✉]), Tomoko Segawa[3], Yuki Murakami[3], and Tetsuya Nakahashi[3]

[1] Research Center for Advanced Science and Technology (RCAST), The University of Tokyo, Tokyo, Japan
[2] Human Augmentation Research Center (HARC), National Institute of Advanced Industrial Science and Technology (AIST), The University of Tokyo, c/o Kashiwa II Campus, 6-2-3 Kashiwanoha, Kashiwa, Chiba 277-0882, Japan
miura-t@aist.go.jp
[3] Hongo Ikinuki Kôbô, Hongo, Bunkyo-ku, Tokyo 113-0033, Japan

Abstract. Rapid improvements in real-world accessibility conditions have enabled greater mobility of people with disabilities as well as senior citizens. Such accessibility information is updated by local volunteers, which leads to further accessibility improvement and community revitalization through the activities of a wide variety of people. However, maintaining the continual activities of these volunteer groups is not always possible, and various regions have various efforts underway. By categorizing these efforts, it is possible to obtain knowledge that leads to effective and sustainable community assessments by local volunteers and to develop a support system for such assessments and collaboration measures. Therefore, this study aimed to categorize the needs and methods of various town tours and strolls (Machi-aruki in Japanese). Based on the holistic multiple case study framework, we first interviewed people who have practiced town tours and strolls in the urban educational district (Bunkyo, Tokyo, Japan). Next, we summarized the details and informatization needs of town tours and strolls. The results indicated that the town tours and strolls were generally conducted for the unified or combined purposes of investigation, sightseeing, and interaction. Also, the needs and expectations for the use of information systems for town tours and strolls can be summarized as three items: prior confirmation of the route, synchronization of information and interactions acquired from the onsite to the online environment, and support for recalling, structuring, and visualizing information related to the map.

Keywords: Interview survey · Town tours and strolls (Machi-aruki) · Informatization needs

© Springer Nature Switzerland AG 2022
V. G. Duffy et al. (Eds.): HCII 2022, LNCS 13521, pp. 599–607, 2022.
https://doi.org/10.1007/978-3-031-17902-0_43

1 Introduction

Mobile and wearable devices such as smartphones and smartwatches have become increasingly omnipresent not only among young people but also among older adults and people with disabilities. Because of their portability and comparable or better functionality relative to personal computers, many people can easily use the advanced functions regardless of location or time. Consequently, a worldwide activation of citizen-based scientific activities, named *Citizen Science*, has been created and distributed [13,15]. Nowadays, various large data collection projects in the fields of astronomy, ecology, cell biology, humanities, and climatology have been conducted via platforms on Zooniverse, and other platforms [2,16].

Various studies have conducted a series of activities that have incorporated the concept of citizen science into mobile applications for volunteers. These studies are to efficiently provide location access conditions for wheelchair users, older adults, and other people with disabilities [4,5,7–9]. Location accessibility information in urban areas and buildings is rapidly improving, which reduces mobility barriers for people with severe and mild physical disabilities. However, there remain places where access to such information is difficult due to nondisclosure or fragmentation of information. We have proposed and implemented an information system that allows many people to share and update the accessibility status of their locations [8,9]. Next, several community-based volunteer groups, including workshop facilitators and participants, used the smartphone-native version and web-based tool of the developed system for facilitating town stroll workshops. Consequently, the developed system facilitated the efficient collection of location accessibility information and enabled participants to organize location information and distribute location accessibility maps more easily.

However, the methodology of mobile-based town stroll workshops has not been established sufficiently in the context of education and other assessment activities. Most educational technologies are mainly used in the classroom, and insufficient knowledge is available on outdoor activities [1,14]. We have proposed a proof-of-concept framework that integrates the designs of events, learning schemes, and applications based on the participatory mapping, problem/project-based learning (PBL), and ADDIE model [18]. However, since there are more and more actual cases of town tours, it may be necessary to analyze and categorize these activities. For constructing a more practical framework that can be adapted to various town tours and strolls (Machi-aruki in Japanese), it is necessary to investigate and analyze the number of these actual cases.

In this paper, we attempt to categorize the methods of town tours and strolls, regardless of whether or not mobile devices have been used. First, we conducted an interview survey of facilitators who have planned and implemented town stroll workshops several times. Next, we attempted to categorize the types of such town tours and strolls and then discuss the informatization needs for the types of town tours and strolls.

2   Method

Based on the design framework of holistic multiple case study [3,19], we conducted a series of online interview surveys to six male expert facilitators who have experienced to design and conduct town tours and strolls over five years in an urban educational district (Bunkyo, Tokyo, Japan), illustrated in Tables 1.

Table 1. Overview of the facilitators of town tours and strolls that we interviewed. Date format is year/month/day. We conducted remote interviews.

No.	Date to interview	Overview of their specialty on town tours and strolls
P1	2021/11/24	An expert who are engaged in disaster prevention and community development activities in various regions
P2	2021/11/27	A researcher with experience in implementing barrier-free maps using mobile devices
P3	2021/12/04	A disaster prevention expert who mainly conducts community development
P4	2021/12/08	A university faculty with extensive experience in community planning related to community interaction and development
P5	2021/12/26	An independent scholar with rich experience in contents tourism (history) in the specific areas
P6	2022/01/23	A Self-employed professional with substantial experience in community development activities as well as mapping parties in the specific area

The reason for this research design is to extract remarkable efforts of the facilitators for designing town tours and strolls rather than those for participants. Moreover, the reason we interviewed them included the fact that some of their initiatives have received awards or have been featured as notable cases in newspapers or research articles.

We employed a semi-structured interview paradigm to survey these people about the methods, positioning, and precautions for town tours and strolls, as well as the use of information systems, if used. Furthermore, they were also asked about the kinds of information systems they would expect to use, regardless of whether or not they use such systems. Table 2 is the overview of the interview items. At least two of the authors were present during the interviews. The interviews were remotely conducted on Zoom platform and lasted approximately two to three hours.

The interview data were recorded using the recording function of a teleconference system (Zoom) and then transcribed individually. These text data were coded by one of the authors using MAXQDA (VERBI Software) to form categories.

At that time, we first added codes such as "designing, planning and managing town tours and strolls" and "ICT-based town tours and strolls" to the relevant part of interview texts and then classified them as findings after additionally coding their specific facilitation methods.

Table 2. Overview of the semi-structured interview items.

No.	Question
Q1	What are the contents of the town tours and strolls conducted so far?
Q2	What motivated you to conduct town tours and strolls?
Q3	Have you ever systematically learned how to do town tours and strolls and how to facilitate it (e.g., workshop methods)? If so, what kind of methods and content?
Q4	What are some of the most memorable experiences you have learned from your activities on town tours and strolls?
Q5	Do you intend or plan to conduct town tours and strolls in the future? If so, what kind of town tours and strolls do you plan to implement? If not, please tell us about your current and future plans for creating places to visit.
Q6	Do you have any ideas about what could possibly improve your current activities in terms of placemaking and town tours and strolls if such technologies were available?

3   Findings

This paper mainly describes the contents, participants, and facilitation methods of the town tours and strolls that we obtained during the interviews, as well as the strategies for informatization of these town tours and strolls. The parentheses at the end of each sentence indicate who stated the information in Table 1.

3.1   Contents, Participants, and Facilitation Methods of Town Tours and Strolls

From the results of interviews with the six facilitators, it was found that the town tours and strolls were generally conducted for the purposes of investigation, sightseeing, and interaction.

Some of the town tours and strolls that were conducted mainly for the purpose of investigation included disaster prevention tours for local residents and their children (P1–P4), and mapping parties using the OpenStreetMap for creating a map of the area itself (P6). Moreover, there were activities to collect local information for the creation of mutual support maps and accessibility maps mainly for frail older adults and wheelchair users, respectively (P1–P2). The purposes of these activities were to promote participants' understanding of people with specific social and physical disabilities and to create maps that would contribute to supporting their self-independence. On the other hand, some of the town tours and strolls with sightseeing as their main purpose introduced the historical background of a specific area (P5). As a method that has both sightseeing and investigation as its main objectives, town strolls and subsequent workshops were conducted to find out the attractiveness of a particular area (P1–P4). A more advanced activity was to make a movie based on the results of town tours and strolls and then upload it to the web (P4). Another example of a town tour and stroll to search for the attractiveness of a town is designed to promote interaction among local residents (P6). In this case, the a town tour and stroll itself was positioned as a means of interaction. There was an attempt to conduct both investigation and interaction by having university students walk through an unfamiliar area and interview local residents they have met (P4), which was positioned as an exercise in community building course.

The participants and facilitation methods were generally different for each of these town tours and strolls. The participants and facilitation methods were generally different for each of these town tours and strolls. Particularly, some of the town tours and strolls aimed for surveys were conducted with interested parties (P1–P2), while others sometimes assumed a minimum level of special knowledge of mappings (P6). The facilitation methods used in these town tours by P6 included measures such as assigning roles to facilitate mapping when the survey results themselves were important, and participants interacted with each other during feedback of the collected results after working silently on the mapping. On the other hand, those that provided learning to participants while obtaining survey results (town strolls for disaster prevention and accessibility mapping) did not require prerequisite special knowledge, but emphasized curiosity and interest (P2, P3). In terms of facilitation methods, the participants were encouraged to make discoveries based on the premise that there are no correct answers, and the facilitators adopted strategies that expected role-sharing to occur spontaneously through interactions among the participants. A good example of a scheme to encourage enjoyment includes a town tour for disaster prevention and crime prevention targeting children by P4. In this case, the adult facilitating the tour intentionally and comically fell down first at a fall-prone place and said to children, "You have to record this point," thereby encouraging discovery in an enjoyable manner.

For the sightseeing and exchange-oriented town tours and strolls, there were no restrictions on the number and the characteristics of the participants. However, some participants, especially in the sightseeing-oriented type, had already learned about the area beforehand, thus the facilitator was required to be flexible in presenting the contents according to the participants' knowledge level (P5). Also, the above-mentioned scheme to encourage enjoyment was mentioned: the facilitator sang a song related to the location shamelessly and took other actions that would leave a lasting impression on the participants (P5). In the interaction-oriented strolls, there was little mention of any facilitation method that should be noted. This fact may be because the town tour for the purpose of interaction was planned as a part of local events such as dinner parties, drinking parties, and local festivals, and was positioned as a means of facilitation for community building.

3.2 Needs for the Use of Information Systems on Town Tours and Strolls

The needs and expectations for the use of information systems for town tours and strolls can be summarized as follows: prior confirmation of the route, synchronization of information and interactions acquired from the onsite to the online environment, and support for recalling, structuring, and visualizing information related to the map.

The advanced check of the route of town tours was especially requested by those who were planning tours for sightseeing purposes (P5), as he wanted to use it when deciding on a meeting place and a rest area. The reason for this opinion was that he had noticed changes in buildings and road conditions when he and participants had actually visited the area and had reflected on the changes. However, the key to achieving this feature is how to regularly reflect the conditions of such potential locations on the web. It is desirable to have at least a record of the date of registration.

Next, the synchronization of information/interactions acquired onsite to the web can be further divided into two main types of information: workshop-related information and map-related information. The former is the information conversion of sticky notes pasted on walls and paper-based maps (P4). The sticky notes on the large sheets of paper were from a workshop that used the KJ method (affinity diagram) [6, 12], and he wanted to use them to review past discussions. He would like to accumulate the information on the sticky notes on a paper-based map in a database so that he can systematically track the changes in the area from the past. Other comments were also received that if children who cannot read a map could use a smartphone to conduct town tours and strolls, it would be easier to conduct the tours and strolls for their learning because they would have photo data linked to GPS data (P2, P4).

Regarding support for recalling, structuring, and visualizing maps and related information, the facilitators reported on content enrichment as well as measures to enhance the accessibility of collected information. In the former, in addition to the smooth presentation of old photographs of existed historically valuable buildings and historic sites that no longer exist, the presentation of virtual reality (VR) models of past situations was requested in some cases (P5). Nakano et al. reported an example of mobile implementation of a virtual time machine that uses VR and augmented reality (AR) technology to present past situations [10, 11, 17]. Based on these technologies and practical examples, it could be easier to conduct town tours as well as workshops to look back on history in various regions. On the other hand, the latter reported a need for support for recalling the context of community development based on the information of tags attached to the information (P6), in addition to the efficiency of recalling information recorded by themselves and others in association with maps (P5). As for the efficiency of information recall, facilitators who conduct town tours for sightseeing purposes would like to use the system for their own pre-study and for presenting information to the participants on the specific spot. Meanwhile, as for the support for contextual recall, other facilitator (P6) suggested that the visualization of the situations that are not recorded directly speculated based on the registered map information including recorded tags and datetime, and registered persons, would help stimulate discussions at a later date. However, in order to improve the availability of the collected information, it is necessary to organize and retrieve the information, as well as to visualize the information to access the required information.

While the above needs and expectations for using information equipment were mentioned, one of the facilitators expressed his fears about becoming accustomed to information technology (P1). This facilitator stated that while we could use information systems very conveniently, it could be difficult to imagine how to facilitate participants of town tours and strolls who are not good with information systems because of over-reliance on them. This is an important point of view for the informatization of town tours and strolls, and suggests that informatization measures are required to encourage participation regardless of the information literacy and skills of the participants.

4   Conclusion and Future Work

By interview surveys based on the holistic multiple case study framework, we collected the activities of town tours and strolls that took place in an urban educational district (Bunkyo, Tokyo, Japan). Then, we summarized the details and needs and informatization needs of town tours and strolls. Our achievements are as follows:

- Town tours and strolls were generally conducted for the unified or combined purposes of investigation, sightseeing, and interaction. Depending on the purposes, different participants are required and facilitators employ different facilitation strategies. Particularly, town tours and strolls for investigation required the participants who have curiosity and interest, while others sometimes assumed a minimum level of special knowledge of mappings.
- The needs and expectations for the use of information systems for town tours and strolls can be summarized as three items: prior confirmation of the route, synchronization of information and interactions acquired from the onsite to the online environment, and support for recalling, structuring, and visualizing information related to the map.

Our future work is as follows:

- Additional interviews and further analysis of the data obtained in this study
- Refining our framework that simultaneously design the mapping events and support application based on the interview data

Acknowledgment. This work was supported by the SECOM Science and Technology Foundation and JSPS KAKENHI Grant Numbers JP21H00915 and JP21H04580. We would also like to thank all those who cooperated in the interview and grateful to Dr. Ryoichi Nitanai for his great help.

References

1. Benavides, F., Dumont, H., Istance, D.: Nature of learning: using research to inspire practice. OECD (2010)
2. Bonney, R., et al.: Next steps for citizen science. Science **343**(6178), 1436–1437 (2014)
3. Creswell, J.W., Poth, C.N.: Qualitative Inquiry and Research Design: Choosing Among Five Approaches. Sage Publications, Thousand Oaks (2016)
4. Goncalves, J., Kostakos, V., Hosio, S., Karapanos, E., Lyra, O.: IncluCity: using contextual cues to raise awareness on environmental accessibility. In: Proceedings of the 15th International ACM SIGACCESS Conference on Computers and Accessibility, ASSETS 2013, pp. 17:1–17:8. ACM, New York (2013). http://doi.acm.org/10.1145/2513383.2517030
5. Holone, H., Misund, G.: People helping computers helping people: navigation for people with mobility problems by sharing accessibility annotations. In: Miesenberger, K., Klaus, J., Zagler, W., Karshmer, A. (eds.) ICCHP 2008. LNCS, vol. 5105, pp. 1093–1100. Springer, Heidelberg (2008). https://doi.org/10.1007/978-3-540-70540-6_164
6. Kawakita, J.: The KJ method-a scientific approach to problem solving. Kawakita Res. Inst. **2** (1975)
7. Miura, T., et al.: Barrier-free walk: a social sharing platform of barrier-free information for sensory/physically-impaired and aged people. In: Proceedings of IEEE International Conference on Systems, Man, and Cybernetics, pp. 2921–2926 (2012)
8. Miura, T., et al.: Sharing real-world accessibility conditions using a smartphone application by a volunteer group. In: Miesenberger, K., Bühler, C., Penaz, P. (eds.) ICCHP 2016. LNCS, vol. 9759, pp. 265–272. Springer, Cham (2016). https://doi.org/10.1007/978-3-319-41267-2_36
9. Miura, T., Yabu, K.I., Ogino, R., Hiyama, A., Hirose, M., Ifukube, T.: Collaborative accessibility assessments by senior citizens using smartphone application ReAcTS (real-world accessibility transaction system). In: Proceedings of the Internet of Accessible Things on - W4A 2018 (2018). https://doi.org/10.1145/3192714.3192826
10. Nakano, J., Narumi, T., Tanikawa, T., Hirose, M.: Implementation of on-site virtual time machine for mobile devices. In: 2015 IEEE Virtual Reality (VR), pp. 245–246. IEEE (2015)
11. Nakano, J., Osawa, S., Narumi, T., Tanikawa, T., Hirose, M.: Designing a walking tour utilizing on-site virtual time machine. Trans. Virtual Reality Soc. Japan **22**(2), 241–250 (2017)
12. Plain, C.: Build an affinity for KJ method. Qual. Prog. **40**(3), 88 (2007)
13. Preece, J.: Citizen science: new research challenges for human-computer interaction. Int. J. Hum.-Comput. Interact. **32**(8), 585–612 (2016)
14. Sawyer, R.K.: The Cambridge Handbook of the Learning Sciences. Cambridge University Press, Cambridge (2005)
15. Silvertown, J.: A new dawn for citizen science. Trends Ecol. Evol. **24**(9), 467–471 (2009)
16. Simpson, R., Page, K.R., De Roure, D.: Zooniverse: observing the world's largest citizen science platform. In: Proceedings of the 23rd International Conference on World Wide Web, pp. 1049–1054 (2014)

17. Tanikawa, T., Nakano, J., Narumi, T., Hirose, M.: Case study of AR field museum for activating local communities. In: Streitz, N., Konomi, S. (eds.) DAPI 2018. LNCS, vol. 10921, pp. 428–438. Springer, Cham (2018). https://doi.org/10.1007/978-3-319-91125-0_34
18. Yabu, K., Miura, T., Segawa, T., Murakami, Y., Nakahashi, T.: Designing local assessment workshops and web-mobile applications for facilitating the workshop. In: Gao, Q., Zhou, J. (eds.) HCII 2021. LNCS, vol. 12786, pp. 114–125. Springer, Cham (2021). https://doi.org/10.1007/978-3-030-78108-8_9
19. Yin, R.K.: Case Study Research: Design and Methods, vol. 5. Sage, Thousand Oaks (2009)

Beyond Age Stereotype: Improving Elderly-Oriented User Experience of Social Media by Value Sensitive Design

Mengqing Yang(✉) and Xintong Bai

School of Journalism and Communication, Nanjing Normal University, Nanjing, China
mqyang@nnu.edu.cn

Abstract. With the increasing use of social media by older adults, age stereotypes have become a problem that cannot be ignored. A lot of studies have shown that age stereotypes have a negative impact on the Internet engagement and performance of the older adults. In order to promote the older adults engage into modern digital life, elderly-oriented social media reform has become an effective means. Value sensitive design is a theoretically grounded approach to the design of technology that accounts for human values in a principled and comprehensive manner throughout the design process. In this study, we try to build an elderly-oriented social media design framework based on value sensitive design. We try to find the exclusive values that the older adults really care about beyond the age stereotype. We hope that this research can provide designers with an idea, that is, breaking the age stereotype and integrating elderly-oriented design into every stage of social media design.

Keywords: Older adults · Age stereotype · Social media · Value sensitive design

1 Introduction

The elderly Internet users in China is not only large-scale, but also the fastest growing group of overall Internet users. By June 2021, the number of Internet users over 60 years old in China accounted for 12.2% of the total number of Internet users (1.011 billion), more than 120 million; Internet users aged 50 and above accounted for 28.0%, an increase of 5.2 percentage points over June 2020 [3]. As one of the most widely used Internet applications, social media has become an important tool for older adults to maintain communication with their families and friends, obtain information and maintain personal social interaction and engagement. With the increasing use of social media by older adults, age stereotypes have become a problem that cannot be ignored. Age stereotypes are characteristics, generalizations or assumptions about how individuals at a particular age are viewed and should behave [25]. For example, in the social media environment, older adults are often defined as lonely, in need of care and with a very aging image. Age stereotypes not only affect other people's cognition of a specific age group, but also affect the self-cognition of a certain age group. A lot of studies have shown that age

© Springer Nature Switzerland AG 2022
V. G. Duffy et al. (Eds.): HCII 2022, LNCS 13521, pp. 608–616, 2022.
https://doi.org/10.1007/978-3-031-17902-0_44

stereotypes have a negative impact on the Internet engagement and performance of older adults [13]. Stereotype threat theory [26] proposes that individuals will underperform or disengage when they feel it will further aggravate other people's negative evaluation of their abilities. With the increasing aging of society, guiding and supporting older adults to actively participate in digital life is an effective way to eliminate a series of problems caused by aging. Therefore, finding the obstacles caused by age stereotypes in the use of social media of the elderly and trying to find solutions are the necessary means for the current society to cope with the aging.

Since 2020, in order to effectively solve the problem of Internet aging, the Chinese government has taken a variety of measures to fully promote relevant work and made remarkable progress. In April 2021, the Ministry of Industry and Information Technology (MIIT) issued the general design specification of websites and mobile Internet applications (APP) for the older adults. These rules have specific requirements in terms of service and technical principles, creating convenient conditions for elderly Internet users to better engage into Internet life and share the benefits brought by the Internet. Many smart phone applications have completed the elderly-oriented reform, and the "elderly mode" with larger font, simpler interface and more convenient operation has been added to the platform. The efforts of the Chinese government have high practical significance and humanistic value. However, we must also admit that most of the current Internet applications are designed for young users, and there is a lack of investigation on the use of elderly users. Even if relevant surveys are conducted, the respondents are often the elderly who are familiar with digital products, and pay less attention to the elderly with poor information literacy. More designers start from their own understanding to design social media 'suitable' for the older adults. The older adults seem to be framed in a certain age stereotype to act as others expect. For example, they are often identified as lacking expressiveness and unable to keep up with the trend, and therefore need special help. However, their real needs and obstacles cannot be understood by the designers.

With the rapid development of modern technology, technical design focuses on the pursuit of efficiency and speed. Although this has brought convenience to people, it often ignores people's requirements for the most fundamental value and meaning of life, causing people to fall into unprecedented spiritual depression and ethical dilemma. The older adults with weak information literacy and technology acceptance bear the brunt. Therefore, designers and technology practitioners should focus on the elderly-oriented information application and service design. Value sensitive design (VSD) advocates putting the technology design process into the social ethics context, and advocates that the stakeholders of technology design consciously take ethics factors into account in the innovative technology design. It especially emphasizes the moral consciousness and ethical responsibility of designers and researchers. This requires technology designers to be aware that their potential or generated decisions or behaviors may affect the interests, happiness and expectations of other stakeholders. Value sensitive design is a formative framework that provides a shaping influence on practice and supports theory and method development [10]. It aims to account for human values throughout the design process by integrating conceptual, empirical, and technical investigations [8]. In view of the difficulty of using social media caused by the age stereotype of the older adults, value sensitive design can provide designers with a more meaningful idea.

In this study, we try to build an elderly-oriented social media design framework based on value sensitive design. We try to find the exclusive values that the older adults really care about beyond the age stereotype which is ubiquitous. Although this is a theoretical discussion, we hope that this research can provide designers with an idea, that is, breaking the age stereotype and integrating elderly-oriented design into every stage of design from the perspective of the older adults, so as to provide real convenience for the older adults to engage into digital life.

2   Literature Review

2.1   Social Media Use of Older Adults

Social participation or maintaining positive social relationships is widely regarded as one of the key elements of health aging [9, 17]. Strong social networks may enhance the quality of life of older adults improving their health, reducing their risks of cognitive decline. In addition, older adults tend to concentrate their social ties upon family interactions [5]. Nef et al. [23] argue that the main benefit of using social media for older adults is to enter in an intergenerational communication with younger family members (children and grandchildren). Therefor social media that helps older adults to connect with family members and other active social networking users is beneficial for them to enhance intergenerational communication and to promote social participation [23].

With an increasing number of older adults using the Internet, social media use among older adults is continuously spreading. In previous studies, researchers are concerned about the motivation of older adults to use social media and their attitude towards social media. And they try to fully understand the impact of social media on the older adults in both physical and mental aspects [17]. The barriers such as privacy concerns, technical difficulties for the older adults in engaging into the social media context are also often discussed by researchers, that reminds stakeholders to take the needs of older users into account when design [23].

2.2   Age Stereotype

Age stereotypes are characteristics, generalizations or assumptions about how individuals at a particular age are viewed and should behave [13], and generally age stereotype has positive and negative valence. It is becoming clear that positive and negative age stereotypes play an important role in health, disease, and disablement processes associated with aging [21]. Although the age stereotypes have different valences, younger individuals tend to hold a prevalence of negative age stereotypes [19] of older adults that lead to prejudice or discrimination. Moreover, due to their own physical or mental condition, older adults do not have dominant discourse power in society, especially in the Internet era [20]. This leads to the fact that ageism has been found to exist throughout a wide variety of social life contexts [19]. People of any age group are inevitably to face a special dilemma caused by ageism [24]. Older adults are more vulnerable to ageism because they have negative stereotypes that cognitive and physical competence decline with age [15, 16]. Brashier and Schacter [2] argue that older adults are especially susceptible to misinformation. Cheng [4] argues that older adults primed with negative age stereotypes reported more negative self-perception of aging. Older adults will make decisions to not use technologies when they perceive the technology as replacing or eroding something of value to them. Moreover, it has become a social consensus that it is acceptable for the elderly to give up using electronic applications, despite being increasingly limiting in digital society [14].

During the COVID-19 pandemic, a significant amount of information has focused on negative stereotypes of aging and stigmatization of older adults increased in mainstream media and social media [1, 11, 28]. Negative information about aging during the pandemic had a detrimental impact on older adults' mental health [18]. The challenges faced by older adults in their use of social media in the present pandemic should be given more attention which can help them live prosperous online lives [22].

2.3 Value Sensitive Design

Value sensitive design is a theoretically grounded approach to the design of technology that accounts for human values in a principled and comprehensive manner throughout the design process. It aims at integrating values of ethical import from the start in the design process of new products and systems [27]. When employing value sensitive design in projects, designers bring together conceptual, empirical, and technical investigations [10]. Conceptual, empirical and technical investigations are called a tripartite methodology of value sensitive design, and they are interdependent and that iteration is the bond between them [29]. In the conceptual investigation, value sensitive design requires first to analyze the ethical value related to specific technology, and fully consider the social impacts of a technical design on direct and indirect stakeholders. A value refers to what a person or a group of people consider important in life [27]. Human welfare, privacy, freedom from bias, universal usability, trust, informed consent, accountability, autonomy, dignity, empathy, feedback are human values often implicated in system design [6–8]. On the basis of conceptual investigation, empirical investigation uses quantitative and qualitative methods such as observations, interviews, surveys, experiments, and user behavior measurement to provide necessary empirical data support for the values discussed in conceptual investigation. Technical investigation focuses on the design of information technology system and the analysis of the performance of existing technology so as to promote a certain value in the specific context of technology design [7, 30].

3   Elderly-Oriented Social Media Design Framework Based on VSD

Value sensitive design can be regarded as a design framework for social media. The tripartite methodology of value sensitive design is shown in Table 1.

Table 1. Tripartite methodology of value sensitive design

Methodology	Main work	Core concerns
Conceptual investigation	Philosophically interpreting core structures and issues Analyzing the values related to specific technical design Fully considering the social impacts of a technical design on direct and indirect stakeholders [12]	Who are the direct and indirect stakeholders affected by the design? How are both types of stakeholders affected? What values are implicated in the design? How to balance the competition between different values in design?
Empirical investigation	The empirical investigation seeks to understand human responses to technical artifacts and to the larger social context of technology use	How do stakeholders understand individual values in the interactive context? How do they make trade-off decisions between different values with competitive relationships? Is there any difference between what people express and their actual practice?
Technical investigation	The technical investigation focuses on the design of information technology system and the analysis of the performance of existing technology	How do existing technologies and mechanisms support (or hinder) the human values? How to involve proactive design of systems to support values identified in the conceptual investigation?

We believe that age stereotypes are the important factors that hinder older adults from engaging into the social media context and in turn led them to abandon their use of social media. However, positive and negative age stereotypes have complex effects on the behavior and psychology of the older adults in social practice. In the design of social media, it is not advisable to both reject negative age stereotype and advocate positive age stereotype too much. Therefore, social media should be designed with sensitivity to values based on the user experience of older adults, namely elderly-oriented design. In this study we propose a social media design framework based on value sensitive design. The framework is shown in Fig. 1.

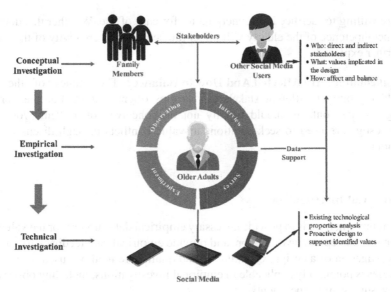

Fig. 1. Elderly-oriented social media design framework based on VSD

3.1 Conceptual Investigation

Who Are the Stakeholders? Value sensitivity design not only emphasizes the direct stakeholders in technology, but also considers the potential indirect stakeholders. Therefore, in conceptual investigation, we should first make an effective distinction between stakeholders. This work helps to reconcile the relationship between different stakeholders, so that direct stakeholders and indirect stakeholders can effectively participate in the process of technology design, and then find solutions to the value conflict and balance arising from the use of technology.

In the context of social media use, all users are direct stakeholders. However, when we put the social media design issue into the perspective of the elderly user experience, there is no doubt that the elderly users are the direct stakeholders. Family and friends who play a major role in the social relations of the elderly are indirect stakeholders. When identifying stakeholders there may be several subgroups within each of these two categories of stakeholders. This requires investigators to always maintain a systematic and comprehensive perspective.

What Values Are Implicated? When identifying the value of stakeholders, we can first identify their benefits and harms. With a list of benefits and harms investigators can have the ability to recognize corresponding values. This work has a tendency to lead to stereotypes because it requires a series of socially coherent attributes to be associated with the "imagined group". Therefore investigators need to ensure that views of stakeholders are fully represented. For example, the older adults are defaulted to have poor digital literacy, so elderly-oriented social media design is required to simplify its functions to facilitate the elderly to learn. This design idea ignores whether the older adults are willing to sacrifice high functionality for ease of use. Whether this default of digital incompetence of the elderly will affect the activity and creativity of them needs to be further explored.

How Stakeholders Are Affected And How to Balance? The values of the same stakeholder group or different stakeholder groups often conflict. For the purposes of design, value conflicts should usually not be conceived of as "either/or" situations. Investigators need to seek solutions to value conflicts through discussion with stakeholders.

3.2 Empirical Investigation

Empirical investigation is to provide necessary empirical data support for the values discussed in the conceptual investigation, and provide empirical data feedback for the technical investigation of a design. Quantitative and qualitative methods used in social science studies is potentially applicable in empirical investigations, including observation, interview, survey and experiment.

This work plays an important role in analyzing the value dilemma caused by age stereotypes. In empirical investigation, investigators can carry out different research designs according to the context of social media use. For example, will the elderly take the initiative to choose the "elderly mode" interface, and what are their attitudes toward this revision? Can the "elderly mode" meet the actual needs of the elderly for social media? If the "elderly mode" does not fully meet the social needs of the elderly, what values should be integrated into the elderly-oriented reform of social media? Is there any potential possibility that the existing elderly-oriented reform may discourage the elderly from engaging into the Internet society?

3.3 Technical Investigation

Existing Technological Properties Analysis. By analyzing the properties of existing technologies, investigators can find out whether existing technologies supports or hinders the identified values. In terms of social media, the "elderly mode" with larger font, simpler interface and more convenient operation has been added to the many websites and platforms. What value demands of the elderly can be supported by these designs? And is there a potential possibility to hinder certain values of older adults? These problems can be solved in this work.

Proactive Design to Support Identified Values. Value sensitive design is a proactive design mode, which actively investigates and summarizes the value appeals of different stakeholders. The advantage of this design method is that it can be planned and adjusted in the early stage of technical design to avoid rectification after problems occur. Based on the research results of conceptual and empirical investigations, elderly-oriented social media can be designed more selectively to provide better user experience for the elderly.

4 Conclusion

Cultural changes under technological innovation can constantly produce new elements. Therefore, even today's young people will have obstacles to accept new technologies in the process of their gradual aging, unless new technologies are designed with sensitivity to values fostered through such experience [14]. In this study, we build an elderly-oriented social media design framework based on value sensitive design. This framework tries to find the exclusive values that the older adults really care about beyond the age stereotypes. Although this is a theoretical discussion, we hope that this research can provide designers with an idea, that is, breaking the age stereotype and integrating elderly-oriented design into every stage of social media design.

In future we will carry out empirical research on elderly-oriented social media design based on the value sensitive design framework. We hope to find more values that the elderly pay attention to in the modern digital society in the research. And we try to provide real convenience for the older adults to engage into digital life.

References

1. Barrett, A.E., Michael, C., Padavic, I.: Calculated ageism: generational sacrifice as a response to the COVID-19 pandemic. J. Gerontol. Soc. Sci. **76**(4), e201–e205 (2021). https://doi.org/10.1093/geronb/gbaa132
2. Brashier, N.M., Schacter, D.L.: Aging in an era of fake news. Curr. Dir. Psychol. Sci. **29**(3), 316–323 (2020). https://doi.org/10.1177/0963721420915872
3. China Internet Network Information Center: The 48th statistical report on China's Internet Dvelopment (2021). http://www.cnnic.net.cn/hlwfzyj/hlwxzbg/hlwtjbg/202109/P020210915523670981527.pdf
4. Cheng, S.T.: The effect of negative aging self-stereotypes on satisfaction with social support. J. Gerontol. Psychol. Sci. **75**(5), 981–990 (2020). https://doi.org/10.1093/geronb/gby113
5. Cornejo, R., Tentori, M., Favela, J.: Enriching in-person encounters through social media: a study on family connectedness for the elderly. Int. J. Hum. Comput. Stud. **71**(9), 889–899 (2013). https://doi.org/10.1016/j.ijhcs.2013.04.001
6. Dadgar, M., Joshi, K.D.: The role of information and communication technology in self-management of chronic diseases: an empirical investigation through value sensitive design. J. Assoc. Inf. Syst. **19**(2), 86–112 (2018). https://doi.org/10.17705/jais1.00485
7. Friedman, B., Kahn, P.H.J., Borning, A.: Value sensitive design and information systems. In: Zhang, P., Galletta, D. (eds.) Human-Computer Interaction in Management Information Systems: Foundations. M.E. Sharpe, New York (2006)
8. Grünloh, C.: Using technological frames as an analytic tool in value sensitive design. Ethics Inf. Technol. **23**(1), 53–57 (2018). https://doi.org/10.1007/s10676-018-9459-3
9. He, T., Huang, C., Li, M., Zhou, Y., Li, S.: Social participation of the elderly in China: the roles of conventional media, digital access and social media engagement. Telematics Inform. **48** (2020). https://doi.org/10.1016/j.tele.2020.101347
10. Hendry, D.G., Friedman, B., Ballard, S.: Value sensitive design as a formative framework. Ethics Inf. Technol. **23**(1), 39–44 (2021). https://doi.org/10.1007/s10676-021-09579-x
11. Jimenez-Sotomayor, M.R., Gomez-Moreno, C., Soto-Perez-de-Celis, E.: Coronavirus, ageism, and twitter: an evaluation of tweets about older adults and COVID-19. J. Am. Geriatr. Soc. **68**(8), 1661–1665 (2020). https://doi.org/10.1111/jgs.16508

12. Johri, A., Venable, J.R., Nair, S.: The role of design values in information system development for human benefit. Inf. Technol. People **24**(3), 281–302 (2011). https://doi.org/10.1108/095 93841111158383

13. Knight, R.L., Chalabaev, A., McNarry, M.A., Mackintosh, K.A., Hudson, J.: Do age stereotype-based interventions affect health-related outcomes in older adults? A systematic review and future directions. Br. J. Health Psychol. (2021). https://doi.org/10.1111/bjhp.12548

14. Knowles, B., Hanson, V.L.: The wisdom of older technology (non)users. Commun. ACM **61**(3), 72–77 (2018). https://doi.org/10.1145/3179995

15. Lamont, R.A., Swift, H.J., Abrams, D.: A review and meta-analysis of age-based stereotype threat: negative stereotypes, not facts, do the damage. Psychol. Aging **30**(1), 180–193 (2015). https://doi.org/10.1037/a0038586

16. Lee, S.Y., Hoh, J.W.T.: A critical examination of ageism in memes and the role of meme factories. New Media Soc. (2021). https://doi.org/10.1177/14614448211047845

17. Leist, A.K.: Social media use of older adults: a mini-review. Gerontology **59**(4), 378–384 (2013). https://doi.org/10.1159/000346818

18. Levy, B.R., Chang, E.S., Lowe, S., Provolo, N., Slade, M.D.: Impact of media-based negative and positive age stereotypes on older individuals' mental health during the COVID-19 pandemic. J. Gerontol. Psychol. Sci. (2021). https://doi.org/10.1093/geronb/gbab085

19. Levy, B.R., Chung, P.H., Bedford, T., Navrazhina, K.: Facebook as a site for negative age stereotypes. Gerontologist **54**(2), 172–176 (2014). https://doi.org/10.1093/geront/gns194

20. Li, Q.: Characteristics and social impact of the use of social media by Chinese Dama. Telematics Inform. **34**(3), 797–810 (2017). https://doi.org/10.1016/j.tele.2016.05.020

21. Meisner, B.A.: A meta-analysis of positive and negative age stereotype priming effects on behavior among older adults. J. Gerontol. Psychol. Sci. **67**(1), 13–17 (2012). https://doi.org/10.1093/geronb/gbr062

22. Moore, R.C., Hancock, J.T.: Older adults, social technologies, and the coronavirus pandemic: challenges, strengths, and strategies for support. Soc. Media + Soc. **6**(3), 1–5 (2020). https://doi.org/10.1177/2056305120948162

23. Nef, T., Ganea, R.L., Muri, R.M., Mosimann, U.P.: Social networking sites and older users - a systematic review. Int. Psychogeriatr. **25**(7), 1041–1053 (2013). https://doi.org/10.1017/S1041610213000355

24. North, M.S., Fiske, S.T.: Modern attitudes toward older adults in the aging world: a cross-cultural meta-analysis. Psychol. Bull. **141**(5), 993–1021 (2015). https://doi.org/10.1037/a00 39469

25. Ory, M., Hoffman, M.K., Hawkins, M., Sanner, B., Mockenhaupt, R.: Challenging ageing stereotypes: Strategies for creating a more active society. Am. J. Prev. Med. **25**(3), 164–171 (2003). https://doi.org/10.1016/S0749-3797(03)00181-8

26. Steele, C.M., Aronson, J.: Stereotype threat and the intellectual test performance of African Americans. J. Pers. Soc. Psychol. **69**(5), 797–811 (1995). https://doi.org/10.1037/0022-3514.69.5.797

27. Poel, I.: Design for value change. Ethics Inf. Technol. **23**(1), 27–31 (2018). https://doi.org/10.1007/s10676-018-9461-9

28. Vervaecke, D., Meisner, B.A.: Caremongering and assumptions of need: the spread of compassionate ageism during COVID-19. Gerontologist **61**(2), 159–165 (2021). https://doi.org/10.1093/geront/gnaa131

29. Winkler, T., Spiekermann, S.: Twenty years of value sensitive design: a review of methodological practices in VSD projects. Ethics Inf. Technol. **23**(1), 17–21 (2018). https://doi.org/10.1007/s10676-018-9476-2

30. Zolyomi, A.: Where the stakeholders are: tapping into social media during value-sensitive design research. Ethics Inf. Technol. **23**(1), 59–62 (2018). https://doi.org/10.1007/s10676-018-9475-3

Author Index